Organising Local Economic Development

THE ROLE OF DEVELOPMENT AGENCIES AND COMPANIES

Greg Clark, Joe Huxley, Debra Mountford

OECD

ORGANISATION FOR ECONOMIC CO-OPERATION AND DEVELOPMENT

The OECD is a unique forum where the governments of 30 democracies work together to address the economic, social and environmental challenges of globalisation. The OECD is also at the forefront of efforts to understand and to help governments respond to new developments and concerns, such as corporate governance, the information economy and the challenges of an ageing population. The Organisation provides a setting where governments can compare policy experiences, seek answers to common problems, identify good practice and work to co-ordinate domestic and international policies.

The OECD member countries are: Australia, Austria, Belgium, Canada, the Czech Republic, Denmark, Finland, France, Germany, Greece, Hungary, Iceland, Ireland, Italy, Japan, Korea, Luxembourg, Mexico, the Netherlands, New Zealand, Norway, Poland, Portugal, the Slovak Republic, Spain, Sweden, Switzerland, Turkey, the United Kingdom and the United States. The Commission of the European Communities takes part in the work of the OECD.

OECD Publishing disseminates widely the results of the Organisation's statistics gathering and research on economic, social and environmental issues, as well as the conventions, guidelines and standards agreed by its members.

This work is published on the responsibility of the Secretary-General of the OECD. The opinions expressed and arguments employed herein do not necessarily reflect the official views of the Organisation or of the governments of its member countries.

ISBN 978-92-64-06081-4 (print)
ISBN 978-92-64-08353-0 (PDF)
DOI 10.1787/9789264083530-en

Series:Local Economic and Employment Development (LEED)
ISSN 1990-1100 (print)
ISSN 1990-1097 (online)

Foreword

The OECD Programme on Local Economic and Employment Development (LEED) has advised governments and communities since 1982 on how to adapt to global trends and tackle complex problems in a fast-changing world. It combines expertise from America, Australasia and Europe into pragmatic task forces that provide rapid responses and targeted advice on specific issues. It draws on a comparative analysis of experience from some 50 countries around the world in fostering economic growth, employment and inclusion.

The work of LEED since 1982 to the present day has played a major part in establishing and gaining acceptance for the notion that local action, local policy flexibility and new forms of local governance in economic development are both desirable and essential. Development agencies and companies have played a fundamental role in the delivery of local economic development since the end of Second World War and they have been an essential partner to the LEED Programme since 1982.

The first development agencies were established in Europe as a response to the place-based crises caused by war damage, industrial decline and dereliction. Development agencies were given the initiative to redevelop devastated districts and regions. They were initially seen as a short-term response to an emergency and even today, closures of major local facilities (such as a defence base, a major factory or a port) can trigger the establishment of a new development agency. Whilst they have become an increasingly popular organisational vehicle for shaping and pursuing development strategies at the sub-national level, there is no common understanding, or rigid formula, of what a development agency is. Nor has there been a global census of there numbers but there are probably now more than 15 000 agencies world wide, with more being created every month. They vary in size, scale, and function and have arisen from different starting points.

As the first international comparative study of development agencies, this book provides unique insights drawn from 16 rich and varied case studies and will be a valuable resource for national policy makers, local practitioners, politicians and stakeholders involved in delivering local economic development. The book draws on 27 years of experience and co-operative action by the LEED Programme Directing Committee members and LEED Partners. It is a collaborative effort between national and local governments, OECD member and non-member countries and global practitioners and stakeholders.

We wish to thank Debra Mountford, Senior Policy Analyst who has led this work stream on behalf of the LEED Programme; Greg Clark, Chair of the OECD LEED Forum on Development Agencies and Investment Strategies and lead author of this book; Joe Huxley, researcher and contributor; Helen Easton, Sheelagh Delf, Lucy Clarke and Elisa Campestrin of the LEED Secretariat; and Julie Harris, who copy-edited and prepared this book for publication. The book would not have been possible without the generous support of the Department of Communities and Local Government (United Kingdom); AucklandPlus (New Zealand); Creative Sheffield (United Kingdom); Invest Toronto and Build Toronto (Canada) and all the contributing agencies that dedicated their time, resources and experience – they are duly thanked.

Sergio Arzeni
Director of the OECD Centre for Entrepreneurship,
SMEs and Local Development

Table of contents

Tables

Preface

I'm delighted the UK Government is supporting publication by the OECD Programme on Local Economic and Employment Development (LEED) of this ground-breaking global review of economic development companies and agencies. I'm also grateful to the development companies and agencies around the world who've made it possible, through their financial support and providing case studies and observations from practice.

Economic development companies and agencies are a key means through which local government can acquire the skills, tools, and resources needed to deliver local economic development. Local authorities have many of the instruments they need to create a sound local platform for economic and business development. Planning, education, housing, infrastructure, amenities and environmental management are all crucial to how a local economy grows and develops.

At the same time, "business and customer-facing" activities like site redevelopment, business support, enterprise promotion, investment facilitation, place branding and marketing, combined with a clear development strategy and communications, are important too in boosting local economic development. Decisions on such activities need to be taken in a market environment, which is why local government companies are being created around the United Kingdom.

We have found that such companies are often the best way for local authorities to pursue economic development, providing both companies and citizens with good support in a contested market. For these reasons we've supported the development of companies such as Prospect Leicestershire, Liverpool Vision, and Creative Sheffield, all featured in this book.

The UK Government is keen to encourage local authorities to use a company structure to define their own solutions to local economic development issues. We've been careful not to insist they follow a set template. The result is that over ten authorities now support an economic development company. Many more are considering doing so.

The book highlights some important features of local development companies and agencies. Local government boundaries often fail to coincide with the real economic geography of places. This means that cross-border collaboration is essential. We've encouraged this in the United Kingdom and found that economic development companies are a good vehicle for promoting cross-border working on economic development issues.

We're continually aware of the need for local economic development to sit well with regional development strategies. In both Sheffield and Liverpool, for example, economic development companies are working to implement the regional economic strategy effectively.

We've been very impressed with the role development companies play in brokering business engagement and private investment in local economic development. The case studies from New York, Hamburg, and Cape Town demonstrate this very well. Major redevelopment and better land use is the key to improving productivity in local economies. We see great examples of this in Johannesburg, New York, Toronto, Bilbao, Hamburg, and Liverpool. We know that place branding and promotion can be important in securing market opportunities. These approaches are used successfully in Auckland, Bilbao, Toronto, Sheffield and Madrid. Lastly, we know local economies must be good places for entrepreneurs to set up companies and to innovate. The cases of Barcelona, Milan, Leicester and Cape Town illustrate this well.

I'd like to congratulate the OECD LEED Programme for preparing this excellent book and to thank LEED and all the agencies and companies involved.

The Rt Hon Rosie Winterton MP
Minister for Local Government
Department for Communities and Local Government
United Kingdom

Communities
and Local Government

Executive summary

Introducing development agencies

The search for the best organisational arrangements to promote local economic development has been a significant task for municipal governments and their partners for several decades now. This book examines the contribution that has been made by agencies, companies, and corporate boards which have proved to be a consistent choice of local government leaders for pursuing local economic strategies.

It reflects an established consensus that economic development activities are unlike the other roles and responsibilities of local governments. It is possible to classify the broad roles of local government into four main categories. They include:

- **Representation**: actions by locally elected officials on behalf of the community which elected them.

- **Services**: the delivery of activities, amenities and infrastructures which are fundamental to the quality of life of the local population.

- **Regulation**: the provision and enforcement of guidelines and rules to maintain order and the well-being of local people.

- **Development and investment**: the stimulation and management of sustainable economic growth and social and environmental well-being for the benefit of residents, workers and visitors in the future. Long-term planning and investment facilitation is critical.

This fourth role of local government is different from its other roles. The development and investment agenda operates with different markets, geographies, timeframes, partners, financing, stakeholders, tools and audiences. As a result, it requires distinctive expertise, skills base and capacity, as well as different structures and organisational arrangements.

One key organisational option for promoting economic development is the use of development agencies, companies, or partnership boards (which we will call "development agencies" for short throughout the rest of this book). Development agencies are primarily "market facing" (labour markets, property markets, investment markets, visitor markets, among others), rather than "citizen facing", and involve market-based transactions, and incentive structures, rather than direct public service delivery (although good public services are critical to wider economic development). They are organisations especially suited to "contested" activities such as locational and investment decisions, or "collaborative/multi-lateral" activities such as cross-sectoral and inter-municipal planning and joint ventures. Such economic development interventions can often be delivered by market-like bodies and business-led development approaches (brokerage, marketing, joint ventures, incentives, capitalisation, competitive recruitment, etc.). It is consistently practiced that these are delivered for local governments and their partners through a corporate, rather than a municipal, or administrative, structure.

Why is this book needed?

Although development agencies have become an increasingly popular organisational vehicle for shaping and pursuing local economic strategies, there is no precise common understanding, or rigid formula, of what a development agency is. No global census of development agencies and companies has been undertaken, but there are probably now more than 15 000 such organisations world wide, with more being created every month. Given their increasingly significant contribution to local economic development, there is a requirement to better understand the factors which underpin their performance and to share best practices.

Methodology

In this book, we examine several important themes in the work of development agencies based on OECD Local Economic and Employment Development (LEED) Development Agency Reviews, an analysis of 16 agencies in 13 locations world wide, as well as drawing from the OECD LEED materials and wider work on the roles of development agencies.

The key focus is on attempting to distil why and how development agencies are established; what they can achieve and what tools they require, what the context is for their success, as well as what can go wrong, or requires attention if success is to be assured.

What do development agencies do?

The range of tasks that development agencies pursue varies enormously. There is a growing menu, and not all development agencies will pursue the same tasks. Though there are others, we have mapped eight of their principal activities in Table 0.1.

Table 0.1. **Development agency functions**

Branding and international promotion	Investment attraction and retention	Business start-ups and growth	Human capital development
② ④ ⑧ ⑩ ⑪ ⑫ ⑬ ⑭ ⑯	② ⑧ ⑩ ⑬ ⑯	③ ⑦ ⑭ ⑯	① ② ③ ⑫
Real estate, urban realm and infrastructure development	Social or green development initiatives	Partnership facilitation, planning and visioning	Urban service provision or management
① ② ⑤ ⑥ ⑧ ⑨ ⑪ ⑮ ⑯	① ⑦ ⑨	③ ④ ⑦ ⑫ ⑭	① ⑦

① Abyssinian Development Corporation		⑨ HafenCity Hamburg GmbH	
② AucklandPlus		⑩ Invest Toronto	
③ Barcelona Activa		⑪ Johannesburg Development Agency	
④ Bilbao Metropoli-30		⑫ Liverpool Vision	
⑤ BILBAO Ría 2000		⑬ Madrid Global	
⑥ Build Toronto		⑭ Milano Metropoli	
⑦ Cape Town Partnership		⑮ New York City Economic Development Corporation	
⑧ Creative Sheffield		⑯ Prospect Leicestershire	

Development agency roles

Not all development agencies play the same role in their local development systems. Indeed, some undertake more. From past reviews the OECD LEED Programme identifies four major organising roles for development agencies:

- economic roles,
- leadership roles,
- governance and co-ordination roles,
- implementation roles.

Development agency typologies

Development agencies vary in size, scale, role and function due to their starting points and the roles they play. To provide structure and for simplicity, it is possible to categories individual agencies in five broad development agency typologies (Table 0.2).

Table 0.2. **Development agency typologies**

Typology	Development and revitalisation agencies	Productivity and economic growth agencies	Integrated economic agencies	Internationalisation agencies	Visioning and partnership agencies
Description	"Place drivers"	"Employment and productivity drivers"	"Place and productivity leaders"	"Place and productivity promoters"	"Place shapers and visioners"
Development agency	BILBAO Ría 2000	Auckland Plus	Creative Sheffield	Invest Toronto	Bilbao Metropoli-30
	Build Toronto	Barcelona Activa	Liverpool Vision	Madrid Global	Cape Town Partnership
	HafenCity Hamburg GmbH		Milano Metropoli		
	Johannesburg Development Agency		New York City Economic Development Corporation		
			Prospect Leicestershire		
			Abyssinian Development Corporation		

Development agencies and the local development system

The "local development system" is a term used in this book to describe the working relationships between public, business and non-governmental sector partners that can create better conditions for economic growth and employment generation. In our approach, a "local development system" can be more or less effective in generating sound public sector co-ordination, effective leverage with business partners, and common agendas amongst multiple actors in support of local economic development.

A key observation of this book is that development agencies perform best within effective local development systems, and many of the problems that development agencies encounter are products of weak or failed local development systems, rather than problems with the development agencies themselves. Where development agencies have not worked well, or have become stuck, it is often because the working relationships or shared agendas with other local bodies have failed.

Identifying the critical relationships of development agencies within the local development system

From the development agency perspective, there are a number of key relationships with other organisations and groups which help form the core of the local development system. Though these relationships vary according to the nature of the system in terms of its scale, focus, aims, politics and legal frameworks, some of the most significant include:

- local and regional political leadership,
- member/stakeholder organisations,
- other development agencies,
- delivery partners,

- the private sector,

- the media,

- the local community.

Development agency strengths and constraints

A number of principal strengths were consistently identified by the development agencies themselves as critical to the success of their organisation. These factors are explored in the book and are illustrated in Table 0.3.

Table 0.3. **Development agency strengths in selected development agencies**

Company type and structure	Agility and flexibility	Spatial focus	Leadership	Focus on outcomes and clients	Talented and experienced staff / focus on quality	Strong revenue-generating capacity
5 8 15	1 2 3 15	2 5	2 3 6 7 9	1 2 3 5 7 9 11	3 5 6 8 9 11 12 13 14	6 9 15

Clear or focussed mandate	Long-term mandate	Strong partnerships	Holistic /integrated approach	Innovation	Apolitical/ low profile/ arm's length positioning	Community/ stakeholder credibility and engagement
2 3 7 11 16	4 5 9	1 2 3 5 6 7 8 9 10 11 13 14 16	1 7 9 12 14	3	4 5 6 9 11 13	1 2 3 5 10 12 14

(1) Abyssinian Development Corporation	(9) HafenCity Hamburg GmbH
(2) AucklandPlus	(10) Invest Toronto
(3) Barcelona Activa	(11) Johannesburg Development Agency
(4) Bilbao Metropoli-30	(12) Liverpool Vision
(5) BILBAO Ría 2000	(13) Madrid Global
(6) Build Toronto	(14) Milano Metropoli
(7) Cape Town Partnership	(15) New York City Economic Development Corporation
(8) Creative Sheffield	(16) Prospect Leicestershire

Successful development agencies are not necessarily agencies which have no challenges. A number of constraints are illustrated in Table 0.4, but more important is how development agencies react and respond. Development agency success therefore is as much about managing the constraints associated with change as it is developing core strengths.

Table 0.4. **Development agency constraints in selected development agencies**

Budget constraints or funding arrangements	Market conditions	Non-enabling governance structures	Lack of autonomy/ executive power	Lack of a socio-economic evidence base	Complex role in complex system of stakeholders	Mission creep
① ② ③ ④ ⑤ ⑦ ⑪ ⑫ ⑬ ⑭	① ⑤ ⑨ ⑩ ⑬ ⑮	② ⑩ ⑭	④	⑦ ⑩	⑦ ⑭ ⑮	⑨

Accountabilities	Focused mandate
⑧ ⑬	⑪

①	Abyssinian Development Corporation	⑨	HafenCity Hamburg GmbH
②	AucklandPlus	⑩	Invest Toronto
③	Barcelona Activa	⑪	Johannesburg Development Agency
④	Bilbao Metropoli-30	⑫	Liverpool Vision
⑤	BILBAO Ría 2000	⑬	Madrid Global
⑥	Build Toronto	⑭	Milano Metropoli
⑦	Cape Town Partnership	⑮	New York City Economic Development Corporation
⑧	Creative Sheffield	⑯	Prospect Leicestershire

Key lessons from the review of development agency experience internationally

The main findings of this review are that development agency-type organisations are significant contributors to the planning and implementation of local development agendas world wide.

They can be instrumental in creating a business-like, and business-facing, operational environment in which local government-led economic development and regeneration can be effectively delivered. As employers, they can attract staff and expertise into local government and regeneration, from a wide range of sectors and backgrounds that might not be attracted to work within a wholly municipal structure. As collaborative organisations, development agencies can often bring together multiple actors in ways which others cannot.

Despite the leading role that development agencies play, a co-ordinated effort is still required across local development systems and their constituent parts. It is important to pursue local development goals through a coherent, seamless, and comprehensive approach local development system.

Of course the roles and activities of development agencies will vary according to the local context and system, but their success appears to be based on the ability to either aggregate different efforts to achieve scale and mass, to focus solely on niche interventions which can be effectively delivered on their own, and/or to address contested markets where more commercial competitive approaches are required to succeed.

Box 0.1 summarises ten key principles for how development agencies can successfully add value to the planning and delivery of local development.

Box 0.1. **OECD LEED principles for development agencies**

- **Focus on implementation at pace and scale**. The development agency pursues development opportunities faster, and at a larger scale, than would normally be possible within a city or local government.

- **Aggregate otherwise separate interventions to add value**. Economic development efforts within cities or regions are often subject to fragmentation of effort due to the multiplicity of funding streams and policy agencies. Development agencies can act to aggregate otherwise disparate efforts, overcoming potential co-ordination failures and information asymmetries.

- **Enhance the capacity and co-ordination of the local development system**. So that it can deliver a greater return on investment and provide a better platform for progress.

- **Focus on the customer**. An important reason for placing economic development activities within a corporate entity such as a development agency rather than a municipal structure is the ability of the development agency to offer a business-like environment and service offering, and the scope to manager customer relationships in a business-to-business model.

- **Adopt flexible spatial scales**. Development agencies can operate at a citywide scale but are also able to function at either more local or wider levels. This is important given that economic development challenges are often focussed at local or sub-regional levels.

- **Achieve confidence of external investors and other businesses**. Confidence of investors, developers and business customers is an important ingredient in maintaining market position for local and sub-regional economies.

- **Become a tool maker and fully utilise existing tools**. Economic development tools need to be fully utilised and new tools need to be made to fit new imperatives. These tools often involve the interplay of public and private interests and assets. Development agencies can be effective tool makers and tool users, combining different powers, resources, and assets to make development happen.

- **Leverage assets and investment**. Assets and private capital are key to reinvestment markets and development agencies can help to leverage them towards city economic development goals. Share risks and costs actively with partners: development agencies can operate as joint venture vehicles between different sectors and between different tiers of government.

- **Refresh image and identity and communicate development progress**. Image and identity is supported by branding and marketing activity which needs to be a focus of concerted action. Co-ordination is essential.

- **Apply leadership to problem solving**. Problem solving is key to making economic development successful. Development agencies are often able to supply the skills and approaches required, unencumbered by other mandates.

This book establishes that there is now clearly substantial confidence in the development agency model across many OECD countries, with a wide range of countries opting to use development agency-type models and seeing this as a preferred means to implement economic development activities at city and sub-regional levels. This book aims to reinforce this confidence by illustrating and disseminating the key lessons learned over 25 years of development agency activity.

Chapter 1

An introduction to development agencies

Following a clear introduction to what local development is and why it is significant, this chapter outlines the importance of effective organisational arrangements for the planning and delivery of local economic development, and of the particular role that development agencies can play. Through a review of the literature the case is made that, despite their proven success and growing prevalence, understanding and appreciation of these flexible, innovative and pragmatic tools for local development are less than what they should be. The chapter concludes suggesting that by drawing on a core evidence base of case studies of 16 agencies in 13 local economies to answer a number of key questions the publication will review how development agencies have contributed as leaders in the local development system.

The nature of local development

The purpose of local development is to build the capacity of a defined territory, often a municipality or region, to improve its economic future and the quality of life for inhabitants. This definition emerges from a consensus between global institutions such as the World Bank, United Nations, and the Organisation for Economic Development and Co-operation (OECD), academics, and from experienced practitioners on the ground.

Local development makes an important contribution to national economic performance and has become more critical with increased global competition, population mobility, technological advances, and consequential spatial differences and imbalances. Effective local development can reduce disparities between poor and rich places, add to the stock of locally generated jobs and firms, increase overall private sector investment, improve the information flows with investors and developers, and increase the coherence and confidence with which local economic strategy is pursued. This can also give rise to better diagnostic assessment of local economic assets and distinctive advantages, and lead to more robust strategy assessment.

Cities have become a focus for renewed efforts to promote local development over the past 20 years. National governments are recognising the need to empower cities and regions so that they can take the decisions and interventions needed to optimise their relative economic performance, and thus contribute more to national growth and development. In some contexts this has led to a renewed impulse for the devolution of power and authority to local governments, and in others it has led to efforts by state, national, and federal governments to better support local and regional initiatives.

To exploit these opportunities, local governments may need to support the adjustment of their local economies, "re-engineer" their offer and leverage their assets to better compete in an internationally open and knowledge-driven economy. This includes fostering the skills of the labour pool as well as improving the productivity of infrastructure, the attractiveness of the business environment and the quality of life available. It can also involve explicit efforts to "reposition" the local economy within contested international markets for locations.

The comparative advantages of having, and using, development tools effectively at the local level include:

- improved alignment of goals and strategies between different public sector players and civic/private partners;
- pace and certainty of the response to investors and developers;
- scale of the development that is simultaneously feasible within the city;
- the quality and conclusiveness of negotiations over how risks and costs will be shared between public and private entities;
- the availability of a mechanism to help capture value and shape benefits of investments and development;
- the unlocking of under-utilised assets;
- increased flexibility, and profitability, in property markets;
- better linkages between property, labour, and investment markets and wider efforts to foster entrepreneurship, and other sources of growth; and

- better co-ordination generally, leading to optimal resource mobilisation against agreed priorities.

Some of these factors are demonstrated in the example from Barcelona Activa in Box 1.1.

Box 1.1. **Signature project: Barcelona Activa and the Glòries Entrepreneurship Centre**

Barcelona Activa is the local development agency of the City of Barcelona which specialises in innovation, entrepreneurship and the knowledge-based economy. Established in 1987 the Gloriès Entrepreneurship Centre acts as a hub for entrepreneurs in Barcelona and encourages all new fledgling businesses to contact the centre and make use of its facilities. It provides professional services for potential entrepreneurs in order to promote the creation of new businesses. It also seeks to encourage an entrepreneurial culture by coaching entrepreneurs and assisting them in taking the step from the business idea to its creation.

The centre forms a central part of Barcelona Activa's overarching strategy, which consists of four fundamental pillars:

1. Business creation and the development of an entrepreneurship culture: the aim is to provide professional services for potential entrepreneurs in order to promote the creation of new businesses, as well as seeking to encourage the development of an entrepreneurial culture.

2. Innovative business consolidation and growth: this aims to generate the conditions that foster the growth of innovative businesses in the city through internationalisation, access to funding, co-operation and innovation.

3. Human capital development and new employment opportunities: this aims to promote Barcelona Activa as the meeting point for human capital in the city of Barcelona, by increasing the professional opportunities that the new work cultures, the new occupations and the emerging economic sectors offer to the population.

4. Access and improvement of employment: Barcelona Activa seeks to inform, orientate, motivate, train and promote employment in Barcelona.

Two of Barcelona Activa's most vaunted objectives are to create an entrepreneurial culture and assist in the creation of innovative new businesses, as well as supporting the growth of existing businesses. One of the key points is its special methodology, which is called the "blended model". It involves the use of cutting edge spaces, such as the Glòries Entrepreneurship Centre, to increase accessibility to the full range of activities which are devoted to entrepreneurs. These activities number over 900 from classical training, dissemination and knowledge pills, personalised coaching, and a powerful website with contents, activities and user-based tools in order to coach the business plan development process on line.

In 2008, Barcelona Activa's entrepreneurship support activities achieved the following:

- 19 387 participants in business creation activities,

- 1 379 business projects coached,

- 60% business creation rate = more than 700 companies created,

- near two employees per created company = 1 500 employment opportunities created,

- 116 innovative start-ups based in the Incubator and Technology Park,

- 711 companies members of Xarxactiva Business co-operation network,

- 350 participant companies in business growth programmes.

Source: Barcelona Activa (2009), "Business Creation Presentation", *www.barcelonanetactiva.com/barcelonanetactiva/en/company-creation/entrepreneurial-initiative-center/index.jsp*.

Local economic development in practice: what is required?

Why is development a distinctive task for local governments?

Given the potential to capture significant benefits from an effective local development agenda, the search for the best organisational arrangements which promote local development has been a significant task for municipal governments and their partners for several decades.

Local development is often led, or facilitated, by local governments, but local development is not like the services that local governments usually provide, of which there are principally three:

- **Representation**: actions by locally elected officials on behalf of the community which elected them.

- **Services**: the delivery of activities, amenities and infrastructures which are fundamental to the quality of life of the local population.

- **Regulation**: the provision and enforcement of guidelines and rules to maintain order and the well-being of local people.

The fourth role of local government is, however, different.

- **Development and investment**: the stimulation and management of sustainable economic growth and social well-being for the benefit of the locality's residents, workers and visitors *in the future*. As a key component of this process, investment attraction and retention is critical.

The "development and investment" agenda is a "market-facing" activity that operates over longer time frames, broader geographies, and wider institutional collaboration than is customary for local government services or regulatory roles. It is a "vision driven" activity that seeks to define a path into the future and to shape the behaviour of other actors, most of whom are not in the control of local government's leaders. It also requires sensitive understanding of external factors such as "contested investment" and "investment returns", "business cycles" and "market forces", as well as a deep appreciation of local assets, endowments, and distinctiveness. Effective local strategies also require deep cross border and cross sectoral collaboration, as well as effective and compelling communication of choices made and investments taken. They must inspire confidence in order to act as co-ordination vehicles.

This requires exceptional leadership skills amongst local government leaders and their partners if local development is to succeed. The skills of visioning, communicating, partnership and alliance building are to the fore. Working with businesses and investors to reduce the risks involved in investing or expanding in a location is a key attribute of local economic leadership.

However, local economic leadership also requires the mobilisation of active support from residents (who have influence through the democratic mandate) for processes that will often involve change, growth, diversification, and the challenge of relinquishing old customs and habits in favour of new ones which may be unfamiliar or even disadvantageous for periods of time.

Local economic leadership must also recognise that many of the economic stakeholders in a local economy do not exercise a vote in local elections. Businesses, commuters, tourists, investors, students, utility, infrastructure and logistics providers are not enfranchised in local elections despite the fact that they are major economic stakeholders.

Important implications arise from this. Local leaders must find a means to engage them in local economic strategies, despite having no mandate to represent them or lead them, and local leaders must seek to reconcile their interests with one another through visioning and agenda building, as well as aligning their needs and interest with those of residents. Reconciling the needs and aspirations of residents with those of economic stakeholders is not usually straightforward, especially in a context where economic growth and quality of life are perceived to have major tensions and trade-offs between them.

Given all of these factors, it is highly desirable that local development is orchestrated as:

- a partnership activity between public, private, and institutional sectors, with substantial vertical and horizontal collaboration on the public sector side, and where stakeholder engagement is both effective and efficient;

- a long-term effort that will also produce important progress and milestones within short time spans;

- an activity that is customer- and investor- facing and utilises appropriate organisational vehicles to deliver this (such as a development agency); and

- an activity that gives rise to its own organisational forms and models, and is able to invent new tools for intervention.

If this is accepted, it becomes clear then that there are two roles for public sector organisations and governments: (1) attending to the fundamentals of delivering economically sensitive public services in a robust and effective way (including infrastructure, education, planning, amenities, etc.). This would also include ensuring that there is the necessary co-ordination of public sector endeavours in place, such as co-ordination of investment in different types of infrastructures or the co-ordination of regulatory regimes; and (2) government should collaborate extensively, and foster co-operation, at a broad regional level with private and public sector actors, to ensure that market sensitive development interventions are delivered in a professional and supported manner. This would include planning and development, branding and promotion, support for businesses and investors, investment facilitation and financial engineering, management of commercial spaces and fostering of entrepreneurship and innovation.

Acknowledging that local development is a specialist activity, many local governments now understand that it requires additional expertise, and new structures and arrangements, beyond the usual activities of municipal government and administration. This book explains and introduces the role of development agencies, and locates them within the idea of a "local development system", as we shall explain.

Development agencies have become an increasingly popular organisational vehicle for shaping and pursuing local economic strategies. However, there is no precise common understanding, or rigid formula, of what a development agency is. No global census of development agencies and companies has been undertaken, but there are currently more than 15 000 such organisations world wide, with more being created every month. Given their increasingly important contribution to local urban development, there is a requirement to better understand the factors which underpin their performance and share best practice.

Although the concept of a local development system is broadly and intuitively understood, it has rarely been defined in isolation and explored. This book attaches more significance to the importance of building a seamless and co-ordinated system of organisations which collaborate to deliver local development activities.

The case study presented in Box 1.2 demonstrates the role of AucklandPlus in the development of the new Auckland brand – a key mechanism to promote the domestic and international success of Auckland.

Box 1.2. **Signature project: Auckland Plus and the Brand Auckland project**

The international promotion of the Auckland region is a key task for the AucklandPlus DA. One of its key projects, Brand Auckland, represents the first attempt in Auckland's history to present a coherent and consistent identity for the Auckland region. Previously, people all over the world were aware that the region has beautiful landscapes, pockets of village culture and a reputation for holding world class sporting events. However, what Auckland lacked was an overall image which would serve as an attraction for investors, large corporates, small and medium-sized enterprises (SMEs), the media, international visitors, domestic travellers, governments, migrants, cultural bodies and other influential organisations.

The brand was launched in September 2008 in response to recommendations in the Auckland Regional Economic Development Strategy and as one of the actions of the Metro Project, which itself was launched in 2006. In the process of the development of the Brand Auckland proposition, thousands of stakeholders were interviewed, including every mayor in the region, the Government, the Leader of the Opposition, a former Governor-General, community and business leaders, members of the public and respondents from as far away as London, Moscow and Shanghai.

As a result of the interview and research process, the Auckland region was identified as having a number of key strengths, such as having one of the highest rated universities in the world, and Auckland's ability to stage world-class events like Pasifika and the Netball World Championships. However, whilst there were many positive individual characteristics of the region, there was no one overarching image of the Auckland regional offering.

Consequently, it was determined that a destination brand was required; a brand which would be used to promote Auckland as a destination to live, work, visit, invest, study and do business. Brand Auckland aims to ensure that people will see a consistent and memorable visual representation of Auckland. This strong consistent image of Auckland will help Auckland to gain recognition and enhance its reputation, thus positively impacting on tourism and business in Auckland. The brand itself has been designed as an umbrella brand for the region so that it can still be used alongside other successful brands, such as the "Eco-City" and "City of Sails" brand, rather than in competition with them. It has been deliberately developed without a strap line so that it does not take away the impact of other, already established brands, but instead adds value.

The brand has already met with considerable success. It has achieved backing at national level through New Zealand Trade and Enterprise, the Ministry of Economic Development and Tourism New Zealand. Tourism New Zealand Chief Executive, George Hickton, commented that, "Auckland is an important part of New Zealand's international tourism scene as it is often the first place many visitors experience when they arrive. The work being done by Brand Auckland will create more awareness of the Auckland region and add real value to the country's overall marketing efforts." AucklandPlus has co-ordinated the development of the brand in line with its "Regional Promotion" activity area. This project contributes to promoting the region, to increasing the pace and scale of development in Auckland and aggregates otherwise separate efforts.

Box 1.2. **Signature project: Auckland Plus and the Brand Auckland project**
(continued)

Key project milestones include:

- October 2002: The Auckland Regional Economic Development Strategy (AREDS) identified the development of a regional brand for Auckland as a key initiative.

- October 2006: The Metro Project Action Plan to deliver key initiatives of AREDS is launched. Objective 3 of the plan "Transform Auckland into a world-class destination" includes the development of a consistent and compelling regional brand identity.

- December 2006: Funding from New Zealand Trade and Enterprise confirmed, brand agency (Designworks Enterprise IG) appointed, and regional steering group established.

- January–April 2008: The brand is visually bought to life using a flexible design.

- July 2008: Brand visuals finalised and presented to the Regional Economic Development Forum.

- September 2008: Regional brand scheduled for roll-out using the regional tourism campaign platform featuring printed media, online and other supporting activities.

- September 2009: One year anniversary of Brand Auckland.

Source: AucklandPlus (2009a), "Brand Auckland", *www.brandauckland.com;* AucklandPlus (2009b), "A Regional Brand Identity for Auckland", *www.aucklandplus.com/subsites/index.cfm?888E0A20-BCD4-1A24-9BAB-C01849ACB189;* AucklandPlus (2009c), "Brand Auckland", *www.brandauckland.com/pdf/Brand%20Auckland%20Q%20and%20As%20v3.pdf.*

A review of the development agency literature

A continually evolving knowledge base, the theme of local development is well treated by a range of authors. For development agencies, the situation is different. The body of work on the subject of these emerging leaders in local development systems is less than exhaustive. Only until more recently, development agencies received indirect and sometimes superficial attention in the literature: at best, as a discrete chapter in a large publication and, at worst, as an afterthought in sections devoted to local development delivery. As appreciation for development agencies as effective tools for local development delivery has grown, and so has the incidence of contributions which offer deeper and more direct insights into their successful deployment in local economies worldwide. To mirror this trend, there has also been a shift from theoretical discussion towards practical principals for development agency success as practitioners seek more tangible explanations of how these instruments can be successfully installed and operated on the ground.

Across the breadth of literature reviewed (Box 1.3), there is convergence around the view that development agencies represent a powerful tool for the planning and delivery of local development. Academics and practitioners have both confirmed development agencies as:

- "Active entrepreneurs, achieving more with less funding, promoting economic development on broader scales geographically, and collaborating creatively within and among organisations" (International Economic Development Council [IEDC], 2006);

- "Excellent vehicle[s] [that] should enjoy strong support from both the public and private sectors" (Blakely and Leigh, 2009);

- "One of the most successful results of the International Links and Services for Local Development Agencies' activity" (ILS LEDA, 2009a).

Box 1.3. **Key development agency texts**

- Regional Development Agencies in Europe (Halkier, Danson and Damborg, 1998)

- "Training Manual for Managing Economic Development Organizations" (IEDC, 2006)

- Planning Local Economic Development: Theory and Practice (Blakely and Leigh, 2009)

- "Setting Up a Development Agency" (EURADA, 1999)

- "Local Economic Development Agencies" (ILS LEDA, 2003)

This précis of existing materials written about development agencies summarises a number of these insights as a means of introducing the main themes, principles and controversies. It shows that while a solid knowledge base exists there is a requirement to present existing theoretical and practical understanding, complemented by additional material, in such a way that these organisations are seen as leaders in the local development system.

ILS LEDA defines development agencies as "legal, none profit structures, generally owned by the public and private entities of the territory" which act as a mechanism through which "local actors plan and activate, in a shared way, initiatives for territorial economic development; identify the most convenient instruments for their realisation; and enhance a coherent system for their technical and financial support" (ILS LEDA, 2007a). Though slightly outdated, this accepted definition captures the essence of what development agencies are as well as their broad purpose. It also introduces a series of significant messages, which are developed well by other authors. The World Bank, Blakely and Leigh, the IEDC, and Halkier, Danson and Damborg all see development agencies as altruistic, business-facing and arm's length vehicles operating in collaboration with other key stakeholders in a wider system of local development and to facilitate local development strategy delivery (World Bank, 2009; Blakely and Leigh, 2009; IEDC, 2006; Halkier, Danson and Damborg, 1998).

Effective collaboration between key stakeholders is seen as fundamental to both the purpose and success of development agencies. Canzanelli and Del Bufalo, for instance, explain that "partnership at the local level gets concrete responses" (Canzanelli and Del Bufalo, 2005). In particular, they argue for public-private collaboration as a means to good local development governance. They suggest that the temporal mandate of government is "absolutely insufficient to assure the necessary continuity" and that development agencies as apolitical, "stable" organisations with "strong time and resource engagements" with business are required (Canzanelli and Del Bufalo, 2005).

The requirement for collaboration and development agencies to facilitate partnership-working is an established conclusion across local development literature. What is less explicit is how the full range of key stakeholders is networked together within a local economy. One of the very latest texts by Blakely and Leigh published in January 2009 comes perhaps the closest to a clear description of why local development planning and delivery should be the result of understanding and appreciation of this stakeholder network. Their book, *Planning Local Economic Development: Theory and Practice*, suggests that "economic development is an institution-building process. As a result, it requires the establishment of planning systems and institutions that can manage the local development process over an extended period of time" (Blakely and Leigh, 2009). Blakely and Leigh then go on to argue that "an institution with specific responsibility to co-ordinate each step of the local development process is essential" and that development agencies are a critical constituent. In other words, only with an appreciation of the entire system of local development can its component parts such as development agencies be designed from scratch or recalibrated effectively. At the same time, only by carefully crafting these component parts to support one another in an efficient way can a seamless and co-ordinated system of local development be established.

In the texts which take a more theoretical approach to development agencies, there is a more obvious convergence of opinion around a number of themes beyond the idea of the local development system. Below, we summarise key contributions on the themes of development agency: activities; roles; territorial spheres of influence and organisational features. We do, however, make a slight distinction between development agencies in the developed and developing worlds.

Many contributions make it clear that development agencies are flexible bodies, capable of performing a range of tasks depending on requirements. According to the texts, development agencies provide several services to local residents, businesses and institutions. A number include: business services and support, entrepreneurial training, territorial marketing, poverty reduction and social initiatives, research, project management and co-ordination, credit provision, innovation support and visioning (Canzanelli and Loffredo, 2008; Canzanelli and Del Bufalo, 2005; Blakely and Leigh, 2009).

It should be noted, here, that development agencies in the developing world undertake activities which differ in their focus to those of development agencies in the developed world. Their projects without doubt reflect a more specific concentration on human development and social concerns. Much of the work in relation to developed world development agencies, on the other hand, describes these organisations as having an economic bias. Productive economic growth is seen as the engine which drives and delivers development. In the developing world, however, both social and economic methods are seen as the means to deliver sustainable local development. In his paper, "The Contribution of the Local Economic Development Agencies Promoted by United Nations to Human Development", Canzanelli outlines a number of the objectives of developing world development agencies which are specific to human development. These include for instance the reduction of poverty and marginality, the improvement of capacities in planning and actions, the safeguarding of the environment, and the empowerment of women capacities in participating to the economic development (Canzanelli, n.d.). Box 1.4 demonstrates the link between strategic human development goals and developing world development agencies in practice.

Box 1.4. **International Links and Services for Local Development Agencies and the Millennium Development Goals**

International Links and Services for Local Development Agencies (ILS LEDA) is a United Nations Development Program which "provides supports to national and territorial actors, and local economic development agencies in order to strengthen territorial economic development processes within the frame of national policies, and to achieve human development and the Millennium Development Goals."

Signed by 147 heads of state and governments during the UN Millennium Summit in September 2000, these Millennium Development Goals represent a strategic set of commitments which shape the activities of the development agencies within the ILS LEDA.

They are defined as "time-bound and quantified targets for addressing extreme poverty in its many dimensions — income poverty, hunger, disease, lack of adequate shelter, and exclusion — while promoting gender equality, education, and environmental sustainability."

Source: ILS LEDA (2009a), "About ILS LEDA", ILS LEDA, *www.ilsleda.org/about/*; United Nations Development Program (2009), "About the Millennium Development Goals", UNDP, *www.undp.org/mdg/basics.shtml*.

The roles of development agencies are seen to differ from the activities they undertake. These roles categorise the way in which development agency activities are delivered. This can help inform a categorisation of development agency types, which is yet to be defined, and which is significant given their diversity of form and function. Though there have been various attempts to categorise the roles of development agencies, there is no agreed single method. Osborne (1999) describes representation, catalytic, direct delivery, facilitation and capacity-building roles. Meanwhile, promotion, technical assistance, strategy-building, diagnosis and service provision roles are described by other authors such as Suarez *et al.* (n.d.). There is considerable space to more clearly define the role of development agencies and for this to inform a categorisation of development agency types. Once a set of development agency types is established, a more coherent analysis of each is possible.

Local development agencies are considered a means of delivering national development policy in decentralised states. More specifically, a number of authors such as the World Bank, Suarez *et al.* and ILS LEDA have approached the question of the optimum spatial scale of operation of development agencies (World Bank, 2009; Suarez *et al.*, n.d.; ILS LEDA, 2009b). Territorial coverage, Suarez *et al.* argue, "has to meet requirements such as stable public-private relationships, within a geographical area equivalent to a decentralised administrative division of the state, the availability of a critical mass of resources for sustainable and competitive development, and the participation of the population in decision making" (Suarez *et al.*, n.d.). As a result, the spatial scale of development agency activities may vary, according to local conditions. Typically, though, the boundary of development agency activity extends beyond the municipality, sometimes towards the provincial or regional level (Suarez *et al.*, n.d.). In rare cases, particularly in developing nations, where population densities are low and poor infrastructure impedes effective coverage, decentralised offices are used to provide direct support (Suarez *et al.*, n.d.).

Development agency organisational forms and features are another commonly addressed theme in the milieu local development writing. Blakely and Leigh (2009) state that "the most important feature of this institutional form is that it can perform all of the tasks local government delegates to it while acting as a private body." The World Bank provides more precision, describing development agencies as: (1) having their own legal structure; (2) being functionally autonomous; (3) not-for-profit; and (4) often multi-stakeholder in their board composition. The organisational designs of development agencies are business-like in their form and should reflect the role the organisation will play in the local development system (Blakely and Leigh, 2009). The requirement for development agencies to reflect local conditions is highlighted by Blakely and Leigh (2009) who explain that "after the type of structure is selected, civic leaders can then 'tailor it' to local circumstances." They go on to suggest that development agency review and evolution is critical. "None of these forms is set in concrete", they argue. "They can evolve in time, with components being added and deleted as the need arises." Whatever the form the development agency adopts, Blakely and Leigh (2009) conclude that "the essential point is that it should have sufficient authority and resources."

As recognition of development agencies as effective mechanisms to stimulate and reinforce sustainable local development has increased, there has been a noticeable trend of the literature to provide more practical insights into the subject. This reflects the increasing appetite of local leaders wanting to establish new agencies or to maximise the performance of those already in operation.

In a 2009 paper called "How to Define the Optimum Administrative and Geographic Boundaries for a Local Economic Development Agency", ILS LEDA defines a method for "identifying the optimum administrative and geographic boundaries" for a development agency based on indicators such as number of resident, proximity, territorial specific personality, and critical mass of resources (ILS LEDA, 2009b).

The subject of development agency operational budget calculation is addressed by another ILS LEDA publication called "Method for Calculating the LEDA Budget and the Credit Fund Requirements" (ILS LEDA, 2007b). The work generates a formula which provides a way to calculate how much funding is required to finance the operational costs of a development agency based on management costs; the number of technicians; annual director costs; technician costs; office space costs; and the human resources cost of director, administrator, and secretary.

Perhaps the most comprehensive practitioners guide to development agencies is found with the 2006 IEDC text, "Training Manual for Managing Economic Development Organisations" (IEDC, 2006). A summary of the structure of this publication is found in Box 1.5.

Box 1.5. **Summary of the "Training Manual for Managing Economic Development Organisations"**

The manual (IEDC, 2006) provides insights into: (1) the different types of development agencies and their relation to other organisations; choosing the development agency that best fits the community's needs; the opportunities and challenges of a changing economy; and the skills and components necessary to manage a development agency, including:

- strategic planning,

- creating and working with a board of directors/city council,

- hiring and managing staff,

- raising finances and budgetary management,

- evaluation,

- issuing requests for proposals (RFPs) and requests for quotations (RFQs),

- selecting consultants,

- collaborating with other development agencies; and

- applying new technology.

A review of the literature shows that understanding of the development agency subject has been driven by an enhanced appreciation of the effectiveness of these organisations to deliver local development objectives. The core knowledge base is now sound, covering many the fundamental pillars of development agency operation in good detail. An enhanced appetite for learning, originating from both the developed and developing worlds, has contributed to a more recent expansion of literature on the subject (since 2000). This body of work has provided many useful, especially more practical, insights to the subject. Blakely and Leigh (2009) argue that "there is no point in re-inventing the wheel ... Adequate institutional experience is available ... for communities to select a development framework to meet their needs." However, we argue that certain gaps and uncertainties do remain and these have contributed to instances of a lack of support for development agencies, which Blakely and Leigh, themselves, admit. Still to be clarified, for instance, is the explicit added value of development agencies; specific roles of development agencies; clear development agency typologies; and the roles of development agencies in the local development system. Even with the IEDC's "Training Manual for Managing Economic Development Organisations", thus far, there has yet to have been published a piece of work which sufficiently punctures through the uncertainties to unequivocally establish development agencies as leaders in the local development system. It is the task of this OECD LEED (Local Economic and Employment Development) publication to do so.

Methodology

This book examines the roles, activities, strengths and constraints, as well as key operational metrics of development agencies within the context of their local development systems.

The core evidence base comprises of a detailed local development analysis of 16 agencies in 13 local economies world wide (Table 1.1). Signature projects of each of the agencies are also showcased to demonstrate, in a more tangible way, the impact of these organisations on the ground. Lasting six months, it draws on written materials provided by the agencies themselves, written analyses of their performance by external sources, as well as detailed interviews and regular correspondence with experienced practitioners on the ground. This evidence also builds on principles established by previous OECD LEED work on development agency reviews (OECD LEED Programme, 2009, 2006).

Table 1.1. **Development agencies profiled in this book**

Development agency	Location
Abyssinian Development Corporation	New York, United States
AucklandPlus	Auckland, New Zealand
Barcelona Activa	Barcelona, Spain
Bilbao Metropoli-30	
BILBAO Ría 2000	Bilbao, Spain
Build Toronto	Toronto, Canada
Cape Town Partnership	Cape Town, South Africa
Creative Sheffield	Sheffield, United Kingdom
HafenCity Hamburg GmbH	Hamburg, Germany
Invest Toronto	Toronto, Canada
Johannesburg Development Agency	Johannesburg, South Africa
Liverpool Vision	Liverpool, United Kingdom
Madrid Global	Madrid, Spain
Milano Metropoli	Milan, Italy
New York City Economic Development Corporation	New York, United States
Prospect Leicestershire	Leicester and Leicestershire, United Kingdom

Terminology

In this book, we cover the activities of organisations that have different names in different countries and localities. Economic development agencies, economic development companies, local development agencies, partnership boards, strategic partnerships, development boards, economic development boards, economic development corporations, local development corporations are just some of the names to describe the organisations that this book covers. For ease of reading, we use the term "development agencies" (DAs) in this book, but all of the organisations listed above are included and we describe in some detail the different functional types of bodies involved. The use of a single term in the book does not imply that the organisations studied are all the same. Rather we will take careful steps to explain how they compare and differ from one another.

DAs add significant value to the local development system by facilitating the effective planning and delivery of development objectives. They are malleable organisations which can be built to contribute effectively in the precise way in which they are needed. As a result, they are often incorporated following the sort of local development system assessment mentioned earlier. Because the nature of local development challenges and opportunities vary from place to place, and over time, DAs also vary. Their objectives, activities, structures, tools, roles and strategies all display a high level of diversity. The common denominators between these organisations are that they: (1) are guided by local governments but operate at arm's length from them; (2) adopt an effective, business-facing approach; (3) are highly collaborative; (4) set clear aims and objectives; and (5) focus on implementation at scale and pace. These features mean that DAs are emerging as powerful tools at the disposal of local leaders to plan and deliver targeted local development.

Key questions

To explore these themes, this book will answer a series of simple questions which have hitherto remained unanswered in a clear and direct way. These questions are based on the requirement to establish a base of uncomplicated understanding around how DAs operate, why they are needed and how they add value. This includes developing an appreciation for the concept of the local development system.

- Why do local governments set up DAs?

- What do DAs do?

- What tools do DAs use?

- What is the link between local government development agendas and DA diversity?

- Which tools are required for what outcomes?

- What does a successful local development system look like?

- What does an unsuccessful local development system look like?

- When is the right moment to and how to start a DA?

- How do DAs evolve?

- What can go wrong and when is the right moment to close DAs?

- How should a DA be led and governed?

To answer these questions, this book proceeds through a structure of eight chapters. It draws extensively on the evidence gathered, particularly that of the 16 DA case studies developed to support this book and the commentary of those experienced practitioners who have been intimately involved in the delivery of excellence in local development across cities world wide.

The example presented in Box 1.6 of the New York City Economic Development Corporation and the New York City Capital Resource Corporation it administers demonstrates how the DA supports the financing of business growth in New York City.

Box 1.6. **Signature project: New York City Economic Development Corporation and the New York City Capital Resource Corporation**

The New York City Capital Resource Corporation (CRC) is a local development corporation administered by New York City Economic Development Corporation (NYCEDC). NYCEDC is a large New York DA which addresses the themes of business, finance, quality of life and real estate in the city. The specific mission of the CRC is to "encourage community and economic development and job creation and retention throughout New York City by providing lower-cost financing programmes to qualified not-for-profit institutions and manufacturing, industrial, and other businesses for their eligible capital projects."

Loan Enhanced Assistance Program (LEAP)

This programme is designed to provide streamlined and cost-effective access to tax-exempt loan financing. LEAP offers the following benefits: transaction costs are reduced, in part due to non-negotiable, streamlined documents; borrowings of as low as USD 1 million may be cost effective; Bond terms are based on debt repayment capacity and useful life of the assets to be financed; the programmes' structure utilises built-in credit enhancement in the form of letters of credit through the programme's letter of credit provider, Bank of America, N.A; borrowers that do not meet the letter of credit provider's credit standards may use an underlying letter of credit to support their participation in LEAP; loans can be repaid over a 20 to 30-year period to limit annual debt service, with capital campaign receipts or other income, subject to satisfaction of tax requirements and continued satisfaction of applicable credit standards.

Nimble

The creation of Nimble, the Small Issuance Bond Program enables CRC to offer tax-exempt industrial development bonds as an alternative to traditional bank loans to finance manufacturing equipment and real estate projects. The programme is designed to provide cost-effective, tax-exempt financing for smaller projects, including equipment only needs in the USD 2 million to USD 5 million range. Key advantages include: (1) expanded eligibility for small companies in the new media, biotechnology, pharmaceutical and related areas to finance capital asset acquisition on a tax-exempt basis; (2) greater flexibility for small manufacturers to finance projects related to their core manufacturing operations, such as the construction of a loading dock, warehouse facility or parking facility on the site of their manufacturing facility; and (3) before 2011, companies will be able to finance office space that is ancillary to the manufacturing operations and is located on the same site without limitation.

Recover NYC Program

This project provides financial assistance to private-sector for-profit companies seeking lower-cost financing for shovel-ready construction projects. Available assistance is mainly in the form of access to triple tax-exempt bond financing authorised under the American Recovery and Reinvestment Act of 2009. Compared with conventional loans, advantages of triple tax-exempt bonds can include reduced interest rates, longer financing terms, lower equity contributions, and, depending on the project, the ability to obtain construction and permanent financing in a single loan.

During the 2008 financial year, CRC completed on three key projects including: Cobble Hill Health Center, Inc. (redevelopment of 46 100 square foot parcel of land, which houses a skilled nursing facility and Cobble Hill's administrative office); Natural Resources Defense Council, Inc. renovation, improvement, furnishing and equipping of an existing 53 500 rentable square foot on five floors in its national headquarters building; and Village Center for Care (64 000 square foot nursing home facility).

During the 2000 fiscal year, NYCCRC delivered USD 98.5 million in financing resulting in USD 22.6 million of private investment.

Source: New York City Economic Development Corporation (2009), "Finance and Incentives: New York City Capital Resource Corporation", *www.nycedc.com/FinancingIncentives/CRC/Pages/CRC.aspx;* New York City Capital Resource Corporation (2008), "Fiscal Year 2008 Annual Report (2008)", New York City Capital Resource Corporation.

References

AucklandPlus (2009a), "Brand Auckland", *www.brandauckland.com.*

AucklandPlus (2009b), "A Regional Brand Identity for Auckland", *www.aucklandplus.com/subsites/index.cfm?888E0A20-BCD4-1A24-9BAB-C01849ACB189.*

AucklandPlus (2009c), "Brand Auckland", *www.brandauckland.com/pdf/Brand%20Auckland%20Q%20and%20As%20v3.pdf.*

Barcelona Activa (2009), "Business Creation Presentation", *www.barcelonanetactiva.com/barcelonanetactiva/en/company-creation/entrepreneurial-initiative-center/index.jsp.*

Blakely, E. and N. Leigh (2009), *Planning Local Economic Development: Theory and Practice*, Sage Publications, Inc.

Canzanelli, G. (n.d.), "The Contribution of the Local Economic Development Agencies Promoted By United Nations To Human Development".

Canzanelli, G. and M. Del Bufalo (2005), "The U.N. Millennium Development Goals and Economic Development", *www.ilsleda.org/usr_files/papers/mdg%20and%20economi920852.pdf.*

Canzanelli, G. and L. Loffredo (2008), "Territorial Systems for Innovation: Hypothesis for the Human Development Programs", United Nations Development Programme.

EURADA (European Association of Regional Development Agencies) (1999), "Setting Up a Development Agency, EURADA.

Halkier, H., M. Danson and C. Damborg (1998), *Regional Development Agencies in Europe*, Jessica Kingsley Publishers, Ltd.

IEDC (International Economic Development Council) (2006), "Training Manual for Managing Economic Development Organizations", IEDC.

ILS LEDA (International Links and Services for Local Economic Development Agencies) Agencies (2003), "Local Economic Development Agencies, ILS LEDA.

ILS LEDA (2007a), "Glossary of Terms related to Territorial Economic Development", ILS LEDA.

ILS LEDA (2007b), "Method for Calculating the LEDA Budget and the Credit Fund Requirements", ILS LEDA.

ILS LEDA (2009a), "About ILS LEDA", ILS LEDA, *www.ilsleda.org/about/.*

ILS LEDA (2009b), "How to Define the Optimum Administrative and Geographic Boundaries for a Local Economic Development Agency", ILS LEDA.

New York City Capital Resource Corporation (2008), "Fiscal Year 2008 Annual Report (2008)", New York City Capital Resource Corporation.

New York City Economic Development Corporation (2009), "Finance and Incentives: New York City Capital Resource Corporation", *www.nycedc.com/ FinancingIncentives/CRC/Pages/CRC.aspx*.

OECD LEED Programme (2006), "Action Space - Local Development Agency Review: The case of Laganside Corporation, Belfast," *www.oecd.org/ document/60/0,3343,en_2649_34455_40417020_1_1_1_1,00.html*.

OECD LEED Programme (2009), "Promoting Entrepreneurship, Employment and Business Competitiveness: The Experience of Barcelona", *www.oecd.org/ document/32/0,3343,en_2649_34461_43504288_1_1_1_1,00.html*.

Osborne, S. (1999), "The Role of Development Agencies", The Joseph Rowntree Foundation.

Suarez, F., *et al.* (n.d), "Local Economic Development Agencies for Governance and Internationalization of Local Economies", International Cooperation Initiative ART - Articulation of Territorial and Thematic Networks of Cooperation for Human Development.

United Nations Development Program (2009), "About the Millennium Development Goals", UNDP, *www.undp.org/mdg/basics.shtml*.

World Bank (2009), "The Role of Local Economic Development Agencies (LEDA)", *http://info.worldbank.org/etools/docs/library/166856/UCMP/UCMP/7_leda.html*.

Chapter 2

The history and diversity of development agencies

This chapter uses an overview of the historical evolution of development agencies and a short profile of each of the 16 development agencies (DAs) which form the core evidence base of this book to introduce how these development organisations compare and why they vary. One consequence of the mix of different factors in the establishment of development agencies is some very basic differences in the purpose, role, structure, scale, shape, size, and resourcing of the agencies. At the same time, while many development agencies are "comprehensive", engaging directly with a wide range of interventions in labour markets, property markets, external investment markets, and with enterprise and innovation drivers, many are more focused, concentrating more on one or two of these activities. Having identified and explained this diversity, the chapter distinguishes five predominant development agency types: development and revitalisation agencies; productivity and economic growth agencies; integrated economic agencies; internationalisation agencies; and visioning and partnership agencies. It concludes that this diversity is evidence of the flexibility of DAs and the different needs of local development systems. The fact that the mandate of each can be tailoured to contribute optimum value to the local development agenda makes them a powerful potential tool for local leaders.

The original development agencies

The first development agencies (DAs) were established in Europe after the Second World War as a response to the place-based crises caused by war damage, industrial decline and dereliction. Development agencies were given the initiative to redevelop devastated districts and regions. They were initially seen as a short-term response to an emergency. In Belgium, France and Germany, DAs were set up with the intention of redeveloping damaged and derelict sites and triggering a process of economic re-stimulation. Even today, closures of major local facilities (such as a defence base, a major factory or a port) can trigger the establishment of a new DA.

While DAs have become an increasingly popular organisational vehicle for shaping and pursuing development strategies at the sub-national level, there is no precise, common understanding, or rigid formula, of what a DA is. No global census of DAs has been undertaken, but there are probably now more than 15 000 DAs world wide, with more being created every month. They vary in size, scale, and function and have arisen from different starting points. Several waves of DAs are identifiable:

- in Europe after the Second World War to aid post-war reconstruction;

- in North America in the 1960s and 1970s to address the impact of de-industrialisation in the "rust belt";

- in East Asia in the 1980s and 1990s to help plan and manage rapid urbanisation and industrialisation; and

- presently in Latin America, South Asia, Africa and Eastern Europe to promote balanced socio-economic development in the newly integrating economies.

There has also been a continued process of evolving and re-inventing DAs in places where they already exist, changing their focus of intervention and altering which tools are applied, or disbanding the old generation of DAs and creating new ones. The shift to city and regional growth policies in many OECD countries and non-OECD countries, rather than the pursuit of "old style" regional policies seeking to address only the challenges of lagging regions, has given rise to a recent expansion in the number of DAs.

Prior to the Second World War, there existed a range of developmental bodies in several parts of the world that had some of the features of DAs today. Transport development bodies and public interest agencies were widely used to promote urbanisation and industrialisation prior to the Second World War, but were not consciously part of a DA peer group, and were usually nationally sponsored projects or enjoyed a national franchise.

Waves of local economic development and waves of development agencies

We can observe several different waves of DA formation. During the 1950s and 1960s, European countries and municipalities set up several DAs, some at municipal and some at regional level. In the 1960s and 1970s, the first waves were set up in North America, many based in the de-industrialising cities of the north, designed to help redevelop old industrial sites and promote new economic futures. In the 1980s and 1990s, new DAs and corporations were set up in many parts of East Asia, in part fuelled by rising industrial and technological developments, and in part by the need to create settlements and urban growth more rapidly to accommodate growing populations.

During the 1990s, many new DAs were set up in Europe, North America, and East Asia, often with broader missions than the original DAs, designed much more to promote economic development in the context of accelerated industrial restructuring, and increasing international and national competition for investment. Also, in the 1990s, and in the past five years, DAs have been established in many developing countries, and their much wider growth is now occurring. Sometimes, DAs are being established as a "bottom-up" process to encourage local development. In other cases, the creation of DAs is being mandated by regional and national governments, or international donors. These are very different kinds of processes that produce very different DAs, as we shall see later.

In all cases, great care is needed to establish how the new DA will achieve sustainability, if efforts and investments are not to be wasted.

Development agencies as a response to local development challenges

The tendency to set up DAs as a response to a crisis still remains today, but DAs have now also been set up for other reasons in many countries. Two major variations are the extent to which DAs are established for all territories as a means of promoting competitiveness and productivity (*e.g.* now in France and the United Kingdom) or whether they are only established for certain particular places that are perceived as needing additional help (*e.g.* in Canada and Germany). In developing countries, such as Brazil and South Africa, we have bottom-up initiatives to create DAs in one or two places, and only a few national governments (*e.g.* Mexico and Bulgaria) have opted to create comprehensive coverage of certain kinds of DAs.

It is important to note that while DAs are the products of national policies in some countries, this is not universally the case. In some countries, Italy and South Africa for example, DAs are the products of local bottom-up efforts which are not subject to national co-ordination or planned programmes of national resourcing. In Canada and the United States, most DAs are fostered by local and state/provincial governments acting with private sector partners, not by federal governments. In Mexico, federal government played a key role in establishing DAs in the past. Equally, whilst DAs at the city-regional level are less common in countries that have rigid regional political geography, they are quite common in countries where there is no political regionalism. The absence of regional government also provides a spur to use DAs as an informal governance arrangement for some development activities that are best pursued at an inter-municipal level. Where regional governments exist this is seen as less necessary.

The core evidence base

To make an assessment of DA experience, we have considered the OECD LEED (Local Economic and Employment Development) experience in reviewing and discussing DAs' roles and functions, undertaken an assessment of the DA literature and examined, in detail, 16 different DAs from 13 localities across Europe, North America and the rest of the world (OECD LEED Programme, 2009, 2006).

The DAs selected reflect: (1) different economic starting points including both extensive industrial dereliction and fast-paced economic growth; (2) different constitutional settings and frameworks from eight different countries; (3) distinctive lead roles for local and national governments; and (4) distinctive spatial scales including local, city-wide, sub-regional, and wider economic spheres.

To develop the evidence base, a combination of techniques were used, including desk research and high-level onsite and offsite interviews and discussions with senior management teams and boards. The case studies were consolidated and fully verified by senior representatives from each DA.

Box 2.1 shows how Milano Metropoli fosters and promotes community–led development innovations.

Box 2.1. **Signature project: Milano Metropoli and the Expo Dei Territori: Verso Il 2015 project**

A key objective for Milano Metropoli is to foster the inclusion of a range of partners in the territorial development process. This is particularly significant in relation to the big drivers of transformation, such as global events and major infrastructure development. With this aim in mind, Milano Metropoli and the Province of Milan, with the support of *Fondazione Banca del Monte di Lombardia*, promoted a competition entitled *Expo dei Territori: Verso il 2015* or "Expo of Territories: Towards 2015". It invited local groups to develop projects to further the development agenda in Milan focussing on the themes of:

- Food and agriculture: the aim is to bring added value to every segment of the food and agriculture chain, improving competitiveness and eliminating the typical weaknesses of the various sectors and compartments involved.

- Energy and the environment: the aim is to promote eco-sustainability by reducing emissions, and by using both renewable and low-impact sources of energy.

- Culture, hospitality and tourism: the aim is to guarantee a full range of tourist services based on economically, socially and environmentally sustainable criteria.

The competition was open to: civil works projects (among which preference will be given to ideas for brownfield redevelopment and derelict building recovery schemes); operative services and instruments (whether new or linked to existing projects); large-scale territorial projects (including those that may have an impact beyond the Milanese Urban Region); local and territorial enhancement projects (especially those involved with food); and international co-operation projects (linked to the three major themes of the competition).

An Appraisal Commission made up of representatives of the Province of Milan, the new Province of Monza and Brianza, Milano Metropoli Development Agency, *Fondazione Banca del Monte di Lombardia*, Milan's Politecnico university and experts in the subjects involved in the three major themes of the competition, were in charge of judging the overall suitability of the projects.

The project has been a success in a number of ways: its extraordinary attendance, quality of the projects submitted and the energy of the participants represent an opportunity for the area as a whole. In addition, the collection of ideas and projects will become a heritage asset for the whole Milanese Urban Region.

Box 2.1. **Signature project: Milano Metropoli and the
Expo Dei Territori: Verso Il 2015 project** *(continued)*

Though the competition does not directly provide funding for the proposed projects, Milano Metropoli is currently supporting the winning proposals to enable their delivery. From the winning groups and organisations, Milano Metropoli is, for instance, fostering the creation of clusters of projects and players. These clusters facilitate synergies and opportunities which can lead to the accelerated development of these winning projects. A number of the project themes developed so far all relate to the forthcoming expo. They include:

- enhanced use of urban-rural relationship and the refurbishment of farmsteads;

- eco-museums; and

- sustainable mobility.

Another form of project support offered by Milano Metropoli relates to fundraising and consists of developing joint applications for public funding (regionally or nationally). At the same time, Milano Metropoli is trying to match the expo masterplan development and the winning projects in order to maximise their chances of implementation. The projects chosen will also visibility posted on the Province of Milan and Milano Metropoli Development Agency websites and within the channels used by the Province of Milan to promote Expo 2015 nationally and internationally.

Source: Milano Metropoli (2009a), "Expo dei Territori: Verso il 2015": extract of the competition, *www.milanomet.it/en/ultime/november-2008.html*; Sala, G. (2009), Written and telephone communication and interviews.

An introduction to the core evidence base of 16 development agencies

Each of our 16 main DA case studies is introduced in the section that follows. They are presented alphabetically.

Abyssinian Development Corporation (New York, United States)

Organisation type

The Abyssinian Development Corporation (ADC) is a locally based, not-for-profit community development corporation dedicated to building the human, social and physical capital of the area of Harlem in New York. ADC offers services to the community through five community development initiatives: (1) affordable housing development; (2) social services; (3) economic revitalisation; (4) education and youth development; and (5) civic engagement.

Mission statement

The organisation's mission is to increase the availability of quality housing to people of diverse incomes; enhance the delivery of social services, particularly to the homeless, elderly, families and children; foster economic revitalisation; enhance educational and developmental opportunities for young people; and build community capacity through civic engagement (ADC, 2009).

The Harlem context

During the late 1980s, Harlem was suffering from unemployment, high levels of violence, AIDS and homelessness. A lack of investment by banks was compounding the problem as building owners who sought to make repairs had difficulty in getting loans. Indeed, between the 1960s and the 1990s, few new commercial or residential buildings were built.

Created by the Abyssinian Baptist Church in 1986, the ADC was a response to the difficulties faced in Harlem. The creation of the organisation was supported principally by encouragement from Reverend Dr. Calvin Butts, III as a way for the congregation to rebuild its community.

What does the Abyssinian Development Corporation do?

ADC runs a number of programmes, all of which aim to stimulate community development in the Harlem area. In particular, it works in the fields of affordable housing development, family services, economic revitalisation, education and youth and civic engagement.

Keynote project or programme: Harlem school and education success

In August 2009, the Abyssinian Development Corporation was chosen as one of four grantees to implement the Deutsche Bank Americas Foundation (DBAF) College Ready Communities initiative for middle and high schools. The DBAF matched funds for a Bill and Melinda Gates Foundation grant they received. ADC was the only public middle school-sponsor selected; the others were from public high schools. This two-year pilot programme will provide the critical resources necessary to achieve high-quality academic support for 423 young Harlem public school students in grades six to eight.

The College Ready Communities initiative is aimed at increasing positive educational outcomes for public school students by reaching beyond classroom walls. The three core objectives for the initiative are to increase: (1) attendance and other measures of improvement in student engagement and school culture; (2) academic performance; and (3) matriculation rates to four-year colleges or college preparatory high schools.

AucklandPlus (Auckland, New Zealand)

Organisation type

AucklandPlus is the Auckland region's economic DA, which specialises in investment promotion and facilitation, including brand building and major project development. AucklandPlus works collaboratively with local, regional and national organisations and business leaders to further develop Auckland's competitiveness. The aim is to increase overall living standards and opportunities, as well as economic performance.

Mission statement

"To be the lead regional agency for economic transformation, and to position Auckland as an international city/region" (AucklandPlus, 2008).

The Auckland Region context

In an international context, the Auckland region is primarily a gateway to New Zealand in terms of trade, tourism, migration and communications. It is by far the largest logistics node for both imports and exports by both air and sea. However, in his presentation at the 2005 "Better by Design" Conference, economic commentator Rod Oram argued that:

> *New Zealand earns its living in a world driven by increasing complexity, homogeneity, rapid change, growth, low cost, high quality, large volumes … yet we are a nation short of human and financial capital with some inherent disadvantages of distance and smallness … To compete in this ever more demanding world, we need to pioneer new business models and skills to capitalise on New Zealand's unique opportunities in global markets. (Oram, 2005)*

What does AucklandPlus do?

AucklandPlus was inaugurated as a business unit of the Auckland Regional Council in 2005. The organisation was built in large part to ensure the effective delivery of the 2002 Auckland Regional Economic Development Strategy (AREDS). The AREDS outlines a vision for the Auckland region to be "an internationally competitive, inclusive and dynamic economy; a great place to live and conduct business; and a place buzzing with innovation, where skilled people work in world-class enterprises" (Auckland Regional Council, 2009).

Its mandate delegates two main tasks to AucklandPlus:

- Inward investment promotion: identifying and promoting the competitive advantage of the Auckland Region (business and lifestyle), establishing the Auckland brand, engagement with businesses domestically and internationally and capitalising on opportunities as a result of emerging trends.

- Facilitating inward investment: brokering between key businesses, their leaders and the relevant networks, bodies and individuals in Auckland to ensure investment in secured and retained. AucklandPlus also advises on market opportunities and where to find specific expertise and sources of support and finance.

As well as providing support to a number of specific business sectors (biotechnology, creative industries, food and beverage, information and communications technology, specialised manufacturing such as marine), AucklandPlus also facilitates large, multi-agency, cross-boundary/council regional economic development projects such as the Metro Project Action Plan (Rogers, 2009).

Keynote project or programme: Brand Auckland

Brand Auckland was launched by AucklandPlus in September 2008 in response to recommendations in the Auckland Regional Economic Development Strategy and as one of the actions of the Metro Project, which itself was launched in 2006. In the process of the development of the Brand Auckland proposition, thousands of stakeholders were interviewed, including every mayor in the region, the Government, the Leader of the Opposition, a former Governor-General, community and business leaders, members of the public and respondents from as far away as London, Moscow and Shanghai.

The brand has met with considerable success given its relative infancy. It has achieved backing at national level through New Zealand Trade and Enterprise, the Ministry of Economic Development and Tourism New Zealand. Tourism New Zealand Chief Executive, George Hickton, commented that, "The work being done by Brand Auckland will create more awareness of the Auckland region and add real value to the country's overall marketing efforts." AucklandPlus has co-ordinated the development of the brand in line with its "regional promotion" activity area. This project contributes to promoting the region and to increasing the pace and scale of development in Auckland and aggregates otherwise separate efforts.

Barcelona Activa (Barcelona, Spain)

Organisation type

Created in 1986, Barcelona Activa is a municipal limited company: a private company, funded and 100% owned by Barcelona City Council (Barcelona Activa, 2009).

Mission statement

The mission of Barcelona Activa is to "transform Barcelona in terms of entrepreneurship, business growth, innovation, professional opportunities, human capital development and quality employment."

The Barcelona context

Barcelona offers a case study of self-determined economic transformation in a city. Set up in 1986, Barcelona Activa was created against the background of a challenging socio-economic climate. Barcelona's unemployment rate was over 20%, the city was suffering post-industrial decline, economic restructuring and the closure of a number of large factories, and there was a lack of entrepreneurial initiative. Entrepreneurship was seen as a key contributor to social cohesion and inclusion and business creation was seen as a means of job creation. Innovation was seen as important due to its ability to contribute to the consolidation of an industrial framework which can adapt and evolve with the changing economic paradigm.

Much is known about how Barcelona's mounting of the Olympic Games in 1992, and the major urban and cultural projects it has undertaken. Much less is known about the major infrastructure investments and the transition to a knowledge-led entrepreneurial economy which has been fostered by Barcelona Activa.

What does Barcelona Activa do?

Initially conceived as a business incubator with 14 projects installed, Barcelona Activa is now a driving force behind entrepreneurial activity, innovation, professional and career development and the creation of employment within Barcelona. A model of successful public-private partnership, each year Barcelona Activa coaches more than 1 400 business projects towards business creation, and more than 350 agencies are helped in the fields of business consolidation and growth (Molero, 2009).

With the 2004-07 Action Plan now completed, Barcelona Activa is today embarking on the 2008-11 period under four main services and two transversal axes:

- business creation and entrepreneurship culture,

- innovative business survival and growth,

- human capital development and new employment opportunities, and

- access to, and improvement of, employment.

The two cross-cutting activities are: (1) innovation promotion; and (2) digital professionalisation and training (OECD LEED Programme, 2009).

Keynote project or programme: the Glòries Entrepreneurship Centre

Established in 1987, the Glòries Entrepreneurship Centre acts as a hub for entrepreneurs in Barcelona and encourages all new fledgling businesses to contact the centre and make use of its facilities. It provides professional services for potential entrepreneurs in order to promote the creation of new businesses. It also seeks to encourage an entrepreneurial culture by coaching entrepreneurs and assisting them in taking the step from the business idea to its creation. One of the key points is its special methodology, which is called the "blended model." It involves the use of cutting-edge spaces to increase accessibility to the full range of activities which are devoted to entrepreneurs. In 2008, Barcelona Activa's entrepreneurship support activities achieved the following results:

- 19 387 participants in business-creation activities;

- 1 379 business projects coached;

- 60% business-creation rate which is more than 700 companies created;

- Nearly two employees per created company which is 1 500 employment opportunities created;

- 116 innovative start-ups based in the Incubator and Technology Park;

- 711 companies members of Xarxactiva Business co-operation network; and

- 350 participant companies in business growth programmes.

Bilbao Metropoli-30 and BILBAO Ría 2000 (Bilbao, Spain)

Organisation type

The Association for the Revitalisation of Metropolitan Bilbao – "Bilbao Metropoli-30" – was established in 1991. It is primarily concerned with strategic planning, research and promotion and is involved in those projects which aim to encourage the recuperation and revitalisation of Metropolitan Bilbao. The Association was recognised as a "Public Utility Entity" by the Basque Government in June 1992. Both public and private bodies who work within Metropolitan Bilbao can become members of the project as founding, full or associate members. In essence, Bilbao Metropoli-30 is an "umbrella organisation" which consolidates and co-ordinates the actions of a disparate range of bodies which operate across the public and private realms and across broad spatial scales.

Mission statement

Bilbao Metropoli-30's mission statement is "to lead the vision of the future through the implementation of the revitalisation process" (Bilbao Metropoli-30, 2009).

Organisation type

BILBAO-Ría 2000 is a non-profit-making inter-institutional company which is responsible for large, urban regeneration initiatives in the Bilbao area, playing a major role in facilitating land consolidation and development. Its shares are held in equal proportions by the central state administration via the *Ministerio de Fomento* (Ministry of Public Works) and a number of dependent companies (SEPES, a public property company; the Bilbao Port Authority; and the Renfe and FEVE railway organisations) and by the Basque administrations (Basque Government, the *Diputación Foral of Bizkaia* [Regional County Council], and the City Councils of Bilbao and Barakaldo) (BILBAO-Ria 2000, 2009a).

Mission statement

BILBAO-Ría 2000's mission is to "recover degraded land or industrial areas in decline in metropolitan Bilbao, thus contributing to balanced development and improvement of urban cohesion" (BILBAO Ría 2000, 2009b).

The Bilbao context

During the industrial era, Bilbao's double blessing of a seaport and vast mineral wealth endowed the city with prosperity. The river's left bank held Spain's largest iron and steel industries and Bilbao's output of iron ore went from 55 000 tonnes in 1861 to 6 496 000 in 1898. Great Britain, the world's imperial power, imported two-thirds of her iron ore from Bilbao. It was the shipping industry, however, that formed the backbone of Bilbao (Centre of Basque Studies, 1998).

Bilbao's success continued until the 1970s, a time when it was the wealthiest region of Spain. All this changed, however, in the late 1980s when its shipyard closed because of low-wage competition from Eastern Europe and Asia. A deep economic crisis developed. There were areas with 35% unemployment and outmigration of 75 000 inhabitants (Harvard Design School, 2009). The urban environment fell into deep decay with 52 industrial ruins that comprised 48 hectares of land, abandoned urban neighbourhoods, and entire valleys and river banks devastated by pollution (Centre of Basque Studies, 1998).

Throughout the 1980s there was a significant effort at renovation and revitalisation, with efforts to build new infrastructure, highways and bridges in particular. By the end of the 1980s, however, it was recognised by Basque officials that what was needed was a new beginning – a new image, a new post-industrial economic base – in short, an entire reinvention of an ancient, declining city.

The solution was an ambitious USD 1.5 billion urban renewal plan. It was prepared by Bilbao Metropoli-30. This organisation formed in 1989 as a public and private institution specifically to formulate the plan. It brought together the town councils and the Provincial Council of Bizkaia, the Basque Government, as well as the major firms in the city (Bilbao City Council, 2009).

The urban regeneration projects are widely seen as a success, because of the visible and tangible impacts they have had on the urban landscape of Bilbao. The perception of Bilbao changed into a modern, cultural city and the whole population benefited from new parks, public places and new roads.

What does Bilbao Metropoli-30 do?

The fundamental role of Bilbao Metropoli-30 is driving forward the implementation of the Strategic Plan for the Revitalisation of Metropolitan Bilbao, which was drawn up in 1992, and the subsequent versions of the document. The original plan was prepared by Bilbao Metropoli-30 in collaboration with more than 300 experts, most of whom were representatives from institutions and companies associated with Bilbao Metropoli-30. Since the conception of the Revitalisation Plan, Bilbao Metropoli-30 has focused its activities on furthering the launch of the revitalisation process through public-private partnerships. In 1999, the Association's efforts were consolidated in the project "Bilbao 2010: Strategic Reflection". Subsequently, and with a view to channelling the strategic reflections, the organisation has focused on projects that will enable Bilbao to make the most of the change already seen, projecting the metropolis as an international world-class city in the knowledge society. On 4 April 2001, the Association presented the strategic plan called "Bilbao 2010: The Strategy".

Bilbao Metropoli-30 also undertakes actions derived from the Strategic Plan with which it is entrusted. In particular, this includes those projects which aim to improve the external and internal image of Metropolitan Bilbao. The Association undertakes studies and research projects related to Metropolitan Bilbao, as well as studies of other cities which can provide useful examples for Bilbao. Another key area of activity is fostering public-private sector co-operation in the hope of finding joint solutions to problems which affect Metropolitan Bilbao.

Keynote project or programme: long-term strategic planning

"From Infrastructures to Values" describes the evolutionary path which Bilbao Metropoli-30 has strategically prescribed for the metropolitan area of Bilbao. Traditionally, interventions focused primarily on the implementation of vast, infrastructural projects. However, as the agency explains, "Cities nowadays no longer compete in infrastructural terms; this means that at international level, we take for granted that cities count on a minimum infrastructural base to be attractive for visitors, inhabitants and investments. What really makes a city competitive and attractive in the 21st century is people and their values." Subsequently, by the end of the 1990s, the organisation began to focus intently on a process of visioning for the city. By creating a coherent vision for Bilbao, Bilbao Metropoli-30 aims to create a unique identity for Bilbao which will serve to attract visitors and businesses alike.

What does BILBAO-Ría 2000 do?

The organisation undertakes complex urban regeneration interventions, usually involving several administrations or agencies (municipalities, local, regional and state administrations and railway or infrastructure companies for instance). As a publicly backed organisation, it is uniquely placed to deliver such strategic interventions – interventions the private sector finds too costly and time-consuming. Its mission is to recover degraded land or industrial areas in decline in metropolitan Bilbao, thus contributing to balanced development and the improvement of urban cohesion. To fulfil this objective, BILBAO-Ría 2000 co-ordinates and executes projects in relation to town planning, transportation and the environment. BILBAO-Ría 2000 does not have planning powers, but the planning authorities (municipalities and *diputacion*) are shareholders in the company and they have the ability to "re-classify" or re-zone land to promote innovative, mixed-use regeneration projects (Centre for Cities, 2005).

Keynote project or programme: the regeneration of Abandoibarra, the Guggenheim district

Abandoibarra and the Guggenheim District is the most emblematic of all the projects carried out by BILBAO-Ría 2000 in its regeneration of metropolitan Bilbao. This area is a waterfront site at the heart of the city, covers 348 500 square metres, and includes the area between the Guggenheim Museum and the Euskalduna Palace. Prior to BILBAO-Ría 2000's intervention, the area was home to harbour facilities, a railway station for containers and a shipyard. The general public was denied access to it for many years. When the *La Ribera* promenade was opened over the *Evaristo Churruca* quays, the people of Bilbao and visitors to the city were able to walk around this area for the first time. The river is no longer a barrier as one of the main objectives is to define the Nervion River as the backbone of the entire city

Build Toronto and Invest Toronto (Toronto, Canada)

Organisation type

In 2008, Toronto Mayor David Miller initiated reviews of both the city's economic development efforts and its use of its own asset base to leverage investment and maintain fiscal health and a strong balance sheet. Through the Agenda for Prosperity, the city has embarked upon a programme to become a successful global player, and some of the city's most recent policies articulate this as a vision for Toronto to become a global business city, a hub of environmental innovation, a beacon of diversity and cohesion, and a centre for global education and training. Although by no means a large city region by international standards, Toronto is becoming a leader in the sectors that are increasingly coming to define the 21st century – sustainability, medical innovation, financial services and education.

The Agenda for Prosperity has a four-pillar approach: (1) Proactive Toronto – Business Climate; (2) Global Toronto – Internationalisation; (3) Creative Toronto – Productivity and Growth; (4) One Toronto – Economic Opportunity and Inclusion.

Following a review of the city's development efforts and agencies, and building upon the Agenda for Prosperity and the Fiscal Blue Print, the City of Toronto has decided to create two new DAs.

- Build Toronto: a predominantly inward-facing organisation with responsibility for property development, institutional investment, urban and asset management, brownfield redevelopment, job creation, and sustainable development.

- Invest Toronto: a predominantly outward-facing organisation with the responsibility for achieving a better presence and market share for Toronto in international markets and contested investments (Invest Toronto, 2009a).

Mission statement

According to the Invest Toronto brochure, the organisation will "engage the private sector in promoting Toronto as a destination for business opportunities, organising strategic trade missions, and co-ordinating economic development initiatives with governments and business" (Invest Toronto, 2009b).

The Toronto context

Faced with the challenges of declining employment in manufacturing in the past 20 years, the city of Toronto has successfully diversified its economy and now exhibits real strengths in the knowledge and creative sectors. It also offers areas of global leadership, including in the green economy, a large and deep pool of talented workers, and is extremely socially diverse, nourished by a high quality of life.

Despite its dynamic economy and evident ambition, the city is suffering from investment and infrastructure deficit, affecting everything from housing to public transport to hospitals, and this has led to concern about the sustainability of economic and population growth. At the same time, despite success in attracting and fostering knowledge and creative sectors, there is growing awareness that the city's economic development efforts do not yet position it effectively to make the most of global opportunities or to leverage its own assets to attract investment.

What will Build Toronto do?

There was no definitive start-up strategy for Build Toronto. With the appointment of the new Chief Executive, Lorne Braithwaite, a strategy to establish Build Toronto as a world-class DA is underway.

It is intended that Build Toronto will contribute to the economic development system in Toronto by increasing the value of lands and implementing projects with specific economic development objectives, including job creation. Build Toronto will work to deliver six key objectives: (1) build value in our lands; (2) revenue generation and prudent financial management; (3) focus on development – joint venture, value-added sale, sole build out; (4) leverage development expertise; (5) return a 'dividend' to the city; and (6) over time, build an organisation that is action oriented, understands the development process and is respected by stakeholders (Braithwaite, 2009; Build Toronto, 2009).

Keynote project or programme: investing in public land

The "Blue Print for Fiscal Stability and Economic Prosperity" is a document which aims to enhance Toronto's competitiveness. The creation and early mandate of Build Toronto will deliver many of the recommendations established in the Blue Print. The process behind the creation of the Blue Print itself began in October 2007 when the Mayor of Toronto formed a City of Toronto Independent Fiscal Review Panel. This panel was asked to report back by February 2008 with: (1) "a high-level, impartial and objective assessment of the City of Toronto's relative competitiveness, financial position, revenue opportunities and savings potential in the near to medium term"; and (2) "a series of comments and recommendations with a view towards helping enable the City to improve its efficiency, effectiveness, economic prosperity, liveability and create opportunity for all." The document is rooted in an evidence base which comprises a thorough literature review and over 200 meetings with City personnel, provincial officials, academics, experts, mayors of other municipalities, as well as other key stakeholders.

What will Invest Toronto do?

Through the start-up process, a list of potential specific roles was identified by the interim board and key stakeholders. They included: (1) investment promotion; (2) investment facilitation; (3) investment retention; (4) city marketing and branding; (5) city intelligence gathering; and (6) building a coherent investment system.

Though the start-up strategy identified a number of issues for Invest Toronto to consider, the precise mandate is to be confirmed shortly (Invest Toronto, 2009c).

Keynote project or programme: Agenda for Prosperity

Invest Toronto is the city's agency for the promotion of the Toronto offer world wide. One of its key guiding documents is the "Agenda for Prosperity". This book represents an attempt "to bring together everyone who can and wants to contribute to Toronto's long-term prosperity around a single, simple agreement on an achievable vision – a vision to which we can all aspire and align our plans and actions." The requirement for Toronto to better tell its story both domestically and abroad, is a constant feature of the Agenda for Prosperity. For instance, the agenda clearly sets out the pillars which support Toronto's unique offer. It describes Toronto as a "global business city'; an "inspiring city"; a "location for new and distinctive cultural products"; a "centre for global education and training"; a "base for open institutions"; a "hub of environmental innovation"; and a "beacon of diversity and cohesion".

Cape Town Partnership (Cape Town, South Africa)

Organisation type

The Cape Town Partnership (CTP) was established in July 1999 by the City of Cape Town and key private sector partners to manage, promote and develop the Cape Town Central City. The Partnership's vision is of an "inclusive, productive and diverse city centre that retains its historic character and reflects a common identity for all the people of Cape Town." A city centre management vehicle, the Central City Improvement District (CCID), was launched by the Partnership in November 2000, as an integrated operation within the CTP, but with a separate board and financing mechanism (Cape Town Partnership, 2006).

The Partnership's bifurcated model has two distinctive, but overlapping operations:

- the CTP itself – a strategic public-private partnership for the long-term development of the Central City; and

- the CCID– a central city urban management organisation delivering services to improve the attractiveness, performance, safety and the sanitation of Cape Town's Central City.

These two entities share a common corporate resource base and institutional arrangements while reporting to distinct boards.

Mission statement

"The Cape Town Partnership strives to develop, manage and promote the Cape Town Central City as a place for all and a leading centre for commercial, retail, residential, cultural, tourism, education, entertainment and leisure activities" (Cape Town Partnership, 2006).

What does the Cape Town Partnership do?

The CTP does not duplicate or replace the role of the public sector, particularly in its statutory and regulatory roles, but seeks to add value to the public services and planning processes. In conjunction with a wide range of stakeholders, the Partnership acts as an initiator, facilitator, co-ordinator and manager of projects. The CTP also manages the CCID, a non-profit organisation that provides complementary services and programmes that make the Central City a cleaner, safer, and more attractive place – conducive for development, investment and growth (Cape Town Partnership, 2008).

The four core CCID functions are: (1) security; (2) urban management and cleansing; (3) social development and job creation; and (4) local marketing and communications (CCID, 2007; Cape Town Partnership, 2009).

Keynote project or programme: the City Centre Development Strategy

The future of the Central City of Cape Town, for the next decade, is being proactively charted through the Central City Development Strategy (CCDS). The CCDS is a joint venture between the City of Cape Town and the Cape Town Partnership, which aims to establish a shared vision for the future of the central city area and a preferred development path and implementation plan. It was laid out in October 2008 and is based on the vision that, "In the next ten years, the Cape Town Central City will grow and greatly enhance its reputation as a dynamic business and people centre." With the focus of this end in mind, the document focuses on five outcomes:

- Cape Town's premier business location, recognised globally,
- a high-quality, sustainable, urban environment,
- a popular destination for Capetonians and visitors,
- a leading centre for knowledge, innovation, creativity and culture, in Africa and the South, and
- a place that embodies the heart and soul of Cape Town.

Creative Sheffield (Sheffield, United Kingdom)

Organisation type

Creative Sheffield was the first of the United Kingdom's new local economic development delivery vehicles – the city development companies and economic development companies (CDCs/EDCs) – to be set up. It was officially formed on 1 April 2007 and was designed to "substantially enhance Sheffield's capacity to develop and deliver economic strategy" (Kerslake and Taylor, 2004). It is a company limited by guarantee, with a high-level board composed of a range of private and public sector representatives, and is owned by Sheffield City Council and the regional DA, Yorkshire Forward. Creative Sheffield has consolidated the city's previously disparate set of development bodies by incorporating "Sheffield One", the investment agency "Sheffield First For Investment" and the "Knowledge Starts in South Yorkshire" project.

Mission statement

Creative Sheffield is tasked with spearheading Sheffield's economic transformation through leading the development and implementation of the Economic Masterplan. Sheffield's Economic Masterplan (2008) provides the strategic framework to guide economic and physical development and investment across the whole city over the next 10-15 years.

The Sheffield context

Sheffield is the fourth largest city in England, with 530 000 inhabitants, while the city region has a population of 1.75 million. Located on the confluence of the River Don and the River Sheaf, the city includes part of the Peak District National Park to the west. As a city region, Sheffield is a hybrid of urban and rural locations, with strong economic potential and distinctive cultural and environmental assets. The city grew rapidly in the 1800s with the expansion of the metal-working industry and the mass production of steel. By the 20th century, the metal industry was flourishing and employed 75 000 by 1911.

The 1973 global oil crisis, however, and the increasing globalisation of trade and manufacturing dealt a major blow to Sheffield's manufacturing base. The city's industrial heartland was unable to adapt sufficiently to market changes. The steel industry in the United Kingdom was privatised and saw significant job losses as the new agencies contracted in an effort to remain globally competitive. The decline in the economy was inevitably accompanied by concomitant social problems. The city witnessed some depopulation and outward migration, though not as much as many other northern UK cities.

Urban regeneration of Sheffield began to occur in the late 1980s under various interventions. Among other interventions, success was achieved through the actions of Sheffield's Development Corporation and Sheffield First Partnership. The latter represented a model adopted by many other cities and by the New Labour Government as best practice.

The widespread perception is that, despite significant challenges, not least the need to attract more high quality agencies, the city is today well positioned to punch above its weight economically. Over the next decade, there is recognition that the city region must increase the proportion of high value-added services in the economy, particularly in the manufacturing sector, where there is a competitive advantage through knowledge and innovation.

In this vein, Creative Sheffield was created as the United Kingdom's first CDC (a new style of DA), to drive forward Sheffield's economic development.

What does Creative Sheffield do?

Creative Sheffield's core activities are to: (1) act as the lead marketing agency for Sheffield and to achieve a positive shift in perceptions of the city's image and reputation;

(2) build on the success of Sheffield First for Investment in the attraction of quality inward investment into the city; (3) follow on from the achievement of Sheffield One in developing the city's physical infrastructure to internationally competitive standards; and (4) develop initiatives that will promote the growth of the city's scientific, creative and cultural knowledge base (Creative Sheffield, 2009a).

Creative Sheffield was also initially tasked with the preparation and management of the city's 2008 Economic Masterplan which provides the framework for the economic and physical development of Sheffield over the next 10-15 years. The Masterplan focuses on enhancing inward investment, developing the city's physical infrastructure, accelerating the growth of knowledge-based businesses and undertaking strategic city marketing.

Compared with the previous disparate model, Creative Sheffield provides synergy by bringing together the various areas of economic development: marketing, regeneration, investment promotion and innovation. For example, the Sheffield Digital Campus began an "E-Campus", one of the original seven projects in the Sheffield One City Centre Master Plan (2001), and was brought forward by Sheffield One, in partnership with Sheffield City Council and Yorkshire Forward, and developed into a physical regeneration project, although its *raison d'être* was to attract and grow the creative industries of the future.

Through Creative Sheffield, the Sheffield Digital Campus has had a natural evolution from physical development through being an inward investment offer, marketing case study and good news story, to an innovation asset at the core of the Digital Region project.

Similar synergies in Creative Sheffield occur from having the innovation and investment teams working together and pitching to the same markets. In the same way, the marketing of Sheffield is directly linked to the target markets for foreign direct investment and the other growth regions of the United Kingdom (Roberts, 2009).

Keynote project or programme: the Sheffield Economic Masterplan.

When Creative Sheffield was launched in 2007, its primary task was to lead the development of the Economic Masterplan. Having made progress over the previous decade, particularly in the city centre, it was clearly recognised that Sheffield needed its underlying economic performance to improve if it were to remain competitive in the 21st century. The Economic Masterplan identified a GBP 1 billion gap in gross value added between what the city actually produced and what it could produce if it operated at the same level as the national average. Closing the gap became the primary target of the city's economic strategy, which itself translated into three main strands of objectives:

- creating an additional 30 000 jobs, over and above the city's normal trajectory;

- bringing at least 16 000 people into the workforce within Sheffield; and

- shifting the economy to a significantly higher level of value-added production and skill levels.

HafenCity Hamburg GmbH (Hamburg, Germany)

Organisation type

The area known as "HafenCity" is Europe's largest inner city urban development zone (HafenCity Hamburg GmbH, 2009a). In 1998, the Free and Hanseatic City of Hamburg entrusted HafenCity Hamburg GmbH (formerly GHS *Gesellschaft für Hafen- und Standortentwicklung mbH*) with the development of HafenCity. Hamburg is one of very few German cities undertaking major urban redevelopment. Unlike many city DAs, who act at the city-wide or metropolitan scale, HafenCity Hamburg GmbH focuses only on a highly specific district – the old port area. HafenCity Hamburg GmbH has been tasked with leading the redevelopment through buying back land and buildings in the project area which are not owned by public authorities and relocating companies from the area to other areas in the city, as well as being responsible for developing the necessary physical infrastructure and required amenities so that new spaces (office, residential, shopping, restaurants, culture and leisure) are developed. It oversees the entire development of the area (Bruns-Berentelg, 2009).

Mission statement

"HafenCity is underlining Hamburg's heritage as a maritime city whilst simultaneously reinterpreting it for the present day and in so doing creating a model for the development of European cities in the 21st century" (HafenCity Hamburg GmbH, 2008). It is the task of HafenCity Hamburg GmbH to deliver this vision.

The Hamburg context

For more than 100 years, Hamburg has been one of the world's ten most important port cities. Following the destruction of approximately 70% of warehouses and 90% of quayside storage facilities in World War II, Hamburg's port facilities underwent significant restructuring. By 1956, the harbour had been rebuilt and modernised, while the arrival of containerised shipping in the late 1960s reshaped the harbour area. As a result of these fundamental changes in the nature of harbour activities, the trans-shipment business moved to more modern facilities south of the River Elbe. While the traditional wharves and quays next to the city centre continued to play host to traditional shipping, it became increasingly clear that they were better suited to modern goods storage. This allowed the City of Hamburg to recover this area for the city centre during the mid-1990s without adversely affecting the port's economic interests (HafenCity Hamburg GmbH, 2009b). On 7 May 1997, the then First Mayor of the Free and Hanseatic City of Hamburg, Dr. Henning Voscherau, presented the HafenCity vision to the public.

What does HafenCity Hamburg GmbH do?

HafenCity Hamburg GmbH is engaged in an integrated process of intensive urban restructuring. It is not only trying to redevelop disused land and buildings, but is trying to create a wholly new economic rationale, housing, leisure and amenities. Simultaneously, the agency is trying to fully integrate this development with the city as a whole. One of the key aims of the work is to create a new distinctive destination. This is to be achieved through a conscious effort to preserve the integration of water and urban land use by preserving the old port structures (*e.g.* harbour basins, quay walls, bridges, etc.) and the neighbouring *Speicherstadt* warehouse district. Six historic buildings in HafenCity will also be preserved and renovated, helping to create a distinct location.

At its core, HafenCity Hamburg GmbH carries out two distinct, but highly inter-related functions. At one level, it is involved in very high-level and complex project management; this involves managing the project of urban restructuring through planning, implementation, development management and promotion, all of which aim to generate real and lasting physical, economic and social change in the area. At the same time, the agency is also concerned with urban management in terms of managing the performance of the district, *e.g.* making the public realm attractive, encouraging people to come to the area and building up new social networks and formal and informal institutions.

More specifically, HafenCity Hamburg GmbH has the following areas of responsibility: marketing and selling municipally-owned real estate in HafenCity (approximately 98% of the total area to be developed); attracting investors and buyers, providing all necessary assistance; developing the location for residential use, service industries and leisure amenities; co-ordinating all planning and construction projects; planning and implementing land development; managing and administering funds (Special Fund "City and Port") used for the development of HafenCity; co-operating with the relevant Hamburg authorities and directly/indirectly with parliamentary committees; location marketing, public relations and citizen involvement (Bruns-Berentelg, 2009).

However, HafenCity Hamburg GmbH offers no financial incentives or tax breaks for developing within the area (Scottish Parliament, 2005). This is in stark contrast to the role of many of the other agencies covered in this book.

Keynote project or programme: leveraging private investment

For the successful delivery of the HafenCity project, Europe's largest inner-city redevelopment zone, the leveraging of private sector investment was essential. It is predicted by HafenCity Hamburg GmbH, the project's DA, that on the project's completion in 2025 between EUR 5 billion and EUR 5.5 billion of private investment will have been secured (78% of the total investment into the project). To facilitate this investment in the early phase of the HafenCity development process, HafenCity Hamburg GmbH was:

- available as an efficient, one-stop-shop agency in charge of the whole development both spatially and thematically;

- able to create and communicate a broad but strong image and vision of what HafenCity was about;

- able to set up a risk-reducing and competition-enhancing framework for private investment;

- able to communicate and co-operate effectively with local and regional developers/investors to create genuine momentum behind the idea of HafenCity as a real investment opportunity; and

- able to offer small individual plots for development to allow a wide range of small, medium and large-sized investors to be targeted.

In terms of investment governance, private investment has been leveraged in a risk-aware manner. Because of this, though the financial crisis has slowed the rate of investment, the project's business model remains robust. The HafenCity investment strategy is sustainable in that it was developed to operate successfully at all parts of the business cycle. It contains the following key features: (1) the project is financed and supported by a diverse range of partners; (2) the development is divided into small segments which can be developed sequentially when finance is available; and the development is mixed use. As a result, HafenCity was as well prepared for a market downturn as one can be for such a situation, much more so than many large-scale international projects, some of which have been seriously affected.

Johannesburg Development Agency (Johannesburg, South Africa)

Organisation type

The Johannesburg Development Agency (JDA) is a wholly-owned agency of the City of Johannesburg Metropolitan Municipality (CoJ). The JDA stimulates and supports area-based economic regeneration and development initiatives throughout the Johannesburg metropolitan area.

Mission statement

"The JDA is an agency of the City of Johannesburg, which stimulates and supports area-based development initiatives throughout the Johannesburg metropolitan area in support of the City's Growth and Development Strategy. As development manager of these initiatives, JDA co-ordinates and manages capital investment and other programmes involving both public and private sector stakeholders" (JDA, 2009a).

The Johannesburg context

Following the liberation elections of 1994 and a new democratic regime, local governments in South Africa strived for economic development, combined with social and spatial integration, and began to take on more responsibility for local development. Following the visit of an international delegation of local development experts in 1999, and in response to ongoing acute challenges in the Inner City of Johannesburg towards the late 1990s, it was decided that a DA was needed in the city to plan and deliver effective local economic development and urban regeneration in Johannesburg.

What does the Johannesburg Development Agency do?

The JDA approaches development through capital investment. It works on the assumption that well-considered investments in public infrastructure will not only provide a direct service, but will also catalyse private investment in the built environment.

The 2006 Growth and Development Strategy (GDS) is "a long-term plan to ensure sustainable delivery of services, deal with social and economic development, involve residents in local government and promote a safe and healthy environment" (JDA, 2009b). The GDS is the City's long-term strategic blueprint for development. It sets down the visioning statement, charts the long-term perspective and maps the development path for achieving the long-term goals. As the development manager for the City's GDS, the JDA's current focus areas include:

- inner city regeneration,
- township and marginalised area development,

- transport systems (BRT) and facilities (transport hubs), and
- World Cup 2010 requirements.

Beyond construction though, the JDA works in a number of other related areas. They include:

- inner city investor liaison and mobilisation;
- joint work on inner city co-ordination and charter;
- city and central business district (CBD) marketing;
- strategic planning projects;
- managing Constitution Hill, as well as overseeing the management and development of Newtown with the Johannesburg Property Company (JPC);
- influencing owners of strategic buildings; and
- land assembly within a precinct upgrade such, as the Bertrams housing project.

In future, the JDA will continue to adjust its role, functions and finance mechanisms to meet the needs of its clients and operating environment (JDA, 2009a).

Keynote project or programme: the Rea Vaya Bus Rapid Transit

In response to the limited provision of high-quality public transportation, the City of Johannesburg has introduced the Rea Vaya Bus Rapid Transit System. The transport system is designed to provide a high-quality and affordable transport system, which is fast and safe. Buses will run in dedicated lanes in the centre of existing roads. Smaller feeder buses will bring people from the outer areas to the stations on the trunk routes. This will extend Rea Vaya's network to areas far beyond the main trunk routes. Buses will be either 75 or 112 capacity vehicles, depending on passenger volumes and will operate from about 150 stations, positioned half a kilometre apart. They will run every three minutes in peak times and every ten minutes in off-peak times and it will be possible to catch a bus from 5am to midnight.

The Johannesburg Development Agency has played a vital role in the construction of the Rea Vaya Bus Rapid Transit System and is involved in "the physical implementation of the bus ways and stations on 14 different contracts which are in various stages of preliminary design, detailed design and implementation." In the 2008/09 financial year, the JDA delivered 24 kilometres of BRT and 26 stations.

Liverpool Vision (Liverpool, United Kingdom)

Organisation type

Liverpool Vision was established in April 2008. It brought together the activities of three companies – Liverpool Vision (a pre-existing organisation of the same name), Liverpool Land Development Company and Business Liverpool – and integrates economic and physical development, investment and business and enterprise support within a delivery-focused, private sector-led company. The establishment of a single economic development company for the city was spearheaded by Liverpool City Council, following consultation with businesses. As well as its support of the business community, the organisation plays a strong role in the domestic and international positioning of Liverpool in conjunction with regional and city regional partners.

Mission statement

Liverpool Vision's mission is to "accelerate the city's economic growth and provide strategic leadership on the economy" (Liverpool Vision, 2009a).

The Liverpool context

In the second part of the 20th century, the Liverpool of the past, with its rich cultural and industrial heritage, was in almost terminal decline as the result of changes in the global and national economies which affected all major British cities. Perhaps because of its exceptional dependence on maritime, port and related manufacturing functions Liverpool experienced particularly significant levels of decline and came to be seen as peripheral and problematic. Between 1950 and 2000, it suffered a 40% population loss and between the 1960s and mid-1980s lost some 43% of its jobs (Liverpool City Council, 2008).

In the latter half of the 1990s, things began to change for the better. Despite its devastation, the city retained its spirit, energy and zeal. With the help of EU Structural Funds and other disparate sources of public investment, Liverpool began to build itself a new future based on a re-orientation towards the service sector economy and improved domestic and international positioning.

The years between 1993 and 2008 saw "considerable public intervention and investment, particularly to redress the effects on long-term under-investment in physical infrastructure, including transport and key gateways across the city and particularly to address shortfalls in quality business premises" (Liverpool City Council, 2008). The European Objective 2 programme represents an important, albeit small, source of ongoing public funding. A decline, however, in both Objective 1-status EU Structural Fund investment and UK Government support through the regional DA means that Liverpool will become increasingly reliant on attracting private sector investment to the city. However, the years of public sector pump-priming had already created a robust climate of private sector investment. Consequently, in the years leading up to Capital of Culture, some GBP 4 billion of private investment was already driving major developments in the city, such as Grosvenor's GBP 1 billion Liverpool One retail centre.

In response to this changing context, Liverpool Vision was incorporated in April 2008. It would consolidate and build upon the achievements of the principal partners behind its creation – Liverpool City Council, Northwest Regional Development Agency (NWDA) and English Partnerships (EP) – and their dedicated delivery mechanisms (the old Liverpool Vision, the Liverpool Land Development Agency and Business Liverpool). The central task for Liverpool Vision would be to initiate and deliver a step change in Liverpool's medium– to long-term economic prospects, primarily by working with markets, to strengthen the environment in which business can expand, thrive and invest in Liverpool. In other words, its aim is not to kick start growth and recovery in Liverpool, but to accelerate it by engaging with and galvanising the private sector into action.

What does Liverpool Vision do?

Liverpool Vision plays a major role in the economic, physical and symbolic regeneration of the city. It also plays a key role in influencing and working with other agencies as a partner on the Liverpool First Economic Development and Enterprise Partnership to help to address issues of enterprise, employment, skills and jobs as well as in other economic partnership arenas in the city and city region.

It also plays a key role in influencing and working with other agencies as a key partner on the Liverpool First Economic Development and Enterprise Partnership to help to address crucial issues of enterprise, employment, skills and jobs.

As part of its mission to "create a world-class city for business" and lead the "next phase of the city's transformation", the organisation has four strategic priorities around which it organises its work (Liverpool Vision, n.d.).

These strategic priorities include: (1) quality of place and "developing an outstanding quality of place, making the most of Liverpool's distinctive assets and potential as a maritime cultural centre, optimising its role as the economic, transport, knowledge and cultural hub of the city region, developing a premier built environment, public realm and effective transport connectivity for business, residents, workers, tourists and visitors" (Liverpool Vision, 2008); (2) vibrant economy and creating "the conditions for a larger city economy which delivers higher up the value chain; supporting a dynamic business space which attracts and retains more leading edge firms, and supports vigorous indigenous growth; optimising and expanding the knowledge and creative economy" (Liverpool Vision, 2008); (3) global connectivity and "developing strong, new international relationships around trade, investment and knowledge, and visitor and tourist markets, strengthening and marketing the Liverpool brand world wide" (Liverpool Vision, 2008); and (4) thriving people and "growing human capital, learning creativity and innovation, embedding learning and skills on the passport for sustainable economic growth for the city and lifelong employability for individuals: attracting skilled and entrepreneurial residents to the city; ensuring economic inclusion through skilled working communities; supporting and celebrating cultural, racial, faith and gender diversity" (Liverpool Vision, 2008, 2009b).

Keynote project or programme: Shanghai Connect

Liverpool's long-established and strong civic relationship with the City of Shanghai led to an invitation to Liverpool to showcase the North West of England at the World Expo 2010 in Shanghai. Liverpool Vision is leading a partnership including the North West Regional Development Agency, the lead investor, the Liverpool Shanghai Partnership, Liverpool City Council, the city's universities, local authorities in the city region and sponsoring organisations from the public and private sectors, to deliver a six-month programme in the Liverpool Pavilion within the Urban Best Practice Area of the World Expo. This is the Shanghai Connect project.

Liverpool will be the only UK city to have a dedicated presence at the expo. Directly supporting UK Government's aim to treble UK exports to China and attract Chinese foreign direct investment, Liverpool Vision's central objectives at Shanghai Expo 2010 are to:

- increase bilateral trade and improve trade relationships;
- increase tourism;

- increase cultural exchanges, research links and student exchanges between Shanghai and Liverpool; and

- increase inward investment opportunities.

Liverpool Vision will showcase the excellence of the Liverpool city region and North West of England through six themes, one for each of the expo months, developed with partners: urban regeneration, energy, sustainability and the environment; advanced technology and science; Liverpool the sea and air gateway to the North; the knowledge sector; professional services and culture; and health and sport.

Madrid Global (Madrid, Spain)

Organisation type

Madrid, the capital of Spain and the largest Spanish-speaking city in Europe, has established Madrid Global as a special office to take forward its international relationships and positioning through municipal diplomacy, co-ordination of international projects and initiatives, and leverage of international activities by leading Madrid-based institutions and companies, including global firms, universities and research centres, and inter-governmental and non-governmental bodies.

Madrid Global is primarily an "internationalisation bureau" rather than a typical DA. Madrid's Strategy and International Action Office (Madrid Global) was created as a response to Madrid's global aspirations and the City Council's recognition of the globalised nature of the world in the 21st century. The municipal government believed that Madrid must have a global and international outlook, both in its management and its strategy, and so the new body was born. Madrid Global collaborates with key public and private bodies to carry out strategic projects to improve international perception of the city, based on its real strengths. It is dependent on the External Relations and Research Co-ordination Division, within the Deputy Mayor's Office. Madrid Global has opted for extending its own "traditional" International Relations measures and projects, and has decided to complement them with new approaches, strategies, programmes and tools to ensure a solid international position for the city of Madrid in the coming decades (Madrid Global, 2009).

Mission statement

Madrid's Strategy for International Positioning states that Madrid Global has the task of: "improving the international position of the Spanish capital by raising awareness of its competitive advantage and reality" (Madrid Global, 2008a).

The Madrid context

Madrid is one of the most rapidly emerging international cities in Europe, and is set to become recognised as a major European metropolis. Following a decade of large scale investment to modernise infrastructure and capacity in the city, Madrid now embarks on a programme of international positioning. The city is shifting from a phase of intensive building and modernisation to a phase of positioning and building international rapport.

The last ten years has been spent improving the product, Madrid must now improve its positioning. A senior official observed that, "there is a gap between perception and reality ... Madrid needs to improve its international image in order to be placed where it should be among the greatest global cities" (Madrid Public Infrastructures and Urban Services Cluster, 2008).

It was for this reason that Madrid Global was created – to close the gap between how Madrid is performing and how it is perceived by leveraging the city's strengths as a capital city, and junction box between the Spanish-speaking world and emerging markets and countries in Asia.

What does Madrid Global do?

One of Madrid Global's primary objectives is to establish and deliver upon a strategy for international positioning. As such, Madrid Global's core business and its specific projects predominantly fall in line with the city's 2008 Strategy for International Positioning (2008-11). Madrid Global, therefore, employs a number of basic types of action to set this strategy in motion:

- international affairs and city diplomacy, *e.g.* participation with international bodies, liaising with other cities and international networks, strategic alliances involving international companies, and projects with the aim of strengthening the city's position and prestige at the international level;

- the management and execution of the international projection of the city, *e.g.* through commissioning major studies of the city, and the formation of catalytic projects such as the urban services cluster of leading firms headquartered in Madrid;

- the planning and development of international positioning plans and strategies, *e.g.* support of the 2016 Olympic Games bid; and

- the fostering of public-private partnerships for internationalisation throughout Madrid, with a goal to leverage resources and know-how between partners in order to optimise the value of all international activities.

Madrid Global is not a typical city-marketing agency. It undertakes key stakeholder liaison handling. Its core role is to foster strategic alliances, effective strategies and collaboration among companies and institutions already in Madrid with key organisations elsewhere in the world. Through this core activity, Madrid Global will raise interest in Madrid across the rest of the world, and position it effectively to contribute to global discourse and action (Madrid Global, 2009, 2008b).

Keynote project or programme: Strategy for International Positioning

Madrid Global is guided by its Strategy for International Positioning (2008-11) – a document which also defines Madrid's plan for strengthening its global position and reputation. Madrid Global has adopted a strategic approach with regards to the development this internationalisation strategy. Nonetheless, the development agency has remained, and intends to continue to remain, pragmatic in its approach. Madrid Global understands that its strengths and objectives may evolve over time, and thus it must react and adjust its strategy accordingly. Madrid Global has established four key objectives as the basis of its Internationalisation Strategy:

- Madrid – the third European Metropolis: Madrid aspires to become Europe's third city, behind London and Paris, but surpassing Berlin, Amsterdam, Stockholm, Frankfurt, Rome and Milan.

- Madrid – focal point of the Spanish-speaking world: Madrid wishes to hold on and develop this position further. Madrid accounts for 71% of Spanish investment in Latin America, but Miami and Florida are emerging as competitors.

- Madrid – a nexus between cultures and continents: Madrid provides a point of entry into Latin American and North African markets and the EU. The City wishes to emphasise this further.

- Madrid – an urban reference for highly dynamic emerging cities: the series of administrations, institutions, companies and research centres that are involved in city management and the improvement of the urban environment represent a cluster of excellence which affords Madrid a competitive advantage in terms of global positioning.

Milano Metropoli (Milan, Italy)

Organisation type

Milano Metropoli is the agency for the promotion and sustainable development of the metropolitan area of Milan and aims to promote economic and social development in greater Milan. It was formed in early 2005 when the corporate purpose and structure of *Agenzia di Sviluppo Nord Milano* (ASNM) (North Milan Development Agency) were redefined. It is, however, not only the name which has changed. ASNM was essentially an urban regional DA for the North Milan area, whilst Milano Metropoli's work not only encompasses a broader geographical area – the metropolitan area of Milan – but also has a wider remit, focusing on territorial marketing and promotion, supporting strategic economic sectors and carrying out reindustrialisation, urban regeneration and development projects.

Milano Metropoli is a joint-stock company and is comprised of mixed public and private capital, with public capital making up the majority. The agency is promoted by the Province of Milan and shareholders include the Province of Milan (majority shareholder), the Milan Chamber of Commerce, *Finlombarda* (the financial holding of the Lombardy Region), *ComuneImprese* (the Rhodense development agency on behalf of 11 municipalities), the municipalities of Sesto San Giovanni, Bresso, Cinisello Balsamo and Cologno Monzese, and private enterprises. All the municipalities in the metropolitan area of Milan, as well as any other public and private bodies interested in promoting the area's economic and social development, can become shareholders in the agency (Sala, 2009).

Mission statement

Milano Metropoli's mission is to "promote sustainable development throughout the Milanese area by means of actions, projects and services. These are designed to increase the competitiveness of local businesses, support growth in strategic industrial sectors and advanced services, and heighten awareness, both in Italy and abroad, of the skills, opportunities and centres of excellence available in the area" (Milano Metropoli, 2009b).

The Milan context

As a response to the deterioration of Milan's socio-economic structure, particularly in North Milan, in 1995, the Municipality of Sesto San Giovanni organised an OECD LEED socio-economic audit. This investigation helped to analyse the situation, draft local development guidelines and transform the industrial crisis into a relevant opportunity. In January 1996, Falck (an industrial agency) closed the last steel factory in the area (pushed also by EU policies), making 1 700 workers redundant. A quick and effective reply was necessary. Following OECD LEED recommendations, the Province of Milan launched a "bottom-up experience of inter-municipal and municipal-provincial co-operation to bolster local economic development" (OECD, 2006). The local municipalities and the Province of Milan set up a local DA which operated on a voluntary basis and was known as *Agenzia di Sviluppo Nord Milano*. The agency aimed to address problems related to de-industrialisation due to the out-movement of many large firms and the dissolution of many traditional manufacturing firms.

Due to its success, the agency increased its membership to other municipalities, important financial institutions and agencies and, in 2005, was restructured as a public-private agency known as Milano Metropoli.

What does Milano Metropoli do?

Milano Metropoli's strategic activities include:

- Promoting the area: the agency plans and develops territorial and communication marketing in order to heighten awareness – both at home and abroad – of local specialisations, skills and opportunities.

- Supporting strategic economic sectors: it devises schemes to support and re-launch businesses in economic sectors that are particularly important for the Milanese economy, such as biotechnology and creative industries.

- Special re-industrialisation and urban regeneration projects: the organisation supports local agencies which have developed plans to reclaim brownfield sites and take steps to boost the manufacturing system. Milano Metropoli creates integrated urban redevelopment schemes to improve territorial, environmental, social and economic interventions.

- Supporting local agencies: the agency devises and co-ordinates strategic planning and participation schemes to help local agencies work out a shared vision of development and improve territorial governance (Sala, 2009).

Keynote project or programme: community innovation

A key objective for Milano Metropoli is to foster the inclusion of a range of partners in the territorial development process, which is particularly significant in relation to significant drivers of transformation such as global events and major infrastructure development. With this aim in mind, Milano Metropoli and the Province of Milan, with the support of *Fondazione Banca del Monte di Lombardia*, promoted a competition entitled *Expo dei Territori: Verso il 2015* or "Expo of Territories: Towards 2015". It invited local groups to develop projects to further the development agenda in Milan focussing on the themes of food and agriculture; energy and the environment; and culture, hospitality and tourism.

The project has been a success in a number of ways: its extraordinary attendance, quality of the projects submitted and the energy of the participants represent an opportunity for the area as a whole. In addition, the collection of ideas and projects will become a heritage asset for the whole Milanese Urban Region. The projects chosen will receive targeted support the Province of Milan and Milano Metropoli development agency in order that they are presented at Expo 2015 and reach the implementation stage.

New York City Economic Development Corporation (New York, United States)

Organisation type

The New York City Economic Development Corporation (NYCEDC) is "responsible for promoting economic growth throughout New York City through real estate development programmes, business incentives and more" (NYCEDC, 2009a).

The organisation works to promote economic growth in New York's five boroughs (the Bronx, Brooklyn, Manhattan, Staten Island and Queens) and to encourage investment in the city in a number of industry sectors. The NYCEDC is concerned with broadening the city's tax and employment base while simultaneously meeting the needs of both large and small businesses.

The aim is to achieve these goals in a socially responsible manner through the revitalisation of neighbourhoods, ensuring that economic development is not pursued to the detriment of local residents. The body is a key driver of the City's three-pronged economic development strategy:

- Make New York City More Liveable: improve the quality of life so that residents, workers and business owners want to be in New York.

- Make New York City More Business-Friendly: create an environment that gives businesses the tools to be competitive and create jobs.

- Diversify the New York City Economy: reduce the City's dependence on financial services and on Manhattan (NYCEDC, 2009b).

The NYCEDC is a local development corporation organised under Section 1411 of the Not-for-Profit Corporation Law of the State of New York. It is a public-private partnership and funding comes from a range of sources, but predominantly from the City of New York.

Mission statement

The organisation's mission statement is "to encourage economic growth in each of the five boroughs of New York City by strengthening the City's competitive position and facilitating investments that build capacity, generate prosperity and catalyse the economic vibrancy of City life as a whole" (NYCEDC, 2009c).

The New York context

The New York City Public Development Corporation, the NYCEDC's predecessor organisation, was founded in 1966 to revitalise New York City's struggling economy. The organisation's primary objective was to retain and create jobs and generate revenue for the City by facilitating the sale and lease of City-owned property.

In 1979, the City created another organisation to focus specifically on the financial elements of the City's economic development initiatives outside of its real estate transactions. This organisation was eventually called the Financial Services Corporation of New York City.

By the early 1990s, New York City had six agencies devoted to economic development. They included the Office of Business Development; the Office of Economic Development; the Office of Labor Services; the Department of Ports and Trade; the Public Development Corporation; and the Financial Services Corporation. The City engaged the consulting firm McKinsey and Co. in the summer of 1990 to deliver recommendations on how to best promote economic development in New York City.

Following this period of consultation, during the spring of 1991, Mayor David Dinkins and Deputy Mayor for Finance and Economic Development Sally Hernandez-Pinero announced that the City would consolidate the agencies into two groups: the NYCEDC and the Department of Business Services.

From 1991, the newly formed body of the NYCEDC has assumed the services previously undertaken by the merged corporations, including overseeing programmes of the New York City Industrial Development Agency. NYCEDC also undertakes services previously performed by the City's Department of Ports and Trade.

What does the New York City Economic Development Corporation do?

To promote comprehensive economic growth, the NYCEDC's overarching aims are to stimulate investment, broaden the city's tax base and increase employment. To achieve these high-level goals, the NYCEDC concentrates its work in the following areas:

- It supervises transport and infrastructure projects which improve the efficiency of tri-state region transit. The corporation also manages redevelopment of freight lines, food markets and maritime and aviation facilities in order to allow better distribution of goods both internally and externally.

- The corporation promotes the city's central business districts to companies looking to relocate. The NYCEDC is able to sell or lease city-owned property and actively encourages those projects which will make use of under-utilised property for economic development purposes.

- The corporation is able to assist redevelopment projects by undertaking planning and feasibility studies, conducting financial analyses, helping companies through public approvals and outlining city programmes and incentives.

- The NYCEDC also offers incentives which enable eligible companies to meet their financing needs for acquiring property, purchasing equipment, undertaking renovation work, working capital and other matters through low-cost tax-exempt bonds.

There is also a focus on revitalising communities by enriching neighbourhoods, publicising new areas of development and opportunity in the five boroughs, and creating local jobs.

The NYCEDC itself states that "to carry out [our] mission, we play many roles – including real estate developer, asset manager, business advocate, policy analyst and programme administrator. We also utilise design, urban planning and construction expertise to build many significant projects across the city" (NYCEDC, 2009d).

Keynote project or programme: long-term investment in job creation

The New York City Capital Resource Corporation (CRC) is a local development corporation administered by the NYCEDC. The mission of the CRC is to "encourage community and economic development and job creation and retention throughout New York City by providing lower-cost financing programs to qualified not-for-profit institutions and manufacturing, industrial, and other businesses for their eligible capital projects." During the fiscal year 2008, NYCCRC delivered USD 98.5 million in financing, resulting in USD 22.6 million in private investment.

Prospect Leicestershire (Leicester and Leicestershire, United Kingdom)

Organisation type

Formally launched on 8 April 2009, Prospect Leicestershire is a new economic development company (EDC). Prospect Leicestershire was set up by the Leicester City Council and Leicestershire County Council to simplify the current economic development arrangements and to drive forward economic growth across the urban area of Leicester and its surrounding county. The new governance arrangements are underpinned by a GBP 1.36 million revenue budget with GBP 250 000 contributions each from the Homes and Communities Agency (HCA), the City and County Councils, GBP 125 000 from the districts and GBP 485 000 from East Midlands Development Agency (EMDA) (I&DeA, 2009). The organisation will primarily be focused on delivering regeneration, economic development and inward investment initiatives, as well has having steering functions. Prospect Leicestershire takes over the responsibilities of the Leicester Regeneration Company (LRC) and the inward investment arm of Leicester Shire Promotions. The majority of board members are from the private sector and legally the Economic Development Company is a company limited by guarantee whose founding members are the City Council and County Councils (Economic Development Company for Leicester and Leicestershire, 2008).

Mission statement

Prospect Leicestershire has the mission to "build on the successful regeneration work already started, seek to extend it to areas around the city and work with organisations across the county to create new jobs, improve skills and promote business and housing growth" (Prospect Leicestershire, 2009).

The Leicester and Leicestershire context

Prospect Leicestershire was set up by Leicester and Leicestershire City and County Councils to simplify the current economic development arrangements and to drive forward economic growth across the urban area of Leicester and its surrounding county.

Leicester City Council, Leicestershire County Council and the county's seven local borough and district councils will all participate in the new agency. Councillor Patrick Kitterick from Leicester City Council stated that "what we found when Labour came to power in 2007, was that the regeneration bodies in Leicester were confusing and it was difficult for any business person or investor to navigate … What we're hoping with [Prospect Leicestershire] is that by concentrating all our efforts and regeneration in one place, we are easier to do business with." (BBC, 2009).

In a meeting of the Cabinet in July 2008, the purpose of setting up Prospect Leicestershire was summarised as putting in place "an effective delivery vehicle to support achievement of the economic development and associated priorities of the County Council and Leicestershire together as set out in the Sustainable Community Strategy (SCS), new Local Area Agreement (LAA) and emerging Multi Area Agreement (MAA)."

What will Prospect Leicestershire do?

Prospect Leicestershire will ensure that there is a co-ordinated approach to the delivery of business growth, investment and regeneration anywhere in Leicester and Leicestershire. This "no boundaries" approach is the first of its kind in the United Kingdom and was made possible by the agreement between Leicester City Council and Leicestershire County Council, with the support of all the district and borough councils across the county.

Prospect Leicestershire will focus on three principal delivery aims:

- Regeneration and Sustainable Economic Growth: delivering physical regeneration, renewal, environmental and infrastructure projects within the Principal Urban Area of Leicester, its Sustainable Urban Extensions and adjoining New Growth Points.

- Inward Investment: promoting both county and city as targets for mobile inward investment opportunities and enquiry handling. Links will be maintained with EMDA's regional investor development project which will collocate into shared office space.

- Business Enterprise: ensuring continuity and integrity of business support provision across the county and city; acting as an advocate for the private sector, joining up delivery of skills and learning activities at all levels, promoting enterprise development and innovation, particularly with the Universities of Loughborough, Leicester and De Montfort, and ensuring an adequate supply of serviced workspace and incubation facilities.

An operational plan for Prospect Leicestershire is currently under preparation. This covers core activities and relevant projects over the first three years of the organisation's operation (Economic Development Company for Leicester and Leicestershire, 2008).

Keynote project or programme: Three Universities for Business (3U4B)

Prospect Leicestershire's Three Universities for Business (3U4B) project is a joint initiative between Leicestershire's three universities – Loughborough, Leicester and De Montfort – and Prospect Leicestershire. The three universities already represent a substantial asset to the local economy; with a total student population of over 50 000, they are producing many of the country's top graduates and generating millions of pounds of revenues from research activities, nurturing spin-off companies and supporting new start-up businesses and job creation. 3U4B was launched in January 2008 to build on the collective capacity within the three universities and increase collaboration with small and larger businesses. It aims to provide benefits to local businesses by exposing them to the wide range of expertise available across the three universities for whom, in its first year alone, 3U4B has generated more than 30 new business enquiries.

The initiative has been led by Prospect Leicestershire to leverage optimal benefit for the local economy of the combined impact of the three universities. Moreover, it recognises that this combined impact exceeds the sum total of its component parts. Central to the philosophy is the whole-area perspective brought to bear in delivery. Such collaboration is believed to be unique.

The range and diversity of development agencies

Diversity of nomenclature

There are many different kinds of DA in many countries. As a result, there is considerable diversity in the range of names which are given to these entities. Among others, these names include: economic development company, city development company, development agency, local development agency, regional development agency, economic development agency, economic development corporation, development authority, city development agency, urban development corporation or city development corporation. The different names do not necessarily suggest distinctive activities. Often, differently named organisations fulfil the exact same roles. At the same time, however, agencies with the same names can often do rather different things. Different legal structures and linguistic preferences tend to determine the names used. Most national governments, however, prefer to promote one named vehicle, especially as national designation to such vehicles often brings specific benefits, incentives, or obligations.

Box 2.2 demonstrates the role Creative Sheffield plays in the development, delivery and evaluation of Sheffield's key strategic development document, the Sheffield Economic Masterplan.

Box 2.2. **Signature project: Creative Sheffield and the Sheffield Economic Masterplan**

When Creative Sheffield was launched in 2007 as the new DA of the City of Sheffield, its primary task was to lead on the development of the Economic Masterplan, which was intended to set the direction of the city's development over the next 10-15 years. Having made progress over the previous decade, particularly in the city centre, it was clearly recognised that Sheffield needed its underlying economic performance to improve if it were to remain competitive in the 21st century.

The Economic Masterplan (EMP) identified a GBP 1 billion gap in gross value added between what the city actually produced and what it could produce if it operated at the same level as the national average. Closing the gap became the primary target of the city's economic strategy, which itself translated into three main strands of objectives:

- creating an additional 30 000 jobs, over and above the city's normal trajectory;

- bringing at least 16 000 people into the workforce within Sheffield;

- shifting the economy to a significantly higher level of value-added production and skill levels.

The EMP was developed through a combination of external consultants working with Creative Sheffield, the City Council and Yorkshire Forward. A large and inclusive steering group met regularly during the development process and would critique early drafts of the plan. The final draft was then widely distributed to ensure all parties bought into both the overall aims and the route map. The EMP was approved by a meeting of the full City Council and by the Sheffield First Partnership.

Box 2.2. **Signature project: Creative Sheffield and the Sheffield Economic Masterplan** *(continued)*

The change in political leadership of the City Council changed in 2008 from a Labour administration to Liberal Democrat. Consequently, Creative Sheffield was quickly endorsed as the main delivery vehicle for the Economic Masterplan, but the Council stressed that future changes of strategy or direction had to be set by those who were directly accountable to the people of Sheffield, the Council's elected members. This division between strategy/policy and delivery has seen Creative Sheffield take on a wider role in its reporting on the progress of the EMP's delivery from all contributing partners, as well as on its own progress. The Strong Economy Board has been established in order to steer the strategic direction of the city and ensure the strategy remains up to date and relevant to any future changes in the wider economy.

Creative Sheffield's dual role as far as delivery of the Economic Master Plan is concerned, is:

- directly delivering projects within its own business plan (city marketing, business investment and innovation promotion, physical regeneration);

- monitoring and reporting on the delivery of the wider economic programme, which includes projects delivered by other organisations.

To fulfil those dual roles, Creative Sheffield and the City Council have established five broad work streams:

- infrastructure, including regeneration schemes, housing and transport;

- skills, including employability, basic and higher level skills;

- enterprise, including enterprise support provision, local economies and the "BiG" (Local Enterprise Growth Initiative);

- innovation and investment, including the city's partnerships with universities, the National Health Service (NHS) and its business investment activities.

- brand management, including leadership on marketing, major events, the city centre retail experience and the leisure economy.

Creative Sheffield reports progress on the economic aspects of these work streams back to the Strong Economy Board and to other partners as appropriate.

Source: Creative Sheffield (2009b), "The Sheffield Economic Masterplan: Transforming the Economy in One Generation", *www.creativesheffield.co.uk/SheffieldEconomicMasterplan*; Hanson, A. (2008), "Sheffield Economic Masterplan Launched", *http://andershanson.wordpress.com/2008/01/17/sheffield-economic-masterplan-launched*; Creative Sheffield (2009c), "The Sheffield Economic Masterplan, 2008", Creative Sheffield; Roberts, P. (2009), Written and telephone communication and interviews.

Diversity of characteristics

DAs display great variety in their characteristics. We will explore and explain this variety as this book proceeds and identify the common features. This includes variation in their: (1) size; (2) role in the development system; (3) key relationships; (4) mission; (5) finance mechanisms and budgets; (6) structure; (7) spatial scale; (8) function; (9) leadership composition and style; and (10) staff expertise.

Table 2.1 showcases some of the diverse characteristics of the 16 development agencies profiled in this book.

Table 2.1. **Development agency diversity: the size, age, spatial scale and annual budget of selected development agencies**

Development agency	Date incorporated	Staff	Primary spatial scale	Annual budget (EUR)
Abyssinian Development Corporation	1989	121	Neighbourhood	6.32 million (2008/9)
AucklandPlus	2004	14	Regional	2.56 million (2008/9)
Barcelona Activa	1986	109	City	24 million (2008)
Bilbao Metropoli-30	1991	9	Metropolitan	2.0 million (2008)
BILBAO Ría 2000	1992	25	Metropolitan with focus areas	111.6 million (2009)
Build Toronto	2008	TBC	City	TBC
Cape Town Partnership	1999	28	City Centre	702 000 (2008)
Creative Sheffield	2007	48	City but in the context of the city region	4.4 million (2008/9)
HafenCity Hamburg GmbH	1997	35	City centre extension	-
Invest Toronto	2008	TBC	City, region and international	TBC
Johannesburg Development Agency	2001	57	Metropolitan with focus areas	108.2million (2009/10)
Liverpool Vision	2008	54	City with focus areas	5.76 million (2008/9)
Madrid Global	2007	Almost 45	City and international	8.48 million (2009)
Milano Metropoli	2005	35	Metropolitan	3.50 million (2007)
New York City Economic Development Corporation	1991	Over 400	City	591.4 million (2008)
Prospect Leicestershire	2009	18	City and county	1.55 million (2009)

What produces development agency diversity?

As flexible, semi-autonomous local development tools, DAs can be designed in a number of ways to reflect the development system of the local economies in which they are found. This starting point, however, reflects only a small dimension of their diversity. In fact, to explain how and why DAs differ more comprehensively, a number of factors emerge. These include: (1) rationale; (2) constitution; (3) stakeholders; (4) mission; (5) status; (6) finance; (7) assets; (8) roles; (9) geography; (10) relationships; and (11) sustainability.

It is the interplay between these characteristics which creates diversity and distinguishes one agency from another. Many of these factors are discussed later in this book, but a number of basic starting points emerge.

Not all DAs will pursue anything like the same tasks, and very few will pursue all of those listed above. Indeed, one of the most interesting aspects of DA activity is that different approaches are used to foster developmental outcomes. The range of tools available to the agency influences the scale of the ambition and the nature of the intervention that is feasible, but it does not determine whether an agency will succeed.

Tools are created by the interplay of resources, rules and regulations, constitutional and institutional arrangements, and the scale of the local assets and the opportunities within local and wider markets. Effective DAs constantly create and build new tools, and use existing tools fully. Less effective DAs may have a range of tools, but not use them as well.

An important, though obvious, observation is that many territories have more than one DA operating within them at any one time, usually with multiple and overlapping geographies. It is important to note that this might be a source of advantage or disadvantage depending upon the clarity of the distinctive roles of the DAs and the readiness of effective means and incentives to collaborate where useful.

For example, even where a large and comprehensive agency has been created, it may well have other specialist agencies operating within its delivery chain for local development. The New York City Economic Development Corporation, for instance, frequently supports the work of smaller and more local development corporations such as the Abyssinian Development Corporation. At same time, many localities have multiple DAs working in a parallel fashion with distinctive tasks; these are illustrated in both the Bilbao and Toronto case studies.

To summarise, not all DAs are the same, and there are very different models in different countries. We have identified that:

- There is a large menu of things that DAs can do, and few do all of these.

- Some DAs are established in response to a crisis, or to a problem of under-development, whilst others are established simply to promote growth, development, and competitiveness in all contexts (both for "successful" and "unsuccessful" places).

- Some are established "bottom up" by local actors, and others "top down" by Governments and donors. Some are wholly private sector sponsored, or the product of public-private joint ventures, and some are bi-lateral or multi-lateral inter-governmental bodies with a focus on enabling neighbouring entities to work together.

One consequence of this mix of different factors in the establishment of DAs is some very basic differences in the scale, shape, size, and resourcing of the agencies produced. To put this simply:

- Some DAs cover very wide geographies of several thousand square kilometres, and others cover very narrow geographies of less than one square kilometre.

- In terms of budget and staff, some DAs are very large and some are very small (more than 2 000 staff in some places and less than 10 in others).

- Some DAs are principally locally accountable and others are accountable to national and international bodies.

- Some DAs have long-term budgets allocated to them by national and international bodies, others have almost no ongoing budgets at all, and are only funded by the projects they run.

- Some DAs have a very wide range of roles, others a very narrow range.

- Lastly, there are major variations and mixtures between these poles and factors.

By way of example, Box 2.3 presents the Johannesburg Development Agency's role in the planning and delivery of the Rea Vaya project, demonstrating how DAs can make significant infrastructure interventions in cities.

Box 2.3. **Signature project: Johannesburg Development Agency and the Rea Vaya/Bus Rapid Transit System project**

The Johannesburg Development Agency stimulates and supports area-based economic regeneration and development initiatives throughout the Johannesburg metropolitan area. In response to the limited provision of high-quality public transportation, the City of Johannesburg has introduced the Rea Vaya Bus Rapid Transit System. The transport system is designed to provide a high-quality and affordable transport system, which is fast and safe. Buses will run in dedicated lanes in the centre of existing roads. Smaller feeder buses will bring people from the outer areas to the stations on the trunk routes. This will extend Rea Vaya's network to areas far beyond the main trunk routes. Buses will be either 75 or 112 capacity vehicles, depending on passenger volumes and will operate from about 150 stations, positioned half a kilometre apart. They will run every three minutes in peak times and every ten minutes in off-peak times and it will be possible to catch a bus from 5am to midnight.

The Johannesburg Development Agency has played a vital role in the construction of the Rea Vaya Bus Rapid Transit System and is involved in "the physical implementation of the bus ways and stations on 14 different contracts which are in various stages of preliminary design, detailed design and implementation." In the 2008/09 financial year the JDA delivered 24 kilometres of BRT and 26 stations.

The specific phases of the construction of the Rea Vaya System are as follows:

- Phase 1: this refers to the construction of the section between the NI Freeway and the M1 freeway. The layer works for this section were completed in May 2008 and is approximately 4.7 kilometres long. In addition to this, BRT stations are to be constructed at Booysens and Nasrec, with related pedestrian bridges, during 2009, with are targeted to be ready for use during the 2010 FIFA World Cup.

- Phase 2A: The construction of this 3-kilometre long section between the M1 freeway and Anderson Street in the CBD began in July 2008. The main layer works have already been completed, but this section is anticipated for completion in May 2009.

- Phase 2B: This section is between the N1 western by-pass freeway and the intersection of Soweto Highway and Mooki/Main Street in Soweto. Construction began in July 2009 on this 4-kilometre long area. This section will have four stations. The target completion date for this phase was May 2009.

The Rea Vaya was officially opened in September 2009, with all construction targets having been completed on time at this point. Indeed, by the middle of October 2009, the system was carrying on average 16 000 passengers per day. However, in addition to the impact that the BRT system has had on congestion and making travelling in the city easier, the system also has planned environmental and economic benefits.

The Rea Vaya Bus Rapid Transit (BRT) system is the single largest climate change initiative ever undertaken by the City of Johannesburg. By replacing poor quality buses, which run on poor quality fuel, with the BRT's new buses, which will run on low-sulphur diesel and are fitted with advanced pollution reduction equipment, air quality will be dramatically improved. Indeed, a study commissioned by the JDA claims that by 2010, the implementation of the system will have resulted in an expected saving of 382 940 tonnes of carbon dioxide. Furthermore, operation of the Rea Vaya system is expected to save 1.6 million tonnes of carbon dioxide emissions by 2020.

The Rea Vaya Bus Rapid Transit system has also had positive economic and regeneration impacts. The new system will, according to the project planners, create a total of 29 000 jobs in various capacities by the end of Stage 1. In addition to job creation, the BRT will also serve to contain urban sprawl, promote densification, promote social inclusion, as well as promoting more general economic development through making the city centre more desirable and accessible.

Source: Rea Vaya (2009), "Rea Vaya", homepage, *www.reavaya.org.za/home.*

What is the link between local development agendas and development agency diversity?

Governmental context

The governmental development agenda varies hugely from the centralised national efforts in certain parts of Europe in the 1940s and 1950s, to the municipal and business efforts in the older industrial cities of the United States in the 1960s and 1970s, to the wide-ranging establishment of DAs in the developing countries of Latin America and the Asia-Pacific region in the 1980s and 1990s. An important issue concerns which tiers of government are the key sponsors of an agency and to what extent financial and fiscal freedom exists for those tiers. For example, DAs that are sponsored directly by national and federal government tend to have much greater financial resources and freedom than those sponsored by municipal governments alone.

Delegation of municipal government powers

Within some national frameworks provision is made for municipal governments to delegate their powers to DAs. Where this does occur, it generally covers some or all of the following:

- certain land-use planning decisions, *e.g.* master-planning and planning approval management in redevelopment areas;

- financial assistance to businesses, *e.g.* loans and grants to firms;

- land acquisition and disposal, *e.g.* rights to buy and sell land in the interest of local development;

- project management, *e.g.* of bid to host an international event;

- raising capital from private sources, *e.g.* through the establishment of special investment funds; and

- marketing of the territory, *e.g.* through the management of a brand platform and marketing alliance.

The benefits of delegating such activities to DAs are assumed to be that a specialist agency might do these things more effectively than a municipal government can. Whilst this may be true in many situations, it will not always necessarily be so. Clear testing of the feasibility of delivering activities directly through a DA needs to be undertaken. It is often the case that a municipal government can attract and retain staff, and can deliver its programme of work from a more stable institutional framework, than a DA can quickly create. The process of delegation needs to be carefully managed so as to help the DA build capacity to deliver, rather than be overwhelmed.

Secondly, the process of delegation needs to be accompanied by clear rules for supervising and overseeing what the DA then delivers. For example, elected municipal leaders need to retain a strong role in setting the policies and frameworks within which the DA is able to operate freely, as they are ultimately accountable for its work. These relationships are rarely easy to organise, and it is for these reasons that delegations have been reversed by municipal leaders who feel that DAs have "gone too far" in acting autonomously. Good preparation and communication can avoid such problems.

Internal liaison within municipal government is a key challenge

One of the most difficult issues concerns the internal liaison within local government which seems to be rife with misunderstandings in many cases. It is clearly important that the role and remit of each part of the local government is clearly articulated and understood by all parts, and that there is authoritative guidance on how joint working should be managed. Equally, it is important for the most senior leaders (council leader, local government chief executive) to pay attention to making such relationships work well, because there are few others within the local government system that can resolve these difficulties.

Legal status is essential for reducing risk and optimising impact

The legal status of DAs is also important. Most DAs are "not-for-profit limited liability" agencies under the various forms of national law that exist. This is often a precondition for them being able to pursue not for profit public purposes and to make use of public sector enhanced tools (*e.g.* tax credits or subsidised debt). The range of such "not-for-profit limited liability" statuses is very large in some countries (*e.g.* Italy, United Kingdom and United States), but in general they have the effects of:

- proscribing the activities such an organisation may not engage in;

- defining how risk and costs will be appraised and apportioned;

- defining the extent of financial and other freedoms;

- defining the tax status of the activities of the agency; and

- providing guidance on the governance and regulatory obligations to which the agency is subject.

The main trends in this regard follow from both the emerging activities of DAs (as law seeks to keep pace with practice and aspiration) and from the precedent of governmental reviews of the functions of particular agencies. Good examples come from many countries. DA activity can become contentious, especially where private sector, or individual, interests appear to have benefited substantially from their participation in DA-related activity. When there is concern that a DA may have achieved public purpose goals at too great a price to public resources, or too great a return to private sector partners, governments will typically initiate a review that results in modifications to the status of the agency and related laws. This is often helpful in terms of exposing to public debate the very nature of the cost and risk (and "return"), sharing dynamics that are central to helping local economic development happen.

Development agency typologies

To deepen understanding, it may be helpful to build a framework which categorises DAs into five main groups, based on the roles that they play in the local development system. Though there is a degree of overlap between each, these categories include: development and revitalisation agencies; productivity and economic growth agencies; integrated economic agencies; internationalisation agencies; and visioning and partnership agencies.

Development and revitalisation agencies

These agencies are responsible for enhancing the competitiveness of place primarily by facilitating and often undertaking or managing investment in "hard" or physical factors such as transport infrastructure, real estate and urban realm. A mission statement typical of this type of agency is found in Table 2.2.

Table 2.2. **Typical development and revitalisation agency mission statement**

Development agency	Mission
BILBAO Ría 2000	To "recover degraded land or industrial areas in decline in metropolitan Bilbao, thus contributing to balanced development and improvement of urban cohesion." (BILBAO Ría 2000 (2009b)

Productivity and economic growth agencies

Primarily responsible for the development of "softer" factors, these DAs tend to focus on branding, skills development, entrepreneurship, business growth and inward business investment and retention. A mission statement typical of this type of agency is found in Table 2.3.

Table 2.3. **Typical productivity and economic growth agency mission statement**

Development agency	Mission
Barcelona Activa	"To coach the transformation of Barcelona in terms of entrepreneurship, business growth, innovation, professional opportunities, human capital development and quality employment."

Integrated economic agencies

Approaching the development agenda in a holistic manner, these agencies tend to focus on both "hard" and "soft" factors. They attempt to link together all aspects of local development in an integrated model or master plan and work closely with the full range of partners required to realise the vision they strive for. A mission statement typical of this type of agency is found in Table 2.4.

Table 2.4. **Typical integrated economic agency mission statement**

Development agency	Mission
The New York City Economic Development Corporation (NYCEDC)	NYCEDC is "responsible for promoting economic growth throughout New York City through real estate development programmes, business incentives and more."

Internationalisation agencies

With the aim of establishing an increased presence on the global stage for their cities, this type of DA focuses primarily on international promotion and branding. Building on the unique assets of their cities, they tend to develop and deliver internationalisation strategies. A mission statement typical of this type of agency is found in Table 2.5.

Table 2.5. **Typical internationalisation agency mission statement**

Development agency	Mission
Madrid Global	"Improving the international position of the Spanish capital by raising awareness of its competitive advantage and reality." (Madrid Global, 2008a)

Visioning and partnership agencies

These agencies tend to facilitate partnerships, research and publish materials, as well as lobby key stakeholders which set and shape the development agendas of their cities. A mission statement typical of this type of agency is found in Table 2.6.

Table 2.6. **Typical visioning and partnership agency mission statement**

Development agency	Mission
Bilbao Metropoli-30	"To lead the vision of the future through the implementation of the revitalisation process." (Bilbao Metropoli-30, 2009)

Table 2.7 shows the distribution, by typology, of the 16 development agencies profiled in this book.

Table 2.7. **Development agency typologies**

Typology	Development and revitalisation agencies	Productivity and economic growth agencies	Integrated economic agencies	Internationalisation agencies	Visioning and partnership agencies
Description	"Place drivers"	"Employment and productivity drivers"	"Place and productivity leaders"	"Place and productivity promoters"	"Place shapers and visioners"
Development agency	BILBAO Ría 2000	Auckland Plus	Creative Sheffield	Invest Toronto	Bilbao Metropoli-30
	Build Toronto	Barcelona Activa	Liverpool Vision	Madrid Global	Cape Town Partnership
	HafenCity Hamburg GmbH		Milano Metropoli		
	Johannesburg Development Agency		New York City Economic Development Corporation		
			Prospect Leicestershire		
			Abyssinian Development Corporation		

Common features

Though these DAs originate from a wide variety of localities and play a variety of different roles, they each support the basic premise that cities and their regional and national partners view a DA model as an effective means to manage economic development and regeneration activities.

DAs also tend to: exhibit a corporate structure and outlook; operate at arm's length from the local government, but have it as the key stakeholder and funder; be accountable to the local government; be relatively autonomous, nimble, responsive and action oriented; display strong leadership; exhibit a skilled and specialised workforce; and be focused on sustainable development. Many of these common traits are also the key strengths of DAs which will be discussed in greater detail later in the book.

Local governments have different powers and duties in respect of economic development and regeneration within the various national contexts described. However, the use of the corporate structures to pursue economic development and regeneration is, in most cases, a means to optimise the responsiveness of the local or regional economy to external and internal drivers, within that framework. It is an organisational means to overcome some of the limitations within the framework. For example, even in situations where local government have few powers of revenue raising and financial competence, DAs can be a means to drive investment innovation through collaboration with the private sector.

Conclusion

Though there are thousands of DAs world wide, the 16 agencies used as the core evidence base for this book demonstrate the breadth of their overarching aims and activities. The previous discussion shows that five categories of DAs can be distinguished. Several of the DAs are "comprehensive", engaging with drivers in labour markets, property markets, external investment markets, and with enterprise and innovation drivers. Some of the DAs are more focused on one or two of these activities. For example, there are several that are largely oriented around property redevelopment and asset management, or around enterprise and innovation drivers, or labour market interventions, or marketing for external investment. However, most of the DAs do include some element of all of these. In several locations, there is more than one developmental entity active (*e.g.* Bilbao, New York and Toronto). For example, there are collaborations between city and regional bodies and there are collaborations between two different DAs both working at city level. There are several examples of sub-regional and regional agencies (*e.g.* Auckland, Bilbao and Milan), some forged by inter-municipal collaborations, others operating as county/regional sponsored bodies. There are also several agencies working at a neighbourhood or district level below that of the municipality (*e.g.* Abyssinian Development Corporation, Cape Town and HafenCity Hamburg GmbH). This diversity is evidence of the flexibility of DAs. The fact that the mandate of each can be tailoured to add maximum value to the local development agenda makes them a powerful potential tool for local leaders.

References

ADC (Abyssinian Development Corporation) (2009), "Abyssinian Development Corporation", homepage, *www.adcorp.org/.*

AucklandPlus (2008), "Business Plan, 2008/9", AucklandPlus.

Auckland Regional Council (2009), "Auckland Regional Economic Development Strategy", *www.arc.govt.nz/albany/index.cfm?1FC20F22-145E-173C-9850-84D85CCEDEF8.*

Barcelona Activa (2009), Written materials provided by and interviews with Barcelona Activa.

BBC (British Broadcasting Corporation) (2009), "Councils Create New Jobs Agency", *http://news.bbc.co.uk/1/hi/england/leicestershire/7846593.stm.*

Bilbao City Council (2009), "Bilbao, A City for Investment: Bilbao Exhibition Centre", *www.bilbao.net/ingles/bilbaonegocios/invertir/eng/2_feria.htm.*

Bilbao Metropoli-30 (2009), "Bilbao Metropoli-30", homepage, *www.bm30.es/homeage_uk.html.*

BILBAO-Ria 2000 (2009a), "BILBAO-Ria 2000 What Is It?", *www.bilbaoria2000.org/ria2000/ing/bilbaoRia/bilbaoRia.aspx?primeraVez=0.*

BILBAO Ría 2000 (2009b), "BILBAO Ría 2000 What Does It Do?", *www.bilbaoria2000.org/ria2000/ing/bilbaoRia/bilbaoRia.aspx?primeraVez=0.*

Braithwaite, L. (2009), "Build Toronto", presentation, Build Toronto.

Bruns-Berentelg, J. (2009), Written and telephone communication and interviews.

Build Toronto (2009), Written materials provided by and interviews with Build Toronto.

Cape Town Partnership (2006), "Cape Town Partnership: A Profile", Cape Town Partnership.

Cape Town Partnership (2008), "Cape Town Partnership Annual Report", Cape Town Partnership.

Cape Town Partnership, (2009), Written materials provided by and interviews with the Cape Town Partnership.

CCID (Central City Improvement District) (2007), "Central City Improvement District Annual Report (2007)", Central City Improvement District, Cape Town.

Centre of Basque Studies (1998), "Post-Industrial Bilbao, the Reinvention of a New City", *http://basque.unr.edu/07/7.3.1t/7.3.1.3t/7.3.1.3.2.lesson1.htm*, University of Nevada.

Centre for Cities (2005), "Bilbao/Bizkaia Visit Report", Centre for Cities.

Creative Sheffield (2009a), "Corporate Information", *www.creativesheffield.co.uk/CorporateInformation.*

Creative Sheffield (2009b), "The Sheffield Economic Masterplan: Transforming the Economy in One Generation", *www.creativesheffield.co.uk/SheffieldEconomicMasterplan.*

Creative Sheffield (2009c), "The Sheffield Economic Masterplan, 2008", Creative Sheffield.

Economic Development Company for Leicester and Leicestershire (2008), "Report of the Chief Executive, Part A", Economic Development Company for Leicester and Leicestershire, July.

HafenCity Hamburg GmbH (2008), "Projects Insights into Current Developments", *www.hafencity.com/upload/files/broschueren/z_en_broschueren_24_Projekte_englisch_09.2008.pdf*

HafenCity Hamburg GmbH (2009a), "HafenCity Hamburg GmbH", homepage, *www.hafencity.com/.*

HafenCity Hamburg GmbH (2009b), "History of a Port", HafenCity Hamburg GmbH, *www.hafencity.com/index.php?set_language=en&cccpage=ueberblick_artikel&show=artikel&item=12&number=2.*

Hanson, A. (2008), "Sheffield Economic Masterplan Launched", *http://andershanson.wordpress.com/2008/01/17/sheffield-economic-masterplan-launched.*

Harvard Design School (2009), "The Vision of a Guggenheim Museum in Bilbao", Harvard Design School, *www.gsd.harvard.edu/people/faculty/pollalis/cases/BilbaoG-CaseA.pdf.*

I&DeA (Improvement and Development Agency) (2009), "Leicestershire Inquiry Visit, 2009", *www.idea.gov.uk/idk/core/page.do?pageId=9898526&aspect=full.*

Invest Toronto (2009a), "Invest Toronto Start Up Strategy Report", Invest Toronto.

Invest Toronto (2009b), "Toronto – Building the New Economy", Invest Toronto.

Invest Toronto (2009c), Written materials provided by and interviews with Invest Toronto.

JDA (Johannesburg Development Agency) (2009a), "Business Plan, 2009-10", Johannesburg Development Agency.

JDA (2009b), "Growth and Development Strategy 2006", Johannesburg Development Agency, *www.joburg.org.za/content/view/139/114/.*

Kerslake, B. and V. Taylor (2004), "Economic Development and Creative Sheffield", Sheffield City Council, *www.sheffield.gov.uk/index.asp?pgid=35768&mtype=print.*

Liverpool City Council (2008), "Liverpool 'New Economic Development Company' Commencement Plan", Revised Working Draft, Liverpool City Council.

Liverpool Vision (n.d.), Liverpool Vision corporate document.

Liverpool Vision (2008), "Business Plan, 2009/10", Liverpool Vision.

Liverpool Vision (2009a), "About Us", *www.liverpoolvision.co.uk/aboutus/aims.asp.*

Liverpool Vision (2009b), Written materials provided by and interviews with Liverpool Vision.

Madrid Global (2008a), "Executive Summary of Madrid: The Strategy for International Positioning, 2008-11", Madrid Global.

Madrid Global (2008b), "Annual Meeting", *www.adb.org/annualmeeting/2008/presentations/jbravo-presentation.pdf.*

Madrid Global (2009), "Who are We?", *www.munimadrid.es/portal/site/munimadrid/menuitem.f4bb5b953cd0b0aa7d245f019fc08a0c/?vgnextoid=a70858fe026de11058fe026de1100c205a0aRCRD&vgnextchannel=8db7566813946010VgnVCM100000dc0ca8c0RCRD&idCapitulo=5211986.*

Madrid Public Infrastructures and Urban Services Cluster (2008), "International Strategy and Development", *www.adb.org/Documents/Events/ (2008)/Madrid-Experience-Sharing-Seminar/Bonifacio.pdf.*

Milano Metropoli (2009a), "Expo dei Territori: Verso il 2015", extract of the competition, *www.milanomet.it/en/ultime/november-2008.html.*

Milano Metropoli (2009b), "Activities", *www.milanomet.it/en/cosa-facciamo/activities.html.*

Molero, A. (2009), Written and telephone communication and interviews.

NYCEDC (New York City Economic Development Corporation) (2009a), "About Us", *www.nycedc.com/Web/AboutUs/AboutUs.htm.*

NYCEDC (2009b), "Annual Investment Projects Report", *www.nycedc.com/AboutUs /FinStatementsPubReports/Documents/LL48_FY08%20_VolumeI.pdf.*

NYCEDC (2009c), "Mission Statement", *www.nycedc.com/Web/AboutUs /WhatWeDo/MissionStatement/MissionStatement.htm.*

NYCEDC (2009d), "New York City: Make it Happen Here", *www.nycedc.com/NR/ rdonlyres/B36DE03D-3ECB-4D51-BD37-3801D68A9AEA/0/NYCEDC_brochure.pdf.*

OECD (2006), *OECD Territorial Reviews: Milan, Italy 2006*, OECD Publishing, DOI: *http://dx.doi.org/10.1787/9789264028920-en.*

OECD LEED Programme (2006), "Action Space - Local Development Agency Review: The case of Laganside Corporation, Belfast," *www.oecd.org/document/ 60/0,3343,en_2649_34455_40417020_1_1_1_1,00.html.*

OECD LEED Programme (2009), "Promoting Entrepreneurship, Employment and Business Competitiveness: The Experience of Barcelona", *www.oecd.org/document/ 32/0,3343,en_2649_34461_43504288_1_1_1_1,00.html.*

Oram, R. (2005), Presentation made at the "Better by Design Conference".

Prospect Leicestershire (2009), "Our Remit", *www.prospectleicestershire.co.uk/about-us/our-remit.*

Rea Vaya (2009), "Rea Vaya", homepage, *www.reavaya.org.za/home.*

Roberts, P. (2009), Written and telephone communication and interviews.

Rogers, C. (2009), Written and telephone communication and interviews.

Sala, G. (2009), Written and telephone communication and interviews.

Scottish Parliament (2005), "Scottish Parliament Business Growth Inquiry Committee Fact-Finding Visit to Germany (Hamburg and Bremen), 23 to 27 October 2005", *www.scottish.parliament.uk/business/committees/enterprise/inquiries/bg/GermanyVisi t.htm.*

Chapter 3

The value-added of development agencies

Given their unique characteristics, development agencies can offer much to local leaders. This chapter links the theoretical discussion of how and where development agencies add value to local development systems to practical examples of the impact of these organisations on the ground in a variety of operating environments. First, the functions of development agencies are divided into eight categories, which range from branding and international promotion to human capital development and social or green initiatives. Then, key performance indicators are used from agencies in each of the five typologies identified in Chapter 2 to demonstrate the depth and breadth of the practical contribution development agencies can make to the local development process.

Because development agencies (DAs) are "special purpose organisations" whose role is to help make development happen, how they are tasked and how their performance is measured and monitored is a key aspect of their success and how well they are understood and how sustainable they become.

This chapter focuses on how DAs add value in practice and how that value-added is measured and understood. It sets out how, where, and to what extent DAs add value to development and investment activities in cities. By doing so, this chapter more clearly and tangibly explains why they are emerging as leading agents for local development planning and delivery in local economies across the world. Through practical examples, the chapter then proceeds to discuss how and why this value-added is measured.

What do development agencies add value to?

The breadth of development agencies' impacts

Given their unique characteristics, DAs can offer much to local leaders. They contribute to local development in ways which go beyond the traditional three roles of local government elaborated in Chapter 1. It is the pursuit of the effective delivery of the fourth "local development and investment" role that stimulates local governments to establish new DAs and re-gear existing DAs. Though we break them down further in the discussion to come, the fundamental goals of DAs, whatever their type, match those of local development as a whole: (1) sustainable economic growth, which produces (2) an enhanced quality of life for local residents, workers and visitors.

The evidence from the 16 core case studies shows that the impact of DAs can have considerable breadth. The local development themes to which they add value ranges widely from, for instance, branding and international promotion, human capital development and hard infrastructure development to investment attraction and retention as well as partnership facilitation and visioning.

Some DAs, such as the Johannesburg Development Agency, specialise in the delivery of one or two types of development activity such as transport infrastructure construction and management. Other DAs, such as Creative Sheffield, have a wider scope. Their mandates inform the delivery of a diversity of interventions such as investment attraction and retention to branding and marketing; and real estate or infrastructure development.

The breadth of development activities within an agency is not clearly linked to the spatial scale at which DAs operate. Larger scales of operation do not necessarily mean broader mandates. HafenCity Hamburg GmbH, for instance, works in a relatively confined location within Hamburg, yet it delivers a holistic form of development accompanied by numerous forms of intervention. BILBAO Ría 2000, for instance, works in key nodes throughout metropolitan Bilbao, yet delivers a deep but relatively narrow form of real estate, urban realm and infrastructure development intervention. Meanwhile, agencies such as Prospect Leicestershire and AucklandPlus work at the metropolitan and even regional scale and deliver on a range of local development activities.

Table 3.1 summarises the main functions of the 16 DAs profiled in this book. Taken as a collective or as individual DAs, the table highlights how flexible a tool these specialist organisations can be. They deliver on a significant range of work streams.

Table 3.1. **Functions and outcomes of selected development agencies**

Branding and international promotion	Investment attraction and retention	Business start-ups and growth	Human capital development
② ④ ⑧ ⑩ ⑪ ⑫ ⑬ ⑭ ⑯	② ⑧ ⑩ ⑬ ⑯	③ ⑦ ⑭ ⑯	① ② ③ ⑫
Real estate, urban realm and infrastructure development	Social or Green development initiatives	Partnership facilitation, planning and visioning	Urban service provision or management
① ② ⑤ ⑥ ⑧ ⑨ ⑪ ⑮ ⑯	① ⑦ ⑨	③ ④ ⑦ ⑫ ⑭	① ⑦

① Abyssinian Development Corporation
② AucklandPlus
③ Barcelona Activa
④ Bilbao Metropoli-30
⑤ BILBAO Ría 2000
⑥ Build Toronto
⑦ Cape Town Partnership
⑧ Creative Sheffield

⑨ HafenCity Hamburg GmbH
⑩ Invest Toronto
⑪ Johannesburg Development Agency
⑫ Liverpool Vision
⑬ Madrid Global
⑭ Milano Metropoli
⑮ New York City Economic Development Corporation
⑯ Prospect Leicestershire

Table 3.2 builds on the analysis above by illustrating how specific DAs have added value to specific development themes.

The depth of development agencies' impacts

The depth of impact of a DA is predominantly a function of the effectiveness of the DA. As will be discussed in Chapter 8, we view DA effectiveness as the net result when strengths and constraints are balanced against one another. Chapter 8 discusses in greater detail both DA strengths (such as company type and structure; agility and flexibility; spatial focus; leadership; focus on outcomes and clients; talented and experienced staff/focus on quality; strong revenue-generating capacity; clear or focussed mandate; long-term mandate; strong partnerships; holistic/integrated approach; innovation; apolitical/low profile/arm's length positioning; and community/stakeholder credibility and engagement) and constraints (such as budget constraints or funding arrangements; market conditions; non-enabling governance structures; lack of autonomy/executive power; lack of a socio-economic evidence base; complex roles in complex systems of stakeholders; mission creep; accountabilities; and focused mandates).

Whatever the scope of their mandates, all agencies aim to achieve development outcomes through their interventions. Though there are other factors, which have been described earlier, if adequately resourced both in terms of finance and staff, most agencies achieve effective progress against their objectives. The fact remains, though, that DA resource bases do vary and this has an impact on their capacity to add value. The level of resources provided to a DA depends on a number of factors such as internal finance expertise and the macroeconomic climate. However, many DAs see it as a core competence to develop a sustainable resource base. This process often involves DAs diversifying income streams and better demonstrating their impact or value-added to city government or other key funders.

Table 3.2. **Development agency impact examples by theme**

Theme	Development agency	Impact
Branding and international promotion	Madrid Global	Madrid Global's enhanced engagement with international networks and partners, such as the committees and forums of the UCCI, Covenant BID and the dialogue between Toronto and Madrid, has deepened and widened this city's global presence.
Investment attraction and retention	Creative Sheffield	Creative Sheffield work closely with companies both already in Sheffield to offer support and also with companies who express interest in relocating their business to the region. A few highlights of this work include: (1) Sandvik Medical Solutions: 112 000 square foot centre of excellence agreed, which will safeguard/create up to 100 jobs; (2) Tomorrow Options: this Portuguese micro-electronics company is to open its first subsidiary in the United Kingdom in Sheffield; and (3) Capita Hartshead, the United Kingdom's largest specialist pensions administration organisation, selected Sheffield for its UK Headquarters.
Business start-ups and growth	Barcelona Activa	In 2008, more than 600 companies were installed in its Business Incubator and Technology Park. Also, in 2008, 350 companies received growth coaching through the agency's business growth programmes.
Human capital development	Barcelona Activa	In 2008, more than 48 000 participants received attention in Porta22.
Real estate, urban realm and infrastructure development	New York City Economic Development Corporation	Introduced an inter-modal train service on Staten Island Railroad for industrial transportation use, eliminating 58 000 truck trips in 2008 through the city.
Social or green development initiatives	HafenCity Hamburg GmbH	There is a mix of district heating and decentralised heat generation plants using fuel cells and solar energy with CO_2 across the HafenCity development.
Partnership facilitation and visioning	Cape Town Partnership	The Cape Town Partnership Chief Executive, Andrew Boraine, was awarded the title of "Business Leader of the Year, 2008" for the contribution he and his team have made towards engaging with the private sector to accelerate investment and development in the central city over recent years.
Urban service provision or management	Abyssinian Development Corporation	Since 2000, the Abyssinian Development Corporation's Harlem Economic Literacy Program has provided homeownership education and counselling to over 1 600 people and is a recognised and approved Housing Counselling Agency by US Department of Housing and Urban Development and the NYC Housing Preservation and Development.

How do development agencies add value?

The preceding section established what themes and to what extent DAs add value. By contrast, this section highlights how these specialist organisations facilitate the effective planning and delivery of development objectives. They are malleable organisations which can be built to contribute effectively in the precise way in which they are needed. Because local development challenges and opportunities vary from place to place, and over time, development agencies also vary. Their objectives, activities, structures, tools, roles and strategies display a high level of diversity. Nonetheless, across the breadth of development agencies that exist, there are a number of fundamental ways in which these organisations add value. They can:

- **Focus on implementation at pace and scale.** Development agencies pursue development opportunities faster, and at a larger scale, than would normally be possible within a city or local government.

- **Aggregate otherwise separate interventions to add value.** Economic development efforts within cities or regions are often subject to fragmentation of effort due to the multiplicity of funding streams and policy agendas that they support. Development agencies can act to aggregate otherwise disparate efforts, overcoming potential co-ordination failures and information asymmetries.

- **Adopt an effective, business-like approach.** An important reason for placing economic development activities within a corporate entity (such as a development agency), rather than a municipal structure, is the ability of development agencies to offer a business-like environment and service offering, and the scope to manage customer relationships in a business-to-business model.

- **Adopt flexible spatial scales.** Development agencies can operate at a city-wide scale, but are also able to function at either more local, or wider, levels, where appropriate. This is a source of significant value added, given that economic development challenges are often focused at local or sub-regional levels.

- **Attain the confidence of external investors and other businesses.** The confidence of investors, developers, and business customers is an important ingredient in maintaining market position for local and sub-regional economies. Development agencies can act as the "commercial attaches" to business for a city.

- **Become a toolmaker and fully utilise existing tools.** Economic development tools need to be fully utilised and new tools need to be made to fit new imperatives. These tools often involve the interplay of public and private interests and assets. Development agencies can be effective toolmakers and tool users, combining different powers, resources and assets to make development happen.

- **Share risks and costs actively with partners.** Development agencies can operate as joint venture vehicles between different sectors and between different tiers of government.

- **Leverage assets and investment.** Assets and private capital are key to reinvestment markets and development agencies can help to leverage them towards city economic development goals.

- **Refresh image and identity and communicate development progress.** Image and identity is supported by branding and marketing activity which needs to be a focus of concerted action; co-ordination is essential.

- **Apply leadership to problem solving.** Problem solving is essential in making economic development successful. Development agencies are often able to supply the skills and approaches required, unencumbered by other mandates.

Box 3.1 demonstrates the role BILBAO Ría 2000 has played in the physical transformation of Bilbao.

Box 3.1. **Signature project: BILBAO Ría 2000 and the *Abandoibarra* and Guggenheim District project**

BILBAO Ría 2000's mission is to recover degraded land or industrial areas in decline in metropolitan Bilbao in order to balance development and improve urban cohesion. To fulfil this objective, BILBAO Ría 2000 co-ordinates and executes complex projects in relation to town planning, transportation and the environment.

Abandoibarra and the Guggenheim District is the most emblematic of all the projects carried out by BILBAO-Ría 2000 in its regeneration of metropolitan Bilbao. This area is a waterfront site at the heart of the city, covers 348 500 m^2, and includes the area between the Guggenheim Museum and the Euskalduna Palace. Prior to BILBAO-Ría 2000's intervention, the area was home to harbour facilities, a railway station for containers and a shipyard. The general public was denied access to it for many years. When the *La Ribera* promenade was opened over the *Evaristo Churruca* quays, the people of Bilbao and visitors to the city were able to walk around this area for the first time. The river is no longer a barrier as one of the main objectives is to define the Nervion River as the backbone of the entire city.

A further example of the agency's work in this area is the *Abandoibarra Ametzola* Southern Routing, known as OAVS, which was the first major task taken on by BILBAO Ría 2000. This work operated simultaneously on the city and the railway systems in order to ensure that available space was being used in the optimum way. As a result of the project's regeneration efforts, *Abandoibarra*, an area covering 345 000 m^2 between the Guggenheim Museum and the Euskalduna Music and Conference Hall, is rapidly becoming the cultural and business heart of Bilbao. Conversely, *Ametzola*, formerly goods train stations, is now a residential area, with a new 36 000 m^2 park built over the old railway tracks. The Southern Rail Routing modified rail access from the left bank of the river to draw these areas closer to the city centre. The operation built four new stations and remodelled two more on the original goods route. This connected Bilbao's southern districts to the city centre and to the entire left bank of the Nervión. It also removed the physical barrier of the previous rail infrastructure, which ran along the river and made it impossible to provide a connection between the city and the banks of the Nervión.

In the *Abandoibarra* area, the *Avenida de Abandoibarra* is now open to the public between the *Palacio Euskalduna* convention centre, concert hall and *Uribitarte* walkway. The riverside promenade has also been completed with the addition of a children's play area and the new cybernetic fountain. It provides a large, tree-lined, mainly pedestrian area with broad pavements, a cycle path and three tram stops. The promenade is linked to the Deusto Bridge via a spiral stairway and the newly opened *Calle Lehendakari Leizaola* provides a thoroughfare for vehicles between the avenue and the bridge.

In addition to these developments, 115 714 m^2 of the total 348 507 m^2 of land will be areas of greenery, which will remain undeveloped and utilised as areas of natural beauty. For example, BILBAO Ría 2000 assigned EUR 10.5 million for the extension work on the *Parque Doña Casilda*, where work began in March 2006. Now, the park extends as far as the Sheraton Hotel and the nearby residential complexes. The operation involves creating 30 000 m^2 of recreational and green areas, including the boulevard and the pedestrian paths between buildings. Some 282 new trees of 19 different species and more than 700 shrubs were planted in the area.

Source: Towns and Town Planners in Europe (2001), "The 4th Biennial of Towns and Town Planners in Europe – Project Reports", *www.planum.net/4bie/main/m-4bie-bilbao.htm;* BILBAO Ría 2000 (2009), "Activity", *www.bilbaoria2000.org/ria2000/ing/zonas/zonas.aspx?primeraVez=0;* European Council of Spatial Planners (2009), "Abandoibarra Regeneration Project and New Southern Railway Line, Bilbao", *www.ceu-ectp.eu/index.asp?id=117.*

How and why is the added-value of development agencies measured?

Being clear about the added value of DAs is a significant step towards the acceptance and utilisation of these tools as effective planners and delivery agents of local development. Indeed, a key message from the reviews and research that underpins this book is that too little broad understanding exists as to the importance of the role played by DAs in local development and, as a consequence, although many are achieving a great deal, much more could be achieved if they were better understood and deployed.

For even the best established DAs, demonstrating tangible impacts remains important. For newly created DAs or those operating in environments experiencing political change or diminishing public resources this requirement becomes more significant. By demonstrating their value in a clear way, DAs are able, for instance, to gain public and political support, secure sustainable finance and build stakeholder support. These factors all influence the success of DAs as later chapters will indicate. Moreover, by demonstrating this value-added, this book intends to showcase the potential utility of these tools to local leaders.

Most DAs have defined hard measurables by which performance can be recorded and reviewed. Chapter 7 explains a number of the methods used with more precision but, essentially, performance monitoring can be divided in two: (1) the internal monitoring of organisational metrics can help the agency drive towards greater operational efficiency and effectiveness; and (2) the measurement of external impact informs stakeholders and senior DA leaders as to the strategic value-added the DA is delivering. This section focuses on the latter.

Quantifiable evidence in the form of these hard measurables gives a robust insight into the impact of DAs. Impact can, however, become difficult to measure when outputs are less tangible. The delivery of thriving communities, a high quality of life, effective facilitation, an enhanced city brand, or symbolic interventions all represent significant DA impacts. More sophisticated forms of social accounting, for instance, have been developed to attach a value to these outputs which are less easily measured. To satisfy stakeholder demand for accurate reporting of DA performance, there is a longer term agenda here to enhance understanding of the intangible impacts of DA activity.

Nonetheless, the most common way to measure DA impact is on a project-by-project basis. Dispersed throughout this book, one-page summaries of signature DA projects (see Table 3.3 for a list) demonstrate the value added of DAs and the fact that figures are collected to evaluate their impact. Data across the scope of the agencies' activities is then collated and presented, often in the form of key performance figures, which are usually published in annual reports.

Table 3.3. **Signature projects and programmes from selected development agencies**

Development agency	Signature project or programme example
Abyssinian Development Corporation	College Ready Communities
AucklandPlus	Brand Auckland
Barcelona Activa	Gloriès Entrepreneurship Centre
Bilbao Metropoli-30	From Infrastructures to Values
BILBAO Ría 2000	*Abandoibarra* and the Guggenheim District
Build Toronto	Blue Print for Fiscal Stability and Economic Prosperity
Cape Town Partnership	Central City Development Strategy
Creative Sheffield	Sheffield Economic Masterplan
HafenCity Hamburg GmbH	Leveraging Private Investment
Invest Toronto	Agenda for Prosperity
Johannesburg Development Agency	Bus Rapid Transport System
Liverpool Vision	Shanghai Connect
Madrid Global	Madrid Internationalisation Strategy
Milano Metropoli	*Expo dei Territori: Verso il 2015*
New York City Economic Development Corporation	New York City Capital Resource Corporation
Prospect Leicestershire	Three Universities for Business (3U4B)

We can now illustrate, for each of the DA types, key performance indicators and, for the newer DAs, key performance targets. Tables 3.4, 3.5, 3.6, 3.7, 3.8 and 3.9 demonstrate clearly how DAs make both tangible and intangible contributions to the local development agendas of their localities. Most DAs have a very broad range of outcomes that they seek to achieve and because relatively high levels of operational freedom are important to enable DAs to undertake their roles, the use of quite elaborate tasking frameworks and systems is important.

To demonstrate the breadth of impacts DAs can have, we profile an agency from each of the agency types introduced in Chapter 2. An example is also chosen to illustrate how relatively new agencies set targets for their performance. These examples include:

- development and revitalisation agencies: Johannesburg Development Agency (Table 3.4);

- productivity and economic growth agencies: Barcelona Activa (Table 3.5);

- integrated economic agencies: New York City Economic Development Corporation (Table 3.6);

- internationalisation agencies: Madrid Global (Table 3.7);

- visioning and partnership agencies: Cape Town Partnership (Table 3.8);

- key performance target setting: Prospect Leicestershire (Table 3.9).

These examples anchor some of the more theoretical discussion in this chapter with practical examples of the impact DAs can deliver. They show both the variety of the ways in which these organisations contribute to local development as well as the depth of impact they have. These tables also offer an insight into what is measured by DAs and through what means.

Table 3.4. Key performance indicators of the Johannesburg Development Agency

Theme (initiative)	Tangible impact	Intangible impact
Catalytic investments	• Between 2001 and 2008, in the High Court Precinct, the JDA invested ZAR 8.3 million which was complemented by total private sector investment of ZAR 2 994.4 million. • 55% of investors thought that JDA interventions were "very important" in encouraging them to invest while 45% saw JDA interventions as "important" (JDA, 2009a).	• The JDA has a continued leadership role in respect of the inner city. In a number of intervention areas in the city, the JDA has made critical interventions which have catalysed further investment. • According to a recent impact review, "there is little doubt that JDA investments in the inner city areas of Johannesburg have had a significant impact on the resurgence of specific development areas, and as a consequence on the reversal of fortunes of the Inner City as a whole" (JDA, 2007).
Job creation	• Short-term jobs created: target (2 650); total achieved (5 788) (JDA, 2009b).	
Economic development and empowerment	• Black Economic Empowerment spend as a percentage of capital expenditure target (70%); total achieved (68%) (JDA, 2009b).	• Creates confidence behind the equal opportunities agenda.
Project management	• City of Johannesburg funded projects: allocated spending ZAR 137 736 000 and total spending ZAR 138 598 000 (100%). • BRT allocated spending 556 453 000 and total spending ZAR 429 945 (77%). • Inner City Fund: allocated spending ZAR 171 500 000 and total spending ZAR 166 174 000 (97%). • Other funds: allocated spending ZAR 28 923 000 and total spending ZAR 27 000 000 (93%). • Project delivery against milestones in service delivery areas: overall Economic Area Regeneration Programme (90%). Constitution Hill (100%); Greater Newtown (87%); Greater Ellis Park (99%); Hillbrow Heath Precinct (55%); and Jewell City (100%) (JDA, 2009b).	• A sense of efficiency and reliability attaches itself to the JDA.
Human resources	• Proportion of female staff employed: target (45%); actual (61%). • Proportion of black staff employed: target (80%); actual (88%). • Proportion of payroll invested in training: target (3%); actual (2.7%) (JDA, 2009b).	• Confidence in equal opportunities and a commitment to staff development is created.

Table 3.5. **Key performance indicators of Barcelona Activa**

Theme (initiative)	Tangible impact	Intangible impact
Barcelona Activa	• In total, Barcelona Activa has handled over 1.3 million participants. • During the 2004 to 2007 Action Plan period, more than half a million participants attended programmes run by the agency. • More than 150 000 participants a year come to Barcelona Activa's premises.	• Creation of a professional agency, with a world-class reputation, charged of the local development of the city. • Strong co-operation with other local and international agents that allows Barcelona Activa to offer more and better programmes.
Boosting entrepreneurship	• In total, 14 500 business projects were coached and 8 000 new companies created. • In 2008, approximately 1 400 businesses received advice. Over 700 companies were created and the estimated new employment from these companies totalled approximately 1 400 new jobs.	• Reference centre for entrepreneurship in Barcelona and model transferred to other international environments (Bogotá, Medellín, Santiago de Chile, Buenos Aires, Rome, Andorra, etc.).
Business growth	• In total, more than 600 companies were installed in its Business Incubator and Technology Park. • More than 115 companies a year in the agency's Business Incubator and Technology Park. • In 2008, 350 companies received growth coaching through the agency's business-growth programmes.	• Hub of business growth initiatives promoted by different agents in the city. • Network of businesses that co-operate amongst each other. • Top-level incubation infrastructures and services.
Human capital development	• In 2008, more than 48 000 participants received attention in the New Jobs Space. In 2009, 72 000 participants in the activities from the Quality Employment Agreement. • In 2008, 6 525 people participated in the Day of the Entrepreneur.	• Reference centre for professional guidance and progress in the metropolitan area of Barcelona. Being transferred to other national environments (Mataró, Bidasoa Region, etc.).
Employment	• In total, 44 486 people have been trained. • In 2008, the agency dealt with over 30 000 participants and the rate of job market insertion reached 72%. • In 2008, more than 800 unemployed people were contracted to develop their skills through apprenticeship arrangements.	• Reference entity in the city for support, coaching and training for the employment. • Co-ordination of the agreement on quality employment in Barcelona 2008-11.
Technological skills acquisition and diffusion	• In total, Barcelona Activa has helped 433 000 participants with technology knowledge and training. • In 2008, 53 784 participants attended Cibernàrium.	• Reference centre for digital literacy and training in Barcelona and model transferred to other international environments (Sao Paolo, Porto Alegre, Brussels, Tampere, San Sebastián, etc.).
Promotion of innovation	• The Barcelona Research and Innovation Map offers comprehensive information about 246 entries, from research centres to entities for Financial and Innovation Support, environments for innovation, and business best practices.	• Spreading the need and spirit of innovation among businesses, entrepreneurs and citizens.

Source: Barcelona Activa (2009), "Barcelona Activa", homepage, *www.barcelonactiva.cat*; Molero, A. (2009), Written and telephone communication and interviews.

Table 3.6. **Key performance indicators of the New York City Economic Development Corporation**

Theme (initiative)	Financial year 2008	Financial year 2009
Transport orientated development	• Introduced inter-modal train service on Staten Island Railroad for industrial transportation use, eliminating 58 000 truck trips in 2008 through the city. • NYCEDC is working to expand the railroad's capacity by 75%, which will create 200 new jobs and generate USD 50 million in wages.	
Physical urban development and revitalisation	• Completed Uniform Land Use Review Procedure (ULURP) approval process in November 2008 for the Willets Point revitalisation project, a 62-acre site which will be re-zoned for 5 000 housing units; new retail, office and open space; convention centre; and school and will create 18 000 construction and 5 000 permanent jobs. • Certified into ULURP in January 2009 for the restoration and revival of Coney Island, a 27-acre amusement and entertainment district, which will create 4 000-5 000 units of housing, 500 000 square feet of new retail space, 25 000 construction, and 6 000 permanent jobs. • More than 15 major construction projects were substantially completed, and an additional 20 designs and construction projects were initiated. • Asset Management's Graffiti-Free NYC program cleaned in excess of 15 million square feet of graffiti (New York City Economic Development Corporation, 2008). • Worked to create nearly 20 million square feet of commercial, cultural, and open space. • Completed more than USD 225 million in capital projects.	• Received approval on five major developments. • Completed construction on almost ten miles of streetscape improvements throughout the city. • Completed construction on almost seven miles of plaza/open space.
Urban management and engagement	• Managed 60 000 square feet of gross property area. • Managed 20 000 square feet of buildings space. • Managed approximately 75 miles of shoreline, including 60 properties across all five boroughs. • Removed 200 000 trucks from the road. • Participated in 276 community and strategic partnership meetings. • Reduced city-wide greenhouse gas emissions by 1 million tonnes annually by facilitating the procurement of cleaner energy for NYC. • Achieved 36% participation rate in Minority- and Women-owned Business Enterprise projects.	
Leveraging private sector investment	• Real estate transactions leveraging almost USD 433.3 million in private investment were completed. These transactions project to create approximately 1 100 construction jobs and 850 permanent jobs (New York City Economic Development Corporation, 2008).	

Economic diversification	• Announced numerous diversification initiatives, including:
	  ○ The Financial Services Initiatives, which will create an estimated 25 000 jobs for the city over the span of ten years.
	  ○ Capital Access Revolving Loan Guaranty Program, which will provide USD 5 million to generate USD 14 million in new business activity, benefiting up to 400 businesses and 700 employees.	

Revenue generation and cost saving	• Achieved USD 24.64 million in land sales.	• Achieved USD 2.1 million in land sales. • Realised almost 20% in decreased operating expenditures.

Source: Olster, S. (2009), Written and telephone communication and interviews.

Table 3.7. **Key performance indicators of Madrid Global**

Theme (initiative)	Tangible impact	Intangible impact
Increased participation in strategic international events, networks and projects	• Madrid Global has been involved in the World Cities Summit, the Program of Urban Development ADB, the World Urban Forum Nanjing, OpenCities, The Dialogue between Young Urban Leaders of Asia and Europe (ASEF), and a number of others. • Madrid's engagement with international networks and partners, such as the committees and forums of the UCCI, Covenant BID and the dialogue between Toronto and Madrid has improved. • As part of the Shanghai 2010 Expo, Madrid has been selected to build a permanent structure. It is predicted that, over the six-month-long event, the structure could be visited by representatives from nearly 200 countries and international organisations – totalling some 70 million foreign and local visitors. • Through the *Árbol Bioclimático* and the Bamboo House at the Shanghai Expo, Madrid has the opportunity to promote its unique advantages to the Chinese market. • Up to 31 March 2009, Madrid Global was working on 40 projects. These projects were divided into 194 actions, of which 65 are still waiting to begin. A total of 103 were underway, with 26 finished.	• Improved international visibility and stature of Madrid. • Entry into Eastern markets.
Formation of key alliances and partnerships	• Key alliances with institutions such as the Japan Foundation in Madrid, House Asia and Community of Cities Arianne have been forged.	• Credibility and trust is being generated between key partners.
Enhanced private sector engagement	• Improved co-ordination with private enterprises by Madrid Global has increased the number of sponsorship deals obtained for the 2016 Olympic candidacy. Two main groups include the Associates of "Club 16" and the Preferential Sponsors of Madrid 2016.	• Engagement with the private sector gains credibility and can improve access to finance.

Source: Vega, B. (2009), Written and telephone communication and interviews.

Table 3.8. **Key performance indicators of the Cape Town Partnership**

Theme (initiative)	Tangible impact	Intangible impact
Tax revenues (combination)	• The Central City accounts for ZAR 50.2 billion out of ZAR 124.37 billion (40.36%) of total city turnover, making it by far the city's largest business node (City of Cape Town, 2006). This represents an increase on the previously measured figure of 33%, even without taking into account growth since 2006 in financial services, asset management, construction, information communication technologies, creative industries and tourism services, all of which have impacted positively on the Central City's position.	• Validates the strategic focus on the central city and claims for more resource support.
Vertical and horizontal co-ordination	• Sustainable public/private partnerships in place.	• Diligent and diplomatic work by the Cape Town Partnership is creating co-operation within the City of Cape Town and with other public/ private agencies.
Crime (CCID)	• Serious crime has fallen in the Central City by 90% since 2000 (Central City Improvement District, 2007).	• The perception/fear of crime in the Central City has fallen. According to a prominent Cape Town Newspaper Editor, "less than ten years ago we were writing stories of Central City abandonment," but thanks to an effective campaign against crime and grime, "the Central City is now a great place to be and a nice place to walk."
Public space improvements (with the City of Cape Town)	• Added value to adjacent buildings. • The conversion of Church Square from a parking lot to an interactive public space. • The completion of Phase 1 of the Grand Parade upgrade. • Pier Place, Jetty Square, Greenmarket Square and St Andrew's Square design and upgrade. • Gradual improvement of the Company's Garden (Cape Town Partnership, 2007). • Many property owners and developers have taken it upon themselves to resurface and "green" pavements adjacent to their properties and to upgrade the facades of their own buildings.	• Shifted the emphasis from a vehicle-dominated to a pedestrian-friendly city. • Provided better access to the Central City to workers and visitors. • Supporting the Creative Cape Town and World Cup 2010 delivery strategies.

Table 3.8. **Key performance indicators of the Cape Town Partnership** (*continued*)

Theme (initiative)	Tangible impact	Intangible impact
Inward investment (combination)	• The Central City has experienced high levels of investment over the past decade. Since 2000, a total ZAR 16-18 billion of investment has been realised from the capital value of current leases, new developments, investment purchases, upgrades and renewals.	• Urban management and development facilitation has significantly enhanced the Central City's reputation among domestic and international investors.
Effective business engagement	• The Cape Town Partnership Chief Executive, Andrew Boraine, was awarded the title of "Business Leader of the Year, 2008" for the contribution he and his team have made towards engaging with the private sector to accelerate investment and development in the Central City over recent years.	
Strong commercial property market	• The Central City has experienced a steady decline in commercial property vacancies over the past decade. By the end of 2007, vacancies in A-grade commercial office units had fallen below 4% (Cape Town Partnership, 2007). • Investments by top property companies such as Growthpoint, Madison and Old Mutual Properties, together with Irish company Eurocape, represent particular highlights. • Around 45% of new Central City apartments have been purchased by black owners. Since 2003, ZAR 2 billion worth of property developments and building purchases have been overseen by black developers. Black property owners now manage 40% of commercial stock in the Central City.	• Increased perceived investment attractiveness.
Employment	• Since 1998, a total of 65 000 construction jobs have been sustained in the Central City (Cape Town Partnership, 2006). • A further 500 jobs have been created in the delivery of basic services linked to the work of the Central City Improvement District (CCID) (Cape Town Partnership, 2006). • Thousands of job opportunities have been created in the retail, tourism and business sectors as a result of the good health of the Central City (Cape Town Partnership, 2006).	
Social development (Caring Cape Town)	• Placement of over 250 homeless young people in care or with their families. • Non-governmental organisations such as Straatwerk, The Haven Night Shelter, Men at the Side of the Road and the Big Issue are now very successful in the Central City (Cape Town Partnership, 2006).	

Table 3.8. **Key performance indicators of the Cape Town Partnership** (*continued*)

Theme (initiative)	Tangible impact	Intangible impact
Cultural resurgence	• Hosting successive stands at the Design Indaba to showcase Cape Town's creative industries. • Establishment of a popular Creative Clusters Networking Forum. • Hosting the Community Jazz Concert with espAfrika on Greenmarket Square as part of the popular Cape Town International Jazz Festival. • A revival of lunchtime entertainment and accessible theatre in public spaces; a renewed use of iconic architecture (Cape Town Partnership, 2007). • Attracted people into public space, in particular the newly-upgraded Church Square. • Provided both physical and e-commerce platforms for local musicians and poets. • Established a Goematronics project. • Contributed to the Cape Town Memory Project by providing living memorialisation to indigenous, slave and African music roots of the people of Cape Town. • Made music production and consumption connections between the Central City, the townships and the Cape Flats (Cape Town Partnership, 2007).	• Cape Town now has a growing reputation as a high potential, high value-added creative economic sector, and the Central City is contributing powerfully to its development.
Event hosting and a growing visitor economy	• In 2006, the Cape Town International Convention Centre alone hosted some 509 events whilst the streets of the Central City have, for instance, hosted the 2006 Homeless World Cup, the Gay Pride March, the Pick 'n Pay Argus Cycle Tour, and the UCI "B" World Cycle Championships (Cape Town Partnership, 2007). The Adderley Street Night Market, the Festive Season Lights and the Cape Town Festival Night Vision attracted 300 000, 50 000 and 35 000 to the Central City respectively (Cape Town Partnership, 2006). • Today, the Central City and its immediate vicinity host an impressive 47% of the total hotel bed capacity in the entire Greater Cape Town region (Cape Town Partnership, 2007). With future hotel projects under development such as the 15 on Orange Hotel (scheduled for completion end 2008) and the Taj Palace Hotel (scheduled for completion end 2009), this offer is set to increase (*The Property Magazine*, 2008; *The Cape Town Magazine*, 2008).	• The Central City is today a genuine visitor destination and gateway in its own right. • The Central City atmosphere is now beginning to bristle with street life.

Table 3.9. **Key performance targets for Prospect Leicestershire**

Theme (initiative)	Target	Associated actions
Economic development	• A reduction of those not in employment, education or training (NEETs). • A reduction of working age people on out-of-work benefits. • An increase in the proportion qualified to Level 2. • An increase in the proportion qualified to Level 4 and above. • Employment growth in small businesses. • An increase in employment floor space. Efficiency savings.	• The government will place a duty on named national and regional partners to co-operate and participate in the MAA. This would be an Multi Area Agreement (MAA) with duties under the Local Democracy, Economic Development and Construction (LDEDC) Bill currently going through Parliament. • The MAA partnership will prepare a sub-regional economic assessment which the regional development agency (RDA) will incorporate into the single regional strategy. • The MAA partnership will prepare a sub-regional investment plan that will provide a commissioning framework and a framework for joint project appraisal by MAA partners and East Midlands Development Agency (EMDA). • The government will ensure that the resources of the Department of Work and Pensions (DWP), Jobcentre Plus (JCP), Learning and Skills Council (LSC) and Connexions are aligned to deliver MAA priorities. • There will be co-commissioning and co-investment in the business support, employment and skills programme. • The government will explore a mechanism for the Higher Education Funding Council for England (HEFCE) to provide additional flexibility to further and higher education institutions to get greater use of LSC funds at Level 4. • Jobcentre Plus Leicestershire and the Northamptonshire District Office will work with the partnership to help people moving from benefits to work (I&DeA, 2009).
Cost savings	• 3% by April 2010, a further 3% by April 2011 and 3.45% by April 2012.	-
Housing	• To be confirmed at a later date – focus on economic development at present.	-
Transport	• To be confirmed at a later date – focus on economic development at present.	-
Environment	• To be confirmed at a later date – focus on economic development at present.	-

Source: Economic Development Company for Leicester and Leicestershire (2008), "Report of the Chief Executive, Part A", Economic Development Company for Leicester and Leicestershire, July.

Box 3.2 shows how Liverpool Vision is capitalising on the Liverpool Capital of Culture '08 success to promote the city world wide, particularly through involvement at the Shanghai Expo.

Box 3.2. **Signature project: Liverpool Vision and the Shanghai Connect project**

Liverpool Vision came into being in the year in which Liverpool hosted the most successful European Capital of Culture to be held since the scheme began (according to the European Commission). The 12-month programme of some 7 000 events, involving 10 000 artists and attracting 15 million cultural visits also showcased the city's renaissance of recent years, a dynamic transformation of the city centre, waterfront and key business and residential areas, achieved through an estimated GBP 4 billion investment of mostly private funding. Capital of Culture '08 placed Liverpool firmly in the global spotlight and established over 100 new international civic relationships. The city's renewed sense of confidence about its role in the international arena has been reinforced by Liverpool Vision's recognition of the vital importance of competing globally for investment and trade, expanding the flow and exchange of knowledge and attracting students, tourists and innovative businesses from across the world. Consequently Liverpool Vision identified "global connectivity" as the fourth of the more traditional economic competitiveness pillars of "place", "economy" and "people" in its economic prospectus "People, Place and Prosperity" (2009).

Complementing Liverpool Vision's physical development, infrastructure, enterprise and business support activities, the ambition for a strong international profile and a wide range of global relationships has been translated into two immediate inter-related deliverables:

- Firstly, Liverpool Vision was tasked to review and update the Liverpool brand created for '08 as the foundations for a major national and international repositioning. Developed in conjunction with business and public sector partners, the launch of the new brand in July 2009 made its own contribution to maintaining the momentum and confidence of the previous years during the difficult months of the global recession.

- Secondly, Liverpool's long established and strong civic relationship with the City of Shanghai led to an invitation to Liverpool to showcase the North West of England at the World Expo 2010 in Shanghai, by far the largest ever with 70 million visitors expected. Liverpool Vision is leading a partnership including the North West Regional Development Agency, the lead investor, the Liverpool Shanghai Partnership, Liverpool City Council, the city's universities, local authorities in the city region and sponsoring organisations from the public and private sectors, to deliver a six-month programme in the Liverpool Pavilion within the Urban Best Practice Area of the World Expo. This is the Shanghai Connect project.

Liverpool will be the only UK city to have a dedicated presence at the expo. Directly supporting the UK Government's aim to treble UK exports to China and attract Chinese foreign direct investment, Liverpool Vision's central objectives at Shanghai Expo 2010 are to: (1) increase bilateral trade and improve trade relationships; (2) increase tourism; (3) increase cultural exchanges, research links and student exchanges between Shanghai and Liverpool; and (4) increasing inward investment opportunities.

Liverpool Vision will showcase the excellence of the Liverpool city region and North West of England through six themes, one for each of the expo months, developed with partners: urban regeneration, energy, sustainability and the environment; advanced technology and science; Liverpool the sea and air gateway to the north; the knowledge sector; professional services and culture, health and sport.

A key priority for Liverpool Vision is the provision of a range of sponsorship packages to support businesses to showcase their expertise to new consumer markets and business partners through participation in the expo in trade missions, business-to-business meetings and sector-based promotion. Similarly the opportunity to present the economic, cultural and tourism "offer" of key locations has been taken up by a number of partner local authorities in the city region.

Source: Krajewska, S. (2009), Written and telephone communication and interviews.

References

Barcelona Activa (2009), "Barcelona Activa", homepage, *www.barcelonactiva.cat.*

BILBAO Ría 2000 (2009), "Activity", *www.bilbaoria2000.org/ria2000/ing/zonas/zonas.aspx?primeraVez=0.*

Cape Town Partnership (2006), "Cape Town Partnership: A Profile, 2006", Cape Town Partnership.

Cape Town Partnership (2007), "Cape Town Partnership Annual Report, 2007", Cape Town Partnership.

Central City Improvement District (2007), "Central City Improvement District Annual Report", Central City Improvement District.

City of Cape Town (2006), "State of Cape Town 2006: Development issues in Cape Town", *www.capetown.gov.za/en/stats/CityReports/Documents/IDP/State_of_Cape_Town_Full_Report_2006_712200610345_359.pdf.*

Economic Development Company for Leicester and Leicestershire (2008), "Report of the Chief Executive, Part A", Economic Development Company for Leicester and Leicestershire, July.

European Council of Spatial Planners (2009), "Abandoibarra Regeneration Project and New Southern Railway Line, Bilbao", *www.ceu-ectp.eu/index.asp?id=117.*

I&DeA (Improvement and Development Agency) (2009), "Leicestershire Inquiry Visit, 2009", *www.idea.gov.uk/idk/core/page.do?pageId=9898526&aspect=full.*

JDA (Johannesburg Development Agency) (2007), "Annual Report, 2007", Johannesburg Development Agency.

JDA (2009a), "Analysis of the Impact of the JDA's Area-Based Regeneration Projects on Private Sector Investments", *www.jda.org.za/2009/pdfs/impact_investments.pdf.*

JDA (2009b), "Business Plan, 2009-10", Johannesburg Development Agency.

Krajewska, S. (2009), Written and telephone communication and interviews.

Molero, A. (2009), Written and telephone communication and interviews.

New York City Economic Development Corporation (2008), "Annual Report, 2008", New York City Economic Development Corporation.

Olster, S. (2009), Written and telephone communication and interviews.

The Cape Town Magazine (2008), "15 on Orange Successfully Attracting Investors", *www.capetownmagazine.com/articles/Accommodation~c2/Western-Cape/Taj-Palace-Five-Star-Hotel-Opening-in-Cape-Town~992~p1.*

The Property Magazine (2008), "15 on Orange Successfully Attracting Investors", *www.thepropertymag.co.za/pages/452774491/articles/2007/May/News/R420-million-5-star-development-15-on-Orange-hotel-development.asp.*

Towns and Town Planners in Europe (2001), "The 4th Biennial of Towns and Town Planners in Europe – Project Reports", *www.planum.net/4bie/main/m-4bie-bilbao.htm.*

Vega, B. (2009), Written and telephone communication and interviews.

Chapter 4

Development agency creation, evolution, performance and review

This chapter assesses when and how a development agency should be set up and how it should be reviewed and encouraged to evolve. It is in the nature of development agencies that they deal with dynamic contexts and constantly changing activities. They must therefore be highly adaptive organisations. Successful agencies continuously evolve and adapt and do not remain rigid, so mechanisms for shaping how they evolve and adapt are essential. Through its discussion, this chapter provides answers to other important issues such as which tasks a development agency should undertake, how to review performance, when to enlarge or contract an agency's roles and activities, how best to deal with process and timing as well as what can go wrong.

In this chapter we assess when and how a development agency (DA) should be set up and how they should be reviewed and evolve. There are important choices to be made here: when to establish a DA, which tasks should a DA take on, when to enlarge or contract their roles, and what is the right timing?

It is in the nature of DAs that they deal with dynamic contexts and constantly changing activities. When local development works (through greater visibility, or external investment, job creation, site redevelopment, and better international positioning, for example) the tasks facing DAs change accordingly. At the same time, the pattern of organisations and competences within a local development system also change and evolve regularly as governments, and others, shift policy and create new implementation tools.

DAs must therefore be highly adaptive organisations. Successful DAs continuously evolve and adapt and do not remain rigid, so mechanisms for shaping how they evolve and adapt are essential.

Setting up development agencies: why and when?

The decision by local government to incorporate a new DA or evolve an existing DA provides a window into how they add value to local development. From city to city, there are many different reasons behind this decision, all of which are outlined below. Whatever the logic, the formation or evolution of a DA represents an acknowledgment that something is missing from the system of local governance.

Kick-starting the development and investment agenda

In some places, DAs are seen as the best means to initiate local economic development and investment activities where none previously existed. This has been common in countries in central and eastern Europe following the political changes of 1991 and looking forwards to their accession to the European Union. It can also be as a result of a crisis or the decision to drive local development forward in a new direction (see Box 4.1.).

Box 4.1. **The origins of Barcelona Activa: leading the city
out of crisis and in a new direction**

Set up in 1986, Barcelona Activa was created against the background of a challenging socio-economic climate. Barcelona's unemployment rates were at over 20%, the city was suffering from post-industrial decline, economic restructuring and the closure of a number of large factories. There was also a lack of entrepreneurial initiative. Barcelona City Council decided to create Barcelona Activa as the main tool to promote entrepreneurship, business creation and innovation and to drive forward the transition from an industrial city to a knowledge city. Entrepreneurship was seen as a key contributor to social cohesion and inclusion and business creation was seen as a means of job creation. Innovation was seen as important due to its ability to contribute to the consolidation of an industrial framework which can adapt and evolve with the changing economic paradigm. Local government also seized the opportunity to recuperate and make use of the empty premises of the Hispano Olivetti factory, which became Barcelona Activa's headquarters.

Simplifying existing arrangements

In many local development systems, the structure in place to lead local economic development is convoluted and complex with many organisations whose agendas taken together can overlap and contradict. DAs offer a means to aggregate existing activities into one corporate body (see Box 4.2 for an example). This tends to take place in systems which are established but need rationalisation.

Box 4.2. **The origins of Prospect Leicestershire: simplifying a complex system**

Formally launched on 8 April 2009, Prospect Leicestershire is a new economic development company (EDC). The organisation was set up by the City and County Councils to simplify the current economic development arrangements and to drive forwards economic growth across the urban area of Leicester and its surrounding county.

Leicester City Council, Leicestershire County Council and the county's seven local borough and district councils will all participate in the new company. Councillor Patrick Kitterick from Leicester City Council stated that, "What we found when Labour came to power in 2007, was that the regeneration bodies in Leicester were confusing and it was difficult for any business person or investor to navigate … What we're hoping with [Prospect Leicestershire] is that by concentrating all our efforts and regeneration in one place, we are easier to do business with."

In a meeting of the Cabinet in July 2008, the purpose of setting up Prospect Leicestershire was summarised as putting in place "an effective delivery vehicle to support achievement of the economic development and associated priorities of the County Council and Leicestershire Together as set out in the Sustainable Community Strategy (SCS), new Local Area Agreement (LAA) and emerging Multi Area Agreement (MAA)."

Source: BBC (British Broadcasting Corporation) (2009), "Councils Create New Jobs Agency", *http://news.bbc.co.uk/1/hi/england/leicestershire/7846593.stm*; Leicestershire Rural Partnership Management Board (2008), "Economic Sub-Regional Arrangements, 2008", Leicestershire Rural Partnership Management Board.

Improving business relations

Elsewhere, DAs have become recognised as a more "business-like" entity to deliver publicly funded services to entrepreneurs and existing and new businesses. This is often true in North America where stress has been placed on creating DAs which operate more like a business-to-business service. The Cape Town Partnership plays this role extensively.

Creating critical mass

In other countries, DAs are seen as the best means for a number of governmental, international, and other entities to invest together in a single effort. This has been true in places as diverse as Portugal, Bulgaria, and Central America. Our case studies in Bilbao show how multiple parties can co-invest through two development bodies.

Fulfilling national policy

In other places, the creation of DAs can be a statutory requirement or guideline. It could, for instance, be a prerequisite for benefiting from resources or incentives (*e.g.* tax credits/efficiencies) that have been made available to help foster local economic development. For example, in Italy and the United States, an organisation has to be registered "not-for-profit", and outside of direct government control if it is to benefit from tax advantages designed to increase the capital available for local investment. In New York City, the New York City Economic Development Corporation operates a number of financial instruments that require a special agency to oversee them.

Start-up time

Starting a DA effectively takes time. Many DAs have been built upon the experience of those that went before them and current roles have gradually evolved. Creative Sheffield represents an excellent example of this.

Local governments should work through a number of considerations when establishing a DA. In particular, it is important that any new organisation fits with the existing fabric and decided future of the city. Some DAs are even articulated locally and created by community actors and so align very well with local needs and objectives (see Box 4.3).

Box 4.3. **Abyssinian Development Corporation: a development agency created bottom up**

The Abyssinian Development Corporation (ADC) is a Harlem, New York City-based DA which was initially conceived of in the 1980s. Created by The Abyssinian Baptist Church, it was a response to encouragement from Reverend Dr. Calvin Butts, III in 1986, for the congregation to rebuild its community. This call was precipitated by the fact that, during the late 1980s, Harlem was suffering from unemployment, high levels of violence, AIDS and homelessness. A lack of investment by banks was compounding the problem as building owners who sought to make repairs had difficulty in getting loans. Indeed, between the 1960s and the 1990s, few new commercial or residential buildings were built.

From simple beginnings, ADC has grown into a nationally renowned community and economic development corporation. In 1989, ADC was officially chartered as a not-for-profit community development organisation and received its first grant for USD 50 000. Amongst other major success stories, in 2007, ADC launched The Abyssinian Neighbourhood project and won national recognition from the US Environmental Protection Agency for Smart Growth in Equitable Development.

Start-up: when and how to start a development agency

There is no fixed time when a DA should be set up, but there appear to be better times to do so than others. It is important to give enough time for the DA to be set up properly – a process which may take many months, or even years. It is also important not to skip important steps in the start-up process.

A DA is never set up overnight. The initiative might come from local, national, or international actors, but the process should have four distinct phases which include:

- **promoting the idea**: creating stakeholder buy-in through, for instance, consultation events, formal and informal networking and meetings, public events, as well as the production and dissemination of publicity materials;

- **establishing the DA**: the consolidation of the mandate and core business; completion of different organisational activities such as the appointment of a board of directors and chief executive; the recruitment of operational staff and administrative teams, the purchase or rental of premises; and the procurement of a suitable information and communication technologies system;

- **starting the activity**: creation of forward momentum by the proactive participation in the local development system as well as relevant institutional networks both domestically and internationally; and

- **consolidation**: constant evaluation and recalibration of activities to ensure the organisation addresses inevitable growing pains and maintains direction and focus.

By way of example, Box 4.4 and Figure 4.1 describe and illustrate the start-up process for the Invest Toronto development agency.

Box 4.4. **Start-up process for Invest Toronto**

The establishment of two new DAs in Toronto provides a window into the practicalities of the start-up process. The following information relates to the creation of Invest Toronto.

- **Purpose**. The re-organisation and re-calibration of Toronto's system of economic development and investment promotion to include the creation of two new DAs aimed at establishing Toronto as a world-class gateway to North America.

- **Evidence**. The process was initiated as a result of two major reports by the City of Toronto about the city's competitiveness.

- **Timescale**. Summer 2008 (conception of idea) to June 2009 (establishment of new chief executive in role).

- **Phase 1**. Began on 14 November 2008 with the appointment of an interim board on the instruction of Mayor David Miller and the City of Toronto Council. Ended with the appointment of a new permanent board on 24 February 2009 by the Mayor. Through (1) an "Investigative Mission to the United States" in December 2008; (2) a three-day "Stakeholder Consultation" session; and the establishment of an "External Reference Group" it was concluded that there was a high level of stakeholder buy-in to the process. It also began to clarify what Invest Toronto's core business should be.

- **Phase 2**. Between February and April 2009, Phase 2 continued to clarify the precise function and role of Invest Toronto into the future. Six streams of activity were undertaken, including: (1) data and evidence – to develop a clear picture of how the economy was performing; (2) system mapping – to identify clearly the entire system of economic development and investment attraction in Toronto; (3) gaps and overlaps – to clearly define gaps and overlaps in the existing system; (4) define core functions - the "who does what" discussion; (5) development of organisational design options; and (6) strategic enabling framework – to develop a viable strategic framework to guide the chief executive and board.

- **Into the future**. The appointment of a new chief executive on 25 May 2009 marked the beginning of the consolidation part of the start-up process in preparation for the future of the DA.

Figure 4.1. **The Invest Toronto start-up process: Phases 1, 2 and the future**

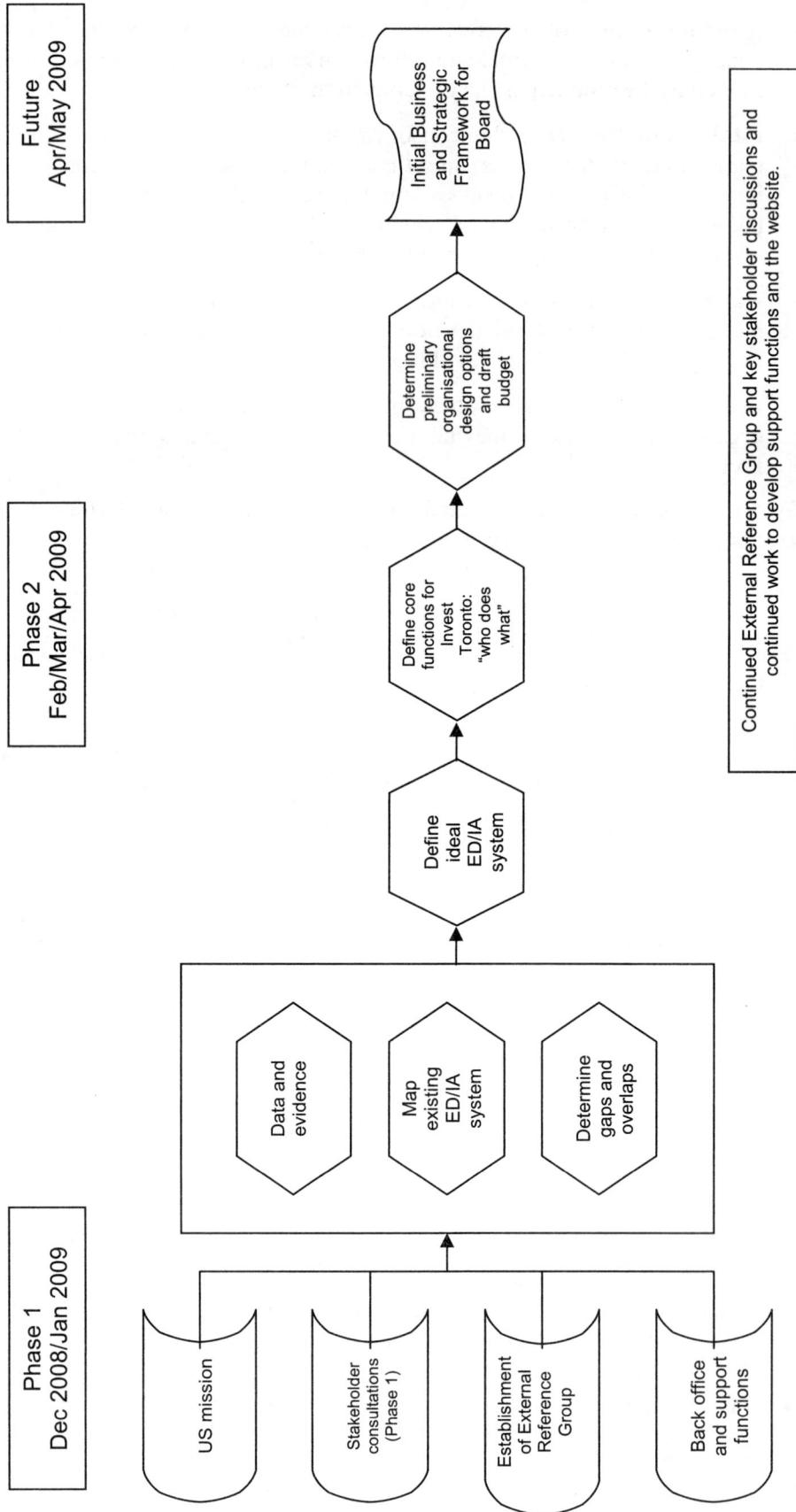

Box 4.5 shows how a new DA can be created to support the delivery of strategic city objectives defined in key guiding documents.

Box 4.5. **Signature project: Invest Toronto and the Agenda For Prosperity**

Invest Toronto is the city's agency for the promotion of the Toronto offer world wide, One of its key guiding documents is the "Agenda for Prosperity". This publication represents an attempt "to bring together everyone who can and wants to contribute to Toronto's long-term prosperity around a single, simple agreement on an achievable vision – a vision to which we can all aspire and align our plans and actions."

The need for Toronto to better tell its story both domestically and abroad is a constant feature of the Agenda for Prosperity. For instance, the agenda clearly sets out the pillars which support Toronto's unique offer. It describes Toronto as a "global business city"; an "inspiring city"; a "location for new and distinctive cultural products"; a "centre for global education and training"; a "base for open institutions"; a "hub of environmental innovation"; and a "beacon of diversity and cohesion".

The delivery of the agenda is framed around four strategic pillars, which have provided guidance to the early mandate of Invest Toronto. They include:

- Proactive Toronto-Business Climate: improving the business climate within the city to enable, accelerate and attract economic growth;

- Global Toronto-Internationalisation: diversifying the city's international portfolio by increasing economic activity with cities beyond North America with a focus on emerging markets;

- Creative Toronto-Productivity and Growth: anchoring and expanding strategic industry sectors through increased competition and collaboration;

- One Toronto-Economic Opportunity and Inclusion: enhancing and expanding Toronto's labour force and ensure that all residents have equitable access to the benefits of Toronto's enhanced economic competitiveness and growth.

The document anchors its strategic discussion with a list of 40 proposed actions and 8 priority activities. Highlights which influence the action of Invest Toronto are illustrated below:

- City-led actions: (1) leadership and organisation; (2) investment in economic development: view economic development as an investment rather than an expenditure and expand budget allocation; and (3) proactive policy development: leverage culture, events and tourism to enhance international presence and expand markets.

- Partner-led actions: (1) cluster development and expansion; (2) global outreach and new market development: enlist business, education and cultural leaders, delegations and touring artists as global business ambassadors to attract investment, skilled labour, conferences, trade shows, meetings, exhibits, performances and visitors to Toronto, Ontario, Canada; tap into locally based international business knowledge by establishing a coalition of business-related international organisations; and (3) labour force development.

- Jointly-led actions: (1) advocacy: identify new policies, tools and incentives that stimulate economic growth; and (2) marketing: take a leadership role in promoting the city and region to the world; develop and implement a strategy to attract lead firms in key sectors; explore opportunities to piggyback on other international marketing efforts with firms in key industry sectors.

The agenda concludes by stating that: "Toronto has choices to make that will define its place in a globalised world. Economic competitiveness must be enhanced through internationalisation, creativity, and inclusion, supported by a business climate that fosters private and public reinvestment. Investment in the future fiscal health of this city is mandatory. By taking action now, through renewed private and public sector investment, Toronto will be bold, energetic, connected and collaborative in the 21st century."

Source: Toronto Mayor's Economic Competitiveness Advisory Committee (2008), "Agenda For Prosperity, 2008", Toronto Mayor's Economic Competitiveness Advisory Committee.

Some of the external indicators that might necessitate the creation of a DA might include: (1) crisis in the local economy which focuses attention on the need for something to be done; (2) the desire to increase the momentum of local economic development activities despite the fact that local partnerships are working effectively; (3) the opportunity to capture local economic benefits from external activities such as an infrastructure investment, increased trade or tourism, or the hosting of a major event; (4) the availability of new tools or incentives/leverage which would be useful for local economic development locally; (5) the presence of a new political climate that offers the opportunity for a stable programme of support (*e.g.* just after an election producing a clear and accepted mandate); and (6) the presence of external organisations that are ready to make a larger investment if the right vehicles are set up.

Of course, other appropriate times may arise for setting up an agency, but these example indicators suggest conditions in which a DA would have a chance of succeeding. Conversely, the absence of these factors might suggest that there would be serious challenges to the success of the DA and some consideration of how to address this is needed.

A clear rationale is essential

A common problem is that the rationale for establishing a DA is often not sufficiently well-defined. As a result, its mission can become unclear, or subject to ongoing debates and controversy. It is therefore desirable to make the rationale for the DA clear from the outset and to communicate it actively. It is also important to use the opportunities of a review to reconsider and consolidate what the rationale is and what the mission should be.

As has been argued throughout this book, essentially, DAs are special purpose vehicles. Justification for creating them, or enhancing their role, rests upon defining how they could achieve more than is possible with pre-existing municipal arrangements.

Intended "value-added", therefore, needs to defined, and DAs should then be designed in such a way as to deliver the additional value that is their remit. The current practice does not emphasise the growth of single purpose/single rationale DAs, although these were more common in the past. Most DAs are now created to fulfil several rationales simultaneously. A DA can review its rationale by reflecting on which of the factors found in the following section would constitute part of its justification, today. This is a good starting point for any conversation about a DA – which of the rationales is it trying to fulfil?

Another important issue is that because there are many potential reasons for setting up a DA, there is often more than one DA in any locality or regional economy. This raises the question about whether the DAs have complementary or conflicting roles, and how they should work together. See Box 4.6 for an example of how such an issue was addressed in Toronto.

Box 4.6. **Invest Toronto and Build Toronto: two new complementary development agencies for Toronto**

Following a review of the city's development efforts and agencies, and building upon the Agenda for Prosperity and the Fiscal Blue Print, the City of Toronto decided to create two new complementary DAs:

- Invest Toronto: a predominantly outward-facing organisation with the responsibility for achieving a better presence and market share for Toronto in international markets and contested investments; and

- Build Toronto: a predominantly inward-facing organisation with the responsibility for property development, institutional investment, urban and asset management, brownfield redevelopment, job creation, and sustainable development. Build Toronto will also finance Invest Toronto to a certain extent.

The mandates for development agency creation

There have been many different starting points for DAs, at different points in time, and in different countries. But understanding the particular purpose, or mixture of purposes, that a DA was established for is both vital in assessing how well it is doing, and essential in estimating how it might contribute to city competitiveness and metropolitan development. A DA is usually set up because one, or more, of the following reasons is suggested.

A DA will be able to quickly address a crisis in the city economy and to organise different actors to take urgent actions together. It is able to respond to a crisis or challenge for which there is no other logical agent (for example, the closure of a key site or facility), and is not distracted by other mandates. This is the "crisis response" mandate (*e.g.* Barcelona Activa).

DAs are also able to act as an organising vehicle for territorial development activities when they are new or under-developed, giving visibility to the economic development work programme, and distinguishing it, organisationally, from other activities. This is the "initiating territorial development" mandate (*e.g.* Prospect Leicestershire).

DAs can potentially be more "investor facing" and "business-like" in their style than a municipal office or department of regional/national government, including the ability to negotiate directly with developers and investors, deliver services to businesses, manage commercial funds, and interface with other commercial actors. In some cases this might include having some delegated local/regional government functions (for example, land use planning or financial assistance decisions) delegated to it. This is the "business interface" mandate (*e.g.* Invest Toronto).

These agencies are also able to focus on the specific needs of an identified redevelopment area or a major project, which may not cover a whole municipality, or may cover several jurisdictions. It may be able to organise a programme for a geographical area, or a new initiative, for which no other "ready" governance structure exists. This is the "special zone, un-served territory" mandate (*e.g.* HafenCity Hamburg GmbH).

DAs can be a new and "independent", and more flexible vehicle for strategy-making, partnership co-investment, and may be capable of integrating the inputs of a diverse range of public and private partners. This is the "aggregator" mandate (*e.g.* the Cape Town Partnership).

DAs can fulfil an "outward facing" or promotional role for the city or region, promoting its appeal and attractiveness for external investment in a targeted manner to key audiences, distinct from the public debate on how the territory needs to be improved. This is the "marketing and promotion" mandate (*e.g.* Madrid Global).

These agencies are also able to develop more flexible procedures and human resource arrangements, enabling it to do things more quickly or efficiently than other organisations. This is the "flexibility" mandate (*e.g.* Abyssinian Development Corporation). DAs tend to undertake a focused task over a defined time-period, unencumbered by other missions and goals. This is the "sole focus" mandate (*e.g.* HafenCity Hamburg GmbH).

Able to achieve a legal or fiscal status which will allow it to utilise or develop additional tools, incentives, investment, asset management and interventions that are otherwise absent, or not available to local governments. This is the "leverage" mandate (*e.g.* New York City Economic Development Corporation).

DAs can manage a transparent process for delivering financial assistance and incentives to businesses, or critical resource allocation decisions, in ways which are not directly politically controlled, and may therefore be seen as more impartial, or not the responsibility of local politicians. This is the "transparency" mandate.

Finally, DAs are able to share risks and costs effectively across a range of interested parties, by negotiating and allocating a clear and novel agreement about how they will be apportioned. This is the "risk and cost sharing" mandate (*e.g.* 22@BCN, Barcelona).

Few DAs will be operating all of these "mandates" simultaneously, but many will have more than one to pursue. This discussion of "mandates" may appear a little arcane, but it is useful in helping to crystallise how DAs may differ from the local, regional, and national governments who sponsor them and why they may be the right new tool for local economic development. The earlier points stress the unique things that are required from a DA, how its impact should be assessed, and whether its mandates should be revised and change over time.

Development agency constitution must reflect rationales and stakeholders

Another important consideration is DA constitution. The constitutional status of DAs varies from one country to another, and many national systems offer more than one alternative status. National or federal legislation has been introduced in many countries to cover a range of DAs, and state/provincial governments have also introduced similar bills and acts. The degree of decentralisation in each country has clearly influenced the constitutional freedoms that local governments may have to introduce their own DAs without recourse to new, or additional, national legislation.

Where national, federal, provincial, or state legislation has been introduced, it tends to define the purposes for which such DAs may be established and the basic rules governing their regulation, management, and governance.

Because national and federal responses to local economic development challenges are both iterative and dynamic, there is an observable legislative "layering" effect in many countries, where initial legislation has been built upon by subsequent additional legislation to further define what is permitted, add new tools and options, or to provide an extended constitutional framework to "catch up" with emerging practices. This is certainly clear in France, the United Kingdom and the United States.

Mission must be clear and verifiable

Another important issue is the mission of DAs. DAs do not all seek to achieve the same things and not all localities require the same contribution from their DAs. Clarity is essential and communication is necessary. At the same time, public sector participation in economic development processes is not particularly well understood, nor accepted in public consciousness or the media. There can thus be an observable "mission creep" that many DAs suffer from, as a vast range of players can often try to dictate to them what they should be doing. Mission statements are therefore a key part of the communications process for maintaining understanding and support for what the DA is trying to achieve.

The establishment of a clear mission for the DA is key to guiding its work and keeping it focused on the core tasks for which it was created. Making the scale and scope of the mission clear at the start is essential. For example, ensuring that some achievable goals are defined early was essential in the start-up processes of Build Toronto, Invest Toronto, Madrid Global and Prospect Leicestershire.

What resources does a start-up process require?

We can distinguish between three type of resources required: start-up costs, core overheads and operational programme funds. All three are needed and they fulfil different functions. An International Links and Services for Local Development Agencies (ILS LEDA) report has detailed sections on each of these that act as a very useful guide. It is important for DAs to develop a clear resourcing strategy from the beginning (see Box 4.7).

Tables 4.1 and 4.2 indicate the sets of strengths, constraints, opportunities and challenges that face start-up DAs. Points to note include the fact that start-up processes involving high levels of stakeholder interaction can establish a solid early foundation from which to build a DA. In addition, though there is a degree of overlap, the disparity between the two, even though they are both new DAs shows that the context in which DAs are created has an important influence on their early development.

Box 4.7. **The origins of the New York City Economic Development Corporation**

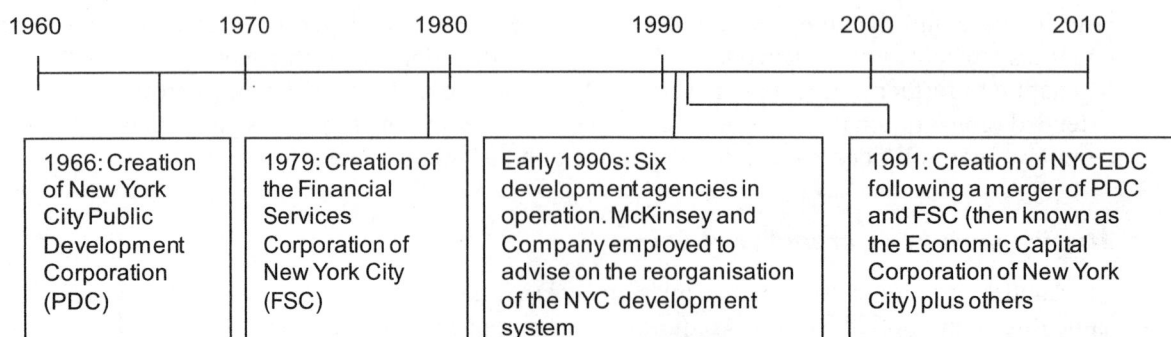

| 1960 | 1970 | 1980 | 1990 | 2000 | 2010 |

| 1966: Creation of New York City Public Development Corporation (PDC) | 1979: Creation of the Financial Services Corporation of New York City (FSC) | Early 1990s: Six development agencies in operation. McKinsey and Company employed to advise on the reorganisation of the NYC development system | 1991: Creation of NYCEDC following a merger of PDC and FSC (then known as the Economic Capital Corporation of New York City) plus others |

The New York City Public Development Corporation, the New York City Economic Development Corporation's (NYCEDC) predecessor organisation, was founded in 1966 to revitalise New York City's struggling economy. The organisation's primary objective was to retain and create jobs and generate revenue for the city by facilitating the sale and lease of city-owned property.

In 1979, the City created another organisation to focus specifically on the financial elements of the City's economic development initiatives outside of its real estate transactions. This organisation was eventually called the Financial Services Corporation of New York City.

By the early 1990s, New York City had six agencies devoted to economic development. They included the Office of Business Development; the Office of Economic Development; the Office of Labor Services; the Department of Ports and Trade; the Public Development Corp.; and the Financial Services Corp. The City engaged the consulting firm McKinsey and Co. in the summer of 1990 to deliver recommendations on how to best promote economic development in New York City.

Following this period of consultation, during the spring of 1991, Mayor David Dinkins and Deputy Mayor for Finance and Economic Development Sally Hernandez-Pinero announced that the City would consolidate the agencies into two groups: The NYCEDC and the Department of Business Services. While the merger was a priority for Mayor Ed Koch, Mayor David Dinkins, the Mayor's Management Advisory Task Force, and the City Council, it was Deputy Mayor Hernandez-Pinero who brought the consolidation effort to fruition.

The 1991 merger that formed the NYCEDC comprised a number of small agencies, plus two large agencies. The two larger agencies included:

- The New York City Public Development Corporation (PDC). The PDC, created in 1966, was primarily charged with retaining and creating jobs and revenue for New York through aiding the sale and leasing of city-owned property. It also managed some of the city's industrial parks and undertook urban planning services.

- The Financial Services Corporation of New York City (FSC). The FSC was created in 1979 and was, at that time, known as the Economic Capital Corporation of New York City (ECC). It complemented the PDC's work and was concerned with overseeing the financial side of urban development work. The FSC acted to promote business expansion by administering finance programmes and overseeing work carried out by the New York City Industrial Development Agency (NYCIDA), a public benefit corporation which encouraged business expansion and employment growth in New York.

From 1991, the newly-formed body of the NYCEDC has assumed the services previously undertaken by the merged corporations, including overseeing programmes of the New York City Industrial Development Agency. NYCEDC also undertakes services previously performed by the City's Department of Ports and Trade.

Table 4.1. **The strengths, constraints, opportunities and challenges of a start-up development agency: Prospect Leicestershire**

Strengths	Constraints
• Designated and expert project manager during start-up. • Multi Area Agreement / "No boundaries approach". • High-level buy-in. • Multi-stakeholder board composition which avoids old tensions. • Clear and manageable mandate.	• Balancing growth across the region. • New organisation with a lack of a track record.
Opportunities	Challenges
• Use the recession as a catalyst to radically improve Leicester and Leicestershire's status as other cities struggle.	• The mandate is too focussed and will need to evolve to include other aspects of social development.

Table 4.2. **The strengths, constraints, opportunities and challenges of a start-up development agency: Invest Toronto**

Strengths	Constraints
• Invest Toronto is supported politically. • It is obvious to all stakeholders that an Invest Toronto-type organisation is required in the city.	• Invest Toronto has no track record at home or abroad. • The Toronto brand and offer is not well understood or known. • There is no evidence-based picture of Toronto's current position to support a thorough marketing campaign. • This city has traditionally not given full attention to its development agenda and role.
Opportunities	Challenges
• Good will generated from the stakeholder engagement process should be utilised. • The chance to form a strong relationship with the City of Toronto Economic Development Department. • The organisation is being created from scratch and has chance to build a fresh reputation and new collaborations. • Emerging from the recession, Toronto could be more marketable than ever, given its resilience in the face of the downturn. • Toronto has never had an investment promotion agency. • Emerging markets could be very fruitful for the city. • Hosting a global event could put Toronto firmly on the world map. • The city's diaspora network could be leveraged. • Build Toronto could unlock the city's underutilised brownfield sites for development.	• Emerging market city competition may make the job of Invest Toronto difficult. • The creation of new organisations risks overlap and friction between the old and the new. • High property taxes could repel new investment. • Looking outwards could leave existing businesses unsupported. • The culture of negativity across the city's system of local development.

Reviewing development agency performance

Healthy and effective DAs undertake regular reviews and make changes to what they do and how they do it as a result. The nature of DA activity demands long-term effort and planning, and yet the context of the activities is changing constantly, especially as economic development activities succeed. This means that it is essential to keep DA activity under active review whilst also supporting the general principle that these are arm's length bodies that do not require minute-to-minute control. It is also essential that DAs are enabled to evolve as the task changes and that the process of DA evolution is guided by stakeholder input and democratic leadership. Indeed, as the previous section suggests, performance review is a key means to being accountable to important stakeholders.

The context of a DA's work can change significantly over small periods of time because: (1) the business cycle can bring new challenges and opportunities; (2) the electoral cycle can deliver different political leadership; (3) the wider policy climate changes the terms of what is possible; (4) public sector reform can trigger wider changes; (5) major projects can arise that have unforeseen impacts; (6) other entities can be created for special purposes; and (7) the business community can become differently organised.

Performance review typologies

There are six main dimensions to DA performance review which ensure that activities can be improved and adjusted to meet a changing operating environment. They include:

- the type of review mechanism, *e.g.* internal monitoring against agreed targets, data analysis, cross-examination meetings, internal colleague discussions, dialogue with external colleagues, external investigation team, public and media opinion;

- the type of output, *e.g.* written reports, presentations, press releases, digital media communications, newsletters, data presentation and performance indicators;

- the formality of the review mechanism, *e.g.* informal dialogues through to legally required report books;

- the provenance of the review mechanism, *e.g.* stakeholders external to the DA such as the City Council and affiliated bodies, clients groups, the community, funders, members, partners;

- the frequency of the review mechanism, *e.g.* regular dialogue with colleagues through to bi-annual external audits; and

- the subject of the review mechanism, *e.g.* the DA as a whole, teams within the DA or individual staff members.

As Table 4.3 shows, DAs review performance in a number of ways, for a number of reasons and bodies, at different frequencies, with a number of outputs and to differing degrees of formality and scale. The exact dimensions of a given review mechanism may vary widely and DAs must choose the most suitable.

Table 4.3. **Summary of development agency performance review mechanisms**

Development agency	Performance review mechanism example	Formality		Provenance		Frequency			
		Formal	Informal	Internal	External	Monthly / bimonthly	Annually	Two-three years	When required / ongoing
Cape Town Partnership	Production and presentation of annual report to board	■		■	■		■		
	Review by external consultants	■			■			■	
	Informal dialogue with City staff		■		■				■
Madrid Global	Simple internal statistical system which measures performance against agreed target	■		■		■			
	Simple external statistical system which measures performance against agreed targets set by the Mayor	■			■				■
New York City Economic Development Corporation	Production of descriptive annual report by law for scrutiny by senior City officials e.g. the Mayor	■			■		■		
	Review of internal operations by in-house Strategic Planning and Strategic Operations departments	■		■					■
	In-house audit of real estate portfolio	■		■		■			
	Project monitoring against agreed aims	■		■					■

Issues of scale commonly arise here. Some of the necessary modes and mechanisms of control and performance review can be costly to undertake in terms of financial and other resources, but there are few shortcuts. This suggests that the issue of critical mass needs to be considered when designing and staffing a DA and when recruiting its Board of Directors. The lack of highly developed understandings of what the economic development process involves, especially the complex risk, cost, and return-sharing elements of the process, is a major communication and performance review challenge to which DAs must attend if they are to succeed.

Though it is also important to keep the rationale and mission of a DA under regular review, frequent review can be disruptive. It is in the nature of the economic development process that new tasks emerge as progress is made and the DA needs a clear procedure for updating such missions. However, frequent review can create a culture of evaluation and self-evaluation to a point which can become obsessive. This can reduce efficiency, the very thing performance reviews are meant to enhance. It is important that a balance between reflection and productivity is maintained.

Box 4.8 and Figure 4.2 showcase two different approaches to development agency performance review.

Box 4.8. An individual approach to performance review and improvement: the Johannesburg Development Agency's "Performance Management System"

The Johannesburg Development Agency "Performance Management System" (PMS) is an essential communication link aimed to provide alignment between the strategies, goals and objectives of the organisation, and the work objectives of teams and individuals in the organisation. The PMS also focuses on the development of soft skills, while managing employees towards the achievement of team and individual goals and objectives. The Johannesburg Development Agency PMS is central to ensuring that every one of its people is competent, motivated and empowered.

During 2007/08 financial year, the Johannesburg Development Agency reviewed its PMS to ensure that it is compatible with that of the City of Johannesburg in terms of content and implementation. The revised PMS informs the Johannesburg Development Agency's reward system to ensure that it is not only market-related, but that it will ensure the success of its retention strategy in line with the determinations and policies of the parent municipality.

The Johannesburg Development Agency has adopted a resolution to continue to spend about 3% of its payroll on training and development of staff.

Figure 4.2. **Liverpool Vision's performance monitoring framework**

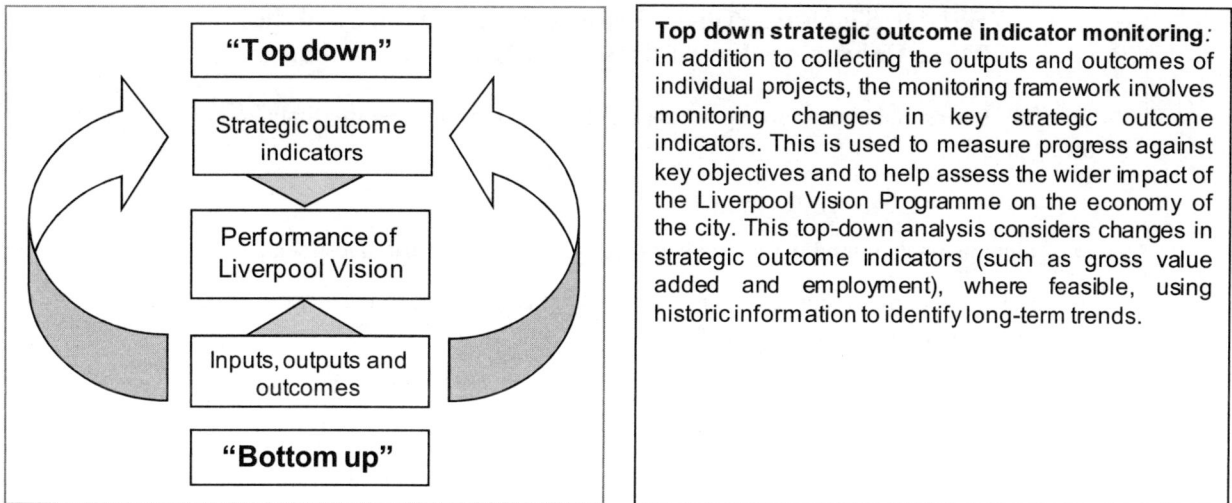

"Top down"

Strategic outcome indicators

Performance of Liverpool Vision

Inputs, outputs and outcomes

"Bottom up"

Top down strategic outcome indicator monitoring: in addition to collecting the outputs and outcomes of individual projects, the monitoring framework involves monitoring changes in key strategic outcome indicators. This is used to measure progress against key objectives and to help assess the wider impact of the Liverpool Vision Programme on the economy of the city. This top-down analysis considers changes in strategic outcome indicators (such as gross value added and employment), where feasible, using historic information to identify long-term trends.

Bottom up individual project monitoring: A clear and simple performance management system has been established to collect monitoring information for each individual project. This involves assembling and updating information on each project identified in the investment programme, including target/forecast data. The system produces the following information for each project.

The next example of Prospect Leicestershire's Three Universities For Business (3U4B) project shows how DAs work with other leaders in the local development system to achieve success (Box 4.9).

Box 4.9. **Signature Project: Prospect Leicestershire and the Three Universities For Business (3U4B) project**

Launched in April 2009, Prospect Leicestershire was set up to drive economic growth forward across the urban area of Leicester and its surrounding county. Its Three Universities for Business (3U4B) project is a joint initiative between Leicestershire's three universities - Loughborough, Leicester and De Montfort, and Prospect Leicestershire. The three universities already represent a substantial asset to the local economy; with a total student population of over 50 000, they are producing many of the country's top graduates and generating millions of pounds of revenues from research activities, nurturing spin-off companies and supporting new start-up businesses and job creation. 3U4B was launched in January 2008 to build on the collective capacity within the three universities and increase collaboration with small and larger businesses. It aims to provide benefits to local businesses by exposing them to the wide range of expertise available across the three universities for whom in its first year alone 3U4B has generated more than 30 new business enquiries.

The initiative has been led by Prospect Leicestershire to leverage optimal benefit for the local economy of the combined impact of the three universities. Moreover, it recognises that this combined impact exceeds the sum total of its component parts. Central to the philosophy is the whole-area perspective brought to bear in delivery. Such collaboration is believed to be unique.

Box 4.9. **Signature Project: Prospect Leicestershire and the Three Universities For Business (3U4B) project** *(continued)*

Prospect Leicestershire is working across the three universities to foster collaboration in the following areas:

- assisting in physical projects linked to the universities;

- joint approach around marketing messages to promote inward investment;

- brokering engagement between the universities and local businesses to encourage innovation, product development and mutual commercial benefit;

- providing support and intelligence to university staff and spin-out businesses; and

- assisting with graduate retention.

The next phase of work will see the three universities, supported by Prospect Leicestershire, establishing a joint venture to:

- integrate the three universities within the Leicester and Leicestershire sub-regional economic development governance arrangements;

- establish governance mechanisms to enable the three universities and the sub-regional partner agencies to build their collective capacity to increase collaboration with small and larger businesses; and

- create more value from growth and innovation in collaboration with small and larger businesses, for example in knowledge transfer and open innovation systems, consultancy services, business management and education, enterprise development, and graduate placements.

The potential deliverables from this new collaboration will be joint ventures between the three universities, Prospect Leicestershire and local authorities:

- developing customer relationship management (CRM) skills and culture within each institution;

- establishing a brokering bureau to diagnose company requirements and match these with capabilities across the three universities;

- improving knowledge transfer and intellectual property (IP) exploitation links between the universities and business;

- developing a shared service approach to the promotion of and support services for early-stage, high-growth businesses; and

- further specific joint ventures, for example to deliver the universities' carbon reduction commitments.

Source: Hughes, D. (2009), Written and telephone communication and interviews.

Outcomes and change as a result of the review process

As has been discussed, the review process is the way in which DAs can establish whether or not there is a need to adapt and evolve. We will now highlight a number of factors which could necessitate the evolution of DA activities. Should these constraints become particularly acute and the DA and its stakeholders fail to, or cannot, respond effectively, the DA risks closure.

Typical problems include:

- A clear mandate is not established for the DA at the outset and there is failure amongst citizens, political leaders and other stakeholders to understand why a more indirectly accountable corporate structure is preferred to a directly accountable municipal structure. This appears to be the most common source of problems. This is, in part, because few local commentators really understand why a corporate structure is desirable. This is often a failure to understand what the local dimension of economic development is.

- One variant on this main source of problems arises when DAs are established by tiers of government higher than the local level. For example, sometimes national ministries or regional governments establish local or regional agencies. This then means that local governments have to work with an agency that is not accountable to them, and may find that it is very hard to reach shared agreements about common objectives or working arrangements. This can then lead to worsened co-ordination failures between different tiers of government on local development issues.

- Sometimes, a clear strategic framework is not set by responsible elected leaders and therefore DAs lack strategic guidance. An important division of labour exists in the DA model whereby the strategic framework is set by policy makers and the DA is asked to implement effectively. A failure to provide the clear strategic framework leaves the DA without the necessary externally imposed discipline.

- On other occasions, scale and critical mass are not achieved. Several DAs operate at too small a scale to impact upon the local economy in a meaningful timeframe. They are seen as irrelevant and end up spending much effort advocating for resources. This is often true where multiple agencies exist in one location or where there is a simple failure to accurately assess the scale of resources required to do a meaningful job.

- In some contexts, DA governance does not work well. DAs may be micro-managed. Local governments do not always have experience in how to both give DAs "arm's length" operational freedom and to make them operationally accountable. This can lead to tensions and to the failure to generate momentum on the economic development tasks.

- At the same time, DA staff may not know how to be fully accountable and operationally innovative. There is an important skill set that DAs require, which is how to be adept at being both accountable and innovative. Much of what is involved here is good planning and anticipation, so that it can predict the kinds of activities and risks it will need to manage and can seek enabling approvals and effective controls in advance of situations.

- In some locations, too many DAs or development bodies co-exist. Multiple development agencies sometimes arise from different historic phases of local development policy or from the different governmental sponsors that exist. Multiple agencies in one location may be an act of design (as in Toronto and Bilbao in our case studies). In these contexts, where they have precise and complementary roles, they can work very well. But too often, multiple agencies in one location are a product of confusion or leadership failure. Public and private sector sponsors may like choice, whereas DAs try to aggregate activities. There can be tension between a desire to achieve critical mass and scale *versus* a desire to have diffused distribution paths and vehicles for activities. Competitors to the DA can be set up or encouraged, thus eroding the potential value added, and fostering confusion about roles and responsibilities.

- Businesses sometimes see DAs as "crowding out" private sector interests in some markets. Activities which were not commercially sustainable at one point in the business or development cycle and needed DA intervention may, at other times, become more attractive to market-based players, and not warrant ongoing intervention. For example, where DAs are involved in the provision of affordable SME accommodation and development finance at one point in a business cycle, they may find that the private sector observes that market opportunity and starts to play the role directly, but sees the DAs as competition. DAs have to be alert to changing market dynamics to know when public sector intervention or subsidy is no longer required. In a variation on this, property owners may refuse to co-operate with DAs, holding out for higher returns on their development lands because they believe the development process will raise values in the future.

- A change of political leadership at the local level can change the preferences about how local development is delivered. Different political parties may take distinctive stances on DAs. It can take DAs more than one electoral cycle to prove their value. Start-up and wind–up costs can be substantial so it is advisable that DAs enjoy some cross-party support and participation and anticipate future changes of local political leadership and be flexible with them.

- It is also observed that municipal colleagues do not always co-operate fully with the DA. It is surprisingly common that municipal staff do not find it easy to co-operate with DAs. This often comes from misunderstandings about the rationale for establishment of a DA or a lack of clarity about roles and division of labour between the DA and municipal departments. Interface with planning departments requires special attention.

- Finally, media and the general public may not fully understand the DA and its role. They may scrutinise individual "deals" done by DAs and not find them appropriate or acceptable, or do not accept the wider benefits. This is particularly challenging where any incentives to business are involved. Often there is a perception that the resources could have been spent on something else. Good media strategy and relations are critical for DAs. Making the case for local development and for the DA is key and defining and illustrating the benefits of local development is essential.

Where and how to evolve development agencies

It is clear that each of these typical problems can be avoided if the right framework is established at the beginning and if good communications are pursued. Regular DA performance reviews are essential. As well as fulfilling accountability requirements, the aim of performance reviews is to identify how operations can be improved to enhance the positive impact of DAs. There a range of typical suggestions for change that arise as a result of DAs reviews. The following discussion outlines such suggestions:

- The focus of the DA needs to change or its mission is somewhat out of date. Sometimes the name and brand need to be revised, or to be re-established. Sometimes DAs need to take on additional tasks or broaden their efforts. Movement from niche, to sectoral or comprehensive DAs is common.

- The communications strategy of the DA needs to be revised and an intensive period of re-communication with stakeholders is needed. Stakeholders change quite regularly, and are often busy people. Keeping up-to-date information about DAs at "front of mind" requires effort.

- Better alignment of DA work with that of local government, business leadership groups, and higher tiers of government is required. Cities need a single development system with multiple entities playing orchestrated roles. This needs constant refreshment.

- The DA needs more vocal and pro-active sponsorship and support in the city at large. DAs need senior elected leaders and senior business figures to continuously give them authority if they are to be effective.

- A new financial or asset management strategy is required. Usually DAs need to move from grant dependency to multiple income streams and sources of revenue if they are to mature over the long term. Usually, assets become more valuable as development proceeds, and this raises questions about whether to hold, endow, or to sell. What is the DA's role?

- New tools are necessary to take developments to a new scale or level of sophistication. As the market matures (in say property redevelopment), DAs need to play more sophisticated roles and they need the tools required to do this.

- A clearer DA "dividend" needs to be communicated to win support from colleagues in other entities. People who work in City Halls are suspicious of the freedom that DAs enjoy and are often wary of attempts to extend their mandate. A clear "dividend" needs to be articulated so that people can focus on the outcomes for the city and for them, not the freedom of the DAs.

- Changes to internal deployment of staff and other resources are warranted. Changes to the mission and role require internal re-engineering. This takes thought, time, and effort.

These outcomes inform stakeholders about the performance of DAs. If positive, reviews can offer an important confidence boost for DAs. If less positive, they act as an indicator that change is required. Many reviews also suggest potential avenues of future direction. Exactly which options are selected, though, remains a decision for the board and senior management team.

Longevity and sustainability

One variable that the literature does not address consciously is the sustainability of DAs. There are two main points to make:

- Where DAs have been given multi-dimensional missions, there tends to be an expectation that their work will need to be ongoing and their organisational development will need to be attended to. However, those DAs that have a more limited or fixed brief are usually expected to close down once their task is largely complete. This latter group tends to rely on short-term organisational practices (such as hiring consultants rather than staff, etc.) and do not easily develop alternative approaches. But many DAs start life as short-term and gradually acquire an additional set of mandates.

- Where a DA has survived through a number of changes to mission and role, and through several turns of the business cycle and political leadership, the agency can acquire a robustness which aids its performance. In effect, the growth of "institutional memory and wisdom" is very valuable and constitutes a "sunk investment" that might otherwise be overlooked.

Table 4.4 and Boxes 4.10 and 4.11 illustrate the adaptability of development agencies as they are reviewed and improved.

Table 4.4. **Responding to change: the adaptability of development agencies**

Organisation	Challenge faced	Approach
New York City Economic Development Corporation	Revenue cost balance during the recession	NYCEDC has taken aggressive steps to maximise its real estate portfolio's assets, while making strategic cuts to its budget. Prior to the fall of 2008, NYCEDC had already engaged an internal team of real estate experts to examine how it could maximise the use of the City's real estate portfolio. The team has made several recommendations to NYCEDC's leadership and has identified ways to save the City and its taxpayers a significant amount of money.
Barcelona Activa	Dependence on external influence	Barcelona Activa competes to attract resources from different public administrations and this allows the organisation to multiply the resources guaranteed to it by the City Council and act more flexibly. At the same time, competition for finance is an added motivation to present projects with highly innovative components and methodologies.
Creative Sheffield	Elongated system of accountability and project commissioning	To improve the speed at which buy-in from key partners is achieved, Creative Sheffield worked closely with key partners such as the City Council and Yorkshire Forward, at the development phase. Achieving earlier buy-in ensures that partners are more likely to have the opportunity to shape initiatives and sign off on new projects. In this way, Creative Sheffield attempts to operate a "No Surprises" philosophy in its work.
Bilbao Metropoli-30	Lack of executive power	Bilbao Metropoli-30 positions itself as a facilitator and works hard to maintain the critical relationships it needs to achieve the necessary buy-in for projects to begin and be delivered. In addition, Bilbao Metropoli-30 only launches its proposals after it has the agreement of its partners. This timing gains it credibility and trust.
Johannesburg Development Agency	Un-sustainability of funding mechanisms	To reduce the reliance on grant funding for capital projects and to re-establish more strategic projects and priorities, the JDA is seeking to diversify its income streams and minimise certain costs where possible. Following a July 2009 board meeting, the organisation is exploring a number of avenues, including: (1) looking for other capital projects in the city; (2) investigating the possibility of charging fees to share expertise gained over recent years; (3) better articulating the value of the JDA to the city to improve levels of grant funding; (4) undertaking a more entrepreneurial real estate development role where a proportion of any surplus created by the JDA is retained to support its operating budget; and (5) exploring funding options from higher tiers of government and international financial institutions.

Box 4.10. **The evolution of the Cape Town Partnership**

The history of the Cape Town Partnership can be broadly set out as such:

- **Establishment (1996-99)**. Discussions take place, mainly between the central business district (CBD) property owners and businesses and the City of Cape Town, around the need for a collective approach to solving the problems of the Central City. Various *ad hoc* initiatives are put in place (*e.g.* CCTV cameras, Broom Brigade), but the decision is taken to initiate a formally structured partnership to sustain efforts. The Partnership was launched in July 1999 and the Central City Improvement District (CCID) in November 2000.

- **Implementation (1999-2002)**. The focus is on improving the performance of the Central City by making the area safe and clean, and *perceived* to be clean and safe, in order to restore business and public confidence, stem capital flight and rescue dwindling municipal revenues.

- **Urban regeneration (2003-05)**. The focus is on attracting private sector investment to regenerate commercial buildings; however, significant conversion of under-utilised B- and C-grade office buildings to residential accommodation occurs. The East City Regeneration Conference takes place in order to promote investment in an under-developed part of the Central City. There is a growing focus on upgrading public spaces to encourage public activities; however, there is still minimal public sector investment in the Central City due to the need to extend basic municipal services to more disadvantaged areas of the city.

- **Broadening the Partnership (2005-07)**. The Partnership's vision and mission is broadened to focus on inclusive development. The CCID's social development and job creation programme is strengthened. New partners from the social, cultural, environmental and educational sectors are drawn onto the Partnership's Board, as well as representation from other public sector bodies such as the Western Cape Provincial Government.

- **Building the long-term agenda (2007-09)**. New programmes, such as Creative Cape Town and the CBD Energy Efficiency Initiative, are established. While the Partnership continues to focus on improving the performance of the Central City through CCID urban management programmes and partnerships, a Central City Development Strategy (CCDS) is drawn up to build a long-term agenda for action. Massive public sector investment begins to take place, mainly due to preparations for the 2010 FIFA World Cup.

Source: Boraine, A. (2009), "Public-Private Partnerships and Urban Regeneration in the Cape Town Central City: Lessons from the First Ten Years of the Cape Town Partnership".

Box 4.11. **The evolution of the Johannesburg Development Agency mandate**

The Johannesburg Development Agency delivered several important phases of inner city regeneration in the first phase of its mandate from 2001-06. Inner city regeneration in Johannesburg is not yet complete and there is more work to be done here which the Johannesburg Development Agency could lead effectively.

The current priority however for the Johannesburg Development Agency is to implement several key components of transport-oriented development intended to better connect Johannesburg internally and to provide a spur for further regeneration and development.

The current priorities associated with transport-orientated development and the FIFA 2010 World Cup provides important deadlines which must be met. After 2010 there is an opportunity to review and develop wider roles for the Johannesburg Development Agency, to enable Johannesburg to better capture the value of current investments.

Looking to the future, the Johannesburg Development Agency is taking the opportunity to conduct a thorough examination of its business model.

What can go wrong and the closure of development agencies

Early warnings or problems

As we have shown above, DAs are not easy organisations to set up and run. This is in part because they try to combine multiple actors from public, private, and community sectors, and also because DAs attempt to achieve public outcomes through market-based interventions and mechanisms. Few DAs go through a lifecycle without some difficulties. It is important that local and other actors support their DAs to come through these challenges and to build a more effective organisation.

As well as the factors detailed earlier in this chapter, some warning signs include: (1) bad news (*e.g.* consistent opposition to what the DA is doing); (2) arguments between partners; (3) delayed projects or implementation; and (4) staff/board retention problems. When these warning signs occur, it is important that the local actors get together to help the DA find a mature solution or way out.

Closing down a development agency

In many countries, DAs have not been closed down when their work is finished. It is important to have regular review processes and to assess the changing needs of locality over time. DAs need to be aware of what is expected of them and how/when they will be judged. If a decision is taken to close down a DA, a plan for closure and asset transfer is needed in just the same way that a start-up plan is required.

It is clear from the outcomes of DA reviews that these are not organisations that can perform well without having effective working relationships with other organisations. Because local development requires integrated inputs in a range of sectors (labour markets, investment markets, business development, infrastructure) and policies (business support, place marketing, skills, land use planning, etc.) effective local development is always the product of the interplay between a range of policies and public sector interventions, and a range of market processes. DAs are only one actor in these processes and their success depends crucially upon other inputs.

Occasionally some DAs are given very broad responsibilities across a range of inputs into local development, often in a tightly defined location. HafenCity in Hamburg is a good example of this. A single company oversees a very wide range of development inputs in a tightly defined area. In this case the development agency is set up in such a way as to internalise many activities that would otherwise be part of a larger and wider local system. This is often the case in intensive redevelopment areas. Even in the case of HafenCity, however, many other public inputs come from other parts of government, and there are many commercial players also involved.

However, this broad responsibility is relatively unusual, and often only occurs on a time-limited basis. In most cases DAs have to work in tandem with many other organisations and are dependent upon them. For example, the OECD LEED (Local Economic and Employment Development) Review of Laganside Development Corporation in Belfast recognised that the employment outcomes of the Laganside redevelopment were at least partially dependent on the success of local colleges in building local skills. The OECD LEED Review of Barcelona Activa noted that the provision of physical space for new economy companies was dependent upon the success of the 22@ District and the role of the planning system in bringing forwards sites for redevelopment. Both of these activities are outside of the role of Barcelona Activa. More broadly, DAs often have roles in promoting their locations for external contested investment. This only works in the long term if wider inputs such as transport, housing, skills are made effectively.

The observation here is simple, but profound. Although DAs are usually expert in local development, there are a wide range of inputs to local development that lie in the hands of other organisations. Understanding this interdependencies is key, and organising the inputs so that they work together is essential. Assessing the performance of DAs requires at least two separate considerations: (1) how well the DA has played the roles for which it is responsible, and (2) how well the rest of the local development system has made its contribution.

In the next chapter of this book we look at the role of these local development systems in DA success.

References

BBC (British Broadcasting Corporation) (2009), "Councils Create New Jobs Agency", *http://news.bbc.co.uk/1/hi/england/leicestershire/7846593.stm.*

Boraine, A. (2009), "Public-Private Partnerships and Urban Regeneration in the Cape Town Central City: Lessons from the First Ten Years of the Cape Town Partnership".

Hughes, D. (2009), Written and telephone communication and interviews.

Leicestershire Rural Partnership Management Board (2008), "Economic Sub-Regional Arrangements, 2008", Leicestershire Rural Partnership Management Board.

Toronto Mayor's Economic Competitiveness Advisory Committee (2008), "Agenda For Prosperity, 2008", Toronto Mayor's Economic Competitiveness Advisory Committee.

Chapter 5

The role of the local development system

This chapter describes how development agencies can lead, shape and facilitate the effective operation of the local development system and are in turn led, shaped and facilitated by it. It defines these systems as networks of public, business and non-governmental sector partners which can work collaboratively within defined areas to create better conditions for economic growth, social cohesion and employment generation. Evidence from the 16 development agency case studies is used to show that local development systems are tightly or loosely organised, precisely orchestrated to deliver a local development strategy, or rather imprecisely oriented. The chapter proceeds with a discussion of how to build a seamless and co-ordinated system giving particular attention to key work streams, key players, features of success and the role of development agencies within it.

Introducing the local development system

The "local development system" is a term which we use here to describe the network of public, business and non-governmental sector partners which work collaboratively within a defined area to create better conditions for economic growth, social cohesion and employment generation. Local development systems might be tightly or loosely organised, precisely orchestrated to deliver a local development strategy, or rather imprecisely oriented.

As we explained in the preceding chapter, a key feature of many reviews of local development is the prevalence of "co-ordination failures" where opportunities to better calibrate and integrate inputs to local economic performance are not taken for a variety of reasons resulting in underperformance. In the context of reviews of the contribution of development agencies to local economic performance, we can observe that the chief issues are:

- Development agencies (DAs) are part of the local development system and the relationship between the development agency and other parts of the system is of critical interest.

- DAs sometimes have explicit roles in co-ordinating or shaping local development systems.

- DAs cannot succeed unless local development systems are effective, unless they seek to internalise many of the aspects of the system itself.

- Many of the challenges that DAs face can be seen as system failures, as much as agency failures.

To illustrate these points, we observe that sometimes there are multiple agencies competing for roles and resources in which we create duplicate, gaps, or waste. Occasionally, there is limited co-operation between the DA and other local bodies, especially is the DA is established by regional or national government. Equally, at certain times there is limited co-ordination between DAs and other parts of the local municipal government.

Local development systems tend to be relatively complex, as they require effective co-ordination between many different types of organisations or stakeholder groups. This potential constraint is also the local development system's most significant strength. It is often the task of local government to construct a system which holds together all its various component parts (public and private sector organisations; citizens and businesses; knowledge-based institutions and DAs) in a positive tension which makes maximum use of all available resources, expertise and experience.

In a review of the literature, which includes sources within cities and relevant institutions, such as the International Labour Organisation, World Bank and the United Nations, there is consensus around local development as the process of building the capacity of a local area to improve its economic future and the quality of life for all. The local development system, therefore, involves both the structure within which development-orientated organisations are organised and the key relationships between them.

These systems are fundamental to local development success. Local development is a multi-disciplinary and integrated practice which requires expertise, experience and delivery capacity that no single organisation has. As a result, organisation and collaboration are essential to deliver effective local development. Without a healthy local development system, therefore, local development progress becomes a far more difficult task. DAs, no matter how effective, cannot easily compensate for weaknesses in the local development system, unless they become very comprehensive managers of all local development activities, which is usually undesirable. An effective DA will not usually take the place of good schools and colleges, responsible employers, an efficient land use planning system, or the local banking sector. Occasionally DAs will do some of these tasks, but rarely for any extended length of time.

At best, these systems involve high levels of vertical and horizontal co-ordination across a multitude of partners to address a number of key themes which support the holistic and sustainable development of a local economy. Relationships are pragmatic and constructive and the application of resources broad, deep, but notably efficient. At worst, key relationships break down through a lack of trust and because of competition for work and resources, personality clashes and other such frictions. Gaps may also exist for key work streams necessary to deliver effective local development. Conversely, some systems are so complex, contested and convoluted that it is not clear who does what and forward momentum dissipates.

Despite their significance, there have been few attempts to describe what comprises a local development system. There remains progress to be made on the understanding of relationships between key stakeholders and the underlying principles for success. Through evidence gathered from the 16 DA case studies, input from experts and practitioners as well as first-hand experience, this chapter will explore these issues.

Building a seamless and co-ordinated local development system

To ensure a holistic and sustainable form of local development, it is essential that all necessary work streams are identified and delivered. But before constructing and populating a local development system, it is first necessary to isolate needs within it and specific organisations to deliver these requirements. Otherwise, delivery arrangements may not dovetail with the delivery requirements.

After mapping local development requirements, a suitable framework that addresses each is necessary. This framework or system should then be populated with the necessary bodies to deliver it effectively. The system should be seamless and co-ordinated and may involve the construction of new bodies, boards and panels, the rationalisation and redefinition of existing bodies or the creation of clear communication channels between key components of the system.

An assessment of local development system capacity and requirements can be undertaken at any time. It tends, however, to be an ongoing process which sees the internal reorganisation of local development arrangements to capture the benefits and avoid the constraints of local and global change. In some cases, a re-evaluation may be stimulated by a period of crisis or because the local area has never formally defined its local development system.

Box 5.2 provides an example of the role that DAs can play in addressing uncertainty and gaps within local economic development.

Box 5.1. **Bridging the gaps in the Toronto local development system**

As a result of stakeholder consultation and reviews of experiences of other cities in 2008, a number of significant gaps and uncertainties were identified in Toronto's system of development and investment promotion. They include: economic intelligence and communication; business, job and investment retention; inward investment facilitation and client handling; identity and brand leadership; network leadership for agencies and stakeholders; co-ordination of promotion in other markets (students, sports, events, institutional investors); business leaders club for promotion; Toronto's lead role in the region; business case for Toronto to the Province and the Federal Governments; and alignment of City, Province and Federal Governments on investment agendas.

These gaps are, in part, the legacy of the city not addressing the theme of economic development directly enough. Awareness of these gaps and uncertainties galvanised the recalibration of the entire system of economic development and investment attraction in Toronto, and has led to establishment of Build Toronto and Invest Toronto.

Key work streams within local development systems

Key work streams comprise all the necessary pillars of activity required for successful urban development. They are many and vary according to place. An examination of city indices in a 2008 book, *City Success: What Do the City Indices Tell Us?* by the Urban Land Institute (Clark, 2008), helps to identify what appear to be the drivers of local development success. They act as an excellent proxy for the pillars of activity which need to be addressed by local development systems. Split into short and longer-term timescales, they are detailed in Table 5.1.

Table 5.1. **Drivers of local development success**

Shorter-term (one or two business cycles)	Longer-term (five to ten business cycles)
Connectivity and accessibility	Openness to international populations
Economic breadth	Power (and adaptability) of the city region identity and brand
Quality of life, place, and amenity	Location and access to growing markets
Skills of labour force	Role in fostering/brokering international trade
Innovation and creativity	Power and influence of language and regulatory/legal/financial systems
Business environment, entrepreneurship and city cost base	Depth of artistic, architectural and cultural endowment
Image and identity	City-regional leadership and effective investment advocacy
Leadership and implementation of strategy	Adaptation to climate change
	Success in adjusting to shocks, and luck/skill in being on the right side of conflicts
	Investment in the city from all sources (including higher tiers of government)

Box 5.2 shows how a DA can add significant value to the planning and objective-setting stage of the development process.

Box 5.2. **Signature project: Bilbao Metropoli-30 and the From Infrastructures To Values project**

"From Infrastructures to Values" describes the evolutionary path which Bilbao Metropoli-30 has strategically prescribed for the metropolitan area of Bilbao. Traditionally, interventions focused primarily on the implementation of vast infrastructural projects. However, as the agency explains, "cities nowadays no longer compete in infrastructural terms; this means that at international level, we take for granted that cities count on a minimum infrastructural base to be attractive for visitors, inhabitants and investments. What really makes a city competitive and attractive in the 21st century is people and their values."

Subsequently, by the end of the 1990s, the organisation began to focus intently on a process of visioning for the city. By creating a coherent vision for Bilbao, Bilbao Metropoli-30 aims to create a unique identity for Bilbao which will serve to attract visitors and businesses alike.

The resulting document, The Strategic Reflection Bilbao 2010, was written in 1999 and the strategy is based in three basic elements:

- People: for high value added business initiatives to develop, it is necessary for the role of leaders to be reinforced in developing metropolitan Bilbao and to design mechanisms for training, keeping and attracting professionals.

- Activity in the City: in order to encourage high value-added business activities, a suitable environment must be created which provides immediate Internet access, support policies for innovative initiatives and the creation of intelligent infrastructures.

- The Appeal of the Metropolis: the city is a vital space, which must be attractive to live and work in.

The Strategic Reflection Bilbao 2010, for the first time, paid special attention to the creation of a new image for Bilbao linked to art and culture and the promotion of business activities of high added value; a theme that the agency dubbed "Cultural Modernity".

In this context, cultural modernity refers to Bilbao as a cultural metropolis which nurtures its traditions in art and culture, but utilises its reputation in a modern and forward-thinking way. The programme aims to raise the level of awareness of all cultural groups in terms of their participation in cultural and leisure activities in Bilbao. By encouraging communities from every background to engage with, and respect, each other, Bilbao Metropoli-30 hopes to create an open, modern, creative and innovative community that residents and the rest of the world will find appealing.

Metropolitan Bilbao continues to develop a vast array of social activities and experiences, and is striving towards producing events of international status. For example, The Guggenheim Museum, Bilbao is establishing itself as the centre of a modern city with a growing international reputation. For this reason, Bilbao Metropoli-30 organised an international Congress in 2006 to define the values for the development of the city. Bilbao recognised five values which are essential for its competitive and sustainable development: innovation, professionalism, identity, community, and openness.

Source: Bilbao Metropoli-30 (2009a), "City and Value Paper", *www.bm30.es/cuadernos_uk.html*; Bilbao Metropoli-30 (2009b), "The Bilbao Case: From Infrastructures to Values", Bilbao Metropoli-30.

Key organisations within local development systems

To plan and deliver the work streams introduced, a myriad of organisations with different aims, objectives and expertise are required.

The precise range of organisations found within a local development system depends on its requirements and other factors such as institutional and legal frameworks. Typically though, maps of local development systems will contain the full range of organisations from the public sector, private sector, civil society as well as higher tiers of government. Specifically, this includes: local government (mayoral offices and other departments); regional government departments; national government departments; community and not-for-profit organisations; business leadership groups, universities and think tanks, infrastructure groups; the media; advisers and consultants; and delivery partners. Without doubt, DAs are a key addition to this network of development-orientated organisations. Flexible, market-facing, business-like, specialist, and innovative, they add value in ways which other organisations in the local development system cannot.

Though it is not one of the 16 case studies used as the core evidence base for this book, the example of the London Development Agency is helpful here. The following diagram or "local development system map" illustrates which organisations are principally networked together to deliver London's local development agenda (see Figure 5.1).

The maps which follow the London local development system map (Figures 5.2 through 5.7) demonstrate the uniqueness of the contexts in which these organisations operate. The London Development Agency plays many important roles in the development of London but must work in tandem with a myriad of other organisations (even in this simplified map) if it is to succeed. The quality and effectiveness of those working relationships are critical to its long-term success.

Figure 5.1. **London's local development system map**

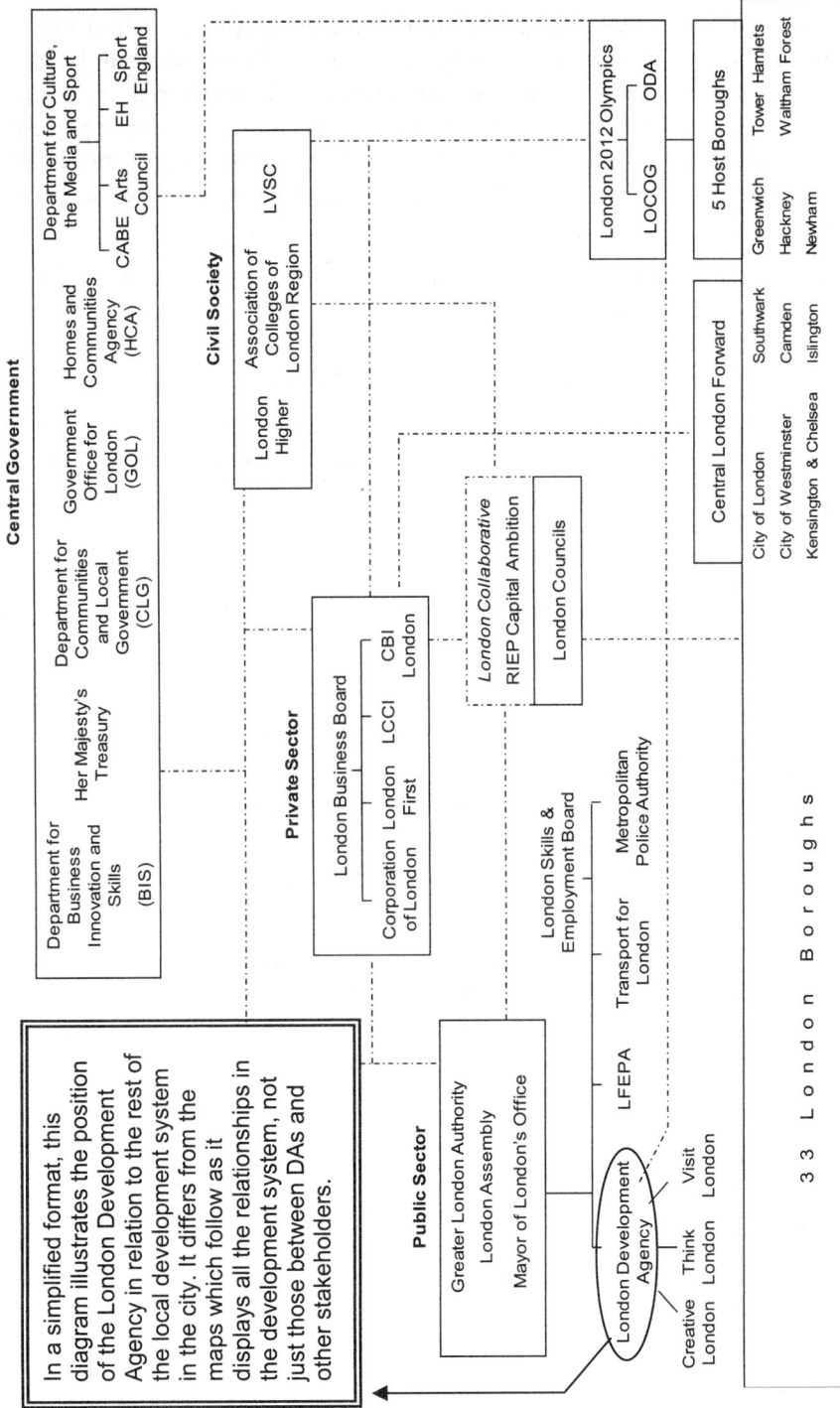

In a simplified format, this diagram illustrates the position of the London Development Agency in relation to the rest of the local development system in the city. It differs from the maps which follow as it displays all the relationships in the development system, not just those between DAs and other stakeholders.

Central Government

Department for Business Innovation and Skills (BIS)

Her Majesty's Treasury

Department for Communities and Local Government (CLG)

Government Office for London (GOL)

Homes and Communities Agency (HCA)

Department for Culture, the Media and Sport

CABE | Arts Council | EH | Sport England

Civil Society

London Higher

Association of Colleges of London Region

LVSC

Private Sector

London Business Board

Corporation of London | LCCI London | CBI London

London Collaborative
RIEP Capital Ambition

London Councils

Public Sector

Greater London Authority
London Assembly
Mayor of London's Office

London Development Agency

Creative London | Think London | Visit London

LFEPA

Transport for London

London Skills & Employment Board

Metropolitan Police Authority

3 3   L o n d o n   B o r o u g h s

Central London Forward

City of London
City of Westminster
Kensington & Chelsea

Southwark
Camden
Islington

London 2012 Olympics

LOCOG | ODA

5 Host Boroughs

Greenwich
Hackney
Newham

Tower Hamlets
Waltham Forest

Source: Travers, T. (2004), *The Politics of London: Governing an Ungovernable City*, Palgrave/Macmillan, Basingstoke.

ORGANISING LOCAL ECONOMIC DEVELOPMENT: THE ROLE OF DEVELOPMENT AGENCIES AND COMPANIES © OECD 2010

The role and positioning of development agencies within the local development system

DAs perform a wide range of significant development activity and their functions within a local system can be many and varied. Functions can include, for instance, investment promotion, business attraction and retention, physical regeneration, international positioning, branding and marketing, relationship brokering, project management, event organisation and delivery, employment, productivity and skills generation, cultural development, environmental sustainability, social development or lobbying.

The roles of DAs within the local development system also vary. Later in this book direct delivery; facilitation and co-ordination; strategic support and promotion; and capacity-building roles are identified. They develop the leadership, economic, implementation and governance; and co-ordination roles which are already well known and accepted.

We first show how integral DAs are to their local development systems by illustrating their position and key relationships in map format. We will then go on to describe the features of local development system success.

Mapping the position of development agencies in the local development system

Through the examples that follow, attempts have been made to map the position of specific DAs within their local development systems. Key relationships these DAs maintain with other stakeholders are identified and codified according to the nature of these relationships.

This mapping exercise is not meant to be exhaustive. Rather it displays the nature and numbers of relationships DAs have within their local development systems. Further work, for instance, should focus particularly on the strength and scale of each linkage. Nonetheless, this provides a basis for further discussion and dialogue on the subject.

A number of interesting examples are illustrated below. They have been chosen to display the diversity of how DAs are positioned within their local development systems. They also illustrate how local development work streams are organised as well as demonstrate the partnership framework which underpins the development of specific local nodes such as city centres. These examples include:

- the New York City Economic Development Corporation: a complex local development system (Figure 5.2);

- Prospect Leicestershire: a two-tier policy and implementation local development system (Figure 5.3);

- Bilbao Metropoli-30 and BILBAO Ría 2000: a multi-agency local development system (Figure 5.4);

- AucklandPlus: a city-regional development system (Figure 5.5);

- Barcelona Activa: an innovation and knowledge economy system with the local development system (Figure 5.6); and

- the Cape Town Partnership: an institutional framework for city centre development (Figure 5.7).

As the maps show, local development systems display a variety of forms. Despite this, they show a number of consistent features, particularly regarding the positioning of DAs within them. DAs have many partnerships with many bodies which are often different in nature. This often depends on the nature of the agency itself and its objectives. They also display high levels of collaboration; a diversity of funding sources and accountabilities; close relationships with other agencies and local government departments; and can operate within either the fields of planning or delivery within the local development system. These themes are explored in greater detail later in this book

Features of a successful local development system

Analysis of the evidence collected from experts on the ground suggests that there are a number of features required for a successful local development system.

A clear understanding of local development requirements is fundamental. To build an effective local development system, there needs to be an appraisal of the exact developmental needs in the city at that time, as well as an appreciation of how these requirements may evolve. Appraisals can take the form of stakeholder consultation sessions, international information exchanges and data analysis, for instance. They are often presented as a formal report to high-ranking officials within the city.

Having relevant bodies to meet identified needs represents another key feature of a successful local development system. Once these appraisals have been completed, the next step is to develop a series of options about how to recalibrate the local development system to address any gaps, weaknesses or opportunities which have been identified. In consultation with key leaders of the city and its urban development agenda, the appropriate option should be chosen and worked up. It should see that there is a strong alignment between the mandates of organisations in the local development system and the needs of the city's local development agenda.

The construction, or evolution, of a local development system does not mean a revolution is required. Leveraging existing strengths is essential. Though the recalibration of a local development system may involve the phasing out of existing, or the creation of new organisations, it is important, however, to strike a balance. Many existing organisations already have the skills and experience to contribute very effectively to local development and investment promotion. The creation of too many new bodies may cause unhelpful tensions which hinder the success of the restructuring effort. It is important, therefore, that though changes may be necessary that the existing apparatus is leveraged to its maximum potential.

Clear lines of communication are also important. Good channels of communication between key bodies are essential to the healthy operation of the local development system. They can prevent organisational jealousies, mission creep and overlaps as well as gaps appearing. On the positive side, they can help foster a very constructive culture between partners where information is shared quickly allowing new opportunities to be identified and seized. These communication channels can be formal in the shape of multi-stakeholder "leadership boards", as in the case of Leicester and Leicestershire, or informal. In Cape Town, for instance, informal networking is a powerful contributor to forward momentum on a range of projects.

Figure 5.2. The position of the New York City Economic Development Corporation in the local development system in New York City

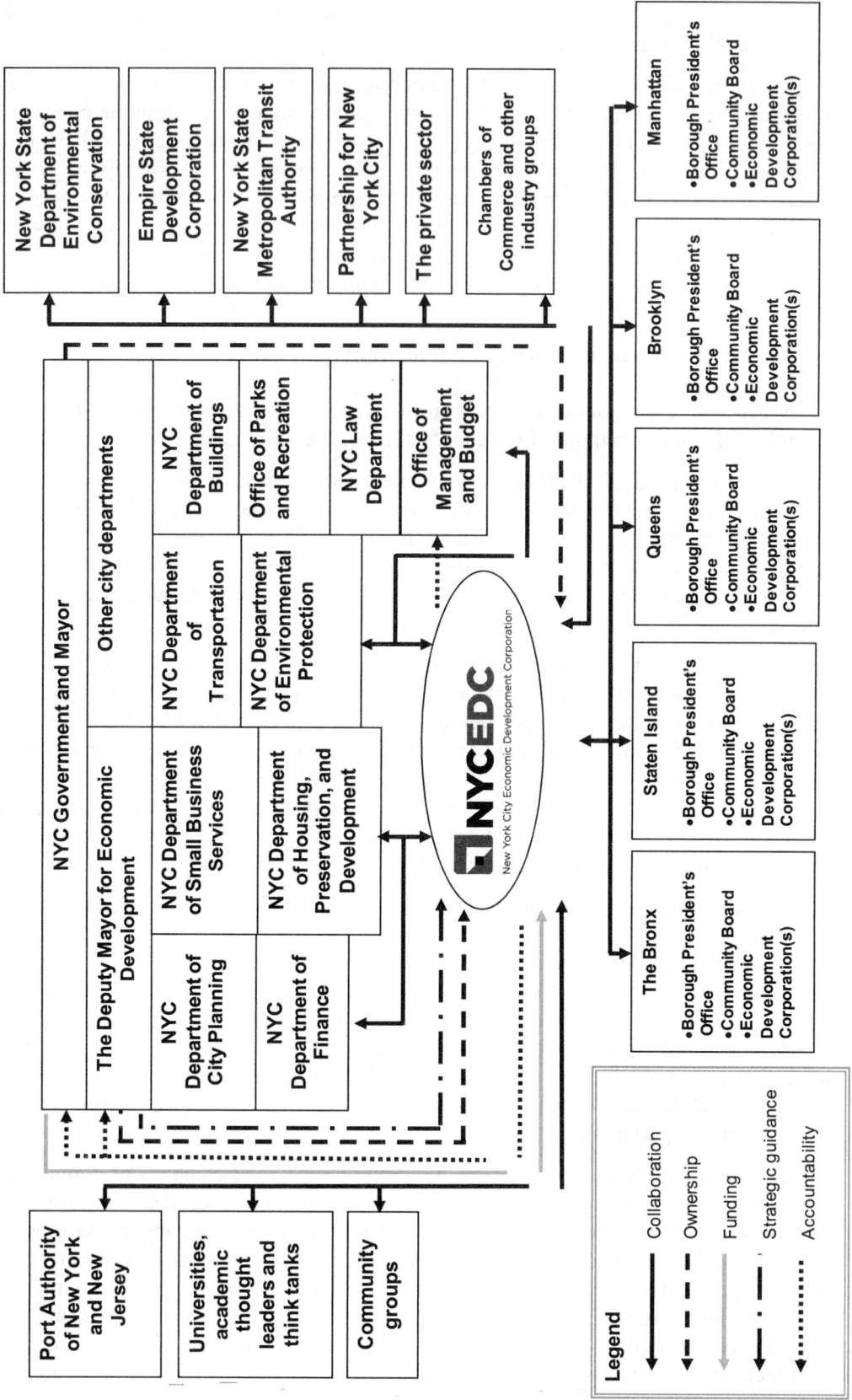

Figure 5.3. **The position of Prospect Leicestershire in the local development system in Leicestershire**

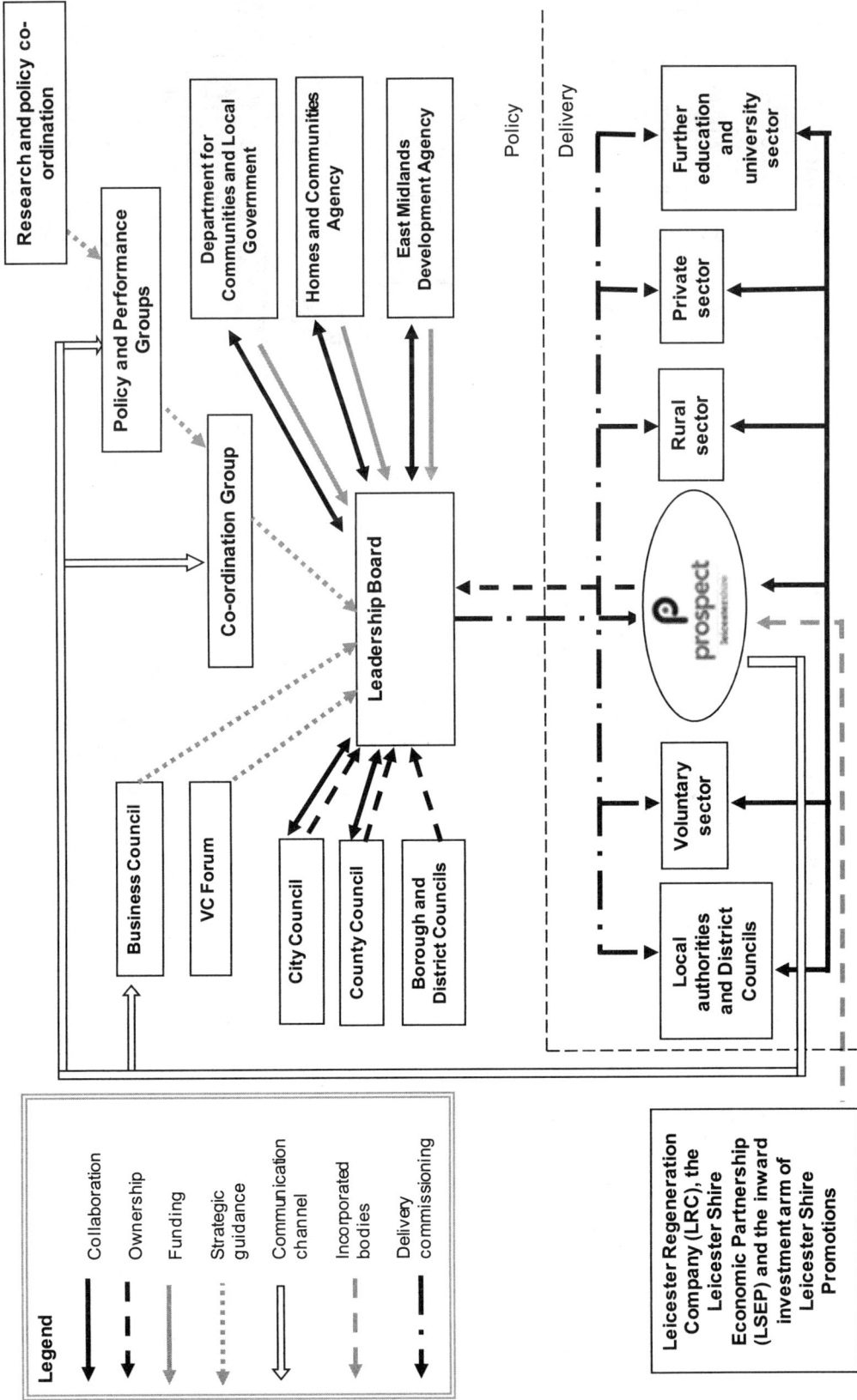

Figure 5.4. **The position of Bilbao Metropoli-30 and BILBAO Ría 2000 in the local development system in Bilbao**

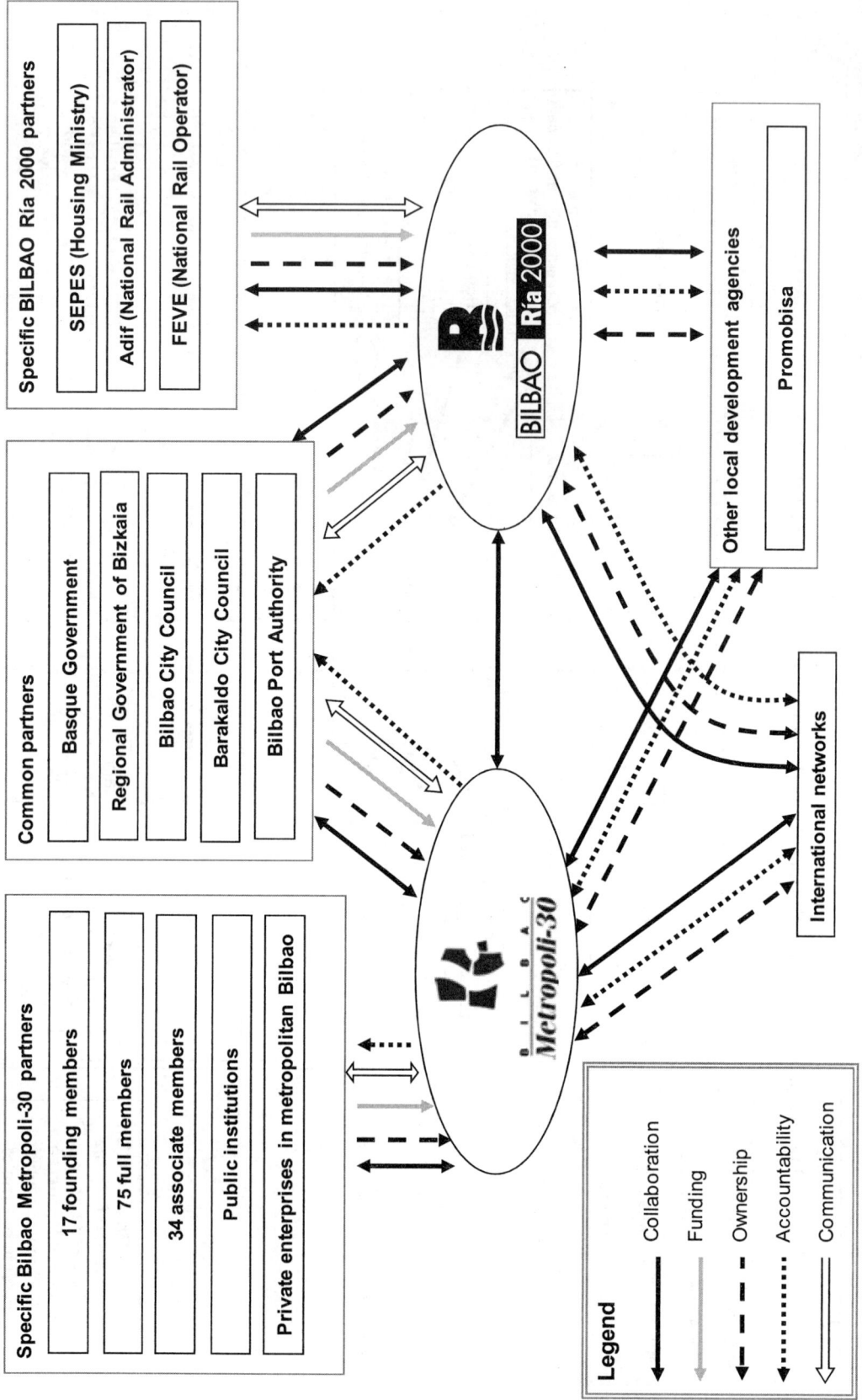

Figure 5.5. **The position of AucklandPlus in the local development system in the Auckland City Region**

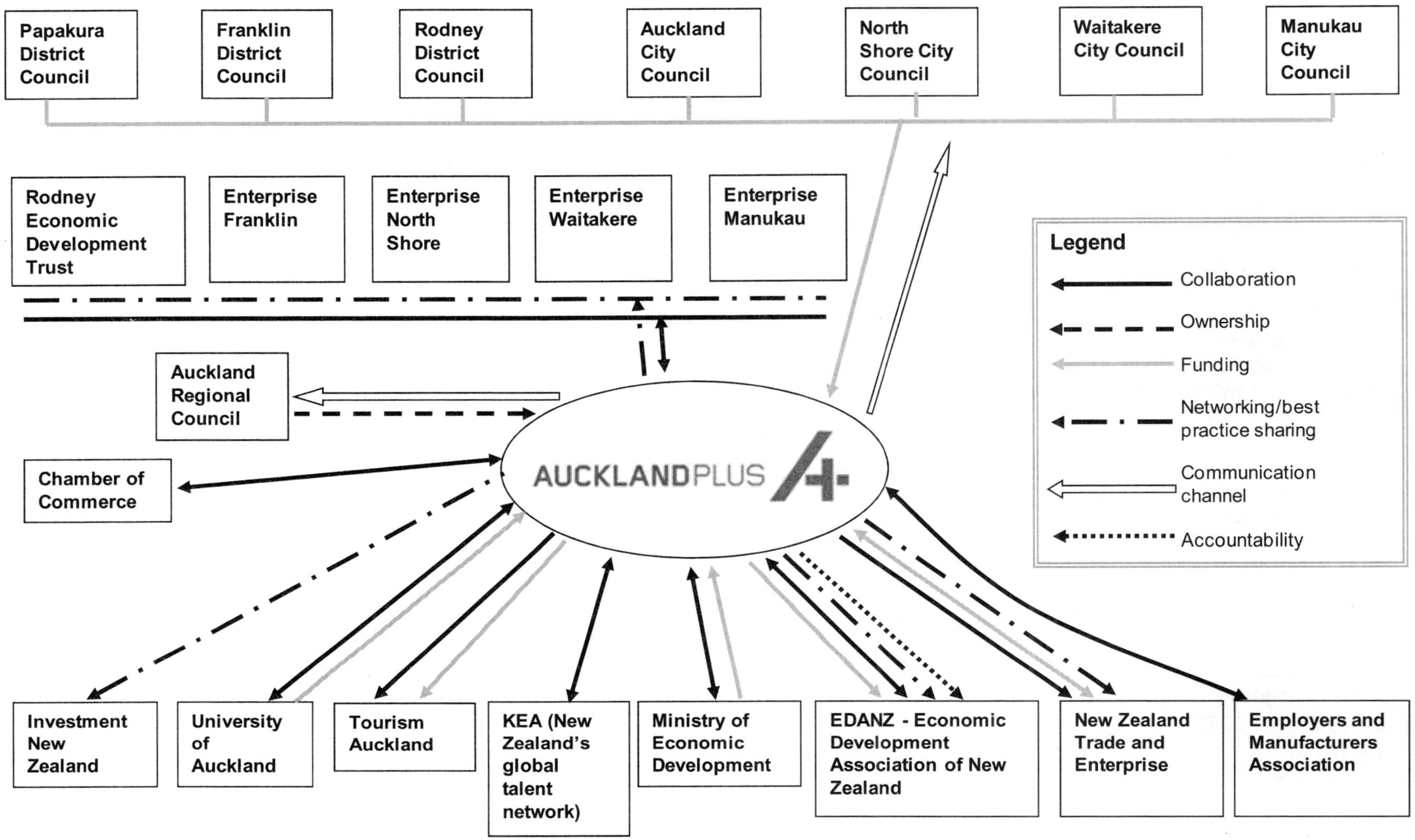

Legend

Collaboration

Ownership

Funding

Networking/best
practice sharing

Communication
channel

Accountability

Figure 5.6. **The position of Barcelona Activa in the local development system in Barcelona**

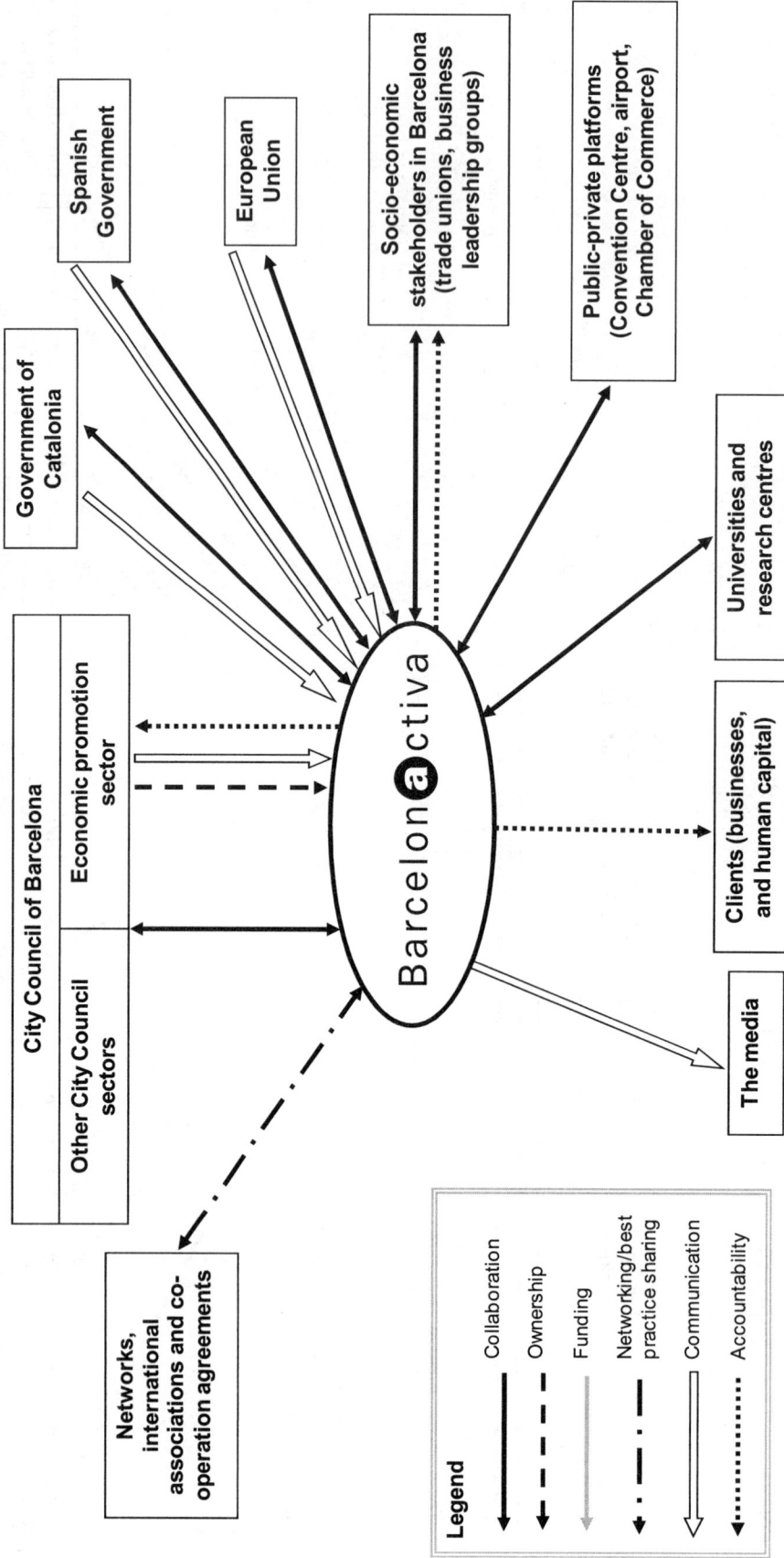

Figure 5.7. **The position of the Cape Town Partnership in the local development system in Cape Town**

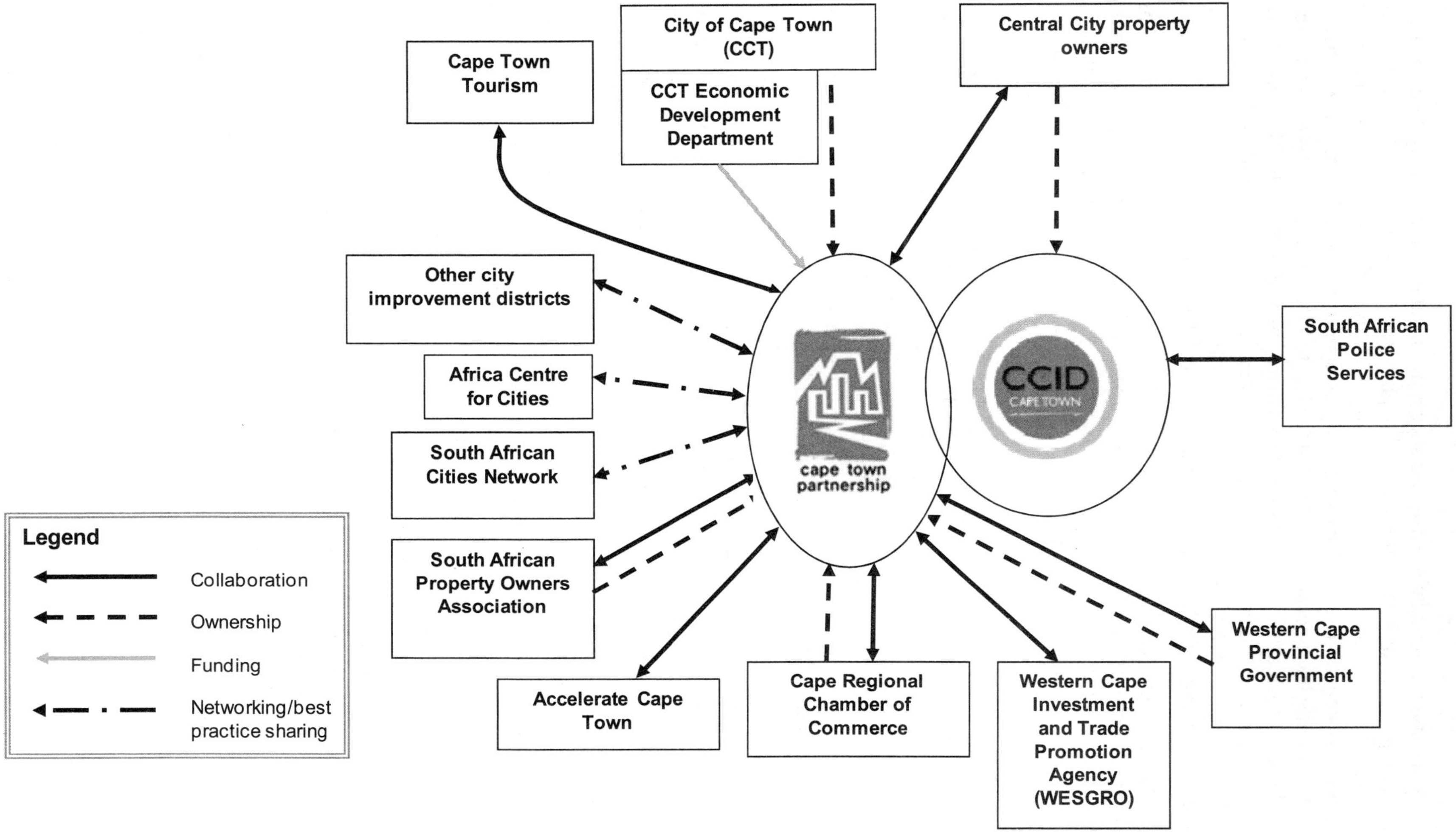

Legend

Collaboration
Ownership
Funding
Networking/best practice sharing

A common denominator across all successful local development systems is that it has an obvious leader or leadership body. Though participation and seamless integration is a key ingredient of success, the involvement of a myriad of bodies can hinder progress unless it is counter-balanced by decisive leadership. Leadership can take many forms. Some systems leave local economic leadership to inclusive, multi-stakeholder and high-level boards such as the "Strong Economy Board" in Sheffield or the "Leadership Board" in Leicestershire. Other systems see City Councils retaining overall authority often via powerful deputy mayors and economic development departments. This is the case in cities such as New York, Barcelona, Auckland and Toronto.

Blurring between policy and implementation can occur in complex systems. This can create frictions and confusion which slow progress. Though some blurring is healthy and natural as it ensures that policy and delivery are continually reviewed and improved, a degree of separation is recommended. Delivery bodies should be given the autonomy to get on with their work without constant redirection from strategy makers, for instance. This approach also avoids unhelpful conflicts of interest and can build an environment where mission creep is minimised by utilising specialist bodies for implementation and strategy making. In Sheffield, for instance, the development system is very much seen as two-tier – one for policy, the other for delivery. As the Sheffield local development system map shows, there is a clear division. Meanwhile, Creative Sheffield provides helpful feedback from the delivery to the policy side. This feedback takes the form of programme evaluations undertaken by Creative Sheffield which help calibrate strategy formulation within the "Strong Economy Board".

The culture of a system is an undervalued asset. The constructiveness of engagements between partners, the robustness of relationships during hard times and the degree of participation are all critical factors which influence the overall effective operation of a system. Positive exchanges, both formal and informal, and all levels between each organisation, or group of organisations, within the system, are important. It breaks down barriers to co-operation, facilitates useful exchanges and consolidates working relationships which can be leveraged later on.

Even with a well-crafted development system, success is not guaranteed in the long term. Local development is a dynamic science, particularly now local economies are plugged into a global system. To function as effectively as possible, local development systems should be reviewed and recalibrated relatively often. Many systems build in a scenario-planning element which foresees and predicts potential change to make the process of readjustment less of a disruption.

There are some excellent examples from the 16 DA case studies which illustrate these points, particularly how local development systems can be created or recalibrated. The relevant case studies are outlined below.

The example of the Cape Town Partnership (Box 5.3) shows how a DA can think strategically about a specific city node and through successful partnership building crystallise thinking into an ambitious document to guide the future development of the area.

Box 5.3. **Signature project: the Cape Town Partnership and the City Centre Development Strategy**

The future of the Central City of Cape Town for the next decade is being proactively charted through the Central City Development Strategy (CCDS). The CCDS is a joint venture between the City of Cape Town and the Cape Town Partnership, which aims to establish a shared vision for the future of the Central City area and a preferred development path and implementation plan. It was laid out in October 2008 and is based on the vision that: "In the next ten years, the Cape Town Central City will grow and greatly enhance its reputation as a dynamic business and people centre."

With the focus of this end in mind, the document focuses on five outcomes and five big ideas.

The five desired outcomes are:

- Cape Town's premier business location, recognised globally,

- a high-quality sustainable urban environment,

- a popular destination for Capetonians and visitors,

- a leading centre for knowledge, innovation, creativity and culture, in Africa and the South, and

- a place that embodies the heart and soul of Cape Town.

While the CCDS contains many different inter-connected strategies, it is based on five "big ideas":

- to reinstate the historical connection of the city to the sea, the mountain and to water, the *raison d'être* of the City of Cape Town (Reclaim Camissa project);

- to bring the people of Cape Town back into the Central City to live, through appropriate residential densification and more affordable housing;

- to improve the public transport system, providing greater accessibility to, from and around the Central City for Capetonians and visitors (with a particular focus on the City's Integrated Rapid Transit System);

- to provide space for future growth and investment in the Central City, in particular through the redevelopment of the Cape Town Station Precinct and the East City Design Initiative; and

- to divide the Central City into 20 neighbourhoods, paving the way for development protocols, based on local characteristics that reinforce the distinctiveness of the Central City, in order to address issues such as appropriate densification, mixed usage, building height, parking ratios, street-frontage, heritage and conservation.

The Cape Town Central City plays an important role within the economic, social, cultural and political life of the region, representing 40% of business turnover in the city. It is a destination for Capetonians and visitors, a place of many education and training institutions, location of important sectors of the regional economy, and the site of all three spheres of Government and the South African National Parliament. Given its significance, the success of the Central City is of the utmost importance.

The purpose of the CCDS is to inspire and to capture the public imagination about what the future of the Central City could potentially be. The aim is to mobilise stakeholders around a shared vision and specific strategies, and to generate a measurable delivery plan, in order to manage growth and change over the next ten years.

Source: Cape Town Partnership (2009), "Central City Development Strategy, 2009", Cape Town Partnership, *http://ctp.wwc.co.za/programmes/centralcitydevelopmentstrategy.html?PHPSESSID=3de09e102e328438dd0039e7550bb328.*

Liverpool's local development system

In 2007, the Liverpool City Council set about a start-up strategy for a new delivery vehicle in Liverpool. This was encapsulated in the "Commencement Plan" for the "Liverpool 'New Economic Development Company'". As well as a review of the changing socio-economic context in the city, it analysed Liverpool's institutional framework. By 2008, the city had three dedicated delivery mechanisms, in the form of Liverpool Vision, Liverpool Land Development Company (LLDC) and Business Liverpool. The Commencement Plan evaluated how best the local development system in Liverpool should be organised to most effectively meet the demands of the new environment.

On the back of its analysis, the Commencement Plan presented four options (Box 5.4) of which the preferred option was the "Integrated approach" which proposed a significant reorganisation of Liverpool's local development system. It was thought that "the integration of all three of the existing vehicles [was] necessary in order to establish a company whose scope reflects the key opportunities and challenges outlined ...., including the need for a more competitive Liverpool" (Liverpool City Council, Northwest Regional Development Agency and English Partnerships, 2008).

Box 5.4. Four options for the future: the results of a review into the future of Liverpool's local development system

The "Commencement Plan" for Liverpool's "New Economic Development Company" evaluated how best the system of economic development and investment promotion in Liverpool should be organised to most effectively meet the demands of the new environment. The Commencement Plan presented four options:

- **Do the minimum**. Under this option the partners would wind up the current vehicles and deliver a service that met the minimum requirements. This would involve Liverpool City Council again establishing an Economic Development Unit, which would seek to work with the Northwest Regional Development Agency, English Partnerships, Business Link, the Merseyside Partnership and other partners as and when possible.

- **Business as usual**. This would involve the continuation of the current vehicles. Business Liverpool would continue to provide business, inward investment and enterprise support services. Liverpool Vision would operate within the wider City Centre and the Liverpool Land Development Company (LLDC) within other key investment locations within Liverpool.

- **Merger of Liverpool Vision and LLDC**. Liverpool Vision and LLDC could be merged to form a new company that combined the skills set of each organisation. Under this option, Business Liverpool would continue to pursue its current activities, but work in partnership with the new company to support the transformation of Liverpool.

- **Integrated approach**. The skills and resources of all three existing vehicles could be brought together to provide an integrated approach to economic development and physical regeneration. This option would combine expertise in procuring, funding and delivering high-quality infrastructure and development projects, with business support, inward investment and enterprise development services to ensure a "joined up" approach to maximising economic growth.

Toronto's local development system

Following a review of the city's development efforts and agencies, which began in the summer of 2008, and building upon the Agenda for Prosperity and the Fiscal Blue Print, the City of Toronto decided to create two new DAs. The creation of Build Toronto and Invest Toronto represents a purposeful step forward in addressing these gaps and weaknesses. Though there is much to do, the City of Toronto took the view that Invest Toronto and Build Toronto should not look to take on too much. And so, though the development of Invest Toronto and Build Toronto will be critical to the future success of the city's development and investment promotion system, there are important roles to be played by other existing, new and yet-to-be-created organisations. According to ex-acting Chief Executive of Invest Toronto and new Vice President of Stakeholder Affairs at Build Toronto, John MacIntyre, "it's all about building a seamless and co-ordinated system across the whole system of economic promotion in the city." This recalibration process also involved the phasing out of a DA known as the Toronto Economic Development Corporation (TEDCO).

Madrid's local development system

The Madrid Global Office for International Strategy and Action (Madrid Global) was created in June 2007 as a dependency of the External Relations and Research Co-ordination Division. It had the explicit aim of responding to the need for improving the international position of the Spanish capital by raising awareness of its competitive advantage and reality. According to the Director General of International Strategy and Development at Madrid Global, whereas the last ten years has been spent improving the product, Madrid must now improve its positioning. He suggested, "there is a gap between perception and reality ... Madrid needs to improve its international image in order to be placed where it should be among the greatest global cities" (Madrid Public Infrastructures and Urban Services Cluster, 2008). It was for this reason that Madrid Global was created, to close the gap between how Madrid is performing and how it is perceived.

Conclusion

The effective performance of all actors in a local development system is critical for success. Each organisation must both play its own roles well and also co-ordinate and collaborate with other organisations in the system. DAs must both deliver their direct activities and also work with others to calibrate, phase, and sequence inputs together. DAs are often established with a remit to rationalise and improve the efficiency of the local development system by aggregating activities that otherwise operate on a "standalone" basis.

The leadership of local development systems becomes very important. Our case studies reveal that the design and co-ordination of the local development system is often led by local governments, frequently with a deputy mayor or similar figure playing the role of arch co-ordinator. As experts in local development processes, DAs are often asked to play a part in the co-ordination of the rest of the system, especially where they are operating over an inter-municipal geography or where they have key roles in defining and setting development strategy.

Long-term economic development strategies play an important role in providing a common agenda across a local development system. The combination of clear strategy, a good DA, and a well-resourced and co-ordinated system for local development are fundamental to success in most places.

The case study in Box 5.5 demonstrates how HafenCity Hamburg GmbH has leveraged private investment by building effective investment strategies and making targeted, high-quality and publicly led interventions.

Box 5.5. **Signature project: HafenCity Hamburg GmbH and leveraging private investment**

For the successful delivery of the HafenCity project, Europe's largest inner-city redevelopment zone, the leveraging of private sector investment was essential. It is predicted by HafenCity GmbH, the project's DA, that on the project's completion in 2025 between EUR 5 billion and EUR 5.5 billion of private investment will have been secured (78% of the total investment into the project). To facilitate this investment in the early phase of the HafenCity development process, HafenCity Hamburg GmbH was:

- available as an efficient, one-stop-shop agency in charge of the whole development both spatially and thematically;

- able to create and communicate a broad but strong image and vision of what HafenCity was about;

- able to set up a risk-reducing and competition-enhancing framework for private investment;

- able to communicate and co-operate effectively with local and regional developers / investors to create genuine momentum behind the idea of HafenCity as a real investment opportunity; and

- able offer small individual plots for development to allow a wide range of small, medium and large-sized investors to be targeted.

As the project progressed, a key feature of HafenCity's success became its communication and marketing process. This process ensured that regional and international awareness of the investment opportunities in HafenCity was established. Investor and public relations such as participation in international real estate fairs were critical here. Furthermore, HafenCity Hamburg GmbH has further enhances the unique offer of HafenCity for investors through various means. For instance, HafenCity fosters investment competition by creating markets and establishing special outstanding features in HafenCity such as an innovative local heating supply system based on dynamic and falling carbon benchmark. The introduction of a special HafenCity sustainability certificate, which is awarded for outstanding buildings, has also enhanced the attractiveness of the project to investors.

Another significant factor behind the private investment success at HafenCity relates to development sequencing. HafenCity was developed as a completely new urban district on the basis of a concept which delivered integrated urban quarters one-by-one in a strongly time-wise and co-ordinated process. This means that private investors can rely on their development being situated in an integrated urban environment and functioning quarter very soon after its completion. This approach is facilitated by the master-developer HafenCity Hamburg GmbH through the provision of high quality and targeted public investments in traffic infrastructures and public spaces, for example. Investments facilities by the City State of Hamburg in the subway as well as cultural, social and educational have also leveraged private investment.

In terms of investment governance, private investment has been leveraged in a risk-aware manner. Because of this, though the financial crisis has slowed the rate of investment, the project's business model remains robust. The HafenCity investment strategy is sustainable in that it was developed to operate successfully at all parts of the business cycle. It contains the following key features: (1) the project is financed and supported by a diverse range of partners; (2) the development is divided into small segments which can be developed sequentially when finance is available; and the development is mixed use. As a result, HafenCity was as well prepared for a market downturn as one can be for such a situation, much more so than many large-scale international projects, some of which have been seriously affected.

Source: Bruns-Berentelg, J. (2009), Written and telephone communication and interviews.

References

Bilbao Metropoli-30 (2009a), "City and Value Paper", *www.bm30.es/cuadernos_uk.html*.

Bilbao Metropoli-30 (2009b), "The Bilbao Case: From Infrastructures to Values", Bilbao Metropoli-30.

Bruns-Berentelg, J. (2009), Written and telephone communication and interviews.

Cape Town Partnership (2009), "Central City Development Strategy, 2009", Cape Town Partnership, *http://ctp.wwc.co.za/programmes/centralcitydevelopmentstrategy.html? PHPSESSID=3de09e102e328438dd0039e7550bb328*.

Clark, G. (2008), *City Success: What Do the City Indices Tell Us?*, Urban Land Institute.

Liverpool City Council, Northwest Regional Development Agency and English Partnerships (2008), "Liverpool 'New Economic Development Company' Commencement Plan", revised working draft, Liverpool City Council, Northwest Regional Development Agency and English Partnerships.

Madrid Public Infrastructures and Urban Services Cluster (2008), "International Strategy and Development", *www.adb.org/Documents/Events/ (2008)/Madrid-Experience-Sharing-Seminar/Bonifacio.pdf*.

Travers, T. (2004), *The Politics of London: Governing an Ungovernable City*, Palgrave/Macmillan, Basingstoke.

Chapter 6

The roles, tools and relationships of development agencies

This chapter addresses what development agencies actually do and the tools they use. A summary of core activities of development agencies is presented and the argument is developed that while what *these agencies do is obviously essential,* how *it is done is equally important. It is established* how *these activities are done by categorising the roles that a development agency might play in a local development system. It is underlined that without a thorough consideration of both what activities are undertaken and how they are undertaken, the contribution of development agencies to sustainable local development may be misunderstood. The chapter begins with an overview of some of the approaches used to categorise development agency roles, and concludes by detailing the roles played by development agencies in the formulation of local development strategy.*

The preceding chapters have illustrated why development agencies (DAs) are established and what value they can add. This chapter addresses what DAs actually do and the tools they use. A summary of core activities of DAs will be presented in this chapter. We observe that while *what* DAs do is obviously essential, *how* it is done is equally important. Without a thorough consideration of both, the contribution of DAs to sustainable local development may be misunderstood.

This chapter will establish *how* these activities are carried out by categorising the roles DAs play in the local development and investment systems. We begin with an overview of some of the approaches used to categorise DA roles, and then conclude by detailing the roles played by DAs in the formulation of local development strategy.

Categorising the roles of development agencies

An introduction to the roles of development agencies

As a "quasi governance vehicle", DAs can offer a unique means to assemble both the resources (assets) and the authorities (or permissions) required to undertake certain economic development activities. In these roles, DAs can become the means to overcome otherwise complex administrative arrangements and or geographies which may not align with the natural economic geographies that are the focus of sound economic development. Neighbouring city and regional governments can work together through the DA, or simply sponsor projects that it undertakes. Equally, DAs may play a role in pooling resources between different "tiers" of government (local, regional, state/provincial, federal or national) and between "spheres" of government (departments, agencies, authorities, commissions, educational institutions and others). Lastly, they can play an important role in bringing together public, private, and civic sectors, through joint ventures, partnerships, service agreements, compacts or other vehicles.

Economic development activity requires the use of economic development tools which can ultimately influence market behaviours through both exogenous and endogenous players. Such tools require careful calibration and management if they are to achieve net positive outcomes without distorting basic market functioning. DAs are seen as capable of designing and implementing such interventions using unique skills and insights from public policy and from market economics/commercial disciplines.

Perhaps most importantly, however, DAs appear to offer a politically acceptable form of co-investment between otherwise disparate partners. This might be for several reasons. For instance, as sole purpose vehicles, there is little chance of resources being used for the wrong purposes, and DAs can be held accountable. At the same time, as corporate entities, DAs can be branded to reflect joint ownership (and joint credit). Finally, as time-limited vehicles, DAs can be closed down if necessary (unlike tiers of government which are hard to close down). This begins to explain why DAs can help develop the collaborative aspects of economic development and develop momentum.

Approaches to categorisation

Not all DAs will pursue anything like the same tasks in the same way and many approaches exist to the categorisation of the role that DAs can play. Indeed, one of the most interesting aspects of DA activity is that different approaches and roles are used to foster developmental outcomes. The range of tools available to the agency does influence the scale of the ambition and the nature of the intervention that is feasible, but it does not determine whether an agency will succeed.

The menu will usually include some of the following roles, which represents a first attempt at categorisation. These strategic, asset and investment; innovation, enterprise, skills and employment; promotional and capacity-building roles are complemented by a further set of roles described later in this chapter.

The following five groups of activities represent the core tasks and functions of most of the DAs in our study. OECD LEED (Local Economic and Employment Development) has noted before that DAs tended to play these roles and they have featured as a framework for thinking about DA roles in OECD DA reviews.

- **Strategic development** roles involve the: (1) fostering of coalitions for growth initiatives; (2) co-ordination/leadership of local actors; (3) co-ordination/leadership of regional, national and international investors/donors; (4) monitoring of the city/metropolitan economy; (5) strategic planning of economic and territorial development; and (6) advocacy of infrastructure and investment.

- **Investment and development** roles involve: (1) land and property redevelopment and management; (2) fund management and direct lending/investment in firms and/or investment projects; (3) other forms of financial intermediation and income/resource generation; and (4) management of grant aid for businesses and other organisations.

- **Innovation, enterprise, skills, and employment** roles involves: (1) the promotion of technology, creativity, and innovation; (2) workforce development and skills development; (3) employment creation and job brokerage; and (4) fostering entrepreneurship and small and medium-sized enterprises (SMEs).

- **Promotional** roles involve: (1) territorial marketing and facilitation of foreign investment promotion of other forms of external investment (tourism, events, trade, sports, etc.); and (2) project management and design of major projects.

- **Capacity building** roles involve: (1) sector and cluster development programmes; and (2) capacity building and technical assistance for other local organisations and identification of good practices and learning models, cross-border, inter-regional, and international co-operation.

The example in Box 6.1 shows how Madrid Global has driven the development of Madrid's internationalisation strategy.

Box 6.1. **Signature project: Madrid Global and the Madrid Internationalisation Strategy**

Madrid Global is the DA for the international positioning and marketing of Madrid. The organisation is guided by its Strategy for International Positioning (2008-11), a document which defines Madrid's plan for strengthening its global position and reputation. Madrid Global has adopted a strategic approach with regards to the development this internationalisation strategy. None the less, the DA has remained, and intends to continue to remain, pragmatic in its approach. Madrid Global understands that its strengths and objectives may evolve over time, and thus it must react and adjust its strategy accordingly.

In developing the strategy, Madrid Global followed a clearly defined methodology which involved a review of the strengths, constraints, opportunities and challenges of the Madrid local development system as a whole.

It included various studies, reports and plans were conducted to discover the gulf between where the city of Madrid wants to be and where it currently is, with regards to the internationalisation process. These included: a study focusing on the Madrid Brand carried out by Millward Brown in 2004; the 2003-07 Plan for Internationalisation issued by the Department for the Economy and Citizen Participation; the Territorial Review on Madrid carried out by the OECD in 2007; international studies focusing on city rankings; and the study to develop the Strategy for the International Positioning of Madrid carried out by Strategy and Focus at the behest of Madrid Global in 2008. An analysis of the city of Madrid was carried out and its competitive advantages were identified. However, in today's constantly changing and globalised world, competitive advantages are not stable and the strategy must therefore incorporate a continuous analysis of the environment in order to adapt to changes and take advantage of new opportunities. Competitive advantages and the potential they offer gave rise to the Vectors for Action and Communication. Taking the city's competitive advantages as a basis, a schematic guide was drawn up to serve as the framework of the discourse employed by Madrid to reinforce its global position. At the same time, the vector serves as a project filter, identifying the essential content or characteristics that a project must possess in order to be in keeping with the strategy and prove capable of achieving the established objectives. In addition to establishing the vectors, it is essential to determine the territory on which they are to be targeted and the actions that will be undertaken by Madrid Global. To this end, having analysed the situation, bearing in mind our capabilities, organisation, possibilities and the strategy to be employed, four strategic objectives have been established.

As a result of the aforementioned research process, and the identification of the city's unique offerings, Madrid Global has established four key objectives as the basis of their Internationalisation Strategy:

- Madrid – the third European Metropolis. Madrid aspires to become Europe's third city, behind London and Paris, but surpassing Berlin, Amsterdam, Stockholm, Frankfurt, Rome and Milan.

- Madrid – focal point of the Spanish-speaking world. Madrid wishes to hold on and develop this position further. Madrid accounts for 71% of Spanish investment in Latin America, but Miami and Florida are emerging as competitors.

- Madrid – a nexus between cultures and continents. Madrid provides a point of entry into Latin American and North African markets and the EU. The city wishes to emphasise this further.

- Madrid – an urban reference for highly dynamic emerging cities. The series of administrations, institutions, companies and research centres that are involved in city management and the improvement of the urban environment represent a cluster of excellence which affords Madrid a competitive advantage in terms of global positioning.

Source: Madrid Global (2008), "Executive Summary: the Strategy For International Positioning, 2008-11", Madrid Global.

The four roles of development agencies: the OECD LEED approach

The OECD LEED Programme has undertaken reviews of many DAs and identified four major organising roles for DAs in economic development and regeneration (OECD, 2006). We suggest that though not all DAs undertake the same activities, it is possible to identify four different, but interlinked, roles played by these organisations:

- **Economic roles**: where DAs seek to build markets within their territories by acting within them. These roles include the DA acting in a risk- and cost- sharing manner using entrepreneurial approaches. This involves intermediating with investment, assets, infrastructure, land, property, finance, planning, and marketing/promotion. The DA derives its unique role by taking on tasks that are normally outside of government due to the nature of commercial disciplines and focus required, the risks that have to be managed and the creativity involved. This often allows fiscally disempowered local governments to sponsor an agency which can operate outside of tight controls and leverage more than the local government is allowed to. Business is frequently the partner and/or client of this activity, and although it is accountable to government, the agency has to mirror the "business-like" behaviour, processes and timescales of commercial players if it is to be successful. This is a case of overcoming policy and investment failures.

- **Leadership roles**: where the DA plays a key role in fostering a long-term plan and vision for the territory, galvanising the interests of multiple leaders, setting out a new future around which resource mobilisation can coalesce. Here, the DA is often an "independent" forum in which distinctive interests can be brought together, and aligned, to shape a long-term purpose beyond the specific limitations of electoral cycles and partisan policies. This is a case of addressing leadership failures.

- **Governance and co-ordination roles**: where the DA helps to facilitate practical co-ordination towards the pursuit of the development strategy, helping to overcome the limitations of fragmented multiple jurisdictions and responsibilities in the public sector, and providing a means for practical engagement with the private and civic sectors. In this role the DA is the chief practical mechanism for co-ordinated multi-lateral action. This is a case of addressing co-ordination failures.

- **Implementation roles**: where the DA can assemble dedicated and capable teams to focus solely on pursuing the development strategy. This will involve complex project management and finance skills, business/investor facing services, and the ability to design and use new tools quickly. The distinctive dimension of this role is often in how DAs can attract and develop expert and specialist staff that are suited to pursuing public goals in a commercially sensitive manner, and are capable of implementing co-operation between public and private sectors in ways which work for both cultures. This is not an insignificant capability, and it frequently distinguishes DA staff from public officials more generally. This is a case of addressing capacity constraints in the public sector.

To develop these categorisations, using the evidence of our case studies, we indentify a further functional categorisation which shows not just what they do, but focuses more directly on how they do it:

- **Direct delivery ("rowing")**: where DAs undertake direct delivery and implementation activities in the city. These activities can vary widely from the delivery of hard infrastructure projects to the implementation of softer skills-based training programmes.

- **Facilitation and co-ordination ("steering")**: where DAs shape and facilitate local economic development with partners. Thought-leadership and visioning activities are core components of this role. Other activities such as formal and informal networking and partnership brokering, can be essential to DAs fulfilling this role in the development system.

- **Strategic support and promotion ("cheering")**: where DAs encourage and support initiatives by a range of other parties involved in the development and promotion of the city. This role involves the use of public relations (PR) methods and activities such as newsletters, press releases and speechmaking to spread the word of success and to lend confidence to the activities underway in the city. This role can create a constructive environment which gives momentum to the city's development agenda.

- **Capacity-building elsewhere ("coaching")**: where DAs build capacity beyond themselves elsewhere in the city. This can take the form of best-practice sharing, formal training sessions or informal knowledge sharing and networking, for instance.

As the examples in Tables 6.1 through 6.5 show, DAs can fulfil a range of roles in the local development system. These illustrations also show how the roles vary by DA type, a concept introduced in earlier chapters. They also show what activities constitute each role to support understanding.

Table 6.1. **Development and revitalisation agency example: Build Toronto's role in the Toronto development system**

	Direct delivery	Facilitation and co-ordination	Strategic support and promotion	Capacity-building elsewhere
Depth and breadth of role	✓✓✓	✓✓	-	-
Specific example	Managing and developing the city's property and land assets.	Working closely with the Economic Department of the City of Toronto and the Facilities and Real Estate Division, Build Toronto has the opportunity to influence agendas.	-	-

Table 6.2. **Integrated economic agency example: New York City Economic Development Corporation in the New York City development system**

	Direct delivery	Facilitation and co-ordination	Strategic support and promotion	Capacity-building elsewhere
Depth and breadth of role	✓✓	✓✓✓	✓✓✓	✓✓✓
Specific example	• Undertakes or oversees transport projects. • Sells or leases city-owned property.	• Conducts planning and feasibility analyses. • Performs financial analyses. • Works with private developers in the field of *e.g.* neighbourhood revitalisation. • Co-ordinates projects *e.g.* Graffiti Free NYC program and the Area Maintenance programme.	• Promotes the city's various central business districts. • Produces the economic snapshot of New York to promote the city. • Chairs the Energy Policy Task Force.	• Guides projects through necessary public approvals. • Packages city incentives. • Helps companies secure financing/ access capital, etc. • Provides support for projects.

Table 6.3. **Productivity and economic growth agency example: Barcelona Activa's role in the Barcelona development system**

	Direct delivery	Facilitation and co-ordination	Strategic support and promotion	Capacity-building elsewhere
Depth and breadth of role	✓✓✓	✓✓✓	✓✓✓	✓✓
Specific example	• Manages spaces and programmes for innovation and employment. • Direct training provider for human capital development and quality employment. • Coaches 1 400 business projects a year. • Coaches more than 30 000 participants to quality employment.	• Works together with the City Council and other city and regional bodies to facilitate local development. • Work on *e.g.* the Agreement for Quality Employment in Barcelona 2008-11, with the two main trade unions and business organisations as well as the Government of Catalunya.	• Promotes the city as a centre for innovation and future-oriented economic activity. • Reference organisation for entrepreneurs in the city and region (such as Day of the Entrepreneur).	• More than 100 visits of institutional delegations a year. • Active members of international networks (EBN, Eurocities, IASP, etc.). • Transfers programmes and methodologies and provide technical assistance to other world cities.

Table 6.4. **Internationalisation agency example: Madrid Global's role in the Madrid development system**

	Direct delivery	Facilitation and co-ordination	Strategic support and promotion	Capacity-building elsewhere
Depth and breadth of role	✓	✓✓	✓✓✓	
Specific example	• Socio-economic intelligence gathering in the city and outside the city.	• Positioning the international promotion agenda at the forefront of the Madrid development agenda.	• Participation in global-scale events. • Participation in collaborative international projects. • Fostering international dialogues amongst target groups.	

Table 6.5. **Visioning and partnership agency example: the Cape Town Partnership's role in the Cape Town development system**

	Direct delivery	Facilitation and co-ordination	Strategic support and promotion	Capacity-building elsewhere
Depth and breadth of role	✓✓	✓✓✓	✓✓	✓
Specific example	• Provision of safety, cleansing, urban management and social development services. • Kerbside parking management. • Management of the Central City Improvement District (CCID).	• Use of local press and media to stimulate public debate and engagement. • Crafting of the Central City Development Strategy (CCDS) – the content driver for the work in the Central City for the next ten years.	• 2010 Central City Partners Forum. • Central City walking tours. • The book of the newsletters *Siyahluma* and *City Views*.	• Business Areas Network • Mentoring a number of the 18 other City Improvement Districts (CIDS) in the city.

Discussion

There are some important points to observe from these simple reviews of the different DA roles by agency types. The first is that many DAs do play this variety of roles. They are not just "delivery organisations" responsible for a narrow set of inputs, but they work to develop the capacity of other entities and they provide a mix roles between direct delivery and shaping the activities of others. Only the redevelopment and re-investment organisations play narrow roles, but this is largely the product of redevelopment cycles, where the first task is to get redevelopment happening before a wider and more complex development process can unfold.

The second observation is that DA roles diversify over time. As a development process matures and the key agencies gain experience, they are more able to play subtle shaping and capacity building roles, and more able to recognise the work that others do. This is one of the important returns that comes from experience and maturity which is highly observable in our case studies. DAs that have succeeded and evolved through various phases of development cycle are more able to play multiple roles later and add much greater value as their experience is leveraged by other bodies.

Lastly, the wider range of roles played by the DA, the more important is systematic communication and good internal management roles. Multiple roles do not necessarily conflict, but they do require both effective and distinctive management as well as clear communication to stakeholders. The Cape Town Partnership (CTP) is both a direct deliverer of urban services and a strategic planner for the future of its city. Both of these roles are played exceptionally well and one of the ways that CTP manages this is to have separate boards and international organisations for each activity within one corporate partnership body.

The roles of development agencies in local development strategy

A preferred model is for all local economic development to be organised around a clear strategic planning process. This section exemplifies how DAs can contribute to this process.

The growth of local economic development strategies is emerging rapidly with the growth of local economic development worldwide. As the desire to promote local economic development has grown, so the necessity to ensure that local economic development is properly formulated has become much more central.

The question arises as to how such strategies should be produced and what role there should be for city DAs. In general, it is important to recognise that a successful economic development strategy at the local, or regional level, has to fulfil a number of purposes, whatever approach is adopted. It should:

1. present a clear analysis of what is happening in the local economy (including demographic and environmental analysis), what the opportunities and constraints are, and how they can be addressed;

2. differentiate between those challenges that can be addressed at the city and regional level and those that cannot;

3. set some clear goals (ambitious and realistic) and be capable of guiding the work of all those who are engaged in economic development;

4. be capable of identifying activity into which other tiers of government and stakeholders can invest;

5. be coherent with other strategies (*e.g.* Land Use and Planning, Transport, Housing, Education, Environment, in particular) and should use the same basic framework of data and analysis;

6. set out a clear picture of what success would look like, either in the form of some precise targets, or some benchmarks; and

7. provide sufficient detail to help inform choices locally.

This seven-point list is not a template for writing an economic development strategy, but rather an indication of what the function of such a strategy needs to be. DAs often lead this strategy-making process, bringing other organisations along in attempts to address each of the seven points elaborated above. However, sometimes DAs are not strategy makers, and they are asked to implement strategies that have been designed by others. Often the creation of a DA is the result of strategy formulation, rather than the start of it. Nonetheless, achieving these seven roles is not easy to do, and it is often not easy for a DA to do them alone, whatever the breadth of its skills and mandate. For these reasons it is often important for DAs to work with others on the formulation of economic development strategies. In particular, these frequently include:

- central policy and economics teams within municipal and regional governments and policy experts from other municipal government functions (*e.g.* Planning, Transport, Housing, Education, etc.);

- community organisations and groups, who are concerned about the economic prospects of their community and municipality and want to be contact for community engagement;

- business groupings, especially those that has access to clear data and analysis about the local economy (*e.g.* banks, utility agencies and real estate);

- universities, especially where there is quality economic analysis taking place; and

- trade unions, who frequently have the best insights into local economic performance, agency dynamics, and possible productivity improvements.

Development agencies as catalysts for collaboration

Stakeholder management: development agencies as a partnership vehicle

Both the International Links and Services for Local Development Agencies (ILS LEDA) and the European Association of Development Agencies (EURADA) point out that it is in the nature of many DAs that they attempt to bring together a diverse range of partners. Indeed, one of the main rationales for creating such DAs is so that they can be a partnership vehicle. This is often crystallised through "stake-holding" arrangements. At a simple level, this produces an agency governance system where different "constituencies" have participation in the board, or other oversight grouping, of the agency with a clear delineation of majority and minority participation.

Typically such an arrangement will see all or any of the following having an effective stake in how the DA is run: (1) municipal governments; (2) state / provincial / national / federal governments; (3) international and multi-lateral investors; (4) business groups and organisations (*e.g.* Chambers of Commerce); (5) financial institutions; (6) infrastructure and utility agencies and facilities (*e.g.* airports, energy/telecom providers); (7) trade unions; (8) community organisations; and (9) higher and vocational education providers.

The balance of authority within any such board will usually reflect the purposes of the initiating institutions. For example, DAs established by a municipal government as the principle sponsor will usually have a majority of appointees made by the municipal council or mayor, whereas a metropolitan DA will usually reflect the wider interests of several municipalities and business groups.

Where a DA owns assets and has a dynamic balance sheet this often results in "stock" or "equity" statements which identify which partners own what portion of the agency's asset value.

Box 6.2 provides an example of how roles and relationships can vary from agency to agency.

Box 6.2. **Flexibility and nimbleness: the roles and relationships of the New York City Economic Development Corporation**

The New York City Economic Development Corporation's (NYCEDC) relationships with the other agencies and actors vary from project to project. At times, NYCEDC acts as a thought partner, providing expertise and research services to agencies. At other times, NYCEDC serves as a facilitator, bringing several stakeholders together to move a project forward. NYCEDC also serves as a project lead in situations where it is the best candidate to complete a project successfully and efficiently.

Variations on the development agency stakeholder model

The vast majority of DAs are "limited liability not-for-profit agencies". However, there are important variations in terms of some DAs which are also financial intermediaries and therefore require a separate legal status and/or supervision. This is generally achieved through a subsidiary DA.

Two other models are worth noting. Firstly, there is the emergence of wholly private sector DAs (although many might not consider "agency" the right word here). Often set up by travel and hospitality businesses, land owners/developers, utility/infrastructure agencies, and financial institutions, the role of these DAs is to build the local economy in such a manner that there are positive benefits for the businesses involved through enlarged customer bases, etc.

In many localities in Europe and North America, this is also undertaken by chambers of commerce and regional tourist boards. This model rests upon a DA or DAs recognising that economic development is a good way to grow their customer base. The Business Improvement District (City Improvement Districts in South Africa) is a variation on this model at a localised level, allowing businesses within a commercial or industrial area to club together to improve the attractiveness of their location for other investors, workers, suppliers and customers. These models are not incompatible with the same organisation also undertaking public, purposeful economic development actions, but great clarity is needed to effectively account for the use of public funds and the benefits to the public at large.

The second model, which is less common, but is now emerging more rapidly, is the publicly owned, but "for-profit" DA. This occurs when a government (at municipal, regional, or state level) identifies the potential to deliver economic development enhancing activity in a commercial manner, with little or no public subsidy, generating revenues from the activity. Frequently, such DAs will provide finance or premises to businesses in ways that the private sector finds less attractive than other alternatives, and thus can operate in a niche market where there is little offering from the market.

These structures offer alternative ways to achieve local economic development goals which may be more sustainable because they do not require ongoing public subsidy.

Working relationships with other entities

Published reports on working relations with other DAs are very limited, even though there is an extensive amount of literature emerging on local economic development partnerships. The literature simply does not address the issue fully from the point of view of how the DA should work with others, and the basic assumption is that the DA is itself the primary partnership vehicle. There are several kinds of distinctive working relationships that need to be attended to by a DA, in addition to its own role of bringing key partners together within its structure and constitution. These include:

- joint work and co-ordination with other parts of local government (*e.g.* Planning, Transport, Policy, Housing, Estates/Real Estate/facilities, Infrastructure, Education, Culture/Amenities/Leisure, etc.);

- joint work and co-ordination with economic development entities in neighbouring municipalities and regions;

- collaborative work with politicians at all levels to give them insights into what the DA is doing for the locality;

- joint work and co-ordination with other parts of the public sector in the city (*e.g.* universities, hospitals, housing, etc.);

- joint work and co-ordination with business leadership groupings and other specialist economic development entities; and

- consultative liaison with community interests and organisations, with trade unions and workers organisations.

None of these are especially easy, but all are important. Much of this relationship management and co-ordination is invisible in terms of the delivery of key programmes of the DA, and yet these are critical relationships to ensure smooth working. DAs are often set up to be "business facing", yet they need to be "partner facing" and "colleague facing" also. Depending upon the local institutional arrangements, there are various ways to address these priorities. Explicit, planned, and agreed mechanisms for managing these relationships are key, and the most senior officials from the entities concerned should be involved.

Identifying development agencies' critical relationships within the local development system

From the DA perspective, there are a number of key relationships between DAs and other organisations which help form the heartbeat of the local development system. Though these relationships vary according to the nature of the development system in terms of scale, focus, aims, politics and legal frameworks, it is nonetheless useful to profile them. The following nine points contain examples which are not definitive. Instead they offer illustrations of each of the points.

Member organisations, e.g. Bilbao Metropoli-30

Bilbao Metropoli-30 has three types of membership organisations: (1) founding members, consisting of 19 institutions which decided to create Bilbao Metropoli-30 in 1992 (these consist of both public and private sector members); (2) associate members, the status of the majority of member organisations; and (3) collaborative members, not-for-profits and consulates which don't pay a membership fee. Tight relationships are formed with these organisations.

The mayor, e.g. Barcelona Activa

The relationship with the mayor is critical to creating the space and the goodwill for Barcelona Activa to support the transformation of Barcelona through entrepreneurship, business growth, innovation, professional opportunities, human capital development and quality employment. Without an open and healthy dialogue with senior city government officials such as the mayor, Barcelona Activa could be judged more critically. With the work of Barcelona Activa being so tightly associated with key themes such as employment, innovation and entrepreneurship, mayoral support is critical to the performance of Barcelona Activa.

City Council (Economic Development Department), e.g. Johannesburg Development Agency

The Johannesburg Development Agency is 100% owned by the City of Johannesburg and is directly accountable the Department of Development Planning and Urban Management (DPUM), insomuch as the Johannesburg Development Agency reports to it strategically. The Johannesburg Development Agency is accountable to the City through the Shareholders Unit which monitors the Johannesburg Development Agency's projects and budgets.

As an agency of the City of Johannesburg, the Johannesburg Development Agency interacts closely with the City's various departments and municipal entities in respect of their functional interest in a development's activities. In this regard, the Johannesburg Development Agency:

- operates in line with the Growth and Development Strategy principles;

- operates within existing agreed plans and frameworks (for instance, in the case of planning, the Johannesburg Development Agency operates within the overall Spatial Development Plan of the City and takes due diligence of Regional Spatial Development Frameworks (RSDF's) and existing precinct plans);

- considers inputs in respect of development design;

- facilitates the development of a management plan in respect of the ongoing operations of the initiative once the development is completed; and

- acts as an implementation agency for other departments including World Cup 2010, Transportation and the DPUM.

Where roles specifically overlap in respect of a particular aspect of a development, the Johannesburg Development Agency will consult with the relevant department or municipal entity accordingly. Given the intensive urban management focus of the City and the DPUM, the Johannesburg Development Agency partners work with regional offices to ensure close operational co-operation (JDA, 2009) (see Figure 6.1).

Figure 6.1. **The Johannesburg Development Agency's relationship with the City of Johannesburg**

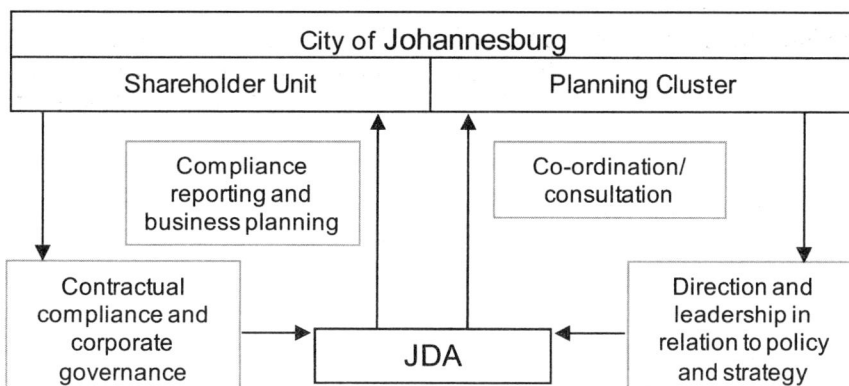

Source: JDA (Johannesburg Development Agency) (2009), "Business Plan, 2009-10", Johannesburg Development Agency.

Regional government, e.g. Cape Town Partnership

Cape Town is the driver of socio-economic growth in the Western Cape and the Central City is a fundamental driver of Cape Town's economic performance. Therefore, the relationship between the Cape Town Partnership and the provincial government is essential. There are also issues and agendas which overlap between the two, such as international investment promotion, which benefit from an integrated approach.

The private sector, e.g. AucklandPlus

AucklandPlus has developed strong links with key private sector organisations across the city region. It maintains formal and informal dialogues with business groups. For instance, the Chair of the AucklandPlus Board is also the President of Auckland's Chamber of Commerce. The AucklandPlus Chief Executive is also a Board member of the Angel Association of New Zealand, an organisation that aims to increase the quantity, quality and success of angel investments in New Zealand. At the same time, AucklandPlus has built strong links with the Committee for Auckland – a group of senior business leaders in the city interested in Auckland's sustainable development agenda.

Community stakeholders, e.g. Abyssinian Development Corporation

Local residents are the Abyssinian Development Corporation's chief customer and the reason the organisation exists. Its entire work programme is informed by and developed in close contact with the community. The Abyssinian Development Corporation interacts and engages with local residents to directly understand their needs. Improving their quality of life is therefore a major objective.

The example in Box 6.3 from the Abyssinian Development Corporation shows how innovative thinking around education can begin to build community development momentum from the ground upwards.

Other development agencies, e.g. Invest Toronto and Build Toronto

Build Toronto and Invest Toronto represent examples of how two agencies can complement one another effectively. Not only is there a sharing of offices and back office resources, the two work together on a project-by-project basis. For instance, when a new firm which has been attracted to the city by Invest Toronto needs a location, Build Toronto will be able to facilitate this process by managing existing real estate holdings effectively or perhaps by constructing a new site. There is also a funding element to this relationship where Build Toronto makes a financial contribution to the ongoing operations of Invest Toronto. The precise dimensions are yet to be decided.

Delivery partners, e.g. Prospect Leicestershire

Prospect Leicestershire will be the chief delivery agent of the county. On many projects, however, it will work in collaboration with other delivery partners. For instance, Prospect Leicestershire meets the Vice Chancellors of the area's three universities to discuss plans and to bring additional skills and expertise to bear.

Box 6.3. **Signature project: Abyssinian Development Corporation and the College Ready Communities Project**

In August 2009, the Abyssinian Development Corporation (ADC) was chosen as one of four grantees to implement the Deutsche Bank Americas Foundation (DBAF) College Ready Communities initiative for middle and high schools. The sponsor of the Thurgood Marshall Academy for Learning and Social Change (TMA) – a Harlem public middle school for grades six to eight – ADC is particularly well-placed to deliver. The DBAF matched funds for a Bill and Melinda Gates Foundation grant they received. ADC was the only public middle school-sponsor selected; the others were from public high schools. This two-year pilot programme will provide the critical resources necessary to achieve high-quality academic supports for 423 young Harlem public school students in grades six to eight. The College Ready Communities initiative aims to increase positive educational outcomes for public school students by reaching beyond classroom walls. The three core objectives are to increase: (1) attendance and other measures of improvement in student engagement and school culture; (2) academic performance; and (3) matriculation rates to four-year colleges or college-preparatory high schools.

The key intervention site for the initiative is the ADC-sponsored public middle/high school TMA. The mission of TMA is to provide students and their families with the experiences they need to meet the challenges of higher education and the workforce in the 21st century. Research shows that investments in middle school academic success are crucial. According to the New York City Department of Education (2008), in New York City, "the repercussions of low middle school performance do not stop when students leave the City's middle schools ... this domino effect continues in high school .... students who show signs of disengagement in middle school (*i.e.* they have low attendance or fail core courses) are less likely to graduate from high school." This theoretical basis led ADC to focus on an early intervention strategy where middle school is a key leverage point to improve academic success.

To achieve full implementation of the Initiative, ADC has formed a collaborative partnership with organisations that were committed to affecting positive change in District 5. They are listed below with their role in project implementation:

- ADC: lead co-ordinator for Initiative programme planning, implementation and evaluation efforts; Steering Committee convener; hire and manage key Initiative staff; provide financial literacy workshops for parents and community at large.

- Thurgood Marshall Academy for Learning and Social Change (Harlem public middle school for grades six to eight): achieve the educational outcomes.

- The Brotherhood/Sister Sol (not-for-profit youth development organisation): provide professional development training for teachers in youth development principles; continue ten-year partnership with TMA by providing youth leadership development activities for students.

- NYC Coalition for Educational Justice (non-profit educational advocacy organisation): train the Parent Organiser for in-house visits, conducting workshops and to execute community building events (town hall meetings, etc.). There is also an emphasis on building a viable parents organisation that functions independently of the schools and focuses on school reform.

- Academy of Collaborative Education (a Harlem public middle school for grades six to eight): achieve the educational outcomes.

The goal of this partnership is to execute a comprehensive approach to creating a holistic college-ready community at the middle school level that engages students, parents, school staff, partners and the community at large. The project will deliver a number of outcomes which include: instruction alignment, school operating standards, academic supports and professional development (for teachers); College Readiness Initiative; parent engagement in education activities; community engagement events; Summer Bridge Transitional Programs; and youth leadership development activities. The ADC sees the College Ready Communities initiative as "a very promising venture that, if adequately funded, can achieve breakthrough educational results for Harlem children."

Source: Abyssinian Development Corporation (2009), "Middle School College Ready Community Initiative, 2009", Abyssinian Development Corporation.

The media, e.g. Cape Town Partnership

Recently, the Cape Town Partnership has concentrated on its digital media strategy. The Partnership has found that a picture is worth a thousand words, and a short video clip on YouTube is worth even more. The Partnership advocates being "accessible to the media at all times" since "they are your friends, even when they don't get the story right. Development walking tours for your own citizens are very effective. Create local ambassadors – if locals don't believe in what you are doing, you will never convince the rest of the world."

International networks, e.g. Milano Metropoli

Milano Metropoli relies on a far-reaching network of national and international contacts and partnerships for knowledge sharing. It also takes an active part in numerous DA networks, such as the Italian Association of Local Development and Territorial Marketing Agencies (AIDA), the EURADA, the LEED programme of the OECD, and the European Learning Network (LNet), to name a few.

References

Abyssinian Development Corporation (2009), "Middle School College Ready Community Initiative, 2009", Abyssinian Development Corporation.

JDA (Johannesburg Development Agency) (2009), "Business Plan, 2009-10", Johannesburg Development Agency.

Madrid Global (2008), "Executive Summary: the Strategy For International Positioning, 2008-11", Madrid Global.

New York City Department of Education (2008), "The Blueprint for Middle School Success: Key Elements and Promising School-Based Practices", a report for the Campaign for Middle School Success, New York, NY.

OECD LEED Programme (2006), "Action Space - Local Development Agency Review: The case of Laganside Corporation, Belfast," *www.oecd.org/document/60 /0,3343,en_2649_34455_40417020_1_1_1_1,00.html.*

Chapter 7

The operational features of development agencies: governance, operations, resources and accountability

Operational features of development agencies are fundamental to their success. This chapter identifies key trends and choices that support organisational effectiveness. Because development agencies are usually not organisations that are statutorily mandated, there are many choices about how they are internally structured, what tools they use, and how they operate. This chapter seeks to illuminate some of these choices giving reference to the 16 development agency case study evidence base. Some of the key issues illustrated in particular include: development agency boards and leadership; organisational structures; financial strategies; resource and asset management; accountabilities; performance review and best-practice sharing.

In this chapter we assess the operational features of development agencies (DAs), seeking to identify key trends and choices that support organisational effectiveness. Because DAs are usually not organisations that are statutorily mandated, there are many choices about how they are internally structured, what tools they use, and how they operate. This chapter seeks to illuminate some of these choices with references to our case study DAs.

Governance and leadership

The role of leadership in the local development system

Local development systems are complex, dynamic, multi-faceted and multi-stakeholder in nature. As a result, the quality of the leadership and governance of local development systems is emerging as a critical factor in how effectively its tools and resources are deployed. Just as weak cities present challenges, success also brings problems like congestion, price rises and shortage of amenities such as housing, green space, high-quality urban realm or office space. How well local and national leaders solve these "growth challenges" is central to success in the longer term.

Consequently, effective leadership and governance are now themselves a factor of comparative advantage that cities and regions compete for. This occurs through the external competitive recruitment of city managers and highly capable civic leaders, such as university vice chancellors, airport chief executives, transport commissioners, chief planners, city architects and many others.

As fundamental elements of local development systems, the effective leadership and governance of DAs is a major contributing factor to city development success. The evidence shows that the leadership style of key individuals both at the management and operational levels of DAs has a significant impact on the effectiveness of the organisation. It is no secret that effective leadership can galvanise an organisation to realise its potential, and DAs are no different.

Key leaders and leadership teams within development agencies

In the paragraphs that follow, we build on accepted principles for effective organisational leadership by isolating a list of principles which are particular and specific to key leaders within DAs.

Before proceeding, it is important to highlight that, though there is considerable common ground, different types of DAs can require different leadership styles to match the necessities of the tasks they perform. Table 7.1 summarises the operational style of DAs by DA type.

Table 7.1. **Operational styles of selected development agencies, by development agency type**

Development agency typology	Development agency	Operational style
Development and revitalisation agencies	HafenCity Hamburg GmbH	Surgical, business-like, ambitious
	Johannesburg Development Agency	Technical, effective, entrepreneurial
Productivity and economic growth agencies	Barcelona Activa	Responsive, innovative, entrepreneurial
	AucklandPlus	Agenda-setting, collaborative, networking
Integrated economic agencies	New York City Economic Development Corporation	Corporate, professional, powerful
	Milano Metropoli	Non-corporate, innovative, entrepreneurial
Internationalisation agencies	Madrid Global	Strategic, networking, savvy
	Invest Toronto	Informed, business-like, nimble
Visioning and partnership agencies	Cape Town Partnership	Diplomatic, inclusive, diligent.
	Bilbao Metropoli-30	Visionary, collaborative, agenda-setting

This table essentially shows that to perform at an optimal level, different DAs require and develop different operational styles. Because the operational style of a DA is tightly linked to the leadership style of its chief executive, and other key individuals, the recruitment of the right leadership team is a prerequisite for success.

It can take time to recruit the right team and secure the right chief executive. Though the start-up process for Invest Toronto was initiated in the summer of 2008, it was not until 24 February 2009 that a new permanent board was appointed by the mayor. Following external advertising and internal searches, the appointment of the new Chief Executive was not announced until 25 May 2009 – almost a year after the idea for Invest Toronto was conceived.

Despite the need for a degree of sensitivity to the style of leadership required, there are a number of common principles which can underline effective DA leadership and the skill set required in a DA chief executive and senior staff. It is recommended that DA leaders:

- **Be open to people, business and ideas**. DA leaders can, for instance, play a key role in attracting the multi-lingual populations that are a competitive advantage of diversity in serving firms in a global economy. The atmosphere a DA leader and his/her organisation can create can permeate through to how the city is viewed from outside – a key feature of city success.

- **Lead through active influence**. Cities have different direct competences and powers. DA leaders must both provide their own inputs well (services, investment, and facilities), but they must also influence those provided by others (such as transport authorities, energy providers, and airports).

- **Understand that leadership teams are key.** Local economies are led by teams, not just by individuals. DA leaders have to galvanise other leaders in business, institutions (such as universities), at higher levels of government around the competitive strategy and performance of the local economy in order to succeed.

- **Tell the story of their city**. Cities increasingly offer a brand platform which is a key part of the branding of firms located there. DA leaders can lead the articulation and co-ordination of the brand and communicate with active commitment and enthusiasm.

- **Communicate with business**. Leadership is at the heart of cities making the most of the opportunities and challenges of a global knowledge-driven economy, and how well cities provide a platform for business success. This involves the DA leaders knowing and communicating what business the city is in. Being clear about the city economic rationale and unique advantages is the first step. DA leaders should be proactive about communicating with business to solve problems and to capitalise on opportunities. This will help attract and retain key employers and productivity drivers to, and in, the city.

- **Organise the "real" economy**. Because local economies are bigger than local boundaries, metropolitan or local regional leadership and co-ordination is key. DA chief executives together with other local, regional and national leaders should look to lead their cities and bring the key business assets of the regional economy together despite multiple authorities. There must be robust mechanisms for doing this.

- **Deliver effective services to business**. Some local services are more important to firms than others, and firms are differently sensitive to local services. So planning, sanitation, education, transport, policing are important to firms in different sectors, and at different points in their lifecycles. DA leaders should be sensitive to the changing needs of their key stakeholders such as the business community.

- **Build investment readiness**. Attracting external investment is a key task for some DA leaders because public finance alone is not enough for local success, either in quantity or orientation. External investment is needed in the productive platform of the local economy. The DA leader should look to provide the investment prospectus and reduce the costs and risks of investing in their local economy by better facilitating external investment and improving the pace and quality of the local and national response to investment. Public assets are also important ingredients in investment attraction and should be managed actively to leverage investment.

- **Pay close attention to key nodes**. City centres, central business districts, airport zones, and major development areas are key places of production, exchange and leisure. They must be led and managed well as they contribute to the productivity of place.

- **Address the climate change agenda**. Investment can be sensitive to the environmental performance of cities. Cities have to adjust to a low carbon economy and enable businesses to accrue the benefits in sustainable investment. DA leaders should look to lead change from within by promoting green work practices.

The chief executive of a DA is the figurehead of the organisation. His, or her, style sets the tone for how the DA operates internally and operates with clients and partners externally. At best they are experienced and knowledgeable and can leverage a wide range of contacts, both domestic and international. Good DA chief executives, like senior members of most organisations, public or private, are talented leaders. They are equally comfortable initiating or shaping new and emerging agendas as well as decisively delivering against existing projects and priorities.

Box 7.1 speaks to the impact effective DA leadership can have.

Box 7.1. **The impact of effective individual leadership
at the Cape Town Partnership**

Qualities such as diplomacy, openness and humility, which have been attributed to the Cape Town Partnership's leadership, have been significant in the DA's success. Not only have these qualities improved the effectiveness of the organisation's steering, cheering and coaching roles as a visioning and partnership DA, they have also helped create a very positive internal culture within the organisation. Staff members are motivated and empowered in this enabling atmosphere, which can, in large part, be associated to excellent leadership.

Given the complex steering function of the Cape Town Partnership against a backdrop of stakeholders which don't often speak the same institutional languages, the style of the Cape Town Partnership's leadership is critical. In many ways the style of the organisation mirrors the leadership styles of Chief Executive Boraine and Deputy Chief Executive Makalima-Ngewana.

It is deliberately designed to be a small organisation focused on a delivering on a clear and concise mandate in a manageable spatial area. In line with the style of its leadership team, the Cape Town Partnership fulfils this role diligently, diplomatically and in an inclusive manner. The notion that all work done is for the betterment of the Central City and the wider City of Cape Town continually underlies the Cape Town Partnership's work and helps contribute to the success of the organisation.

Board of Directors

A DA's Board of Directors plays an important role in both supervising the work of the organisation, and in communicating its impact and effectiveness to the wider community in which it operates. The International Economic Development Council (IEDC) isolates a range of important roles for Boards of Directors and for individual officers of the board. It considers key board roles to be: (1) financial oversight; (2) strategic planning; (3) raising funds; (4) developing policy; (5) community relations; (6) monitoring and evaluation; (7) hiring/firing the executive director; and (8) providing counsel.

Additionally, IEDC views the Board of Directors as potentially bringing a vast array of other skills and knowledge to the organisation. These range from expertise in economic development to leadership and management techniques, to clout and persuasion.

IEDC also provides a wide range of guidance on how to recruit and develop the role of the board, including the designation of committee roles and the effective management of oversight. It stresses the importance of the composition of the board in achieving representativeness and accountability. It also identifies particular roles for the chair of the board including that of leading on community relations, and ensuring compliance of the agency with its constitutional and legal framework. There are specific roles identified for deputy chair, treasurer, secretary, and the executive director (or chief executive).

Table 7.2 and Box 7.2 display the diversity of DA board structures, compositions and sizes.

Table 7.2. **Board composition and size in selected development agencies**

Development agency	Composition						Number			
	Public sector: local	Public sector: regional	Private sector	Third sector	Mayor or Council CEO	DA CEO	0-5	6-10	10-15	15+
Abyssinian Development Corporation	■		■	■						■
AucklandPlus	■		■			■		■		
Barcelona Activa	■		■		■				■	
Bilbao Ria-2000	■	■			■	■				■
Creative Sheffield	■	■	■	■	■	■				■
Liverpool Vision	■	■	■		■			■		
Prospect Leicestershire	■	■	■		■				■	

Box 7.2. **Dual boards with dual responsibilities: HafenCity Hamburg GmbH**

HafenCity Hamburg GmbH's Supervisory Board consists of five ministers (for urban development, economics, finance, culture and education) plus the State Councillor at the Senate Chancellery. In 2005, an Advisory Board was set up. Its nine members include the President of the Chamber of Commerce, the President of the Chamber of Architects, the president of the Chamber of Crafts and four academic members.

Operations

Organisational structure

Comment can be made on DA organisational structures in two particular ways. Firstly, there are a range of prescriptions about the internal organisation of DAs. These principally focus on good management principles, such as the separation of audit functions from expenditure functions; the need for clear accountability for risk management; the responsibility for cost control; and effective techniques of project management. Secondly, there are no principles that are unique to DAs *per se*, but the basic principles common to all not-for-profit public-purpose organisations apply to DAs.

What is difficult for DAs is to generate effective understanding from external sponsors and "overseers" of what the economic development business is. Therefore, the need for DAs to pay attention to communication and liaison functions is paramount.

In practice, the structure of a DA tends not to vary a great deal between organisations. In many ways it mirrors private sector companies in that it tends to:

- be two-tiered with a strategic Board of Directors above an operational team;

- be run by a chief executive who reports to the board on a regular basis through clear channels of communication;

- have a senior management team to support the chief executive;

- divide personnel into separate teams to reflect different work streams and priorities;

- have a clear chain of command and communication with each team having a clear leader; and

- provide capacity for business support and administration.

Figures 7.1, 7.2 and 7.3 present the organisational structures of selected DAs, pointing out, if relevant, interesting features. We have chosen three examples which display the diversity of structures which can be found:

- **Prospect Leicestershire**: conventional two-tier structure with clear divisions and chains of command as well as sufficient administrative capacity.

- **New York City Economic Development Corporation**: two-tier structure but with a defined senior leadership team operating between board and operational levels. High level of labour division and administrative capacity, including an internal and external policy, strategy and public relations teams.

- **Bilbao Metropoli-30**: conventional two-tier structure, but the strategic board level of the organisation is divided into three units which have some overlap. They include: (1) the General Assembly, which comprises all the founding, full and associate members that attend its meetings. It is the supreme debating and decision-making body of the association and its resolutions govern the life of Bilbao Metropoli-30. The General Assembly is composed of all the members, with one representative per member. It meets once or twice a year; (2) the Board of Trustees, which acts as the governing body of the association, and sets it specific aims and targets. Its members are designated by the General Assembly, but some of them are proposed by the Basque Government, the Regional Government of Bizkaia, the Bilbao City Council and the Association of Basque Municipalities. It meets twice a year, often organised at the same as the General Assembly, to allow the presence of top leaders such as the mayor; and (3) the Board of Directors – using power delegated to it by the Board of Trustees, the Board of Directors is the association's administrative and management body. It is made up by delegation among founding and full members and is designated by the General Assembly.

Boxes 7.3 and 7.4 demonstrate the approach taken in Toronto.

Box 7.3. **Building a new senior leadership structure: options for Invest Toronto**

Two main options were considered for the leadership structure of Invest Toronto: (1) a conventional board and operational team model; and (2) a distinctive two-tier board.

Option 2 involved the strategic level of the board being populated by a range of Torontonian chief executives, acting as champions of the city through the mechanism of Invest Toronto. The other board tier would oversee the strategic direction of Invest Toronto as an organisation.

Option 1 – a conventional board and operational team model – was chosen.

Box 7.4. **Building an organisational structure from scratch: imperatives for Build Toronto**

Key objectives for the new organisational structure included:

- Structure is designed to achieve major shareholder goals.

- Provides ability to develop and effectively manage public-private partnerships.

- Capital-intensive business requires additional resources and expertise in Development, Finance and Treasury functions.

- Provides capacity to engage stakeholders effectively.

- Ensures that primary focus is on real estate development and maximising financial and non-financial value from surplus lands.

- Cohesive and "lean-launch" management structure that can build in the future.

The size, composition and quality of the staff base are three fundamentals which underpin the successful operation of a DA.

Staff size, composition and quality

Staff size

Though they can display a degree of overlap, the scale of the human resource base of DAs is representative of a number of factors: (1) the scale of activities undertaken; (2) how labour intensive these activities are; (3) how institutionally mature the DA is; and (4) the level of funding available. Of the 16 DAs profiled in this book, the range of staff employed varied between 9 and over 400.

Staff numbers tend to stay relatively stable for mature organisations. However, should any of these four factors show variation, numbers may change. The following examples are not definitive; the case studies are merely illustrative.

Change in the scale and labour intensiveness of activities

As a nimble and responsive organisation, Barcelona Activa is able to be highly flexible and responsive to the rapidly changing needs of the city. The DA exhibits a fluid and constantly evolving organisational structure according to the scale of the most-needed and tailor-made programmes. As a result, though Barcelona Activa has a permanent staff of 109, it purposefully builds in a degree of human resource flexibility which allows it to employ temporary staff according to the demands of its work streams. This can increase staff numbers by up to 221 people.

Figure 7.1. **The organisational structure of Prospect Leicestershire**

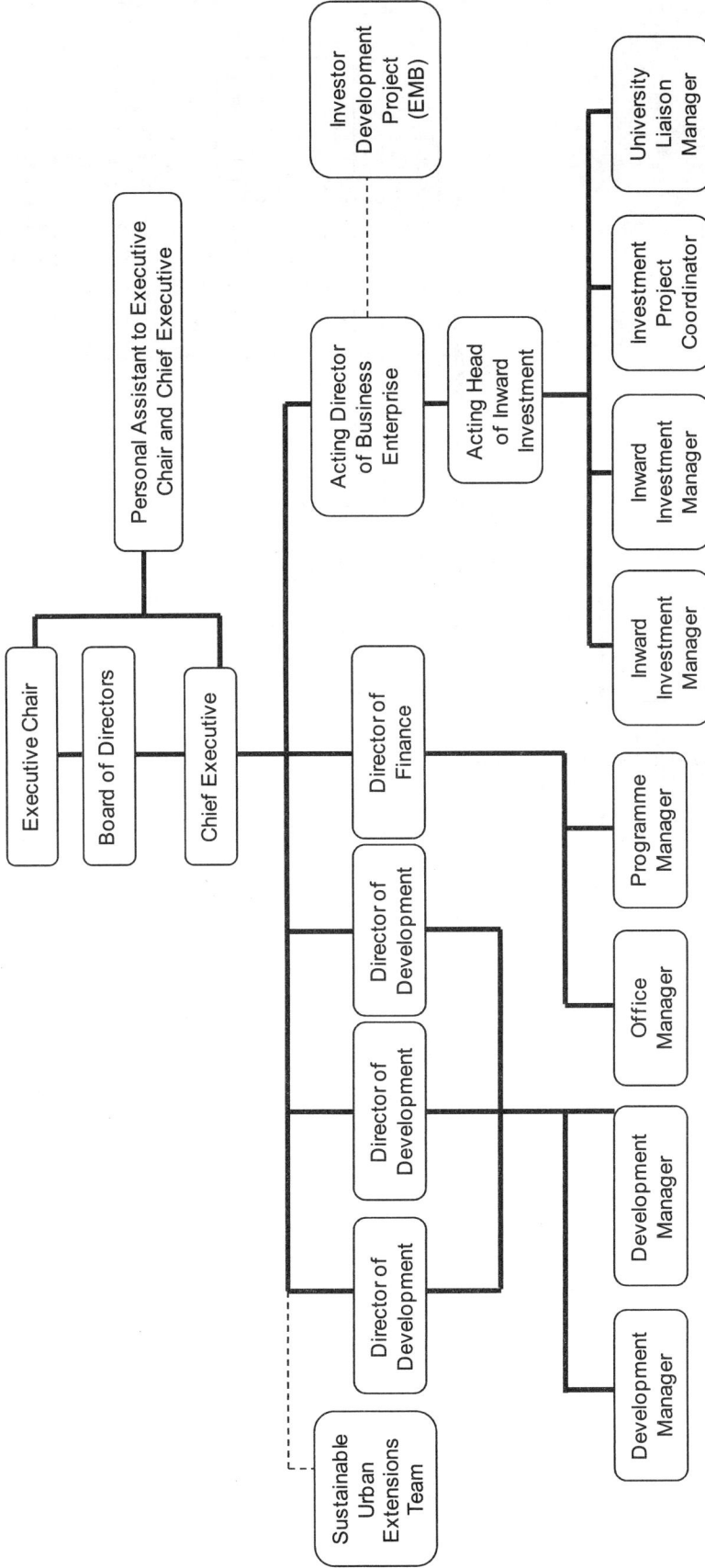

Figure 7.2. **The organisational structure of the New York City Economic Development Corporation**

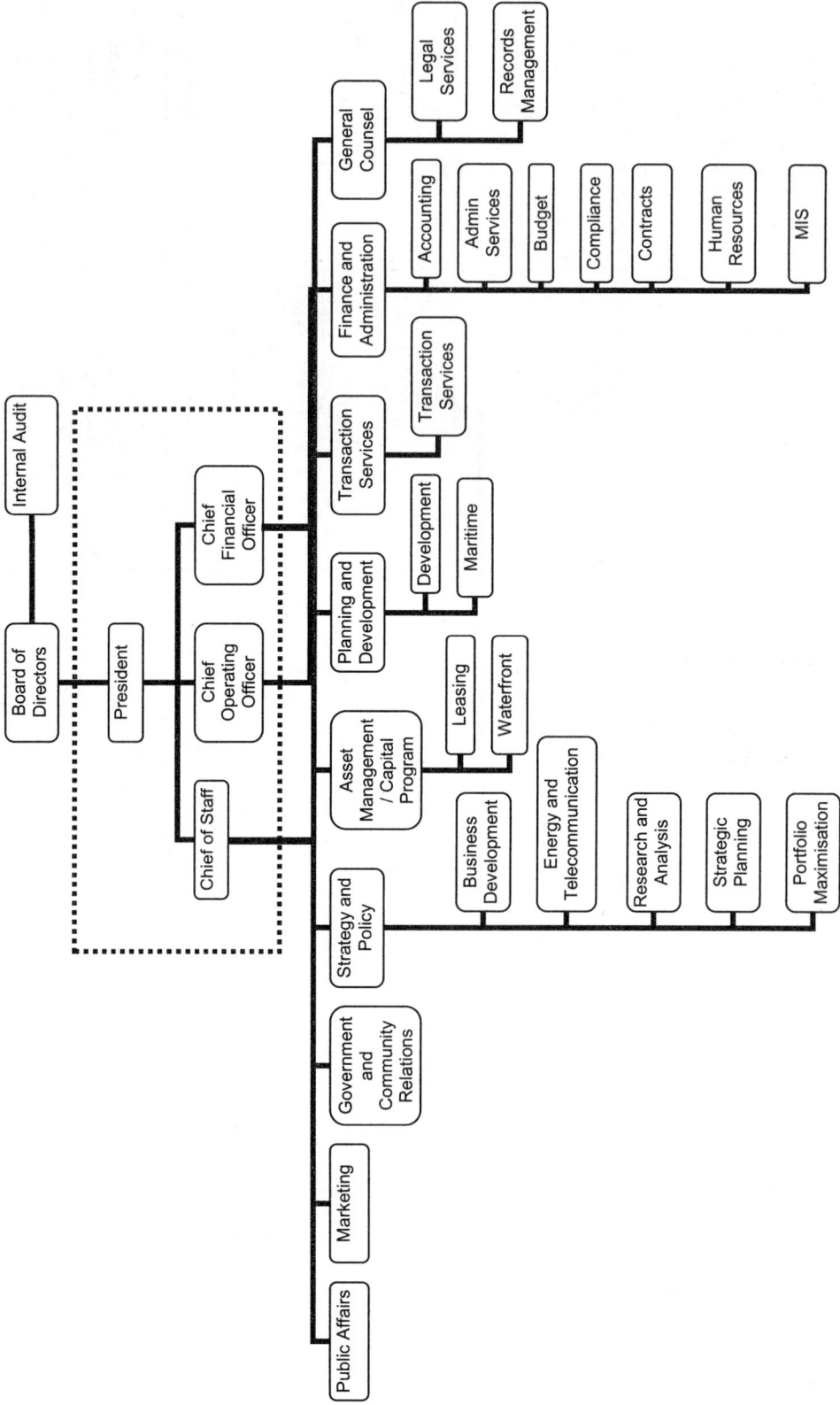

Figure 7.3. **The organisational structure of Bilbao Metropoli-30**

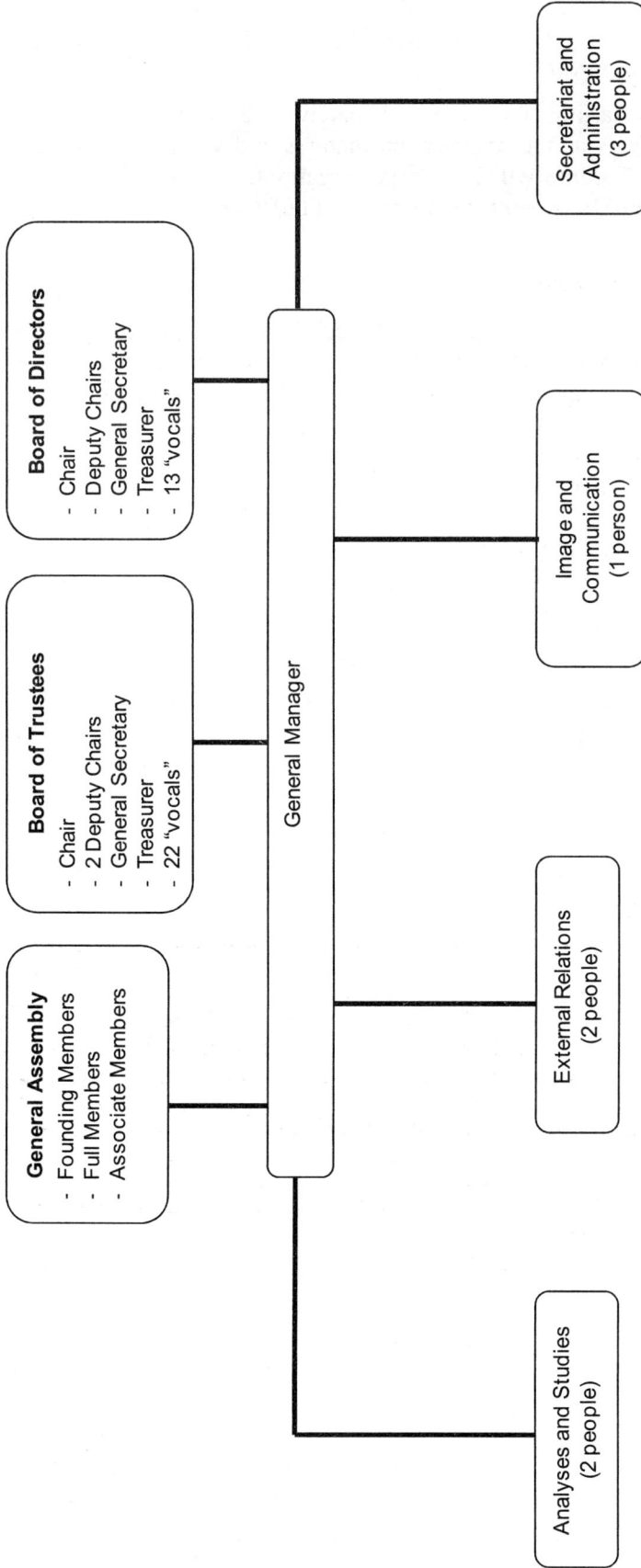

General Assembly
- Founding Members
- Full Members
- Associate Members

Board of Trustees
- Chair
- 2 Deputy Chairs
- General Secretary
- Treasurer
- 22 "vocals"

Board of Directors
- Chair
- Deputy Chairs
- General Secretary
- Treasurer
- 13 "vocals"

General Manager

Analyses and Studies
(2 people)

External Relations
(2 people)

Image and
Communication
(1 person)

Secretariat and
Administration
(3 people)

178 – 7. THE OPERATIONAL FEATURES OF DEVELOPMENT AGENCIES: GOVERNANCE, OPERATIONS, RESOURCES AND ACCOUNTABILITY

Changes in institutional maturity

Build Toronto has a starting staff of approximately 30-35 people. This could rise to around 50 within two years as the organisation matures and workloads increase. These figures show that Build Toronto will be a larger organisation than both Invest Toronto and the Toronto Economic Development Corporation (TEDCO).

Changes in the level of funding

Operational costs such as staff wage costs of the Johannesburg Development Agency are met predominantly by both a year-on-year City of Johannesburg operating grant and the retention of 5% of all capital spend. As a result, the amount of funding available depends on the nature of the projects undertaken. Towards the future, there will likely be a shift away from capital intensive projects as the Bus Rapid Transit System and the 2010 World Cup as these projects move to completion. Because 5% of capital expenditure is retained for costs, this shift will erode an important pillar of revenue for the organisation. This could stimulate a change in staff numbers.

Staff composition

As has been discussed earlier in this chapter, the divisions of labour within a DA are an important component of how well it functions. There is very little here which is distinctive to the operational success of DAs compared to many other organisations. It is important, however, that DAs have clear priorities, objectives and work streams which are reflected by the composition of the workforce and the way the DA divides and allocates its labour.

Nonetheless, such divisions can provide a clarity of purpose within the DA and a single point of contact for other organisations when they want to liaise with the DA on a particular subject. Dividing human resources in this was can also facilitate the hire of specialist staff which can drive forward the success of the DA as a whole. Another positive aspect of division is that it can create smaller, more cohesive communities within a larger structure. This can boost morale.

As organisations grow, however, it is important that functions which support the smooth operation of the organisation also grow. Auxiliary support teams such as public relations, legal, administrative, internal strategy, human resources and accounting teams, among others, can develop. It is also essential as the organisation grows that lines of communication between departments remain clear and open. This can avoid work duplication to maximise resource use. It also facilitates information exchange and the cross-fertilisation of ideas.

Staff quality

It is a consistent feature of DA success that these organisations recruit the highest quality individuals they can find. Given the complexity and diversity of the roles and functions that DAs undertake, attracting and retaining talent and experience can underpin the impact a DA has within its local development system.

It is, therefore, important that DAs develop effective human resource strategies, both internal and external. Some of these will be discussed in later chapters. The following examples highlight the importance of human resources to successful DAs.

Johannesburg Development Agency

The Johannesburg Development Agency has built up a highly skilled and experienced team of strategists and practitioners over a number of years. In a highly pressurised working environment (due to budget and time constraints and demands), the quality of its staff are a key reason why the Johannesburg Development Agency is considered effective.

Creative Sheffield

Creative Sheffield recruits the best talent it can find. This process has been aided by the fact that the organisation is semi-autonomous, dynamic and action-orientated. The fact the organisation recruited a foreign-born chief executive with excellent links to networks outside the United Kingdom facilitated the identification, attraction and acquisition of talented individuals.

New York City Economic Development Corporation

New York City Economic Development Corporation is able to effectively contribute to local economic development because of the broad range of expertise and commitment of its leadership and staff. New York City Economic Development Corporation has real estate professionals, engineers, management consultants, economic analysts and attorneys, among several other professionals on its staff, allowing it to look at a policy or real estate challenge across several different dimensions, which allows it to tackle economic development challenges in a thoughtful and innovative way. In these ways, the organisation has a breadth and depth of talent.

The relationships between the operational teams and the board within development agencies

Effective communication between the strategic and operational sides of a DA is a regular feature of the internal operation of these organisations. Strong relationships here can cause tight alignment behind a series of objectives which maximises the potential for effective delivery against them. Weak relationships can cause an internal tension which can have a destabilising effect on the DA.

Table 7.3 lists a number of mechanisms which DAs commonly employ to ensure strong relationships between operational teams and strategic boards. Figure 7.4 presents a schema of the relationships between the Johannesburg Development Agency, its board and key stakeholders, by way of example.

Table 7.3. **Internal communications between strategic and operational teams in selected development agencies**

Development agency	Mechanism	Frequency					
		Weekly	Bi-weekly	Monthly	Bi-monthly	Less often than bi-monthly	When the need arises
Bilbao Metropoli-30	CEO discussions with the board			■			
	Production of written reports			■			
Bilbao Ria-2000	Meetings on the strategic direction of the organisation					■	
	Presentation of projects by staff for approval						■
Madrid Global	Meeting of a "Direction Committee"	■	■				
	Meeting of "Direction Committee" Madrid Global Departments			■			
Milano Metropoli	CEO presentation to the board				■		
	Review of working budgets				■		
Prospect Leicestershire	Transactional discussions between the board and senior management team			■			
	Formation of board member-led working groups						■

Development agency resources

Business strategy and financial models

The business model a DA employs will clearly incorporate its financial strategy. Depending on the regulatory framework, DAs more or less have the freedom to develop a model which is more than an income and expenditure account. Most DAs do seek to find ways to generate additional income and there are a range of economic development interventions which offer scope for the DA to generate some income. The European Association of Development Agencies (EURADA) list these as: (1) participating in the capitalisation of SMEs; (2) invoicing small and medium-sized enterprises (SMEs) for consultancy and support; (3) real estate and property management/development; (4) consultancy services to municipal and national governments; (5) providing training; (6) organising seminars; (7) attracting sponsorship; (8) management fees; (9) trade missions; (10) services for foreign investors; (11) management of incubators and industrial parks; and (12) sale of books.

Figure 7.4. **The relationships between the Johannesburg Development Agency, its board and key stakeholders**

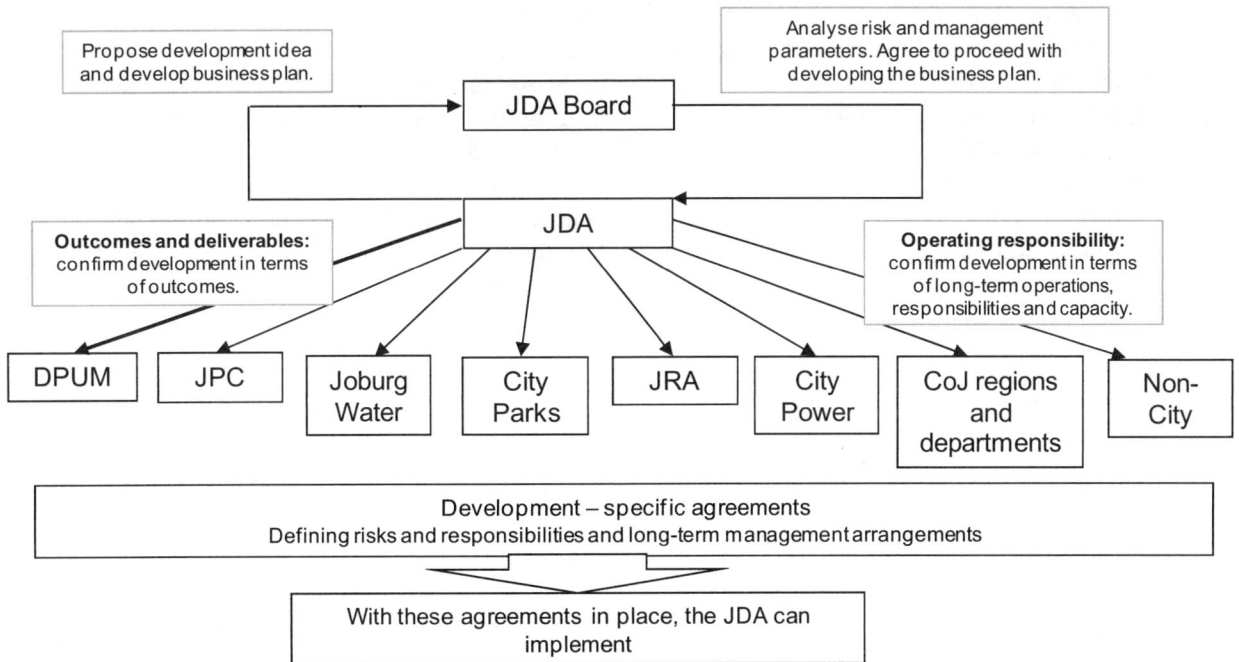

JDA: Johannesburg Development Agency
DPUM: Department of Planning and Urban Management
JPC: Johannesburg Property Company
JRA: Johannesburg Roads Agency
CoJ: City of Johannesburg

Source: JDA (2009), "Business Plan, 2009-10", Johannesburg Development Agency.

In some countries, where DAs have been recently established (*e.g.* Poland), they have been designed so as to build commercial income strategies from the outset. There are some examples of DAs that are wholly commercial in their approach, but these are not alternatives to the comprehensive public DA function, they are complementary.

The building of greater investment and financing capacity is very important in order to move from a low-investment/low-return equilibrium to a high-investment/high-return equilibrium through engagement with the private sector, better use of financial innovations and assets, and the capturing of value to support long-term investment. In many cases, it also requires raising additional levies and taxes for specific purposes. But it often also requires using existing economic development tools better and more confidently.

Implementation capability has to be built at a scale required to make decisive interventions on the major challenges facing the locality or sub-region. This may require the development of new DAs or entities, the disposal of existing ones or more ambitious priorities for those that exist already. It nearly always involves using existing tools in bolder and more imaginative ways, as well as creating new ones. It is helpful to identify catalysts that can accelerate progress on solving key problems and utilise them to foster momentum fully.

These might be projects or events that have the ability to deliver immediate and short-term outcomes, but can also foster momentum on longer term goals – for instance, the hosting of major events. A further issue is to measure and benchmark progress regularly against agreed goals and engage media attention in the long term on issues and trends facing the locality or sub-region. Support should be given to those leaders that have taken the longer term, bigger picture view of what is in the best interests of the interdependent region and celebrate success. And it is important to build a local or sub-regional identity that represents the essence of the region and promote it effectively through major channels. This may involve building champions for the region, from both within and outside, and encouraging them to present the region positively through key media channels. The region should be open to the world and ready to make adjustments to benefit from international opportunities.

Financing development agencies

While a myriad of arrangements exist for financing DAs, five basic approaches suggest themselves, with a range of hybrids between them.

These five approaches to financing DAs include:

1. The DA is wholly public-sector funded/owned, and its balance sheet is tightly publicly controlled through either detailed control of budget lines and project finances, or annualised budgeting and resources accounting processes.

2. The DA is wholly public-sector funded and owned but has freedom to vary the use of capital receipts, trading income, fees, and levies (for example) to generate an "internal financial engine" which is subject to public sector accounting rules, but provides for a complementary commercial strategy to help achieve public policy goals.

3. The DA is funded from a range of public and private sector sources and there are clear rules and processes for setting financial strategy and for the reapportioning of income and expenditure to different sponsors.

4. The DA is largely, or wholly, private-sector funded and operates principally as a not-for-profit business with extensive control over its internal financial strategy.

5. The DA has created its own "subsidiary" or "intermediary" for engaging in more complex financial transactions/arrangements and this is separately governed and accounted for within approved rules. Freedom may, or may not, exist to wire resources between the parent agency and the additional vehicle.

Many DAs are hybrids of more than one of these approaches and it is not at all uncommon for a DA to gradually acquire the features of several of these as it makes progress on its key mission. Indeed, it is often a necessity that the DA should do so in order to take forward the particular requirements at specific stages of the redevelopment effort.

Building on the theory introduced earlier in this chapter, the Tables 7.4 through 7.8 illustrate these funding mechanisms in practice and by DA type. They highlight that: certain agencies are better financed than others; some have more diversified funding sources and mechanisms; there is innovation around DA finance; and many agencies are underfunded, yet still deliver very effectively.

Table 7.4. **The financing and balance sheets of development and revitalisation agencies**

Development agency	Budget	Key income source	Key expenditure	Finance mechanism
Abyssinian Development Corporation (2008/09)	EUR 6.01 million	Government contracts EUR 2.47 million (41%)	Salaries EUR 3.15 million (52%)	• Government contracts (41%) • Grants and contributions (5.5%) • Development fees (24.9) • Special events (6.1%) • Management fees (4.2%) • Social service fees (0.8%) • Equity investment (1.1%) • Net gain on sales (5.5%) • Rental incomes (0.9%)
BILBAO Ria 2000 (2009)	2009 budget forecast of EUR 116.60 million. Managing over EUR 83 million of development	-	-	• Original contribution of EUR 1.8 million by the shareholders. • Receipt of land in areas it operates from company shareholders for free. • BILBAO Ria 2000 upgrades the plots of land and the company then invests in building and infrastructure work. • Resultant plots are then sold off, generating surpluses which are used to purchase more land. • Develop-sell-purchase model is then repeated. • European Union subsidies have accounted for approximately 9% of the budget in recent years. • Occasional contributions from shareholders in return for specific investments complementary to the main intervention.
Build Toronto	Long-term budget TBC	TBC	TBC	• Initial start-up grant and free donation of high-quality land assets from the city. • Nominally self-funded recycling surplus from a purchase-develop-sell or rent model to cover operational costs. • Surplus likely also to fund Invest Toronto.

Table 7.4. **The financing and balance sheets of development and revitalisation agencies** *(continued)*

Development agency	Budget	Key income source	Key expenditure	Finance mechanism
HafenCity Hamburg GmbH (1997-2025)	EUR 6.53-7.03 billion	EUR 5 - 5.5 billion private sector investment (78%)	• Special "City and Port" fund expenditure EUR 800 million (11%) on business relocation and selected infrastructures. • Grants from Hamburg government ministries to cover site remediation U4 subway link, infrastructure links to CBD and public amenities EUR 730 million (11%) • EUR 5-5.5 billion private sector expenditure (78%)	• Initial "City and Port" fund established. • Stream of land donated to the fund by municipality free of charge. • Lend against "City and Port" fund a public sector loan rates to finance infrastructure (EUR 750 million) (10%). • Sale of land as freehold to repay loans. • Grants from Hamburg government ministries (EUR 1.13 billion excluding "City and Port" Fund Contributions) (15%). • Private sector investment leveraged (75%).
Johannesburg Development Agency (2009/10)	EUR 116.64 million (Capital: EUR 109.35 million. Operating: EUR 7.29 million)	• City of Johannesburg Transportation (BRT and non-BRT) (EUR 90.21 million) • City of Johannesburg capex allocation (EUR 2.64 million) • Inner city fund (EUR 3.82 million) • 2010 Office (EUR 10.85 million) • Neighbourhood Development grant (EUR 2.14 million) • City of Johannesburg operating grant (EUR 1.81 million). • Retention of 5% capital expenditure (EUR 5.47 million)	Employee costs (2007) EUR 1.54 million	Capital: • Yearly City of Johannesburg capital expenditure grant (2.3%) • Inner City Fund grant (3.3%) • City of Johannesburg Transportation grant (77%) • 2010 Office grant (9.3%) • Yearly Neighbourhood Development Programme Grant (NDPG) (1.8%) Operating: • City of Johannesburg operating expenditure grant (2.1%) • Retention of 5% total capital spend (4.7%) • NDPG cost recovery allowance of one salary per project per year

Table 7.5. **The financing and balance sheets of productivity and economic growth agencies**

Development agency	Budget	Key income source	Key expenditure	Finance mechanism
AucklandPlus (2008/09)	EUR 2.57 million	Private sector and university sponsorship (54%)	Key regional projects (61%)	• Local and national government grants (46%) • University and private sector sponsorship (54%)
Barcelona Activa (2008)	EUR 24 million (2008)	City Council (51.8%)	Access to and improvement of employment (19%)	• Public funding from the European Union, Spanish Government, Catalonian Government, City Council and other through winning open tenders (86.5%) • Management of own assets (13.5%)

Table 7.6. **The financing and balance sheets of integrated agencies**

Development agency	Budget	Key income source	Key expenditure	Finance mechanism
Creative Sheffield (2008/09)	EUR 4.83 million	Government grants EUR 3.3 million	Salaries and wages EUR 2.31 million	• Government grants (Yorkshire Forward and Local Enterprise Growth initiative) (68%) • Member contributions (Sheffield City Council and English Partnerships) (30%) • Other income (ERDF objective one) (0.7%)
Liverpool Vision (2008/09)	EUR 5.46 million	Liverpool City Council EUR 4.07 million	-	• Liverpool City Council (74.7%) • Northwest Regional Development Agency (12.1%) • English Partnerships/HCA (9.9%) • Working Neighbourhood Fund (3.2%)
Milano Metropoli (2007)	EUR 3.5 million	-	-	• Match funding from EU programmes and initiatives, the Italian national government and public local authorities (70%) • Provision of services directly to clients such as SMEs, local municipalities, local agencies and other public bodies (30%). (New EUR 1.5 million sponsor for 2008-2010 is a private not-for profit foundation in the Lombardy region)
New York City Economic Development Corporation (2008)	EUR 562.77 million	Reimbursements and other city grants EUR 391 million	Project and programme costs EUR 410.63 million	• Real estate sales, property rentals (14.4%) • Power sales (8%) • Reimbursements and other city grants (69%) • Fees and other income (9%)
Prospect Leicestershire (2009)	Approximately EUR 1.49 million	TBC	TBC	• National government, regional DA, and Homes and Communities agency grants.

Table 7.7. **The financing and balance sheets of internationalisation agencies**

Development agency	Budget	Key income source	Key expenditure	Finance mechanism
Invest Toronto	Long-term budget TBC	Build Toronto donation	TBC	• High proportion intended to come from Build Toronto surplus. Exact dimensions TBC.
Madrid Global (2009)	EUR 8.48 million excluding private sector contributions	City Hall grant EUR 8.48 million	• EUR 3.1 million for human resources • EUR 3.9 million for existing projects • EUR 1.4 million for operational costs	• Grant from City Hall (100% of EUR 8.48 million) • Funding from the private sector in support of the Madrid 2016 Olympic bid

Table 7.8. **The financing and balance sheets of visioning and partnership agencies**

Development Agency	Budget	Key income source	Key expenditure	Finance mechanism
Bilbao Metropoli-30	-	• Member organisations. • 50% public and 50% private.	-	• Core funding from member organisations. • Additional income achieved by approaching Regional Government with innovative projects which are commissioned.
Cape Town Partnership (2008)	CTP EUR 0.75 million CTP and CCID combined EUR 3.61 million	City of Cape Town grant EUR 0.5 million (66%)	Salaries and wages (52%)	• City of Cape Town annual grant (66%) • Management fee from the CCID (9.8%) • Annual donations from private corporations • Parking and filming (14.8%) • Sea Point improvement district fees (3.2%) • Interest

Asset management

The role and remit of a DA with regards to asset holding often reflects the position on financing. In order to promote local economic development, most DAs need to own or manage land and redevelopment processes. It is in the nature of local economic development that the promotion of the re-use of land and sites for new purposes (as the old ones have become obsolete) is a critical aspect of how well the locality is responding to new economic realities.

However, DAs do not always own the land they are redeveloping outright; it is frequently in the ownership of the main sponsoring authorities. Where a DA is largely owned by municipal government, it is typically the case that the municipal government itself remains the owner. How far a municipal government goes in endowing its lands to the ownership of the DA usually reflects a considered decision to empower that agency to both manage redevelopment and to secure internal capital receipts, rents, and other revenues from doing so. Equally, the re-organisation of municipal and metropolitan government, or the agreement to consolidate the control of publicly owned lands in one place, often results in DAs owning land themselves. A municipal government should generally review which option will best suit long-term purposes.

Financial strategies of development agencies

The various approaches to assets and financing of DAs were defined earlier. We noted five basic approaches as being distinguishable, but not mutually exclusive. The fundamental issue for DAs that are largely sponsored by municipal governments is how to develop a long-term business model and financial strategy in the context of annualised funding agreements, or even the individual appraisal and approval of projects and initiatives. This is difficult to do. The basic challenges can be summarised as follows:

- Local economic development requires multi-annual strategies and programmes, but these are hard to develop and deliver within annualised funding.

- DAs have to prepare and develop more initiatives than will go ahead each year, and the precise timing of implementation may be effected by market conditions outside of the agency's control (making annualised spend targets a problem). Local economic development implementation is not usually linear and does not conform very well to annual budget settlements, or equally to monthly expenditures.

- Risk cannot be mitigated totally, and indeed risk sharing is a requirement for many local economic development initiatives.

- Assessing value for money is extremely difficult as most local economic development interventions are unique, and therefore unit cost comparisons are rarely available.

- Over the long term, local economic development activity should be classed as an investment rather than anexpenditure, but the systems of public finance and accounting models required to do this are not readily available.

These challenges combine to make life hard for DA staff and municipal finance officers alike.

In its reports, EURADA advocates a strategy of financial diversification for DAs. This is built on analysis that shows that DAs with several sponsors are more likely to achieve long-term sustainability. They cite DAs with up to six basic income lines, including the: (1) municipality; (2) province; (3) region; (4) state; (5) sales; and (6) others.

Of the 16 DAs surveyed for this book, over half had income lines from three sources or more.

A second strategy is to try to move towards a multi-annual funding programme set against a business plan or investment plan for the locality. This is the settlement that most of the mature DAs have come to. In this scenario, a budget is proposed by the agency within a business planning document that has a detailed one-year programme, but a clear three-to-five-year horizon, showing the links between the programmes and expenditures over the whole cycle. Fundamentally, financial strategy is linked to business planning in DAs that are largely public sector sponsored. The general model for this among DAs in Europe includes the following elements:

- The DA develops and proposes: (1) a multi-annual local economic development strategy; and (2) an annual corporate plan/business plan incorporating multi-annual financial and investment strategy.

- Municipal government provides an annual approval of corporate plan budget and programme with indicative commitments made to future year budgets.

This model has the benefits of separating the local economic development strategy from the business plan of the DA, recognising that the DA may not be the only organisation that is delivering the plan.

Accountabilities

The overall thrust of the current practices is not to suggest that one model of a DA is necessarily more accountable and effective than any other, but it does indicate that sound management of the DA's business and its relationships is essential in achieving both. Differing accountability regimes exist, related, in particular, to the range of stakeholders engaged in the DA and the public finance system in which it operates.

Most often these regimes follow the form of annual reporting against the business plan combined with sound monitoring and evaluation systems, effective communication and relationship management throughout the operational year, and a performance management system which allows for activities to be monitored in a timely manner and then recast if they are not performing well. Good consultation mechanisms are also highlighted as essential to achieve accountability so that there are ways for stakeholders to engage in:

- setting the overall economic development strategy for the locality;

- building the annual and multi-annual plans for programmes of work;

- considering the impacts or consequences that certain actions may have; and

- enabling those directly affected by developments to register their position.

Of the 16 DAs profiled in this book, the range of stakeholders to which these organisations are accountable varies greatly from the local community and other key clients to government regulatory bodies and members. By far and away the most important body to which DAs are accountable is the City Council in the form of the Mayor's Office, the City Manager's Office, the Deputy Mayor for Economic Development's Office or Planning Clusters. Because most DAs are funded by City Councils and many have their priorities set by them this is unsurprising. The example of the Johannesburg Development Agency shows the tight relationship of co-ordination, compliance and reporting that this DA has with its City Council (see Figure 6.1 in Chapter 6).

Overall, an effective DA has to undertake quite a wide range of effectiveness and accountability activities in order to maintain momentum and support. These mechanisms will be explored in the next section about performance review, but almost half of the DAs we studied were accountable to more than one type of body. Details can be found in Table 7.9.

Key performance indicators and responding to change

Before discussing the topic of performance in greater detail, it is important, first, to distinguish between operational effectiveness (a measure of the day-to-day efficiency of the DA) and strategic impact (a measure of the value-added of the DA to the development activities in the local development system).

Operational effectiveness and strategic impact measures

The importance of creating a clear rationale, mission, strategic framework, and some deliberate choices of tools and programmes for any DA is clear (as discussed in Chapter 4). This is, in part, important because DAs need to demonstrate their effectiveness, and this is hard to do without clear measures of progress.

It is desirable to have both measures of progress (milestones), as well as ultimate goals in terms of the outputs and impacts of the interventions of the DA against which to measure performance. Each of these (milestones, outputs, impacts) requires careful specification and definition. A basic process of quarterly (milestones) and annual review (outputs and impacts), with multi-annual assessment (impacts and achievement of mission) is key to keeping DA performance well monitored.

Tables 7.10 and 7.11 highlight how different DAs can report performance indicators over different timescales: Barcelona Activa on an annual basis and HafenCity Hamburg GmbH since project inception and guaranteed future success. It is important also to complement tangible performance with the intangible impacts of the work of a DA to achieve a true sense of the total impact of the organisation. Intangible success is often not well articulated or understood.

Table 7.9. **Development agency accountabilities and performance review mechanisms**

Typology	Development agency	Accountable to	Performance review mechanism
	Abyssinian Development Corporation	• Board members • Local community and clients • Funders and partners • Government regulatory bodies	• Management Dashboard and Operations Overview Report • Annual executive team retreats and quarterly business reviews • Performance management reviews
Development and revitalisation agencies	BILBAO Ria 2000	• Board members - comprises members of various tiers of government	• Board involvement in strategic decisions • External reviews every two to three years • Audited externally for accounts, in quality assurance and from institutions such as FEDER (European) or *Tribunal de Cuentas Vasco*
	Build Toronto	• City Council	• Success measured against financial and non-financial key performance metrics
	Johannesburg Development Agency	• City Council (Department of Development Planning and Urban Management), Planning Cluster (Member of the Mayoral Council) and Shareholder Unit • Central Government (National Treasury's Neighbourhood Partnership Development Grant) and Board	• Contractually obliged to the Department of Development Planning and Urban Management to undertake compliance reporting in respect of key performance indicators • Co-ordination and alignment with Planning Cluster on strategic development issues • Annual report and key performance area setting and reporting • City-wide integrated performance scorecard
Productivity and economic growth agencies	AucklandPlus	• Auckland Regional Economic Development Forum	• "Level of Service" targets accompanied by a more precise set of "Measures" • Performance also measured against Metro Project objectives
	Barcelona Activa	• City Council (Economic Promotion Sector – Deputy Mayor for Economic Promotion is Barcelona Activa's President) • Clients and citizens • Management Board	• Internal performance review and monitoring system measured against Action Plan aims • OECD LEED Programme review • Measurement of activity indicators for project impact • Benchmarking against other DAs worldwide

Table 7.9. **Development agency accountabilities and performance review mechanisms** *(continued)*

Typology	Development agency	Accountable to	Performance review mechanism
	Creative Sheffield	• Board members (City Chief Executive, two Senior City Council and two Regional DA representatives) • Funders (Regional DA and City Council) • City Council and Government regulatory bodies	• Funders undertake regular audits of activities, financial management and outputs. • Statutory audit • Annual report on performance against the Economic Masterplan
Integrated economic agencies	Liverpool Vision	• Three public sector membership organisations	• Bottom-up individual project monitoring • Strategic outcome indicator monitoring (progress measured against key objectives and to help assess wider impact of the Liverpool Vision Programme on the economy of the city)
	Milano Metropoli	• Internal Board of Control	• End of Mandate Board Report • Project specific review mechanism based on parameters set at project initiation
	New York City Economic Development Corporation	• The Mayor, City Controller and City Council • Public advocate • Boroughs presidents	• Under Local Law 48, an annual report which profiles selected projects is obligatory • Performance against internal and project-based benchmarks is reviewed every 90 days • Internal Strategic Planning and Strategic Operations departments evaluate progress • Internal research group to audit the company's real estate portfolio
	Prospect Leicestershire	• Two founding members (Leicester City and Leicestershire County Councils)	• Performance measured against business plan targets which incorporate the MAA targets plus other funding partner targets
Internationalisation agencies	Invest Toronto	• City Council	• Internal key performance indicators • Annual report and external review every two to three years
	Madrid Global	• City Council (Deputy Mayor's Office)	• City-wide and integrated review system based on mayoral policy goals and objectives • Results reviewed and acted upon on a month-by-month basis
Visioning and partnership	Bilbao Metropoli-30	• Members	• All funding and project information offered through governing bodies
	Cape Town Partnership	• Board and city leaders • Wider partners	• Annual reports and open dialogues with City of Cape Town staff • Company reviews by external consultants

Table 7.10. **Key performance indicators for Barcelona Activa in 2008**

Theme (initiative)	Tangible impact	Intangible impact
Boosting entrepreneurship	• c.1 400 businesses received advice. Over 700 companies were created and the estimated new employment from these companies was c.1 400 new jobs per year.	• Reference centre for entrepreneurship in Barcelona and model transferred to other international environments (Bogotá, Medellín, Santiago de Chile, Buenos Aires, Rome, Andorra, etc.)
Business growth	• 350 companies received growth coaching through the agency's business growth programmes.	• Hub of business growth initiatives promoted by different agents in the city. • Network of businesses that co-operate amongst each other. • Top level incubation infrastructures and services
Human capital development	• More than 48 000 participants received attention in Porta22.	• Reference centre for professional guidance and progress in the metropolitan area of Barcelona. Being transferred to other national environments (Mataró, Bidasoa Region, etc.)
Employment	• The agency dealt with over 30 000 participants and the rate of job market insertion reached 72%. • More than 800 unemployed people were contracted to develop their skills through apprenticeship arrangements.	• Reference entity in the city for support, coaching and training for the employment • Co-ordination of the agreement on quality employment in Barcelona 2008-11
Technological skills acquisition and diffusion	• 53 784 participants attended Cibernarium.	• Reference centre for digital literacy and training in Barcelona and model transferred to other international environments (Sao Paolo, Porto Alegre, Brussels, Tampere, San Sebastián, etc.)

Source: Barcelona Activa (2009), "Barcelona Activa", homepage, *www.barcelonactiva.cat.*

Table. 7.11. **Key performance indicators for HafenCity Hamburg GmbH since project inception**

Theme (initiative)	Tangible impact	Intangible impact
Investment leverage	• For EUR 1.53 billion of public funding, HafenCity Hamburg GmbH has managed to leverage EUR 5.5 billion of private sector investment.	• High visibility of the project in the international arena.
High-quality public space	• 20% of HafenCity's space will be developed as open areas, and public access rights exist for an additional 20%. 34 hectares of water surface will be used to a certain extent as well (HafenCity Hamburg GmbH, 2008). • A range of waterfront urban spaces has been open since autumn 2007: Marco Polo Terraces, Vasco da Gama Plaza and Dalmannkai Promenades. They were joined by the Tall Ship Harbour in autumn 2008. Large pontoons form a floating walkway over the water, with permanent moorings for about 20 historic tall ships and steamers (HafenCity Hamburg GmbH, 2009).	• Improved quality of urban space. • Serve as public encounter spaces due to different character and allow for a high degree of social integration.
Linkages with the City Centre	• Construction of the new U4 underground railway line is of extreme importance, as its two stops - Überseequartier and HafenCity University - will provide the connecting link to Hamburg's underground and urban railway network.	• Opening up the development opportunities in the Speicherstadt area and the southern inner city. Pushing also competition to improve existing buildings. • Socially and economically integrating lower profile urban quarters via employment opportunities and new traffic links.

Achievement of mission

Initial missions established for DAs should have concrete goals. The vision for local economic development might stress a 20-year horizon, but a mission should be broadly achievable within five to ten years. Where a mission focuses on redevelopment of a specific area, this can often be achieved in five years.

It is important to have an explicit process for reviewing the DA comprehensively every five years. This will enable some reflection on how far the mission has been achieved, and the work that remains to be done. It can also address the extent to which: (1) the DA has completed its task and should be closed down; (2) the DA needs additional or new tools and resources to complete its task; and (3) certain achievements have been made and it is time for the DA to develop new or additional goals, as demonstrated in Box 7.5.

Box 7.5. **Completing the mandate: the evolving functions of the Cape Town Partnership**

The case of the Cape Town Partnership provides an excellent example of how DA roles and functions can evolve to fulfil mandates.

A comprehensive review process in September 2008 in preparation for the tenth anniversary of the organisation's incorporation produced a series of performance indicators. It suggested that in ten years, the Cape Town Partnership has fulfilled its core business of stabilising the Central City by reducing crime and grime to make the area an attractive investment proposal. In doing this the Cape Town Partnership has crafted and delivered a number of strategic initiatives that add significant value to the Central City and foster a strong future for the city as a whole.

The present moment represents an evolution in the activities of the Cape Town Partnership. Having fulfilled its *management* and *promotion* role (as mandated) in the Central City, the Cape Town Partnership is moving to fulfil the third pillar of its core mandate – the *development* of the Central City. Seeing the 2010 World Cup as a potential catalyst the Partnership adapted and promptly formalised its new 45-page Central City Development Strategy, the details of which can be found in Chapter4 of this book.

Nonetheless, the organisation recognises that Central City management and promotion is an ongoing task and, without continued regular attention, the work completed in the past ten years could be undone. The role of Central City management and promotion also becomes more important given the global recession. If the Central City is not occupied fully there is a risk, for instance, that vacant buildings will otherwise become obsolete – something which the Cape Town Partnership should focus strongly on avoiding.

Sharing best practices

Sharing of best practice is now common for most DAs. DAs tend to undertake best practice sharing on an as-needed and project-specific basis and through the regular participation in networks. Information sharing can enhance the operation of a DA, particularly when faced by difficult challenges or significant opportunities such as global economic recession, regional de-industrialisation or the hosting of major events, for instance. Below we have codified a number of the principal ways in which DAs share best practice, giving practical examples from a range of DAs. The examples aren't prescriptive; they are illustrative.

Participation in national networks

Economic Development Company (EDC) Network, Department for Communities and Local Government (CLG), UK Government

CLG has established an EDC national network to "share knowledge, best practice and discuss issues and concerns that may arise throughout the process of establishing and operating an EDC. The network meets approximately every three months and is open to any authority with an interest in EDCs" (Department for Communities and Local Government, 2009). A number of UK DAs participate, such as Hull Forward, Creative Sheffield, Prospect Leicestershire, Plymouth City Development Company and Liverpool Vision. Regional DAs also participate in these meetings to reinforce relationships and facilitate exchanges of helpful information.

Participation in international networks

The International Economic Development Council (IEDC)

IEDC is the "world's largest professional organisation for economic development practitioners" (IEDC, 2009). IEDC has more than 4 500 members world wide and many DAs have taken up membership to collaborate, share information and learn from best practice cases.

Participation at strategic events

Bilbao Metropoli-30

Since its incorporation, one of the main objectives of Bilbao Metropoli-30 has been to study other metropolis and regions that could be of interest for the metropolitan area's Revitalisation Plan. As a consequence, a long list of international networks and contacts has been developed and has proven to be very fruitful in the definition of the future vision of metropolitan Bilbao. Of particular importance have been conferences and forums. At these events, Bilbao Metropoli-30 attempts to tell the Bilbao story as a way of building contacts with other regions and cities and to promote the case of Bilbao as a symbol of urban success.

Participation in keynote publication

Liverpool Vision

Liverpool Vision was the lead contact for the preparation of a Liverpool City case study for the OECD LEED book, *Recession, Recovery and Reinvestment: The Role of Local Economic Leadership in a Global Crisis* (Clark, 2009). This book showcased how 41 local economies had been impacted by, and were recovering from, the economic recession.

Hosting visiting delegations

Barcelona Activa

Hundreds of delegations (33 national, 26 from the European Union and 41 from the rest of the world – a total of more than 750 representatives to date) have visited Barcelona Activa since its creation in 1986. They look to learn and exchange ways of doing things to improve and extend their own services to the public in relation to providing support to entrepreneurs, policies for business growth, promoting innovation and boosting quality employment (Barcelona Activa, 2007).

Bilateral collaboration

HafenCity Hamburg GmbH

This DA has clearly stated its wish to be a reference point for urban development for other European cities. As part of attempts to share its best practice, the organisation signed co-operation agreement with Stadshavens Rotterdam and the Thames Gateway in March 2009.

AucklandPlus

Box 7.6 is an example of the effectiveness of bilateral agreements between DAs and governments.

Box 7.6. **The partnership agreement between AucklandPlus and the Ministry of Economic Development "directorate" located in the Government Urban and Economic Development Office in Auckland**

This agreement seeks to provide a firm foundation for the mutually supportive relationship to continue to develop and mature between Ministry of Economic Development "directorate" located in the Government Urban and Economic Development office in Auckland, and AucklandPlus, the region's/Auckland Regional Council's economic development unit.

Both parties wish to recognise their shared agenda of positioning and supporting Auckland to be a truly world-class city and their existing strategic relationship. By adopting this partnership agreement they wish to galvanise their strategic partnership by agreeing:

- shared values,

- operating principles,

- priorities for actions / focus of collaboration, and

- supporting processes.

It is intended that each organisation maintains a strong individual identity and mandate while gaining strength in their delivery efforts by working in partnership.

References

Barcelona Activa (2007), "Annual Report, 2007", *www.barcelonactiva.cat/barcelonactiva/images/en/Memoria_ (2007)_tcm84-38949.pdf.*

Barcelona Activa (2009), "Barcelona Activa", homepage, *www.barcelonactiva.cat.*

Clark, G. (2009), *Recession, Recovery and Reinvestment: The Role of Local Economic Leadership in a Global Crisis*, OECD LEED Programme, *www.oecd.org/document/28/0,3343,en_2649_34461_43550172_1_1_1_1,00.html.*

Department for Communities and Local Government, (2009), "Economic Development Companies", *www.communities.gov.uk/citiesandregions/cities/economicdevelopment/.*

HafenCity Hamburg GmbH (2008), "Brochure", *www.hafencity.com/upload/files/broschueren/z_en_broschueren_24_Projekte_englisch_09. (2008).pdf.*

HafenCity Hamburg GmbH (2009), "Current State of Affairs", *www.hafencity.com/index.php?set_language=en&cccpage=ueberblick_artikel&show=artikel&item=84.*

IEDC (International Economic Development Council) (2009), "Frequently Asked Questions About IEDC", *www.iedconline.org/?p=FAQs.*

JDA (Johannesburg Development Agency) (2009), "Business Plan, 2009-10", Johannesburg Development Agency.

Chapter 8

Learning from international development agency experience

The final chapter in this book makes the case that although development agencies of all kinds have become a global phenomenon, there has been limited international exchange on how and why such organisations work. It explains that though the codification and sharing of practice is inherently difficult, the purpose of this book is to attempt to bridge part of that gap and promote understanding within a shared framework and the learning of precise lessons across borders. To conclude, a series of development agency strengths and constraints are defined and illustrated which inform the OECD LEED Programme's ten principles for development agencies.

Although development agencies of all kinds have become a global phenomenon, there has been limited international exchange on how and why such organisations work. The huge variety of national and regional institutional frameworks, coupled with the very wide range of development agency (DA) roles makes codification and sharing of practice inherently difficult. This book attempts to bridge part of that gap. We have observed that despite the many differences, key common features and common challenges arise that can best be addressed within some shared framework of understanding and learning of precise lessons across borders.

Development agency strengths, constraints, opportunities and challenges analysis

Development agency strengths

Though others are described briefly below, this section identifies and discusses a total of 14 principal strengths which were regularly identified by the DAs themselves as critical to their success. These factors are listed in the Table 8.1.

Table 8.1. **Development agency strengths in selected development agencies**

Company type and structure	Agility and flexibility	Spatial focus	Leadership	Focus on outcomes and clients	Talented and experienced staff / focus on quality	Strong revenue-generating capacity
⑤ ⑧ ⑮	① ② ③ ⑮	② ⑤	② ③ ⑥ ⑦ ⑨	① ② ③ ⑤ ⑦ ⑨ ⑪	③ ⑤ ⑥ ⑧ ⑨ ⑪ ⑫ ⑬ ⑭	⑥ ⑨ ⑮

Clear or focussed mandate	Long-term mandate	Strong partnerships	Holistic / integrated approach	Innovation	Apolitical/ low profile/ arm's length positioning	Community/ stakeholder credibility and engagement
② ③ ⑦ ⑪ ⑯	④ ⑤ ⑨	① ② ③ ⑤ ⑥ ⑦ ⑧ ⑨ ⑩ ⑪ ⑬ ⑭ ⑯	① ⑦ ⑨ ⑫ ⑭	③	④ ⑤ ⑥ ⑨ ⑪ ⑬	① ② ③ ⑤ ⑩ ⑫ ⑭

① Abyssinian Development Corporation
② AucklandPlus
③ Barcelona Activa
④ Bilbao Metropoli-30
⑤ BILBAO Ría 2000
⑥ Build Toronto
⑦ Cape Town Partnership
⑧ Creative Sheffield

⑨ HafenCity Hamburg GmbH
⑩ Invest Toronto
⑪ Johannesburg Development Agency
⑫ Liverpool Vision
⑬ Madrid Global
⑭ Milano Metropoli
⑮ New York City Economic Development Corporation
⑯ Prospect Leicestershire

In addition to this list, other strengths were recorded, including: (1) an intelligence and analysis-based approach; (2) global benchmarking and building a global perspective; (3) creation from crisis; (4) board composition; (5) tackling social concerns; (6) leveraging culture for regeneration; (7) effective communication; (8) co-ordination capacity and project management expertise; (9) having a foreign direct investment (FDI) function; and (10) operating in a politically stable environment.

We explore the strengths introduced in Table 8.1 in the following discussion.

Company type and structure

Strength in practice: Creative Sheffield

City development company status and structure. The creation of Creative Sheffield saw the amalgamation of a number of existing development organisations. This process of consolidation means that it is both far more efficient and simpler with which to work for individuals, potential investors and other agencies. Other advantages of Creative Sheffield are that it is a quasi-independent body which can operate in a way that a City Council cannot. The company has the independence and multi-partnership style of an urban regeneration company (URC), with the added benefit of the full range of tools to achieve the economic transformation of the city.

Agility and flexibility

Strength in practice: Milano Metropoli

Autonomous and nimble. Milano Metropoli is an "agile" and "ready-to-use" tool at the disposal of public authorities in its operating area. Its legal status as an organisation operating under private law but with a clear public mission makes it responsive and flexible enough to support local authorities in particular tasks. For example, Milano Metropoli is effective at interfacing between, and co-ordinating, public or private players, as well as securing community involvement.

Spatial focus

Strength in practice: AucklandPlus

Regional scope. By being regionally focused, AucklandPlus meets its strategic objectives from building strong cross-border alliances and working co-operatively. To this end, its focus remains on the greater regional needs of the cities and districts within the Auckland region. It is not about borders, it is about the performance of the entire city region and Auckland's contribution to the national performance.

Leadership

Strength in practice: HafenCity Hamburg GmbH

Management approach. The management team's openness, entrepreneurial attitude and traditional style of business are what have made the project a success so far. The team are also given the flexibility to adopt innovative approaches. For instance, they are able to develop new ideas and frameworks which produce an innovative and distinctive approach to city development.

Focus on outcomes and clients

Strength in practice: Abyssinian Development Corporation (ADC)

A commitment to achieving tangible change. It is critical to ADC that its "theory of change" creates concrete and measurable progress on the ground. ADC sees it as a concrete statement of plausible, testable, and tested pathways of change that both guide its actions and explain its input.

Talented and experienced staff / focus on quality

Strength in practice: Johannesburg Development Agency (JDA)

High-quality human capital. The JDA has built up a highly skilled and experienced team of strategists and practitioners over a number of years. In a highly pressurised working environment (due to budget and time constraints and demands) the quality of its staff are a key reason why the JDA has been considered successful.

Strong revenue-generating capacity

Strength in practice: New York City Economic Development Corporation (NYCEDC)

Strong revenue generating and maximising capability. NYCEDC has been able to successfully meet its increased financial commitment to the City, cut its expenses where possible and, with the help of its internal consulting departments, optimally leverage its assets to produce additional revenue.

Clear or focussed mandate

Strength in practice: Prospect Leicestershire

Clear and manageable mandate. Many (new) organisations take on more than they are capable of delivering to a very high standard. To avoid mission creep and becoming over-stretched, Prospect Leicestershire has defined for itself a clear and concise mandate. As a result, it is manageable enough to deliver to a very high standard.

Long-term mandate

Strength in practice: Bilbao Metropoli-30

Strategic and long-term in nature. The role of Bilbao Metropoli-30 is more strategic than practical and more long-term than short-term. Members and politicians tend to be so absorbed by short-term concerns that Bilbao Metropoli-30 has the chance to think about the future of Bilbao and its metropolitan area. For instance, even during prosperous times of the late 1990s and earlier 2000s Bilbao Metropoli-30 took the opportunity to vision the area's future despite its relative economic good health. More specifically, since 1999 Bilbao Metropoli-30 has worked with stakeholders on the area's "values" in order to construct an accurate and representative long-term vision for the city. To facilitate this approach, Bilbao Metropoli-30 has organised a number of meetings and workshops on the subject. This approach is justified by the view that cities no longer compete on hard factors such as infrastructure. According to Bilbao Metropoli-30, cities now compete in intangibles, such as knowledge, people, quality of life and leadership.

Strong partnerships

Strength in practice: the Cape Town Partnership (CTP)

Partnership quality. The CTP model is fundamentally based on partnership building. Indeed, the quality of the relationships built across public, private and non-governmental organisations is internationally renowned. These quality partnerships have enabled the CTP to provide the City Council a high return on investment in the Central City.

According to the CTP Chief Executive, "the Cape Town Partnership is only as good as its partners." In a recent speech, he hailed the regular partner support of "the Cape Town City Council, Western Cape Provincial Government, Cape Regional Chamber, South African Property Owners Association, Central City property owners and developers represented on the CCID [Central City Improvement District], and many more" as fundamental to the CTP effort. "Our success is your success," he said, adding, "We value the trust and commitment to common principles that we have patiently built over these years" (CTP, 2008).

Holistic/integrated approach

Strength in practice: HafenCity Hamburg GmbH

High-quality and comprehensive urban design. HafenCity Hamburg GmbH has a variety of mechanisms in place to allow comprehensive, and socially and ecologically responsible, development to proceed. For instance, land available for residential development is subject to competitive tenders. This is less to do with achieving a high price for the land, indeed the offer price is usually fixed before the start of the tender process, and more to do with the quality of the concept and the possibilities for a diverse mix of uses. After the decision for a bidder, architectural competitions take place. Through this process, HafenCity Hamburg GmbH aims to set and develop international standards for conceptual and architectural quality. Unlike in other places, developer incentives have not been pursued to the detriment of quality urban development, and the agency states that, "it is important not only to attract powerful and financially strong investors, but also to find building partners willing to co-operate in setting quality standards and in treading new and innovative paths" (HafenCity Hamburg GmbH, 2008).

In addition, the HafenCity Hamburg GmbH Chief Executive suggests that, "HafenCity is different. Economic development is not the centre of our focus, but rather the urban development process in the broadest sense. We want to join economic, social, cultural, and architectural forces in a way that translates into lasting urbanity" (Steinborn, 2007).

Innovation

Strength in practice: Barcelona Activa

Developing the entrepreneurial capacity. The promotion of an innovative culture in the city is an essential part of the support programmes for entrepreneurs. Creating an entrepreneurial culture among Barcelona's citizens can guarantee innovation and sustainable economic growth. In this way, Barcelona Activa performs the task "entrepreneurship diffusion and encouragement" in order to awaken new capabilities and to generate innovation, employment and new economic activity with global vision.

Apolitical / low profile / arm's length positioning

Strength in practice: Bilbao Metropoli-30

Perceived lack of power. One of the secrets to Bilbao Metropoli-30's success is that the organisation has no real power, either economic or political. Everything that is proposed needs to be first backed by its members, who are the key stakeholders in the metropolitan area's future. These same members deliver the project, leaving Bilbao Metropoli-30 to shape the process and "play Cupid" from the background. For instance, in the preparation of any draft proposal, Bilbao Metropoli-30 would first create a working group related to the subject. The working group would then be invited to examine and enrich the proposal with its input. Once the proposal is finished, Bilbao Metropoli-30 disappears and the members, who have already bought into the proposal, then deliver the work. Bilbao Metropoli-30 also has a limited public image. Most people have not heard of the organisation, which is a positive given the quite confusing mix of agencies in the city and their struggle for position. Bilbao Metropoli-30's low profile and non-threatening position helps to make partners more confident in the organisation.

Community/stakeholder credibility and engagement

Strength in practice: Abyssinian Development Corporation (ADC)

Deep community engagement and empowerment. From its inception, it has been ADC's practice to support the empowerment of the community to address the myriad of issues it faces. As a result, engaging and developing a rapport with the community has been a priority. It is an ADC priority to work with the community it serves.

Development agency constraints

Evidence from the 16 DAs also reveals a number of DA constraints. Successful DAs are not agencies which have no challenges. Constraints and challenges are an inevitable outcome of the dynamic and complex operating environment within which DAs operate. Recession conditions, for instance, have had a significant impact on many of the DAs that we have profiled in this book. What is important is how DAs react and respond. DA success therefore is as much about managing the constraints associated with change as it is developing core strengths.

The constraints illustrated in Table 8.2 are explained in the following discussion.

Table 8.2. **Development agency constraints in selected development agencies**

Budget constraints or funding arrangements	Market conditions	Non- enabling governance structures	Lack of autonomy/ executive power	Lack of a socio-economic evidence base	Complex role in complex system of stakeholders	Mission creep
① ② ③ ④ ⑤ ⑦ ⑪ ⑫ ⑬ ⑭	① ⑤ ⑨ ⑩ ⑬ ⑮	② ⑩ ⑭	④	⑦ ⑩	⑦ ⑭ ⑮	⑨

Accountabilities	Focused mandate
⑧ ⑬	⑪

① Abyssinian Development Corporation
② AucklandPlus
③ Barcelona Activa
④ Bilbao Metropoli-30
⑤ BILBAO Ría 2000
⑥ Build Toronto
⑦ Cape Town Partnership
⑧ Creative Sheffield

⑨ HafenCity Hamburg GmbH
⑩ Invest Toronto
⑪ Johannesburg Development Agency
⑫ Liverpool Vision
⑬ Madrid Global
⑭ Milano Metropoli
⑮ New York City Economic Development Corporation
⑯ Prospect Leicestershire

Budget constraints or funding arrangements

Constraint in practice: Johannesburg Development Agency

Un-sustainability of funding mechanisms. Operational costs of the JDA are met predominantly by both a year-on-year City of Johannesburg operating grant and the retention of 5% of all capital spend. This is problematic for a number of reasons: (1) it is difficult to anticipate year-on-year staffing fluctuations, and therefore costs; (2) if capital funding (and thus spending) falls, then the operating budget falls, undermining the financial viability of the organisation; (3) to retain the necessary operating funding to cover costs, the JDA would be forced to take on more capital intensive projects narrowing the organisation's role. At the same time, the number of capital intense projects in the city is likely to fall post-BRT (Bus Rapid Transport system project) and the 2010 World Cup.

Market conditions

Constraint in practice: New York City Economic Development Corporation

Revenue cost balance during the recession. Because of NYCEDC's unique 501(c) 3 non-profit status and its significantly smaller size compared with other city agencies, the corporation has been able to flexibly respond to the changing economic climate. NYCEDC has taken aggressive steps to maximise its real estate portfolio's assets, while making strategic cuts to its budget. Prior to the fall of 2008, NYCEDC had already engaged an internal team of real estate experts to examine how it could maximise the use of the city's real estate portfolio. The team has made several recommendations to NYCEDC's leadership and has identified ways to save the city and its taxpayers a significant amount of money.

Non-enabling governance structures

Constraint in practice: AucklandPlus

Regional governance structures. A recent review by the Royal Commission on Auckland Governance raised a range of concerns that impact on AucklandPlus' ability to maximise opportunities around Auckland's economy and, in particular, to assist effectively with New Zealand's recovery from the current global economic crisis. Issues highlighted included the current governance structures which allow territorial authorities to operate independently from each other on economic development matters, encourage a lack of regional focus and intra-regional rivalry, increase regulatory impediments through multi-consenting parties and processes, impair regional co-ordination of infrastructure priorities and have worked against the development of the city centre and waterfront in a co-ordinated or strategic way. The Commission went on to recommend structures that enabled delivery mechanisms with funding and mandate to implement, and the ability and authority to marshal, resources behind transformative projects which have the potential to deliver multiple economic outcomes that provide long-term legacy.

Lack of autonomy/executive power

Constraint in practice: Bilbao Metropoli-30

Lack of executive power. Bilbao Metropoli-30's lack of power is simultaneously a strength and a constraint. Though the organisation has received strong support for its projects so far, because of its lack of executive power, should disagreements amongst members arise, Bilbao Metropoli-30 would face a difficult and complex situation.

Lack of a socio-economic evidence base

Constraint in practice: the Cape Town Partnership

Research into the key dimensions of and trends within the Central City. One reason why articulating the strategic importance of the Central City is so difficult is that the area and its trends are not fully understood, at least in a quantitative sense. Though the CTP is flexible, responsive and effective, performance is hampered by a lack of precise and detailed knowledge of Central City flows in relation to and impacts on businesses, residents, visitors, other locations and other themes.

Complex role in complex system of stakeholders

Constraint in practice: Milano Metropoli

Territorial complexity. The second challenge relates to the complexity of Milano Metropoli's operating area in terms of players, roles, responsibilities. These are not often clear and can overlap, making it harder for Milano Metropoli to make synergies where they should be found. It is also difficult for Milano Metropoli to help the governance processes on some issues that require, by their nature, a multi-stakeholder approach and an area-wide perspective. These can include, for example, public transport, public utilities, employment and local job market interventions.

Mission creep

Constraint in practice: HafenCity Hamburg GmbH

Mission creep and divisions of labour. There is a question about where HafenCity Hamburg GmbH as a development company ends and where the municipal actors as providers of public services begin. There is a risk of mission creep here and that agendas will overlap. While the quality of spaces developed and the intensity of use is very high (specifically from visitors) the municipal authorities may not be fully equipped to keeping the quality of environment and services. Representatives of HafenCity Hamburg GmbH are lobbying for an extended role of HafenCity Hamburg GmbH beyond the completion of physical construction. There is a perception that high-quality urban management should be the way in which HafenCity Hamburg GmbH continues its association with the development area.

Accountabilities

Constraint in practice: Creative Sheffield

System of accountability and project commissioning. To improve the speed at which buy-in from key partners is achieved, Creative Sheffield works closely with key partners such as the City Council and Yorkshire Forward, at the development phase. Achieving earlier buy-in ensures that partners are more likely to have the opportunity to shape initiatives and sign off on new projects. In this way, Creative Sheffield attempts to apply a "No Surprises" philosophy to its work.

Focussed mandate

Constraint in practice: Johannesburg Development Agency

Focused mandate and project handover. The JDA recognises capital intervention is only one part of the urban development challenge for many places. It is understood that an integrated approach is critical to solving challenging urban problems. The JDA is discussing whether its role should extend more explicitly beyond project management and implementation, especially given the decreasing requirement for large and capital intense interventions. It works hard to build relationships across the city to ensure the long-term sustainability of the projects it completes.

Lessons

The use of city-wide, county-wide, and sub-regional economic DAs in OECD and non-OECD countries is common. Confidence in this organisational approach has been built up over time in these countries, and the roles of such bodies have evolved and expanded. This review highlights the lessons from this international experience.

The OECD Programme on Local Economic and Employment Development (LEED) undertakes reviews of local DAs internationally, and insights from those reviews are incorporated into this assessment.

The main findings of this review are that DA-type organisations are potentially important contributors to the implementation of the sub-national review of economic development and regeneration. Development agencies can:

- be instrumental in creating a business-like and business-facing operational environment in which local government-led economic development and regeneration be effectively delivered;

- as employers, attract staff and expertise into local government-led economic development and regeneration, from a wide range of sectors and backgrounds who might not be attracted to work within a wholly municipal structure;

- operate effectively in tandem with strategic regional bodies and do not need to compete for role or resources with regional bodies. In general, the local bodies can focus on implementing the specific goals of regional strategies in their local or sub-regional area;

- be an effective means to facilitate multi-area collaboration and co-ordination on economic development and regeneration between neighbouring municipalities;

- be an effective means for local governments to place economic development activity on a more a formal or statutory footing;

- be successful in attracting private sector partnership and leadership into local economic development; and

- help to identify local economic investment priorities and to assess the best means to finance them including managing costs and risk mechanisms with the private sector, involving for example, incremental tax levies or supplementary business rates.

Conclusion

From our review of international experiences, we can identify a number of key principles that will underline success for DAs. These are set out in Box 8.1.

Box 8.1. **OECD LEED principles for development agencies**

- **Focus on implementation at pace and scale**. The development agency pursues development opportunities faster, and at a larger scale, than would normally be possible within a city or local government.

- **Aggregate otherwise separate interventions to add value**. Economic development efforts within cities or regions are often subject to fragmentation of effort due to the multiplicity of funding streams and policy agencies. Development agencies can act to aggregate otherwise disparate efforts, overcoming potential co-ordination failures and information asymmetries.

- **Enhance the capacity and co-ordination of the local development system**. So that it can deliver a greater return on investment and provide a better platform for progress.

- **Focus on the customer**. An important reason for placing economic development activities within a corporate entity such as a development agency rather than a municipal structure is the ability of the development agency to offer a business-like environment and service offering, and the scope to manager customer relationships in a business-to-business model.

- **Adopt flexible spatial scales**. Development agencies can operate at a citywide scale but are also able to function at either more local or wider levels. This is important given that economic development challenges are often focussed at local or sub-regional levels.

- **Achieve confidence of external investors and other businesses**. Confidence of investors, developers and business customers is an important ingredient in maintaining market position for local and sub-regional economies.

- **Become a tool maker and fully utilise existing tools**. Economic development tools need to be fully utilised and new tools need to be made to fit new imperatives. These tools often involve the interplay of public and private interests and assets. Development agencies can be effective tool makers and tool users, combining different powers, resources, and assets to make development happen.

- **Leverage assets and investment**. Assets and private capital are key to reinvestment markets and development agencies can help to leverage them towards city economic development goals. Share risks and costs actively with partners: development agencies can operate as joint venture vehicles between different sectors and between different tiers of government.

- **Refresh image and identity and communicate development progress**. Image and identity is supported by branding and marketing activity which needs to be a focus of concerted action. Co-ordination is essential.

- **Apply leadership to problem solving**. Problem solving is key to making economic development successful. Development agencies are often able to supply the skills and approaches required, unencumbered by other mandates.

There is clearly substantial confidence in the DA model across many OECD countries, with a wide range of countries opting to use DA-type models and seeing this as a preferred means to implement economic development activities at city and sub-regional levels. There is a primary need to fully define what the intended value-added of the DA is before it is established. It needs very clear goals and roles.

Local government and regional partners must set a clear strategic and institutional framework for DAs they create. This will be greatly aided by the existence of clear local and regional economic strategies, but it will still require co-ordinated effort. DAs work within local development systems of many organisations which must be carefully co-ordinated and systemically organised. DA success appears to be based on the ability to either aggregate different efforts to achieve scale and mass or to focus solely on niche interventions which can be effectively delivered on their own. In both cases, DAs need to be collaborative organisations, and other organisations need to collaborate with them.

Guidance for local governments on how to effectively sponsor and oversee DAs, and, at the same time, gives DAs substantial operational freedom appears to be required. This is a major skills' requirement for local government leaders that should not be overlooked. In a context, where there is strong regional strategic leadership of economic development and regeneration, guidance for on how to delegate to DAs and how to ensure that DAs meet the goals of regional strategies may be helpful.

Regular reviews of DAs are desirable. An annual assessment is probably best with careful deliberation over multi-annual corporate plans.

The best DAs diversify income streams and support cross-funded activities. DAs should become vehicles that multiple stakeholders are content to invest in and therefore it is important that they seek and secure a mix of funding and resourcing. Networking and knowledge/know-how exchanges are useful. These are widely supported in Europe and North America and appear to be an essential mechanism to improving DA skill sets and know-how.

Lastly, some activities are most efficiently performed at regional and national levels and it is important that these are defined so that DAs understand what they are to achieve. For example, economic intelligence and international promotion may be best done at higher levels than smaller cities or towns, even if other local delivery is best done locally. If so, this should be explicitly set out at the commencement of a DA's activities.

References

CTP (Cape Town Partnership) (2008), "Cape Town Partnership", homepage, *www.capetownpartnership.co.za.*

HafenCity Hamburg GmbH (2008), "Brochure", *www.hafencity.com/upload/files/ broschueren/z_en_broschueren_24_Projekte_englisch_09. (2008).pdf.*

Steinborn, D. (2007), "Hamburg's City Within a City Takes Shape", *The Wall Street Journal.*

Annex A

Sixteen development agency case studies

**Abyssinian
Development
Corporation**
BELIEVE.BUILD.EMPOWER.

Abyssinian Development Corporation
New York, United States

Organisation type

Abyssinian Development Corporation (ADC) is a locally based, non-profit community development corporation dedicated to building the human, social and physical capital of the area of Harlem in New York. ADC offers services to the community through five community development initiatives: (1) affordable housing development; (2) social services; (3) economic revitalisation; (4) education and youth development; and (5) civic engagement.

Mission statement

The organisation's mission is to:

- increase the availability of quality housing to people of diverse incomes;
- enhance the delivery of social services, particularly to the homeless, elderly, families and children;
- foster economic revitalisation;
- enhance educational and developmental opportunities for young people;
- build community capacity through civic engagement (ADC, 2009a).

History, origins and ownership

ADC was founded in 1989 by the Abyssinian Baptist Church, in response to a call from the pulpit by Reverend Dr. Calvin O. Butts, III in 1986 for the congregation to rebuild its community. This call was precipitated by the fact that, during the late 1980s, Harlem was suffering from unemployment, high levels of violence, drug abuse, AIDS and homelessness. A lack of investment by banks was compounding the problem as building owners abandoned their properties and left them in disrepair. Indeed, between the 1960s and the 1990s, few new commercial or residential buildings were built. The City of New York owned 60% of the property in Harlem.

In 1989, ADC was officially chartered as a not-for-profit community development organisation and received its first grant for USD 50 000. In 1991, the Abyssinian Towers senior citizens housing facility opened and ADC organised the Central Harlem Local

Development Corporation to promote neighbourhood small business development. In 1997, ADC formed a partnership to develop the Harlem Centre, a USD 85 million mixed-use retail and commercial complex on 125th Street, whilst in 2004, the Thurgood Marshall Academy for Learning and Social Change – the first public school facility to be built in Harlem in 50 years – was completed and housed 580 students. In 2007, ADC launched the Abyssinian Neighbourhood Project and won national recognition from the US Environmental Protection Agency for Smart Growth in Equitable Development. Other significant projects include: (1) Pathmark – a 65 000 square foot grocery superstore in Harlem that anchored the revitalisation of the 125th Street commercial corridor in 1997; and (2) Abyssinian House – a tier II transitional homeless family residence (ADC, 2009b).

What does the Abyssinian Development Corporation do?

ADC runs a number of programmes, all of which aim to stimulate community development in the Harlem area. In particular, it works in the fields of affordable housing development, family services, economic revitalisation, education and youth and civic engagement.

What is the spatial scale of operation and influence of the Abyssinian Development Corporation?

ADC works at the local scale, focusing on Harlem in the borough of Manhattan and including Manhattan Community Districts 9, 10 and 11 (see Figure A.1 and A.2). More specifically, current projects, programmes and services range, geographically, from 110th Street to 155th Street, from the Hudson River to the west and Harlem River to the east. ADC also recognises that it needs to work with organisations outside its locality to initiate and deliver sustainable change.

Figure A.1. **Manhattan Community District 9**

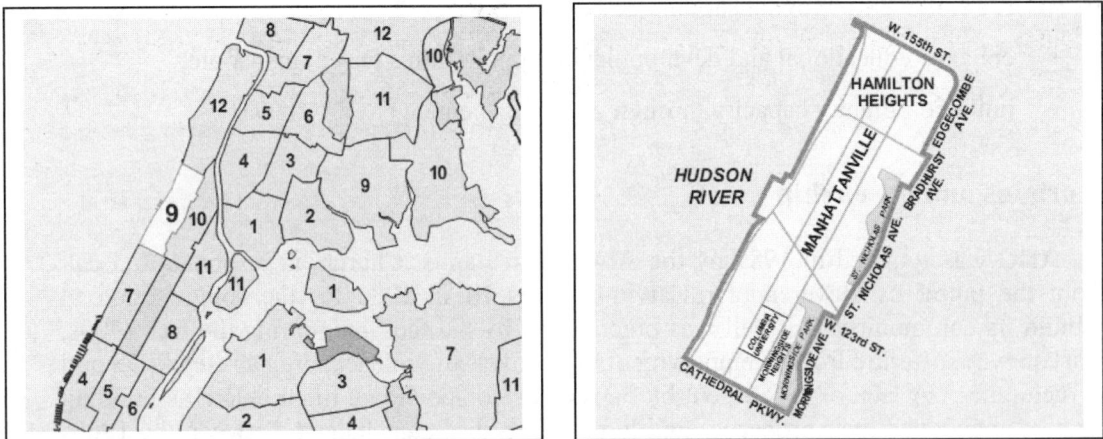

Figure A.2. **Manhattan Community District 10**

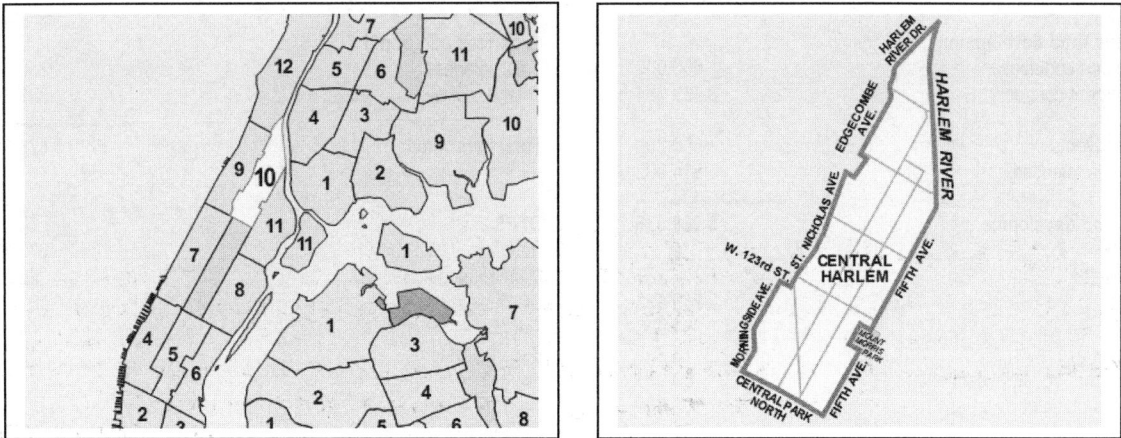

How is the Abyssinian Development Corporation financed?

In 2008/09, the ADC had a total budget of USD 9.07 million. The most significant contribution is that of government contracts which are worth USD 3.72 million. The total 2008/09 expenditure reached USD 8.70 million with the most significant cost being the salary expenditure of USD 4.75 million (ADC, 2009b).

A more detailed breakdown of the 2008/09 budget is detailed in Table A.1.

The organogram that follows (Figure A.3) reveals the local development system within which ADC operates.

Who are the Abyssinian Development Corporation's partners?

The ADC's partner organisations can vary depending on the project being undertaken. For instance, in the Abyssinian Neighbourhood Project, ADC worked with the New York City Department of Housing Preservation and Development (HPD), the Urban Technical Assistance Project (UTAP) at Columbia University and the Office of the Manhattan Borough President, as well as a host of private and public supporters. Across the range of their projects, however, the following three partners are fundamental to the ADC.

Government agencies

At the city, state and federal levels, the ADC interfaces with a variety of government partners. The organisation works closely with these agencies to preserve and maintain affordable housing for local residents to prevent the displacement of local residents. The HPD, for instance, acts as a partner to the ADC. HPD provides ADC with financing and technical assistance to deliver on its objectives and to leverage private resources.

Table A.1. **The Abyssinian Development Corporation's 2008/09 budget**

INCOME	USD
Revenue fund development	
Grants and contributions	500 000
Government contracts	3 723 384
Special events	550 000
Revenues released	814 992
Total fund development	**5 588 376**
Real estate	
Developers fee	2 259 422
Management fee	381 996
Social service fee	73 300
Income from equity investment	99 996
Net gains on sales	500 000
Rental income	84 000
Total real estate revenue	**3 398 714**
Other income	
Other income	57 311
Investment income	22 657
Interest income	2 899
Total other income	**82 867**
Total revenue	**9 069 957**

EXPENDITURE	USD
Expenses personnel	
Total salaries	4 750 345
Total benefits	923 372
Total personnel	**5 673 716**
OTPS	
Rent	673 422
Maintenance and repair	42 309
Utilities	102 300
Telephone	44 370
Security system	19 377
Equipment leasing	96 091
Network leasing	51 260
Insurance	67 283
Consultants	96 473
Professional fees	85 000
Membership, dues and affiliation	7 998
Catering	192 457
Printing	7 947
Equipment	1 500
Postage and delivery	12 510
Staff development and training	33 270
Contribution to affiliates	36 241
Fees	7 855
IT HW and SW	41 324
Miscellaneous	41 879
Community outreach	122 813
Supplies	198 047
Travel and conference	52 096
Total OTPS	**2 033 822**
Programme expense	
Programme expenses	422 249
Programme consultant	451 328
Total programme expense	**873 577**
Debt service	**114 348**
Total expenses	**8 695 463**
Net direct surplus / (deficit)	**374 494**

Figure A.3. **The position of the Abyssinian Development Corporation's in the system of economic development and investment promotion in New York City**

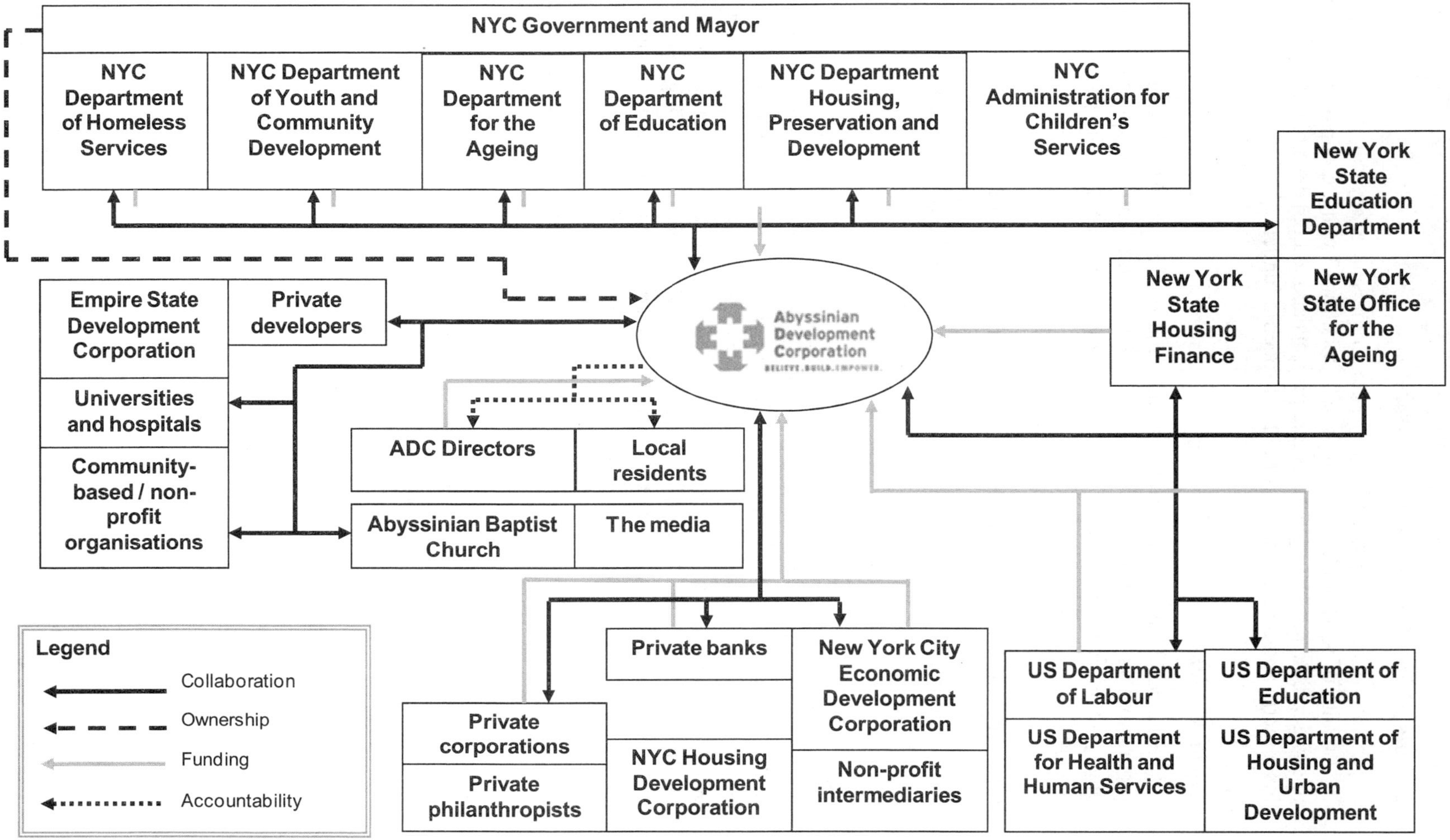

Legend

— Collaboration

- - - Ownership

— Funding

···· Accountability

Private philanthropists and corporations

Private philanthropists and corporations represent a key donor group which support the breadth of work undertaken by ADC. Donations by this group allow the organisation to develop innovative programmes and projects and to plan development projects over the longer term and outside the constraints of specific funders.

Local residents

Local residents are the chief customer and the reason ADC exists. The entire work programme is informed by and developed with the community. ADC interacts and engages with local residents to hear directly their needs. Improving their quality of life is a major objective for ADC.

How is the Abyssinian Development Corporation governed?

The corporation has a board which is composed of 21 members and there are currently 121 employees working for the corporation.

Board level

The ADC Board of Directors are involved in fundraising activities, planning efforts and policy development through their participation on committees and presence at quarterly board meetings. Every year, the board participates in an all-day, off-site retreat where members revisit the mission, vision and proposed planning efforts for the year. Additional engagement efforts include each board member serving on one of eight committees: audit, executive, finance, human resources, nominating and board development, programme, real estate, and resource development. Members of the board advise on high-level strategy issues and regularly review budget and programmatic data. Finally, the board participates in staff-led presentations on ADC's programme priorities that share the latest developments and overarching objectives on an ongoing basis.

Chief executive officer

Sheena Wright is the president and chief executive officer (CEO) of Abyssinian Development Corporation (ADC) (ADC, 2009b).

Organisational style

ADC has been described as locally sensitive, faith-based and effective.

What are the Abyssinian Development Corporation's key services and programmes within the system of local development and investment promotion?

Affordable housing development

ADC believed that upgrading Harlem's physical infrastructure was important as a first step towards revitalisation. During the organisation's first full year of operation, 60% of the housing in Central Harlem was city-owned, due largely to abandonment. In comparison, less than 1% of the housing stock is now owned by the city. This shift has been achieved by ADC and other community development corporations in the area, developing rental housing and homeownership opportunities for the residents of Central Harlem. Over the past 20 years, ADC has developed over 1 244 units of affordable housing in 82 buildings. The majority of this has been targeted at very-low and low-income families, the homeless and senior citizens. Over 100 homeownership opportunities for moderate-income families have also been created. ADC believes that home ownership is vital to a neighbourhood's success and growth and there is still a significant gap between levels of home ownership in Harlem and levels of home ownership in New York as a whole, with Harlem consistently lagging behind. Over the next three years, ADC is set to focus on completing major preservation, rehabilitation and revitalisation efforts in the immediate neighbourhood – "the Abyssinian Neighbourhood" – and there are plans to develop over 200 units of affordable housing that will be available to homeowners of all income brackets. In fact, this project has begun with the construction of almost 50 units near completion. Despite downturn conditions, ADC remains focussed on delivering all 200 units.

Social services

ADC provides a wide range of services to families within the Central Harlem community. ADC offers a broad range of family strengthening activities including crisis intervention, case management and housing assistance. For over 17 years, ADC has operated Abyssinian House – a transitional family residence for the homeless – where families receive counselling and intensive case management. ADC is currently working to further develop its service delivery to senior citizens at Abyssinian Towers and the greater Central Harlem community through expanded case management and social services.

Economic revitalisation

ADC has worked to strengthen and rebuild the community through economic development initiatives that support entrepreneurial activity, develop and promote local businesses, and create employment opportunities for residents. The organisation has developed projects such as Pathmark, which employs over 200 local residents, and the Harlem Centre, a mixed-use development with retail commercial space and an office tower which has generated over 500 jobs for local residents. ADC also administers the Harlem Economic Literacy Programme (HELP) which provides residents with the financial tools and resources necessary to participate in Harlem's economic system and homeownership opportunities. Through workshops and one-to-one sessions HELP delivers personal finance, budgeting, home ownership and debt repayment advice.

Education and youth

ADC provides educational opportunities by developing programmes and creating institutions that serve the young people of Central Harlem. ADC sponsors the Abyssinian Head Start Programme, which provides 144 preschool children with early childhood education, social skills, nutrition, and medical, dental and developmental screenings. ADC also sponsors and developed the Thurgood Marshall Academy (TMA) for Learning and Social Change, a public middle and high school, with partners of New Visions for Public Schools and the NYC Department of Education. The curriculum education at

TMA emphasises social change and community involvement. ADC opened the Thurgood Marshall Lower School in 2004, a public elementary school. Another programme developed by the ADC is the Gateway Builders Leadership Programme, which serves young people between 13 and 18 years of age in after-school and summer programmes that foster academic enhancement, cultural discovery, recreational engagement and leadership for transitions to college, work, and civic involvement.

Civic engagement

Through its Displacement Prevention Campaign, ADC works with residents to enhance and improve their quality of life and increase their participation in community life. To date, ADC has helped to organise and/or provide technical support to a total of 22 tenant associations and 13 block associations. In addition, 2 000 housing units have been saved and preserved since 2006. As a result, hundreds of community residents are actively managing quality-of-life issues and effectively communicating with civic leaders, police precincts, and legislators to solve problems (ADC, 2009c).

Keynote project

ADC has embarked on the Abyssinian Neighbourhood Project, a comprehensive community development initiative that will have an impact on the Central Harlem community and beyond. These community development activities are focused on a neighbourhood bounded by Adam Clayton Powell Boulevard to the west, Malcolm X Boulevard to the east, West 139th Street to the north and West 137th Street to the south. ADC will deploy its mission of community development in this neighbourhood by:

- developing approximately 200 additional units of housing;

- building a major educational facility for approximately 450 children and their families;

- developing approximately 15 000 square feet of commercial space, 33 000 square feet of community facility/arts and culture space and much-needed open space (Franqui, 2009).

What role has the Abyssinian Development Corporation played in the system of local development and investment promotion?

Table A.2 summarises the role ADB has played in the system of local development and investment promotion.

Table A.2. **Conceptualising the role of the Abyssinian Development Corporation**

	Direct delivery	Facilitation and co-ordination	Strategic support and programmes	Creating capacity elsewhere
Depth and breadth of role	✓✓✓	✓✓✓	✓✓	✓✓
Specific example	• Develop and preserve affordable housing for low to moderate income families. • Provide services and shelter to homeless families through Abyssinian House. • Provide services and affordable housing to seniors through Abyssinian Towers and the NNORC. • Provide workforce development and GED prep to out-of-school youth. • Provide quality educational institutions: Abyssinian Head Start, TMALS, and TMA. • Provide quality enrichment programmes for students such as Extended Learning Time, College Prep and creating a college-ready culture.	• Constructed state-of-the-art facility for TMA, the first public high school in 50 years. • Developed Pathmark. • Developed Harlem Centre.	• Housing Policy Advocacy. • Education Reform Advocacy.	• Civic Engagement and Technical Assistance for Organising and Campaigning. • The convening of non-profit organisations into networks e.g. as part of the Harlem Neighbourhood Naturally Occurring Retirement Community (NNORC) project 28 organisations are brought together to act as a clearing house for senior services. • CEO constantly asked to sit on advisory panels and boards. • Presentations to worldwide visitors interested in best practices in community development.

What enables the Abyssinian Development Corporation to contribute to the local development and investment promotion system so effectively?

The grassroots nature of the organisation and its rooting within and throughout the community it serves means that ADC can effectively identify problems, formulate solutions, and access resources to implement them.

Technical expertise, particularly around funding

The ADC makes every attempt to streamline its operations, minimise expenditure and maximise revenues. As a result, the ADC has developed in-house technical expertise. In particular, ADC has specialist knowledge around accessing funding. It works to identify funding opportunities and craft funding applications which are skilfully adapted to meet the strict requirements of various funding bodies and programmes. This requires a solid understanding of the relevant rules and regulations. This keeps costs low, which significantly benefits the community ADC serves.

An integrated plan and vision

ADC's "Theory of Change" suggests that, to maximise the likelihood of creating sustainable solutions to problems of chronic poverty, neglect and disenfranchisement, an integrated approach is required. There must be a comprehensive and simultaneous focus on bolstering the social, physical and human capital within the community in a holistic and interconnected way. ADC also has a commitment to achieving tangible change. It is critical to ADC that its "Theory of Change" creates concrete and measurable progress on the ground. ADC sees it as a concrete statement of plausible, testable, and tested pathways of change that both guide its actions and explain its input.

Deep community engagement and empowerment

From its inception, it has been ADC's practice to support the empowerment of the community to address the myriad of issues it faces. As a result, engaging and developing a rapport with the community has been a priority. It is an ADC priority to work with the community it serves.

Collaborative approach

To achieve tangible change within its operating area, ADC ensures that it pro-actively engages with elements outside of the community that cause, control or inform the conditions within the boundaries of the community.

Community-based leadership

The ADC has built a reputation for leadership excellence in the community across its various work streams. As a result, the organisation has received a range of awards from bodies such as the US Environmental Protection Agency for excellence in neighbourhood leadership.

Responsive, intelligence-based activities

ADC engages with its community clients with the goal of better understanding their needs and challenges. ADC has a number of formal and informal mechanisms to do this, such as surveys, interviews, focus groups, and/or conversations. For instance, several of ADC's programmes have advisory committees. ADC's Neighbourhood Naturally Occurring Retirement Community (NNORC) was derived from extensive engagement with, and outreach to, senior citizens in the community.

What constraints make Abyssinian Development Corporation less able to effectively contribute to the local development and investment promotion system?

Budget constraints

Like many non-profit organisations, ADC must balance programme delivery with administrative expenses, but still remain responsive to the increasing difficulty of both securing and sustaining a stable and diversified revenue stream, and administering it to the rising need.

Competition in the real estate market

In a tough real estate market, it has become increasingly difficult for non-profit community development corporations to compete. There is competition to acquire property and opportunities against relatively well-off, for-profit actors in an unstable and market rate housing environment. ADC has found it challenging to keep up with this market without a financial cushion that would allow it to more effectively participate in this market.

How has, or how is, the Abyssinian Development Corporation approached/approaching these problems?

Budget constraints

ADC has been successful in maintaining a healthy balance by effective planning – diversifying its funding base so as not to rely heavily on income from one particular funding stream, and recruiting specialised staff, who are able to maximise philanthropic and earned income opportunities.

Competition in the real estate market

Under the guidance of the Board of Directors, ADC has recently addressed this issue by establishing its own real estate acquisition fund. With the expertise of staff and professionals on the board that have experience in finance and real estate transactions, ADC is poised to position itself favorably to participate in this difficult new market environment. ADC has also prioritised the establishment of a reserve fund for real estate (Franqui, 2009).

How has the Abyssinian Development Corporation performed in relation to its key performance indicators?

Table A.3 summarises how the ADC has performed in relation to its key performance indicators.

Accountabilities, performance review mechanisms and best-practice sharing

Accountabilities

ADC is accountable to the community it serves, its board, funders, partners, clients, government regulatory bodies, and other stakeholders.

Performance review mechanisms

ADC adopts an approach to measuring organisational performance that looks at the efficiency and effectiveness of its: (1) internal infrastructure by assessing its systems, processes and procedures; (2) ability to meet its programmatic goals; and (3) impact on the community.

Table A.3. **Key performance indicators of the Abyssinian Development Corporation**

Theme (initiative)	Tangible impact	Intangible impact
Affordable housing development	• Over the past 20 years, ADC has developed over 1 244 units of affordable rental housing in 82 buildings. • 100 units for private homeownership have been created. • Homeownership has stimulated a process of wealth creation as many homes were purchased at a value considerably lower than today.	• Creates a deeper sense of community.
Economic revitalisation	• ADC has leveraged over USD 600 million of investments in the Harlem community. • They created 15 000 square feet of commercial space for five local businesses, which has helped revitalise the central Harlem business corridors. 750 000 square feet of commercial space. • Developed the first PathMark grocery superstore in Harlem, a 65 000 square foot retail centre that anchored the revitalisation of the 125th Street commercial corridor in 1997, and built the Harlem Centre, a 375 000 square foot retail and office building on Lenox Avenue and 125th Street whose commercial tenants include Marshall's Department Store, CVS, Washington Mutual and H&M. • Supports small business development, such as developing the first IHOP on the island of Manhattan, and has made significant and broad economic impact, such as the creation of over 1 000 jobs for local residents. • The revolving loan fund, which was in operation from 1991 to 2003 to finance start-up SMEs, lent over USD 300 000.	• Civic pride: "As a client of ADC and a resident of the Abyssinian Neighbourhood, watching the transformation taking place here is truly inspiring. To be able to live, work and shop in my neighbourhood, gives me and other residents a renewed sense of engagement, ownership and most importantly, community" - Kisha Spence, Harlem Community resident. • Shaun Donovan, Former Commissioner of New York City's Department of Housing Preservation and Development and new Secretary of the US Department of Housing and Urban Development (HUD), stated that the ADC "has been instrumental to the continuing revitalisation of the surrounding community" (ADC, 2009a).
Civic engagement	• To date ADC has helped to organise and/or provide technical support to a total of 22 tenant associations and 13 block associations. • 2 000 units saved and preserved through ADC's community organising efforts.	• Enables residents to have a deeper stake in their community. • Fosters sense of personal agency and control over change in their neighbourhood.
Education and youth	• ADC provides educational opportunities through numerous programmes, such as the Thurgood Marshall Academy for Learning and Social Change, the first high school built in Harlem in over 50 years, the award-winning Abyssinian Head Start Programme, and the recently opened elementary school - Thurgood Marshall Academy Lower School.	• Exemplifying the successful development of quality public school opportunities in partnership with community-based organisations.
Resident services	• Since 2000, ADC's Harlem Economic Literacy Programme (HELP) has provided homeownership education and counselling to over 2 700 people and is a recognised and approved Housing Counselling Agency by the US Department of Housing and Urban Development (HUD) and the NYC Housing Preservation and Development. • Provides a broad range of services, including crisis intervention, case management, housing assistance and programmes for homeless families, senior citizens, and residents in transition from welfare to work. 620 homeless families transitioned to permanent housing from 1992 to May 2009. • 1 303 children served by the Head Start programme (3-5 years old) from 1994 to May 2009.	• Improved quality of life.

Source: ADC (2007), "The Abyssinian Development Corporation Wins the 2007 EPA Award for Smart Growth in Equitable Development", *www.adcorp.org/U.S.%20EPA%202007%20Award%20Press%20Release.pdf*; ADC (2009d), "Highlights and Accomplishments", Abyssinian Development Corporation.

ADC reviews itself by:

- Management Dashboard and Operations Overview Report: a crucial quarterly tracking and monitoring tool that describes the agency's performance against projected goals.

- Annual executive team retreats and quarterly business reviews: the retreat and quarterly business reviews are a valuable planning and evaluation process that allow for executive management to review previous year accomplishments, track emerging issues, monitor and plan for upcoming year goals.

- Performance management reviews: enhance organisational management through employee retention and development.

The third component, measuring impact on the community, is tracked through an outcome evaluation strategy. ADC's efforts in this area include the creation of a system that supports and effectively measures the impact that ADC services and programmes have on the ever-changing needs of the Harlem community.

ADC gathers anecdotal data on overall impact by: conducting community planning meetings; presenting plans to community boards; and incorporating input, meetings, surveys, interviews, focus groups, and/or conversations.

Best-practice sharing

Moreover, ADC creates model systems and strategic plans that can be replicated across the nation, such as the Abyssinian Neighbourhood Project, ADC's Education Initiative, and most recently, ADC's Displacement Prevention Strategy (Franqui, 2009).

What progress has the Abyssinian Development Corporation made?

According to an ADC press release:

For almost 20 years, ADC has helped to strengthen and rebuild the socio-economic fabric of the Harlem community by developing housing, spearheading commercial development, stimulating the local economy, fostering education, strengthening families and building community capacity through civic engagement. ADC has grown into a USD 600 million, 120+ person agency with significant accomplishments, playing a key leadership role in the current "Harlem Renaissance. (ADC, 2007)

What are the Abyssinian Development Corporation's strengths, constraints, opportunities and challenges?

The ADC's strengths, constraints, opportunities and challenges are summarised in Table A.4.

Table A.4. **The Abyssinian Development Corporation's strengths, constraints, opportunities and challenges**

Strengths	Constraints
• High level of development skills within a locally oriented organisation. • Responsiveness to the community's needs. • Clear and persuasive vision. • An integrated plan and vision. • Fosters a genuinely collaborative approach. • Intelligence gathering function. • A commitment to achieving tangible change.	• Budget constraints. • Competition from commercial real estate developers.
Opportunities	Challenges
• Purchase property at recession prices to use for community development.	• Diversification of resources through philanthropic sources due to market conditions. • Credit crisis and impact on banks lending for affordable housing.

References

ADC (Abyssinian Development Corporation) (2007), "The Abyssinian Development Corporation Wins the 2007 EPA Award for Smart Growth in Equitable Development", *www.adcorp.org/U.S.%20EPA%202007%20Award%20Press%20Release.pdf.*

ADC (2009a), "Abyssinian Development Corporation", homepage, *www.adcorp.org/.*

ADC (2009b), "About ADC", *www.adcorp.org/about.html.*

ADC (2009c), "Programs and Services", *www.adcorp.org/programs.html.*

ADC (2009d), "Highlights and Accomplishments", Abyssinian Development Corporation.

Franqui, M. (2009), Written and telephone communication and interviews.

AUCKLANDPLUS /4·

AucklandPlus
Auckland, New Zealand

Organisation type

AucklandPlus is the Auckland region's economic development agency, which specialises in investment promotion and facilitation, including brand building and major project development. AucklandPlus works collaboratively with local, regional and national organisations and business leaders to further develop Auckland's competitiveness. The aim is to increase overall living standards and opportunities, as well as economic performance.

Mission statement

Vision

AucklandPlus is a driving force in the transformation of Auckland into an international city region (AucklandPlus, 2008).

Mission

To be the lead regional agency for economic transformation, and to position Auckland as an international city region.

Values

AucklandPlus is underpinned by a series of values:

- results-driven,
- regionally focussed,
- globally connected,
- nationally and locally linked,
- forward-thinking (AucklandPlus, 2008).

History, origins and ownership

In an international context, the Auckland region is primarily a gateway to New Zealand in terms of trade, tourism, migration and communications. It is by far the largest logistics node for both imports and exports by both air and sea. However, in his presentation to the 2005 "Better by Design Conference", economic commentator Rod Oram argued that:

New Zealand earns its living in a world driven by increasing complexity, homogeneity, rapid change, growth, low cost, high quality, large volumes ... yet we are a nation short of human and financial capital with some inherent disadvantages of distance and smallness .... .although New Zealand has worked hard in the past 20 years to halt our economic decline, the economic challenges ahead only get harder. To compete in this ever more demanding world, we need to pioneer new business models and skills to capitalise on New Zealand's unique opportunities in global markets. (Oram, 2005)

To this end, AucklandPlus was created.

AucklandPlus was inaugurated as a business unit of the Auckland Regional Council in 2005. The organisation was built in large part to ensure the effective delivery of the 2002 Auckland Regional Economic Development Strategy (AREDS).

The AREDS outlines a vision for the Auckland region to be "an internationally competitive, inclusive and dynamic economy; a great place to live and conduct business; and a place buzzing with innovation, where skilled people work in world-class enterprises" (Auckland Regional Council, 2009).

AucklandPlus's agenda overlaps with many of the AREDS core themes, which include:

- **Promote the Auckland region.** Raise international awareness and recognition of the Auckland region as a great place to live, work, play and visit.

- **Encourage innovation and excellence.** Foster an environment in which new ways of thinking are encouraged.

- **Develop overseas markets.** Gain international recognition for Auckland as a dynamic Asia-Pacific leader in trade and investment. Encourage businesses to build relationships and succeed in overseas markets. Maximise opportunities from expatriate and migrant networks.

- **Support exports.** Encourage dynamic, well-prepared companies that are exporting successfully. Support companies and sectors with the potential to lead improved export success. Exceptional people, cultures, environment and infrastructure.

- **Provide a high-quality living environment.** Take steps to create a region rich in arts and culture, vibrant, cosmopolitan, safe and attractive, offering a wide variety of choices for living, working, playing and visiting.

- **Build an entrepreneurial culture.** Foster an environment in which people are motivated to look for opportunities and are willing to take risks.

- **Produce a skilled and responsive labour force.** Create a virtuous cycle of business growth and skills development that increases productivity and participation in education, training and the labour force, creating a community able to respond to changing opportunities.

- **Deliver a high-quality and responsive government.** Foster effective relationships between business and the government by facilitating a sound regulatory environment in which business can operate efficiently, and which will attract new businesses to the region (Auckland Regional Council, 2009).

What does AucklandPlus do?

AucklandPlus undertakes two main tasks:

- Inward investment promotion: identifying and promoting the competitive advantage of the Auckland Region (business and lifestyle), establishing the Auckland brand, engagement with businesses domestically and internationally and capitalising on opportunities as a result of emerging trends.

- Facilitating inward investment: "playing Cupid" between key businesses, their leaders and the relevant networks, bodies and individuals in Auckland to ensure investment is secured and retained. AucklandPlus also advises on market opportunities and where to find specific expertise and sources of support and finance.

As well as providing support to a number of specific business sectors (biotechnology, creative industries, food and beverage, information and communications technology (ICT), specialised manufacturing such as marine), AucklandPlus also facilitates large, multi-agency, cross-boundary/council regional economic development projects such as the Metro Project Action Plan (Rogers, 2009).

What is the spatial scale of operation and influence of AucklandPlus?

AucklandPlus is regional in focus. Specifically, it works across the seven districts and cities which make up the Auckland region (Rodney District, North Shore City, Auckland City, Waitakere City, Franklin District, Papakura District and Manukau City) (see Figure A.4). As a major development player, the influence of AucklandPlus extends beyond its regional operating boundary. The organisation, for instance, lobbies central government in Wellington on important issues and projects such as the Rugby World Cup 2011, major infrastructure such as improved broadband and for support to sectors key to Auckland's economy. The organisation also reaches internationally to attract business and share best practice.

Figure A.4. **Map of the Auckland region**

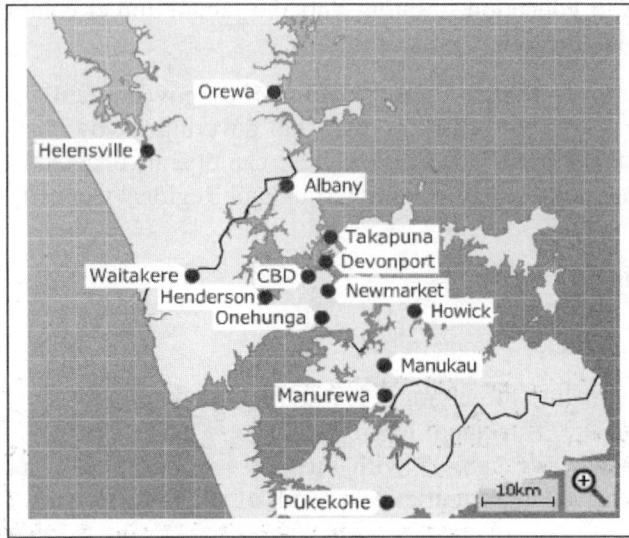

Source: AucklandPlus (2009a), "Interactive Regional Map", www.aucklandplus.com/interactive-map.cfm.

How is AucklandPlus financed?

The AucklandPlus 2008/09 budget states that the organisation will both receive and spend NZD 5 357 000. Revenue is comprised of a combination of central government and local government funding with some sponsorship from the universities and the private sector. The majority of the expenditure focuses on "key regional projects" such as the Marine Industry Action Plan (Rogers, 2009). Table A.5 for a summary of AucklandPlus' funding model.

The organogram that follows (Figure A.5) reveals the local development system within which AucklandPlus operates.

Who are AucklandPlus' partners?

The organisation works with local, regional, national and international agencies on a range of projects and initiatives (see Table A.6). Within the region, relationships with the various city and district councils and business leadership groups are fundamental to the success of AucklandPlus and it works hard to maintain them. The organisation also engages in national debates, often through national government departments.

Table A.5. **The AucklandPlus funding model**

AucklandPlus activities 2008/09	Description	External funding (NZD)	Expenditure (NZD)	Rate funded (NZD)
Regional promotion	Bringing the world to Auckland.		500 000	500 000
	Build on Auckland's distinctiveness.		235 000	235 000
	Position Auckland as a major event destination and use the 2011 Rugby World Cup to create long-term benefits.	190 000	215 000	25 000
Single point of contact	Promote and showcase Auckland region as a great place to live, work, invest and do business in.		100 000	100 000
	Benchmark services globally.		25 000	25 000
	Gain more value from networks.		22 000	22 000
	Digital Content Sector Innovation Programme.	900 000	1 080 000	180 000
	Marine Sector Development Programme.	600 000	720 000	120 000
Key regional projects	Sector-specific actions – MRIs, food and beverage, advanced materials and health technologies.	1 000 000	1 015 000	15 000
	Take an integrated, region-wide approach to tackling Auckland's skill issues.	150 000	250 000	100 000
	Accelerate innovative business in Auckland.		150 000	150 000
	Improve workplace productivity.	30 000	60 000	30 000
Corporate and marketing services	Internal capability and resource.		750 000	750 000
	AucklandPlus communications, marketing and advocacy.		205 000	205 000
	Research and information.		30 000	30 000

Source: Rogers, C. (2009), Written and telephone communication and interviews.

Figure A.5. The position of AucklandPlus in the local development system in the Auckland City Region

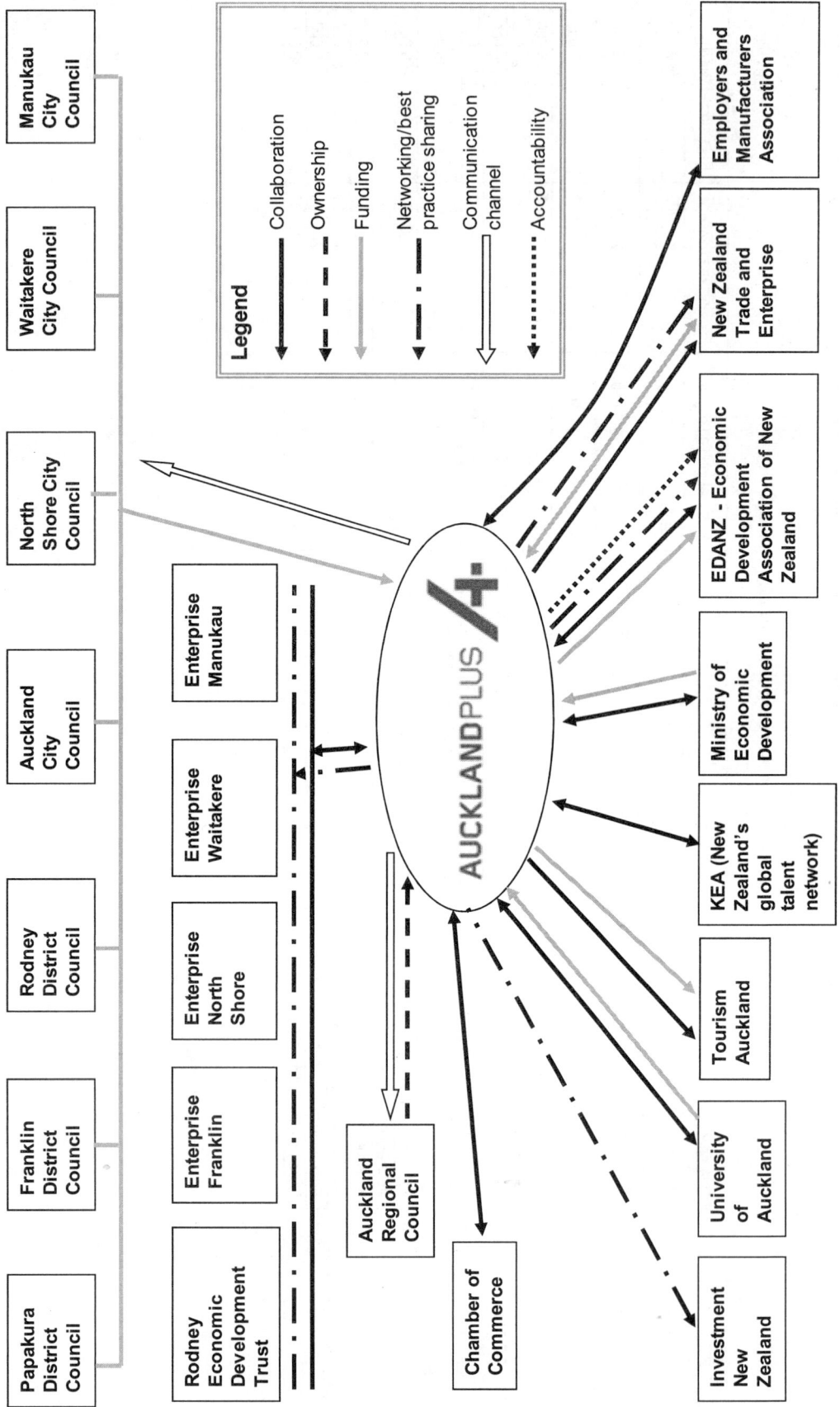

Table A.6. **Key partners of AucklandPlus**

Regional	National
Auckland City Council	EDANZ - Economic Development Association of New Zealand
North Shore City Council	New Zealand Trade and Enterprise
Enterprise North Shore	Investment New Zealand
Waitakere City Council	Ministry of Economic Development
Enterprise Waitakere	Department of Labour
Manukau City Council	Kiwi ExPat Association (KEA)
Enterprise Manukau	Angel Association of New Zealand
Rodney District Council	
Rodney Economic Development Trust	
Papakura District Council	
Franklin District Council	
Enterprise Franklin	
Chamber of Commerce	
Employers and Manufacturers Association	
Tourism Auckland	
Committee for Auckland	
Universities (UOA, AUT, Massey and Unitec)	
Pacific Business Trust	

AucklandPlus is also a member of a number of key networks, which it uses to build the relationships and credibility it needs to work effectively. One such group is the Economic Development Association of New Zealand (EDANZ), the national networking body which promotes economic development, best practice and knowledge in New Zealand. Another is the Kiwi Ex-Pat Association of New Zealand (KEA) – New Zealand's global talent network, which exists to help connect with, and leverage, the knowledge and contacts of talented New Zealanders around the world.

How is AucklandPlus governed?

Board level

AucklandPlus is governed by a board of seven high-calibre business leaders who provide leadership, energy and expertise, ensuring effective partnership with a wide range of industries and agencies across Auckland.

Staff

At the operational level, 14 staff members work for AucklandPlus – a full complement.

Figures A.6 and A.7 set out AucklandPlus' governance and organisational structures.

Figure A.6. **AucklandPlus' governance structure**

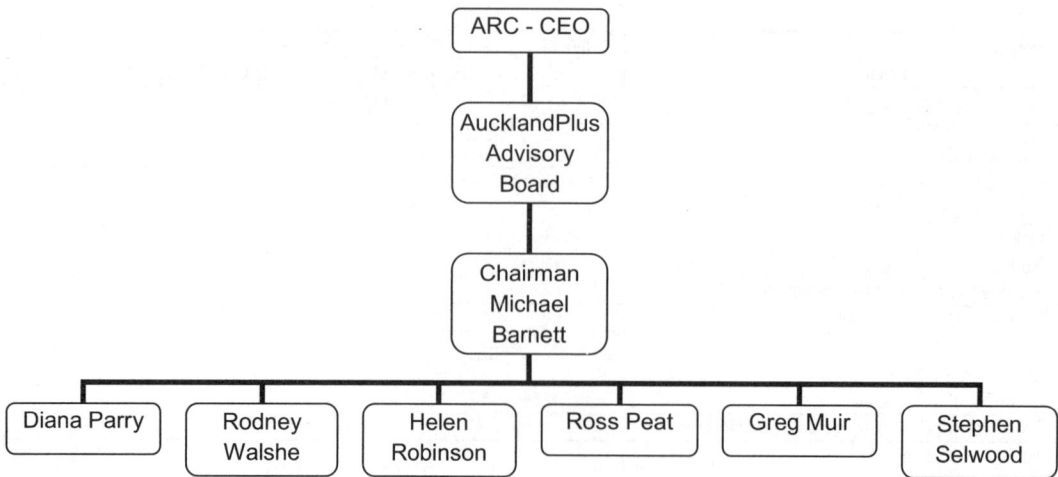

```
                    ┌──────────────┐
                    │  ARC - CEO   │
                    └──────┬───────┘
                    ┌──────┴───────┐
                    │  AucklandPlus │
                    │   Advisory   │
                    │    Board     │
                    └──────┬───────┘
                    ┌──────┴───────┐
                    │   Chairman   │
                    │   Michael    │
                    │   Barnett    │
                    └──────┬───────┘
  ┌──────────┬──────────┬──┴───────┬──────────┬──────────┐
┌─────────┐┌─────────┐┌─────────┐┌─────────┐┌─────────┐┌─────────┐
│ Diana   ││ Rodney  ││ Helen   ││ Ross    ││ Greg    ││ Stephen │
│ Parry   ││ Walshe  ││ Robinson││ Peat    ││ Muir    ││ Selwood │
└─────────┘└─────────┘└─────────┘└─────────┘└─────────┘└─────────┘
```

Source: AucklandPlus (2008), "Business Plan, 2008/9", AucklandPlus.

Figure A.7. **AucklandPlus organisational structure**

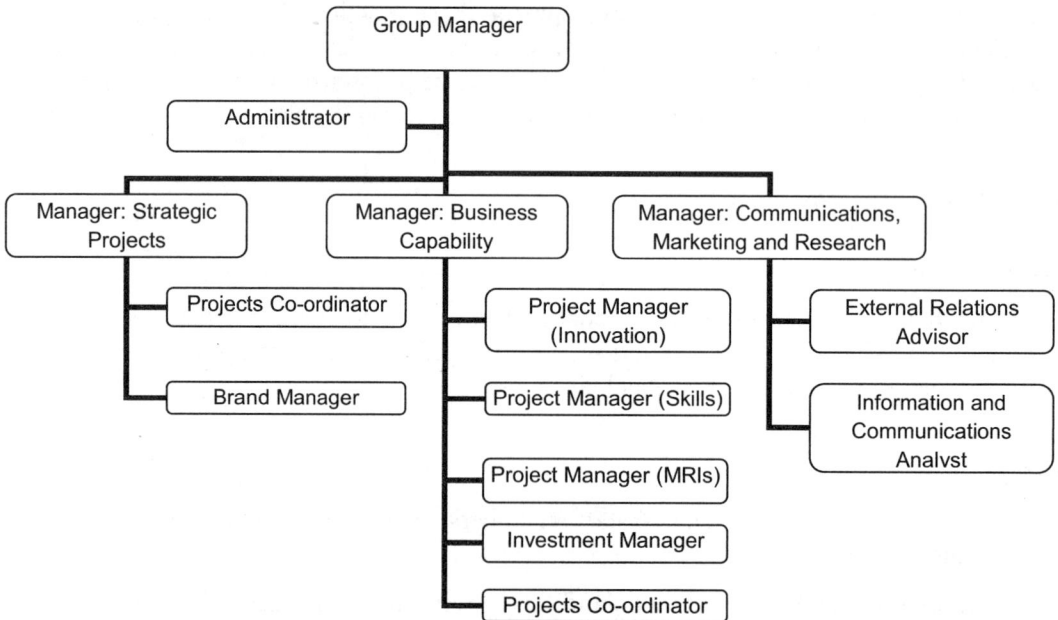

```
                        ┌──────────────────┐
                        │  Group Manager   │
                        └─────────┬────────┘
        ┌─────────────────┐       │
        │  Administrator  ├───────┤
        └─────────────────┘       │
  ┌──────────────────┬────────────┴──────────────┐
┌──────────────┐ ┌──────────────┐ ┌────────────────────┐
│ Manager:     │ │ Manager:     │ │ Manager:           │
│ Strategic    │ │ Business     │ │ Communications,    │
│ Projects     │ │ Capability   │ │ Marketing and      │
│              │ │              │ │ Research           │
└──────┬───────┘ └──────┬───────┘ └─────────┬──────────┘
   ┌───┴──────────┐ ┌───┴──────────┐    ┌───┴───────────┐
   │ Projects     │ │ Project      │    │ External      │
   │ Co-ordinator │ │ Manager      │    │ Relations     │
   └──────────────┘ │ (Innovation) │    │ Advisor       │
   ┌──────────────┐ └──────────────┘    └───────────────┘
   │ Brand        │ ┌──────────────┐    ┌───────────────┐
   │ Manager      │ │ Project      │    │ Information    │
   └──────────────┘ │ Manager      │    │ and           │
                    │ (Skills)     │    │ Communications│
                    └──────────────┘    │ Analyst       │
                    ┌──────────────┐    └───────────────┘
                    │ Project      │
                    │ Manager(MRIs)│
                    └──────────────┘
                    ┌──────────────┐
                    │ Investment   │
                    │ Manager      │
                    └──────────────┘
                    ┌──────────────┐
                    │ Projects     │
                    │ Co-ordinator │
                    └──────────────┘
```

Source: AucklandPlus (2008), "Business Plan, 2008/9", AucklandPlus.

How is AucklandPlus led?

Board level

All the board members are renowned for business and political acumen in Auckland, New Zealand and globally. The status, experience and talents that they bring lend credibility and muscle to AucklandPlus. Moreover, with strengths in branding, marketing, sports, tourism, infrastructure advocacy and ICT, as a team they have a wide and relevant knowledge base from which to contribute.

Organisational style

AucklandPlus is an organisation which provides regional economic leadership and vision. It has been described as agenda-setting, collaborative and as an interface between key participants in the Auckland regional system of economic development and promotion.

What are AucklandPlus' key services and programmes within the system of local development and investment promotion?

AucklandPlus organises its work in line with its overarching vision to transform Auckland into an international "city region". Its strategic objectives, over a three-to-four-year timescale, are delivered through services and activities which are organised at the one-to-two-year intervals. These activities are further broken down into sets of strategic initiatives to give the work of AucklandPlus real focus (see Table A.7 and details below).

Activity area 1: Regional promotion

Strategic Initiative 1.1: Bringing the world to Auckland

- Ongoing management funding agreement with Tourism Auckland, the regional visitor organisation.

- Encourage an increased focus on destination management.

Strategic Initiative 1.2: Build on Auckland's distinctiveness

- Demonstrate optimal use of Brand Auckland in AucklandPlus communications and marketing activities.

- Develop rules to guide the implementation of Brand Auckland.

- Identify existing, and create new, opportunities for AucklandPlus to showcase Brand Auckland and lead by example.

- Build AucklandPlus's capacity to facilitate the use of the brand by other agencies.

Table A.7. **AucklandPlus' strategic direction alignment matrix**

Vision 2012+	Strategic objectives 2008-11	Services	Activities 2008/09	Strategic initiatives
AucklandPlus has been the driving force in the transformation of Auckland into an international "city region".	(1) Be the Auckland region's lead agency and point of contact for economic development implementation, developing international connections and export strength and in matters of strategic economic importance to the region.	Management/ brokering	Regional promotion	Strategic Initiative 1.1 – Bringing the world to Auckland. Strategic Initiative 1.2 – Build on Auckland's distinctiveness. Strategic Initiative 1.3 – Position Auckland as a major event destination. Strategic Initiative 1.4 – Use the 2011 Rugby World Cup to create long-term benefits.
			Single point of contact for investors	Strategic Initiative 2.1 – Promote and showcase the Auckland region as a great place in which to live, work, invest and do business. Strategic Initiative 2.2 – Benchmark services globally. Strategic Initiative 2.3 – Gain more value from offshore networks. Strategic Initiative 2.4 – Develop and maintain local network.
	(2) Play the lead role of economic capacity and capability builder, collaborator, facilitator and broker of economic activities in the Auckland region. Work with key policy makers to create the environment for economic success.	Project facilitation	Key regional projects	Strategic Initiative 3.1 – Accelerate innovative businesses in the Auckland region. Strategic Initiative 3.2 – Take an integrated and region wide approach to tackling Auckland's skills issues. Strategic Initiative 3.3 – Improve work place productivity. Strategic Initiative 3.4 – Deliver the Digital Content Development Programme. Strategic Initiative 3.5 – Deliver the Marine Sector Development Programme. Strategic Initiative 3.6 – Sector specific action in food and beverage, advanced materials and health technologies.
	(3) Leverage resources from others in the public, private, voluntary and community sectors and guide the activity of its partners with economic evidence, professional advice and best practice learning.	Support services	Corporate and marketing services	Strategic Initiative 4.1 – AucklandPlus communications and marketing. Strategic Initiative 4.2 – Advocacy and relationship management. Strategic Initiative 4.3 – Internal communications – AucklandPlus and the Auckland Regional Council. Strategic Initiative 4.4 – Information and research. Strategic Initiative 4.5 – Identification and development of internal capability.

Strategic Initiative 1.3: Position Auckland as a major events destination

- Continue regional advocacy for major events.
- Work towards establishing a regional major events office.
- Bid for 2010 international competitiveness conference.
- Investigate the feasibility of hosting the 2018 Commonwealth Games.

Strategic Initiative 1.4: Use the 2011 Rugby World Cup (RWC) to create long-term benefits.

- Co-ordination and delivery of the economic development objectives for the RWC 2011.
- Business-ready kit.
- Investor attraction programme.
- Ensure there is a skilled pool of talent to support the event.
- Business showcasing and networking opportunities.
- Co-ordination and management of the regional communications objectives (AucklandPlus, 2008).

Activity area 2: Single point of contact for investors

Strategic Initiative 2.1: Promote and showcase the Auckland region as a great place to live, work, invest and do business

- Respond to investment enquiries, prepare investment proposals and host visits by potential investors.
- Maintain information and communication databases, aftercare records and protocols.
- Review and update the AucklandPlus website regularly in accordance with international benchmarks.
- Lead regional approach to the co-ordination of the promotion of Auckland as an investment destination and optimise response and aftercare effort.

Strategic Initiative 2.2: Benchmark service delivery against global competitors

- Complete a detailed GAP analysis (a tool that helps a company to compare its actual performance with its potential performance) of current services.
- Undergo GDP Global benchmark exercise.
- Establish a monitor for regional investment activity in accordance with international benchmarks.

Strategic Initiative 2.3: Gain more value from offshore networks

- Leverage international networks and strengthen connections between existing networks and sector programmes.

Strategic Initiative 2.4: Develop and maintain local and national networks

- Establish and support regional investment group.

- Encourage best practice behaviours and processes (AucklandPlus, 2008).

Activity area 3: Key regional projects

Strategic Initiative 3.1: Accelerate innovative business in the Auckland region

- Delivery of online innovation road map and toolkit.

- Establish national Angel Association, to grow New Zealand companies through angel investment.

Strategic Initiative 3.2: Take an integrated and region wide approach to tackling Auckland's skills issues

- Support the delivery of the skills observatory (Knowledge Auckland website) and career pathways programme in schools.

- Regional presence at UK Job Expos.

- Delivery of Auckland pilot for PLATO learning and capability network.

Strategic Initiative 3.3: Improve workplace productivity

- Launch of sector-based productivity pilots in the region.

Strategic Initiative 3.4: Delivery of Digital Content Sector Innovation Programme

- Digital content entity for Auckland region established and funding secured.

- Skills action package delivered to support the digital sector.

- Globally competitive business capability programme in place.

Strategic Initiative 3.5: Delivery of Marine Sector Development Programme

- Establish project scope and brief for marine industry study.

- Engage in broad sector consultation.

- Provide ongoing sector support to develop a clear and actionable regional strategy.

- Identify performance measures for the sector.

- Secure funding and implement programme of actions based on findings of feasibility study.

Strategic Initiative 3.6: Sector-specific actions in food and beverage, advanced materials and health technologies

- Contribute to regional project teams/taskforces in target sectors (AucklandPlus, 2008).

Activity area 4: Corporate and marketing services

Strategic Initiative 4.1: AucklandPlus communications and marketing

- Ensure that all AucklandPlus communications, marketing and sponsorship activity is driven by, and models, best practice in the use of Brand Auckland.

- Provide strategic advice and manage resources to support the communications, marketing and stakeholder requirements of all AucklandPlus projects.

- Maximise opportunities to demonstrate and promote AucklandPlus' role and how we are adding value and getting results.

- Utilise national and international networks to promote Auckland and AucklandPlus.

- Build relationships with key global agencies to ensure that AucklandPlus activity is in line with international best practice.

Strategic Initiative 4.2: Advocacy and relationship management

- Maintain and enhance AucklandPlus's position as the partner of choice for central government in Auckland.

- Ensure that communications with stakeholders is action and implementation focused.

- Maximise opportunities to collaborate with government at all levels.

- Ensure that AucklandPlus remains globally focused with strong international connections.

Strategic Initiative 4.3: Internal communications – AucklandPlus and Auckland Regional Council

- Ensure that AucklandPlus team is kept informed of projects and initiatives underway.

- Maximise opportunities to keep the wider Auckland Regional Council (ARC) group informed of AucklandPlus projects and initiatives.

Strategic Initiative 4.4: Information and research

- Identify, source and develop high-quality, timely and relevant information to support the activities of AucklandPlus and its stakeholders.

- Build and maintain relationships with other research providers and information networks to enhance AucklandPlus' research capacity.

Strategic Initiative 4.5: Identification and development of internal capability

- Building a high-performing team environment through empowerment, clear communication and strong lines of accountability.

- Promoting best practice, team satisfaction and cohesion and a culture that celebrates success.

- Developing employee capability through a targeted leadership and skills training programme.

Strategic Initiative 4.6: Develop our economic development transformation approaches and refine our systems

- Development of processes and project management systems that support targeted outcomes.

- Intervention Logic Guidelines applied (AucklandPlus, 2008).

Key projects

Brand Auckland

Developing a comprehensive approach to promoting Auckland as a region by establishing a publicly engaging brand used by the visitor and events sector, as well as business. The brand has been used for all offshore marketing activities.

Rugby World Cup 2011

AucklandPlus is leading the business leverage programme surrounding the Rugby World Cup, including opportunities for business, networking and international connections.

PLATO™ New Zealand

This international business-mentoring and peer-support programme was introduced for the first time in mid-2008. The two-year pilot in Auckland offers owners and managers of small and medium-sized businesses a unique opportunity to receive comprehensive training and mentoring alongside like-minded companies.

Digital Content Project

Building on the USD 1.7 billion of gross domestic product (GDP), Auckland's digital content sector already directly contributes to the economy, the initiative aims to increase productivity, growth and export reach.

Marine Industry Project

By enhancing future infrastructure, research and development, capability training and collaborative marketing efforts, the Marine Industry Project aims to support the further development of the marine industry.

Food and Beverage Project

The Manukau Food Innovation Centre is a state of the art research and development centre for processed foods which is being developed as a public-private partnership with Massey University.

Screen Production Project

The project will further boost Auckland's popularity as a screen production location with a new state-of-the-art sound stage, a high-end training programme and an international marketing campaign promoting Auckland and New Zealand's screen production capability.

Productivity Pilot

A programme aimed at up-skilling local business advisors to identify, diagnose and direct companies towards appropriate productivity training and resources to ensure continuous learning (AucklandPlus, 2009b).

What role has AucklandPlus played in the system of local development and investment promotion?

Table A.8 summarises the role AucklandPlus has played in the system of local development and investment promotion.

Table A.8. **Conceptualising the role of AucklandPlus**

	Direct delivery	Facilitation and co-ordination	Strategic support and programmes	Creating capacity elsewhere
Depth and breadth of role	✓✓	✓✓	✓✓✓	✓
Specific example	• Delivery of key strands of the Auckland Regional Economic Development Strategy (AREDS). • Investment facilitation. • AucklandPlus was heavily involved in Brand Auckland, which was launched in December 2008.	• The Metro Project. • The Marine Industry project. • The Food and Beverage project. • The bio-science initiatives.	• Publication of the *Bringing the World to Auckland* report. • The AucklandPlus website. • The International RWC Ball.	• PLATO™ New Zealand. • Productivity pilot.

What enables AucklandPlus to contribute to the local development and investment promotion system so effectively?

City regional scope

AucklandPlus meets its strategic objectives of building strong cross-border alliances and working co-operatively through its city-regional focus. It is not about borders, it is about the performance of the entire city region and Auckland's contribution to the national performance.

Leadership

AucklandPlus provides city-regional economic leadership and vision. It has been described as agenda-setting, collaborative and as an interface between key participants in the Auckland region system of economic development and promotion.

Credibility

The reputation of AucklandPlus has been established by its commitment to benefit the region whilst balancing priorities locally, nationally and internationally. This has been supported by a clear view of Auckland's unique and dynamic characteristics and requirements. AucklandPlus demonstrates capability in the management and delivery of regional projects, ensures actions are evidence-based, and maintains and develops good relationships within and at the national, regional and local level through strategic oversight and a clear understanding of roles, coupled with a high level of communication.

Independence

AucklandPlus aims to maintain its position as an advice- and solution-offering organisation.

Flexibility and agility

The work programme of AucklandPlus is holistic, systemic and focused on delivering economic wellbeing within an inevitably dynamic and evolving context. In a politically charged operating environment it must remain agile.

Collaboration

To achieve its objectives and to ensure they are sustainable, AucklandPlus works co-operatively with local and national government agencies and other private and public organisations. At times, AucklandPlus manages competing stakeholder demands in the delivery of regional work programmes. High levels of communication and relationship building are encouraged to develop and maintain cohesion between the public and private sectors. Auckland Plus' partnership agreements for best practice are a clear demonstration of how the organisation has responded to the structural and systemic issues present in the region's current governance arrangements. They don't necessarily secure resources but they do achieve alignment around common/shared objectives.

Focus on outcomes and delivery

AucklandPlus remains focussed on achieving agreed outcomes and delivering measurable results.

Clear intervention framework

AucklandPlus has developed a framework to help it make decisions about how best to utilise resources to achieve its outcomes (Figure A.8). The framework is based on a series of key questions: What is the opportunity? Does it contribute to agreed priorities? Is AucklandPlus the most appropriate or most efficient provider of the solution? Is it appropriate for AucklandPlus to be involved? Is the project viable? What difference will AucklandPlus' involvement make?

Figure A.8. **AucklandPlus' intervention framework**

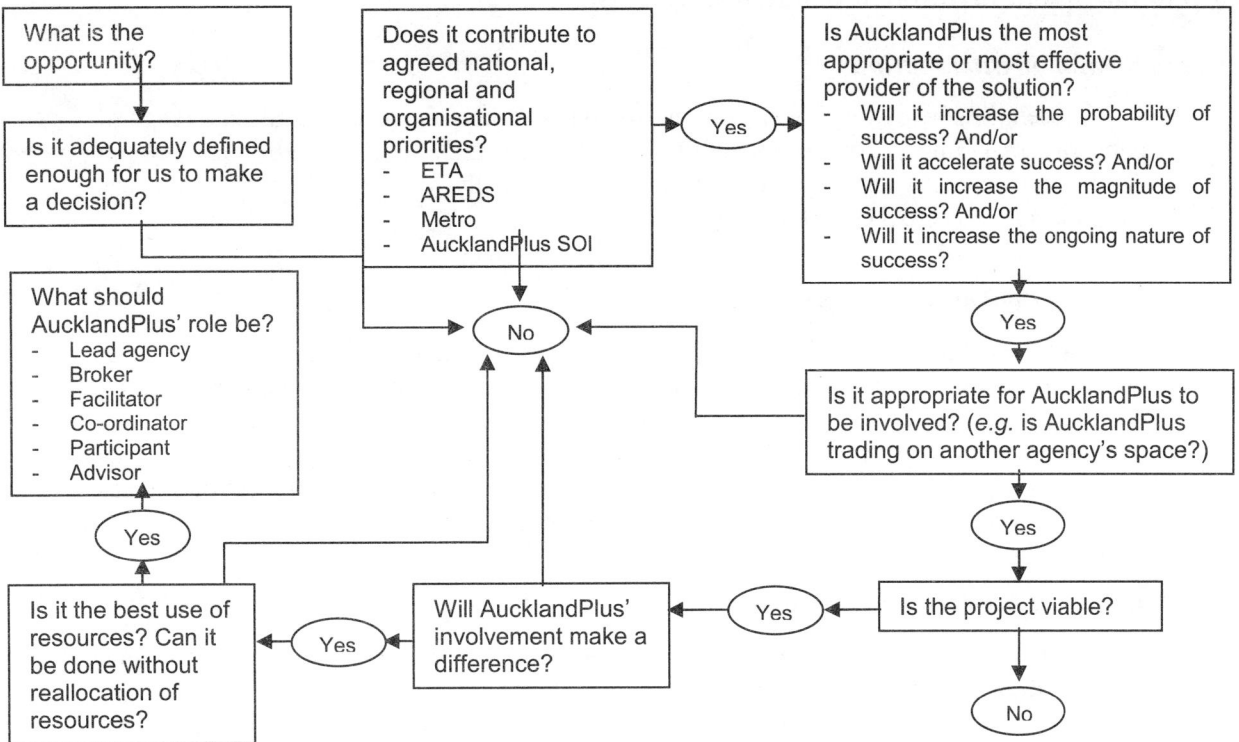

Source: AucklandPlus (2008), "Business Plan, 2008/9", AucklandPlus.

Figure A.9 illustrates AucklandPlus' organisational capabilities and competitive advantage.

Figure A.9. **Organisational capabilities and competitive advantage**

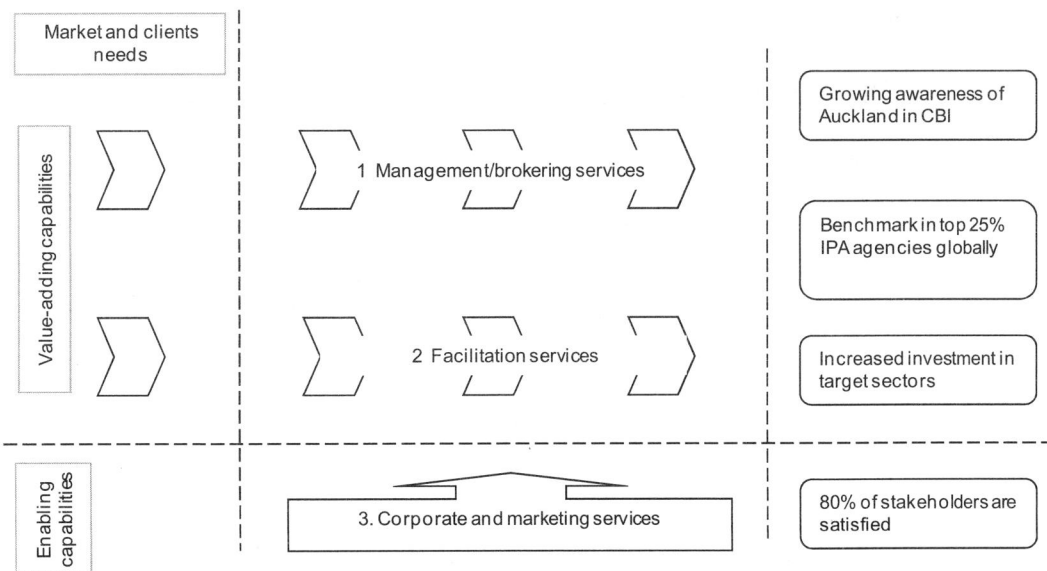

Source: AucklandPlus (2008), "Business Plan, 2008/9", AucklandPlus.

What constraints make AucklandPlus less able to effectively contribute to the local development and investment promotion system?

Economic interventions

A recent review by the Royal Commission on Auckland Governance raised a range of concerns that impact on AucklandPlus' ability to maximise opportunities around Auckland's economy and, in particular, to assist effectively with New Zealand's recovery from the current global economic crisis.

Regional governance structures

Issues highlighted included the current governance structures which allow territorial authorities to operate independently from each other on economic development matters, encourage a lack of regional focus and intra-regional rivalry, increase regulatory impediments through multi-consenting parties and processes, impair regional co-ordination of infrastructure priorities and have worked against the development of the city centre and waterfront in a co-ordinated or strategic way.

Regional funding arrangements

The Commission further recommended structures that enabled delivery mechanisms with funding and mandate to implement, and the ability and authority to marshal, resources behind transformative projects which have the potential to deliver multiple economic outcomes that provide long-term legacy.

How have, or how are, AucklandPlus approached/approaching these problems?

To meet these challenges, AucklandPlus is working with the Royal Commission's Report of Auckland Governance, the national government, the Auckland Transition Agency and private and public partners to develop an economic plan and implementation strategy for the proposed new Auckland Council.

How has AucklandPlus performed in relation to its key performance indicators?

AucklandPlus collects the following data to evaluate its performance (as summarised in Table A.9):

- customer satisfaction with access to, and quality of, regional economic and labour market information;

- percentage of enquiries from potential investors interested in investing in the Auckland region;

- growth in dollars invested in business sectors of importance to the region (current sectors of focus are food and beverage, screen, digital, marine and bioscience);

- benchmarking by global investment benchmarking group (GDP Global);

- stakeholder satisfaction with relationship and services received from AucklandPlus.

Table A.9. **Key performance indicators of AucklandPlus**

Theme (initiative)	Tangible impact	Intangible impact
Rate of inward investment	• Auckland is home to two-thirds of the country's top 200 companies and nearly a quarter of the world's Fortune 500.	• Global profile, networks and connections.
Auckland's innovation and export strength	• May 2009, the Government announced a NZD 9.6 million technology and research grant to a materials accelerator at the University of Auckland's Tamaki campus.	• Research and development-based innovation in key sectors.
Quality business environment	• IMD World Competitiveness Yearbook's survey of 215 cities, Auckland was ranked fourth, equal with Vancouver, rising from fifth last year.	• Auckland is seen as a great place to live, visit, study work and invest.
Effective business engagement	• New Zealand has improved three places to 15th in a survey of economic competitiveness and also ranks well on a measure of resilience in a recession.	• Improved perception of Auckland as a destination to do business.
Event hosting	• The Louis Vuitton Pacific Series, sailed on the Waitemata Harbour earlier this year, injected at least NZD 16.1 million of additional cash into the Auckland economy according to an independent economic impact report.	• Live cast to 100 countries and 600 million people.
Visitor economy	• In 2007 there were 5 million overnight visits to the Auckland region, split between 2.1 million international overnight visits and 2.9 million domestic overnight visits.	• Growth of Auckland as an international visitor destination.

Source: Rogers, C. (2009), Written and telephone communication and interviews.

Accountabilities, performance review mechanisms and best-practice sharing

Accountabilities

AucklandPlus is accountable to the Auckland Regional Economic Development Forum. The forum was established by the Auckland Regional Council, but is a confederate body comprising representatives from business, unions, Maori, the pacific community, infrastructure providers, educators, economic development associations (EDAs) and territorial authorities.

AucklandPlus is accountable for outcomes related to the objectives in the Metro Project, detailed below.

The Metro Project

Public and private sector organisations are bringing the region's economic development strategy to life through the Metro Project Action Plan. Its objectives are to:

- take effective and efficient action to transform Auckland's economy;

- develop world-class infrastructure and urban centres;

- transform Auckland into a world-class destination;

- develop a skilled and responsive labour force;

- increase Auckland's business innovation and export strength (AucklandPlus, 2009b).

Performance review mechanisms

For each activity strand, AucklandPlus sets a "level of service" target which is accompanied by a more precise set of "measures". It is against these dimensions that AucklandPlus evaluates the success of its initiatives.

Best-practice sharing

A relatively large proportion of the organisation's initiatives relate to best-practice sharing and the enhanced participation in networks. These include: (1) Strategic Initiative 2.2: Benchmarking service delivery against global competitors; (2) Strategic Initiative 2.3: Gaining more value from offshore networks; and (3) Strategic Initiative 2.4: Developing and maintaining local and national networks.

More precisely, AucklandPlus makes bilateral partnership agreements on a needs-based basis. For instance, AucklandPlus recently made a partnership agreement with the Ministry of Economic Development "directorate" located in the Government Urban and Economic Development office in Auckland.

The partnership agreement between AucklandPlus and Ministry of Economic Development "directorate"

This agreement seeks to provide a firm foundation for the mutually supportive relationship to continue to develop and mature between the Ministry of Economic

Development "directorate" located in the Government Urban and Economic Development office in Auckland, and AucklandPlus, the region's/ARC's economic development unit.

Both parties wish to recognise their shared agenda of positioning and supporting Auckland as a truly world-class city. By adopting this partnership agreement they wish to galvanise their strategic partnership by agreeing:

- shared values,

- operating principles,

- priorities for actions / focus of collaboration,

- supporting processes.

It is intended that each organisation maintains a strong individual identity and mandate whilst gaining strength in their delivery efforts by working in partnership (AucklandPlus, 2009c).

What progress has AucklandPlus made in relation to its original mandate?

Significant achievements in relation to the Metro Project include:

- a review of regional governance;

- an infrastructure plan for Auckland;

- a new regional brand;

- a visitor plan;

- a major events strategy;

- Rugby World Cup 2011 and a possible bid for the Commonwealth Games;

- new funding and governance structure for Tourism Auckland;

- international marketing efforts in Paris and London;

- a skills and labour-market knowledge hub;

- PLATO and productivity pilots;

- a review of Auckland's innovation system;

- the development of a materials accelerator at the University of Auckland;

- the establishment of the NZ Angel Investment Association;

- sector projects in marine, food and beverage and bioscience.

What are AucklandPlus' strengths, constraints, opportunities and challenges?

AucklandPlus' strengths, constraints, opportunities and challenges are summarised in Table A.10.

Table A.10. **AucklandPlus' strengths, constraints, opportunities and challenges**

Strengths	Constraints
• Credibility within the private sector, in particular those companies and people involved with current projects. • Preferred partner in Auckland for government. • Primarily an outward focus to all projects. • Strong brand that already has a presence within certain sectors. • Strong focus on action. • Access to numerous public and private sector networks. • Advisory board with experienced and credible individuals. • Visible and well-connected chair of the Board of Directors.	• Lack of awareness of and understanding about who the organisation is and what it does. • Lack of understanding about economic development and what it is/means. • Strength and role of the Regional Economic Development Forum. • Resources and how this impacts meeting and managing expectations.
Opportunities	**Challenges**
• Relationships with agencies, businesses and individuals who are not already engaged with AucklandPlus and Metro. • Maximising role of advisory board members *vis-à-vis* AucklandPlus strategic goals and reputation. • Identifying and tapping into other/more "key influencers". • Balance between promoting AucklandPlus and promotion of partners. • Build general awareness of AucklandPlus – who and what. • Exploring new communications channels (*e.g.* new media, innovative online approaches which reflect involvement in innovation).	• Metro project turning into yet more talk and moving away from action. • AucklandPlus seen as empire-building (especially with changes to governance arrangements). • Too many committees/working groups – shift to strategy rather than action. • Over-promising and under-delivering (taking on too many projects). • Not keeping it simple – perpetuating rather than dispelling the myths about action in Auckland and about economic development.

Source: Rogers, C. (2009), Written and telephone communication and interviews.

References

AucklandPlus (2008), "Business Plan, 2008/9", AucklandPlus.

AucklandPlus (2009a), "Interactive Regional Map", *www.aucklandplus.com/interactive-map.cfm.*

AucklandPlus (2009b), "About Us", *www.aucklandplus.com/about-us/.*

AucklandPlus (2009c), "Partnership Agreement between AucklandPlus and Ministry of Economic Development "Directorate", located in the Government Urban and Economic Development Office in Auckland".

Auckland Regional Council (2009), "Auckland Regional Economic Development Strategy", *www.arc.govt.nz/albany/index.cfm?1FC20F22-145E-173C-9850-84D85C CEDEF8.*

Oram, R. (2005), Presentation made at the "Better by Design Conference".

Rogers, C. (2009), Written and telephone communication and interviews.

Barcelon**a**ctiva

Barcelona Activa
Barcelona, Spain

Organisation type

Barcelona Activa is the local development agency (DA) of Barcelona City Council and was created in 1986. Initially conceived as a business incubator with 14 projects installed, the agency is now the main actor in developing entrepreneurial activity, innovation, professional and career development and employment creation within Barcelona. Each year Barcelona Activa coaches more than 1 400 new business start ups, and more than 350 existing companies are given further consolidation and growth support (European Commission, 2006). The agency is a municipal limited company; a private company, funded and 100% owned by Barcelona City Council.

Mission statement

The mission of Barcelona Activa is to transform Barcelona in terms of entrepreneurship, business growth, innovation, professional opportunities, human capital development and quality employment.

The 2004-07 Action Plan has been completed and Barcelona Activa is today embarking on the 2008-11 period under four main services and two transversal axes:

- business creation and entrepreneurship culture,
- innovative business survival and growth,
- human capital development and new employment opportunities,
- access to, and improvement of, employment.

The two cross-cutting activities are: (1) innovation promotion; and (2) digital professionalisation and training (OECD LEED Programme, 2009).

History, origins and ownership

Established in 1986, Barcelona Activa was created as a reaction to the challenging socio-economic climate. Barcelona's unemployment rates were at over 20%, the city was suffering post-industrial decline, economic restructuring and the closure of a number of large factories, and there was a lack of entrepreneurial initiative. Barcelona City Council created Barcelona Activa as the main tool to promote entrepreneurship, business creation and innovation, as well as to transform it from an industrial city to a knowledge city. Entrepreneurship was seen as a key contributor to social cohesion and business creation was seen as a means of job creation. Innovation was deemed important due to its ability to contribute to the consolidation of an industrial framework which can adapt and evolve with changing economic theory. Local government also seized the opportunity to make use of the empty premises of the Hispano Olivetti factory, which became Barcelona Activa's headquarters (UK Government, 2008).

Table A.11 presents a synopsis of Barcelona's development phases from 1975 through to the future.

Table A.11. **Barcelona's development phases**

Development phase	Period	Key ingredients
1	1975 to 1992	• Goal was to stop decline and begin to restore confidence. Key idea is to build some confidence internally and attract external interest. • Requires the beginnings of physical redevelopment from the derelict industrial mode to a new mode of urbanism. • Physical and infrastructure-led regeneration. • Required detailed master planning and a new urbanism. • Required an urban DA or similar. • Focused on larger sites and urban infrastructure. • Iconic projects at local scale with international visibility. • Attempt to address unemployment directly and begin to foster future entrepreneurial role with focus on business incubation.
2	1992 to 2004-07	• Goal was to become a significant European city. • Increasing economic diversification through foreign direct investment, entrepreneurship, innovation, building competitiveness and building a new supply of jobs. • Attracting internal talent and reversing population decline. • The beginning of sectoral and knowledge-economy strategies. • Requires a balanced focus between urban development and economic development. • Continuity of large sites, but also market-led development of smaller sites. • Need for additional and modernised infrastructure. Connectivity becomes very important. • Success triggers wider metropolitan growth, and thus initial metropolitan co-ordination requirements. • Private sector becomes a more important actor in development and begins to share some elements of leadership with city government.
3	2005-08 to 2020	• Goal is to become a globally important city with leading continental and sub-continental roles (Mediterranean capital, gateway to Latin America, etc.) and to sustain growth through high-quality urban environment and connectivity/infrastructure. • Growth management challenges emerge. Need for continuous flow of new sites and development opportunities. Need to contain/control negative externalities, e.g. congestion, inflation, conflict over land uses and conflict between diverse populations. • Increased focus on high value-added knowledge economy, but also on quality of place and creative economy. Greater embedding of local and international businesses. • Requires proactive image and identity building to highly segmented markets/audiences. • Requires economic DAs which are able to work with complex international businesses, foster business-to-business collaboration, provide advanced technologies and attract and retain human capital. • Private sector co-leadership becomes more critical to attract and retain leading firms in clusters and provide competitive business-to-business services. • Strategic co-ordination of wider range of players required (e.g. universities, banks, infrastructure providers) and between tiers of government and neighbouring municipalities. • Metropolitan growth strategy becomes more critical and co-ordination is essential to reinforce strategic goals. • Connectivity is important to ensure hub and gateway status.
4	2020 onwards	• Will be about maintaining "world-class" international success. • Will require continuous reinvention and reinvestment and active problem solving, including ongoing growth management. • Major companies and institutions are very demanding clients of the city. • Requires continuous pro-active marketing and customer care with major investors. • Metropolitan governance must be very effective. Vertical and horizontal co-ordination is the norm and organisations are highly flexible and adaptive. • Presence of world class development organisation(s), which are jointly owned and governed by major stakeholders as partners.

Source: OECD LEED Programme (2009), "Promoting Entrepreneurship, Employment and Business Competitiveness: The Experience of Barcelona", *www.oecd.org/document/32/0,3343,en_2649_34461_43504288_1_1_1_1,00.html.*

How has Barcelona Activa contributed to Barcelona's redevelopment success?

Enterprise and incubation

Barcelona Activa has undertaken systematic leadership of the entrepreneurship and incubation agenda and has had many successes. It is a leading provider of support to new companies and to entrepreneurs.

Employment

Barcelona Activa has successfully innovated employment promotion, with the "New Occupation Space" (Porta22) initiative. These are state-of-art services to link people with employment and to help them understand the requirements and orientation of different forms of work. This has proved particularly useful for people re-entering work; those seeking to develop their careers by entering new fields with higher levels of responsibility; or for migrants needing support orienting into Barcelona's labour market. In times of economic crisis, Barcelona Activa has also developed an action plan for the guidance and professional improvement of the unemployed in the city of Barcelona. Indeed, the "Activate for Work" plan has been developed together with the regional government and in the framework of the Agreement for Quality Employment in Barcelona 2008-11, which itself is subscribed to by the city's two main trade unions and business organisations as well as the Government of Catalunya.

Innovation

Barcelona Activa's work on entrepreneurship and incubation has put the organisation at the heart of Barcelona's drive for an innovative and creative economy. In the next phase of growth Barcelona will need to have a clear city-wide innovation system with a wider range of existing organisations operationalising a common agenda. This will require at least one organisation to take a lead in working with the partners to define and articulate the common framework and standards of service and support required, and to continuously map and review changing needs and expectations. It is logical that Barcelona Activa should play such a role.

Attraction of talent

Barcelona Activa offers an integrated framework of support for international people wishing to develop their careers, in employment or as an entrepreneur, in Barcelona. The specific initiative is named "Do it in Barcelona". Many of these people have already set up businesses or lead business growth processes. This in has created job opportunities for local people and additional investment from outside the city.

Business growth

Barcelona Activa has developed and implemented innovative programmes to support businesses once established, such as incubation facilities, programmes in support of internationalisation, access to finance, business co-operation and strategic growth management. These programmes have engaged leading business schools, investors, and business organisations as partners.

Education

Barcelona Activa has begun work to promote entrepreneurship and professional guidance to become part of the curriculum in the city's schools (OECD LEED Programme, 2009).

What does Barcelona Activa do?

It began as an organisation focused on business incubation, whilst during the most recent Action Plan period 2008-11, the agency focuses on the aforementioned four strategic lines of activity and the two transversal programmes. In essence, Barcelona Activa: (1) manages spaces and programmes for people to find and enhance employment, network and develop business ideas; (2) provides business support and services to entrepreneurs and start-ups through the management of business incubators and other tailor-made programmes and facilities; (3) promotes the uptake of technology and innovative practices; and (4) provides training and skills upgrading for the human capital in the city.

What is the spatial scale of operation and influence of Barcelona Activa?

The agency is concerned with the city of Barcelona, but also with the metropolitan area of Barcelona. With more than 1.6 million inhabitants, which represent 23% of the total Catalan population, Barcelona accounts for more than 1 million jobs, 33% of the total of Catalonia (Barcelona Activa, 2008).

How is Barcelona Activa financed?

In 2008, Barcelona Activa's income was approximately EUR 24 million (see Figure A.10). It is important to note that the funds received by Barcelona Activa from the different public institutions and administrations are gained through the submission of innovative projects to public tenders and calls for proposal to different regional, national and international administrations and, therefore, are gained under a process of open competition (OECD LEED Programme, 2009).

Figure A.11 presents Barcelona Activa expenditures per activity line in 2008.

Figure A.10. **Sources of funding for Barcelona Activa, 2008**

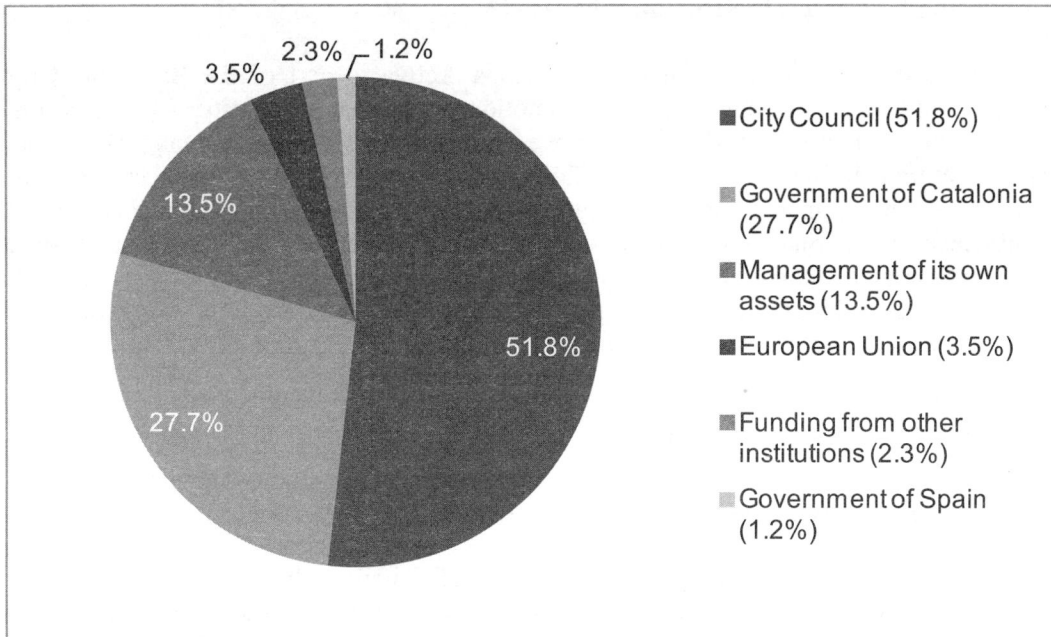

Legend:
- City Council (51.8%)
- Government of Catalonia (27.7%)
- Management of its own assets (13.5%)
- European Union (3.5%)
- Funding from other institutions (2.3%)
- Government of Spain (1.2%)

Source: Molero, A. (2009), Written and telephone communication and interviews.

Figure A.11. **Barcelona Activa expenditures per activity line, 2008**

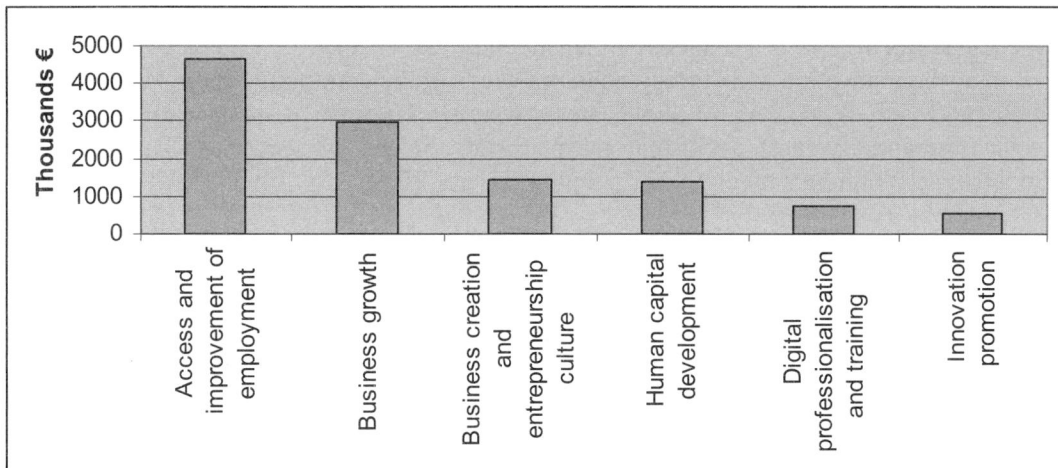

Source: Molero, A. (2009), Written and telephone communication and interviews.

What is Barcelona Activa's institutional context?

Despite its operational autonomy, Barcelona Activa is part of the Barcelona City Council and now acts as the Economic Promotion Counsellor of the city. The promotion of the local economy is a shared objective between the City Council and Barcelona Activa. Within the City Council, Barcelona Activa is in charge of business creation, business growth, human capital development, innovation promotion, digital literacy and employment. Barcelona Activa collaborates with other services in the City Council, such as the international economic promotion department, the tourism agency and the research and innovation programme. The key actions undertaken by Barcelona Activa are co-ordinated with the overall strategy of the city (OECD LEED Programme, 2009).

The organogram that follows (Figure A.12) reveals the local development system within which Barcelona Activa operates.

Who are Barcelona Activa's partners?

Barcelona Activa not only works closely with affiliated public sector bodies, but has also collaborated with private institutions in order to better understand the needs of the community and create an environment in which entrepreneurship, quality employment and innovation can thrive. To date, more than 370 collaboration agreements have been signed that work jointly with Barcelona Activa to deliver programmes and services in the community.

How is Barcelona Activa governed?

Barcelona Activa works under a Board of Directors and the Managing Director, Ms. Anna Molero, leads the agency independently and ensures that the activities carried out meet the innovation and entrepreneurship needs of the community in line with the city strategy (Figure A.13). As of 2008, there were 109 permanent staff and the agency engages temporary staff according to the needs of the current work streams. This increases staff numbers by up to 221 people (Molero, 2009).

How is Barcelona Activa led?

Ms. Maravillas Rojo, who chaired Barcelona Activa for over ten years, was vital in the establishment and development of Barcelona Activa and its innovative programme of work. Today, the chair is Mr. Jordi William Carnes, Deputy Mayor for the Treasury and Economic Promotion.

Board level

The members on the management board come from the different political parties in the city and from the system of economic promotion and local innovation (European Union Knowledge Network, 2009). The *Consell d'Administració* is presided over by the Deputy Mayor for Economic Promotion. The vice president is the Chief Executive of Economic Promotion. Currently there are nine other councillors who represent the different parties in the Chamber of Commerce and the City Council (Molero, 2009).

Figure A.12. **The position of Barcelona Activa in the local development system in Barcelona**

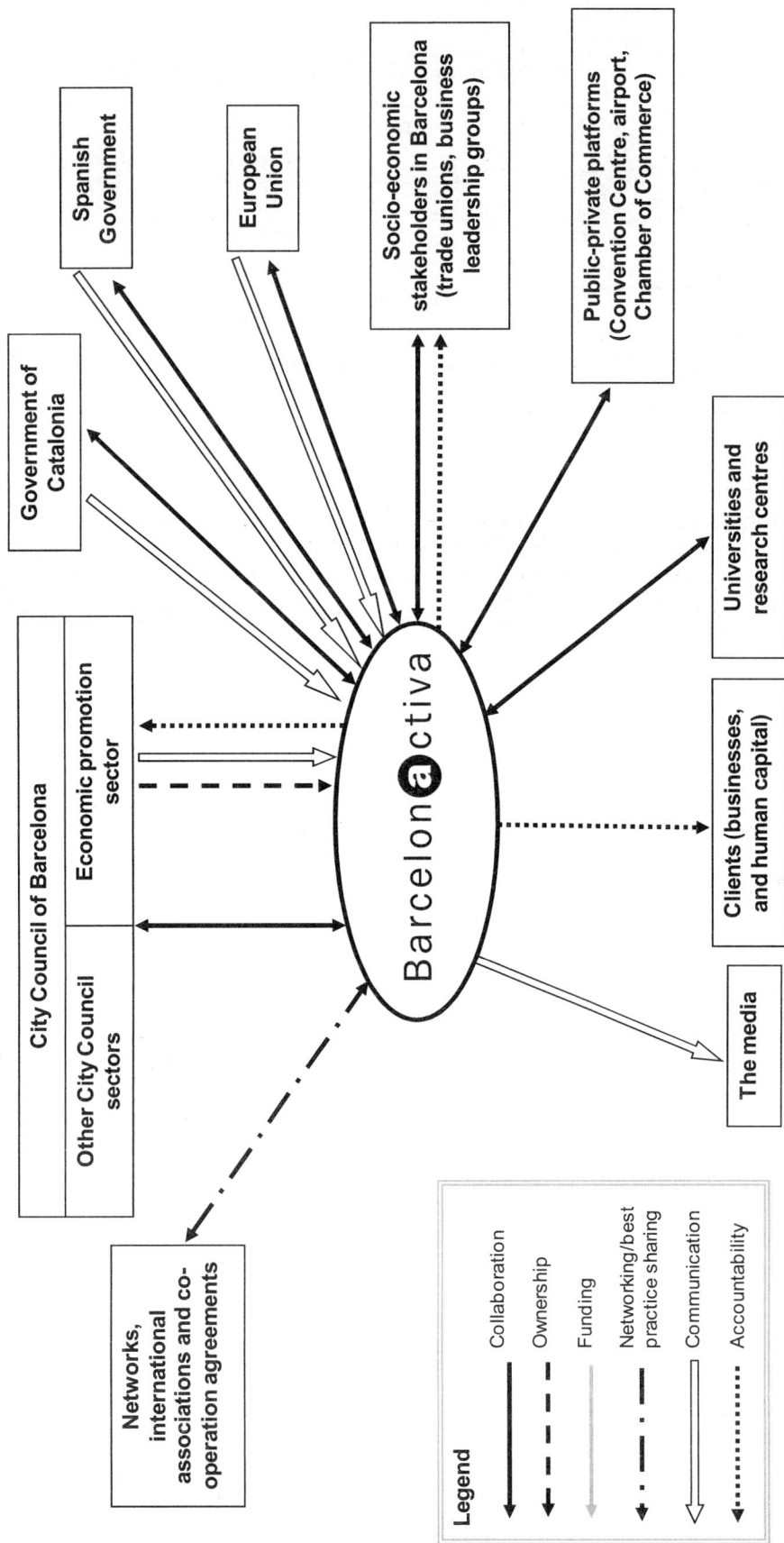

Figure A.13. **The organisational structure of Barcelona Activa**

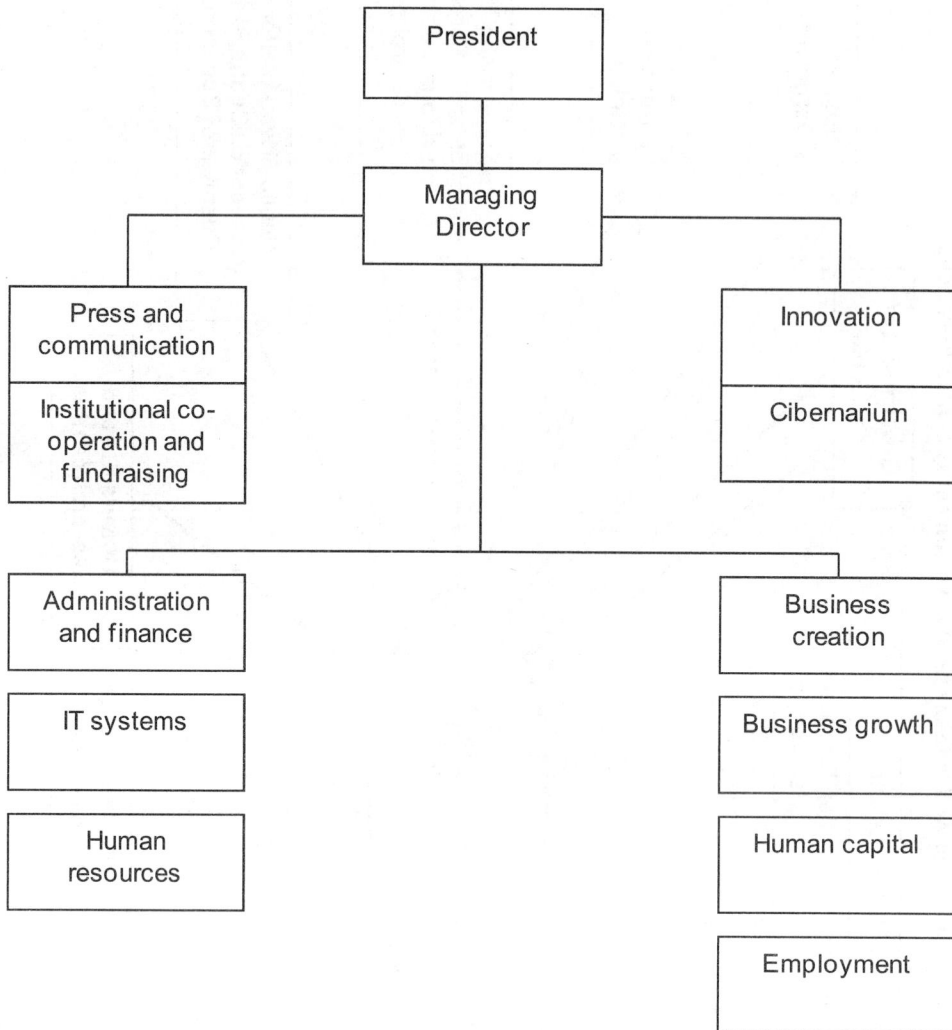

Organisational style

Barcelona Activa is a relatively small organisation, but this allows it to be highly flexible and responsive to the changing needs of the city. The agency exhibits a constantly evolving organisational structure according to the most needed and tailor-made programmes.

What are Barcelona Activa's key services and programmes within the system of local development and investment promotion?

Barcelona Activa is now embarking on the 2008-11 period through four major services and two transversal axes, as follows.

Service 1: Business creation and entrepreneurship culture

The aim is to provide professional services for potential entrepreneurs in order to promote the creation of new businesses (Figure A.14). It also seeks to encourage an entrepreneurial culture by coaching entrepreneurs and assisting them in taking the step from the business idea to its creation. One of the key points is its special methodology, which is called the "blended model". It involves the use of cutting-edge spaces to increase accessibility to the full range of activities which are devoted to entrepreneurs. These activities number over 900 from classical training, dissemination and knowledge pills, personalised coaching, and a powerful website with contents, activities and useful self tools in order to coach the business plan online. The main initiatives carried out under this line of action include: (1) the Gloriès Entrepreneurship Centre; (2) BarcelonaNETactiva; and (3) the Day of the Entrepreneur (Molero, 2009).

Figure A.14. **Barcelona Activa: supporting the business-creation process**

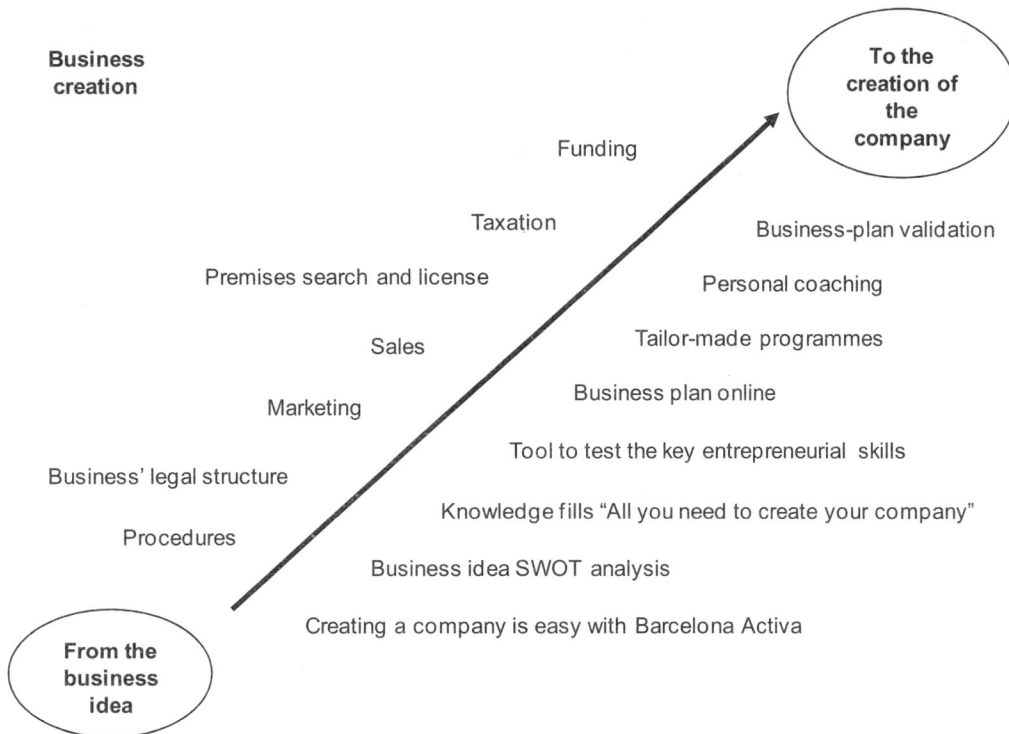

Service 2: Innovative business consolidation and growth

This aims to generate the conditions that foster the growth of innovative businesses in the city through internationalisation, access to funding, co-operation and innovation (Figure A.15). The specific activities carried out are: (1) business co-operation programmes; (2) technology and innovation bridges; (3) investment readiness programmes, such as Ready for Growth; (4) strategic business growth programmes; (5) Barcelona Nord Technology Park: and (6) the Business Incubator (Molero, 2009).

Figure A.15. **Barcelona Activa: supporting the business-growth process**

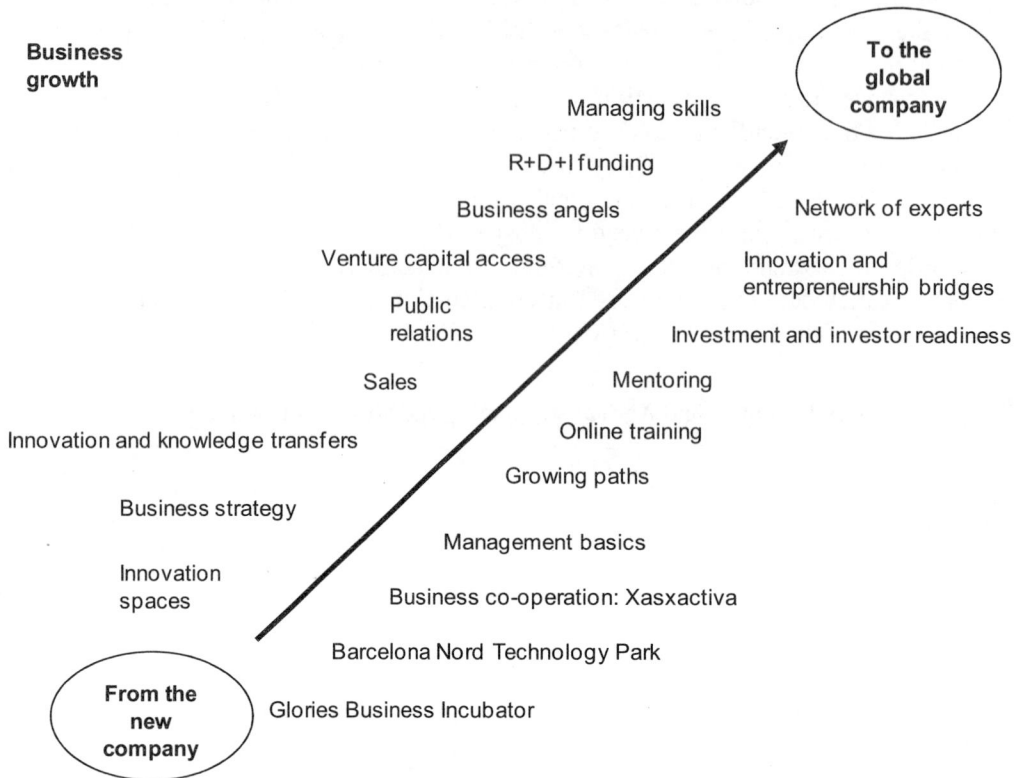

Business growth

To the global company

Managing skills

R+D+I funding

Business angels

Network of experts

Venture capital access

Innovation and entrepreneurship bridges

Public relations

Investment and investor readiness

Sales

Mentoring

Innovation and knowledge transfers

Online training

Growing paths

Business strategy

Management basics

Innovation spaces

Business co-operation: Xasxactiva

Barcelona Nord Technology Park

From the new company

Glories Business Incubator

Service 3: Human capital development and new employment opportunities

This aims to promote Barcelona Activa as the meeting point for human capital in the city of Barcelona, by increasing the professional opportunities that the new work cultures, the new occupations and the emerging economic sectors offer to the population. The programmes are defined based on the prospective labour and skills demands of the economic sectors. The activities seek to develop the workforce in the evolving context of the labour market and to reduce the mismatch between the supply and demand of skills in the labour market. They also aim to improve local production processes and better harness the skills available locally, thereby leading to higher quality jobs and a more competitive local economy. The main activities are: (1) the "Space of New Occupations" (Porta22) (Box A.1); (2) the programme of professional progress; and (3) the meeting point of talent (Molero, 2009).

Box A.1. **Porta22: "Space of New Occupations"**

Porta22 is a reference centre about new occupations and emerging and transforming sectors. The amenity is designed as an open, free-access space, aimed at people looking for new jobs, opportunities, employment orientation, and orientation about the future of professional evolution. It provides:

- 730 new professional profiles analysed in depth through 12 multimedia interactive applications and 150 visuals;

- 50 000 pages of digital content;

- personal advice and a twice monthly activities' programme.

Service 4: Access and improvement of employment

Barcelona Activa seeks to inform, orientate, motivate, train and promote employment in Barcelona (Figure A.16). This axis contributes to updating the professional skills of the jobseekers or those wanting to improve their professional career, and also promotes labour inclusion by responding to the needs of the companies. The facilities are: (1) Can Jaumandreu; (2) Sant Agustí convent; (3) Ca n'Andalet; and (4) Cibernarium (Molero, 2009).

Figure A.16. **Barcelona Activa: supporting human capital and access to quality employment**

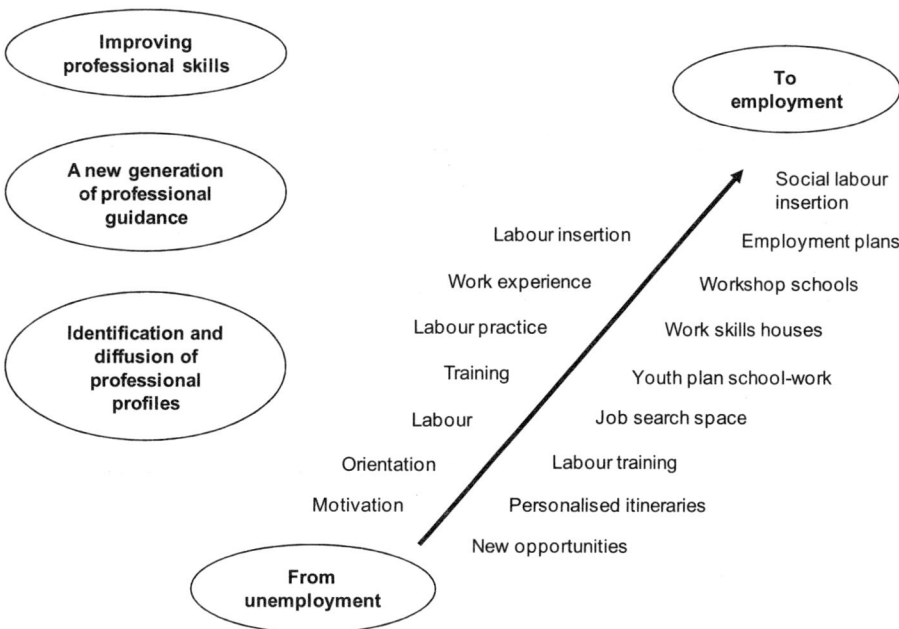

The two transversal activities identified by Barcelona Activa are: (1) innovation promotion; and (2) digital professionalisation training at the Cibernarium facility. Each of these areas has several cutting-edge programmes and initiatives that were thought to meet the overall objective of the Barcelona Activa Action Plan.

What role has Barcelona Activa played in the system of local development and investment promotion?

Table A.12 summarises the role Barcelona Activa has played in the system of local development and investment promotion.

Table A.12. **Conceptualising the role of Barcelona Activa**

	Direct delivery	Facilitation and co-ordination	Strategic support and programmes	Creating capacity elsewhere
Depth and breadth of role	✓✓✓	✓✓✓	✓✓✓	✓✓
Specific example	• Manages spaces and programmes for innovation and employment. • Direct training provider for human capital development and quality employment. • Coaches 1 400 business projects a year. • Coaches more than 30 000 participants to quality employment.	• Works together with the City Council and other city and regional bodies to facilitate local development. • Work on e.g. the Agreement for Quality Employment in Barcelona 2008-11, with the two main trade unions and business organisations as well as the Government of Catalunya.	• Promotes the city as a centre for innovation and future-oriented economic activity. • Reference organisation for entrepreneurs in the city and region (such as Day of the Entrepreneur).	• More than 100 visits of institutional delegations a year. • Active members of international networks (EBN, Eurocities, IASP, etc.). • Transfers programmes and methodologies and provide technical assistance to other world cities.

What enables Barcelona Activa to contribute to the local development and investment promotion system so effectively?

Effective programmes within a clearly defined strategic action plan

Barcelona Activa defines its strategic action plans in line with the guidelines of the City Council. This allows the organisation to contribute very effectively to the city's economic growth model. To operationalise this strategy, there are two key issues: (1) effective collaboration with the main economic and social actors in Barcelona with respect to the strategic action framework; and (2) effective public-private co-operation and complementarities. The OECD LEED Programme gave a glowing report, stating that "Barcelona Activa is an exceptional agency by international standards .... and is dynamic and effective in contributing to reshaping the city and regional economy in which it is located. But it is an agency that recognises the need to evolve" (OECD LEED Programme, 2009).

Client-oriented

The organisation works on a client-oriented basis, providing real and direct services to entrepreneurs, professionals, unemployed and citizens, to whom the agency is also accountable. Because of this accountability, Barcelona Activa is implored to ensure the provision of high-quality services and facilities to its users.

Developing the entrepreneurial capacity to allow Barcelona to compete

The promotion of entrepreneurial culture in the city is an essential part of the support programmes for entrepreneurs. Creating an entrepreneurial culture among Barcelona's citizens can contribute towards innovation and sustainable economic growth. Barcelona Activa performs the task of "entrepreneurship diffusion and encouragement" in order to awaken new capabilities and to generate innovation, employment and new economic activity with global vision.

Good rates of business creation and growth

Barcelona Activa has built an excellent track record of delivery which has given the organisation the credibility to operate more flexibly to meet previously unmet and new demands. High-quality service delivery also lends the organisation the necessary levels of political and financial support to expand and improve service and programme delivery.

Barcelona Activa is well known locally and credible in relation to the community

It is also able to contribute successfully to local development due to the public's positive perception of the organisation and its strong brand. This adds credibility to the organisation's products and services, which make them highly in demand among policy makers and practitioners.

Top quality infrastructures, well-trained service providers, state-of-the-art technology and e-services

Barcelona Activa is a leader in the use and provision of services through new technologies. The agency makes online content available to citizens and companies to facilitate autonomous work and business creation, the development of the strategic business growth plans, job searches, skills development and information technology (IT) knowledge acquisition. Simultaneously, Barcelona Activa provides an online company constitution service in less than 48 hours.

High levels of public-private collaboration

The agency's open communication with its stakeholders and a collaborative approach with other partner institutions have been essential in ensuring the agency is an innovative and effective tool of the City Council.

Global vision

The success of Barcelona Activa has meant that it has become a reference point for development agencies on an international scale. It aims to both be the best and to share good practice with the best in the world.

What constraints make Barcelona Activa less able to effectively contribute to the local development and investment promotion system?

Dependence on external influence

Barcelona Activa is dependent on external financial resources. At the same time, the organisation has to wait to be selected to deliver proposals, thus making it more difficult to make long-term strategic plans.

How has, or is, Barcelona Activa approached/approaching these problems?

Barcelona Activa competes to attract resources from different public administrations which allows the organisation to multiply the resources guaranteed to it by the City Council. At the same time, competition for finance is an added motivation to present projects with highly innovative components and methodologies.

How has Barcelona Activa performed in relation to its key performance indicators?

The performance of Barcelona Activa is best measured against the four strategic activity lines and the two transversal activity lines (Table A.13).

The agency's strong performance is reflected in it winning a number of awards including: "World Best Practice in Local Development, Habitat Initiative" from the United Nations; "Excellence in Innovation and Entrepreneurship, Paxis Region" from the European Commission; and "Best Local Project Supporting Entrepreneurship" from Eurocities and EBN best tools.

Accountabilities, performance review mechanisms and best-practice sharing

Accountabilities

As well as its clients, Barcelona Activa is accountable to the Economic Promotion Sector of the Barcelona City Council led by the deputy mayor responsible for this sector, who is also its president. The organisation is also accountable to its management board and to the citizens and users of its services and programmes.

Performance review mechanisms

As well as benchmarking its performance against other development agencies worldwide, Barcelona Activa is committed to monitoring its performance. It not only measures its activity indicators, but also their impact on the economy and job creation in the city. Its own internal performance review and monitoring systems showed it to have achieved and exceeded the expectations of the 2004-07 Action Plan. In addition, in 2008, Barcelona Activa commissioned an OECD LEED Programme review to examine its strengths and weaknesses. This review, called "Promoting Entrepreneurship, Employment and Business Competitiveness: The Experience of Barcelona" was published in March 2009 (OECD LEED Programme, 2009).

Table A.13. **Key performance indicators of Barcelona Activa**

Theme (initiative)	Tangible impact	Intangible impact
Barcelona Activa	• In total, Barcelona Activa has handled over 1.3 million participants. • During the 2004-07 Action Plan period, more than 500 000 participants attended programmes run by the agency. • More than 150 000 participants a year come to Barcelona Activa's premises.	• Creation of a professional agency, with a world-class reputation, charged with the local development of the city. • Strong co-operation with other local and international agents that allows Barcelona Activa to offer more and better programmes.
Boosting entrepreneurship	• In total, 14 500 business projects were coached and 8 000 new companies created. • In 2008, c. 1 400 businesses received advice. Over 700 companies were created and the estimated new employment from these companies was c. 1 400 new jobs per year.	• Reference centre for entrepreneurship in Barcelona and model transferred to other international environments (Bogotá, Medellín, Santiago de Chile, Buenos Aires, Rome, Andorra, etc.)
Business growth	• In total, more than 600 companies were installed in its Business Incubator and Technology Park. • More than 115 companies a year in the agency's Business Incubator and Technology Park. • In 2008, 350 companies received growth coaching through the agency's business growth programmes.	• Hub of business growth initiatives promoted by different agents in the city. • Network of businesses that co-operate among each other. • Top level incubation infrastructures and services.
Human capital development	• In 2008, more than 48 000 participants received attention in Porta22.	• Reference centre for professional guidance and progress in the metropolitan area of Barcelona. Being transferred to other national environments (Mataró, Bidasoa Region, etc.).
Employment	• In total, 44 486 people have been trained. • In 2008, the agency dealt with over 30 000 participants and the rate of job-market insertion reached 72%. • In 2008, more than 800 unemployed people were contracted to develop their skills through apprenticeship arrangements.	• Reference entity in the city for support, coaching and training for the employment. • Co-ordination of the agreement on quality employment in Barcelona 2008-11.
Technological skills acquisition and diffusion	• In total, Barcelona Activa has helped 433 000 participants with technology knowledge and training. • In 2008, 53 784 participants attended Cibernàrium.	• Reference centre for digital literacy and training in Barcelona and model transferred to other international environments (Sao Paolo, Porto Alegre, Brussels, Tampere, San Sebastián, etc.)
Promotion of innovation	• The Barcelona Research and Innovation Map offers comprehensive information about 246 entries, from research centres to entities for financial and innovation support, environments for innovation, and business best practices.	• Spreading the need and spirit of innovation among businesses, entrepreneurs and citizens.

Source: Barcelona Activa (2009), "Barcelona Activa", homepage, *www.barcelonactiva.cat;* Molero, A. (2009), Written and telephone communication and interviews.

Best-practice sharing

Barcelona Activa has been pro-active in transferring its programmes and advising other regions on how to develop tools and policies for local economic development. For example, Barcelona Activa has supported the creation of the Santiago Innova Business Incubator (Chile), the Serda Business Incubator in Sarajevo (Bosnia), the organisation of the European Day of the Entrepreneur (Eurocities), the initiative Bogotá Emprende in Colombia and the Initiative Cerne in Brasil, and transferred the Online Business Plan portal to Buenos Aires, Montevideo, La Plata, Santiago, Bogotá, Rome and Bilbao.

The agency also leads or takes part in a number of co-operation programmes such as @lis, Urb-AL, Detect-It, Invesat, EurOffices and Equal. Hundreds of delegations (33 national, 26 from the European Union and 41 from the rest of the world – a total of more than 750 representatives to date) have visited Barcelona Activa. They look to learn and exchange ways of doing things to improve and extend their own services to the public in relation to providing support to entrepreneurs, policies for business growth, promoting innovation and boosting quality employment (Barcelona Activa, 2007).

What progress has Barcelona Activa made over its lifetime?

In 2007, Barcelona Activa reached the final stretch of its Action Plan 2004-07, surpassing the targets set for it, both with regards to the volume of users and the new dimension of its service to the public and the territory.

What are Barcelona Activa's strengths, constraints, opportunities and challenges?

Barcelona Activa's strengths, constraints, opportunities and challenges are summarised in Table A.14.

Table A.14. **Barcelona Activa's strengths, constraints, opportunities and challenges**

Strengths	Constraints
• The agency has become a reference point for development agencies internationally due to its dynamism, ability to anticipate change, flexibility and responsiveness and innovative policies. • Effective programmes within a clearly defined strategic action plan. • Develops entrepreneurial capacity to allow Barcelona to compete in the future. • Good rates of business creation and growth. • Barcelona Activa is well known locally and credible in relation to the community. • Top-quality infrastructures, well-trained service providers, state-of-the-art technology and e-services. • Strong position between the public vision and the private priorities. • Global vision.	• Enterprises created have been mainly small. • Businesses created by Barcelona Activa have disconnection with academic researchers. • The "Barcelona Activa brand" is not exploited enough internationally. • The communication strategy of Barcelona Activa does not reach minority groups. • Barcelona Activa is lacking commercial products, tools and infrastructures to reach out to new markets nationally and internationally.

Table A.14. **Barcelona Activa's strengths, constraints, opportunities and challenges** *(continued)*

Opportunities	Challenges
• Barcelona Activa benefits from strong support from the public authorities and goodwill across the city. • Tourism development is a window for Barcelona Activa to the international sphere. • Quality employment and entrepreneurship tools and services are demanded internationally and there are few providers of such services. • Well placed to join networks and expand the reach of partnerships with cities abroad to attract human and financial capital. • Could make use of the international community in Barcelona as a bridge to other innovative cities to explore new collaborations. • Could actively seek to attract and coach talented entrepreneurs from abroad. • Could develop specific training programmes to support business creation among the immigrant community.	• International competition from emerging cities toughens the process of talent attraction and retention. • Should make sure that the demographic diversity of the city is taken into account in the programmes and tools offered to avoid social disruptions. • Innovative culture among companies outside Barcelona Activa and in universities is low.

Source: OECD LEED Programme (2009), "Promoting Entrepreneurship, Employment and Business Competitiveness: The Experience of Barcelona", *www.oecd.org/document/32/0,3343,en_2649_34461_43504288_1_1_1_1,00.html.*

References

Barcelona Activa (2007), "Annual Report, 2007", *www.barcelonactiva.cat/barcelonactiva/images/en/Memoria_(2007)_tcm84-38949.pdf.*

Barcelona Activa (2008), "Agreement for Quality Employment, 2008-11", Barcelona Activa.

Barcelona Activa (2009), "Barcelona Activa", homepage, *www.barcelonactiva.cat.*

European Commission (2006), "Barcelona Activa, 20 Years Promoting Entrepreneurship", European Commission.

European Union Knowledge Network (2009), "Barcelona Activa Case Study", *www.eukn.org/binaries/eukn/eukn/practice/2006/11/barcelona-activa.pdf.*

Molero, A. (2009), Written and telephone communication and interviews.

OECD LEED Programme (2009), "Promoting Entrepreneurship, Employment and Business Competitiveness: The Experience of Barcelona", *www.oecd.org/document/32/0,3343,en_2649_34461_43504288_1_1_1_1,00.html.*

UK Government (2008), "International Events and Local Development", UK Government.

B I L B A O
Metropoli-30

Bilbao Metropoli-30
(The Association for the Revitalisation of Metropolitan Bilbao)
Bilbao, Spain

Organisation type

The Association for the Revitalisation of Metropolitan Bilbao – "Bilbao Metropoli-30" – was established in 1991. It is primarily concerned with strategic planning, research and promotion and is involved in those projects which aim to encourage the recuperation and revitalisation of metropolitan Bilbao. The association was recognised as a "public utility entity" by the Basque Government in June 1992. Both public and private bodies who work within metropolitan Bilbao can become members of the project as founding, full or associate members. In essence, Bilbao Metropoli-30 is an "umbrella organisation" which consolidates and co-ordinates the actions of a disparate range of bodies which operate across the public and private realms, and across broad spatial scales.

Mission statement

Bilbao Metropoli-30's mission statement is "to lead the vision of the future through the implementation of the revitalisation process" (Bilbao Metropoli-30, 2009).

This is achieved by developing the vision together with the members of the association. Subsequently, this allows those members to implement their own strategies, taking into consideration the visions provided by Bilbao Metropoli-30 (Bilbao Metropoi-30, 2008).

Tied up with Bilbao Metropoli-30's mission statement is its vision for the city. The organisation states that, "our vision of the future is a city capable of identifying, attracting and materialising good ideas in benefit of all the community" (Bilbao Metropoi-30, 2009). This vision is based on five strategic points:

- Active and committed leadership.

- People and their values: the vision of Bilbao is made up of people capable of visualising a future community, people with ideas about how to design that future, and people with the expertise to put the ideas into practice.

- Knowledge and innovation: knowledge is the seed for new ideas. Innovation is the process of tapping ideas and applying them in ways that benefit the whole community.

- Networking: networks offer a global perspective. Individuals can join forces and strengthen the competitive edge.

- Quality of life: as an element that attracts qualified professional people, it is vital for the city's competitiveness. Promoting the city's appeal will generate wealth and competitiveness and sustained growth (Bilbao Metropoi-30, 2008).

History, origins and ownership

In the 1980s, the city of Bilbao experienced economic decline in terms of the steel industry and industrial port activities. This situation "encouraged leaders to look towards a large-scale urban renewal to start a change of economic strategy" (Bilbao Metropoi-30, 2008). The economic situation brought leaders together and they were forced to make bold decisions regarding the city's future direction. Political leaders saw that it would not be possible for the public sector to bring about the necessary change alone. This realisation led to the incorporation of the private sector into the project, and Bilbao Metropoli-30 was set up in 1991, with 19 members.

The Strategic Plan for the Revitalisation of Metropolitan Bilbao was launched in 1992 as a response to requests by the Basque Government, the County Government of Bizkaia and the City of Bilbao. Eight critical issues identified in the plan were: human resources, advanced services, mobility and accessibility, environmental regeneration, urban regeneration, cultural centrality, public-private partnerships and social welfare. These issues were envisaged to produce homogenous development of the city. The plan has subsequently been developed through a series of emblematic projects and these are seen to have "made the difference" (Bilbao Metropoi-30, 2008).

The Revitalisation Plan itself has gone through various amendments and ancillary and updated documents have been produced, including "Strategic Reflections" (1999) and the more recent "Bilbao 2010: The Strategy" (2001). These recognise that progress has been made with regards to the original plan and set the stage for action moving forwards.

Furthermore, the process of city development is achieved through the coalescence of Bilbao-Metropoli 30 and BILBAO Ría 2000, whose aim is to reclaim deteriorated areas or industrial areas in decline.

The two organisations work together in the following manner:

- Bilbao Metropoli-30 develops plans and forwards long-term strategies for the metropolitan area.

- BILBAO-Ría 2000 manages specific urban revitalisation projects, often on disused public lands within the city of Bilbao, working on behalf of the public sector land owners.

This case study highlights the work of both organisations.

What does Bilbao Metropoli-30 do?

Bilbao Metropoli-30 implements the Strategic Plan for the Revitalisation of Metropolitan Bilbao, which was drawn up in 1992, and the subsequent versions of the document. The original plan was drawn up by Bilbao Metropoli-30 in collaboration with more than 300 experts, most of whom were representatives from institutions and companies associated with the association. Since the conception of the Revitalisation Plan, Bilbao Metropoli-30 has focused its activities on furthering the launch of the revitalisation process through public-private partnerships. In 1999, the association's efforts were consolidated in the project "Bilbao 2010: Strategic Reflection", which was presented on 25 November 1999. Subsequently, and with a view to channelling the strategic reflections, the organisation has focused on projects that will enable Bilbao to make the most of the change already seen, projecting the metropolis as an international world-class city in the knowledge society. On 4 April 2001, the association presented the strategic plan called "Bilbao 2010: The Strategy" (Cearra, 2009).

Bilbao Metropoli-30 also undertakes actions derived from the Strategic Plan with which it is entrusted. In particular, this includes those projects which aim to improve the external and internal image of metropolitan Bilbao. The association carries out studies and research projects related to metropolitan Bilbao, as well as studies of other cities which can provide useful lessons for Bilbao. Another key area of activity is fostering public-private sector co-operation in the hope of finding joint solutions to problems which affect metropolitan Bilbao.

Bilbao Metropoli-30's five main roles have been summarised by its Director, Alfonso Martínez Cearra:

- identify opportunities,
- long-term issues,
- economy and community,
- collaborative leadership,
- monitor the process (Bilbao Metropoli-30, 2008).

What is the spatial scale of operation and influence of Bilbao Metropoli-30?

The work of the Bilbao Metropoli-30 is broadly focused on metropolitan Bilbao, which comprises 30 municipalities. In fact, the organisation has no specific administrative limits. The area in which it operates is better defined as an area linked by its culture and industrial heritage (Cearra, 2009).

How is Bilbao Metropoli-30 financed?

Bilbao Metropoli-30 is a non-profit partnership and the core of its budget comes from its members, of which there are around 140. Funding is split roughly 50:50 between public and private sector stakeholders which comprise the Basque government, its regions, municipalities and many other organisations that contribute to the life of the area. The majority of this small budget is devoted to pay Bilbao Metropoli-30 staff and to generate reports and undertake analysis and studies.

In 2008, Bilbao Metropoli-30 had a total budget of EUR 1 995 818, comprising the fees of its members and co-operation agreements.

However, because of the limited budget, Bilbao Metropoli-30 is always looking for new ways to maximise its resources. For instance, the organisation tries to develop activities in co-operation with its members through collaborative agreements. In particular, Bilbao Metropoli-30 has also found innovative ways to work with its members, by presenting them with ideas and potential roles it can play in projects to relieve them of its workload. In this regard Bilbao Metropoli-30 has developed for itself an additional grant funding source (Cearra, 2009).

The organogram that follows (Figure A.17) reveals the local development system within which Bilbao Metropoli-30 and BILBAO Ría 2000 operate.

Key members

Firstly, Bilbao Metropoli-30 has three types of members: (1) founding members: consisting of 19 institutions who in 1992 decided to create Bilbao Metropoli-30. These consist of both public and private sector members; (2) associate members: the status of the majority of member organisations; and (3) collaborative members: not-profits and consulates which don't pay.

Other local development agencies

There are two other development agencies of mention which operate in the same territorial area: (1) Promobisa is a company that belongs to the City Council which was created to promote Bilbao primarily in economic and other terms; and (2) BILBAO Ría 2000 is a public organisation responsible for the urban regeneration of Bilbao.

Local partners

Thirdly, Bilbao Metropoli-30 has a number of local and international partner organisations. For example, Uniport Bilbao; Association for the implementation of Benchmarking (AiB); Bilbao Convention Bureau; Parekatuz – a flexible network open to all socio-economic organisations in Bizkaia that wish to be involved in promoting gender equality; and Xertatu – an initiative of the Department of Innovation and Economic Promotion of the Regional Government of Bizkaia for the promotion of corporate social responsibility of companies in Bizkaia.

International partners

Bilbao Metropoli-30 works with the British Urban Regeneration Association (BURA); Urban Forum Network; International Institute of Administrative Sciences; the Internet Society; Standing Committee on Urban and Regional Statistics; the System Dynamics Society; the World Future Society, Internet Corporation for Assigned Names and Numbers; the European Urban Research Association; the International Network for Urban Research and Action; and the World Development Federation (Cearra, 2009).

Figure A.17. **The position of Bilbao Metropoli-30 and BILBAO Ría 2000 in the local development system in Bilbao**

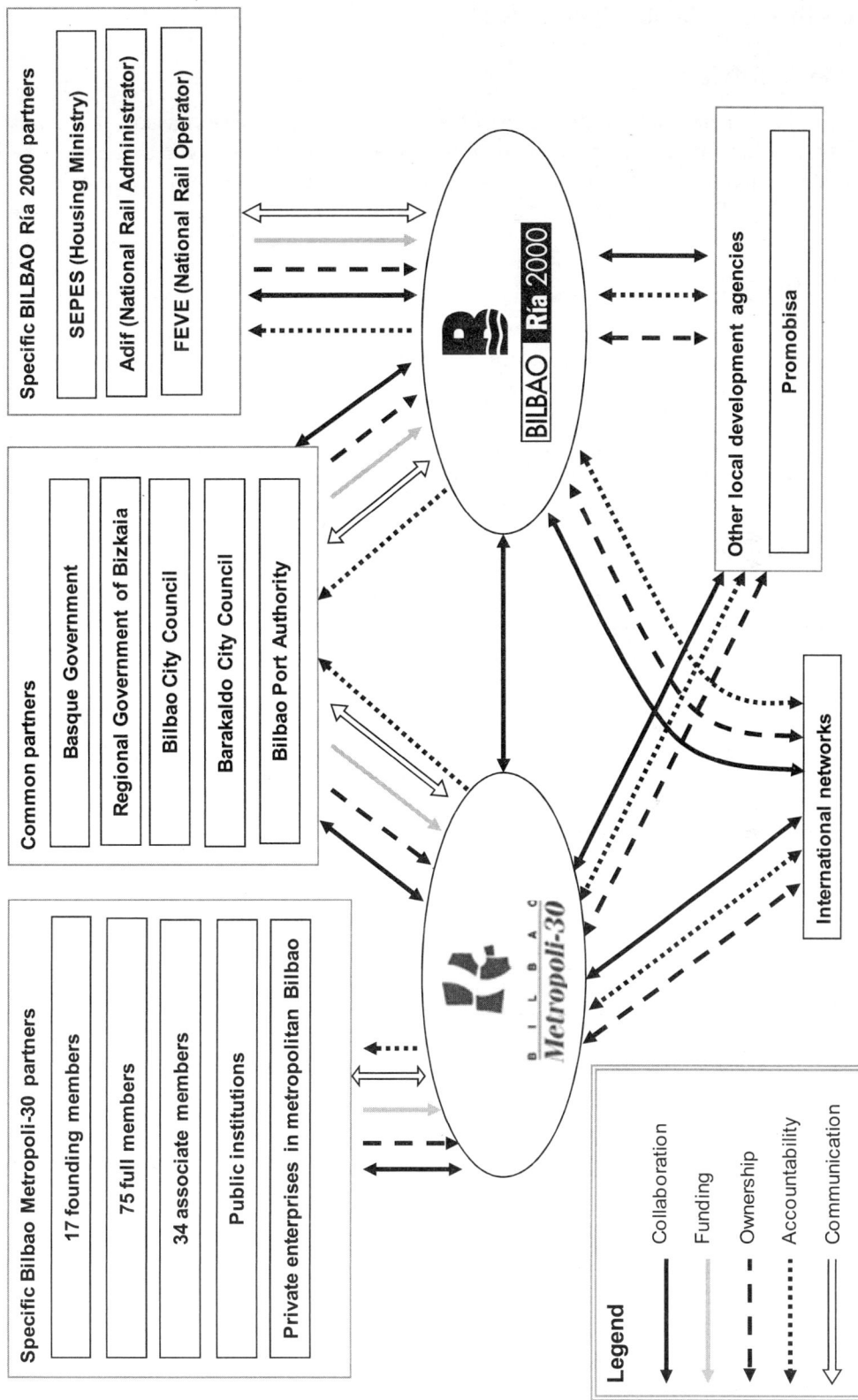

How is Bilbao Metropoli-30 governed?

General Assembly

The General Assembly comprises all the founding, full and associate members, with one representative per member, that attend its meetings. It is the supreme debating and decision-making body of the association and its resolutions govern the life of Bilbao Metropoli-30. The General Assembly meets once or twice a year.

Board of Trustees

The Board of Trustees (founding members) acts as the governing body of the association, and sets it specific aims and targets. Its members are designed by the General Assembly, but some of them are proposed by the Basque Government, the Regional Government of Bizkaia, the Bilbao City Council and the Association of Basque Municipalities. The Board of Trustees meets twice a year, often organised at the same time as the General Assembly, to allow the presence of top leaders such as the mayor.

Board of Directors

Using power delegated to it by the Board of Trustees, the Board of Directors is the association's administrative and management body. It is made up by delegation among founding and full members and is designated by the General Assembly (Cearra, 2009) (Figure A.18).

Figure A.18. **The organisational structure of Bilbao Metropoli-30**

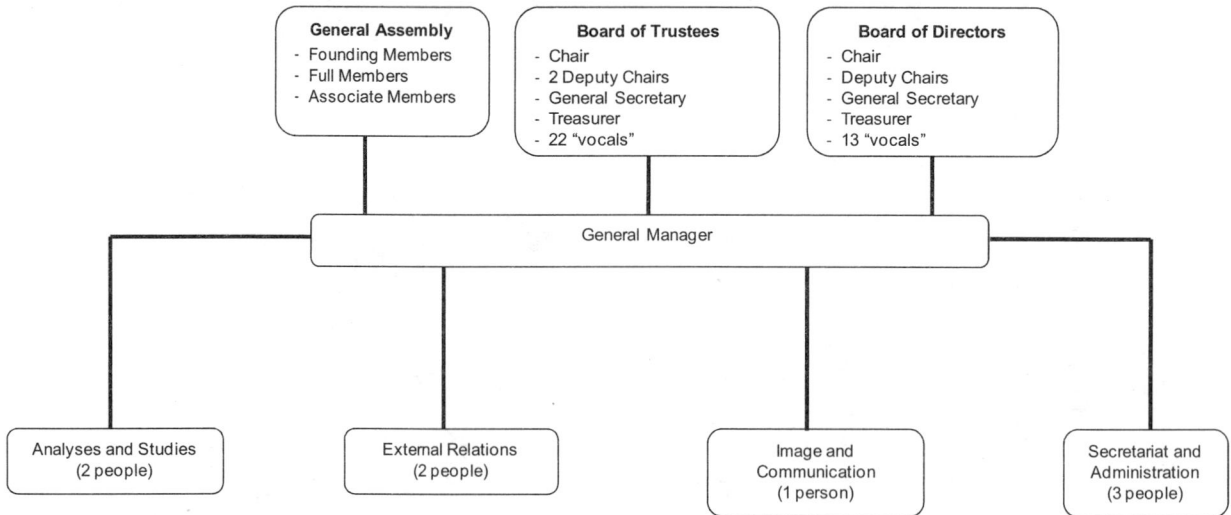

Who are Bilbao Metropoli-30's leaders?

Board level

The Board of Directors, which has 17 members, usually meets once a month and are responsible for making decisions with the Director General, Alfonso Martinez Cearra, about the day-to-day life of the organisation. Planning reports and analysis are produced to control the work the organisation undertakes. They tend to originate from the *Junta de Patronato* and often from important founding members (Cearra, 2009).

Organisational style

Bilbao Metropoli-30 has been described as visionary, collaborative, ambitious, agenda-setting, nimble, niche and focussed.

What are Bilbao Metropoli-30's key services and programmes within the system of local development and investment promotion?

Services

Bilbao Metropoli-30 primarily carries out planning, research and promotion. It also organises workshops with international experts to show the challenges that metropolitan Bilbao is facing and to offer ideas for Bilbao moving forwards. The organisation has also arranged a variety of events to increase the city's appeal. These include the World Forum of Values for City Development, held in Bilbao in 2006, which aimed to highlight the strategic values inherent in metropolitan Bilbao's development. Other events include the European Institute for City Development in 2008 and the training of 150 leaders between 2005 and 2009, which constitutes one more way for Bilbao Metropoli-30 to identify and attract leaders. Bilbao Metropoli-30 is organising a programme dealing with subjects such as company projects, government and management, property and the generation of wealth, shared leadership and strategic reflection.

Key programmes

Bilbao Metropoli-30 has been involved in a number of flagship projects designed to promote the revitalisation of metropolitan Bilbao. Some of these projects are discussed below. However, despite these impressive and wide-ranging projects, it is important to note that Bilbao Metropoli-30 suggests that it has now moved from the creation of infrastructure to the creation of values.

Infrastructure projects

Abandoibarra area

Cesar Pelli was charged with drawing up the master plan for the development of this area of the city. The physical regeneration of the area began in 1997 with the inauguration of the Guggenheim Museum. The area encompasses 350 000 square meters and is now home to new districts, a business area and a Sheraton hotel, a leisure and commercial centre, a university building and library, a skyscraper and numerous green areas and riverside promenades. The project has meant that the actual centre of Bilbao has moved geographically towards the Nervion River, finally integrating this area into the city. The project will be completed in 2011, when the Pelli Tower has been finished. This project has only been made possible through effective public-private partnership. The area is managed by BILBAO-Ría 2000, a public society of the Central and Basque Administration, but requires the collaboration of private entities.

Guggenheim Museum Bilbao

This flagship cultural project, which has involved significant levels of public-private collaboration, was designed to provide an economic boost for the city and act as an "image maker". This development has given Bilbao a cultural dimension by "rendering it as a point of reference in cultural circuits and industries at an international scale." Between 1997 and 2004, over 8 million people visited the museum and in 2006, museum activities contributed over EUR 223 million to the Basque economy (Bilbao Metropoli-30, 2008). Other cultural projects include the Euskalduna Conference and Music Hall, which will further enhance Bilbao's cultural offering and image.

Zorrozaurre Masterplan

This was formerly a peninsula which had been left to decay. Zaha Hadid's Masterplan will bring about housing construction, new industries and service industries and the development of urban and recreational spaces. The development will occupy 72 hectares and contain 6 000 new houses, two technology centres, a private hospital and a four-hectare park. The Basque regional government has estimated the total cost at EUR 1.43 billion, including transport links, business development and other infrastructures. Plans are in place for work to begin in 2010 and to be completed between 2025 and 2030.

New Bilbao airport and effective underground system

This is the main airport in northern Spain and work involved a new terminal and control tower. On the other hand, the underground system has improved internal connectivity in Bilbao and carried 32 million passengers in its first year (1995), 80 million in 2006 and reduced travel time by 30 million hours/year.

Enlargement of Bilbao Port

The port is the main element of the metropolitan area and has a huge impact, both in economic and strategic terms. The port's enlargement means that there is now more space for activities and port facilities could be moved from their old inner city riverside locations. It was this which made the development of *Abandoibarra* possible.

Technology Park

This is now home to 182 high-technology enterprises, 6 000 highly qualified employees and has aided the development of the tertiary sector.

Bilbao Exhibition Centre (BEC)

This includes a leisure and congress room, up-to-date technology, economic activity of EUR 480 million and 8 000 jobs. It is a major promoter of economic, social and cultural development in Bilbao. In 2006, BEC's activity had an economic impact on the Basque Country's gross domestic product (GDP) of over EUR 76 million.

Water treatment of the river

The Integral Clean-Up Plan of the River for the treatment of waste and polluted land started in 1981 and is now complete, enhancing the city's environmental quality and attractiveness (Cearra, 2009).

Visioning Bilbao: value and perception projects

As capital is more mobile and free to choose where to locate than ever, softer factors such as the way a city is perceived and branded are critical to its success. Consequently, Bilbao Metropoli-30 is increasingly undertaking long-term visioning work for the metropolitan area. Using value and perception-based analysis, Bilbao Metropoli-30 is constructing a vision of the city's future. Once established it will create a target towards which stakeholders in the economic development system in Bilbao can work.

Looking forward, important programmes outlined in "Bilbao 2010: The Strategy" are shown in Figure A.19.

What role has Bilbao Metropoli-30 played in the system of local development and investment promotion?

Bilbao Metropoli-30's website clearly states that "Bilbao knows that it must work together with institutions and companies in planning the future of the city" (Bilbao Metropoli-30, 2009). Its success is dependent upon its "capacity to convert itself into a meeting point for all sectors, which warrants its ability to unite the public and private forces" (Bilbao Metropoli-30, 2008) (Table A.15).

Table A.15. **Conceptualising the role of Bilbao Metropoli-30**

	Direct delivery	Facilitation and co-ordination	Strategic support and programmes	Creating capacity elsewhere
Depth and breadth of role	✓✓	✓✓✓	✓✓✓	✓✓
Specific example	• Involved in the definition of the long-term vision for metropolitan Bilbao.	• Produces the Revitalisation Plan and other such documents which guide urban development. • Conducts research and organises workshops.	• Promotes the city internationally. • Attempts to promote the image of the city internally.	• Encourages public-private collaboration.

Figure A.19. **Bilbao 2010: strategic projects**

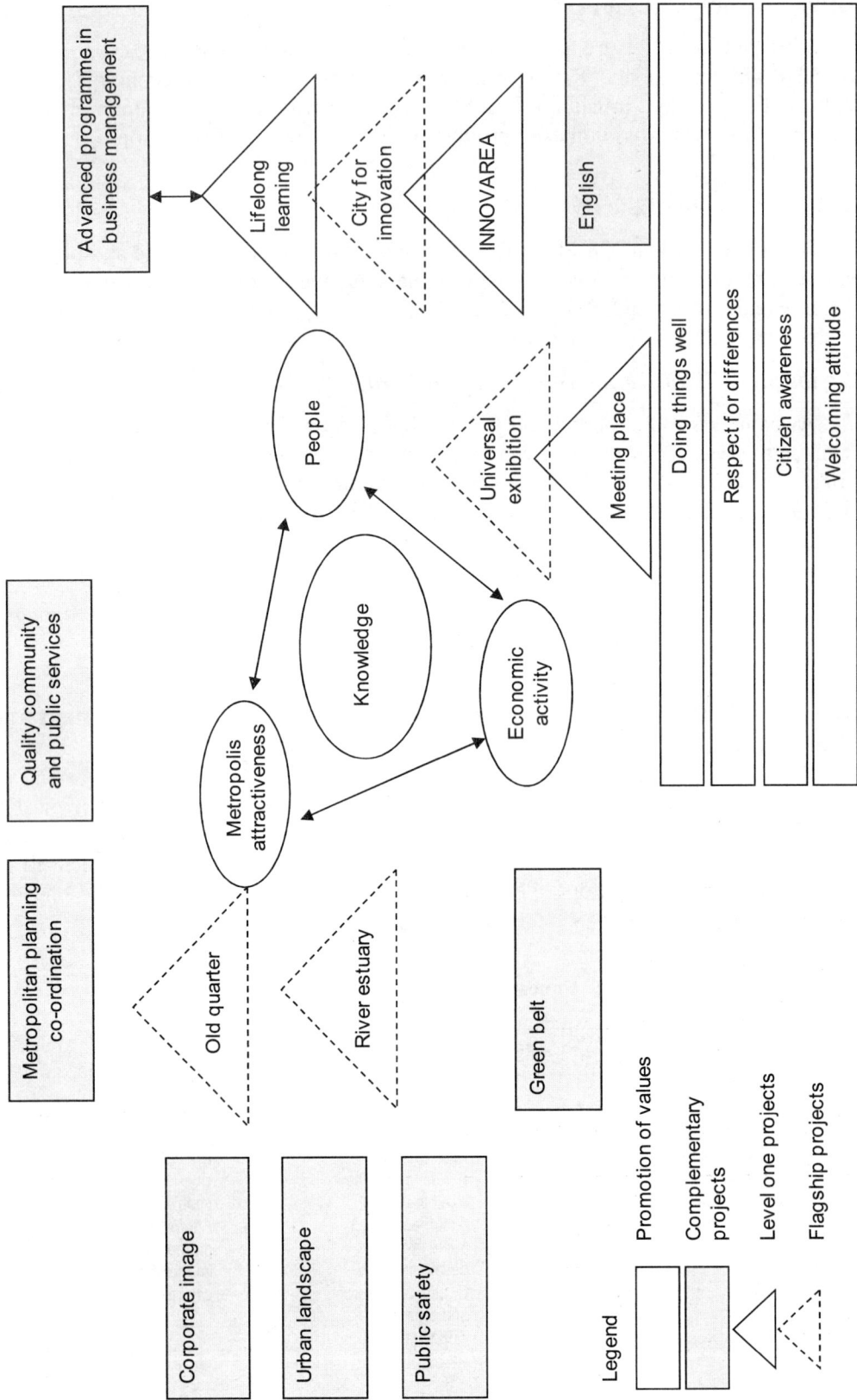

Source: Eurocities (2006), "The Liveable Cities Project Theme: The Open Planning Process and Public Private Partnership – The Case of Bilbao", *www.eurocities.org/liveablecities/site/IMG/pdf/Presentation_M30.pdf.*

ORGANISING LOCAL ECONOMIC DEVELOPMENT: THE ROLE OF DEVELOPMENT AGENCIES AND COMPANIES © OECD 2010

What enables Bilbao Metropoli-30 to contribute to the local development and investment promotion system so effectively?

Part of Bilbao Metropoli-30's success is due to its capacity to position itself as a meeting point for all sectors, which warrants its ability to unite the public and private sectors (Eurocities, 2006).

Perceived lack of power

One of the secrets to Bilbao Metropoli-30's success is that the organisation has no real power, either economic or political. Everything that is proposed needs to be first backed by its members, who are the key stakeholders in the metropolitan area's future. These same members deliver the project, leaving Bilbao Metropoli-30 to shape the process and "play Cupid" from the background. For instance, in the preparation of any draft proposal, Bilbao Metropoli-30 would first create a working group related to the subject. The working group would then be invited to examine and enrich the proposal with its input. Once the proposal is finished, Bilbao Metropoli-30 disappears and the members, who have already bought into the proposal, then deliver the work.

Low profile

Bilbao Metropoli-30 has a limited public image. Most people have not heard of the organisation, which is a positive given the quite confusing mix of agencies in the city and their struggle for position. Bilbao Metropoli-30's low profile and non-threatening position helps to make agents more confident in the organisation.

The context of its creation

Bilbao Metropoli-30 was created at a time of acute environmental and socio-economic crisis in the 1970s and 1980s. The area was suffering from serious land and river industrial pollution, as well as unemployment levels of up to 25%. The depth of this crisis ensured that buy-in to Bilbao Metropoli-30 from the public and private sector was high. This initial commitment ensured that the initial momentum has continued.

Apolitical in nature

Every time political changes take place in the electoral cycle, its members change. Its neutral role is reinforced by the fact that its members fulfil a largely technical role in relation to the organisation's activities.

Strategic and long-term in nature

Members and politicians tend to be so absorbed by short-term concerns that Bilbao Metropoli-30 has the chance to think about the future of Bilbao and its metropolitan area. For instance, even during prosperous times of the late 1990s and earlier 2000s, Bilbao Metropoli-30 took the opportunity to vision the area's future despite its relative economic good health. More specifically, since 1999 Bilbao Metropoli-30 has worked with stakeholders on the area's "values" in order to construct an accurate and representative long-term vision for the city. To facilitate this approach, Bilbao Metropoli-30 has organised a number of meetings and workshops on the subject. This approach is justified by the view that cities no longer compete on hard factors such as infrastructure. According to Bilbao Metropoli-30, cities now compete in intangibles, such as knowledge, people, quality of life and leadership.

International benchmarking and experience

The knowledge and expertise acquired in relation to urban strategic planning through a long process of international benchmarking has been a key ingredient of Bilbao Metropoli-30's success.

What constraints make Bilbao Metropoli-30 less able to effectively contribute to the local development and investment promotion system?

Lack of executive power

Bilbao Metropoli-30's lack of power is a strength, whilst simultaneously a limitation. Although the organisation has been lucky to achieve healthy support for its projects so far, because of its lack of executive power, should disagreements among members arise, Bilbao Metropoli-30 would have to face a complex situation.

Thin budget

Working in partnership, Bilbao Metropoli-30's small budget stretches a relatively long way. The limited resources it has, however, present a barrier to growth and working capacity.

How has, or is, Bilbao Metropoli-30 approached/approaching these problems?

Lack of executive power

Bilbao Metropoli-30 positions itself as a facilitator and works hard to maintain the critical relationships it needs to achieve the necessary buy-in for projects to begin and be delivered. In addition, Bilbao Metropoli-30 only launches its proposals after it has the agreement of its partners. This timing gains the organisation credibility and trust.

Thin budget

Bilbao Metropoli-30 innovates and works in partnership to fill its funding and capacity gaps. By building robust and two-way partnerships, the organisation is well positioned and trusted to suggest new collaborative projects and to sometimes deliver such initiatives.

How has Bilbao Metropoli-30 peformed in relation to its key performance indicators?

Table A.16 summarises how Bilbao Metropoli-30 has performed in relation to its key performance indicators, as measured against the eight critical themes identified previously.

Table A.16. **Key performance indicators of the Revitalisation Plan of Metropolitan Bilbao (Bilbao Metropoli-30)**

Theme (initiative)	Tangible impact	Intangible impact
Human resources	• Improved co-operation between universities, research centres, enterprises and the wider community.	• Development of a professional and skilled workforce.
Advanced services	• The development of advanced technology centres and of an industrial economy with a strong service sector.	• Development of a knowledge-based economy built on innovation and creativity.
Mobility and accessibility	• Facilitated the construction of a new underground railway network, expansion of the port, new airport terminal, tramway and bike ways.	• Improving city appeal as well as the development of an intelligent transport system.
Environmental regeneration	• Facilitated the construction of a water treatment plant and recycling centre.	• Improved quality of life built on sustainability.
Urban regeneration	• Aided the regeneration of the waterfront and traditional industrial sites.	• Promoted new economic activities.
Cultural centrality	• Facilitated the construction of the Guggenheim Museum, Euskalduna Conference and Concert Hall and enlargement of the Fine Arts Museum.	• Development of cultural industries, tourism, city image and identity.
Public-private partnership	• Opened communication channels between institutions and enterprises.	• Developed a long-term shared vision and increased business sponsorship.
Social action	• Ensured integrated development, inclusive immigration, corporate social responsibility and gender equity.	• Encouraged openness and community spirit.

Source: Cearra, A. (2009), Written and telephone communication and interviews.

Accountabilities, performance review mechanisms and best-practice sharing

Accountabilities

Bilbao Metropoli-30 offers all the necessary information about future projects and its work to its members, through its governing bodies.

Performance review mechanisms

In 1999, Bilbao Metropoli-30 conducted a study of advanced international models of urban strategy development with 133 participating members and the support of more than 300 local and international experts. Using scenario analysis, a methodology was set for the vision of the future of metropolitan Bilbao.

Since its creation until 2003, Bilbao Metropoli-30 developed and used a progress report which measured the development of the Revitalisation Plan against eight critical themes. This performance review mechanism used a set of statistical indicators, as well as a perception report from residents and visitors about how they feel about the revitalisation effort in Bilbao. From 2004, Bilbao Metropoli-30 signed a collaboration agreement with the Bilbao City Council to jointly develop a socio-economic annual report that includes progress against these indicators. These reviews indicate where future efforts should be directed.

Best-practice sharing

Since its incorporation, one of the main objectives of Bilbao Metropoli-30 has been to study other metropolis and regions that could be of interest for the metropolitan area's Revitalisation Plan. As a consequence, a long list of international networks and contacts has been developed and has proven to be very fruitful in the definition of the future vision of metropolitan Bilbao. Conferences and forums have been particularly important events where Bilbao Metropoli-30 attempts to build contacts with other regions and cities and to promote the case of Bilbao as a symbol of urban success. Simultaneously, Bilbao Metropoli-30 looks to learn about other examples of success in similar areas such as Pittsburgh, Newcastle and Singapore. The organisation also looks beyond its boundaries for examples from different areas and to other Spanish and Latin American cities for examples of how to carry out work on urban values (Cearra, 2009).

What progress has Bilbao Metropoli-30 made over its lifetime?

In terms of progress, the original Strategic Plan for the Revitalisation of Metropolitan Bilbao (1992) has been added to by Strategic Reflection (1999), the City and Values Forum (2006) and the 2001 Strategy as well as the end document "Now, the People" (2005). Progress has been made from a focus on infrastructure development to the introduction of a comprehensive set of values which are now guiding future development.

What are Bilbao Metropoli-30's strengths, constraints, opportunities and challenges?

Bilbao Metropoli-30's strengths, constraints, opportunities and challenges are summarised in Table A.17.

Table A.17. **Bilbao Metropoli's strengths, constraints, opportunities and challenges**

Strengths	Constraints
• Flexibility. • Non-political organisation. • Public and private members. • Its work is in the background of the urban development system. Because it is not a protagonist it can operate more freely. • Skilled workforce. • Benchmarking. • Networking and contacts. • Member buy-in.	• The organisation has no executive role. • It has a limited budget. • Highly dependent on members.
Opportunities	Challenges
• Enabling improved communication channels could stimulate more effective collaboration. • The creation of a long-term strategy could unite stakeholders behind a common goal. • Advanced methodologies represent the chance to deliver more effectively. • World-wide expertise and knowledge sharing can enhance work in the metropolitan area. • The involvement of citizens can create momentum and civic buy-in to projects. • Leadership. • The creation of a Basque-wide organisation called Basque Metropoli Foundation could unite the separate territories within the Basque region behind a common and purposeful vision.	• The economic crisis. • Uncertainty about the area's future. • Overconfidence about the future. • Other institutions with a similar role could appear.

References

Bilbao Metropoli-30 (2008), "Successful Urban Regeneration – The Case of Bilbao: From Infrastructures to Values", Bilbao Metropoli-30, *www.galway.ie/en/Services/ CommunityEnterpriseEconomicDevelopment/FormsDownloads/TheFile,8250,en.pdf.*

Bilbao Metropoli-30 (2009), "Bilbao Metropoli-30", homepage, *www.bm30.es/ homeage_uk.html.*

Cearra, A. (2009), Written and telephone communication and interviews.

Eurocities (2006), "The Liveable Cities Project Theme: The Open Planning Process and Public Private Partnership – The Case of Bilbao", *www.eurocities.org/liveablecities/ site/IMG/pdf/Presentation_M30.pdf.*

BiILBAO-Ría 2000
Bilbao, Spain

Organisation type

BILBAO-Ría 2000 is a non-profit-making, inter-institutional company which is responsible for large urban regeneration initiatives in the Bilbao area, playing a major role in facilitating land consolidation and development.

Mission statement

BILBAO-Ría 2000's mission is to "regenerate degraded or disused industrial sites, port areas and railway infrastructures within the metropolitan Bilbao, co-ordinating and undertaking developments that integrate urban design, transport infrastructure and the environment." Its mandate is to achieve maximum efficiency through financial self-sufficiency.

History, origins and ownership

In 1987, Bilbao Town Hall drew up the first General Urban Plan, which set out opportunities for development in Bilbao. To push forward and manage development, in areas such as *Abandoibarra* and *Ametzola*, a non-profit entity was created in 1992, owned equally by the Basque Administration and the State Administration. This was BILBAO-Ría 2000.

The creation of a specific development agency was necessary for this job because of a combination of three critical factors. First, there was an emerging consensus regarding the need to concentrate efforts and carry out co-ordinated actions for the revitalisation of Bilbao. A second factor was the recognition of the extraordinary land management difficulties related to the land ownership structure of derelict sites that required agreement among the different agents involved. A third factor was the extremely high costs of renewal operations and the imperative of financial self-sufficiency as a condition for urban renovation initiatives – a factor that called for more entrepreneurial forms of management (Swyngedouw, Moulaert, and Rodríguez, 2003).

BILBAO-Ría 2000's shares are held in equal proportions by the central state administration via the *Ministerio de Fomento* (Ministry of Public Works) and a number of dependent companies (SEPES, a public property company; the Bilbao Port Authority; and the Renfe and FEVE railway organisations) and by the Basque administrations (Basque

Government, the *Diputación Foral of Bizkaia* (Regional County Council), and the City Councils of Bilbao and Barakaldo (BILBAO-Ria 2000, 2009a) (Figure A.20).

Figure A.20. **The ownership of BILBAO-Ría 2000**

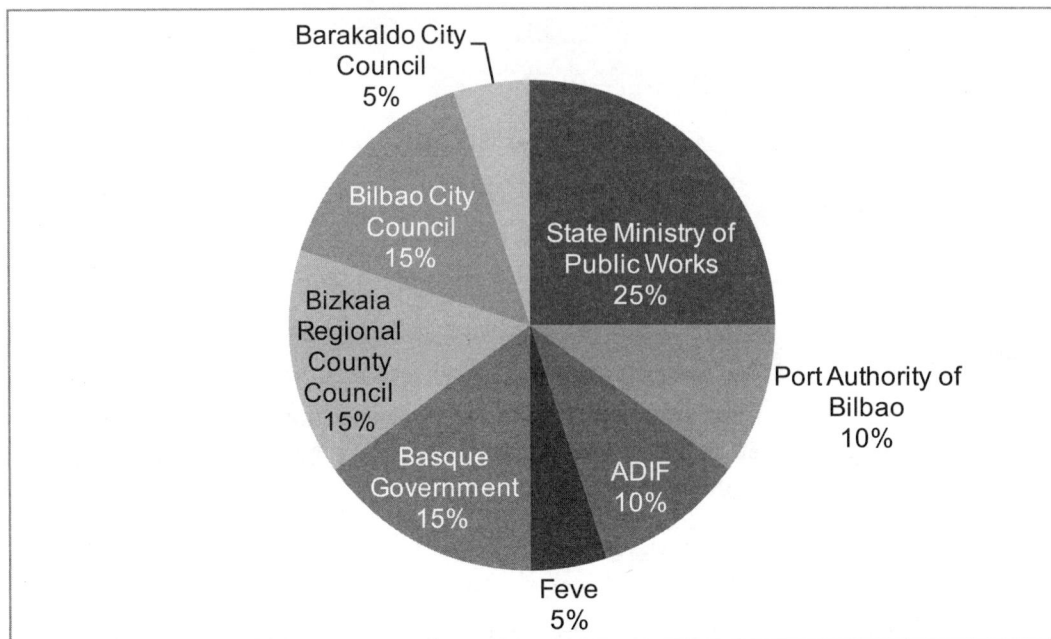

Source: BILBAO-Ria 2000 (2009a), "BILBAO-Ria 2000 What Is It?", *www.bilbaoria2000.org/ria2000/ ing/bilbaoRia/bilbaoRia.aspx?primeraVez=0*.

What does BILBAO-Ría 2000 do?

The organisation undertakes complex urban regeneration interventions, usually involving several administrations or agencies (municipalities, local, regional and state administrations and railway or infrastructure companies, for instance). Its mission is to recover degraded land or industrial areas in decline in metropolitan Bilbao, thus contributing to balanced development and the improvement of urban cohesion. To fulfil this objective, BILBAO-Ría 2000 co-ordinates and executes projects in relation to town planning, transportation and the environment. BILBAO-Ría 2000 does not have planning powers, but the planning authorities (municipalities and *Diputación*) are shareholders in the company and they have the ability to "re-classify" or re-zone land to promote innovative, mixed-use regeneration projects (Centre for Cities, 2005).

Key projects

Abandoibarra

Abandoibarra is at the heart of the city and covers 348 500 square metres, and includes the area between the Guggenheim Museum and the Euskalduna Palace. The area was in the past, the home to harbour facilities, a railway station for containers and a shipyard. The general public was denied access to it for many years. When the *La Ribera* promenade was opened over the *Evaristo Churruca* Quays, the people of Bilbao and visitors to the city were able to walk around this area to discover it for the first time. The river is no longer a barrier because one of the main objectives is to define the Nervion River as the backbone of the entire city (Towns and Town Planners in Europe, 2001).

In the *Abandoibarra* area, the *Avenida de Abandoibarra* is now open to the public between the *Palacio Euskalduna* Convention Centre and Concert Hall and *Uribitarte* walkway. The riverside promenade has also been completed with the addition of a children's play area and the new cybernetic fountain. It provides a large, tree-lined, mainly pedestrian area with broad pavements, a cycle path and three tram stops. The promenade is linked to the *Deusto* Bridge via a spiral stairway and the newly opened *Calle Lehendakari Leizaola* provides a thoroughfare for vehicles between the avenue and the bridge.

Barakaldo

Operación Galindo, as the *Barakaldo* project was known, began in 1998. It aimed to move the *Barakaldo* area closer to the waterline by salvaging an area of over 600 000 square metres once operated by the iron and steel industry. Most of the land was handed over to BILBAO-Ría 2000 by the Provincial Council of Bizkaia (*Diputación Foral de Bizkaia*), one of the institutions represented on its board. The development project removes physical barriers which had previously hampered any efforts in *Barakaldo* to play the preponderant role assigned to it in view of the strategic location at the heart of metropolitan Bilbao. At Galindo, the structures prolong the area down to the river, and the plan includes the construction of more than 2 000 dwellings, a leisure area, a business facility, and a brand new sports complex. Half the space is taken up by areas of greenery, and the road infrastructure has improved traffic links between districts and the A8 motorway.

Bilbao la Vieja

Bilbao la Vieja is one of Bilbao's original historical districts which had fallen victim to considerable physical and social deterioration. A regeneration plan was prepared to draw it back into the city, in conjunction with the Basque Government and the Provincial Council of Bizkaia. BILBAO-Ría 2000's contribution to this task was a number of urban regeneration and development projects to make improvements to specific areas and mitigate the problem of physical isolation. The funds made available by BILBAO-Ría 2000 for work to be carried out in *Bilbao la Vieja* were earned from the *Abandoibarra* project (BILBAO-Ría 2000, 2009b).

What is the spatial scale of operation and influence of BILBAO-Ría 2000?

The agency operates at the metropolitan level (Bilbao, Barakaldo and Basauri), working within similar geographies as Bilbao Metropoli-30. The scale of operation has expanded since the agency was inaugurated when it concentrated on only one zone: *Abandoibarra*. After *Abandoibarra*, the agency spread its influence to the old steel factory land and more recently opportunities have been around railway infrastructure.

How is BILBAO-Ría 2000 financed?

Besides an original contribution of EUR 1.8 million by the shareholders, the way the company operates, primarily, is by receiving the lands in the areas it operates from the company shareholders for free. These are typically municipal lands or lands used for infrastructure that can either be dismantled or moved to more suitable locations. BILBAO-Ría 2000 is then responsible for the planning, design and infrastructure work to upgrade the whole area and generate plots of land that can then be sold to private or public sector developers to generate sufficient income to cover the investment. BILBAO-Ría 2000 has also received European Union subsidies, which in recent years have accounted for approximately 9% of its investment budget, and occasional contributions from shareholders for add-ons or additional works. Since it is a non-profit making entity, the capital gains obtained are invested in the regeneration of further projects. BILBAO-Ría 2000 is presently managing over EUR 115 million of development per year (2009 budget) on sites across the metropolitan area – in addition to projects completed in central Bilbao – with an overall investment target (as per 2008 forecasts) of EUR 1 110 million, 80% of which have already been realised since 1992 (BILBAO-Ría 2000, 2009a).

What is the institutional context of BILBAO-Ría 2000?

It is an entity owned by public institutions, participated in by all the administration levels (from central to municipal government and all the layers in between). The company has a very "physical" rather than "economic" oriented role, however, the mix of land uses to occupy the redeveloped areas is decided jointly with the various authorities.

Who are BILBAO-Ría 2000's partners?

As a key agency in the transformation of the metropolitan area of Bilbao, and because of the complex nature of the developments the organisation undertakes, BILBAO-Ría 2000 works with a wide range of actors across Bilbao.

In particular, BILBAO-Ría 2000 works closely with:

- Shareholders: according to one of its directors, BILBAO-Ría 2000 "could not do what it does without working closely with its shareholders" (Alayo, 2009). The relationship between the two is flexible and understanding. This enables BILBAO-Ría 2000 to work with more confidence and within clearly defined parameters and to plan more ambitiously and over longer time scales. This is made possible because its shareholders are powerful entities within the Bilbao metropolitan area. They can provide capital when necessary, influence key stakeholders if required and provide a high level of support throughout the project process.

- Municipalities' planning departments: planning departments of individual municipalities are effectively the clients of BILBAO-Ría 2000. BILBAO-Ría 2000 works as an appointed consultant to translate the ambitions of planners and politicians into reality on the ground. The relationship is two-way. Though planners and politicians set the agenda for BILBAO-Ría 2000, the organisation can influence planning by bringing added level experience and expertise to the process. Meetings are held weekly between BILBAO-Ría 2000 and the municipalities to ensure that the relationship is kept strong.

- Railway agencies: because most development schemes involve railway infrastructures, the relationship between BILBAO-Ría 2000 and the railway agencies is fundamental. The two work closely together. BILBAO-Ría 2000 regularly updates the railway agencies about objectives and orientates them as to project progress.

- Government: BILBAO-Ría 2000 works with all levels of government in the Bilbao metropolitan area to ensure that work is completed effectively and aligned to political ambitions. In this way, the Basque Government, the regional government of Bizkaia, and the various city councils with which it works are all significant partner organisations.

- Bilbao Metropoli-30: the relationship between BILBAO-Ría 2000 and Bilbao Metropoli-30 becomes strong when the metropolitan area undertakes substantial redevelopment projects which capture the entire development community. The key strategic development of *Abandoibarra*, for instance, involved the close collaboration of a range of agencies and organisations from across the local development system of Bilbao. At other times, the relationship between the two agencies remains strong, if less intense. Though Bilbao Metropoli-30 provides the visioning for the development of the Bilbao metropolitan area and BILBAO-Ría 2000 is charged with realising development on the ground, there is not necessarily frequent overlap between the two. Nonetheless, when the two agencies do occupy the same space – a practical and tight collaboration often results.

How is BILBAO-Ría 2000 governed?

BILBAO-Ría 2000's Board of Directors consists of 20 members. These board members are made up of top-level public sector representatives and officials who are engaged with the work of BILBAO-Ría 2000. The chair is the Mayor of Bilbao, Iñaki Azkuna, and the vice chair is the Secretary of State for Infrastructures and Planning at the Ministry of Economic Promotion, Víctor Morlán (BILBAO-Ría 2000, 2009a).

Operational level

BILBAO-Ría 2000's team of experts is made up of 25 people, university graduates for the most part. It also has external technical assistance to carry out the various surveys and projects and deal with site management (BILBAO-Ría 2000, 2009a) (Figure A.21).

Figure A.21. **The organisational structure of BILBAO-Ría 2000**

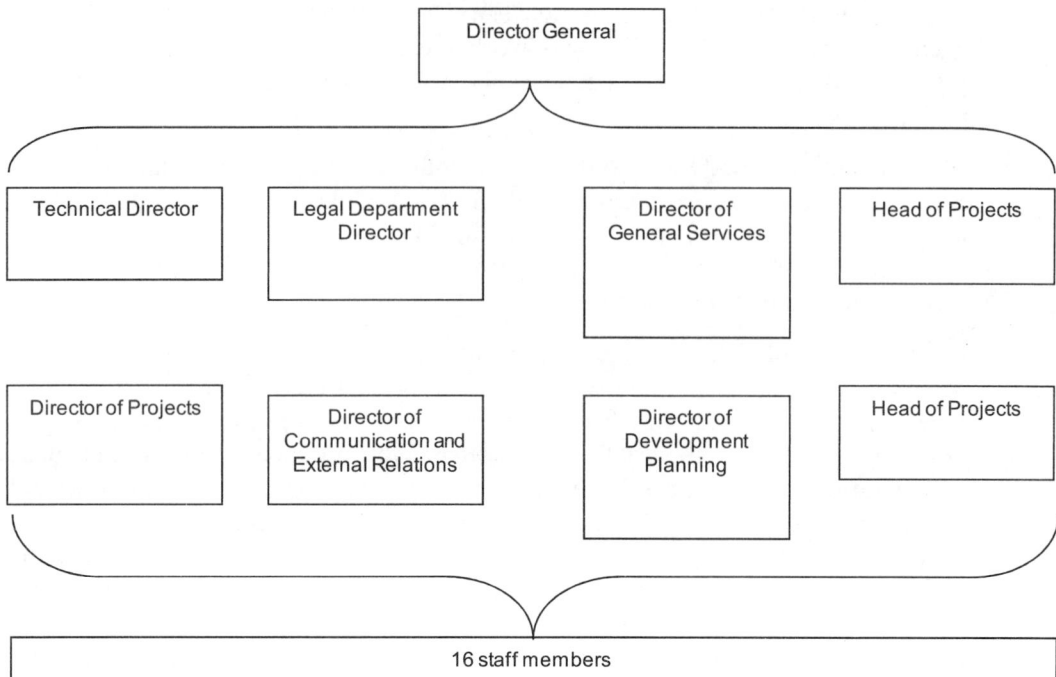

```
                          ┌─────────────────────┐
                          │  Director General   │
                          └─────────────────────┘

┌──────────────────┐  ┌──────────────────┐  ┌──────────────────┐  ┌──────────────────┐
│ Technical Director│  │ Legal Department │  │   Director of    │  │ Head of Projects │
│                  │  │    Director      │  │ General Services │  │                  │
└──────────────────┘  └──────────────────┘  └──────────────────┘  └──────────────────┘

┌──────────────────┐  ┌──────────────────┐  ┌──────────────────┐  ┌──────────────────┐
│Director of Projects│ │   Director of    │  │   Director of    │  │ Head of Projects │
│                  │  │ Communication and │  │  Development     │  │                  │
│                  │  │ External Relations│  │   Planning       │  │                  │
└──────────────────┘  └──────────────────┘  └──────────────────┘  └──────────────────┘

┌──────────────────────────────────────────────────────────────────────────────────┐
│                              16 staff members                                      │
└──────────────────────────────────────────────────────────────────────────────────┘
```

How is BILBAO-Ría 2000 led?

Board level

The president is Bilbao's mayor. BILBAO-Ría 2000's director general sits on the board, but is not a member of it.

The board meet four to five times per year and decisions are made throughout the year as to the strategic direction of the company. The board is also responsible for approving all contracts above a minimum threshold. A characteristic of the board's operation is that it works on the basis of consensus. This means that for significant or strategic decision there are a number of preparatory meetings with the various stakeholders to reach a common understanding (Alayo, 2009).

What are BILBAO-Ría 2000's key services and programmes within the system of local development and investment promotion?

The company's main areas of activity are *Abandoibarra*, *Ametzola*, *Bilbao La Vieja*, *Barakaldo* and *Basurto-San Mamés-Olabeaga* and *Basauri*. BILBAO-Ría 2000 is also involved in restructuring the railway system and integrating the trains into the new urban framework. Here its main projects have been the southern Bilbao rail routing, covering over the FEVE line in *Basurto*, and construction of new Renfe and FEVE stations.

Although the agency is known as the "execution agency", it is in fact only one player amongst many others whom have been involved in developing the city in a physical sense. BILBAO-Ría 2000's particular niche was in dealing with those projects which in physical terms were complex in nature and were composed of many components. Board composition in 1992 reflected this: 50% central government dependent agencies, 10% rail, 10% port authority, 5% national rail organisation; 50% local/Basque governance.

The key development activities of the organisation are summarised as follows:

- Project planning: BILBAO-Ría 2000 defines the brief for the master planning team, which often consists of architects which have won the tender. With a vision of the final product in mind, BILBAO-Ría 2000 creates the business model with clearly defined planning objectives and budgets.

- Delivery management: BILBAO-Ría 2000 is responsible for the physical change to the face of Bilbao. Its interventions span urban regeneration, environmental regeneration as well as transport infrastructure delivery. For instance, there is a civil engineering team within the organisation which dedicates most of its time to infrastructure development. The team is "on site" every day meeting contractors. The technical competencies within the organisation can add expertise to projects on the ground. The high level of experience and expertise of the staff means the organisation is able to liaise with contracts effectively (Alayo, 2009).

What role has BILBAO-Ría 2000 played in the system of local development and investment promotion?

There is a complex distribution of competencies, powers, and funds in Bilbao created by the decentralisation of the Spanish state during the transition to democracy. The administrative/political division of labour creates a constant arena of conflict and negotiation. In the case of urban regeneration in *Abandoibarra*, this dynamic is further complicated by the location of urban planning powers at the local level and fiscal powers at the regional one, while landownership is overwhelmingly held by public firms and institutions of the central administration (Swyngedouw, Moulaert and Rodríguez, 2003).

What enables BILBAO-Ría 2000 to contribute to the local development and investment promotion system so effectively?

Commitment

The pro-active commitment of all bodies involved in BILBAO-Ría 2000 has allowed many major projects to be carried forward effectively.

Apolitical timescales

The agency has a certain degree of autonomy and continuity in terms of the way it functions. This is aided by the fact that planning has a longer timeframe than those involved in electoral timescales.

Board composition and approach

The high level and mixed political Board has a great degree of autonomy to take and implement strategic decisions. Board consensus also avoids rifts and divisions that could damage BILBAO-Ría 2000's image or reputation.

Experience in delivering complex projects with a range of stakeholders

BILBAO-Ría 2000 has nearly two decades of experience in complex projects. This experience stretches to dealing with a myriad of partners both public and private at a range of levels. Maintaining smooth and strong relationship with the various administrative powers is a key feature of the organisation's success.

Strong public support

High opinion ratings from the general public towards BILBAO-Ría 2000 gives the organisation the credibility to operate more flexibly and autonomously.

High levels of autonomy

Design schemes for the sites are established by BILBAO-Ría 2000 before being offered to investors who are committed to implementing the scheme. This gives the organisation a high level of control over the final project (Thomas, 1999).

What constraints make BILBAO-Ría 2000 less able to effectively contribute to the local development and investment promotion system?

Declining revenues

The downturn in the housing market is undermining BILBAO-Ría 2000's main source of income.

Complexity of the market

Pressure and competition in the market have increased. Some land parcels are in the public domain which prohibits BILBAO-Ría 2000 from acting on them. In some cases, changes in land use are prohibited by the public.

Financial sufficiency and model

As it is a not-for-profit company, the need to balance the books can be challenging, especially in the preliminary stages when it is necessary to have the foresight to design the schemes to pay for themselves. In addition, as a non-profit, the organisation has no "cash reserve", or similar, to ride out difficult periods like the current one. It lives on credit until it sells finished plots of land.

Neglect of economic factors

The question remains whether this form of property-led regeneration will provide a sufficient basis for sustained growth. It is assumed that economic recovery is an automatic outcome of physical renewal, but critical decisions are made on the basis of very partial views on economic restricting and growth processes.

Finite number of projects

Across the city there is an ever-diminishing pool of potential projects, particularly given that BILBAO-Ría 2000 deals with especially complex locations.

How has, or how is, BILBAO-Ría 2000 approached/approaching these problems?

Declining revenues

With the need to be aware of increased expenditure at all times, BILBAO-Ría 2000 has developed some conservative accounting techniques. The organisation is also looking to its partners, particularly the government members on its board, to back up its financial obligations allow it to achieve higher debt levels than usual and contain financing costs.

How has BILBAO-Ría 2000 performed in relation to its key performance indicators?

Operational efficiency

BILBAO-Ría 2000 has sustained low operational costs, compared to the amounts invested.

Increasing investment levels

BILBAO-Ría 2000 is experiencing an increasing level of investment on a yearly basis. Even against the backdrop of the economic crisis, a record of more than EUR 100 million of investment is expected for 2009. This suggests that there is still a large amount of work to be completed in Bilbao but also that BILBAO-Ría 2000 is increasingly entrusted to do it (Alayo, 2009).

High rates of approval

Regular surveys of public opinion (as part of BILBAO-Ría 2000 Q&A system) show extremely high approval ratings. In June 2008, BILBAO-Ría 2000 commissioned an independent company to undertake a public survey. The results showed that 77.6% of respondents knew the work of BILBAO-Ría 2000. Furthermore, 82% of respondents believed that BILBAO-Ría 2000 undertakes developments that contribute positively to the evolution of the metropolitan area (Alayo, 2009).

Sharing of best practice

The constant stream of visitors and invitations to events underlines the success of BILBAO-Ría 2000's work. In 2008, the organisation received 27 organised (and prearranged) visits, comprising about 200 people (from single visitors to groups of up to 30 people). There was a coarse geographical distribution of these groups, with few from Spain. They include: 13 from Europe; 7 from Asia; 6 from the Americas; and 1 from Australia. The individuals involved varied greatly, often being municipal leaders and government officials or planning officers/professionals. Visitors also comprised, however, of student groups and a South Korean TV channel. With regards to being invited to specific events (generally as speakers), BILBAO-Ría 2000 has records of seven events, all of them in Europe (with two in Madrid and Murcia, Spain).

Prize-winning

BILBAO-Ría 2000 has been awarded high profile prizes from a range of external and international organisations. They include: (1) *Venice Bienale* in 2004; (2) ISOCARP in 2005; and (3) Best Basque Company in 2006. Each of these awards reflects BILBAO-Ría 2000's high-quality approach to the urban development and regeneration process (Alayo, 2009).

Accountabilities, performance review mechanisms and best-practice sharing

Accountabilities

BILBAO-Ría 2000 is accountable directly to the board, but this includes top-level representatives from all the local authorities where it works, the provincial government (*Diputación*), the Basque Government and the Central Government.

Performance review mechanisms

Besides a "Question and Answer" system with regular audits, the board is directly involved in all strategic decisions and management embarks on strategic reviews every few years (updating the strategic plan), typically with the help of specialised consultants.

Best-practice sharing

BILBAO-Ría 2000 hosts presentations for visitors (several dozen per year) of a generic, as well a technical, nature and attends forums and symposia on a regular basis (at national and international level). Additionally, the organisation publishes a well-documented and profusely illustrated magazine biannually. Occasionally BILBAO-Ría 2000 participates in publications by third parties.

What progress has BILBAO-Ría 2000 made?

As the organisation charged with realising complex and strategic infrastructure projects that private sector developers are unlikely to undertake, BILBAO-Ría 2000 has made a significant contribution to transforming the metropolitan area. Since its creation in 1992, the organisation has played a key role in a number of projects that have changed the face of the city. *Abandoibarra*, *Barakaldo* and *Bilbao la Vieja* have all had a clear and substantial socio-economic and symbolic impact on the metropolitan area of Bilbao.

The more recent success of the organisation is substantiated by the number of institutional visitors it receives, its high approval ratings, the presentations it delivers across the world and the awards it has won. The fact that the organisation was created to deliver the *Abandoibarra* project alone, and has since delivered a range of other projects represents another sign of the organisations success. It is now a tool for wider intervention. BILBAO-Ría 2000 is today seen as a key tool in the local development system of Bilbao to work with partners to plan and deliver transformation on the ground.

The statistics confirm the progress outlined above. Since its incorporation in 1992, more than EUR 1 billion of development has been planned, of which approximately EUR 800 million has been realised through direct investment. Since 1992, the total investment target has grown year on year. This suggests that there is still a large amount of work to be completed in Bilbao but also that BILBAO-Ría 2000 is increasingly entrusted to do it (Alayo, 2009).

What are BILBAO-Ría 2000's strengths, constraints, opportunities and challenges?

BILBAO-Ría 2000's strengths, constraints, opportunities and challenges are summarised in Table A.18.

Table A.18. **BILBAO-Ría 2000's strengths, constraints, opportunities and challenges**

Strengths	Constraints
• Commitment. • Experience in delivering complex projects with a range of stakeholders. • Strong public support. • Board composition and approach. • Apolitical timescales. • High levels of autonomy. • High opinion ratings.	• Complexity of the market. • Financial model and sufficiency. • Neglect of economic factors.
Opportunities	Challenges
• The organisation has a flexible business model which is backed by strong shareholders. This means that the model still operates in difficult market conditions. For instance, should the organisation need to generate more "revenue" to support a development it can: (1) ask shareholders for support; (2) adjust the proportion of social housing constructed to meet financial requirements (though there is a legal requirement to develop 40% social housing, BILBAO-Ría 2000 typically builds 50% social housing. This leaves room for manoeuvre.); and (3) time the sale of assets held to secure reasonable returns. • There are also a number of specific development opportunities available at the present moment: (1) *Garellano*- the master planning is underway for a 1 000 dwelling development which involves the diversion of existing railway lines into a tunnel 2.5 km in length; and (2) *Basauri* – a municipality within the metropolitan area where BILBAO-Ría 2000 has not worked before. At the centre of the town there is a railway yard and a railway trench. Master planning is underway to relocate the rail lines and close the trench with connecting infrastructure. Some 600 new dwellings are planned for this EUR 70–75 million development which will be realised within six to eight years (Alayo, 2009).	• There are a finite number of complex projects left in the city. • Declining revenues. • Lack of a cash reserve due to non-profit status makes difficult times more difficult.

References

Alayo, J. (2009), Written and telephone communication and interviews.

BILBAO-Ria 2000 (2009a), "BILBAO-Ria 2000 What Is It?", *www.bilbaoria2000.org/ ria2000/ing/bilbaoRia/bilbaoRia.aspx?primeraVez=0.*

BILBAO Ría 2000 (2009b), "Activity", *www.bilbaoria2000.org/ria2000/ing/zonas/ zonas.aspx?primeraVez=0.*

Centre for Cities (2005), "Bilbao/Bizkaia Visit Report", Centre for Cities.

Swyngedouw, E., F. Moulaert and A. Rodríguez (2003), *The Globalized City: Economic Restructuring and Social Polarization in European Cities*, Oxford University Press.

Thomas, M. (1999), *Study Visits and Travellers' Tales*, Oxford Brookes University, *www.brookes.ac.uk/other/aesop/roving.htm.*

Towns and Town Planners in Europe (2001), "The 4th Biennial of Towns and Town Planners in Europe – Project Reports", *www.planum.net/4bie/main/m-4bie-bilbao.htm.*

BUiLD   iNVEST
TORONTO TORONTO

Build Toronto and Invest Toronto
Toronto, Canada

Organisation type and origins

In 2008, Toronto Mayor David Miller initiated reviews of both the city's economic development efforts and the use of its own asset base to leverage investment and maintain fiscal health and a strong balance sheet. Through the Agenda for Prosperity, the city has embarked upon a programme to become a successful global player, and some of the city's most recent policies articulate this as a vision for Toronto to become a global business city, a hub of environmental innovation, a beacon of diversity and cohesion, and a centre for global education and training. Although by no means a large city region by international standards, Toronto is becoming a leader in the sectors that are increasingly coming to define the 21st century – sustainability, medical innovation, financial services and education.

The Agenda for Prosperity has a four-pillar approach:

- Proactive Toronto – Business Climate,

- Global Toronto – Internationalisation,

- Creative Toronto – Productivity and Growth,

- One Toronto – Economic Opportunity and Inclusion.

Following a review of the city's development efforts and agencies, and building upon the Agenda for Prosperity and the Fiscal Blueprint for Fiscal Stability and Economic Prosperity – A Call to Action, the City of Toronto has decided to create two new development agencies.

1. Invest Toronto: predominantly outward-facing organisation with the responsibility of achieving a better presence and market share for Toronto in international markets and contested investments.

2. Build Toronto: predominantly inward-facing organisation with responsibility for property development, institutional investment, asset management, brownfield redevelopment, job creation, and sustainable development agencies (Invest Toronto, 2009a).

Are there any gaps and uncertainties in the system of economic development and investment promotion in Toronto?

Despite the fact that for two decades Toronto has been delivering municipal economic services, including: support for business improvement areas, support for start-up services and the redevelopment of land for other uses by organisations such as the Toronto Economic Development Corporation (TEDCO, see Box A.2). There was consensus that these did not add up to a comprehensive approach to economic development in the city. As a result of stakeholder consultation and reviews of experiences of other cities, a number of significant strategic gaps and uncertainties were identified in Toronto's system of development and investment promotion. They include:

- economic intelligence and communication,

- business, job and investment retention,

- inward investment facilitation and client handling,

- identity and brand leadership,

- network leadership for agencies and stakeholders,

- co-ordination of promotion in other markets (students, sports, events, institutional investors),

- Business Leaders Club for promotion,

- Toronto's lead role in the region,

- business case for Toronto to the Provincial and the Federal Governments,

- alignment of City, Provincial and Federal Governments on investment agendas.

These gaps are, in part, the legacy of the city historically significantly under-resourcing its economic development division relative to comparable municipalities with global ambitions. Awareness of these gaps and uncertainties has galvanised the re-calibration of the entire system of economic development and investment attraction in Toronto.

The creation of Build Toronto and Invest Toronto represents a purposeful step forwards in addressing these gaps and weaknesses. The City of Toronto took the view that Invest Toronto and Build Toronto should not look to take on too much. And so, though the development of Invest Toronto and Build Toronto will be critical to the future success of the city's development and investment promotion system, there are important roles to be played by other existing, new and yet-to-be-created organisations.

John Macintyre, Build Toronto, summarises the task ahead by commenting that, "It's all about building a seamless and co-ordinated system across the whole system of economic promotion in the city" (Invest Toronto, 2009a).

Councillor Kyle Rae, of the Invest Toronto and Build Toronto Board and City of Toronto, further emphasised the point suggesting that, "We need to step up to the plate now because Toronto has been coasting on old momentum for too long" (Invest Toronto, 2009a).

Box A.2. The Toronto Economic Development Corporation (1986-2009)

The Toronto Economic Development Corporation (TEDCO) was incorporated in 1986 as an economic development corporation (EDC), after provincial legislation was passed to allow the City of Toronto to create TEDCO as a company under the Ontario Business Corporations Act. Whilst a wholly-owned subsidiary of the City of Toronto, the organisation was self-financing, which gave it a large degree of operational autonomy. Nonetheless, it was aligned with the City's Economic Development Division and worked to advance various elements of the City's Economic Development Strategy.

TEDCO has today been repositioned as a property steward of contaminated lands and the lands awaiting development in the Portlands area of Toronto. Many of the staff from TEDCO have and will migrate to Build Toronto over time, as Build Toronto now has the mandate to deliver on the property agenda in Toronto, as a result of the redesign process of the local system of economic development and promotion. The new working name for the remnant TEDCO operation is the "Toronto Portlands Company".

Invest Toronto start-up strategy

Phase 1

Phase 1 of the Invest Toronto start-up process, which began officially with the appointment of the interim board in November 2008, lasted until the appointment of the permanent board in February 2009. It consisted of three main strands of activity. They included:

1. Investigative mission to the United States: the Steering Committee engaged 17 different groups over three and a half days of meetings in Chicago, Washington and New York City in December 2008. These groups represented all the elements of the overall system of economic development and investment attraction in each city and included representatives from the city government, political leadership, investment agency, economic development agency, Chamber of Commerce and other stakeholders.

2. External Reference Group: an External Reference Group was formed to provide advisory input to the Steering Committee. The Steering Committee and External Reference Group met on Thursday, 8 January 2009 and reviewed the role and mandate of the group, provided an overview of the findings of the US investigative mission, and had extensive input on the stakeholder consultation sessions.

3. Stakeholder consultation: over three days in January 2009, Invest Toronto invited a variety of leaders representing key stakeholders to an extensive consultation session hosted by the Steering Committee. The participants were senior representatives of major stakeholder groups, academic and institutional partners, specific business sectors, ethno-cultural chambers of commerce and other leaders. The third day of consultations included senior staff from the City of Toronto. While the consultation programme had specific outcomes and conclusions, it also served the purpose to introduce the Invest Toronto proposition to a range of senior

partners and set the bar in terms of the quality of discussion and the expectations for the organisation following its launch.

This phase of consultation concluded that:

- There are significant gaps in the economic development system in Toronto.

- Success will include more than just improving the inward investment role or foreign direct investment (FDI) role.

- Toronto needs to take the lead in the current climate, as there are many opportunities on which to capitalise.

- The mandate of Invest Toronto should be highly focused and not attempt to be "all things to all people".

- There was a strong consensus that Invest Toronto's core business should be to effectively market and promote Toronto regionally, nationally and internationally.

- The role and priorities of the organisation need to be further refined and focused in the next stage of work (Invest Toronto, 2009a).

Phase 2

Building on the conclusions of Phase 1, the next stage of development lasted from February to around April 2009 and the appointment of the new board. It comprised six strands of activity:

- data and evidence: develop a clear picture of how the economy is performing – ongoing work with the Economic Development, Culture and Tourism (EDCT) Division of the City of Toronto;

- system mapping: identify clearly the entire system of economic development and investment attraction in Toronto;

- gaps and overlaps: clearly define gaps and overlaps in existing system;

- define core functions: the "who-does-what" discussion;

- develop organisational design options;

- strategic enabling framework: develop a viable strategic framework to guide the chief executive officer (CEO) and board (MacIntyre, 2009).

Figure A.22 presents Phases 1 and 2 of Invest Toronto's start-up process– and looks to the future. Figure A.23 sets out who does what with regard to the direct sources of incremental private sector investment in Toronto. Figure A.24 sets out who does what with regard to indirect methods of economic development in Toronto.

Figure A.22. **The Invest Toronto start-up process: Phases 1, 2 and the future**

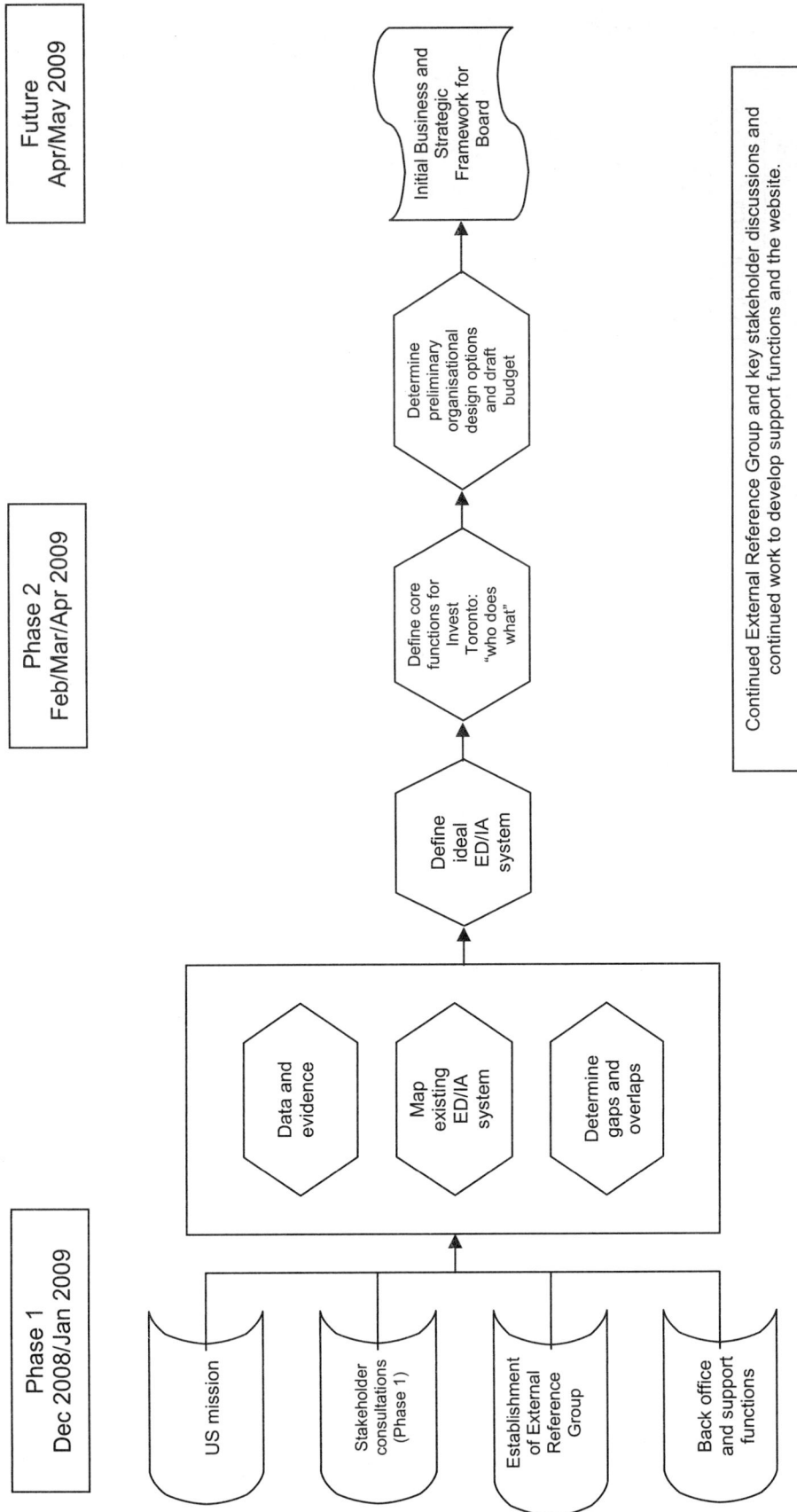

| Phase 1 Dec 2008/Jan 2009 | Phase 2 Feb/Mar/Apr 2009 | Future Apr/May 2009 |

US mission

Stakeholder consultations (Phase 1)

Establishment of External Reference Group

Back office and support functions

Data and evidence

Map existing ED/IA system

Determine gaps and overlaps

Define ideal ED/IA system

Define core functions for Invest Toronto: "who does what"

Determine preliminary organisational design options and draft budget

Initial Business and Strategic Framework for Board

Continued External Reference Group and key stakeholder discussions and continued work to develop support functions and the website.

Source: MacIntyre, J. (2009), Written and telephone communication and interviews.

Figure A.23. **Who does what? Direct sources of incremental private sector investment in Toronto**

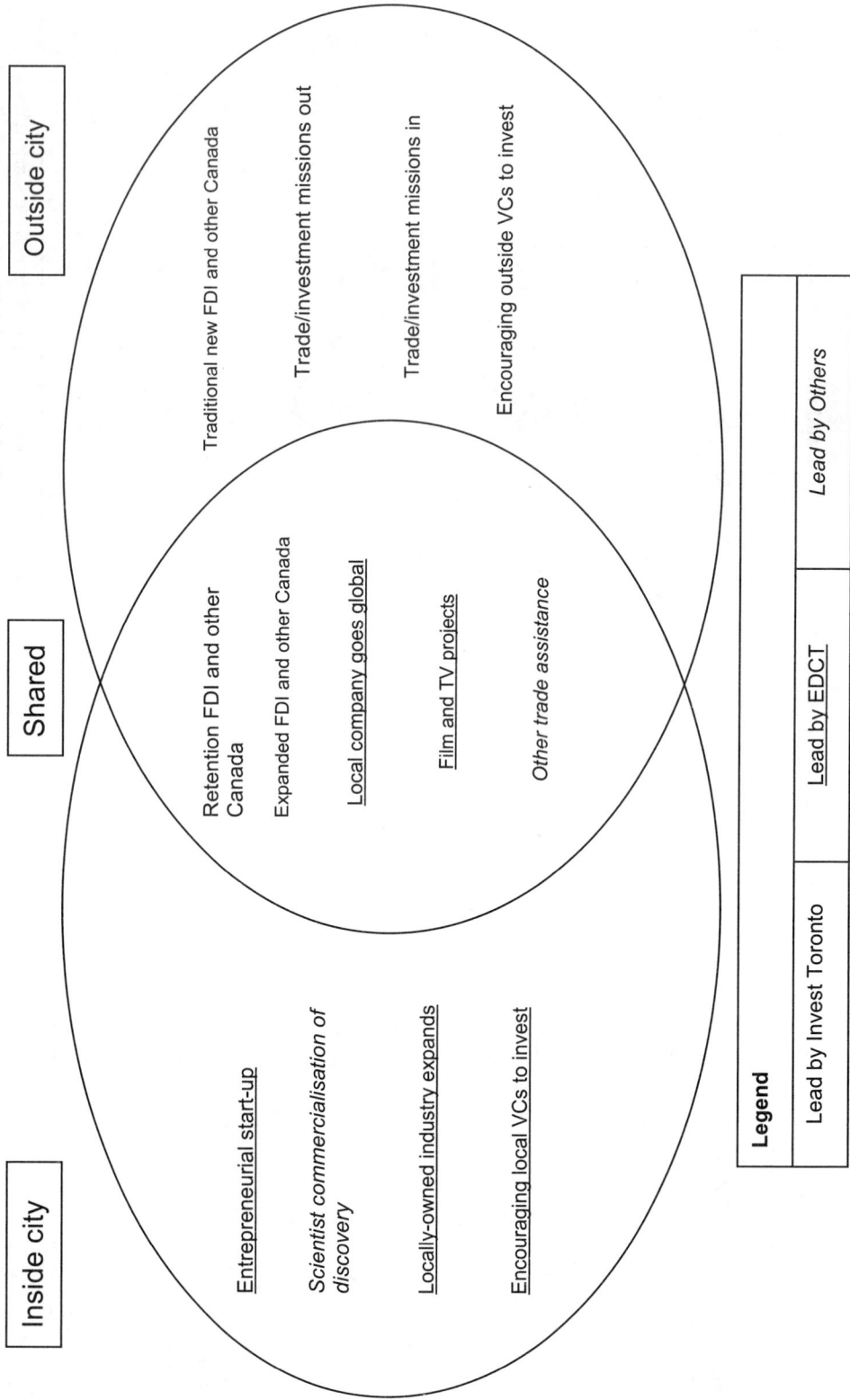

Inside city

Shared

Outside city

Entrepreneurial start-up

Scientist commercialisation of discovery

Locally-owned industry expands

Encouraging local VCs to invest

Retention FDI and other Canada

Expanded FDI and other Canada

Local company goes global

Film and TV projects

Other trade assistance

Traditional new FDI and other Canada

Trade/investment missions out

Trade/investment missions in

Encouraging outside VCs to invest

Legend

Lead by Invest Toronto	Lead by EDCT	Lead by Others

Source: MacIntyre, J. (2009), Written and telephone communication and interviews.

Figure A.24. **Who does what? Indirect methods of economic development in Toronto**

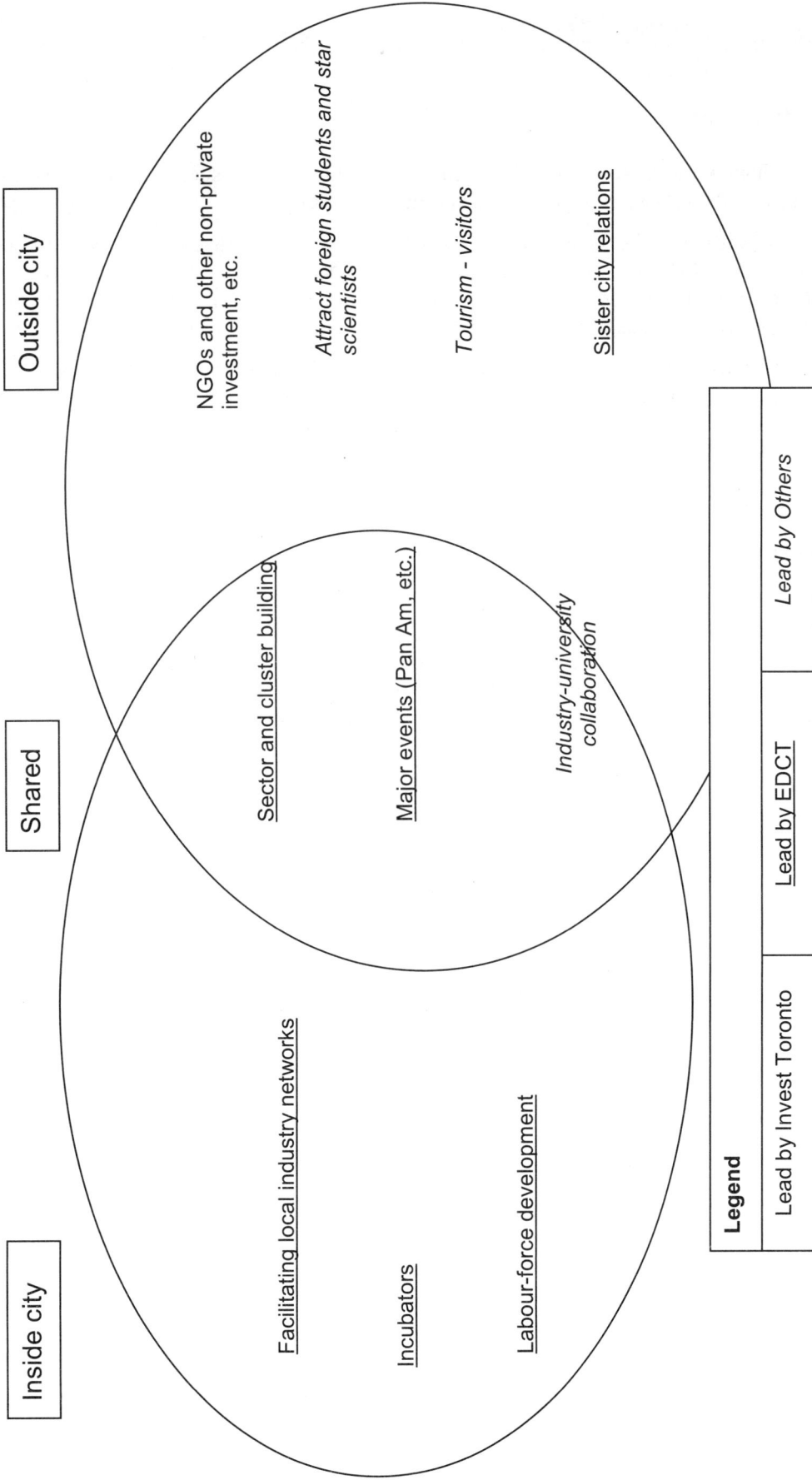

| Inside city | Shared | Outside city |

NGOs and other non-private investment, etc.

Attract foreign students and star scientists

Tourism - visitors

Sister city relations

Sector and cluster building

Major events (Pan Am, etc.)

Industry-university collaboration

Facilitating local industry networks

Incubators

Labour-force development

Legend

| Lead by Invest Toronto | Lead by EDCT | *Lead by Others* |

Source: MacIntyre, J. (2009), Written and telephone communication and interviews.
ORGANISING LOCAL ECONOMIC DEVELOPMENT: THE ROLE OF DEVELOPMENT AGENCIES AND COMPANIES © OECD 2010

Mission statement

Though the start-up strategy identified a number of issues for Invest Toronto to consider, the precise mandate is to be confirmed shortly.

According to the Invest Toronto brochure, the organisation will "engage the private sector in promoting Toronto as a destination for business opportunities, organising strategic trade missions, and co-ordinating economic development initiatives with governments and business" (Invest Toronto, 2009b).

To make Toronto the world-class gateway to North America it wants to be, the city initiated a process of re-organisation and recalibration of its system of economic development and investment promotion in the summer of 2008. It was initiated as a result of two major reports by the City of Toronto about the city's competitiveness. The process gathered pace towards the end of the year.

Invest Toronto's history, origins and ownership

On 14 November 2008, on the instruction of Mayor David Miller and the City of Toronto Council, an interim board for Invest Toronto was appointed. The interim board appointed John Macintyre as the Acting CEO and oversaw the development of a start-up strategy for the organisation. There was a target for completing the process and providing strategic guidance to the inaugural CEO and Board of Directors by March 2009.

In fact, the inaugural Board of Directors for Invest Toronto was confirmed by the Toronto City Council on 24 February 2009. The Board of Invest Toronto is comprised of 15 directors. The new CEO of Invest Toronto, Michael Bryant, was confirmed by Mayor Miller and the Invest Toronto Board on 25 May 2009 (Invest Toronto, 2009c).

What will Invest Toronto do?

Through the start-up process, a list of potential specific roles was identified by the interim board and key stakeholders. They included:

- investment promotion,
- investment facilitation,
- investment retention,
- city marketing and branding,
- city intelligence gathering,
- building a coherent investment system.

To refine this list, Invest Toronto worked with partners in the wider system of economic development promotion in the city to address gaps and weaknesses in the Toronto offer and decide who does what. Discussions with the Economic Development Department of the City of Toronto (EDCT) and other partners resulted in a clearer understanding of what the Invest Toronto role in the city might be. The potential themes which Invest Toronto is likely to lead are described below.

Direct sources of incremental private sector investment (Figure A.23):

- retention FDI and other Canada,
- traditional new and other Canada,
- trade/investment missions out,
- trade/investment missions in,
- encouraging outside venture capitalists to invest.

Indirect methods of economic development:

- NGOs and other non-private investment (Invest Toronto, 2009a).

How will Invest Toronto achieve its objectives?

As result of the start-up process, it began to become clear what style Invest Toronto would adopt to become most effective. The following list describes what was agreed:

- exercise leadership,
- be informed and intelligent,
- be apolitical, autonomous and nimble,
- be galvanising and entrepreneurial,
- be reliable and professional,
- be open, communicative and inclusive,
- be results-orientated and focussed,
- have a customer orientation,
- have a stakeholder orientation,
- have a strategic orientation,
- be a collaborative body that leads networks,
- have operational independence,
- be built around a sustainable financial model.

John Macintyre, Acting President and CEO Invest Toronto, summarised these points by stating that, "Toronto must build and implement a co-ordinated and effective system for international promotion" (Invest Toronto, 2009a).

What is the likely role that Invest Toronto will play in the system of local development and investment promotion?

Table A.19 summarises the anticipated role that Invest Toronto will play in the system of local development and investment promotion.

Table A.19. **Conceptualising the role of Invest Toronto**

	Direct delivery	Facilitation and co-ordination	Strategic support and programmes	Creating capacity elsewhere
Depth and breadth of role	✓	✓✓	✓✓✓	
Specific example	• Visiting Toronto's large employers to ensure that their needs are being met.	• Lobby businesses to locate in Toronto. • Facilitating deals between key players to achieve this objective.	• Trade missions, brand development, brand dissemination, international promotion.	

What is the spatial scale of operation and influence of Invest Toronto?

Invest Toronto will be based locally, but operate internationally. To increase Toronto's presence and share in global markets, it must become visible both within and outside the City of Toronto. This means it will likely operate a series of projects at the international scale.

Despite Toronto being Canada's economic engine and largest city, regional arrangements are still not as coherent as they need to be for the city to succeed internationally. There is a need for Invest Toronto to upscale and collaborate regionally to improve the level of co-ordination in the area. Specifically, the Provincial Government is powerful and holds significant resources. Invest Toronto is likely to look to build bridges here.

How is Invest Toronto financed?

A draft budget and set of assumptions have been developed and forwarded to the interim Board of Directors for input and discussion. These assumptions are based on a shared service model with Build Toronto, with common delivery of finance, legal, human resources, information technology and communications services. The organisation received a start-up grant from the City to be shared with Build Toronto. While the long-term budget will need to be further informed by the detailed organisational design process that is proposed, the initial estimates and assumptions were put to the board on 25 February 2009. Now that the permanent CEO has been named, Mr. Bryant will be developing these budget estimates in a more detailed way and will provide a revised budget to the board later in the autumn of 2009 (Invest Toronto, 2009a; MacIntyre, 2009).

Who are Invest Toronto's partners?

Build Toronto

As the partner of Invest Toronto in the newly formed, two-pronged development agency approach in the city, collaboration with Build Toronto will be essential. An effective relationship will healthily link the city building agenda to the city promotion agenda. As a result of this, one agency will support the other towards the joint goal of making Toronto a world-class gateway to North America.

The City of Toronto Economic Development Department

A preliminary "who-does-what" framework and division of labour between the City of Toronto Economic Development, Culture and Tourism (EDCT) Department and Invest Toronto has been developed. This framework will serve as an interim guide towards how Invest Toronto will set its priorities and further the working relationship with the City. There is no doubt, though, that this relationship will be fundamental to the future success of urban development and investment promotion in Toronto. With the goodwill created from the stakeholder engagement meetings and with the appointment of a new general manager at EDCT (Mike Williams), there is a window of opportunity now to create a robust and positive working relationship between the two. It is likely that the City of Toronto Economic Development Department will facilitate the relationships required for Invest Toronto to do its job.

Waterfront Toronto

The aim of Waterfront Toronto is "to put Toronto at the forefront of global cities in the 21st century by transforming the waterfront into beautiful, sustainable new communities, parks and public spaces, fostering economic growth in knowledge-based, creative industries and ultimately: re-defining how the city, province and country are perceived by the world" (Waterfront Toronto, 2009). In 2007/08, the organisation expanded its mandate from planning and smaller-scale project management to implementation and development. Invest Toronto will have to think carefully about how to manage this relationship (MacIntyre, 2009).

What is Invest Toronto's leadership structure and who are its personnel?

Leadership structure

Two main options were presented for the leadership structure of Invest Toronto: (1) a conventional board and operational team model; and (2) a distinctive two-tier board.

The latter would have seen the strategic level of the Board of Directors populated by Torontonian CEOs, acting as champions of the city through the mechanism of Invest Toronto. The other board tier would oversee the strategic direction of Invest Toronto as an organisation.

In fact, the first option – a conventional board and operational team model – was chosen.

Board

A new permanent Board of Directors was appointed on 24 February 2009 by the mayor. The new CEO, Michael Bryant, was announced on 25 May 2009. The majority of the board is made up of private citizens but, to meet public policy objectives, the mayor will chair the board and will be supported by the Chair of the Economic Development Committee of City Council and the General Manager of EDCT (Invest Toronto, 2009c).

Staff

A small number of staff members have been appointed. More staff will be confirmed as the role for Invest Toronto becomes clearer and the specialties it will require from its staff are decided.

How will Invest Toronto proceed?

Over the coming months, Invest Toronto has a number of priority areas it will focus on to ensure it is given the best opportunity to succeed (Invest Toronto, 2009a). These priority areas are listed in Table A.20.

Table A.20. **Invest Toronto's priority areas**

Priority Area	Description	Tasks	Responsibility
Data and evidence	Develop an evidence-based picture of Toronto's current position. Define what targets might be for the next five years. Use this data to prioritise these markets and hold an in-depth discussion about what matters most.	• Gather existing benchmark data for the city economy with comparisons to other jurisdictions. • Determine gaps in the data set and determine how this information can be gathered and at what cost. • Develop case studies on why companies come to Toronto and why they might leave Toronto. • Determine how the city government is doing in terms of its own performance metrics, such as processing times for applications and ability to co-ordinate the system of investment attraction.	EDCT Division, General Manager Mike Williams
Gaps and overlaps	Determine the gaps and any overlaps in the system that need to be addressed.	• Using information from the stakeholder consultation and other sources, identify the gaps and overlaps in activity, workflow and responsibility within the overall system of economic development and investment attraction in Toronto.	GM, EDCT and CEO and Invest Toronto Board
System mapping	Identify the existing system of economic development and investment attraction In Toronto.	• Using the information from the stakeholder consultation and the existing evidence, map out and identify the existing system in Toronto. Include graphic representation and resource allocations to each function.	GM EDCT Division and CEO and Invest Toronto Board
	Design the ideal system of economic development and investment attraction for Toronto.	• Using the information and the gap analysis, determine the ideal system for Toronto given the available resources. It should include both the City EDCT Division and the external agencies, including Invest Toronto and Build Toronto as well as other key delivery agents and stakeholders.	GM EDCT Division and CEO and Invest Toronto Board
Define core functions and priorities for Invest Toronto	As a result of the gap analysis and system design, define the core priorities for Invest Toronto for the next 24 months, to be validated by the incoming board and CEO.	• Determine how much delivery capacity *vs.* how much co-ordination capacity is required in Invest Toronto. Determine initial priorities that must be addressed first in allowing Toronto to be well positioned when the economic situation eases, and share those priorities with other partners.	CEO and Invest Toronto Board

Table A.20. **Invest Toronto's priority areas** *(continued)*

Priority Area	Description	Tasks	Responsibility
Organisational design	Develop organisational design options for Invest Toronto.	• Using the input and budget process, design a minimum of three organisational design options for Invest Toronto, with an analysis of strengths and weaknesses of each option. Core budget assumptions to be included and the permanent CEO should assess them with the Invest Toronto Board.	CEO and Invest Toronto Board Acting CFO assistance and input
Initial business plan and strategic framework	Develop a one-year business plan to get the Invest Toronto Corporation established and focused on its key priorities.	• By April 2009, develop a one-year business plan for provision to the permanent CEO and the board.	CEO and Invest Toronto Board

Invest Toronto's accountabilities, performance review mechanisms and best-practice sharing

Accountabilities

Invest Toronto is accountable to the City Government.

Performance review mechanisms

As well as its own internal key performance indicators and the requirement to produce an annual report which will be scrutinised by the City Council and members of the public, it is likely that Invest Toronto will commission external reviews when appropriate. These could be large institutional reviews, such as those of the OECD, or could be smaller and more specialised.

Best-practice sharing

Invest Toronto will look to learn from examples of best practice from overseas, domestically and within the City of Toronto itself through participation in networks and through bilateral co-operation agreements.

What are Invest Toronto's strengths, constraints, opportunities and challenges?

Invest Toronto's strengths, constraints, opportunities and challenges are summarised in Table A.21.

Table A.21. **Invest Toronto's strengths, constraints, opportunities and challenges**

Strengths	Constraints
• Invest Toronto is supported politically. • It is obvious to all stakeholders that an Invest Toronto-type organisation is required in the city.	• Invest Toronto has no track record at home or abroad. • The Toronto brand and offer is not well understood or known. • There is no evidence-based picture of Toronto's current position to support a thorough marketing campaign. • Toronto has traditionally not given full attention to its economic development agenda and role.
Opportunities	Challenges
• Goodwill generated from the stakeholder engagement process should be utilised. • The chance to form a strong relationship with EDCT with the appointment of Mike Williams. • The organisation is being created from scratch and has a chance to build a fresh reputation and new collaborations. • Emerging from the recession, Toronto could be more marketable than ever, given its resilience in the face of the downturn. • Toronto has never had an investment promotion agency. • Emerging markets could be extremely fruitful for the city. • Hosting a global event could put Toronto firmly on the world map. • The city's diaspora network could be utilised.	• Emerging market city competition may make the job of Invest Toronto difficult. • The creation of new organisations risks overlap and friction between the old and the new. • High property taxes could repel new investment. • Looking outwards could leave existing businesses unsupported. • The culture of negativity across the city's system of economic development.

Build Toronto start-up strategy

Though not a specific start-up "business plan", a strategy for the development of Build Toronto was approved by City Council. Part of the strategy involved transitioning TEDCO, principally a real estate development and management agency, to a more robust development agency (Build Toronto) and a passive port lands lease administration agency. The "old" TEDCO is now called the Toronto Port Lands Corporation. At the same time, an interim board, led by an interim CEO (Joe Casali, Director in the City's Facilities and Real Estate Division) presided during the transition phase. With the appointment of the new permanent CEO, Lorne Braithwaite, a strategy for the establishment of Build Toronto as a world-class development agency is underway. This strategy identifies the need to:

- design organisational structure to deliver on mandate;

- develop risk, financial and non-financial benchmarks, and performance metrics;

- assess existing lands for disposition;

- resolve role in residential development;

- develop stakeholder engagement strategy;

- increase development expertise;

- provide services to Invest Toronto and Toronto Portlands Company;

- succession planning/leadership development;

- develop a branding strategy for Build Toronto that supports, and is aligned with, corporate and City interests;

- establish a balanced governance framework;

- lay framework for a performance-based organisation (Braithwaite, 2009).

Mission statement

Build Toronto is evolving at the time of writing in July 2009. Its early mission statement, however, suggests that:

Build Toronto will be the City's primary real estate developer that, partners with a range of private and public sector organisations, satisfies the needs of its various stakeholders and acts as a trusted advisor to the City. It will maximise the value and economic development potential of lands under its management and act as a catalyst for the development of infrastructure and sustainable services in Toronto. (Braithwaite, 2009)

History, origins and ownership

The rationale behind the development of Build Toronto is the same as that of Invest Toronto.

What will Build Toronto do?

Build Toronto will work to deliver six key objectives:

- build value in city lands,

- revenue generation and prudent financial management,

- focus on development – joint venture, value added sale, sole build out,

- leverage development expertise,

- return a "dividend" to the city,

- over time, build an organisation that is action-oriented, understands the development process and is respected by stakeholders (Braithwaite, 2009).

What is the likely role that Build Toronto will play in the system of local development and investment promotion?

Table A.22 summarises the anticipated role that Build Toronto will play in the system of local development and investment promotion.

Table A.22. **Conceptualising the role of Build Toronto**

	Direct delivery	Facilitation and co-ordination	Strategic support and programmes	Creating capacity elsewhere
Depth and breadth of role	✓✓✓	✓✓	✓	
Specific example	• Managing and developing the City's property and land assets that are surplus to City programme needs.	• Working closely with the EDCT and the Facilities and Real Estate Division, Build Toronto has the opportunity to influence agendas. • Working with private sector real estate developers on joint ventures, with banks and pension funds on financings, and with the construction industry on new developments.	• Brand development and dissemination to broad real estate community. • City Council and Community engagement on specific projects.	

What is the spatial scale of operation and influence of Build Toronto?

Build Toronto will focus its work within the city of Toronto.

How is Build Toronto financed?

Though the organisation received a small start-up grant to be shared with Invest Toronto and will receive a stream of high-quality land assets from the City, Build Toronto will be nominally self-funded. It will utilise surplus from development projects to cover its running costs. In addition, there is scope for this surplus to be invested in Build Toronto's sister organisation, Invest Toronto. The exact dimensions of this arrangement are to be decided (MacIntyre, 2009).

Who are Build Toronto's partners?

The City of Toronto

Build Toronto will play an arm's length, real estate development role for the City. Essentially, Build Toronto will be the repository for the City's surplus real estate assets, which it will then manage and develop in line with the City's building targets. The City of Toronto is also the principal shareholder in the organisation, and partners within the City include:

- Economic Development Department (EDCT): within City Council, the EDCT is a key partner. Build Toronto will respond to and incorporate the key aims and objectives around economic development, such as job creation and the preservation of employment lands into its agenda.

- Facilities and Real Estate Division: this organisation is the "in-house" city resource for real estate. Build Toronto represents the external repository for real estate in Toronto. The two will have to co-ordinate their activities to ensure that real estate management occurs effectively in the city.

The City is likely to benefit fiscally from the work of Build Toronto.

Invest Toronto

There is much scope for Build Toronto and Invest Toronto to complement one another effectively. Not only is there a sharing of offices and back office resources, the two can work together on a project-by-project basis. For instance, Invest Toronto might identify a business wishing to locate in Toronto that needs a large block of office space or wishes to construct a plant on remediated port lands. Build Toronto could satisfy this need. There is likely to be a funding element, where Build Toronto makes a financial contribution to the ongoing operations of Invest Toronto, but the dimensions are yet to be decided.

The real estate and development community

Build Toronto will nurture healthy relationships with real estate developers, property owners, pension funds, development financiers and investors to facilitate its work.

Institutional land owners

Build Toronto will build relationships with institutional land owners such as universities, school boards, community colleges, the Housing Corporation, the Parking Authority, the Transit Commission and the Provincial and Federal Governments, including their land development agencies, Ontario Realty Corporation, and Canada Lands Corporation.

Waterfront Toronto

There will be lands that are near the waterfront area, but not necessarily in the area, that Build Toronto will inherit. Build Toronto will collaborate with Waterfront Toronto to making sure that the plans of both organisations align and strategic objectives are met (MacIntyre, 2009).

How is Build Toronto's leadership structured and who are its personnel?

Board level

The inaugural Board of Directors for Build Toronto was confirmed by the Toronto City Council on 24 February 2009. It is made up of 12 members.

In late April 2009, following a lengthy and competitive recruitment process, Canadian development executive Lorne Braithwaite was named CEO. The following day, the Board of Directors for Build Toronto then named Derek Ballantyne, who was CEO of Toronto Community Housing Corporation, as its first chief operating officer (Build Toronto, 2009).

Staff

Build Toronto will have a starting staff of approximately 30-35 people. This could rise to around 50 within two years. These figures show that Build Toronto will be a larger organisation than both Invest Toronto and Toronto Economic Development Corporation (TEDCO).

At present, apart from the CEO, the senior management team numbers four highly qualified and experienced individuals in the field of real estate development.

A full organogram is under current development and so cannot yet be reproduced. The structure of the organisation is underpinned by several important factors, which include:

- Structure is designed to achieve major shareholder goals.

- Provides ability to develop and effectively manage public-private partnerships.

- Capital-intensive business requires additional resources and expertise in Development, Finance and Treasury functions.

- Provides capacity to engage stakeholders effectively.

- Ensures that primary focus is on real estate development and maximising financial and non-financial value from surplus lands.

- Cohesive and "lean-launch" management structure that can build in the future (MacIntyre, 2009).

Build Toronto's accountabilities, performance review mechanisms and best-practice sharing

Accountability

At present, Build Toronto is solely accountable to the City. As the organisation develops, however, it will become accountable to its employees, shareholders and the wider community.

Performance review mechanisms

Build Toronto's success will be measured against financial and non-financial key performance metrics which have yet to be decided.

Best-practice sharing

It is too early in Build Toronto's development for the organisation to be sharing best practice widely. Though its start-up process has been captured in this book, Build Toronto will share its experiences more widely as it evolves (MacIntyre, 2009).

What are Build Toronto's strengths, constraints, opportunities and challenges?

Build Toronto's strengths, constraints, opportunities and challenges are summarised in Table A.23.

Table A.23. **Build Toronto's strengths, constraints, opportunities and challenges**

Strengths	Constraints
• The start-up process has been structured to see that a stream of property assets come to the organisation. • Expertise, understanding and clarity when dealing and partnering with the private sector. • Arm's length positioning from the City allows Build Toronto to take advantage of added nimbleness, independence and flexibility. • Expertise and experience of the management team.	• Performance measures need to be defined quickly. • The organisation needs early wins. • There is a need to demonstrate that the organisation is credible. • In the current economic downturn, it is difficult to obtain capital funding.
Opportunities	Challenges
• Differentiating itself from former TEDCO will give Build Toronto the opportunity to flourish. • Rich inventory of property will be under Build Toronto's auspices. • There is an increasing desire on the part of the City to be more pro-active and effective in the area of real estate and development. • The senior ranks within City Council are embracing this agenda. • The quality of the board and senior management team allow Build Toronto to tap into excellent networks. • New relationships can be formed and existing relationships can be consolidated. • With falling land prices, now is an excellent time to buy and develop land, if sufficient capital can be secured.	• Balancing the potential conflict between generating revenue, creating economic activity, social objectives and environmental issues. • Establishing a sustainable partnership culture in a public environment. • Create an effective working relationship with the shareholder. • Developing a competitive and transparent joint venture selection process. • Develop effective strategy for subsidiaries. • Financing and establishment of debt mechanisms. • Initial working capital and equity funding requirements. • Ability to attract and retain appropriate talent for the organisation.

Concluding remarks

In early 2010, Toronto has now fully established Invest Toronto and Build Toronto as the two lead organisations for the development of the city. They will work closely with the City Council and EDCT in particular. These two new development agencies have rapidly helped to develop the capacity and partnerships to enable Toronto to deliver an enhanced scale of economic development intervention and to broker a more complementary approach between the City, the private sector and other public sector partners.

The organogram that follows (Figure A.25) reveals the local development system within which Invest Toronto and Build Toronto operate.

Figure A.25. **The position of Invest Toronto and Build Toronto in the system of economic development and investment promotion in Toronto**

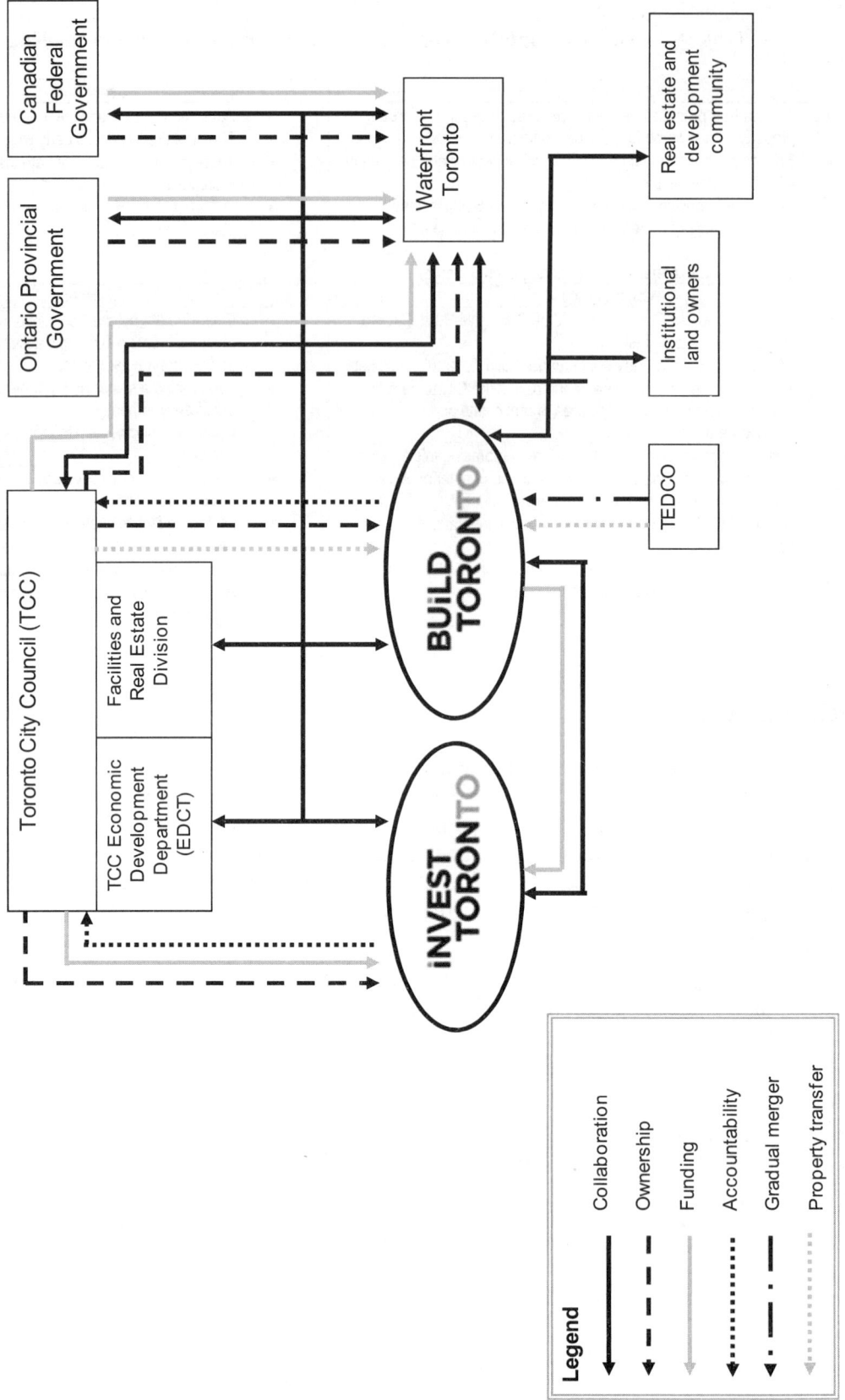

Legend

Collaboration	
Ownership	
Funding	
Accountability	
Gradual merger	
Property transfer	

References

Braithwaite, L. (2009), "Build Toronto", presentation, Build Toronto.

Build Toronto (2009), "About Us", *www.buildtoronto.ca/about-build-toronto.shtml.*

Invest Toronto (2009a), "Invest Toronto Start Up Strategy Report", Invest Toronto.

Invest Toronto (2009b), "Toronto – Building the New Economy", Invest Toronto.

Invest Toronto (2009c), "About Us", *www.investtoronto.ca/about-invest-toronto.shtml.*

MacIntyre, J. (2009), Written and telephone communication and interviews.

Waterfront Toronto (2009), "About Us", *www.waterfrontoronto.ca/dynamic.php? first=43fa759348c04.*

cape town
partnership

Cape Town Partnership
Cape Town, South Africa

Organisation type and origins

The Cape Town Partnership (CTP) was established in July 1999 by the City of Cape Town and key private sector partners to manage, promote and develop the Cape Town Central City. The Partnership's vision is of an "inclusive, productive and diverse city centre that retains its historic character and reflects a common identity for all the people of Cape Town." A city centre management vehicle, the Central City Improvement District (CCID) was launched by the Partnership in November 2000, as an integrated operation within the CTP, but with a separate board and financing mechanism (CTP, 2006).

The Partnership's bifurcated model has two distinctive but overlapping operations:

- the CTP itself: a strategic public-private partnership for the long-term development of the Central City;

- the Central City Improvement District: a Central City urban management organisation delivering services to improve the attractiveness, performance, safety and the sanitation of Cape Town's Central City.

These two entities share a common corporate resource base and institutional arrangements whilst reporting to distinct boards.

Mission statement

The aims, goals and focus of the CTP are split into three categories: "vision", "mission", and "core functions".

Vision

"An inclusive, productive and diverse city centre that retains its historic character and reflects a common identity for all the people of Cape Town." (CTP, 2006)

Mission

"The Cape Town Partnership strives to develop, manage and promote the Cape Town Central City as a place for all and a leading centre for commercial, retail, residential, cultural, tourism, education, entertainment and leisure activities." (CTP, 2006)

Core functions

The core functions of the CTP are to:

- mobilise the public and private sectors and other stakeholders around common development objectives;

- consolidate the Central City as the economic, social and cultural heart of the Cape Town metropolitan region;

- broaden access to the benefits, services and opportunities in the Central City for all the people of Cape Town;

- co-ordinate and facilitate urban regeneration programmes;

- guide decision making and direct resources into solving the economic and social challenges facing the Central City;

- contribute to the overall economic and social development of the city of Cape Town (CTP, 2007).

History, origins and ownership

The CTP was established as a Section 21 Company in July 1999 by the City of Cape Town, the South African Property Owners' Association (SAPOA), the Cape Town Regional Chamber of Commerce and Industry, and other stakeholders. It was inaugurated in response to rising concerns about commercial disinvestment in the Central City as a result of perceived high levels of crime and as a result of pursuing the agenda of developing other, non-Central City, locations. There was a perception that Central City failure would lead to significant and negative economic, fiscal and social consequences. In response to this, the CTP was created to arrest decline before it became irreversible.

The history of the Cape Town Partnership can be described roughly as follows:

- Establishment (1996-99): discussions took place, mainly between central business district (CBD) property owners and businesses and the City of Cape Town, around the need for a collective approach to solving the problems of the Central City. Various *ad hoc* initiatives were put in place (*e.g.* CCTV cameras, Broom Brigade) but the decision is taken to initiate a formally structured partnership to sustain efforts. The Partnership is launched in July 1999 and the CCID in November 2000.

- Implementation (1999-2002): the focus was on improving the performance of the Central City by making the area safe and clean in order to restore business and public confidence, stem capital flight and rescue dwindling municipal revenues.

- Urban regeneration (2003-05): the focus was on attracting private sector investment to regenerate commercial buildings; however, significant conversion of under-utilised B- and C-grade office buildings to residential accommodation occurs. The East City Regeneration Conference took place in order to promote investment in an under-developed part of the Central City. There was a growing focus on upgrading public spaces to encourage public activities; however, there was still minimal public sector investment in the Central City due to the need to extend basic municipal services to more disadvantaged areas of the city.

- Broadening the Partnership (2005-07): the Partnership's vision and mission was broadened to focus on inclusive development. The CCID's social development and job creation programme was strengthened. New partners from the social, cultural, environmental and educational sectors were drawn onto the Partnership's board, as well as representation from other public sector bodies such as the Western Cape Provincial Government.

- Building the long-term agenda (2007-09): new programmes, such as Creative Cape Town and the CBD Energy Efficiency Initiative, are established. While the Partnership continues to focus on improving the performance of the Central City through CCID urban management programmes and partnerships, a Central City Development Strategy (CCDS) is drawn up to build a long-term agenda for action. Massive public sector investment begins to take place, mainly due to preparations for the 2010 FIFA World Cup (Boraine, 2009).

What does the Cape Town Partnership do?

The CTP does not duplicate or replace the role of the public sector, particularly its statutory and regulatory roles, but seeks to add value to the public services and planning processes. In conjunction with a wide range of stakeholders, the Partnership acts as an initiator, facilitator, co-ordinator and manager of projects. The CTP also manages the Central City Improvement District (CCID), a non-profit organisation that provides complementary services and programmes that make the Central City a cleaner, safer, and more attractive place – conducive for development, investment and growth (CTP, 2008a).

The four core CCID functions are:

- security,

- urban management and cleansing,

- social development and job creation,

- local marketing and communications (CCID, 2007).

What is the Cape Town Partnership's spatial scale of operation and influence?

The CTP has had an explicit focus on the Central City of Cape Town. The Central City includes the traditional central business district of Cape Town. It also includes the historical 350-year-old "Old Town", the East City and the Foreshore, as well as Woodstock, District Six, Gardens, the Bo Kaap, Green Point, the V&A Waterfront and the Port (Figures A.26 and A.27). The CCID more specifically focuses on the CBD.

Figure A.26. **The Cape Town Partnership operating areas: the Central City Development Strategy boundary**

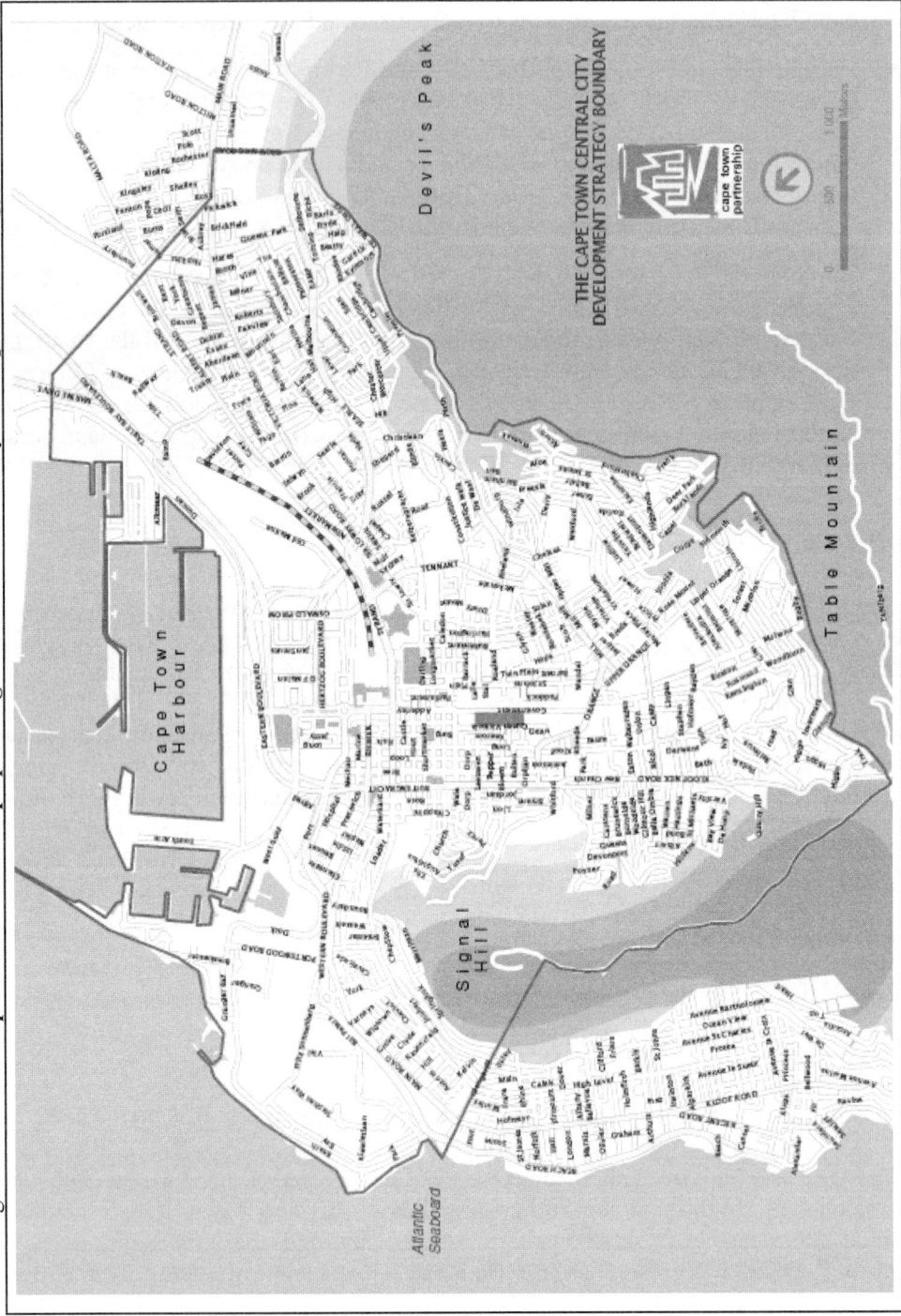

Source: Boraine, A. (2009), Written and telephone communication and interviews.

Figure A.27. **The Cape Town Central City area**

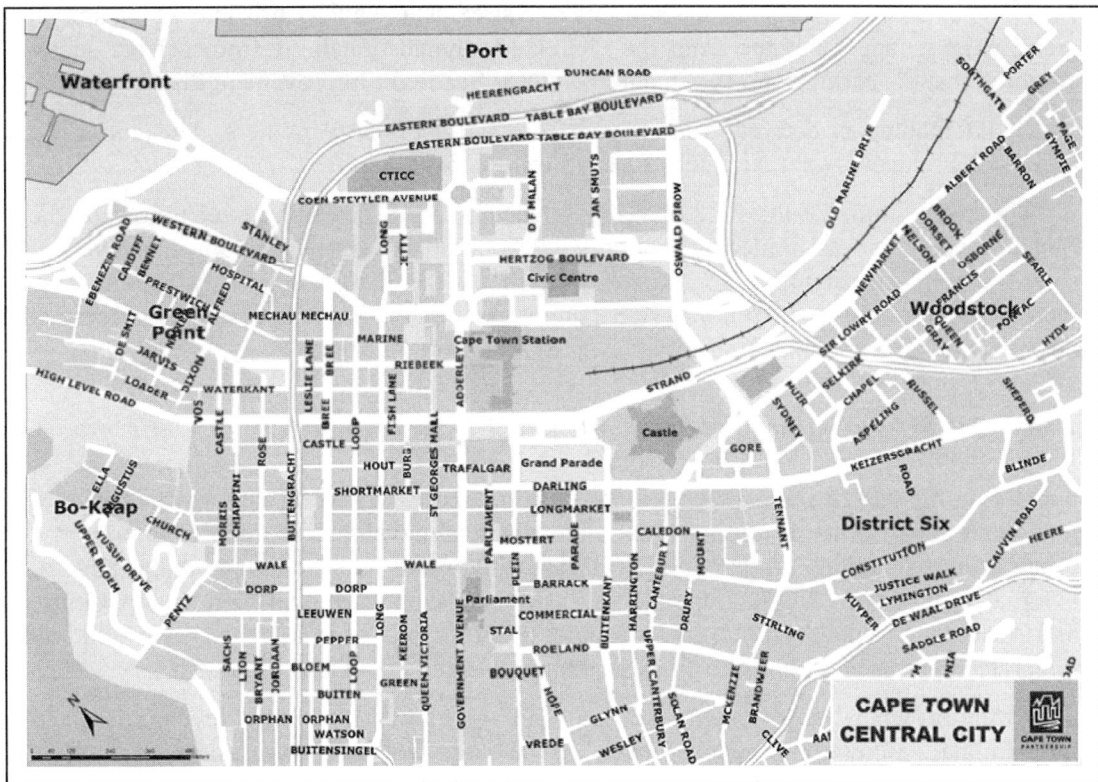

Source: Boraine, A. (2009), Written and telephone communication and interviews.

Increasingly, there has been a draw to expand the activities of the CTP to the city scale for two main reasons: (1) development activities are not always neatly confined to the Central City; and (2) there is no present organisation which co-ordinates city-wide development and investment promotion in Cape Town.

One example of a tangible intervention outside the Central City includes the coaching and mentoring of a number of the 18 City Improvement Districts and emerging development partnerships across Cape Town.

In short, the core business of the CTP has been and is currently confined to the Central City despite there being a natural pull to operate in more areas city-wide. There are a number of reasons for this including: (1) the lack of resources to operate at a larger spatial scale; (2) the fact there still remains a sizeable task in the Central City; (3) the job of maintaining the health of the Central City is critical; (4) there is a real risk of mission creep if the spatial mandate of the CTP is expanded; and (5) the spatial focus of the CTP is a real strength.

John Bielich, Director of Ingenuity Property Investments, commented that, "The Cape Town CBD has unique features that very few worldwide CBDs have and that no decentralised commercial nodes can provide. We have a lot of faith in the successful future of the Cape Town CBD and hence are preparing to make a significant investment in its future" (Boraine, 2009).

How is the Cape Town Partnership financed?

CTP revenue is principally made up of five streams: (1) a City of Cape Town annual grant; (2) a management fee from the CCID; (3) annual donations from private sector corporations; (4) parking and film income; and (5) Sea Point improvement district fees.

CCID income is derived from levies from CBD property owners. The combined CTP/CCID budget is approximately ZAR 40 million per annum.

The contribution of the City of Cape Town has been increasing over time. For the first few years, it was limited to around ZAR 500 000 million per annum. However, in recent years, in recognition of the role played by the Partnership, City funding has increased to around ZAR 6.5 million per annum, paid on the basis of a three-year contract between the Partnership and the City (CTP, 2007) (Table A.24).

What is the institutional context of the Cape Town Partnership?

Within the city of Cape Town, the Partnership and CCID work with a wide range of municipal departments, including economic and social development, municipal property, urban design, planning, tourism, policing, cleansing, roads and sanitation, and a range of external agencies, including Cape Town Tourism, the International Convention Centre and Accelerate Cape Town, to draw together a wide range of stakeholders and build an integrated approach to Central City management, promotion and development.

At the provincial government level, the CTP works with economic development and international promotion agencies such as Wesgro (official investment and trade promotion agency for the Western Cape) and Cape Town Routes Unlimited (tourism) to ensure that strategies are aligned.

The organogram that follows (Figure A.28) reveals the local development system within which CTP operates.

Who are the Cape Town Partnership's main partners?

Because of the Cape Town Partnership's limited size and budget, it relies heavily on partnership working and relationship building to make an impact in the Central City and for benefits to carry beyond its boundaries. As Andrew Boraine, the Chief Executive of the CTP, suggests, "the Cape Town Partnership is only as good as its partners" (CTP, 2008b).

In this regard, there are three key relationships upon which the CTP relies.

The city government

The relationship with the mayor and the City's own Economic Development Department is critical to creating the space and goodwill for the CTP to manage, promote and develop the Central City. Without an open and healthy dialogue with the City Government, the CTP could be judged more critically. With the City Government having such a widespread involvement in the business of the Central City, its support is critical to the performance of the CTP.

Table A.24. The Cape Town Partnership's financial statements for the year ending 30 June 2008

Income statement (top left); Detailed revenue (bottom left); Detailed expenditure (top right)

Income statement

	2008 ZAR	2007 ZAR
Revenue	7 826 822	8 194 459
Operating expenses	(7 296 057)	(8 922 151)
Other income	490 340	805 478
Surplus from operations	1 021 105	77 786
Finance income	20 852	29 966
Net surplus for the year	1 041 957	107 752

Detailed revenue

	2008 ZAR	2007 ZAR
Revenue	7 826 822	8 194 459
City Improvement District administration fees	816 610	3 885 714
Sea Point Improvement District fees	270 344	394 320
City of Cape Town revenue	5 500 000	2 650 000
Parking and film income	1 239 868	1 264 425
Other income	511 213	835 444
Interest	20 873	29 966
Sundry Income	490 340	805 478
	8 338 035	9 029 903
Expenditure	7 296 078	8 922 151
Net surplus	1 041 957	107 752

Detailed expenditure

	2008 ZAR	2007 ZAR
EXPENDITURE	(7 296 078)	(8 922 151)
Administration fees	11 500	-
Advertising and promotions	28 068	-
Auditors remuneration	71 806	84 150
Bank charges	11 328	10 138
Cleaning	7 124	-
Computer expenses	15 004	38 570
Depreciation	151 467	103 496
Donations	516	-
Electricity and water	48 471	61 532
Entertainment	11 796	12 514
Events	45 950	-
General expenses	48 268	41 754
Gifts	697	954
Insurance	12 429	13 014
Interest	21	-
Internet costs	45 761	49 343
Lease costs	22 980	2 200
Legal costs	126 124	7 324
Marketing	167 893	582 853
Office equipment	217 695	25 218
Parking	5 072	9
Photographic	22 352	-
Postage	1 965	3 595
Subscriptions	6 318	2 098
Telephone and fax	80 017	119 122
Training	18 296	33 376
Travel	169 457	192 591
Printing and stationery	73 630	140 665
Project costs	1 642 083	892 915
Public relations	13 512	162 902
Reimbursements paid	7 901	-
Rent	324 004	428 050
Repairs and maintenance	420	-
Salaries and wages	3 793 887	5 913 768

Source: CTP (2008a), "Cape Town Partnership Annual Report, 2008", Cape Town Partnership.

Figure A.28. The position of the Cape Town Partnership in the local development system in Cape Town

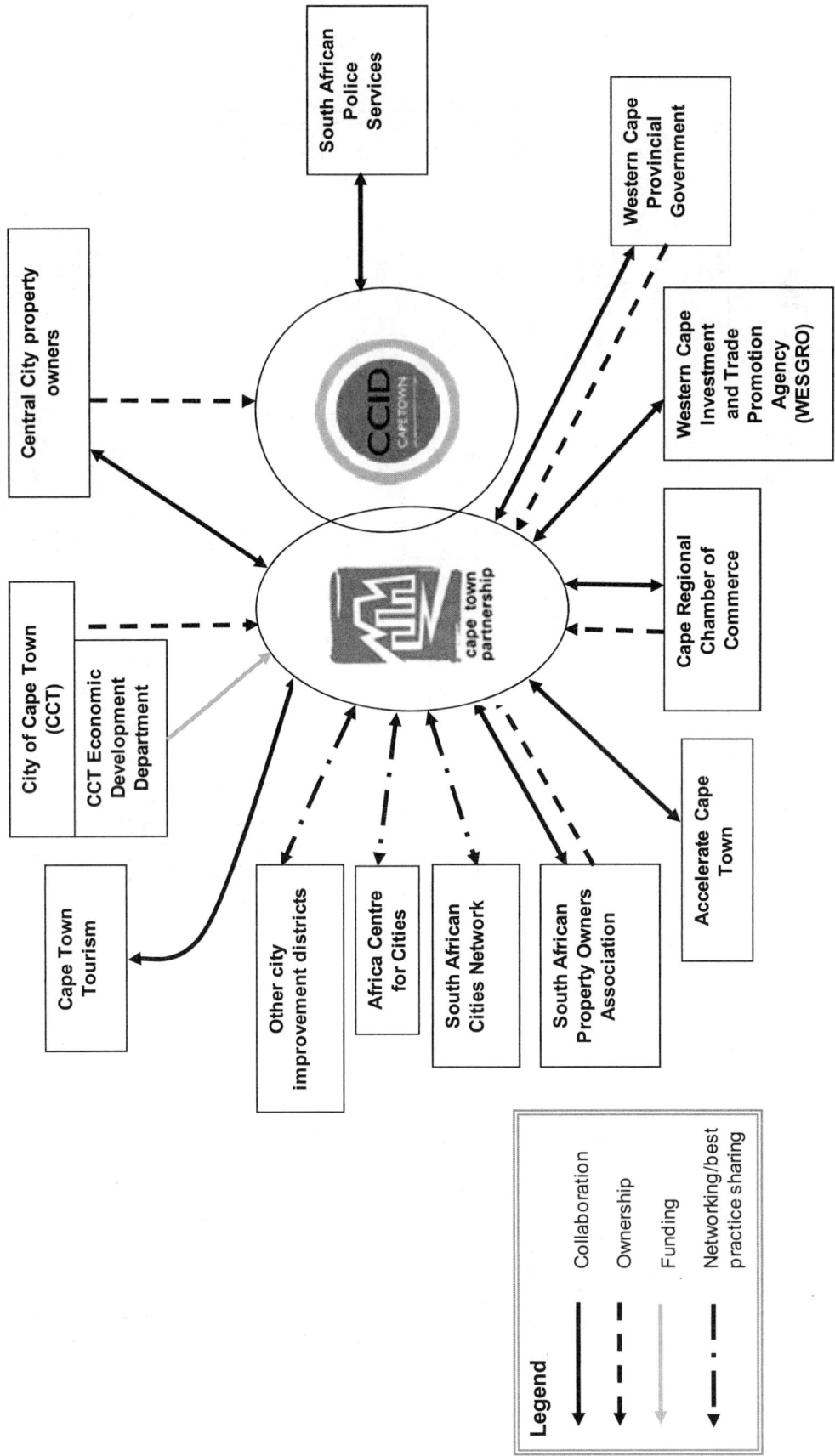

Provincial government

With Cape Town driving socio-economic growth in the Western Cape, and with the Central City a fundamental driver of Cape Town's economic performance, the relationship between the CTP and the Provincial Government is essential. There are also issues and agendas which overlap between the two, such as international investment promotion, which will benefit from an integrated approach.

Business community

There are a number of reasons why the CTP engages actively with the business community in Cape Town: (1) the key role of the Central City in the important task of city-wide development and investment promotion; (2) the unique contribution of the business community to Central City (and city-wide) development and investment promotion and facilitation; (3) the fact that businesses are important and paying CTP/CCID clients; and (4) the fact that businesses are a key pillar of Central City success. To facilitate the relationship, the CTP has representation from the Chamber of Commerce, the South African Property Owners Association and Business Against Crime, while the CCID Board is constituted of a number of key property owners and developers and retailers in the Central City. Business leaders are also invited to regular events, where they can contribute and be kept informed of progress and emerging agendas.

How is the Cape Town Partnership governed?

Board level

At the strategic level, the CTP is run by a board which is composed of a number of key stakeholders from the public and private sectors which have an interest in the Central City agenda. The CCID Board is predominantly made up of key property owners and developers from the Central City.

Operational level

With a staff of 28, the CTP/CCID is a relatively lean development agency. It should be noted that each staff member has his/her role clearly defined. The CCID arm of the CTP is very much considered part of the operating structure of the CTP (Boraine, 2009).

How is the leadership of the Cape Town Partnership structured?

Board level

There is an excellent relationship between the CTP and CCID boards and operational staff, both in a formal and informal sense. Each will go out of its way for the other – an effort underlined by a genuine commitment to the CTP's task.

The composition and work of the board also provides a springboard to develop working relationships with leaders in the city such as the mayor, other business leaders, newspaper editors, decision makers and thought leaders.

Chief executive officer

The chief executive officer (CEO) of the CTP is Andrew Boraine and the deputy chief executive officer is Bulelwa Makalima-Ngewana.

Organisational style

Given the complex steering function of the CTP, against a backdrop of stakeholders who don't often speak the same language, the style of the CTP's leadership is critical. It is deliberately designed to be a small organisation focused on delivering on a clear and concise mandate in a manageable spatial area. The CTP fulfils this role diligently, diplomatically and in an inclusive and warm manner. The notion that all work is done for the betterment of the Central City and the wider city of Cape Town continually underlies its work.

What are the Cape Town Partnership's key services and programmes within the system of local development and investment promotion?

The following section details the services/work themes that the CTP delivers as part of its mandate (CTP, 2008c; Boraine, 2009).

Safety and security

The CCID's security partnership, working with the Central City's business community, the South African Police Services, Metro Police and other security organisations and stakeholders, has formed a tight security net around the Central City. Due to this co-operative effort, the crime rate has dropped significantly. The complementary services provided by the CCID security partnership ensures that additional patrol officers are being deployed in the Central City 24 hours a day, 7 days a week.

Urban management

The CCID's four precinct managers monitor the streets and public spaces in Cape Town on a daily basis. Defects are reported and regular follow-up meetings with local authorities take place to develop urban management solutions. The CCID provides a top-up cleansing service in the Central City. Streets and public spaces are kept clean and graffiti-free by 63 cleaners – 24 hours a day, 7 days a week. The CCID works together with various non-governmental organisations (NGOs), such as the organisation *Straatwerk*, on urban management projects that have a strong social development and job-creation focus.

Social development

The CCID's Social Development department focuses on assisting homeless people in the Central City as well as alleviating poverty by supporting skills training and job-creation projects. It works in partnership with NGOs and other stakeholders. The CCID formed partnerships with the following organisations to assist them in the Central City:

- *Straatwerk*: an NGO that employs previously homeless people and assists them in rebuilding their lives on a daily basis. They are used for special projects such as graffiti removal, removal of posters, drain cleaning and any other cleaning projects (see below).

- Men on the Side of the Road: an NGO that helps unemployed people find work by creating special projects, such as a waterless carwash project in public parking spaces and training scheme for tourist assistants in the Central City.

- The Haven, Homestead, *Ons Plek* and Home of Hope: shelters for homeless people and children in the Central City area.

Development facilitation

The CTP is particularly effective in the area of development facilitation. The CTP both provides the quality of place and brokers the key relationships required to make the Central City investment attractive and investment-ready.

Key programmes

City Centre Development Strategy (CCDS)

The Partnership and the City of Cape Town published a ten-year framework for action, entitled the CCDS in October 2008. The CCDS is based on the following vision: "In the next ten years, the Cape Town Central City will grow and greatly enhance its reputation as a dynamic business and people centre, and focuses on five outcomes and five big ideas."

Five outcomes

- Cape Town's premier business location, recognised globally;

- a high-quality sustainable urban environment;

- a popular destination for Capetonians and visitors;

- a leading centre for knowledge, innovation, creativity and culture, in Africa and the South;

- a place that embodies the heart and soul of Cape Town.

Five big ideas

- to reinstate the historical connection of the city to the sea, the mountain and to water, the *raison d'être* of the city of Cape Town (Reclaim Camissa project);

- to bring the people of Cape Town back into the Central City to live, through appropriate residential densification and more affordable housing;

- to improve the public transport system, providing greater accessibility to, from and around the Central City for Capetonians and visitors (with a particular focus on the city's Integrated Rapid Transit System);

- to provide space for future growth and investment in the Central City, in particular through the redevelopment of the Cape Town Station Precinct and the East City Design Initiative;

- to divide the Central City into 20 neighbourhoods, paving the way for development protocols, based on local characteristics that reinforce the distinctiveness of the Central City, in order to address issues such as appropriate densification, mixed usage, building height, parking ratios, street-frontage, heritage and conservation (Boraine, 2009; CTP, 2009d).

Creative Cape Town

Creative Cape Town aims to support the more than 1 000 creative and cultural firms and organisations based in the Central City. These include individuals and companies involved in architecture, advertising and communication, media, jewellery, fashion, crafts, visual arts and photography and the heritage, music, performance and film sectors. Creative Cape Town is a social, economic and spatial strategy to promote an active, vibrant and diverse Central City by using culture to accelerate urban regeneration.

Green City Initiative

Since February 2007, the Cape Town Partnership has hosted the "Energy Efficiency Initiative" (EEI) which is the first South African city-level public-private partnership created to reduce energy consumption within commercial buildings. It was established jointly with the Sustainability Institute (linked to the University of Stellenbosch) with seed funding from Dutch foundation CORDAID. This has now been broadened into a more comprehensive "Green City" programme, promoting urban densification, public transport, affordable housing and sustainable use of scarce resources.

Public Space for Public Life

The Partnership aims to foster a high-quality urban environment in the Central City that is a popular destination for locals and visitors. Particular emphasis is placed on the upgrade, use and management of public space and increased after-hour and weekend activity. Improved access, with an emphasis on safety and security, and good urban design are key.

Living in Town

One of the weaknesses of the Central City is its relative lack of a residential population – approximately 5 000 people live in the CBD and around 55 000 in the Central City. It is the CTP's opinion that it is both possible, and socially and economically desirable, to double the residential population of the Central City within the next ten years. The Partnership wishes to achieve this through a combination of small-scale densification in existing suburbs (a trend which is already happening) and large-scale densification on public land.

What role has the Cape Town Partnership played in the system of local development and investment promotion?

As Table A.25 shows, it is possible to conceptualise the role of the CTP in the system of local development and investment promotion. This description shows that the CTP has a strong "cheering" and "steering" function, whilst the CCID delivers the rowing function of the CTP as a whole.

Table A.25. **Conceptualising the role of the Cape Town Partnership**

	Direct delivery	Facilitation and co-ordination	Strategic support and programmes	Creating capacity elsewhere
Depth and breadth of role	✓✓	✓✓✓	✓✓	✓
Specific example	• Provision of safety, cleansing, urban management and social development services. • Kerbside parking management. • Management of the CCID.	• Use of local press and media to stimulate public debate and engagement. • Crafting of the Central City Development Strategy - the content driver for the work in the Central City for the next ten years.	• 2010 Central City Partners Forum. • Central City walking tours. • The publication of the newsletters *Siyahluma* and *City Views*.	• Business Areas Network. • Mentoring a number of the 18 other City Improvement Districts (CIDS) in the city.

What enables the Cape Town Partnership to contribute to the local development and investment promotion system so effectively?

Hon Helen Zille, former Executive Mayor of Cape Town, now Premier, Western Cape Provincial Government commented that, "I am delighted with the CTP. I think it has helped to turn Cape Town around," (CTP, 2008b).

There are twelve key principles that demonstrate why CTP has been a successful partnership body:

1. **Get the basics right.** For the first five years, the focus of the Partnership, via the work of the CCID, was on sound management of the urban environment, including safety and security, cleansing and precinct management (addressing issues such as graffiti, potholes and illegal posters). The CCID pays attention to detail, with no problem being too small. The importance to the CTP of the work of the CCID to provide a clean, safe, well-managed, well-marketed and socially responsible Central City cannot be underestimated. Just as the CTP creates the relationships for the CCID to function, the CCID has built a high-quality, investment-attractive urban environment which has provided an essential foundation from which a more strategic and effective approach by the CTP to Central City development may be taken.

   This is not a privatisation model. The CCID does not substitute the role of the City of Cape Town or other public bodies, but provides complementary (top-up) services, funded through an additional levy on property owners. This mechanism allows public sector service providers to be held accountable and for additional services to be delivered.

   A defined spatial focus for urban regeneration is helpful, but boundaries should not be allowed to become rigid borders. Crime, for example, has no borders, so collaboration across boundaries is important. Issues such as housing, public transport and employment have to addressed over a wider area.

2. **Combine strategic planning and operations.** One of the CTP/ CCID mantras is "Strategy without action is futile, action without strategy is blind." There are

benefits of having a "two-in-one" organisational structure. On the one hand, the CCID focuses on the "here and now". Its strength is its attention to detail, and its ability to provide immediate responses to problems and have a visible presence on the streets. On the other hand, the Partnership concentrates on "what happens tomorrow". Its strength is that it provides the broader socio-economic context, brings diverse partners (and points of view) together and is able to initiate new ideas and longer-term programmes.

3. **The importance of providing a "translation service".** The role of a partnership is to bring different "worlds" together through shuttle diplomacy and by "playing Cupid", *i.e.* public/private, different levels of government, city departments, owners and tenants, developers and heritage practitioners and formal and informal retailers.

   A public-private partnership is not a municipal or public entity, nor is it a business lobby. In the view of the Partnership, "A strategy of 'name, blame and shame' does not work with the public sector (or anyone else for that matter) and can be counter-productive. Do not fight your battles via the media."

   The Partnership has adopted a networking approach, and does not just rely on formal structures and leaders. It creates multiple entry points into organisations and government administrations, and has a keen understanding of who deals with what, and who can make things happen. The Partnership finds it necessary to have an intuitive understanding of the political, social and commercial environment, and values the relationships that it establishes.

   Indeed, Alan Winde, MEC of Finance, Economic Development and Tourism, Western Cape Provincial Government commented that, "The success of the Cape Town Partnership is a sterling example of what can result from a well-run, well managed, public-private partnership."

4. **The quality of the CTP's partnerships**. The CTP model is fundamentally based on partnership building. Indeed, the quality of the relationships built across public, private and non-governmental organisations is internationally renowned. These quality partnerships have enabled the CTP to provide the City Council a high return on investment in the Central City.

   According to Andrew Boraine, the CEO of the CTP, "the Cape Town Partnership is only as good as its partners." In a recent speech, he hailed the regular partner support of "the Cape Town City Council, Western Cape Provincial Government, Cape Regional Chamber, South African Property Owners Association, Central City property owners and developers represented on the CCID, and many more" as fundamental to the CTP effort. "Our success is your success," he said, adding that, "we value the trust and commitment to common principles that we have patiently built over these years" (CTP, 2008c).

5. **Leadership and vision.** The CTP's leadership and vision have helped establish the organisation as a "unifying force" in the Central City. The CTP has been able to both create a vision of what can be achieved in the Central City and Cape Town, and strategise in such a way that plugged gaps in the Central City's development pathway. For instance, the CTP has been able to create a sense of commitment to urban renewal that investors are willing to buy into. According to Boraine, "while the well-known 'bottom line' of business is fundamental to the efficiency of the market, it is not the only thing that matters." Just as important is

the tremendous responsibility the new South African generation has "to get more South Africans into jobs and work, and to spread income" (CTP, 2008c).

Leadership qualities such as tact, diplomacy, openness and humility, often attributed to the CTP's leadership, have also been important. Not only have these qualities improved the effectiveness of the organisation's steering, cheering and coaching roles, they have also helped create a very positive internal culture within the CTP. Staff members are motivated and empowered by this enabling atmosphere.

The fact the CTP has gained extensive knowledge of what works for other world cities has enabled it to set agendas and provide visionary leadership with a high degree of credibility.

6. **Lean, efficient and concise mandate.** The CTP has a clear and concentrated mandate in terms of its core business roles and geographic sphere of influence, which means that it can specialise and build the necessary skills and experiences to fulfil its mandate.

Though the CTP's budget has grown from ZAR 1 million in the 1999/2000 financial year to approximately ZAR 8 million in the 2007/08 financial year, it remains modest. However, this tight budget means that for the CTP to succeed, waste and red tape have to be minimised, quality partnerships have to be constantly created and maintained, and quality staff have to be employed.

Furthermore, the fact that CTP is small in size and budget means that it is usually not seen as a threat to other stakeholders and that its sole agenda is the betterment of the Central City and wider Cape Town. Currently, no one can accuse the CTP of being politically or profit motivated, which helps the organisation play its steering and diplomacy role more effectively.

7. **Social development is a core principle of urban regeneration.** Because CTP and CCID deal with street-level activity, they have to address issues of poverty, homelessness, unemployment, substance and alcohol abuse, mental illness, school absenteeism, dysfunctional homes, physical and sexual abuse, personal trauma, and many other social issues, as well as "crime and grime." In the view of the CTP, "'Zero tolerance' can sometimes be misinterpreted to mean 'get the poor and the homeless off the streets' without regard of where they go or what happens to them. Urban regeneration is about people, all people, including the most marginalised."

The CTP and CCID believe that there is a need to differentiate between criminal activities and anti-social behaviour, and that two different strategies are required. There need to be consequences for unacceptable behaviour; however, diversion programmes via a Community Court are preferable to clogging the criminal justice system. It is helpful to differentiate between needs of different groups, for example homeless children, homeless youth and homeless and unemployed adults. They need different support programmes. Having fieldworkers on the streets, particularly at night and on weekends, is essential. Social development is not a "9 to 5" issue.

Cape Town, like other South African cities, faces the challenge of high levels of unemployment and poverty. This is why the Partnership and CCID have for some years focused on linking urban management programmes to employment creation and social development.

In 2001, the CTP/CCID, together with the City of Cape Town, introduced a parking marshal system that regularised most informal car parkers into a legal parking management system. The system now incorporates hand-held meters. This project created over 300 permanent jobs, to date one of the most successful job creation projects.

In 2006, the CCID managed the Western Cape Provincial Government "Walking Bus" programme, a nine-month project which created over 70 new employment opportunities.

Subsequently, the CTP/CCID have been on a drive to develop sustainable job-creation programmes within the Central City. The CCID has partnered with *Straatwerk*, a faith-based NGO, to develop urban management programmes that complement the social upliftment projects that *Straatwerk* has in place. These programmes are for people who are not yet able to act productively in society. These projects help desperate (and often destitute) individuals to earn cash in hand by means of work as an alternative to begging, theft or other criminal activities.

The CCID has assisted *Straatwerk* in developing two levels of service: basic and technical services. Some of the projects provide employment at a basic level while others require additional training and skills. The CCID has also assisted in developing supervisory, administrative and management structures as the programme has grown from strength to strength. The system currently employs over 200 people per month; over 60 people are employed at any one point during a typical day. There are over 130 four-hour shifts per month. A shift normally accommodates four people, one of which is a supervisor. Remuneration is close to double the minimum wage for basic, entry-level services. A higher rate is paid to supervisory and technical staff.

The following programmes are currently in place.

Entry-level programmes:

- General cleaning: this includes both street and pavement sweeping and occurs on a daily basis. On any one day about 20-30 people are involved in this activity.

- High-level specialised cleaning: this is usually confined to a relatively small area, but with a high concentration of cleansing on a specific task *i.e.* broken glass or cigarettes.

- Hot-spot cleaning: reactive/emergency cleaning service.

- Big drain and gulley cleaning: this task occurs twice a year and involves the cleaning of all drains in the city centre (over 1 300 drains) to ensure that there are no blocked drains and to prevent flooding during the rainy season.

- Pavement channels and small drain cleaning: this task occurs every three months and ensures that all litter and blockages are cleared.

- Illegal poster, sticker and string removal: this task is performed weekly and ensures that the Central City is clear of any illegal posters and stickers on all lamp poles, electrical boxes and any other surface.

- Public squares and events: dedicated cleaning teams assigned to specific public spaces and events on a daily, weekly and monthly basis.

- Community Court programme: dedicated supervisory capacity to individuals sentenced to community service three times a week.

- Entrances and exits to the Central City cleaning programme: dedicated teams ensure that they are maintained on a daily basis.

- Dawn cleaning patrol (graveyard shift): dedicated early morning cleaning within the entertainment district to ensure that Central City is clean when office workers arrive.

- Weeding programme: a twice-a-year programme that ensures that the Central City is weed-free.

- General distribution services: weekly and monthly distribution of the CCID newspapers and social awareness campaign pamphlets and other marketing collateral.

- Bakkie Brigade: a monthly service that ensures that rubbish, junk and rubble that cannot be removed by the City's Cleaning Department is removed.

- Recycling project: eight positions were created through the CCID's primary cleaning service provider, as one of their conditions of contract, to recycle all waste collected in the Central City before being taken to landfill.

- General *ad hoc* services.

Technical services:

- Graffiti Squad: two highly-trained graffiti removal teams (eight members) ensure that the Central City is graffiti-free. This team has become so specialised the City Council also uses them for other areas throughout the city on a contract basis.

- Electrical light pole repair team: this service is conducted on a weekly basis on behalf of the Electricity Department whereby all electrical poles with missing or vandalised and exposed wiring are covered up with special aluminium flaps provided by the department. This is another public-private partnership with a skill-transfer component.

- Environmental rodent inspectors ("Rat Pack"): a dedicated team working closely with the city's Health Department to ensure the city centre is rodent-free. This is a labour-intensive programme where over 1 300 drains are baited in a two-week period.

- Beautification and gardening services: services such as tree trimming, bush clearing, irrigation, tree planting, flower maintenance and general maintenance of green spaces. This service is conducted on a monthly basis.

- Technical team: this team, another example of a joint partnership with the City Council, provides the following services:

- secondary street maintenance tasks, *i.e.* brickwork and levelling of pavements,

- signage replacement and pole straightening,

- painting of street and road signs,

- minor building alterations and repairs.

A number of new programmes are under consideration:

- cigarette cleansing team (specialised cleansing service),

- maintenance and technical team – dedicated team per CCID precinct,

- public space maintenance,

- management of public amenities (*i.e.* public toilets),

- 2010 Visitor Ambassadors.

The Partnership has approached the national government's Extended Public Works Programme (EPWP) for funds in order to double the impact of job-creation projects in the Central City.

8. **Role of Central City within city region as a whole.** The Partnership recognises that the Central City is part of a wider, multi-nodal, metropolitan economy, that all economic nodes are important, and that to "be competitive" does not necessarily mean being "in competition" with one another. The Partnership believes that a healthy Central City means a healthy city, *i.e.* in terms of city image and identity, as a visitor destination and gateway, as a business, employment, investment, government, cultural attractions, infrastructure and logistics and educational institutions hub, and a source of tax revenue.

The Partnership has found it necessary to address constantly what it sees as a false "town" *vs.* "suburbs" dichotomy (which is understandably very prevalent in the context of historically divided cities). The Partnership believes that city development is about bringing resources and job opportunities to where people have been historically located and bringing people closer to jobs and economic opportunities, for example through better public transport and well-located affordable housing, and that it is not "either/or". In the long run, the Partnership believes that low density urban sprawl, and the continued location of poor people towards the urban periphery, as is the case in Cape Town, is not sustainable, and that there is a need for a clear and strong public policy of appropriate urban densification, particularly near public transport routes.

9. **Role of culture in urban regeneration**. The Partnership strongly believes that urban regeneration is about people, not just buildings and infrastructure, and that people express themselves through their culture. This is why history and memory, and the shaping of a new common city identity, often form an integral part of successful urban regeneration strategies. Understanding of culture often varies amongst city stakeholders – it's not just about art and entertainment.

Culture has economic value within the global knowledge economy. The creative and knowledge economies include the full range of creative and cultural industries, educational institutions, the developmental and non-profit sectors, as well as related organisations and businesses which can contribute to make the city a place of innovation, dynamism and inclusivity. This is why the Partnership established its Creative Cape Town Programme in 2007, which aims to provide a platform for the creative industries and enterprises that have clustered in the Central City. These include communication and advertising agencies, architectural firms, the craft sector, the broad design sectors, the publishing, music, fashion, film, visual arts and performance industries, as well as the print and electronic media industries, galleries, museums, festivals, performing arts and live music venues, educational institutions, libraries and archives, software and information technology (IT) companies – the broadest range of innovators, creators and knowledge makers the city has to offer.

10. **The role of the city centre in building a new common identity.** South Africa is known for conducting an extensive and formal "truth and reconciliation" process in response to the issues it has faced over the past three centuries. In Cape Town, there has also been a strong emphasis on finding ways to address the divisions of the past through historical projects.

Many people and communities who made a contribution to the construction of the city were previously "written out" of the city's history. This included the way in which the public realm was historically constructed to portray only one side of the story (*i.e.* through names of streets and buildings, types of statues in public squares). Ways are now being found to portray the "hidden histories" and "intangible memories" of indigenous people, slaves, dispossessed communities, and leaders of anti-apartheid struggles, including through "living memorialisation" projects such as *Goemarati*, which refers to a traditional grassroots form of Cape Town musical performance.

In addition, ways are being found to make the city centre a "neutral space" where previously divided communities can interact in a variety of ways in order to create a new, more inclusive, identity for the city. Therefore, a Public Space for Public Life strategy which can address the quality of the public realm, and which welcome people into public spaces, is very important.

11. **Communicate, communicate, and communicate.** CTP seeks to communicate constantly and become a trusted source of information and an authority on Central City issues. Information collection, collation, analysis and dissemination are the lifeblood of a networked organisation. A commitment to knowledge management and knowledge sharing, internally and externally, is essential.

More recently, the Partnership has concentrated on its digital media strategy. The Partnership says, "Be accessible to the media at all times. They are your friends, even when they don't get the story right. Development walking tours for your own citizens are very effective. Create local ambassadors – if locals don't believe in what you are doing, you will never convince the rest of the world."

12. **Using large events to leverage urban regeneration** Cape Town has a strong tradition of hosting large events (cycle tours, marathons, carnival, jazz festival, international cricket and rugby) and is one of nine South African host cities for the 2010 FIFA World Cup. The Partnership has put together a strategy for leveraging urban regeneration impact from the World Cup in the Cape Town Central City.

The overall aim of the Partnership's 2010 programme is getting citizens to feel that they live in a great city. Specific goals are to:

- *Enhance citizen participation.* A 2010 Central City Partners Forum has been established to ensure communications with all Central City stakeholders. This is enhanced through regular Fan Walk tours from the CBD to the new stadium in Green Point. The Partners Forum promotes 2010 business opportunities for retailers, suppliers, event organisers, performers, advertisers, and so on. Another way of promoting citizen participation is to use existing events in the Central City, but with a football "twist", *e.g.* the Twilight Run, Switching on Festival Lights, Design Indaba and International Jazz Festival. During the World Cup, an official FIFA Fan Park, catering for 30 000 people, will operate in the Central City. The City of Cape Town will provide an additional three public viewing areas at decentralised locations.

- *Organise a unique and authentic Cape Town experience for visitors.* The Fan Walk will follow the traditional route of the annual Cape Minstrels Carnival, an event stretching back to the era just after the emancipation of slaves in 1834. Fan activation zones, where fans can meet before a match, will happen in traditional public squares in the Central City. The Fan Park will take place on the Grand Parade, Cape Town (and South Africa's) oldest public square, where Nelson Mandela first addressed the world on his release from 27 years in jail.

- *Contribute to a well-organised and efficient event.* The Central City is strategically located between the new Green Point Stadium and the main event transport hubs. It is also the location of approximately 50% of available bed space. If the Central City is not well organised and managed, it will impact negatively on the ability of Cape Town to successfully host a memorable World Cup. Existing security and cleansing partnerships can be strengthened to deliver additional services. The Partnership is also part of a communication effort to explain how access to and from the stadium will be organised on match days.

- *Leave a lasting economic, social and cultural legacy.* The 2010 World Cup has unlocked national government expenditure on public infrastructure that would not normally be available to Cape Town. The main legacy for the city will be an upgraded rail network (including a ZAR 440 million upgraded CT Station) and the first phase of a new Integrated Rapid Transit System, including a connection to the CT airport (which itself is being rebuilt). Significant investment has also been made by the City Council into improved pedestrian environments, better public spaces and dedicated cycle routes. Key interchanges on the highways connecting the Central City are also being upgraded. The new stadium itself will leave a legacy, together with the new 16.5 hectare Green Point Urban Park. Less tangible but equally important legacies will include additional jobs, training and skills development, and partnerships to organise major events.

- *Enhance business branding and marketing of Cape Town.* Cape Town already has a strong leisure tourism brand, based on its natural attributes and its flora and fauna. In addition, Cape Town has established itself as an event and festival city, a place of music, entertainment and urban culture, as well as a place for meetings, conventions and exhibitions (the Cape Town International Convention Centre hosts 50% of all international events in Africa and 67% of international events in South Africa).

> – *Use 2010 infrastructure preparations to mitigate the effects of global recession and speed recovery.*The Partnership has put forward a plan to address the effects of the recession in the Central City and to speed up recovery. This includes: (1) doing the basics well and maintaining high standards of urban management (clean, safe, attention to detail) to offset the negative visual impact of ground-floor vacancies and to-let signs. The business area must be seen to be cared for, especially during a recession. Strong operational partnerships between the City and CCID are essential to address urban defects; (2) encouraging building owners to ensure that vacant ground-floor spaces are decorated and well-maintained; (3) enhancing communications on development trends, including articles on business and development trends and the launch of new developments, including 2010 public infrastructure; (4) organising Central City Investment seminars to get best business minds together; (5) expanding impact of CCID job creation opportunities through partnership with the Department of Public Works Extended Public Works Programme, focusing on maintenance of public facilities and management of the public environment; and (6) seeing the crisis as an opportunity and planning now for a future economic upturn, including a 2020 CBD retail strategy, Central City Development Strategy infrastructure capacity study, and key projects such as the expansion of the Convention Centre, Cape Town Station Phase 2 upgrade and the Cape Town Cruise Liner Terminal (CTP, 2008c; Boraine, 2009).

What constraints make the Cape Town Partnership less able to contribute effectively to the local development and investment promotion system?

Complex roles in a dynamic situation

The distinctions between the roles of the CTP, the CCID and other stakeholders sometimes become blurred. Though overlap is inevitable to an extent due to the complexity of the Central City operating environment, tensions can occur particularly in areas which overlap closely such as the responsibility for public infrastructure maintenance and investment facilitation.

Equally, with some weaknesses in the delivery capability on other aspects of development policy (*e.g.* affordable housing and urban regeneration), there is a tendency to suggest that CTP should take on areas of activity outside of its founding mandate. This pressure for "mission creep" is not easy to negotiate. There is much experience internationally of development partnerships and agencies finding it difficult to define their core roles.

The CTP's working environment would be greatly aided should other organisations support it more effectively and immediately. For example, where organisations such as the City of Cape Town are restricted in terms of its own mandate by legislation such as the Local Government: Municipal Finance Management Act (MFMA), Act No. 56 of 2003, it could be useful to permit CTP, and other partners, to get on with matters and projects that are in the interest of the greater public good.

The Cape Town Partnership is under and unsustainably resourced

Though being tightly resourced can have its advantages, there is little doubt that the CTP could perform its Central City roles more comprehensively if it were better funded. An increase in funding would allow the CTP to develop expertise outside its current mandate and hire more staff to better contribute to the wider system of city development and investment promotion in Cape Town.

CTP funding is also not yet sustainable as it is reliant on both short-to-medium term City Council contributions and the strength of Central City corporate balance sheets, both of which are affected by the recessionary climate.

Messaging and communication

The CTP have to balance the need to advocate for change and inspire new thinking, whilst not overstepping their own mandate. At the same time, the need to promote success and co-operation has to be balanced with the desire of some stakeholders, in the wider system of city development and investment promotion, to seek much of the credit for the CTPs work.

The CTP achieves this balance, but there are some concerns that, on occasion, the CTP does not get this fine balance quite right. The CTP is both a Central City evelopment Partnership and a Central City Improvement District and these two complementary roles might occasionally need to speak with different voices. To a large extent this is inevitable, given the role of the CTP in a complex system with so many stakeholders. What is required to improve the situation though is a sound communications strategy and a clear differentiation between the roles being played by the CTP and its partners. It is important to share and discuss such a communications strategy with partners in order to avoid surprises.

One important area for clear messaging is the contribution made by the Central City and the CTP to city-wide and provincial success. This needs to be very fully articulated and updated regularly.

Research into the key dimensions of and trends within the Central City

One reason why articulating the strategic importance of the Central City is so difficult is that the area and its trends are not fully understood, at least in a quantitative sense. Though the CTP is flexible, responsive and effective, performance is hampered by a lack of precise and detailed knowledge of Central City flows in relation to and impacts on businesses, residents, visitors, other locations and other themes.

How has the Cape Town Partnership approached these problems?

The CTP conducts regular reviews to understand its position and the challenges it faces. As a result it seeks to evolve and adjust to the requirements and restraints of its operating environment.

In more general terms, the CTP has, for ten years, responded and reacted to Central City challenges and opportunities. More recently, the CTP has moved to a longer term framework and has taken steps towards creating a ten-year agenda on the form of the Central City Development Strategy. This has enabled the CTP to better tackle the challenges of: (1) the complexity of its role in the dynamic situation; (2) the fact it needs to be more sustainably resourced; (3) messaging and communication; and (4) intelligence gathering (Boraine, 2009).

At the same time, its continued focus on nurturing healthy relationships and building capacity elsewhere in the city help it function as effectively as possible given its constraints.

Neil Fraser, Citychat, commented on the success of the CTP by stating that, "There is a renewed sense of place and a sense of pride that I certainly haven't experienced in the iKapa (Cape Town) inner city for years ... Ten years ago I was very critical of the way the Cape Town Partnership was structured but there can be little doubt that it has been responsible, to a very large measure, for the turnaround of the inner city." (Boraine, 2009)

How is the Cape Town Partnership performing in relation to its key performance indicators?

As discussed in Table A.26, the CTP is performing well across a number of themes, both tangible and intangible.

Accountabilities, performance review mechanisms and best-practice sharing

Accountabilities

As a not-for-profit company, the CTP is primarily accountable to its board. At the same time, the CTP takes steps to make it accountable to city leaders and wider partners and does this by being open and communicating extensively in what it is engaged.

Performance review mechanisms

The CTP regularly reviews itself both internally and by external parties. At times which are critical to the development of the organisation, reviews are more likely.

Best-practice sharing

Both within Cape Town and across the world, the CTP is involved in sharing its best practice and learning from others. Momentum is created by the organisation of forums, speeches, conferences, publishing and the review process itself. A Cape Town Business Areas Network has been especially established for this purpose (Boraine, 2009).

What progress has the Cape Town Partnership made over its lifetime?

Over a ten-year period, the CTP has fulfilled its core business of stabilising the Central City by reducing crime and grime to make the area an attractive investment proposal. Subsequently, the CTP has crafted and delivered a number of strategic initiatives that add value to the Central City and foster a strong future for the city as a whole.

Table A.26. **Key performance indicators of the Cape Town Partnership**

Theme (initiative)	Tangible impact	Intangible impact
Tax revenues (combination)	• The Central City accounts for ZAR 50.2 billion out of ZAR 124.37 billion (40.36%) of total city turnover, making it by far the city's largest business node (City of Cape Town, 2006). This represents an increase on the previously measured figure of 33%, even without taking into account growth since 2006 in financial services, asset management, construction, information and communication technologies, creative industries and tourism services, all of which have impacted positively on the Central City's position.	• Validates the strategic focus on the Central City and claims for more resource support.
Vertical and horizontal co-ordination	• Sustainable public/ private partnerships in place.	• Diligent and diplomatic work by the CTP is creating co-operation within the City of Cape Town and with other public/ private agencies.
Crime (CCID)	• Serious crime has fallen in the Central City by 90% since 2000 (CCID, 2007).	• The perception/fear of crime in the Central City has fallen. According to a prominent Cape Town Newspaper Editor, "less than ten years ago we were writing stories of Central City abandonment", but thanks to an effective campaign against crime and grime, "the Central City is now a great place to be and a nice place to walk"
Public space improvements (with the City of Cape Town)	• Added value to adjacent buildings. • The conversion of Church Square from a parking lot to an interactive public space. • The completion of phase one of the Grand Parade upgrade. • Pier Place, Jetty Square, Greenmarket Square and St Andrew's Square design and upgrade. • Gradual improvement of the Company's Garden (CTP, 2007). • Many property owners and developers have taken it upon themselves to resurface and "green" pavements adjacent to their properties and to upgrade the facades of their own buildings.	• Shifted the emphasis from a vehicle-dominated to a pedestrian-friendly city. • Provided better access to the Central City to workers and visitors. • Supporting the Creative Cape Town and World Cup 2010 delivery strategies.
Inward investment (combination)	• The Central City has experienced high levels of investment over the past decade. Since 2000, a total ZAR 16-18 billion of investment has been realised from the capital value of current leases, new developments, investment purchases, upgrades and renewals.	• Urban management and development facilitation has significantly enhanced the Central City's reputation amongst domestic and international investors.
Effective business engagement	• The CTP Chief Executive, Andrew Boraine, was awarded the title of "Business Leader of the Year, 2008" for the contribution he and his team have made towards engaging with the private sector to accelerate investment and development in the Central City over recent years.	

Table A.26. **Key performance indicators of the Cape Town Partnership** (*continued*)

Theme (initiative)	Tangible impact	Intangible impact
Strong commercial property market	• The Central City has experienced a steady decline in commercial property vacancies over the past decade. By the end of 2007, vacancies in A- grade commercial office units had fallen below 4% (CTP, 2007). • Investments by top property companies such as Growthpoint, Madison and Old Mutual Properties, together with Irish company Eurocape, represent particular highlights. • Around 45% of new Central City apartments have been purchased by black owners. Since 2003, ZAR 2 billion worth of property developments and building purchases have been overseen by black developers. Black property owners now manage 40% of commercial stock in the Central City.	• Increased perceived investment attractiveness.
Employment	• Since 1998, a total of 65 000 construction jobs have been sustained in the Central City (CTP, 2006). • A further 500 jobs have been created in the delivery of basic services linked to the work of the CCID (CTP, 2006). • Thousands of job opportunities have been created in the retail, tourism and business sectors as a result of the good health of the Central City (CTP, 2006).	
Social development (Caring Cape Town)	• Placement of over 250 homeless young people in care or with their families. • NGOs such as *Straatwerk*, the Haven Night Shelter, Men at the Side of the Road and the Big Issue are now very successful in the Central City (CTP, 2006).	
Cultural resurgence	• Hosting successive stands at the Design Indaba to showcase Cape Town's creative industries. • Establishment of a popular Creative Clusters Networking Forum. • Hosting the Community Jazz Concert with espAfrika on Greenmarket Square as part of the popular Cape Town International Jazz Festival. • A revival of lunchtime entertainment and accessible theatre in public spaces; a renewed use of iconic architecture (CTP, 2007). • Attracted people into public space, in particular the newly upgraded Church Square. • Provided both physical and e-commerce platforms for local musicians and poets. • Established a *Goematronics* project. • Contributed to the Cape Town Memory Project by providing living memorialisation to indigenous, slave and African music roots of the people of Cape Town. • Made music production and consumption connections between the Central City, the townships and the Cape Flats (CTP, 2007).	• Cape Town now has a growing reputation as a high potential, high value-added creative economic sector, and the Central City is contributing powerfully to its development.

Table A.26. **Key performance indicators of the Cape Town Partnership** *(continued)*

Theme (initiative)	Tangible impact	Intangible impact
Event hosting and a growing visitor economy	• In 2006, the Cape Town International Convention Centre alone hosted some 509 events whilst the streets of the Central City have, for instance, hosted The 2006 Homeless World Cup, The Gay Pride March, The Pick 'n Pay Argus Cycle Tour, and The UCI 'B' World Cycle Championships (CTP, 2007). The Adderley Street Night Market, the Festive Season Lights and the Cape Town Festival Night Vision attracted 300 000, 50 000 and 35 000 to the Central City respectively (CTP, 2006). • Today, the Central City and its immediate vicinity host an impressive 47% of the total hotel bed capacity in the entire Greater Cape Town region (CTP, 2007). With future hotel projects under development such as the 15 on Orange Hotel (scheduled for completion end 2008) (*The Property Magazine*, 2008) and the Taj Palace Hotel (scheduled for completion end 2009) (*The Cape Town Magazine*, 2008), this offer is set to increase.	• The Central City is today a genuine visitor destination and gateway in its own right. • The Central City atmosphere is now beginning to bristle with street life.

The CTP is currently going through a process of evolution. Having fulfilled its management and promotion role (as mandated) in the Central City, with the publication of the Central City Development Strategy, the CTP is moving to fulfil the third pillar of its core mandate – the development of the Central City.

Nonetheless, it recognises that Central City management and promotion is a constant task and, without regular attention, the work completed in the past ten years could be undone. The role of Central City management and promotion also becomes more important given the global recession. If the Central City is not occupied fully there is a risk, for instance, that vacant buildings will otherwise become obsolete – something which the CTP should focus strongly on avoiding (Boraine, 2009).

What are the Cape Town Partnership's strengths, constraints, opportunities and challenges?

The Cape Town Partnership's strengths, constraints, opportunities and challenges are summarised in Table A.27.

Table A.27. **The Cape Town Partnership's strengths, constraints, opportunities and challenges**

Strengths	Constraints
• Non-partisan and apolitical stance allows the organisation to succeed. • Lean, nimble and flexible. • Populated with talented and committed team. • Strong leadership from the senior management team. • Wide buy-in and goodwill towards the organisation has been built up through diligent and high-quality work. • Clear and concise mandate gives the organisation and its employees focus. • Openness to ideas and review shows a willingness to learn and become even better. • Strength of the organisation's partnerships allows the organisation to accomplish a variety of tasks to a high standard.	• Unsustainable and small budget. • Small team for the volume of work. • Lack of deployable data on trends, activity and impact. • Lack of political buy-in about why a city centre focus is needed. • Seen to be business- rather than people-orientated. • Some blurring between the understanding of the role of the CTP and the CCID.
Opportunities	Challenges
• Feeling that Cape Town is about to enter a new phase of socio-economic development. • End of rebuilding following the 1994 generation. • 2010 World Cup. • With problems in the resource use sector, a renewed focus on green development and energy efficiency could be a practical and a symbolic differentiating factor for the city. • A strengthening visitor economy could boost Central City development. • Political stability could make Central City management easier. • Effective management, planning and implementation of the CCDS have the potential to secure Cape Town's long-term development future. • The CCDS could provide the vision for city-wide development, which could galvanise many stakeholders into action towards specific targets. • If harnessed, cultural activities could be a visible and powerful development mechanism. • Affordable transportation to and housing in the Central City could reduce the town/township dichotomy.	• Competition from decentralised business nodes for investment. • Economic progress could damage the Cape Town USP and accentuate inequalities. • There is currently no Cape Town City Development Strategy or organisation to oversee city-wide development. This vacuum could be de-motivating and encourage conflicting and unfocussed action by individual stakeholders. • The perception of the Central City as being apart from, and not a part of, the rest of the city could deepen. • Change of leadership in the CTP may disrupt the organisation's balance. • Raised expectations could make the job of effective management more difficult. • Rising market prices could make the Central City more and more unaffordable. • Increased resource use could overstretch supply. • Heavily reliant on partnership. • Increased global financial connectivity could make the Cape Town economy at the mercy of other economies.

Table A.27. **The Cape Town Partnership's strengths, constraints, opportunities and challenges** *(continued)*

Opportunities	Challenges
• Use of this ten-year anniversary review to focus on the core tasks for the future and to renew targets and a support base in order develop the Central City to help Cape Town succeed.	• Unbridled party political contestation makes Central City management more difficult. • Competition from out-of-town shopping malls could "trip out" the Central City retail offer. • Skills exodus to other city regions. • A lack of infrastructure development (virtual, transport and so on) could damage Cape Town's long-term competitiveness. • Investment regimes and the Cape Town visitor economy could collapse in the face of the global economic recession. • Reduced investment in the Central City will reduce the CCID levy yield and damage the CTP balance sheet.

References

Boraine, A. (2009), "Public-Private Partnerships and Urban Regeneration in the Cape Town Central City: Lessons from the First Ten Years of the Cape Town Partnership".

CCID (Central City Improvement District) (2007), "Central City Improvement District Annual Report, 2007", Central City Improvement District, Cape Town.

City of Cape Town (2006), "State of Cape Town 2006: Development Issues in Cape Town", *www.capetown.gov.za/en/stats/CityReports/Documents/IDP/State_of_Cape_Town_Full_Report_2006_712200610345_359.pdf.*

CTP (Cape Town Partnership) (2006), "Cape Town Partnership: A Profile, 2006", Cape Town Partnership.

CTP (2007), "Cape Town Partnership Annual Report, 2007", Cape Town Partnership.

CTP (2008a), "Cape Town Partnership Annual Report, 2008", Cape Town Partnership.

CTP (2008b), "Cape Town Partnership Review", Cape Town Partnership.

CTP (2008c), "About Us", *www.capetownpartnership.co.za/.*

CTP (2008d), "Central City Development Strategy", Cape Town Partnership.

The Cape Town Magazine (2008), "15 on Orange Successfully Attracting Investors", *www.capetownmagazine.com/articles/Accommodation~c2/Western-Cape/Taj-Palace-Five-Star-Hotel-Opening-in-Cape-Town~992~p1.*

The Property Magazine (2008), "15 on Orange Successfully Attracting Investors", *www.thepropertymag.co.za/pages/452774491/articles/2007/May/News/R420-million-5-star-development-15-on-Orange-hotel-development.asp.*

Creativesheffield.
Transforming Sheffield's Economy

Creative Sheffield
Sheffield, United Kingdom

Organisation type

Creative Sheffield was the first of the United Kingdom's new local economic development delivery vehicles – the city development companies and economic development companies (CDCs/EDCs) – to be set up. It was officially formed on 1 April 2007 and was designed to "substantially enhance Sheffield's capacity to develop and deliver economic strategy" (Kerslake and Taylor, 2004). It is a company limited by guarantee, with a high-level board composed of a mix of private and public sector representatives, and is owned by Sheffield City Council and the regional development agency, Yorkshire Forward. Creative Sheffield has consolidated the city's previously disparate set of development bodies and, as such, incorporated "Sheffield One", the investment agency "Sheffield First for Investment" and the "Knowledge Starts in South Yorkshire" project.

Mission statement

Creative Sheffield is tasked with spearheading Sheffield's economic transformation through leading the development and implementation of the Economic Masterplan. Sheffield's Economic Masterplan (2008) provides the strategic framework to guide economic and physical development and investment across the whole city over the next 10-15 years.

When Creative Sheffield was launched, it set itself a series of targets, including the creation of 30 000 new jobs over the next ten years; the development of specific industrial sectors that would attract further companies to invest in the region, including manufacturing and materials, medical equipment and nanotechnology; and the emergence of a "city region" to draw on the talents of people from the surrounding areas to ensure the region is able to compete on the global business stage in terms of size and skills mix (Creative Sheffield, 2007).

History, origins and ownership

In a paper by Bob Kerslake, Chief Executive of Sheffield City Council, and Vince Taylor, Director of Sheffield First Partnership (2004), it was suggested that the recent history of Sheffield can be summarised into three distinct stages, each of which required a different organisational capacity to meet its needs.

The three stages were outlined as (Kerslake and Taylor, 2004):

1. Survival: arresting the decline from the mid-1980s to 1998. Early partnership structures were developed that brought together public and private agencies to set priorities and encourage joint working. An urban development corporation was established during the 1990s to lead the regeneration of the Lower Don Valley – the location of much of Sheffield's former industry. The Heart of the City project was secured in order to launch the city centre's renaissance.

2. Revival: producing a clear improvement in the main economic indicators (from 1999 to 2006). This stage saw the formation of much stronger and simpler business support arrangements within the city, with the collocation of the Chamber, Business Link services, Enterprise agency and the International Trade Centre. Sheffield First for Investment was created as the primary port of call for new investment enquiries for local companies and inward investors. Sheffield One – one of three first round urban regeneration companies (URCs) – was also set up to lead the implementation plan for the economic and physical regeneration of the city centre. The City's partnership arrangements were significantly strengthened through the creation of the Sheffield First "family" of partnerships, covering the entire regeneration activity arena.

3. Transformation: 2006 onwards. It was decided by the Sheffield First Partnership Board and Sheffield City Council that new arrangements were required. In particular, it was felt that the future development and delivery of Sheffield's economic strategy required fundamental capacity improvement, in terms of stronger inputs from individuals and organisations with a track record of private sector experience and success in external markets where Sheffield had the potential to do much better, and in cities that had previously overcome the hurdles Sheffield was facing. The Partnership Board saw the changes as "critical for the City's ability to discharge its Core City economic responsibilities to its city region and to the regions covered by the 'Northern Way'" (Kerslake and Taylor, 2004). Once these initial factors had been identified, the entire process took three years and culminated in the launch of Creative Sheffield, a city development company, on 1 April 2007. The aim of Creative Sheffield is to produce a shift in the nature of the economy to one that is knowledge-driven, of high value and with Sheffield becoming a true core city, raising the prosperity of the city region as well as the City itself (Roberts, 2009).

What does Creative Sheffield do?

Creative Sheffield's core activities are:

*   to act as the lead marketing agency for Sheffield and to achieve a positive shift in perceptions of the city's image and reputation;

*   to build on the success of Sheffield First for Investment in the attraction of quality inward investment into the city;

*   to follow on from the achievement of Sheffield One in developing the city's physical infrastructure to internationally competitive standards;

*   to develop initiatives that will promote the growth of the city's scientific, creative and cultural knowledge base (Creative Sheffield, 2009a).

Creative Sheffield was also initially tasked with preparation and management of the city's Economic Masterplan which provides the framework for the economic and physical development of Sheffield over the next 10-15 years from 2008. The Masterplan focuses on enhancing inward investment, developing the city's physical infrastructure, accelerating the growth of knowledge-based businesses and undertaking strategic city marketing.

Compared with the previous disparate model, Creative Sheffield provides synergy by bringing together the various areas of economic development: marketing, regeneration, investment promotion and innovation. For example, the Sheffield Digital Campus (SDC) began as an "e-campus", one of the original seven projects in the Sheffield One City Centre Master Plan (2001), and was brought forward by Sheffield One, in partnership with Sheffield City Council and Yorkshire Forward, and developed into a physical regeneration project, although its *raison d'etre* was to attract and grow the creative industries of the future.

Through Creative Sheffield, the SDC has had a natural evolution from physical development through being an inward investment offer, marketing case study and good news story to an innovation asset at the core of the Digital Region project.

Similar synergies in Creative Sheffield occur from having the innovation and investment teams working together and pitching to the same markets. In the same way the marketing of Sheffield is directly linked to the target markets for foreign direct investment and the other growth regions of the United Kingdom (Roberts, 2009).

What is the spatial scale of operation and influence of Creative Sheffield?

Creative Sheffield is a predominantly city-based organisation which operates within the context of the city region. Sheffield has a population of 530 000, making it England's fourth largest city, while 1.75 million people live in the Sheffield city region (Creative Sheffield, 2008a). The Economic Masterplan, led by Creative Sheffield, states:

> *While the Masterplan is for the whole of the City of Sheffield, it has been developed in the context of the Sheffield City Region, which includes the South Yorkshire towns of Barnsley, Doncaster and Rotherham as well as the areas to the south of the city, Bassetlaw, Bolsover, Chesterfield, Derbyshire Dales and North East Derbyshire. Administrative boundaries very rarely match the economic reality of labour markets and investment flows. The Sheffield economy impacts upon, and is directly influenced by, neighbouring locations and as such the future success of the City Region economy requires all areas to work collaboratively. (Creative Sheffield, 2009b)*

How is Creative Sheffield financed?

Creative Sheffield's core funding comes from Sheffield City Council and Yorkshire Forward (the region's development agency). In order to leverage private sector support, Creative Sheffield brought in a highly experienced chief executive whose reputation means that he can leverage financial support.

Creative Sheffield's annual budget is approximately GBP 4 million. As a not-for-profit, its annual total income matched its total expenditure. The budget is shown in Table A.28.

Table A.28. **Creative Sheffield's income and expenditure account, 2008/09**

	2008/09 Programme	2008/09 Company
Turnover	£	£
Government grants	2 998 022	827 947
Member contributions	1 320 568	1 649 367
Other income	85 910	58 189
Total income	**4 404 501**	**2 535 503**
Administrative expenses		
Salaries and wages	2 147 582	939 733
Programme expenditure	1 820 811	1 350 458
Other administrative costs	436 108	245 313
Irrecoverable VAT	-	-
Total expenditure	**4 404 501**	**2 535 503**

	2008/09 Programme	2008/09 Company
Government grants		
Yorkshire Forward grants	£	£
Single programme core funding	1 968 364	-
Key account management	148 393	148 393
RSY Joe Anwyls salary	30 000	-
Single programme transitional funding	-	-
JOBMatch South Yorkshire	-	-
Advanced Manufacturing Park Marketing Programme	32 204	-
Other grants		
South Yorkshire Inward Investment Programme	-	-
South Yorkshire Investor Support Aftercare Programme	-	-
Local Enterprise Growth Initiative	819 062	679 554
Total grants	**2 998 022**	**827 947**

	2008/09 Programme	2008/09 Company
Contributions from members		
Contributions from members	£	£
Sheffield City Council	1 070 568	1 649 367
English Partnerships	250 000	-
Total contributions	**1 320 568**	**1 649 367**

	2008/09 Programme	2008/09 Company
Other income		
Other income	£	£
ERDF Objective One (Regeneration Delivery Vehicle RDV)	30 122	30 122
Other misc income	55 788	28 067
Total other Income	**85 910**	**58 189**

Source: Roberts, P. (2009), Written and telephone communication and interviews.

An examination of the accounts also highlights an intimate and sometimes complex relationship with the City Council.

The "Company" column relates to costs that are run through the limited company. This accounts for direct employees and approximately 85% of the activity costs. Value-added tax (VAT) cannot be reclaimed on this part of the activity, resulting in part of the funding being "recycled" back to central government.

The "Programme" column describes the Council's activity in regards to the company. These activities include, for example, staff that are employed by the Council but seconded to the company; rent and service charges on the lease that the Council holds; and costs of contracts tendered by the Council.

The organogram that follows (Figure A.29) reveals the local development system within which Creative Sheffield operates.

Who are Creative Sheffield's partners?

Strong and successful partnerships with a wide range of bodies throughout the city are vital for the success of the city's Economic Masterplan, which states that:

Creative Sheffield is the lead organisation in terms of setting the ambition and monitoring progress against the plan. But it will lead only on a proportion of the programmes and projects – those most closely and directly linked to the economic agenda. Complete success depends on all partners delivering their part of this ambitious programme. The performance of our schools, the delivery of the right volume and type of housing, the achievement of successful neighbourhoods, are essential elements in the transformation programme. (Creative Sheffield, 2009b)

Governance

The Board of Directors is made up of a number of representatives from both the private and public sectors. As of 2009, it had 17 members including the Leader of Sheffield City Council, a Shadow Cabinet Member, representatives from the regional development agency, universities, and a variety of private firms.

Figure A.30 presents the organisational structure of Creative Sheffield's senior management team.

Figure A.29. **The position of Creative Sheffield in the system of economic development and investment promotion in Sheffield**

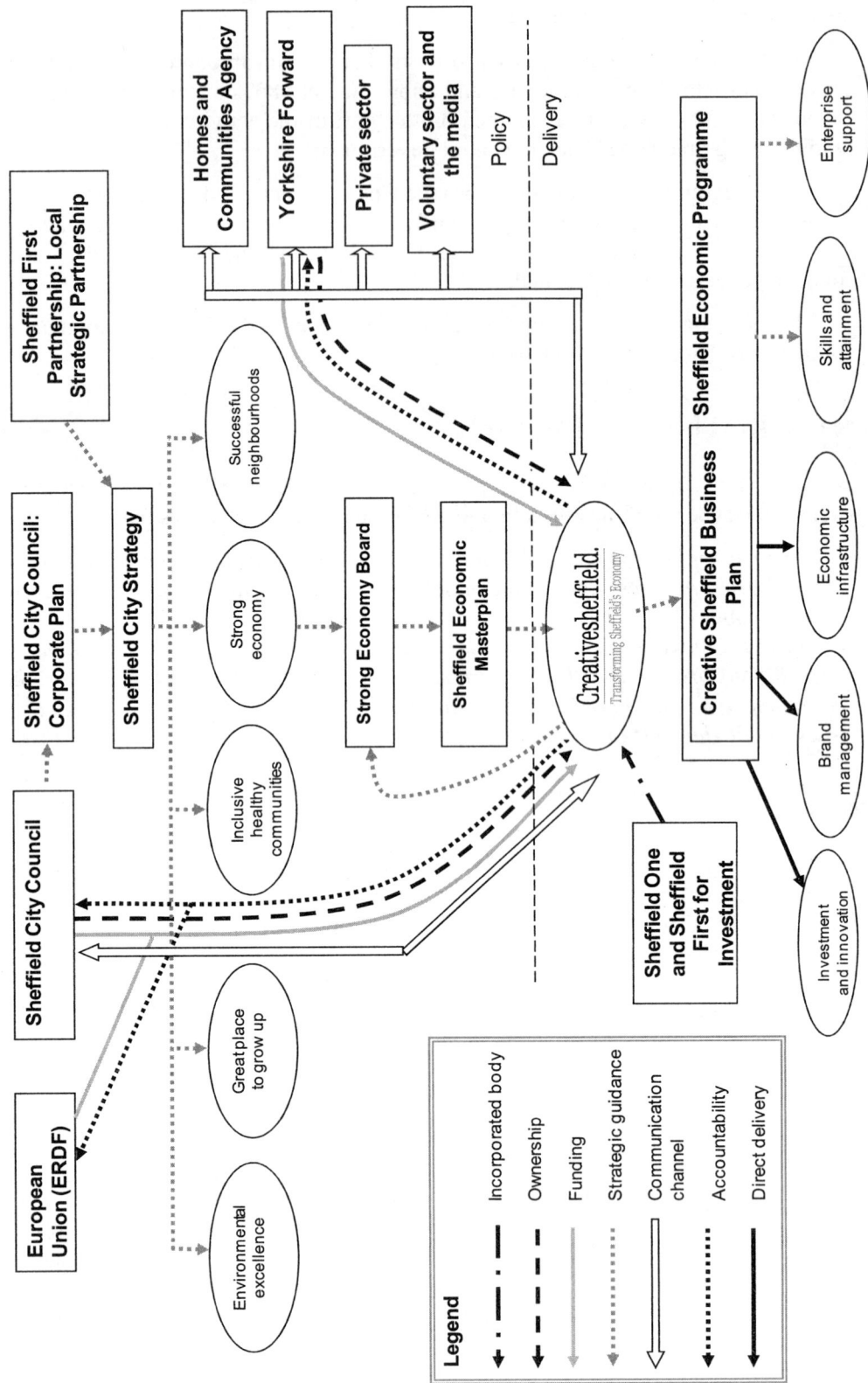

Figure A.30. **The organisational structure of Creative Sheffield's senior management team**

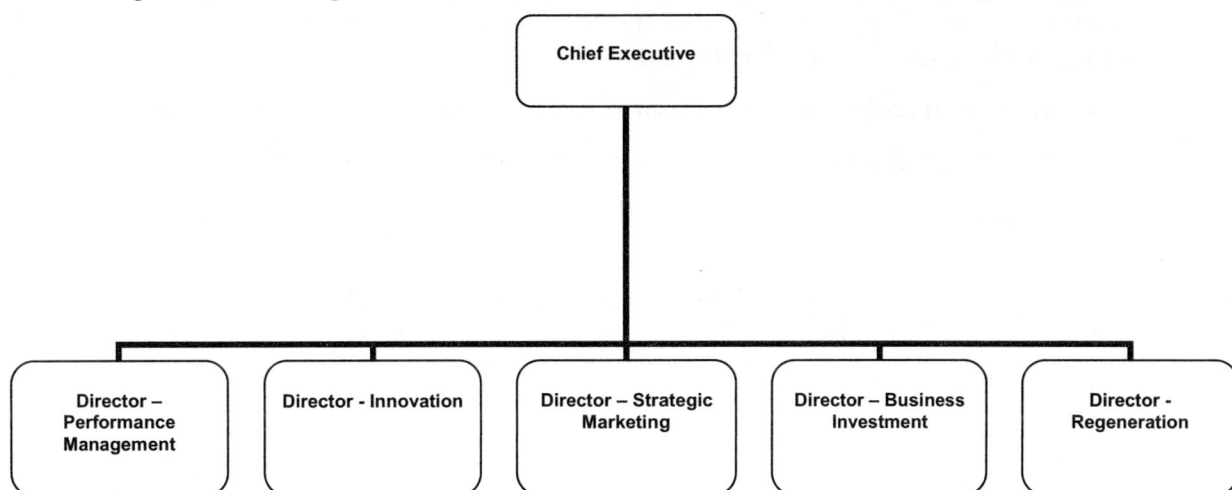

```
                        ┌──────────────────┐
                        │ Chief Executive  │
                        └──────────────────┘
                                 │
   ┌──────────┬──────────────┬───┴──────────┬──────────────┬──────────┐
┌──────────┐┌──────────┐┌──────────────┐┌──────────────┐┌──────────────┐
│Director –││Director -││Director –    ││Director –    ││Director -    │
│Performance││Innovation││Strategic     ││Business      ││Regeneration  │
│Management ││          ││Marketing     ││Investment    ││              │
└──────────┘└──────────┘└──────────────┘└──────────────┘└──────────────┘
```

Source: Roberts, P. (2009), Written and telephone communication and interviews.

How is Creative Sheffield led?

Board level

The board is charged with the delivery of its own business plan and reporting on the performance of the economy and the delivery of all aspects of the Economic Programme.

The board communicates with the operational team in two main ways: (1) the Creative Sheffield chief executive officer (CEO) sits on the board; and (2) board members actively work with Creative Sheffield officers, as board members lead each work stream of the Sheffield Economic Programme and Creative Sheffield Business Plan.

Chief executive officer

The first CEO of Creative Sheffield was appointed in September 2006.

What are Creative Sheffield's key services and programmes within the system of local development and investment promotion?

Strategy and delivery

When Creative Sheffield was launched in 2007, its primary task was to lead on the development of the Economic Masterplan (EMP), which was intended to set the direction of the city's development over the next 10-15 years. Having made progress over the previous decade, particularly in the city centre, it was clearly recognised that Sheffield needed its underlying economic performance to improve if it were to remain competitive in the 21st century.

The EMP identified a GBP 1 billion gap in gross value added (GVA) between what the city actually produced and what it could produce if it operated at the same level as the national average. Closing the gap became the primary target of the city's economic strategy, which itself translated into three main factors:

- creating an additional 30 000 jobs over and above the city's normal trajectory;

- bringing at least 16 000 people into the workforce within Sheffield;

- shifting the economy to a significantly higher level of value-added production and skill levels.

The EMP was developed through a combination of external consultants working with Creative Sheffield, the City Council and Yorkshire Forward. A large and inclusive steering group met regularly during the development process and would critique early drafts of the plan. The final draft was then widely distributed to ensure all parties bought into both the overall aims and the route map.

The EMP was approved by a meeting of the full City Council and by the Sheffield First Partnership.

Political leadership of the City Council changed in 2008 from a Labour administration to Liberal Democrat. Paul Scriven, the Leader of the Council, was quick to endorse Creative Sheffield as the main delivery vehicle for the Economic Masterplan, but stressed that future changes of strategy or direction had to be set by those who were directly accountable to the people of Sheffield, the Council's elected members. This division between strategy/policy and delivery has seen Creative Sheffield take on a wider role in its reporting on the progress of the EMP's delivery from all contributing partners, as well as on its own progress. The Strong Economy Board has been established in order to steer the strategic direction of the city and ensure the strategy remains up to date and relevant to any future changes in the wider economy (Roberts, 2009).

Delivery work streams

Creative Sheffield's dual role as far as delivery of the Economic Master Plan is concerned, is:

- directly delivering projects within its own business plan (city marketing, business investment and innovation promotion, physical regeneration);

- monitoring and reporting on the delivery of the wider economic programme, which includes projects delivered by other organisations.

To fulfil those dual roles, Creative Sheffield and the City Council have established five broad work streams:

- **infrastructure**, including regeneration schemes, housing and transport;

- **skills**, including employability, basic and higher level skills;

- **enterprise**, including enterprise support provision, local economies and the "BiG" (Local Enterprise Growth Initiative);

- **innovation and investment**, including the city's partnerships with universities, the National Health Service and its business investment activities;

- **brand management**, including leadership on marketing, major events, the city centre retail experience and the leisure economy.

Each of these work streams is led by one Creative Sheffield board member and one officer, either from Creative Sheffield or Sheffield City Council. Creative Sheffield reports progress on the economic aspects of these work streams back to the Strong Economy Board and to other partners as appropriate.

A more detailed summary of Creative Sheffield's activities and key projects is found below.

Leading the delivery of the Economic Masterplan

Creative Sheffield leads the delivery of the city's Economic Masterplan. The Masterplan was unveiled in January 2008 and provides the vision for a transformed city by 2020.

Evaluation of the Economic Masterplan delivery

It is the responsibility of Creative Sheffield to report on progress of how the city's Economic Masterplan is delivered.

City marketing and promotion

Creative Sheffield promotes the city globally by, for instance, raising its profile at global events such as MIPIM, the world's leading property exposition. In local terms, there is also the concept of "Wednesday Night Live": Sheffield city centre tended not to be seen as a lively hub. People returned home after work. This project attempts to create a buzz in the city centre to hold workers in the area for longer. On Wednesdays, restaurants and shops are encouraged to stay open longer and a series of events are promoted. The initiative has been so successful that retailers have asked for more of the same. As a result, making the case for investment in the city centre has also improved significantly.

Business investment and retention services

The Business Investment team at Creative Sheffield: (1) helps businesses find appropriate sites, using a database of available property in the city, and can also help guide businesses through the various planning and regulatory requirements; (2) helps identify sources of funding for businesses via a number of options; (3) helps businesses recruit staff; (4) provides relocation support for incoming employees; and (5) helps existing Sheffield businesses expand their workforce, move to larger premises, access expert help from the universities or seek suppliers. For example, the Creative Sheffield team worked on the investment of Capita Hartshead UK headquarters in Sheffield. The outsourcing company is developing a new high-profile site at the gateway to the city.

Innovation

Creative Sheffield has seen an increasing focus on innovation, particularly over the past 12 months. One of the programmes it is looking to develop focuses on innovation accelerators. These are specialist companies that create and nurture businesses developed from university and other research sources and invests in them to bring them to market.

Nanotechnology and new energy firms are an excellent example of the areas they work in. The programme, when developed, will assist the accelerators through a range of interventions, assisting them to provide a pipeline of new and innovative businesses in the city (Roberts, 2009).

Urban regeneration

Creative Sheffield has delivered and co-ordinated a number of key projects across the city; for example, Digital Campus. The new Digital Campus is now a key part of Sheffield's infrastructure offer. According to the Digital Campus website, "The Digital Campus, located in front of Sheffield's train station, will be home to more than 3 000 creative and digital industries sector workers." Phase 1 – Electric Works – is already attracting companies to its 50 000 square feet of flexible workspace (Sheffield Digital Campus, 2009). The campus is at the heart of the city's plans to become the e-learning capital of Europe.

What enables Creative Sheffield to contribute to the local development and investment promotion system so effectively?

City development company status and structure

The amalgamation of a number of existing development agencies under one banner, Creative Sheffield, has ensured that it is far more efficient and simpler to work for individuals, potential investors and other agencies. Other advantages of Creative Sheffield are that it is a quasi-independent body which can operate in a way that a City Council cannot. The company has the independence and multi-partnership style of a URC, with the added benefit of the full range of tools to achieve the economic transformation of the city.

Partnership working

Effective relationship working is reinforced because Creative Sheffield is intimately involved in all parts of Sheffield's economic development system.

Co-ordination capacity

Creative Sheffield has the capacity to co-ordinate its activities at the city scale, involving the full range of key partners. For instance, Creative Sheffield works to develop a co-ordinated approach to brand marketing. The creation of the City Marketing Group allows all key partners to be linked into the process of building the city's brand which ensures a consistent approach to the marketing; something which is illustrated by the "Event Sheffield" website.

Talented staff

Creative Sheffield recruits the best talent it can find. This process has been aided by the fact that the organisation is autonomous, dynamic and action-orientated. The fact the organisation recruited a foreign-born CEO with excellent links to networks outside the United Kingdom has facilitated the identification, attraction and acquisition of talented individuals.

Foreign direct investment function

In 2005, Sheffield First for Investment (SFFI) was rated in the top ten agencies in the world for foreign direct investment (FDI) marketing and account management by GDP Global Consultancy. In 2006, SFFI was ranked number one. Creative Sheffield has built on the strength of SFFI expanding the team and focussing more closely on target sectors. Creative Sheffield points out that, as well as quality of life and locational assets, the process of dealing with a prospective investor well is part of a place's unique selling point. Building the necessary network within the city to provide potential investors with the bespoke information they request in a rapid and reliable way is key here. Because a large proportion of FDI goes to places where there is an existing link, Creative Sheffield attracts further investment from organisations which are currently tied to the city. In this way, intense account management of the top 100 employers in the city is a critical task. Creative Sheffield is quick to assign this task to talented relationship managers and ensures senior staff have regular meetings with the top employers.

Discipline of private sector property development

Creative Sheffield sees project management expertise as critical to the organisation's success. Not only does it improve efficiency and quality, it also gives the organisation the solid base from which it can think creatively and do things that haven't been done before. For instance, master planning from a holistic point of view has been made possible by operating with private-sector-type discipline. Without the added capacity project management expertise offers, unexpected events such as the loss of a key funder would have serious implications.

What constraints make Creative Sheffield less able to effectively contribute to the local development and investment promotion system?

System of accountability and project commissioning

The City Council's chief executive is the company secretary and the board has two automatic members, the Leader of the Council and the Shadow Cabinet Member for Economic Development. Creative Sheffield is also open to call in to the Council's Scrutiny Committees. Yorkshire Forward also has two automatic board members, the executive Directors of Business and Environment. As funders, the City Council and Yorkshire Forward carry out regular audits of activities, financial management and outputs. As a limited company, Creative Sheffield is also subject to a statutory audit.

Reporting on own delivery

Responsible for reporting on the delivery of the Economic Masterplan, Creative Sheffield, to a certain extent, evaluates its own work on behalf of the City. Though this has not been an issue thus far, conflicts of interest could occur.

How has, or how are, Creative Sheffield approached/approaching these problems?

System of accountability and project commissioning

To improve the speed at which buy-in from key partners is achieved, Creative Sheffield works closely with key partners such as the City Council and Yorkshire Forward, at the development phase. Achieving earlier buy-in ensures that partners are more likely to have the opportunity to shape initiatives and sign off on new projects. In this way, Creative Sheffield attempts to apply a "No Surprises" philosophy to its work.

Reporting on own delivery

To date, this risk is reduced by the engagement of external independent programme managers, who assess projects and programme progress for Creative Sheffield, City Council and Yorkshire Forward projects in the city in an equal and objective manner (Roberts, 2009).

How has Creative Sheffield performed in relation to its key performance indicators?

Table A.29 summarises how Creative Sheffield has performed in relation to its key performance indicators.

Accountabilities, performance review mechanisms and best-practice sharing

Accountabilities

Creative Sheffield is accountable in many ways. As previously stated, the City Council's chief executive is the company secretary and the board has two automatic members, the Leader of the Council and the Shadow Cabinet Member for Economic Development. Creative Sheffield is also open to call in to the Council's Scrutiny Committees. Yorkshire Forward also has two automatic board members, the executive Directors of Business and Environment. As funders the City Council and Yorkshire Forward carry out regular audits of activities, financial management and outputs. As a limited company, Creative Sheffield is also subject to a statutory audit.

Performance review mechanisms

In order to review performance continually, it has been decided that Creative Sheffield will produce an annual report on performance against the Economic Masterplan, both to the Council and to the City as a whole (Roberts, 2009).

Table A.29. **Key performance indicators of Creative Sheffield**

Theme	Tangible impact

Innovation and investment	• Business investments: Creative Sheffield offers support to those companies already in Sheffield and also to companies who express interest in relocating their business to the region. A few highlights of this work are:
	   ○ Sandvik Medical Solutions: 112 000 square foot centre of excellence agreed, which will safeguard/create up to 100 jobs.
	   ○ Tomorrow Options: this Portuguese micro-electronics company is to open its first subsidiary in the United Kingdom in Sheffield.
	   ○ Capita Hartshead, the United Kingdom's largest specialist pensions administration organisation, selected Sheffield for its UK Headquarters.
	   ○ HR Forum: a quarterly forum for businesses is being run by Creative Sheffield's qualified human resource (HR) consultants to provide businesses with information relevant to the current economic circumstances. These events also allow businesses a chance to talk with others who are facing the same problems and share experiences.
	• Advanced manufacturing and materials sector: a strategy for the development of this critical sector has been endorsed by Yorkshire Forward and other South Yorkshire partners.
	• Electric Works: recently completed, this building is being marketed towards the digital and new media industries. The building has received positive worldwide media attention and has been voted as one of the best office spaces in the world in which to work. It is a huge asset in further developing the sector and its successful delivery is a major achievement for the city.
	• Sheffield China relations: ongoing work on developing strong relations with the Chinese government to pursue long-term partnerships and trade opportunities with a number of regions.

Economic infrastructure	• City Centre Masterplan: approved by Creative Sheffield and Sheffield City Council in February 2008, the City Centre Masterplan is the roadmap to which all development in the city centre will follow for the foreseeable future. The changes were endorsed by the City Council Cabinet in January 2009. • Sevenstone (new retail quarter): this is one of the major projects in the next stage of the city's development. Hammerson who are developers for the project continue to progress the project with close involvement from partners: Sheffield City Council, the Housing and Communities Agency and Yorkshire Forward. Whilst there have been delays in getting the project started, other schemes in other cities have been scraped during the last year due to the economic downturn. It is great success keeping this flagship project moving forwards so that work can commence as soon as is viable. • Castlegate: the construction of the second office building on the site has been completed with 50 000 square feet of office space being made available. Take up by quality occupiers has been swift. • The Crucible: this project is now complete. The new Crucible will be formally opened in early 2010. In conjunction with the refurbishment is the redevelopment of Tudor Square, which the Crucible fronts onto. This work is also near completion and will provide a high-quality setting for the cluster of theatres in this part of the city centre.

Table A.29. **Key performance indicators of Creative Sheffield** (*continued*)

Theme	Tangible impact
	• Vivienne Westwood: bringing the Westwood exhibition to Sheffield and supporting the late night opening. As a result of the success of this project and the increased numbers in the city centre, Wednesday Night Live was developed.
	• Wednesday Night Live: a project that targets the evening economy to drive footfall in the city centre. Throughout 2008, a number of events were scheduled to bring people back into the city centre or to keep the office workers later into the evening by working with shops, bars and restaurants to stay open late. The project was a resounding success, with a year-on-year increase in city centre footfall on a Wednesday night of 89%. The initiative generated intensive media coverage including two live television broadcasts and frontpage leads in local media.
Brand management	• Sheffield Stories: with a number of media outlets focusing on too many negative stories, Creative Sheffield have launched a Sheffield Stories bulletin to get people talking about all the amazing positive stories that are coming out of our city. The bulletin has been met with extremely positive feedback and has resulted in a number of positive media articles in local and regional press.
	• UK Cities Monitor: each year, Cushman and Wakefield publish the results of their survey on UK cities. Sheffield's perception has been raised since 2007, with many areas showing significant improvement including lively city centre environment, best city to locate to and availability of office space.
	• Growing Sheffield's reputation: one of the key marketing strategies has been to find great city stories and amplify them nationally and internationally. Tony Christie's "Made in Sheffield" album is a good example of this in action where, with a small investment, a huge level of media value has been generated, all talking about Sheffield.
	• Strategic Events Group: Developed to prioritise the city's events, this group ensures that the key events gain the full support from all the connected partners to maximise the impact on the city.
Enterprise support	• Enterprise Match: offering companies and individuals help, advice and training in all aspects of their sales and marketing needs. This is one project in a series being run under the BiG project within the city.

Source: Roberts, P. (2009), Written and telephone communication and interviews.

Best-practice sharing

In November 2008, a delegation from two Chinese cities visited Sheffield to see what they could learn from Sheffield's regeneration. Further links with China include the Sheffield-China Business Network. Ian Bromley, the Chief Executive of Creative Sheffield, stated at the time, "These increased connections with China are fast putting Sheffield on the global map. This worldwide interest in Sheffield's economic and physical development can only bring benefits through an improved city image, increased inward investment, knowledge transfer, global collaborations and trade" (Creative Sheffield, 2008b).

What are Creative Sheffield's strengths, constraints, opportunities and challenges?

Creative Sheffield's strengths, constraints, opportunities and challenges are summarised in Table A.30.

Table A.30. **Creative Sheffield's strengths, constraints, opportunities and challenges**

Strengths	Constraints
• As a CDC, Creative Sheffield offers a holistic and less fragmented approach to development. • Dedicated and highly focused organisation. • Repays business investment by being competitive, focused on the bottom line and providing clear decision-making lines through its management. • Partnership working is a clear strength of Creative Sheffield.	• Incorporation as an arm's length company. • Complex system of accountability and project commissioning. • Reporting on own delivery.
Opportunities	Challenges
• Regional development agencies will likely delegate more funds to city regions such as Sheffield. • The approval to install a super high-speed broadband network across the whole of South Yorkshire is a significant opportunity to develop a digital region. It will be paid for by Yorkshire Forward ERDF transition funds and by the four local authorities of South Yorkshire and is now confirmed. The project will be delivered over the next three years and the private sector is already very interested, particularly those with a track record in e-learning and film. • The "New Retail Quarter" project: the developer Hammerson, which named it "Sevenstone", is on board and the Council, Homes and Communities Agency and Yorkshire Forward are now carrying it forward.	• Regional development agencies and councils are not able to give long-term funding. Three years is the funding timescale for both. The political change that accompanies public spending can disrupt longer term planning. • South Yorkshire straddles two regional development agencies, which can cause complexities.

References

Creative Sheffield (2007), "Creative Sheffield Sets out Stall with Target of 25 000 New Jobs in Next Ten Years", *www.creativesheffield.co.uk/MarketingSheffield/News/Launch.htm?p=2&y=2007.*

Creative Sheffield (2008a), "Sheffield Means Business", *www.quebec innovation2008.com/documents/presentations/Andy_Curtis.pdf.*

Creative Sheffield (2008b), "International Recognition for Sheffield's Regeneration", *www.creativesheffield.co.uk/MarketingSheffield/News/SheffChina.htm?p=1&y=2008.*

Creative Sheffield (2009a), "Corporate Information", *www.creativesheffield.co.uk/CorporateInformation.*

Creative Sheffield (2009b), "The Sheffield Economic Masterplan: Transforming the Economy in One Generation", *www.creativesheffield.co.uk/SheffieldEconomicMasterplan.*

Kerslake, B. and V. Taylor (2004), "Economic Development and Creative Sheffield", Sheffield City Council, *www.sheffield.gov.uk/index.asp?pgid=35768&mtype=print.*

Roberts, P. (2009), Written and telephone communication and interviews.

Sheffield Digital Campus (2009), "New Digital Campus Signals Push by Sheffield to Be the E-Learning Capital of Europe", *www.sheffielddigitalcampus.com/news/new_digital_campus_signals_push_by_sheffield_to_be_the_e-learning_capital_of_europe/.*

HAFENCITY HAMBURG GMBH – **359**

HAFENCITY
HAMBURG

HafenCity Hamburg GmbH
Hamburg, Germany

Organisation type

The area known as "HafenCity" is Europe's largest inner city urban development zone (HafenCity Hamburg GmbH, 2009a). In 1998, the Free and Hanseatic City of Hamburg entrusted HafenCity Hamburg GmbH (formerly GHS *Gesellschaft für Hafen- und Standortentwicklung mbH*) with the development of HafenCity. Hamburg is one of very few German cities undertaking major urban redevelopment. Unlike many city development agencies who act at the city-wide or metropolitan scale, HafenCity Hamburg GmbH focuses only on a highly specific district – the old port area. HafenCity Hamburg GmbH has been tasked with leading the redevelopment through buying back land and buildings in the project area which are not owned by public authorities and relocating companies from the area to other areas in the city, as well as being responsible for developing the necessary physical infrastructure and required amenities so that new spaces (office, residential, shopping, restaurants, culture and leisure) are developed. It oversees the entire development of the area (Bruns-Berentelg, 2009).

Mission statement

No explicit mission statement could be found, but the organisation does state that "HafenCity is underlining Hamburg's heritage as a maritime city while simultaneously reinterpreting it for the present day and in so doing creating a model for the development of European cities in the 21st century" (HafenCity Hamburg GmbH, 2008a).

History, origins and ownership

On 7 May 1997, the then First Mayor of the Free and Hanseatic City of Hamburg, Dr. Henning Voscherau, presented the HafenCity vision to the public. The formal decision to develop HafenCity was made by the City Parliament in August 1997. The Masterplan for the project was drafted in 1999 by the Ministries for Urban Development and Economics together with HafenCity Hamburg GmbH (at that time named *Gesellschaft für Hafen- und Standortentwicklung*, GHS). This Masterplan outlined goals for the metropolitan city of Hamburg as a whole, density and land use of redeveloped areas, flood protection, transport and traffic, industrial operations to be retained and social infrastructure (HafenCity Hamburg GmbH, 2009b).

Since the Masterplan was conceived as a flexible reference framework for developing HafenCity, the Masterplan is able to change and respond as necessary. The Masterplan was reprinted in 2006 with a new editorial summing up various new developments. However, with the exemption of these new developments, there were no changes or updates made to the Masterplan itself. This is scheduled for the end of 2009 for the second phase of HafenCity development.

Other issues which have developed over time have been incorporated into the realisation strategy for sub-areas and projects in HafenCity, and were developed on the basis of the content of the Masterplan. These issues include: the need for clearance and relocation of land uses of formerly restricted areas to allow the development of HafenCity to proceed; changes in the process of land acquisitions; increased urban density to improve the urban character of living and forge closer social interaction; a doubling of the number of jobs created by the development; the cancellation of a streetcar network plan; the subsequent development of a subway connecting HafenCity to the existing railway based public transport network; the development of HafenCity University; culture, which has become a fundamental aspect of the project's development despite not playing a key role in the Masterplan; and, lastly, development timeframes, which have shifted due to a brisker than expected pace of work (HafenCity Hamburg GmbH, 2006).

What does HafenCity Hamburg GmbH do?

HafenCity Hamburg GmbH is engaged in an integrated process of intensive urban restructuring. It is not only trying to redevelop disused land and buildings, but is trying to create a wholly new economic rationale, housing, leisure and amenities. Simultaneously, the agency is trying to fully integrate this development with the city as a whole. One of the key aims of the work is to create a new distinctive destination. This is to be achieved through a conscious effort to preserve the integration of water and urban land use by preserving the old port structures (e.g. harbour basins, quay walls, bridges, etc.) and the neighbouring *Speicherstadt* warehouse district. Six historic buildings in HafenCity will also be preserved and renovated, helping to create a distinct location.

At its core, HafenCity Hamburg GmbH carries out two distinct, but highly inter-related functions. At one level, it is involved in very high-level and complex project management; this involves managing the project of urban restructuring through planning, implementation, development management and promotion, all of which aim to generate real and lasting physical, economic and social change in the area. At the same time, the agency is also concerned with urban management in terms of managing the performance of the district, *e.g.* making the public realm attractive, encouraging people to come to the area and building up new social networks and formal and informal institutions.

More specifically, HafenCity Hamburg GmbH has the following areas of responsibility:

- market and sell municipally owned real estate in HafenCity (approximately 98% of the total area to be developed);

- attract investors and buyers, providing all necessary assistance;

- develop the location for residential use, service industries and leisure amenities;

- co-ordinate all planning and construction projects;

- plan and implement land development;

- manage and administer funds (special fund "City and Port") used for the development of HafenCity;

- co-operate with the relevant Hamburg authorities directly and indirectly with parliamentary committees;

- location marketing, public relations and citizen involvement (Bruns-Berentelg, 2009).

However, HafenCity Hamburg GmbH offers no financial incentives or tax breaks for developing within the area (Scottish Parliament, 2005). This is in stark contrast to the role of many of the other agencies covered in this book.

Figure A.31 details the timeline of HafenCity since inception to major project realisation.

What is HafenCity Hamburg GmbH's spatial scale of operation and influence?

The geographical scale at which HafenCity Hamburg GmbH operates is comparatively small. Its work is concerned only with a particular area within the city, namely the former harbour areas near to the city centre which cover an area of 157 hectares. Development of this area will extend and enlarge Hamburg's city centre by nearly 40%. As of 2009, the eastern part of HafenCity was still primarily in the planning phase; the centre was a huge construction site and the western side was increasingly becoming an urban environment.

Within this scale of operation, different areas are being developed in different ways, as illustrated in Figure A.32. HafenCity Hamburg GmbH does not impose top-down, homogenous urban planning but instead ensures that the quarters identified below are appropriately and sensitively developed in a physically and conceptually differentiated manner (Bruns-Berentelg, 2009).

How is the HafenCity project financed?

In 1997, a law was passed to create a special fund called "City and Port" to provide a financial basis for the development of HafenCity and a container terminal. Municipal land within the HafenCity area was contributed to the fund free of charge. This was vital in facilitating redevelopment of the former port area, as political consensus between port and urban development was achieved by also lending against the newly established "City and Port" special fund in order to finance the new port infrastructure required for the container terminal in *Hamburg-Altenwerder* (total investment approximately EUR 335 million).

Figure A.31. **HafenCity: a timeline of key development events**

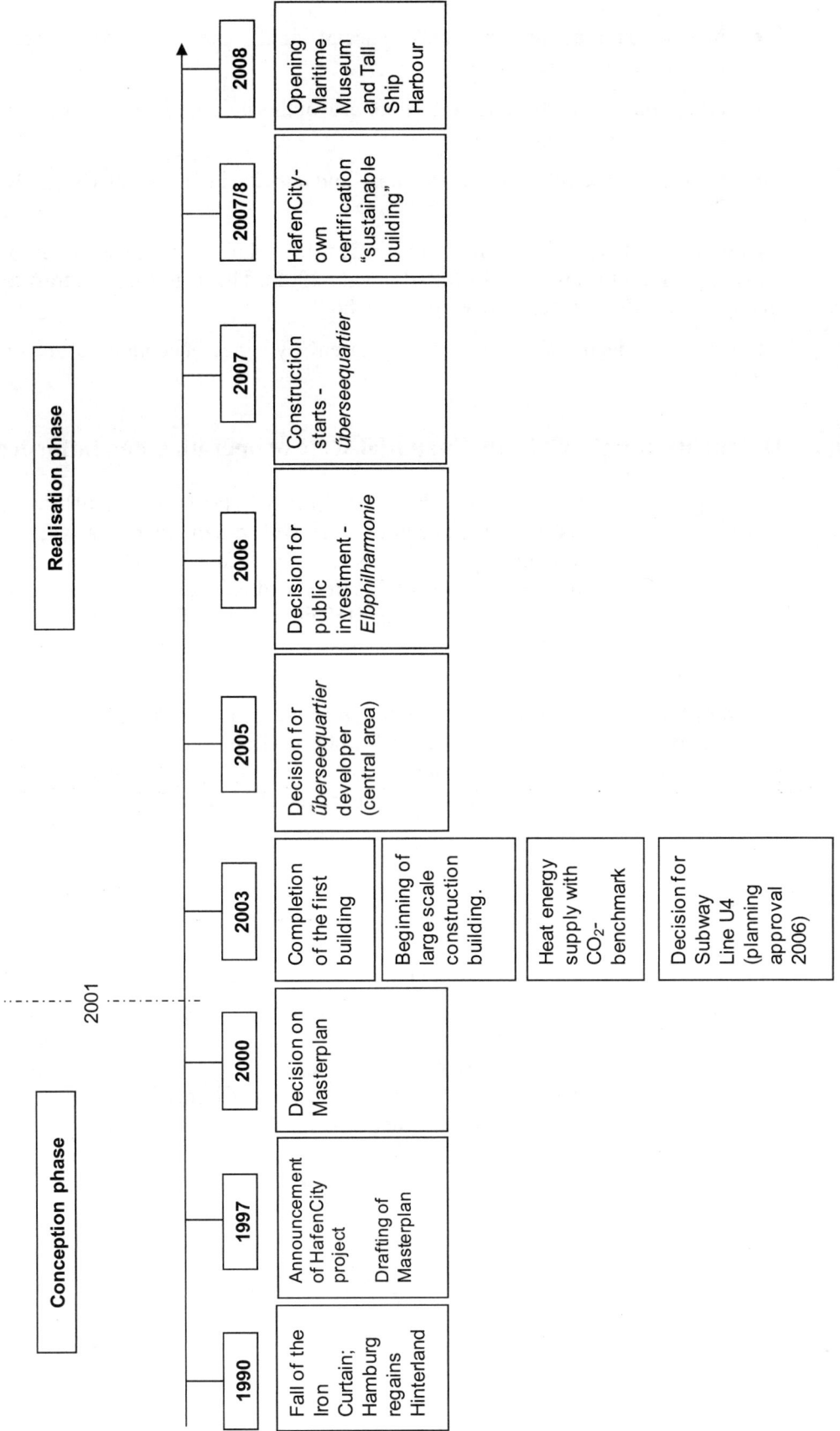

Conception phase				Realisation phase				

2001

1990	**1997**	**2000**	**2003**	**2005**	**2006**	**2007**	**2007/8**	**2008**
Fall of the Iron Curtain; Hamburg regains Hinterland	Announcement of HafenCity project Drafting of Masterplan	Decision on Masterplan	Completion of the first building Beginning of large scale construction building. Heat energy supply with CO_2-benchmark Decision for Subway Line U4 (planning approval 2006)	Decision for *überseequartier* developer (central area)	Decision for public investment - *Elbphilharmonie*	Construction starts - *überseequartier*	HafenCity-own certification "sustainable building"	Opening Maritime Museum and Tall Ship Harbour

Figure A.32. **Aerial view of the HafenCity development**

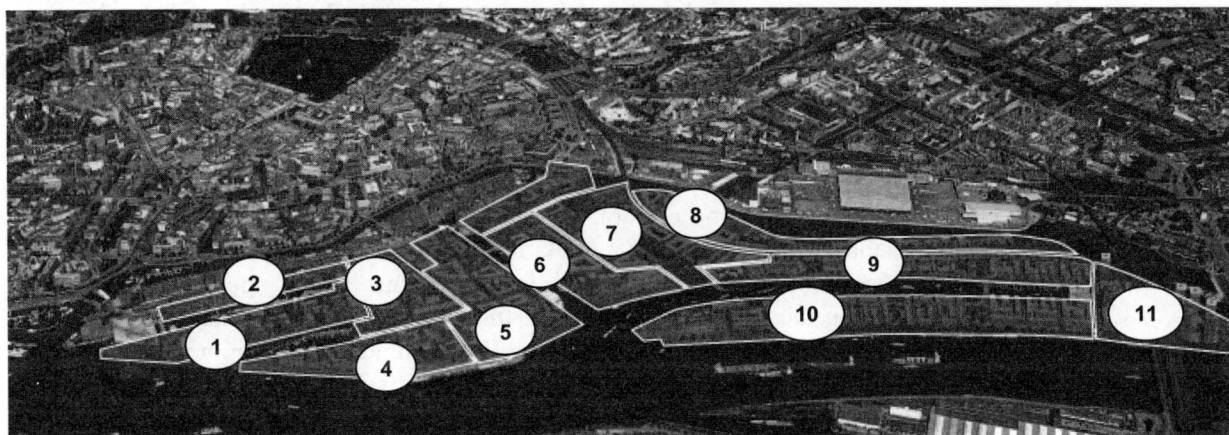

Legend

1. *Dalmannkai*: this includes rental apartments and condominiums, joint building ventures, co-operative building associations and luxury projects in addition to office space, cafés and restaurants whilst retaining maritime charm. The site has become a "leisure mile" and is home to roughly 1 100 people. This site was completed by the beginning of 2009.

2. *Am Sandtorkai*: this was the first quarter in HafenCity to be completed in 2005. It includes three mixed-use buildings, two residential and three office buildings and companies recently settled here include Drees and Sommer Group, Wölbern bank and China Shipping, with its European Head Office.

3. *Am Sandtorpark/Grasbrook* quarter: comprises corporate head offices, schools, kindergarten and homes and constitutes part of the open space for the western part of HafenCity, around which buildings are gathered. The quarter should be completed by 2011.

4. *Strandkai*: this offers rivers views providing space for service industries (Unilever moved in during 2009) and apartments. The design will include seven 55-metre-high towers.

5. *Uberseequartier*: this will be the new heart of HafenCity. Construction started in 2007 with major buildings and will be completed by 2012. The site was sold in December 2005 to a Dutch-German investor consortium. The quarter covers 7.9 hectares, 6 000-7 000 people will work here and residences, catering and retail will also be present. The site will also include the Science Centre, the cruise ship terminal, a hotel and the *Überseeboulevard* and shopping spread over the whole area.

6. *Elbtorquartier*: this site is home to HafenCity University, the German headquarters of Greenpeace; a design cluster with exhibition spaces, museums and a socially responsible hotel development in addition to residential units (*e.g.* special apartments for professional musicians).

7. *Brooktorkai*: office site housing *Germanischer* Lloyd headquarters and one of the largest German publishers.

8. *Lohsepark*: a new park connecting the eastern sector of the Wallring strip, which encircles Hamburg's historic city centre, with the Elbe riverbank walkway at *Baakenhafen*, effectively completing Hamburg's "green belt". The central part of the site is not available until 2018, but development started in 2009.

9. *Oberhafen*: creative industries and combined work-live concepts, sport facilities. A new bridge will act as a link with the city centre.

10. *Baakenhafen*: this is a mixed-use zone with focus on residential uses and a leisure and sports emphasis. All structures will be south facing and provide waterfront living. The site was originally zoned as the Olympic Village for the city's 2012 bid.

11. *Elbbrückenzentrum*/Chicago Square: a new multi-storey complex will be developed and the site has excellent linkages to interstate transport. It has potential as a high-value service hub.

Source: Bruns-Berentelg, J. (2009), Written and telephone communication and interviews.

A majority of public expenditure in the HafenCity development is advanced by the special fund, which borrows money on terms and conditions similar to those for public sector loans. The loans are repaid by the sale of land as freehold. Special fund expenditure amounts to some EUR 750 million, from which most of the funds are required for relocating business enterprises, clearing land, public flood defences, main and access roads, bridges, quaysides, promenades, parks, planning, communications and marketing. Other public infrastructures (namely underground train lines, road intersections and bridges outside of HafenCity), educational facilities, academic institutions (HafenCity University) and cultural facilities (*Elbphilharmonie* Concert Hall, Science Centre, International Maritime Museum Hamburg) are funded from the budgets of various Hamburg government ministries. Public expenditure totals approximately EUR 1.53 billion (including the City and Port special fund) and is more than matched by private investment of approximately EUR 5.5 billion. The HafenCity development does not receive any public financing from the central government (except EUR 135 million according to legal obligations for the subway) or European Union (HafenCity Hamburg GmbH, 2008b).

Figure A.33 sets out the projected capital investment requirements for HafenCity to 2025.

Figure A.33. **Projected capital investment requirements for HafenCity to 2025**

In EUR millions

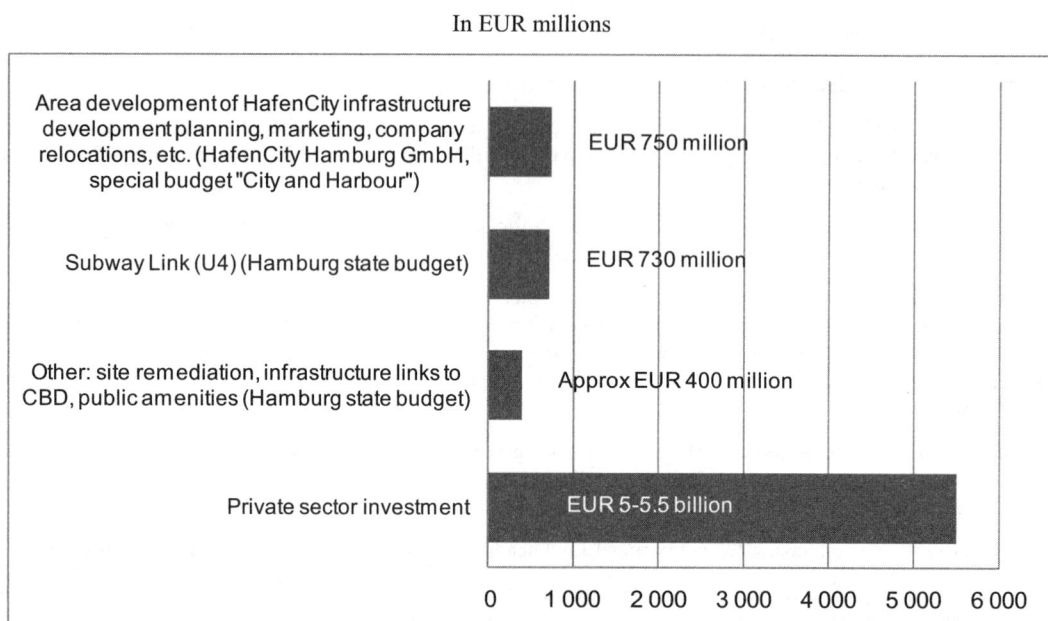

Source: Urban Land Institute (2007), "HafenCity Models of Development Success: Unlocking Regeneration Opportunities", Jürgen Bruns-Berentelg CEO, ULI European Trends Conference, Hamburg, *www.uli.org/sitecore/content/ULI2Home/Events/Conferences/Europe/Trends/Hamburg2007/Cities%20Transformed%20Pr ofiting%20from%20Urban%20Development.aspx*

What is the institutional context of the HafenCity project?

HafenCity Hamburg GmbH is a wholly owned subsidiary of Hamburg City State Government and works with both public bodies and the private sector. For instance, it collaborates with the city's ministries and interacts with a wide range of predominantly German and international companies acting as investors and occupiers of land. As a master developer, HafenCity Hamburg GmbH is the partner for all private sector developers and investors to participate in development and supports the newly established local communities regarding the development of the new urban spaces. The City State creates the enabling framework of the right policies and incentives and acts as a sponsor. Indeed, HafenCity Hamburg GmbH is operationally dependent on the City State.

In terms of the extent of autonomy and external influence in the development process, whilst HafenCity Hamburg GmbH is the organisation responsible for the development of the area and the trustee for the special fund "City and Port", the Ministry for Urban Development and the Environment has its own working group covering building approval and development planning.

Since 1 October 2006, HafenCity has been a priority project which means that Hamburg's City Parliament will debate the development plans in a city development committee especially created for this purpose. All contracts offered to developers by HafenCity Hamburg GmbH must be ratified by the Land Use Committee.

Other ministries of the City State of Hamburg are involved in the development process of HafenCity with respect to special projects like educational and cultural facilities (financed also from their budgets) or to a co-ordinated real estate policy and joint economic promotion efforts or city marketing of the City State (Figure A.34).

Who are HafenCity Hamburg GmbH's partners?

In order for HafenCity to act as a stimulus for broader development in Hamburg, the Masterplan recognised that it is necessary to build a broad consensus regarding the objectives and measures involved. This was achieved through wide-ranging dialogue early on in the planning process and, as such, the Masterplan is the result of an interdisciplinary exchange of ideas, whereby results of an international town planning competition, the outcome of a public planning debate and political decision making played an equal part.

In the realisation process of HafenCity, the involvement of important stakeholders, such as the Chambers of Commerce, architects, and the Retail Association, is assured by their representation in the advisory board. HafenCity is also a member of some of these organisations and their commissions such as the Urban Development Committee of the Chamber of Commerce.

Figure A.34. **HafenCity Hamburg GmbH project management and governance structure**

City State of Hamburg	Private/public sector HafenCity Hamburg GmbH (wholly-owned State of Hamburg subsidiary)	Private sector
1. Provides public guidelines **2. Prepares and grants:** (Ministry of Urban Development and Environment) - development plans - urban design (guidelines) - building permits **3. State Commissions approvals:** - development plans - land sales or acquisition **4. Finances and builds,** partly as public-private joint venture: - schools - university - concert hall - science centre - subway **5. Finances and builds external infrastructure linkages:** - streets and bridges - subway (partly financed from federal government)	**1. Acts as land owner** - special asset "City And Port" - finances all its activities from land sales **2. Activities:** - master developer - development planning - plans and builds infrastructure (streets, bridges, quay walls) - plans and builds public spaces (promenades, parks) - acquires investors, property sales - organises communication, marketing	**1. Private and institutional developers and investors** - development of individual sites - exception of central quarter *Überseequartier* where a guided area development takes place by a private consortium

Source: HafenCity Hamburg GmbH (2009a), "HafenCity Hamburg GmbH", homepage, *www.hafencity.com/*.

There are very close working relationships between the City State of Hamburg, HafenCity Hamburg GmbH and the private sector. The agency is supposed to bring the private sector to the table and make development happen in a way which shares risks and costs. In order to induce private sector success, Jürgen Bruns-Berentelg, Chief Executive of HafenCity Hamburg GmbH, states that the important factors are: relating the project to the overall strategy of the City; an appropriate spatial strategy; reducing risk; increasing competition; increasing transparency; reducing free rider strategies/co-ordination time wise; increasing innovation and quality; and increasing diversity and creating market niches in addition to producing appropriate infrastructure environments and a favorable mental map of HafenCity (Urban Land Institute, 2007). The private sector firms involved are mainly property firms, large corporate companies, investors and smaller companies which will be tenants as well as co-operative building societies and joint building associations.

Other organisations have also been set up to support the HafenCity development. For instance, the Cultural Co-ordination Committee jointly headed by the Ministry of Cultural Affairs and HafenCity Hamburg GmbH. HafenCity is also represented on the Board of Trustees of Hamburg Maritime Foundation which operates the Tall Ship Harbour in

HafenCity and on the board of Hamburg Harbour Marketing GmbH, the cruise ship marketing organisation supporting cruise ship terminal operations in HafenCity.

Universities and research institutes, as well as networking and co-operation agreements with other cities and waterfront projects, and the media are also partners for developing and promoting HafenCity.

How is HafenCity Hamburg GmbH governed?

The leadership team and staff members of HafenCity, including their specificities and numbers, are set out in Figure A.35.

Figure A.35. **The organisational structure of HafenCity Hamburg GmbH**

Managing Director Economist		**Chief Executive Officer** Geographer Real estate economist	
Assistant (1) (Architecture, sustainability)		**Assistant (1)** (Advisory Board, culture, R&D)	
Urban development fund / Corporate planning / Administration	**Area development**	**Communication / Marketing**	**Infrastructure**
Managers - Finance and controlling (4) - Facilities, property, contract management (2) - Assistants (5) (controlling/receptionists/pe rsonal assistants)	Senior managers (5) - Project management	Senior managers, managers (7) - PR, media relations - InfoCenter operations - Internet, publications - Event marketing - Investor relations - Social relations	Senior managers, managers (8) - Waterways - Road engineering - Transport planning - Landscape planning - Public space management - Construction management - Draftsman, data management
In addition many functions are accomplished by commissioning to the private sector/outsourcing			
1) **Immediate outsourcing (regular co-operation)** - Accounting - HR - Legal	- Master planning - Sub-area planning	- Ca. 15 part-time employees in addition to those listed - Copywriters, design agencies	- Infrastructure planning - Project management and quantity surveying for individual infrastructure measures
2) **Markets (based on individual tenders)** - Other support functions	- Architects, engineers, and consultants - Developers	- Research (universities and private companies)	- Consultancy (engineering) - Construction

Source: Bruns-Berentelg, J. (2009), Written and telephone communication and interviews.

The organogram that follows (Figure A.36) reveals the local development system within which HafenCity operates.

Figure A.36. **The position of HafenCity in the system of economic development and investment promotion in Hamburg**

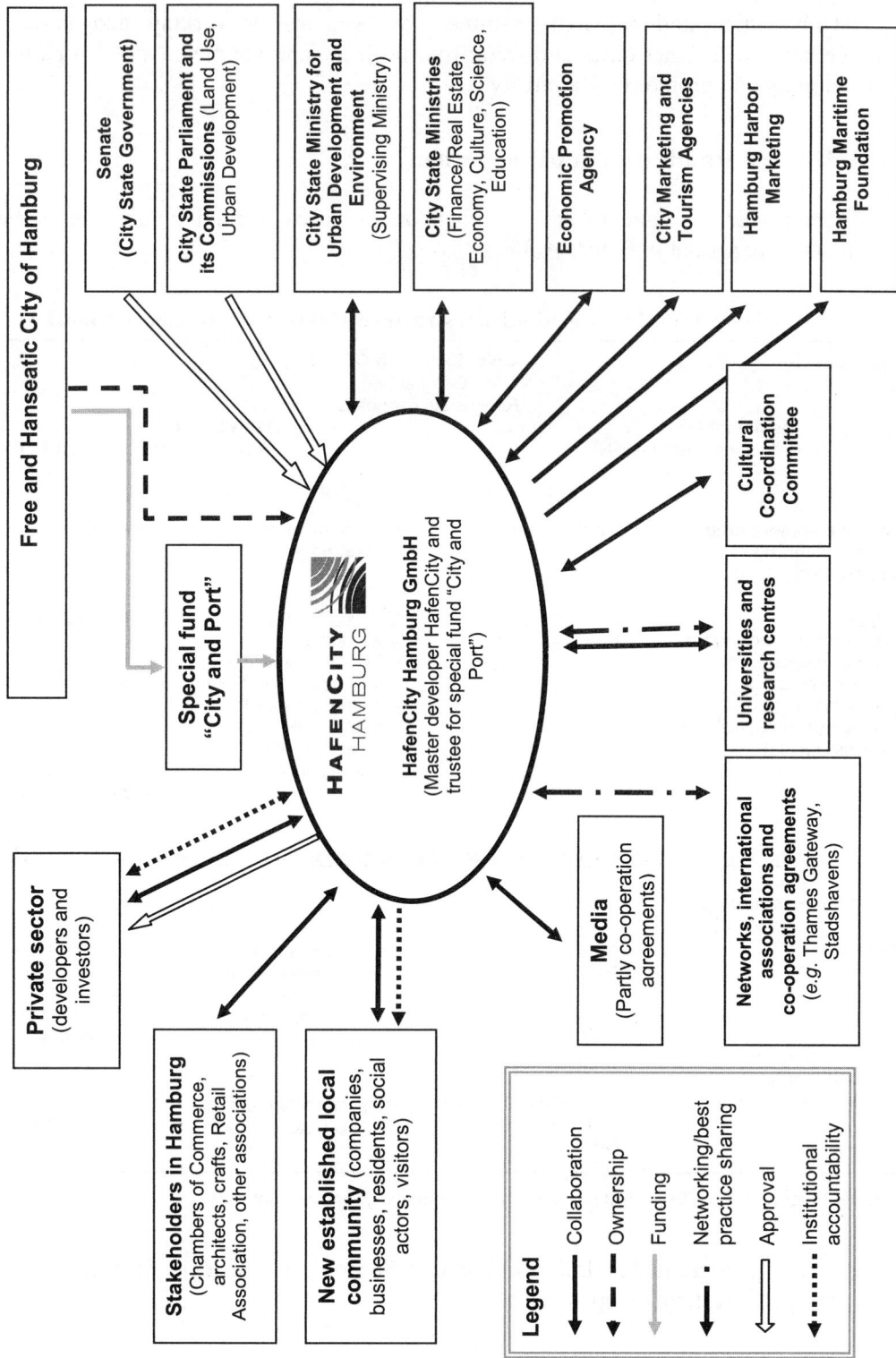

Free and Hanseatic City of Hamburg

Senate (City State Government)

City State Parliament and its Commissions (Land Use, Urban Development)

City State Ministry for Urban Development and Environment (Supervising Ministry)

City State Ministries (Finance/Real Estate, Economy, Culture, Science, Education)

Economic Promotion Agency

City Marketing and Tourism Agencies

Hamburg Harbor Marketing

Hamburg Maritime Foundation

HAFENCITY HAMBURG

HafenCity Hamburg GmbH (Master developer HafenCity and trustee for special fund "City and Port")

Special fund "City and Port"

Private sector (developers and investors)

Stakeholders in Hamburg (Chambers of Commerce, architects, crafts, Retail Association, other associations)

New established local community (companies, businesses, residents, social actors, visitors)

Media (Partly co-operation agreements)

Networks, international associations and co-operation agreements (e.g. Thames Gateway, Stadshavens)

Universities and research centres

Cultural Co-ordination Committee

Legend

→ Collaboration
--→ Ownership
→ Funding
·→ Networking/best practice sharing
⇒ Approval
·····→ Institutional accountability

How is HafenCity Hamburg GmbH governed?

Board level

HafenCity Hamburg GmbH's Supervisory Board consists of five ministers (for urban development, economics, finance, culture and education) plus the State Councillor at the Senate Chancellery. In 2005 an advisory board was set up. Its nine members include the President of the Chamber of Commerce, the President of the Chamber of Architects, the President of the Chamber of Crafts and four academic members (Bruns-Berentelg, 2009).

Chief executive officer

The current chief executive officer (CEO) of HafenCity Hamburg GmbH is Jürgen Bruns-Berentelg. Prior to taking on this position in 2003, he was a member of the board of a major listed real estate company headquartered in Hamburg and worked as Managing Director (Germany) for New York-based real estate developer Tishman Speyer in Berlin (Bruns-Berentelg, 2009).

Organisational style

HafenCity Hamburg GmbH is a high-level project management and master planning development agency which is seen as surgical, effective, businesslike and ambitious. The organisation is also highly orientated towards the private sector. Of the 34 paid positions at HafenCity Hamburg GmbH, most are occupied by individuals with high-level private sector experience across a number of different disciplines.

What are HafenCity Hamburg GmbH's key services and programmes within the system of local development and investment promotion?

Services

HafenCity Hamburg GmbH has bought back land in the project area which was not owned by public authorities, and is responsible for developing the necessary physical infrastructure before new spaces are developed and implementing public amenities.

The tasks on the left-hand side of Figure A.37 are HafenCity Hamburg GmbH's responsibility. The black dotted line marks those tasks that could potentially (and in the institutional context does) shift to private sector responsibility, but are not in the Hamburg context, which prefers public-private area development which focuses strongly on public goods generation and quality aspects over more quantity.

Figure A.37. **HafenCity: public-private and private development responsibilities**

HafenCity responsibilities (public-private tasks)	Interface	**Private development responsibilities**
- *Master developer* Setting the frame for real estate development		*Individual projects/project development*
- Relocation of companies		(*Überseequatier* area is a special concept of guided area development)
- Site clearance concept - Remediation - Infrastructure: road construction, quay walls, promenades, squares, parks (without subway "U-Bahn") - Location marketing - Communication		
- Acquisition of developers and owner occupiers for the properties - Pre- and post-contractual co-operation: quality development and controlling - Planned generation of economic, social and cultural capital - Production of other public commodities, *e.g.* climate protection or heating supply.	Public / Private	

Source: HafenCity Hamburg GmbH (2009a), "HafenCity Hamburg GmbH", homepage, *www.hafencity.com/*.

Key programmes

The key areas in which HafenCity Hamburg GmbH is active is the former harbour area, divided into the districts shown earlier in this chapter (Figure A.32). Each site has an individual character and focus. Table A.31 presents the percentage of square metre floor space per building volume.

Table A.31. **Hafencity: size of building volume**

Total building volume	2 million square metres gross floor space
Offices	~ 52 %
Residential	~ 33%
Culture (museum, science centre, concert hall), leisure (hotels, cruise terminal), and education	~ 7%
Retail and gastronomy	~ 5%

One key theme which runs through its work is the role of culture in site development. Until 2003, the Harbour Development Law set specific zoning terms for the harbour and free port area, which prohibited cultural activities on the site where HafenCity is now emerging; the same applied to many other harbours throughout the world. The area was barred from having any other than port activities. There are now, however, a number of new venues for culture: the *Elbephilharmonie* Concert Hall, the International Maritime Museum and the Science Centre. These new venues, along with the extension of

Hamburg's "Art Mile" into HafenCity, and culture being also an important use in public spaces, are providing an international artistic focus for the city.

What role has HafenCity Hamburg GmbH played in the system of local development and investment promotion?

Table A.32 summarises the role HafenCity Hamburg GmbH has played in the system of local development and investment promotion.

Table A.32. **Conceptualising the role of HafenCity Hamburg GmbH**

	Direct delivery	Facilitation and co-ordination	Strategic support and programmes	Creating capacity elsewhere
Depth and breadth of role	✓✓✓	✓✓✓	✓✓✓	✓
Specific example	• Buying back land. • Developing infrastructure.	• Working with a multiplicity of private investors. • Overseeing general development with a combination of market and non-market approaches.	• Fostering new social networks and informal institutions. • Strong support for the cities attractiveness and competitiveness. • Encouraging new concepts on the outreach of existing ones. • Setting incentives for new economic approaches. • Supporting the sustainable city Hamburg.	• "Cross border" social network and institutional setting.

What enables HafenCity Hamburg GmbH to contribute to the local development and investment promotion system so effectively?

High-quality and comprehensive urban design

HafenCity Hamburg GmbH has a variety of mechanisms in place to encourage comprehensive, and socially and ecologically responsible, development to proceed. For instance, land available for residential development is subject to competitive tenders. This is less to do with achieving a high price for the land, indeed the offer price is usually fixed before the start of the tender process, and more to do with the quality of the concept and the possibilities for a diverse mix of uses. After the decision for a bidder, architectural competitions take place. Through this process, HafenCity Hamburg GmbH aims to set and develop international standards for conceptual and architectural quality. Unlike in other places, developer incentives have not been pursued to the detriment of quality urban development, and the agency states that, "it is important not only to attract powerful and financially strong investors, but also to find building partners willing to co-operate in setting quality standards and in treading new and innovative paths" (HafenCity Hamburg GmbH, 2008c).

In addition, the CEO of HafenCity Hamburg GmbH, Jürgen Bruns-Berentelg, suggests that, "HafenCity is different. Economic development is not the centre of our focus, but rather the urban development process in the broadest sense. We want to join economic, social, cultural, and architectural forces in a way that translates into lasting urbanity" (Steinborn, 2007).

People-centred

There is also a people-centred approach to development, as illustrated in efforts made for social integration. Moreover, many institutions and networks have been established, with HafenCity Hamburg GmbH playing a vital role in supporting different initiatives (Figure A.38).

Figure A.38. **Hafencity: building social institutions and networks in the first phase**

Formal institutions Expanding the cohesive capacity	Networks/communication Face-to-face informal institutions	Clubs/associations
1. **Elementary school HafenCity** (*Am Sandorpark*) - Morning and afternoon classes. - Serving as a community centre. - Opening Spring 2009.	1. *Nachbarschaftstreff* - Monthly events with external guests in the common room at Bergedorf-Bille Foundation. 2. *Anwohnerstammtisch* - Monthly regulars' table at Kaiser's restaurant.	1. *Störtebeker* SV Sports Club - Sports club for HafenCity and old/new city. - Using the gym of *Katharinenkirche* school and, from 2009, *Katharinenschule* school in HafenCity.
2. **Day-care facility for children located in elementary school** - Also open on Saturdays and in emergencies. - Pilot project. - Opening spring 2009.	3. *Poldergemeinschaft Sandtorkai* - Digital networks/delocalised place identity generation.	2. *Kunstkompanie* HafenCity e.V. - Art projects and musical concerts in HafenCity.
3. *Brücke* – **Ecumencial Forum (with Laurentius Convent)** - Start-up project at Kaiserkai; recently launched.	4. *HafenCity-News.de* - District magazine 5. *HafenCityben.de* - Discussion forum	3. **Sponsoring committee for** *Katharinenschule* **school in HafenCity**
4. *Stadthaushotel* **HafenCity** - Hotel and catering services. - 40 workplaces for people with a handicap. - Opening 2010.	6. *Am-Keiserdai.net* - Platform for Bergedorf-Bille residents. - Communication projects. 7. *Quartier* magazine (Published by Elbe and Flut Vertag) 8. **Public cultural events**	

Source: HafenCity Hamburg GmbH (2009a), "HafenCity Hamburg GmbH", homepage, *www.hafencity.com/.*

An integrated approach

HafenCity Hamburg GmbH addresses both hard and soft elements of city development together. In other words, according to its CEO Jürgen Bruns-Berentelg, "Urban quality is characterised not just by physical quality, appeal or attractiveness of the place, but also inclusivity and diversity and its sustainability and mix. It should be open and accessible to lots of people."

To pursue this model of holistic and integrated development, HafenCity Hamburg GmbH pursues a diverse and heterogeneous involvement in the project from groups often outside the development process. For instance, disabled, children or affinity groups are encouraged to contribute to the development process. HafenCity Hamburg GmbH also delivered one of the first schools in Germany according to very high green building standards, as well as supported the development of a green university building.

Arm's-length positioning

The company can do things that the market and policy framework alone will not deliver. It can make market-based institutions deliver social objectives and encourage public actors to incentivise the market. In other words, it delivers a high internal rate of return for the market and high rate of external return for the public sector. For instance, HafenCity Hamburg GmbH convinced public-private joint venture partners that building the "green school" and using the school as a community centre was essential. It builds momentum behind such projects by organising and supporting applied research projects, discussion groups, focus groups discussions, *e.g.* to help specifying the requirements of young families in the new urban environment. In the case of the school, it took two years to develop the idea and roughly 35 people were involved in bringing ideas to focus. The school has now been finished and was handed over to the Ministry of Education in April 2009.

Public and private sector collaboration

The EUR 1.53 billion of investment from the public sector is being matched by EUR 5.5 billion from the private sector. Many large multi-nationals such as Unilever are working closely with the public sector to deliver the project. Many, such as the publisher *Der Spiegel and Germanischer Lloyd*, are relocating their company to the HafenCity complex using specific high HafenCity standards such as sustainability and public spaces to create positive externalities beyond using new efficient office space.

Pursuing a long-term growth strategy

According to Hamburg's first Mayor Ole Von Beust, the secret to the project's success is the fact that it is "pursuing a long-term growth strategy based on innovation, quality and sustainability [whilst] exploring new avenues too" (Freudewald, 2008).

Management approach

The management team's openness, entrepreneurial attitude and traditional style of business are what have made the project a success so far. The team are also given the flexibility to adopt innovative approaches. For instance, they are able to develop new ideas and frameworks which produce an innovative and distinctive approach to city development.

Partnership and collaboration

HafenCity Hamburg GmbH is able to achieve more by better involving existing partners and attracting new partners.

Financial sustainability

Even if the national government doesn't invest a single Euro for the next ten years, HafenCity Hamburg GmbH would operate successfully. This sustainability creates a level of certainty and confidence that infuses the organisation's activities. It also enables longer term planning, increased effectiveness (less time chasing funding), more apolitical decision making and more flexibility. In addition, the Urban Development Fund gives

HafenCity Hamburg GmbH the flexibility and capacity to implement plans effectively reflecting private sector demand.

Politically stable operating environment

In spite of changes in government from the Social Democratic to the Christian Democrats and a Christian Democratic and Green Party coalition the operating environment has been successful since 1997.

What constraints make HafenCity Hamburg GmbH less able to effectively contribute to the local development and investment promotion system?

At present, HafenCity Hamburg GmbH cites three constraints:

- **Bringing partners together.** HafenCity has strong boundaries with regard to responsibilities and weak overlapping institutional exchange.

- **Recession conditions**. Momentum behind the project is continuing yet small adaptations are being made due to tighter financial constraints of the private sector. The hotel sector and office demand are a particular concern of the private sector in 2009.

- **Mission creep and divisions of labour.** There is a question about where HafenCity Hamburg GmbH as a development company ends and where the municipal actors as providers of public services begin. There is a risk of mission creep here and that agendas will overlap. While the quality of spaces developed and the intensity of use is very high (specifically from visitors), the municipal authorities may not be fully equipped to keeping the quality of environment and services. People in HafenCity are arguing for an extended role of HafenCity Hamburg GmbH beyond the completion of physical construction. There is a perception that high-quality urban management should be the way in which HafenCity Hamburg GmbH continues its association with the development area.

How has, or how are, HafenCity Hamburg GmbH approached/approaching these problems?

Recession conditions

Certain projects have been readjusted to allow for changes in population driven growth and investment form. Due to the fact that the recession has only affected a small range of developers and its core areas are under construction and qualities have been achieved, only minor adjustments seem necessary. There has also been a diversification in the sources of investment as some investors not proceeding at same pace and style. Flexibility in the HafenCity Hamburg GmbH model has allowed the organisation to respond.

Mission creep and divisions of labour

HafenCity occupies itself with this question on a regular basis and is in ongoing discussion (Bruns-Berentelg, 2009).

How has HafenCity Hamburg GmbH performed in relation to its key performance indicators?

Table A.33 summarises how HafenCity Hamburg GmbH has performed in relation to its key performance indicators.

Accountabilities, performance review mechanisms and best-practice sharing

Accountabilities

HafenCity Hamburg GmbH is primarily accountable to the City State as its sole shareholder.

Performance review mechanisms

The organisation pursues benchmark-setting implementation processes.

Best-practice sharing

HafenCity Hamburg GmbH has clearly stated its wish to be a reference point for urban development for other European cities. A co-operation agreement was signed with *Stadshavens* Rotterdam and The Thames Gateway in March 2009 (Bruns-Berentelg, 2009).

Progress

With the exception of the amendments made in the 2006 Masterplan, the development is proceeding largely as it was initially conceptualised. Indeed, in many cases work has progressed faster and with higher quality than expected. The first quarter was completed in 2005, the second in 2009, two others will be completed in 2011 and the central one in 2012. The whole project is envisaged to be completed between 2020 and 2025. Hamburg has been elected European Green Capital 2011 by the European Union, in part based on HafenCity's performance (Bruns-Berentelg, 2009).

Table A.33. **Key performance indicators of HafenCity Hamburg GmbH**

Theme (initiative)	Tangible impact	Intangible impact
Investment leverage	• For EUR 1.53 billion of public funding, HafenCity Hamburg GmbH has managed to leverage EUR 5.5 billion of private sector investment.	• High visibility of the project in the international arena.
High quality of public space	• 20% of HafenCity's space will be developed as open areas, and public access rights exist for an additional 20%. Some 34 hectares of water surface will be used to a certain extent as well (HafenCity Hamburg GmbH, 2008c). • A range of spectacular waterfront urban spaces has been open since autumn 2007: Marco Polo Terraces, Vasco da Gama Plaza and Dalmannkai Promenades. They were joined by the Tall Ship Harbour in autumn 2008. Large pontoons form a floating walkway over the water, with permanent moorings for about 20 historic sailboats and steamers (HafenCity Hamburg GmbH, 2008c).	• Improved quality of urban space. • Serve as public encounter spaces due to different character and allow for a high degree of social integration.
Linkages with the City Centre	• Construction of the new U4 underground railway line is of extreme importance, as its two stops - *Überseequartier* and HafenCity University - will provide the connecting link to Hamburg's underground and urban railway network.	• Opening up the development opportunities in the *Speicherstadt* area and the southern inner city. Pushing also competition to improve existing buildings. • Socially and economically integrating lower profile urban quarters via employment opportunities and new traffic links.
Creating an attractive destination	• By mid-2009, 4 000 people worked in 200 companies in HafenCity. • By the end of 2008, approximately 1 500 people lived in HafenCity. • *Elbphilharmonie* Concert Hall, a new superstructure with two auditoriums, a five-star hotel and 45 residential apartments will follow in 2012. • Thousands of visitors have used the area's public spaces and amenities.	• According to a Pricewaterhousecoopers, LLP and an Urban Land Institute survey, Hamburg is now considered a prime location for investment in Europe. It was placed third behind Moscow and Istanbul (Freudewald, 2008).
Social and ecological development	• Ecological sustainability there is a mix of district heating and decentralised heat generation plants using fuel cells and solar energy with carbon dioxide. • HafenCity awards an Ecolabel for especially sustainable buildings. This is groundbreaking in Germany, where there was until 2009 no environmental certification process. The HafenCity Ecolabel, silver for special and gold for extraordinary achievements, can be applied for and awarded even in the early planning stages. Investors can then use this in their marketing and can profit from measures which normally take many years to accumulate.	• Tenants and users benefit strongly from environmental quality and are pushing investors to offer high ecological standards. • Is becoming an employment argument for companies in many sectors (*e.g.* media or creative industries).

What are HafenCity Hamburg GmbH's strengths, constraints, opportunities and challenges?

HafenCity Hamburg GmbH's strengths, constraints, opportunities and challenges are summarised in Table A.34.

Table A.34. **HafenCity Hamburg GmbH's strengths, constraints, opportunities and challenges**

Strengths	Constraints
• Very effective division of labour between public and public/private sector. • Flexibility of the Masterplan and its ability to respond to external changes. • Ability to respond quickly and effectively, meaning development has proceeded at a brisker than expected pace. • Mixed use development will allow HafenCity to respond to future changes in demand and circumstances. • People-centred approach to development efforts to build social integration, meaning it is not purely economics driven.	• High costs of regeneration and infrastructure development in a spatially segmented waterfront location with the risk of not meeting "break even" between income from land sales and expenditure at the end of the project period.
Opportunities	Challenges
• Built on principles of ecological sustainability – increasingly popular with developers and companies, so can leverage this. • Based on a large number of market participants and a strategy of spatial segmentation, competition and innovation have been held high and thus quality could be raised significantly.	• Development of a new balance of the public and the private realm in order to shape a sustainable urbanity between neighbourhood and visitor/employers aspirations. • Avoiding an exclusionary character of the area in spite of high costs and quality standards.

References

Bruns-Berentelg, J. (2009), Written and telephone communication and interviews.

Freudewald, J. (2008), "Hamburg's HafenCity Attracts International Firm", *German American Trade*, Volume 19, Number 5.

HafenCity Hamburg GmbH (2006), "The Masterplan: New Edition 2006", *www.hafencity.com/upload/files/broschueren/z_en_broschueren_19_Masterplan_end. pdf*.

HafenCity Hamburg GmbH (2008a), "Projects Insights into Current Developments", *www.hafencity.com/upload/files/broschueren/z_en_broschueren_24_Projekte_englisch_09.2008.pdf*

HafenCity Hamburg GmbH (2008b), "Financing and Organisation", *www.hafencity.com/*.

HafenCity Hamburg GmbH (2008c), "Projects: Insights to Current Developments", *www.hafencity.com/upload/files/broschueren/z_en_broschueren_24_Projekte_englisch_09.2008.pdf*.

HafenCity Hamburg GmbH (2009a), "HafenCity Hamburg GmbH", homepage, *www.hafencity.com/*.

HafenCity Hamburg GmbH (2009b), "Planning History", *www.hafencity.com /index.php?set_language=en&cccpage=staedtebau_artikel&show=artikel&item=70*.

Scottish Parliament (2005), "Scottish Parliament Business Growth Inquiry Committee Fact-Finding Visit to Germany (Hamburg and Bremen), 23 to 27 October 2005", *www.scottish.parliament.uk/business/committees/enterprise/inquiries/bg/GermanyVisit.htm*.

Steinborn, D. (2007), "Hamburg's City Within a City Takes Shape", *The Wall Street Journal*.

Urban Land Institute (2007), "HafenCity Models of Development Success: Unlocking Regeneration Opportunities", Jürgen Bruns-Berentelg CEO, ULI European Trends Conference, Hamburg, *www.uli.org/sitecore/content/ULI2Home/Events/ Conferences/Europe/Trends/Hamburg2007/Cities%20Transformed%20Profiting%20from%20Urban%20Development.aspx*.

Johannesburg Development Agency
Johannesburg, South Africa

Organisation type

The Johannesburg Development Agency (JDA) is a wholly-owned agency of the City of Johannesburg Metropolitan Municipality (CoJ). The JDA stimulates and supports area-based economic regeneration and development initiatives throughout the Johannesburg metropolitan area.

Mission statement

The JDA vision

The JDA aims to be "a world-class, area-based development agency for the City of Johannesburg, constantly striving towards developing best practice in its projects and operations" (JDA, 2009a).

The JDA mission

"The JDA is an agency of the City of Johannesburg, which stimulates and supports area-based development initiatives throughout the Johannesburg metropolitan area in support of the City's Growth and Development Strategy. As development manager of these initiatives, JDA co-ordinates and manages capital investment and other programmes involving both public and private sector stakeholders." (JDA, 2009a)

The JDA's objectives are to:

- promote economic growth through the development and promotion of efficient business environments in defined geographic areas;
- regenerate decaying areas of the city;
- unlock public and private sector investment in marginalised areas;
- undertake area-based regeneration projects in areas in the city not meeting their potential;
- promote economic empowerment through the structuring and procurement of JDA developments;

- promote productive partnerships and co-operation between all relevant stakeholders on area-based initiatives;

- develop and implement best practice and organisational expertise in respect of area-based development management (JDA, 2009a).

History, origins and ownership

Following the analysis of economic development and urban problems and the apartheid spatial form, along the recommendations made by an international delegation of urban experts, and in response to acute challenges of disinvestment in the inner city of Johannesburg towards the late 1990s, it was decided that a development agency was needed in the city. The JDA was established in April 2001 to facilitate area-based economic development in Johannesburg. Since then, the JDA has successfully undertaken a range of capital-based projects throughout the city and the organisation's development can be split into three distinct stages (JDA, 2009a).

Phase 1 (2001-06)

Overview

The intervention of the JDA began the process of the transformation of the inner city from a dangerous and decaying area with little hope of success or investment opportunity to a safe, clean and vibrant place with huge potential.

Interventions during this period were big, bold and symbolic. They were characterised by iconic area-based regeneration projects, many organised and financed on a public/private partnership basis, such as Constitution Hill, Newtown and the Fashion District as well as flagship projects such as the Nelson Mandela Bridge. The JDA also led a number of major public space upgrades over the decade, in particular: Gandhi Square, the Main Street Upgrade, Metro Mall, Mary Fitzgerald Square, Faraday Taxi Rank, and the *Braamfontein* retail district.

Many of these initiatives were planned and implemented in conjunction with stakeholders and partners from other spheres of government, business or civil society. Many other regeneration achievements have been realised because private sector players took the lead and established the conditions for further private investment through upgrading and improving the management of urban spaces. The creation of management arrangements through city improvement districts (CIDs) has been critical to the ongoing maintenance of these spaces (Bethlehem, 2009).

Inner City policy framework

This phase of intervention built on a series of policy frameworks developed in relation to the Johannesburg Inner City. Some highlights include:

- Vision for the Inner City (1997): in mid-1997, (then Deputy President) Thabo Mbeki launched a new vision for the inner city – "The Golden Heartbeat of Africa." The vision was the product of months of intensive dialogue between representatives of provincial and local government, business, the community and other stakeholders.

- An Inner City Economic Development Strategy (1999).

- An Inner City Spatial Framework (1999): it focused on 12 parallel strategies.

- A City Centre Development Framework (2000): it focused on precinct development plans (Bethlehem, 2009).

The Inner City Office (1998-2001)

These strategies and plans guided the work of the City of Johannesburg Inner City Office (ICO), established in 1998, which reported to an Inner City Committee, comprising the representatives of government, business and community who had formulated the vision. The ICO initiated a wide range of interventions and projects aimed at halting and reversing the decline that had become apparent over the previous decade. Upgrading initiatives included Constitutional Hill, Newtown, Joubert Park Precinct Pilot Project and the Better Building Programme. This work prepared the ground for the establishment of the JDA (Bethlehem, 2009).

A continued focus on the Inner City

A new five-year mayoral term starting in December 2000 saw increased importance and urgency given to the regeneration of the Inner City. Inner City renewal was declared one of six mayoral priorities. Key strategies and actions included:

- Creation of the JDA and incorporation of ICO Inner City functions (2001): much of the preliminary work of the ICO was institutionalised in the JDA, established in 2001 by the City of Johannesburg as its implementation authority.

- An Inner City Regeneration Strategy (February 2003): it interpreted the aims of the metropolitan-wide long-term economic strategy "Joburg 2030" into a five-pillar Inner City strategy that would "raise and sustain private investment leading to a steady rise in property values." The five pillars were: address sinkholes; intensify urban management; maintain and upgrade infrastructure; pursue ripple-pond investments; and support strategic economic sectors.

- An Inner City Regeneration Strategy Business Plan (March 2004): the business plan translated the strategy into concrete projects. This was a three-year business plan for the period July 2004 to June 2007.

- Urban Development Zone (2004): this tax incentive had a positive effect: property owners redeveloped their properties and new investors initiated new developments. The upswing in building refurbishments for middle and upper-income rental accommodation reflected this.

- City improvement districts: CIDs demonstrated physically what could be done when non-government stakeholders are also energised and are enabled to enter into collaboration with government. The city improvement district is a geographic focus area where property owners pay a levy to fund top-up services such as security, cleaning, and environmental upgrading to keep the area clean and safe (Bethlehem, 2009).

Phase 2 (2005 to present)

The Inner City

The executive mayor, on 13 November 2006, in reaction to concerns that the Inner City had appeared to have lost its priority status, announced a programme to "refocus and re-energise interventions and initiatives around the regeneration of the Inner City." This multi-dimensional intervention would be driven through an "Inner City Regeneration Charter" and Inner City Summit process.

The Inner City Regeneration Charter (2007–present)

The Inner City Regeneration Charter was agreed between public and private sectors at an Inner City Summit held in May 2007. The first meeting of the "Inner City Charter Partnership Forum" (ICCPF) was held on 7 November 2007. The ICCPF has been designed as the oversight platform for the examination, review, monitoring and measurement of the regeneration efforts of the City. It is a forum which holds the City accountable for ensuring that the commitments made in the Inner City Charter are met. To this end the charter sets out commitments that are to be pursued within a dedicated time frame in the following focus areas:

- urban management, safety and security,
- public spaces, arts, culture and heritage,
- economic development,
- social development,
- transportation,
- residential development.

The Inner City Fund Programme

The JDA has been mandated by the Department of Development Planning and Urban Management (DPUM) to implement projects under the Inner City Fund (ICF). The ICF is a ring-fenced fund specifically focussed on realising the objectives of the Inner City Regeneration Charter. In the 2009/10 financial year, a total of ZAR 100 million was initially anticipated, but owing to financial constraints in the City, a total of ZAR 43 million has been allocated through the ICF to undertake public environment upgrades in the Inner City. As such, the ICF is one of the JDA's core funding streams. Through this fund, the JDA will undertake a public environment upgrade of the core Inner City, redevelop the Ernest Oppenheimer Park and focus on rejuvenating the walkable core in Fordsburg, a historic mixed use area on the western side of the city.

The JDA's deliverables in the Inner City during this phase include the: core retail area upgrade; Fordsburg public environment upgrade; Bertrams/Greater Ellis Park public environment and housing intervention; preparations for the redevelopment of Chancellor House (which hosted Mandela and Tambo's offices in the 1960s); upgrades in old Chinatown; the development of taxi/bus facilities; as well as non-capital interventions.

Transit-oriented development and bus rapid transport

Johannesburg's urban form is influenced by the flat topography and the drive to build quickly and inexpensively. This has resulted in urban areas that spread widely across the landscape. In addition, the city has always had poor public transport, with a large percentage of transport being provided by mini-bus taxis. This has been overlaid by apartheid geography which has distorted development in ways that confine the poorest residents to areas furthest away from employment opportunities. In response, the City of Johannesburg has adopted an urban development policy which strongly focuses on the need to create compact cities and limit urban sprawl. The aim is to better utilise urban infrastructure and land, and connect different parts of the city. At present, the primary measure to support this policy is transport-orientated development. The principal project for the delivery of this policy is the Rea Vaya – Bus Rapid Transit (BRT) system.

Township and marginalised area development

The JDA has also developed a role in planning and implementing regeneration initiatives in developing townships and marginalised areas.

World Cup 2010 requirements

As part of the World Cup 2010 project, the JDA has been commissioned to implement a series of strategic public space upgrades, particularly around the two host stadiums and their gateway areas (Bethlehem, 2009).

Phase 3 (ongoing from present)

In response to progress made, to the future development requirements of the city and to changing operational and funding circumstances, the JDA has initiated, in conjunction with DPUM, a process of evaluating what its future role and functions should be within the city development system (Bethlehem, 2009).

What does the Johannesburg Development Agency do?

The JDA approaches development through capital investment. It works on the assumption that well-considered investments in public infrastructure will not only provide a direct service, but will also catalyse private investment in the built environment.

The 2006 Growth and Development Strategy (GDS) is "a long-term plan to ensure sustainable delivery of services, deal with social and economic development, involve residents in local government and promote a safe and healthy environment" (JDA, 2009b). The GDS is the City's long-term strategic blueprint for development. It sets out the visioning statement, charts the long-term perspective and maps the development path for achieving the long-term goals. As the development manager for the City's Growth and Development Strategy, the JDA's current focus areas include:

- Inner City regeneration,
- township and marginalised area development,
- transport systems (BRT) and facilities (transport hubs),
- World Cup 2010 requirements.

Beyond construction though, the JDA works in a number of other related areas. They include:

- Inner City investor liaison and mobilisation,

- joint work on Inner City co-ordination and charter,

- city and central business district (CBD) marketing,

- strategic planning projects,

- managing Constitution Hill as well as overseeing the management and development of Newtown with the Johannesburg Property Company (JPC),

- influencing owners of strategic buildings,

- land assembly within a precinct upgrade such as the Bertrams housing project.

In future, the JDA will continue to adjust its role, functions and finance mechanisms to meet the needs of its clients and operating environment (JDA, 2009a).

What is the spatial scale of operation and influence of the Johannesburg Development Agency?

The JDA operates across the Johannesburg metropolitan area, with particular concentrations of work regenerating the Inner City, developing transit areas in the city as well as working in townships.

How is the Johannesburg Development Agency financed?

JDA's finances are structured in terms of development (capital) financing and operating (non-capital) financing.

JDA draws its development-based capital budgets from:

- the City of Johannesburg (in respect of City-defined developments);

- other innovative (both public and private) options defined in respect of specific development initiatives such as the Inner City Fund.

Capital funding in 2009/10 broke down into: (1) City of Johannesburg capex allocation of ZAR 29.2 million; (2) Inner City Fund contribution of ZAR 42.3 million; (3) City of Johannesburg Transportation (BRT and non-BRT) of ZAR 998 million; (4) 2010 Office of ZAR 120 million; and (5) Neighbourhood Development Programme Grant (NDPG) of ZAR 23.7 million.

The JDA draws its operating budget from:

- a year-on-year operating grant;

- recovering a 5% development fee on the total capital spent and 4% on capital spent on BRT and transportation-related projects.

Operating funds in 2009/10 broke down into: (1) a City of Johannesburg operating grant of ZAR 20 million; (2) recovering a 5% development fee on the total capital spent; and (3) NDPG cost-recovery allowance of one salary per project per year.

Table A.35 sets out, by way of example, the JDA cash flow statement for 2007.

The JDA is currently pursuing a revenue diversification strategy. One option is for JDA to be financially self-sustainable in future, such that its management fees cover all operational expenses. This is dependent on the quantum of developments offered by the City to JDA to implement. Another option is for the JDA to follow a purchase-develop-sell model where the JDA acts as a public developer and can retain a proportion of surplus to cover operational costs (Bethlehem, 2009).

The organogram that follows (Figure A.39) reveals the local development system within which JDA operates.

Table A.35. **The Johannesburg Development Agency cash flow statement, 2007**

	2007 ZAR	2006 ZAR
CASH FLOW FROM OPERATING ACTIVITIES		
Receipts		
Rendering of services	-	11 673 207
Government grants	25 050 000	10 028 947
Interest received	4 448 558	3 285 331
Other income	593 964	1 394 660
Payments		
Employee costs	(17 164 765)	(15 504 902)
Other payments	(22 619 949)	(11 503 288)
Net cash flows from operating activities	(9 692 192)	(626 045)
CASH FLOW FROM INVESTING ACTIVITIES		
Acquisition of property, plant and equipment	(1 290 406)	(226 034)
Proceeds from sale of plant and equipment	4 912	-
Development of intangible asset	(434 627)	(354 175)
Increase in investment in associates	-	(7 500 000)
Net cash flows from investing activities	(1 720 121)	(8 080 209)
CASH FLOW FROM FINANCING ACTIVITIES		
Proceedings from borrowings	35 266 133	36 797 693
Repayment of borrowings	-	(3 001 491)
Decrease/(increase) in project debtors	(179 519 938)	11 669 093
Increase/(decrease) in project creditors	87 537 633	13 898 533
Net cash flows from financing activities	(56 716 172)	59 363 828
Net increase/(decrease) in cash and cash equivalents	(68 128 485)	50 657 574
Cash at the beginning of the year	68 968 527	18 310 953
Total cash at the end of the year	840 042	68 968 527

Source: JDA (2007), "Annual Report, 2007", Johannesburg Development Agency.

Figure A.39. **The position of the Johannesburg Development Agency in the system of area-based regeneration and investment promotion in Johannesburg**

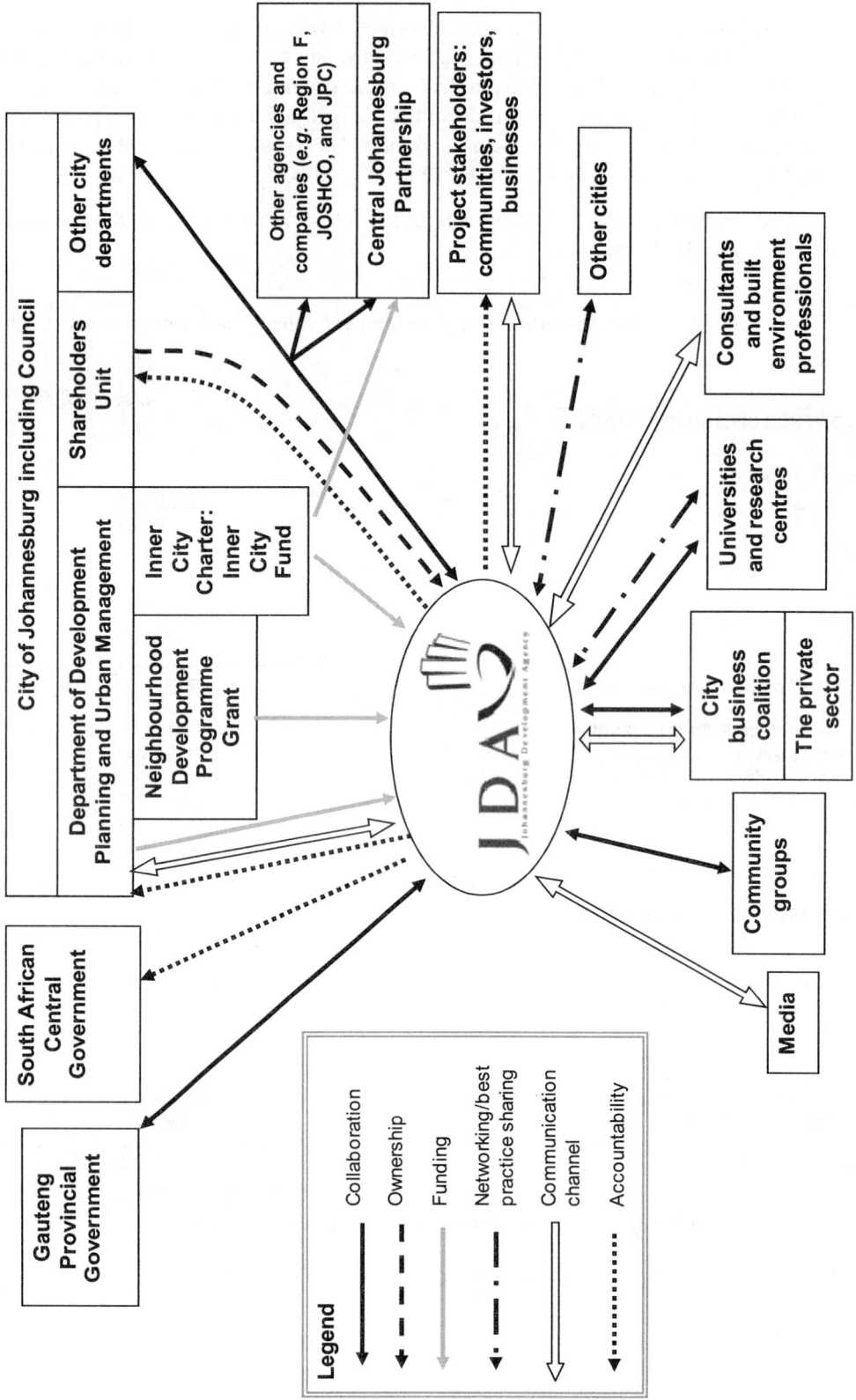

Legend

Collaboration	
Ownership	
Funding	
Networking/best practice sharing	
Communication channel	
Accountability	

Who are the Johannesburg Development Agency's partners?

City of Johannesburg

The JDA is 100% owned by the City of Johannesburg and is directly accountable the Department of Development Planning and Urban Management, insomuch as the JDA reports to it strategically. The JDA is accountable to the City through the Shareholders Unit which monitors the JDA's projects and budgets (Figure A.40).

As an agency of the City of Johannesburg, the JDA interacts closely with the City's various departments and municipal entities in respect of their functional interest in a development's activities. In this regard, the JDA:

- operates in line with the Growth and Development Strategy principles;

- operates within existing agreed plans and frameworks (for instance, in the case of Planning, the JDA operates within the overall Spatial Development Plan of the City and takes due diligence of Regional Spatial Development Framework's [RSDF's] and existing precinct plans);

- considers inputs from City departments in respect of development design;

- facilitates the development of a management plan in respect of the ongoing operations of the initiative once the development is completed;

- acts as an implementation agency for other departments including 2010, Transportation and the DPUM.

Where roles specifically overlap in respect of a particular aspect of a development, the JDA will consult with the relevant department or municipal entity accordingly. Given the intensive urban management focus of the City and the DPUM, the JDA partners work with regional offices to ensure close operational co-operation (JDA, 2009a).

Figure A.40. **The Johannesburg Development Agency's relationship with the City of Johannesburg**

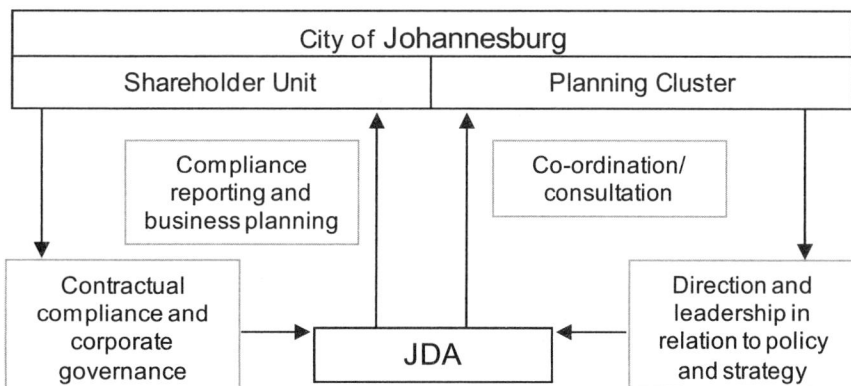

Source: JDA (2009a), "Business Plan, 2009-10", Johannesburg Development Agency.

The Central Johannesburg Partnership

The JDA collaborates with the Central Johannesburg Partnership (CJP) and shares experiences and best practice around projects and visions of the Inner City.

Universities, research centres and other cities

The JDA shares its experiences and best practice with universities, research centres and other cities through its staff and via consultants and urban development experts.

Central government

The JDA is also partially funded and accountable to central government, insofar as the JDA is a recipient of funding from National Treasury's Neighbourhood Partnership Development Grant. Under normal circumstances the JDA does not directly receive funding from national government.

Gauteng provincial government

The JDA collaborates with the Gauteng Government on projects of mutual interest. Currently, the JDA does not receive funding for activities from the Gauteng Government although it has done in the past.

The media, the private sector and other stakeholders

The JDA is in constant communication with the media regarding its projects. The JDA also communicates with its stakeholders in each area through a proactive and participatory process and the JDA is accountable to them in terms of the product. An example of a communication platform might be the City Business Coalition.

How is the Johannesburg Development Agency led?

Board

According to the JDA's Annual Report, "The Board of Directors is committed to business integrity, transparency and professionalism in all its activities. As part of this commitment, the board supports the highest standards of corporate governance and the development of best practice" (JDA, 2007).

Moreover, the board "retains full control over the JDA, its plans and strategy; acknowledges its responsibilities as to strategy, compliance with internal policies, external laws and regulations, effective risk management and performance measurement, transparency and effective communication both internally and externally by the company" (JDA, 2007) (Figure A.41).

Figure A.41. **The relationships between the Johannesburg Development Agency, its board and key stakeholders**

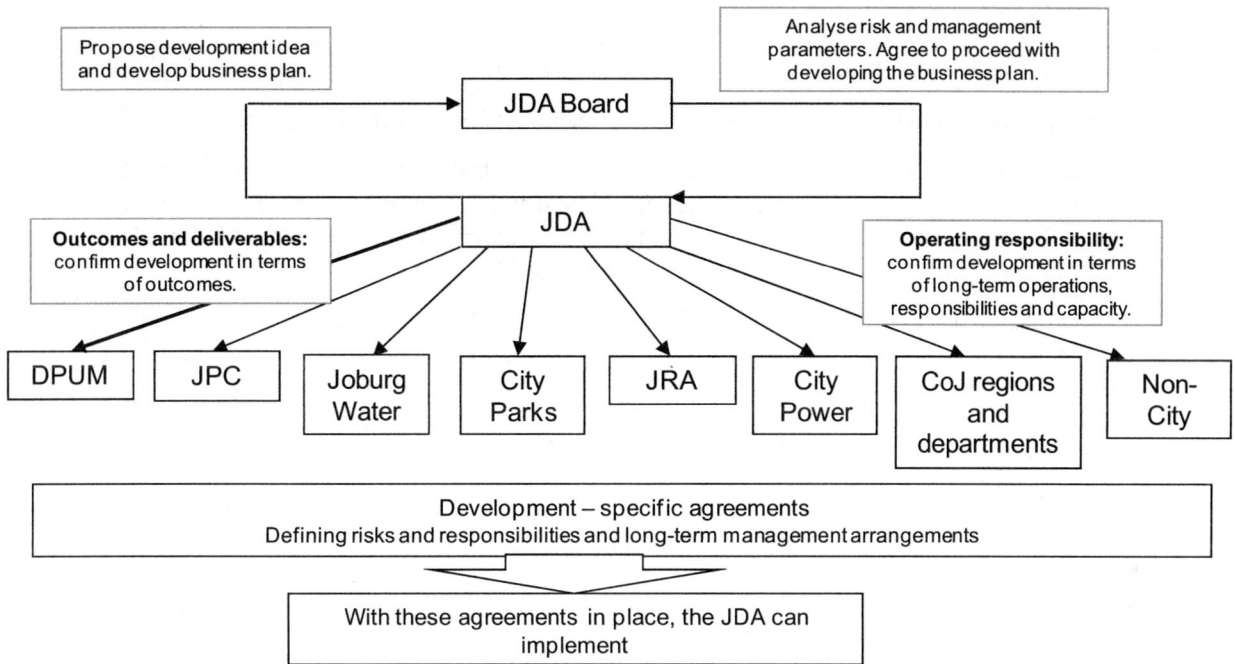

```
┌─────────────────────────────┐                              ┌──────────────────────────────┐
│ Propose development idea    │                              │ Analyse risk and management  │
│ and develop business plan.  │        ┌─────────────┐       │ parameters. Agree to proceed │
└─────────────────────────────┘        │  JDA Board  │       │ with developing the          │
                                        └─────────────┘       │ business plan.               │
                                                              └──────────────────────────────┘

                                        ┌─────────────┐
                                        │     JDA     │
                                        └─────────────┘

┌──────────────────────────┐                                 ┌──────────────────────────────┐
│ Outcomes and deliverables:│                                │ Operating responsibility:    │
│ confirm development in    │                                │ confirm development in terms │
│ terms of outcomes.        │                                │ of long-term operations,     │
└──────────────────────────┘                                 │ responsibilities and capacity.│
                                                              └──────────────────────────────┘
```

| DPUM | JPC | Joburg Water | City Parks | JRA | City Power | CoJ regions and departments | Non-City |

Development – specific agreements
Defining risks and responsibilities and long-term management arrangements

With these agreements in place, the JDA can implement

JDA: Johannesburg Development Agency

DPUM: Department of Planning and Urban Management

JPC: Johannesburg Property Company

JRA: Johannesburg Roads Agency

CoJ: City of Johannesburg

Source: JDA (2009), "Business Plan, 2009-10", Johannesburg Development Agency.

Chief executive officer

Lael Bethlehem is chief executive officer (CEO) of the JDA.

Organisational style

The JDA has been described as pragmatic, effective, professional, entrepreneurial and technical.

How is the Johannesburg Development Agency governed?

Staff and organisational structure

The JDA currently employs 57 staff of whom:

- 20 are directly involved in developments as development managers and administrators.

- 30 are corporate (CEO, finance, risk and compliance, human resources, information and communications technology (ICT), procurement, marketing, planning and so on).

- 7 are cleaners or drivers.

- (2 additional contractors: construction specialist and facilities manager).

The JDA has grown as an organisation in the last few years in line with the exponential increase of its capital budget. This trend will remain stable for the next financial year because of the implementation requirements of the hosting of the FIFA 2010 Soccer World Cup and the completion of Phase 1B of the BRT.

Beyond 2010 and the completion of the BRT, the JDA is well aware that its growth in relation to the implementation of current projects will be checked as these projects are completed. In addition, the JDA is impacted by financial stresses in the wider economy and in the finances of the City of Johannesburg. The JDA is being pro-active about planning for future changes in its functions and the knock-on effects this may have on the way its human resources are organised.

The JDA's organisational structure (Figure A.42) is largely based on the following principles:

- Small specialist teams focusing on developments in specific areas and various departments supporting the operations of the entity and the developments.

- Outsourcing of specific tasks and functions, such as internal audit. JDA, however, retains responsibility and full accountability for the outsourced functions.

- JDA has five departments interacting together in pursuit of both JDA and development-based objectives.

- JDA operates with a series of development-based teams each with a senior development manager (SDM) who is responsible for overseeing the development managers' (DMs) operational performance and securing strategic input from the CEO. The SDM is fully accountable for all aspects of the development.

The Board of Directors is made up of one executive director and seven non-executive directors, all of whom are independent. The board has three sub-committees: (1) Audit; (2) Development and Risk; and (3) Human Resources and Remuneration (JDA, 2009a).

Figure A.42. **The organisational structure of the Johannesburg Development Agency**

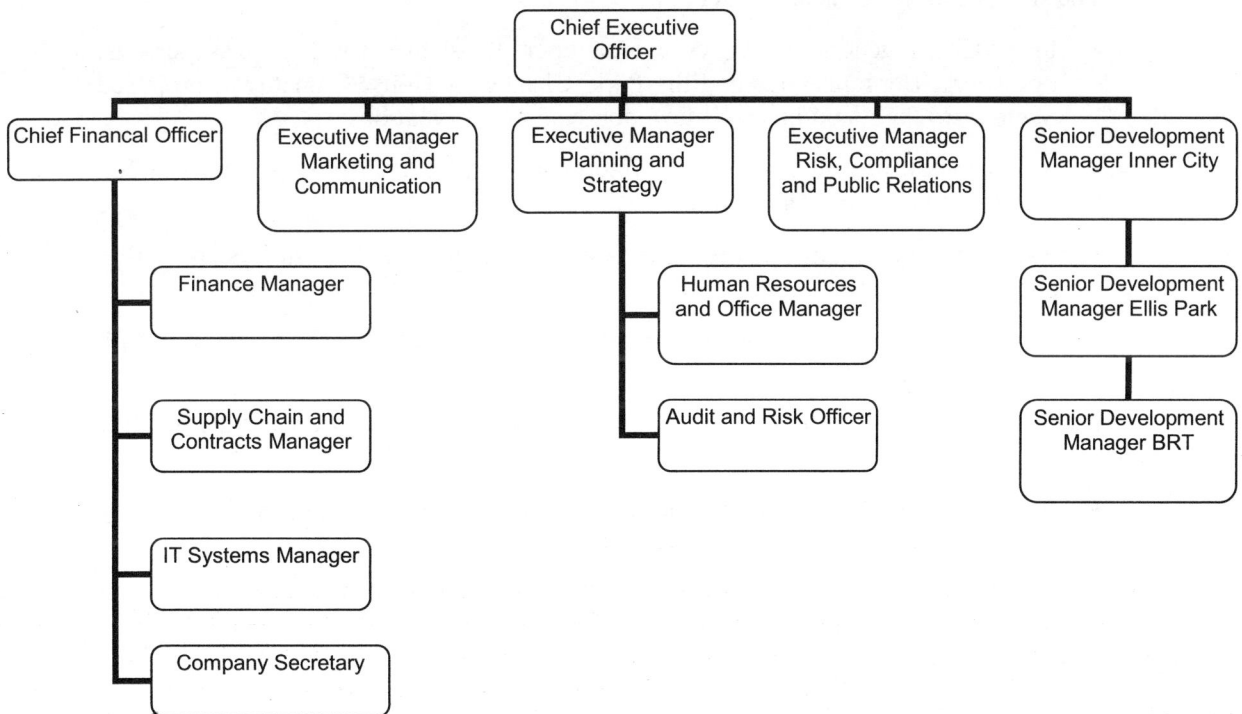

Source: JDA (2009a), "Business Plan, 2009-10", Johannesburg Development Agency.

What are the Johannesburg Development Agency's key services and programmes within the system of local development and investment promotion?

Services

As the development manager for the City's Growth and Development Strategy, the JDA's development management service involves:

- Development and project packaging: this involves identifying strategic opportunities for responding to the JDA's focus area by bringing together all the relevant stakeholders and parties to the initiative and developing a plan for implementation.

- Development and project facilitation and co-ordination: this involves working with the various stakeholders and parties involved in an initiative and ensuring they are undertaking their roles as expected and required.

- Overall development implementation: this involves ensuring the development is implemented as planned. In this regard, the JDA may outsource specific project management functions within a development, while retaining its overall development management role (JDA, 2007).

Specific focus areas and projects

The JDA's current focus areas include:

- Inner City regeneration, *e.g.* core area upgrade, shelter for homeless persons, Fordsburg, Bertrams/Greater Ellis Park, Chancellor House/Chinatown, proposed Skateboard Park, taxi/bus facilities, non-capital interventions;

- township and marginalised area development, *e.g.* Orlando East, Vilakazi Street, Stretford Station and Diepsloot;

- transport systems and facilities, *e.g.* Rea Vaya/ Bus Rapid Transit System (BRT) and transport hubs;

- World Cup 2010 requirements, *e.g.* public space upgrades to the north and south gateways of Ellis Park.

Beyond construction though, the JDA works in a number of other related areas. They include:

- Inner City investor liaison and mobilisation, *e.g.* Inner City Business Community coalition and Halala;

- joint work on Inner City co-ordination and Charter, *e.g.* collaboration with DPUM and Region F, Central Strategy Unit;

- city and CBD marketing, *e.g.* media walkabout, media comment, development launches, and public art;

- strategic planning projects, *e.g.* long distance transport facility near Park Station, decking over railway lines, Discovery : "Walking the City", and Metro Inner City Park;

- development management, *e.g.* Constitution Hill and Newtown with the Johannesburg Property Company;

- influencing owners of strategic buildings, *e.g.* the Barracks near Ghandi Square and the Barbican;

- land assembly within a precinct upgrade, *e.g.* the Bertrams Housing Project.

JDA marketing function

The JDA also runs a pro-active marketing programme. Its aims and objectives for 2009/10 are detailed below.

Five-point marketing lever programme

There are five areas around which the JDA marketing framework finds expression:

- Marketing of JDA developments: every development completed by the JDA is offered a high-profile launch event, media coverage, production of branded collateral and any other *ad hoc* marketing services required (*i.e.* social-consciousness campaigns, public meetings, press conferences, stakeholder engagement, etc.).

- Marketing the JDA as a whole: this strategy involves the positive positioning of the JDA brand and contextualising the JDA as a delivery agent of the City of Johannesburg. This includes the design, production and distribution of brand collateral and the hosting of events which are not necessarily linked to a specific development (*i.e.* tree planting, presentations and requested tours to specific sectors).

- Building confidence in the main development areas: here the strategy is to raise awareness of and confidence in JDA's major development areas, with special emphasis on Soweto and the Inner City. The aim here is to work beyond JDA's own specific developments and to market the areas as a whole, as well as any positive developments that may be taking place in these areas. This will include bringing audiences to the development areas through targeted activities and events.

- Giving recognition and injecting momentum into the City's regeneration effort: the JDA alone can clearly not rejuvenate all areas of decay, hence the need to identify those (private, non-governmental organisation) stakeholders who through their investments and effort are contributing to significant regeneration in the Inner City and elsewhere through the Halala Joburg Awards Programme.

- Public relations / communications management: the aim is to develop, maintain and project the JDA as an organisation that delivers innovative projects effectively and efficiently. This contributes to positive brand equity in the media, attracting talented staff as well as keeping morale high among staff. It also helps to ensure buy-in and support for work within the City and its entities. This work is split between internal and external communications in order to break it into manageable chunks.

  - Internal communications: this work targets JDA staff, the Mayoral Committee, Section 79 Committees, Shareholder Unit, other CoJ entities and the JDA Board. Delivery mechanisms include regular briefings, walkabouts, an internal newsletter and special events (*i.e.* monthly staff training day).

  - External communications: communication with stakeholders who may be directly affected by the developments, as well as residents of Johannesburg as a whole and the investment community, especially property investors. Delivery mechanisms include the JDA website, regular media briefings, walkabouts and tours, as well as pro-active and reactive media releases (JDA, 2009a).

Integration with DPUM plans

Table A.36 shows how JDA projects are integrated and aligned with the City's plans. As described below, the key programme areas and the delivery agenda for the JDA in 2009/10 in relation to DPUM sector planning are split into three plans: (1) the Spatial Form and Urban Management Sector Plan; (2) the Transportation Sector Plan; and (3) the Community Development Sector Plan (JDA, 2009a).

Table A.36. **Johannesburg Development Agency project alignment with the Department of Planning and Urban Management**

Five-year strategic objectives	IDP Programme	2009/10 delivery agenda
Spatial Form and Urban Management Sector Plan		
Corridors and mobility routes planned, developed and managed in the way that supports the overall development framework of high-intensity nodes on a lattice of connecting routes.	Mobility Routes Development Programme	Continued implementation of the BRT busways and stations (JDA045)
Implementation of all public sector infrastructure investment to support priority nodal development, movement, urban renewal and other city priorities.	Integrated Public Investment Programme	JDA034/1: Vilakazi Street Precinct JDA048: Orlando East Phase 1
Increased investor confidence in declining and under-performing areas. Public investment in marginalised areas to facilitate crowding in of private sector spending.	Economic Area Regeneration Programme	JDA022/01: NASREC Precinct Development JDA052: Fordsburg Public Environment Upgrade JDA047: Bertrams Neighbourhood Development Programme
Increased investor confidence in declining and under-performing areas. Public investment in marginalised areas to facilitate crowding in of private sector spending.	Upgrading of Marginalised Areas Programme	JDA036: Stretford Station
Increased investor confidence in declining and under-performing areas. Public investment in marginalised areas to facilitate crowding in of private sector spending.	Inner City Regeneration Programme	JDA035 Inner City Fund Core Projects JDA035/6: Skateboarding Plaza JDA051: New Chancellor House design JDA035/7: Chinatown Precinct Upgrade (incorporated into JDA051)
Transportation Sector Plan		
Phase 1 of Rea Vaya BRT implemented. Reduced average public transport travel times on selected BRT routes as measured by a five-yearly survey or improvement on a mobility index to be finalised.	Bus Rapid Transit – Rea Vaya infrastructure Programme	Continued implementation of the BRT busways and stations (JDA045)
All bid-book commitments in respect of transport services and times delivered in terms of the approved high-level 2010 Transport Plan. World Cup 2010 transport infrastructure and services designed so as to ensure lasting value for the City.	World Cup 2010 Transportation Programme	Continued implementation of the BRT busways and stations (JDA045) JDA022/01: NASREC Precinct Development

Source: JDA (2009a), "Business Plan, 2009-10", Johannesburg Development Agency.

What enables the Johannesburg Development Agency to contribute to the local development and investment promotion system so effectively?

Arm's length implementation body

The JDA has a pro-active and entrepreneurial organisational culture, which is propagated because it is an agency; not a municipal department of the City of Johannesburg. It is less procedural and more nimble as a result. The JDA can, for instance, call a committee at 24 hours' notice if deemed necessary.

High-quality human capital

The JDA has built up a highly skilled and experienced team of strategists and practitioners over a number of years.

Robust relationships

Strong, long-term relationships with the private sector and community organisations, in particular, have ensured that the JDA is guided effectively and kept in touch with what is needed. Over a number of years, the JDA has nurtured an alliance of Inner City investors. The "City Business Coalition", for example, is an informal partnership between Inner City businesses with which the JDA liaises.

Strong analytical capacity

The JDA operates an effective intelligence-gathering project which allows it to report on project impact and highlight emerging trends in the city in such a way that they can be tackled or reinforced effectively.

Strong marketing capacity

The JDA generates positivity around given themes and agendas, building trust between relevant stakeholders and facilitating the urban development process. This marketing also indirectly promotes the work of the JDA, lending it credibility and presence, which could lead to more funding and responsibility.

Focused mandate

The JDA's limited mandate aids the delivery of its projects. It provides clarity, reduces bureaucracy and politics, and creates a sense of purpose behind delivery.

What constraints make the Johannesburg Development Agency less able to effectively contribute to the local development and investment promotion system?

Focused mandate

Though a simultaneous strength, the JDA's focused mandate also represents a challenge. The JDA approaches development through the built environment. Its involvement in management and social environment interventions are limited. This can skew approaches and sees the JDA tend towards more of an engineering consultancy and project management organisation than a pure development agency *per se*. There are also a number of other agencies working in the built environment within the city, which can constrain its role.

Project handover

On the completion of a development project, the JDA hands over assets to other agencies for their management and maintenance. The JDA has little influence over what happens afterwards. Sometimes the results are very poor.

Un-sustainability of funding mechanisms

Operational costs of the JDA are met predominantly by both a year-on-year City of Johannesburg operating grant and the retention of 5% of all capital spend. This is problematic for a number of reasons: (1) it is difficult to anticipate year-on-year staffing fluctuations and therefore costs; (2) if capital funding (and thus spending) falls, then the operating budget falls, undermining the financial viability of the organisation; (3) to retain the necessary operating funding to cover costs, the JDA would be forced to take on more capital-intensive projects, narrowing the organisation's role. At the same time, the number of capital-intense projects in the city is likely to fall post-BRT and 2010 World Cup.

How have, or how is, the Johannesburg Development Agency approached/approaching these problems?

Focused mandate and project handover

The JDA understands that an integrated approach is critical to solving challenging urban problems. The JDA is discussing whether its role should extend more explicitly beyond project management and implementation, especially given the decreasing requirement for large and capital-intense interventions. It works hard to build relationships across the city to ensure the long-term sustainability of the projects it completes.

Tensions between funding mechanism and strategic objectives

To reduce the reliance on grant funding for capital projects and to re-establish more strategic projects and priorities, the JDA is seeking to diversify its income streams and minimise certain costs where possible. The organisation is exploring a number of avenues here including: (1) looking for other capital projects in the city; (2) the possibility of being leverage fees to share expertise gained over recent years; (3) better articulating the value of the JDA to the city to improve levels of grant funding; (4) undertaking a more entrepreneurial real estate development role where a proportion of any surplus created by the JDA is retained to support its operating budget; and (5) exploring funding options from higher tiers of government and international financial institutions.

How has the Johannesburg Development Agency performed in relation to its key performance indicators?

Table A.37 summarises how JDA has performed in relation to its key performance indicators.

Figures A.43 and A.44 detail the overall public and private sector investment in the JDA area between 2001-08 and present an assessment of the importance of the public sector investment to stimulate private sector investment.

Table A.37. **Key performance indicators of the Johannesburg Development Agency, 2007/08**

Theme (initiative)	Tangible impact	Intangible impact
Catalytic investments	• Between 2001-08, in the High Court Precinct, the JDA invested ZAR 8.3 million which was complemented by total private sector investment of ZAR 2 994.4 million. • 55% of investors thought that JDA interventions were "very important" in encouraging them to invest whilst 45% saw JDA interventions as "important" (see Figure A.44) (JDA, 2009c).	• The JDA has a continued leadership role in respect of the Inner City. In a number of intervention areas in the city, the JDA has made critical interventions which have catalysed further investment. • According to a recent impact review, "there is little doubt that JDA investments in the Inner City areas of Johannesburg have had a significant impact on the resurgence of specific development areas, and as a consequence on the reversal of fortunes of the Inner City as a whole" (JDA, 2007).
Job creation	• Short-term jobs created: target (2 650); total achieved (5 788) (JDA, 2009a).	
Economic development and empowerment	• Black Economic Empowerment spend as a percentage of capital expenditure target (70%); total achieved (68%) (JDA, 2009a).	• Creates confidence behind the equal opportunities agenda.
Project management	• City of Johannesburg funded projects: allocated spend ZAR 137 736 000 and total spend ZAR 138 598 000 (100%). • BRT allocated spend 556 453 000 and total spend ZAR 429 945 (77%). • Inner City Fund: allocated spend ZAR 171 500 000 and total spend ZAR 166 174 000 (97%). • Other funds: allocated spend ZAR 28 923 000 and total spend ZAR 27 000 000 (93%). • Project delivery against milestones in service delivery areas: overall Economic Area Regeneration Programme (90%). Constitution Hill (100%); Greater Newtown (87%); Greater Ellis Park (99%); Hillbrow Heath Precinct (55%); and Jewell City (100%) (JDA, 2009a).	• A sense of efficiency and reliability attaches itself to the JDA.
Human resources	• Proportion of female staff employed: target (45%); actual (61%). • Proportion of black staff employed: target (80%); actual (88%). • Proportion of payroll invested in training: target (3%); actual (2.7%) (JDA, 2009a).	• Confidence in equal opportunities and a commitment to staff development is created.

Figure A.43. **Total private *vs.* public investment expenditure per intervention area in Johannesburg, 2001-08**

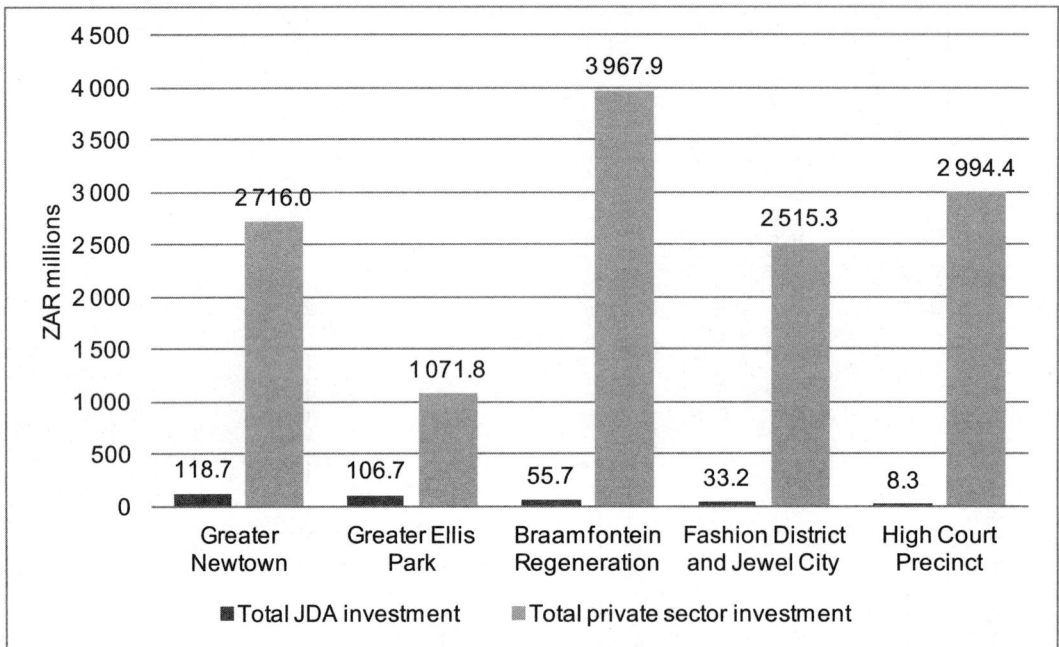

Note: JDA DIMS data was only analysed to December 2007 and is not reflected for the 2008 period.

Source: JDA (2009c), "Analysis of the Impact of the JDA's Area-Based Regeneration Projects on Private Sector Investments", *www.jda.org.za/2009/pdfs/impact_investments.pdf*.

Figure A.44. **The importance of Johannesburg Development Agency area-based interventions in encouraging investment in the Inner City according to relevant investors**

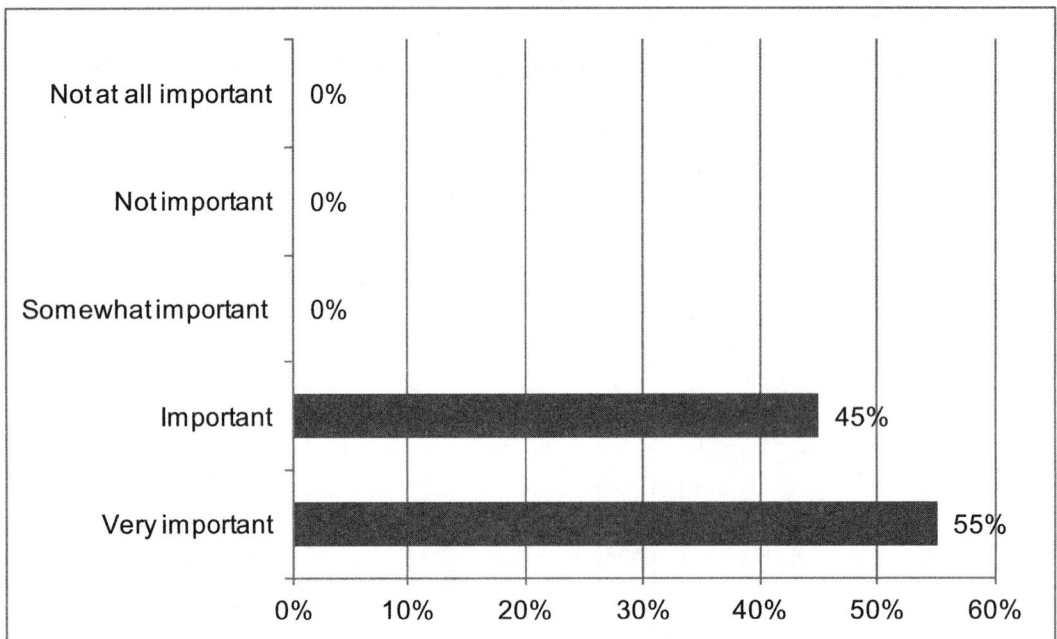

Source: JDA (2009c), "Analysis of the Impact of the JDA's Area-Based Regeneration Projects on Private Sector Investments", *www.jda.org.za/2009/pdfs/impact_investments.pdf*.

Accountabilities, performance review mechanisms and best-practice sharing

Accountabilities

The JDA receives its mandate from the City and is contractually accountable to the Department of Development Planning and Urban Management and the members of the Mayoral Council within the Planning Cluster, to whom it undertakes compliance reporting in respect of its key performance indicators. The JDA relies on the DPUM for support, in terms of its contractual obligations. In respect of operational matters, the JDA management is accountable to the JDA's Board of Directors. The JDA is strategically accountable to the Planning Cluster, with whom it co-ordinates its area-based development initiatives. The JDA relies on the Planning Cluster for direction and leadership in respect of development in Johannesburg (JDA, 2009a).

It is also accountable to central government insofar as the JDA is a recipient of funding from National Treasury's Neighbourhood Partnership Development Grant.

Performance review mechanisms

Individual performance

The JDA Performance Management System (PMS) is a communication link aimed to provide alignment between the strategies, goals and objectives of the organisation, and the work objectives of teams and individuals in the organisation. The PMS also focuses on the development of soft skills, whilst managing employees towards the achievement of team and individual goals and objectives. The JDA PMS is central to ensuring that every one of its people is competent, motivated and empowered.

During the 2007/08 financial year, the JDA reviewed its PMS to ensure that it was compatible with that of the CoJ in terms of content and implementation. The revised PMS informs the JDA's reward system to ensure that it is not only market-related, but that it will ensure the success of its retention strategy in line with the determinations and policies of the parent municipality.

JDA has adopted a resolution to continue to spend about 3% of its payroll on training and development of staff (JDA, 2009a).

Company performance

At the organisational scale, the JDA gathers intelligence to evaluate its year-on-year performance. The JDA collects data against a series of key performance areas which include: (1) job creation; (2) economic development and empowerment; (3) project management and delivery; (4) human resource management and development; and (5) effective financial management and effective corporate governance. The theme of human resources stands out as a unique performance indicator and relates to South Africa's apartheid past.

Performance is measured against targets stated at the beginning of the year. A traffic light system is used for evaluation (Figure A.45). The results of the evaluation are published each year in the JDA's Annual Report.

Figure A. 45. **The Johannesburg Development Agency's traffic light evaluation system**

Source: JDA (2007), "Annual Report, 2007", Johannesburg Development Agency.

The City is also now implementing an integrated scorecard which will measure the performance of its affiliated department and agencies including the JDA against a set of predetermined standards.

Best-practice sharing

The JDA shares examples of best practice with universities and research centres, as well as other cities, through its staff members, conferences, consultants and built environment specialists.

What progress has the Johannesburg Development Agency made?

The JDA delivered several important phases of Inner City regeneration in the first phase of its mandate from 2001-06. Inner City regeneration in Johannesburg is not yet complete and there is more work to be done which the JDA could lead.

The current priority set for the JDA is to implement several key components of transport-oriented development intended to better connect Johannesburg internally and to provide a spur for further regeneration and development.

The current priorities associated with transport-orientated development, township renewal and the FIFA 2010 World Cup provide important deadlines which must be met. After 2010, there will be an opportunity to review and develop wider roles for JDA, to enable Johannesburg to better capture the value of current investments. This evolutionary step is being planned for now (Bethlehem, 2009).

What are the Johannesburg Development Agency's strengths, constraints, opportunities and challenges?

The Johannesburg Development Agency's strengths, constraints, opportunities and challenges are summarised in Table A.38.

Table A.38. **The Johannesburg Development Agency's strengths, constraints, opportunities and challenges**

Strengths	Constraints
• Focussed mandate. • Proven track record of delivery in regeneration. • Highly professional and experienced staff with key skills in development and project management. • Strong intelligence-gathering and marketing capacities. • Robust and long-term working relationships have been fostered over many years.	• Narrow current mandate focused on project management and implementation. • Pressure to take on a capital-intensive work load which stretches the capacity of the organisation to secure finance.
Opportunities	Challenges
• By the end of World Cup 2010 and the end of the Bus Rapid Transit project, the JDA will be better positioned to make the case for diversifying its mandate from that of hard infrastructure project delivery. • New funding mechanisms may be developed which allow the JDA to operate more strategically and to take on additional roles in the development system. • The JDA could play a role in the creation, delivery and management of Africa's first truly global city. • The JDA could develop world-class intervention programmes in townships which could be emulated globally. • The JDA could complete the transformation of the Inner City. • The JDA could collapse the town/township divide through transport-orientated developments. • The JDA could share its current and future expertise worldwide.	• Local elections at the beginning of 2011 could stall important restructuring and reorientation work. • The current CEO's contract expires on 31 July 2010. • A decline in capital intensive-projects could undermine the current financial model. • As the organisation re-orientates, staff morale could be impacted. • With the completion of the BRT and World Cup 2010, the JDA budget will get smaller and the JDA will be required to diversify its deliverables.

References

Bethlehem, L. (2009), Written and telephone communication and interviews.

JDA (Johannesburg Development Agency) (2007), "Annual Report, 2007", Johannesburg Development Agency.

JDA (2009a), "Business Plan, 2009-10", Johannesburg Development Agency.

JDA (2009b), "Growth and Development Strategy, 2006", *www.joburg.org.za/content/ view/139/114/*.

JDA (2009c), "Analysis of the Impact of the JDA's Area-Based Regeneration Projects on Private Sector Investments", *www.jda.org.za/2009/pdfs/impact_investments.pdf*.

Liverpool Vision
Liverpool, United Kingdom

Organisation type

Liverpool Vision was established in April 2008. It brought together the activities of three companies – Liverpool Vision (a pre-existing organisation of the same name), Liverpool Land Development Company and Business Liverpool – and integrates economic and physical development, investment and business and enterprise support within a delivery-focused, private-sector-led company. The establishment of a single economic development company for the city was spearheaded by Liverpool City Council following consultation with business. As well as its support of the business community, the organisation plays a strong role in the domestic and international positioning of Liverpool in conjunction with regional and city regional partners.

Mission statement

Mission

Liverpool Vision's mission is to "accelerate the city's economic growth and provide strategic leadership on the economy" (Liverpool Vision, 2009a).

Aims

Liverpool Vision's aims are to:

- create an outstanding quality of place, with a premier environment, public realm, cultural assets, high-quality developments and effective transport connections for businesses, residents, workers, tourists and investors;

- build a dynamic, competitive business base, which has a strong knowledge base and is high value-added;

- strengthen the Liverpool brand worldwide and attract inward investment, entrepreneurs and highly skilled knowledge workers;

- become a city of talented, highly skilled and innovative people (Liverpool Vision, 2009a).

History, origins and ownership

The Liverpool context

In the second part of the 20th century, the Liverpool of the past, with its rich cultural and industrial heritage, was in almost terminal decline as the result of changes in the global and national economies which affected all major UK cities. Perhaps because of its exceptional dependence on maritime, port and related manufacturing functions, Liverpool experienced particularly significant levels of decline and came to be seen as peripheral and problematic. Between 1950 and 2000, it suffered 40% population loss and between the 1960s and mid-1980s lost some 43% of its jobs (Liverpool City Council, 2008).

In the latter half of the 1990s, things began to change for the better. Despite its devastation, the city importantly retained its spirit, energy and zeal. With the help of EU structural funds and other disparate sources of public investment, Liverpool began to build itself a new future based on a re-orientation towards the service sector economy and improved domestic and international positioning.

Indeed, from 1999 onwards, Liverpool began to drive a coherent and focused development strategy and established a series of dedicated delivery mechanisms which included the following three companies (Liverpool City Council, 2008):

- Liverpool Vision: Liverpool Vision was established in 1999 as the first of three pilot urban regeneration companies. The creation of the company was a joint initiative by Liverpool City Council, the Northwest Regional Development Agency (NWDA) and English Partnerships (EP). The decision to establish the company represented a common recognition that the city centre is of critical importance for the economic and social prosperity of Liverpool and the city region, and that previous efforts to regenerate the city centre had failed because of a lack of focus and co-ordination of public resources, as well as the lack of engagement of the private sector.

- Liverpool Land Development Company (LLDC): LLDC was created in 2003 as a joint initiative by the NWDA, EP and Liverpool City Council. It was the succession vehicle of the Speke and Garston development company established in 1997 to regenerate the southern "gateway" area of the city. Its remit was implementing major physical regeneration projects in the four strategic investment areas of Liverpool outside the city centre. It achieved this by working with its members to invest in land that is derelict, underdeveloped, contaminated or under-utilised in order to create serviced, accessible industrial and commercial sites for sale to developers or end-users. Acting as a catalyst, LLDC worked to build business confidence and market areas in the rest of the region, the United Kingdom and beyond.

- Business Liverpool: Business Liverpool was established in 2005 by Liverpool City Council, Liverpool Chamber of Commerce and Greater Merseyside Business Link as the principal partners. Key imperatives were to establish a business-facing and business-driven model of delivery, moving away from traditional local authority economic development, to provide a single access point for business in the city and better integration of partners' business support, inward investment and enterprise programmes. From the outset, Business Liverpool's role in serving the city's business community was reflected in its private sector chair and board members, representing a range of firms and sectors and a chief executive recruited from the private sector.

As a result of the overall city regeneration strategy, including the contribution made by the three regeneration companies, between 1995 and 2006, Liverpool's gross value added (GVA) grew by 6.9% per annum; the stock of jobs increased by 12% to 226 514 (Figure A.46); and the number of businesses increased by 11% (see also Figure A.47). Most symbolic of this transformation was the rejuvenation of the City Centre, Waterfront and South Liverpool, together with the growth of Liverpool John Lennon Airport (Liverpool City Council, 2008). The successful hosting of the 2008 European Capital of Culture (the most successful ever according to the European Commission) should also not be forgotten as a symbol of the city's new-found confidence, renewed leadership, delivery capacity and socio-economic progress.

Figure A.46. **Liverpool employment growth, 1980-2006**
Index 1980 = 100

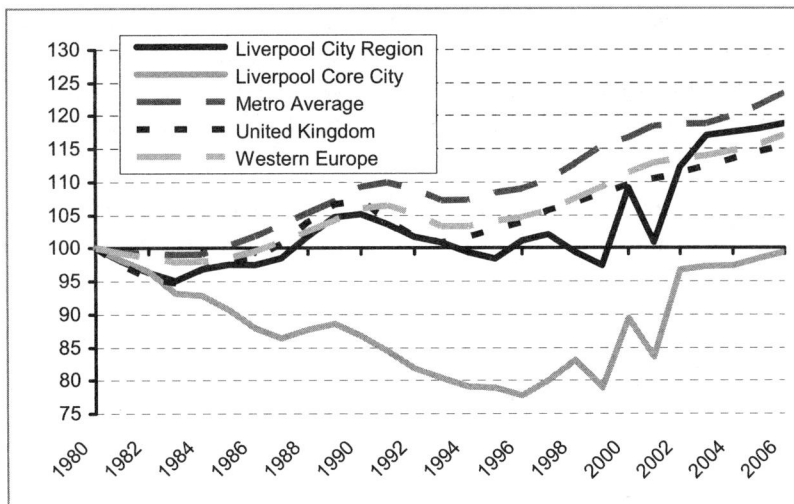

Source: BAK Basel Economics (2008), "Liverpool Employment Growth Between 1980-2006", BAK Basel Economics.

Figure A.47. **Liverpool's productivity level and growth, 1980-2006**

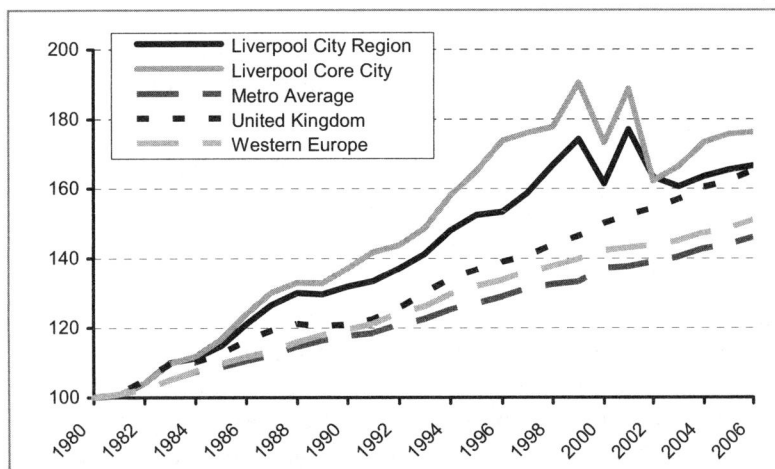

Source: BAK Basel Economics (2008), "Liverpool Employment Growth Between 1980-2006", BAK Basel Economics.

New context and a fresh approach

The years between 1993 and 2008 saw "considerable public intervention and investment, particularly to redress the effects on long-term under-investment in physical infrastructure, including transport and key gateways across the city and particularly to address shortfalls in quality business premises" (Liverpool City Council, 2008). The European Objective 2 programme represents an important, albeit small, source of ongoing public funding. A decline, however, in both Objective 1-status EU Structural Fund investment and UK Government support through the regional development agency means that Liverpool will become increasingly reliant on attracting private sector investment to the city. However, the years of public sector pump-priming had already created a robust climate of private sector investment. Consequently, in the years leading up to Capital of Culture, some GBP 4 billion of private investment was already driving major developments in the city, such as Grosvenor's GBP 1 billion Liverpool One retail centre.

Liverpool's response to this new context was four-fold. It acknowledged the need:

- for increased added value and better returns on reducing levels of public investment, through more effective strategic interventions via its Local Strategic Partnership, Liverpool First, and the delivery of the Sustainable Communities Strategy (SCS) and Local Area Agreement (LAA) to deliver greater multiple outcomes;

- to start making the transition from public sector, subsidy-dependent intervention to a new, strengthened model of business-facing, private sector-led delivery and investment;

- to recognise that the overarching imperative for the next decade is the city's international competitiveness;

- to re-organise and reform its development tools and delivery vehicles to ensure that Liverpool succeeded against its new set of priorities (Liverpool City Council, 2008).

Following the identification of these priorities, the City Council set about a start-up strategy for a new delivery vehicle in Liverpool. This was encapsulated in the "Commencement Plan" for the "Liverpool 'New Economic Development Company', essentially a proposal to Government, the Northwest Regional Development Agency and English Partnerships in January 2008 for the establishment of a new economic development company for the city." It proposed a significant re-organisation of Liverpool's system of economic development and investment promotion.

As well as a review of the changing socio-economic context in the city, it analysed Liverpool's institutional framework. The Commencement Plan evaluated how best the system of economic development and investment promotion in Liverpool should be organised to meet the demands of the new environment most effectively. The Commencement Plan presented four options:

- Do the minimum: under this option the partners would wind up the current vehicles and deliver a service that met the minimum requirements. This would involve Liverpool City Council again establishing an Economic Development Unit, which would seek to work with the Northwest Regional Development Agency, English Partnerships, Business Link, The Merseyside Partnership and other partners as and when possible.

- Business as usual: this would involve the continuation of the current vehicles. Business Liverpool would continue to provide business, inward investment and enterprise support services. Liverpool Vision would operate within the wider City Centre and LLDC within other key investment locations within Liverpool.

- Merger of Liverpool Vision and LLDC: Liverpool Vision and LLDC could be merged to form a new company that combined the skills set of each organisation. Under this option, Business Liverpool would continue to pursue its current activities, but work in partnership with the new company to support the transformation of Liverpool.

- Integrated approach: the skills and resources of all three existing vehicles could be brought together to provide an integrated approach to economic development and physical regeneration. This option would combine expertise in procuring, funding and delivering high-quality infrastructure and development projects, with business support, inward investment and enterprise development services to ensure a "joined up" approach to maximising economic growth.

As a result of the analysis in the "Liverpool 'New Economic Development Company' Commencement Plan", the "Integrated approach" option was chosen as the preferred way forward. It was thought that "the integration of all three of the existing vehicles [was] necessary in order to establish a company whose scope reflects the key opportunities and challenges outlined …, including the need for a more competitive Liverpool" (Liverpool City Council, 2008).

Subsequently, Liverpool Vision was incorporated as a company limited by guarantee in April 2008, as the best vehicle to support the delivery of these ambitions. As suggested, it incorporated the skills and resources of all three existing delivery vehicles, which were disbanded (Liverpool City Council, 2008).

Summary

The inauguration of Liverpool Vision was not therefore to kick-start growth and recovery in Liverpool. It was to accelerate it by engaging with, and galvanising, the private sector into action. Liverpool Vision would consolidate and build upon the achievements of the principal partners behind its creation – Liverpool City Council, Northwest Regional Development Agency and English Partnerships – and their dedicated delivery mechanisms in the form of Liverpool Vision, Liverpool Land Development Company and Business Liverpool. The central task for Liverpool Vision would be to initiate and deliver a step change in Liverpool's medium– to long-term economic prospects, primarily by working with markets, to strengthen the environment in which business can invest in Liverpool. In the event, Liverpool Vision came into being just as the global credit crisis and recession were unrolling. This inevitably resulted in some change of priorities with increased focus on supporting the city's business through the more difficult operating conditions, in conjunction with regional and local partners, and on maintaining the regeneration momentum, particularly in the city's investment areas.

What does Liverpool Vision do?

Liverpool Vision plays a major role in the economic, physical and symbolic regeneration of the city. It also plays a key role in influencing and working with other agencies as a partner on the Liverpool First Economic Development and Enterprise

Partnership to help to address issues of enterprise, employment, skills and jobs as well as in other economic partnership arenas in the city and city region.

As part of its mission to create a world-class city for business and lead the next phase of the city's transformation, the organisation has four strategic "pillars" around which it organises its work.

They include:

- quality of place,
- vibrant economy,
- global connectivity,
- thriving people.

Approach

Liverpool Vision seeks to maximise the leverage of private sector resources and the creative use of public powers and resources in realising value for money. This involves working with key partners, especially Liverpool City Council, NWDA and the Home and Communities Agency (HCA). Liverpool Vision delivers a number of roles and functions, including:

- **Co-ordination and alignment of programmes and policies**. Liverpool Vision co-ordinates and aligns existing projects and programmes to maximise their effectiveness and contribution to the Liverpool vision. These services and projects also form part of the corporate planning systems of NWDA and EP (now HCA). They are also aligned with those of The Mersey Partnership (TMP) – the sub-regional partnership which is a key partner for activities such as inward investment. Where appropriate, the physical regeneration proposals are embedded within the statutory planning framework.

- **Partnering with Business Link.** It works in partnership with Business Link to encourage the city's businesses to access the available publicly-funded support services and programmes. All business support and enterprise interventions are aligned with the principles of Business Support Simplification. A joint working protocol with Business Link provides the operational framework for business support and enterprise activities. Liverpool Vision's Business Support and Enterprise programme are developed in conjunction with NWDA and Business Link.

- **Inward investment.** Liverpool Vision works with TMP, which takes the lead, and with the NWDA to attract and deliver high-quality inward investment projects, in line with the sub-regional inward investment protocol. Liverpool Vision's inward investment activities form part of the body of local authority economic development functions funded by Liverpool City Council, to enable the Council itself to deliver its own obligations under the inward investment protocol.

- **Marketing and image.** It markets and promotes Liverpool, in conjunction with TMP, and leads on the City's brand and image.

- **Delivery of business support and enterprise support**. Liverpool Vision delivers a range of business and enterprise support services to businesses throughout

Liverpool. In order to maximise its impact, however. Liverpool Vision works collaboratively with Business Link North West and NWDA on key enterprise and business-support priorities for the city.

- **Accessing external public sector funding.** Liverpool Vision leads and supports bids for external funding for economic development programmes and projects and, where appropriate, helps to deliver any resulting programmes, such as LEGI.

- **Master planning, project management and procurement**. Liverpool Vision undertakes feasibility, appraisal and master planning work. It procures and lets contracts and manages projects in agreement with Liverpool City Council.

- **Direct development**. In appropriate circumstances, where there are significant market failures, Liverpool Vision works with the public sector partners to reclaim and service sites for development.

- **Gap funding / negative tendering**. One important tool is gap funding of private sector developments which enables the public sector to outline standards in terms of design and sustainability – within the specified intervention rates. However, with reducing availability of traditional gap funding mechanisms, Liverpool Vision is working with national and regional partners on the identification of new financial models and approaches.

- **Compulsory Purchase Order (CPO) powers.** To support land assembly in order to facilitate the comprehensive development of an area in multiple ownership, Liverpool City Council will make use of its CPO powers where appropriate, potentially supported by private sector partners. HCA's and NWDA's CPO powers are also potential tools.

- **Section 106 (S106).** Planning gain will be used to contribute towards the costs of relevant works and projects.

- **Public-private partnerships.** As part of the development of a new approach to funding development, Liverpool Vision is examining the potential of strategic linkages to private sector development interests through appropriate vehicles, such as joint ventures or special purpose vehicles, or agreements which embrace the concept of sharing risk and reward and take a long-term view.

- **Public sector assets**. Liverpool Vision will work with Liverpool City Council, NWDA and HCA, and, where appropriate, utilise their property assets to provide a catalyst for development through appropriate means. For example, the current work in the Baltic Triangle has assessed how best to use NWDA land holdings.

- **Acquisition of assets, recycling of receipts**. Liverpool Vision will, where appropriate and possible, acquire, through its partners, strategic land and property holdings to give it greater control and influence and to tackle specific problems or issues.

- **Cross-subsidisation within a mixed-use development/consent.** In identified locations, the value generated by residential development may be used to subsidise the commercial elements of a project in order to reduce the need for public sector support. In addition, such an approach can potentially be highly sustainable.

- **Infrastructure development incorporating developer contributions.** The unlocking of sites through the early funding of major infrastructure works by the public or private sectors, some or all of the costs of which are subsequently "recovered" from the development of sites that benefit from the works.

Many of the above roles/powers proposed for Liverpool Vision were already being used by Liverpool Vision (the 1999 company) and LLDC in the delivery of agreed projects. Consequently, the skill sets required to effectively use these powers were already in place to be applied within the first three years of operation.

What is the spatial scale of operation and influence of Liverpool Vision?

Liverpool Vision adopts a twin-track approach to prioritising intervention in terms of spatial focus. It focuses on:

- Existing commitments: the city sees it as essential that momentum is maintained in delivering existing priorities and programmes included in the Regional Economic Strategy, the Action Plan for the City Region the Sub-Regional Action Plan and the Liverpool First Sustainable Communities Strategy.

- New priorities: Liverpool Vision focuses in particular on the City Centre, the Knowledge "Crescent", Northshore and the North Liverpool area as well as the other strategic regional sites. The chief executive and board are working to develop appropriate strategies and action plans for the new priorities for the medium term and. These include, for instance, a Strategic Regeneration Framework for Northshore/North Liverpool and a Strategic Investment Framework for the Knowledge Crescent.

In this way, Liverpool Vision's Business Plan identifies a number of priority investment areas and projects designed to concentrate related activity, create a co-ordinated approach to project delivery and to generate the maximum regeneration and economic benefits for the city. The priority investment areas include the:

- City Centre,

- Knowledge Quarter / Crescent,

- Northshore/ North Liverpool,

- Eastern Gateway,

- International Gateway,

- Approach A580 Gateway (Liverpool Vision, 2009b).

How is Liverpool Vision financed?

Operational budget

The Business Plan for 2009/10 assumed that the running costs of the company would be met from financial contributions made by the three member organisations: Liverpool City Council (GBP 4.095 million), the Northwest Regional Development Agency (GBP 0.494 million) and English Partnerships/the Housing and Communities Agency (GBP 0.469 million).

In addition to these main sources, Liverpool Vision is able to bid into the Area-Based Grant (ABG), which is administered through Liverpool First (the Local Strategic Partnership), for activities to support local enterprise. The breakdown of these figures is detailed in Table A.39.

Table A.39. **Liverpool Vision's indicative budget: financial contributions (income) and running costs (expenditure), 2008-12**

In GBP thousands

Income	2008/09 (11 months)	2009/10	2010/11	2011/12
Liverpool City Council	3 714	4 095	4 095	4 095
Northwest Regional Development Agency	600	494	494	494
English Partnerships/HCA	494	469	446	446
Area-Based Grant	160	188	192	197
Other	90	20	20	20
Total	5 058	5 266	5 247	5 252

The organogram that follows (Figure A.48) reveals the local development system within which Liverpool Vision operates.

The main elements of the budget include:

- The contributions of member organisations for 2009/10 which total GBP 5.058 million. The ABG contribution of GBP 188 000 for 2009/10 and the contributions for future years are to be confirmed.

- Staffing costs assume the initial staff structure and reflect the outcome of the exercise to produce an integrated set of employment terms and conditions. Overall salary costs were assumed to rise at 2.25% – the assumed rises in the "cost of living". Employee contributions to pensions are assumed to be 14% for each of the plan years.

- Direct salary-related costs for 2009/10 are forecast at GBP 2.87 million, which compares with a figure of GBP 2.79 million (GBP 2.93 million inflated) for the pre-merger position in 2007/08. This reflects a small, real net reduction of salary costs following non-replacement of staff leaving in 2008/09 and their replacement by new posts in 2009/10. The cost estimates for 2009/10 assume that all posts are filled from 1 April.

- The marketing budget for 2009/10 has been reduced compared to 2008/09, reflecting the completion of a number of "one-off" activities. Marketing expenditure is then marginally increased in 2010/11 in anticipation of additional requirements associated with the Shanghai 2010 Expo.

- The consultancy budget enables the procurement of additional professional services for the development of the company's work programmes such as area-based analysis, development frameworks, particularly Northshore initial feasibility studies and market analysis. The budget also covers external costs involved in appraising major projects. The profile reflects the increased level of programme/project development in 2009/10 reducing in subsequent years.

Figure A.48. The position of Liverpool Vision in the system of economic development and investment promotion in Liverpool

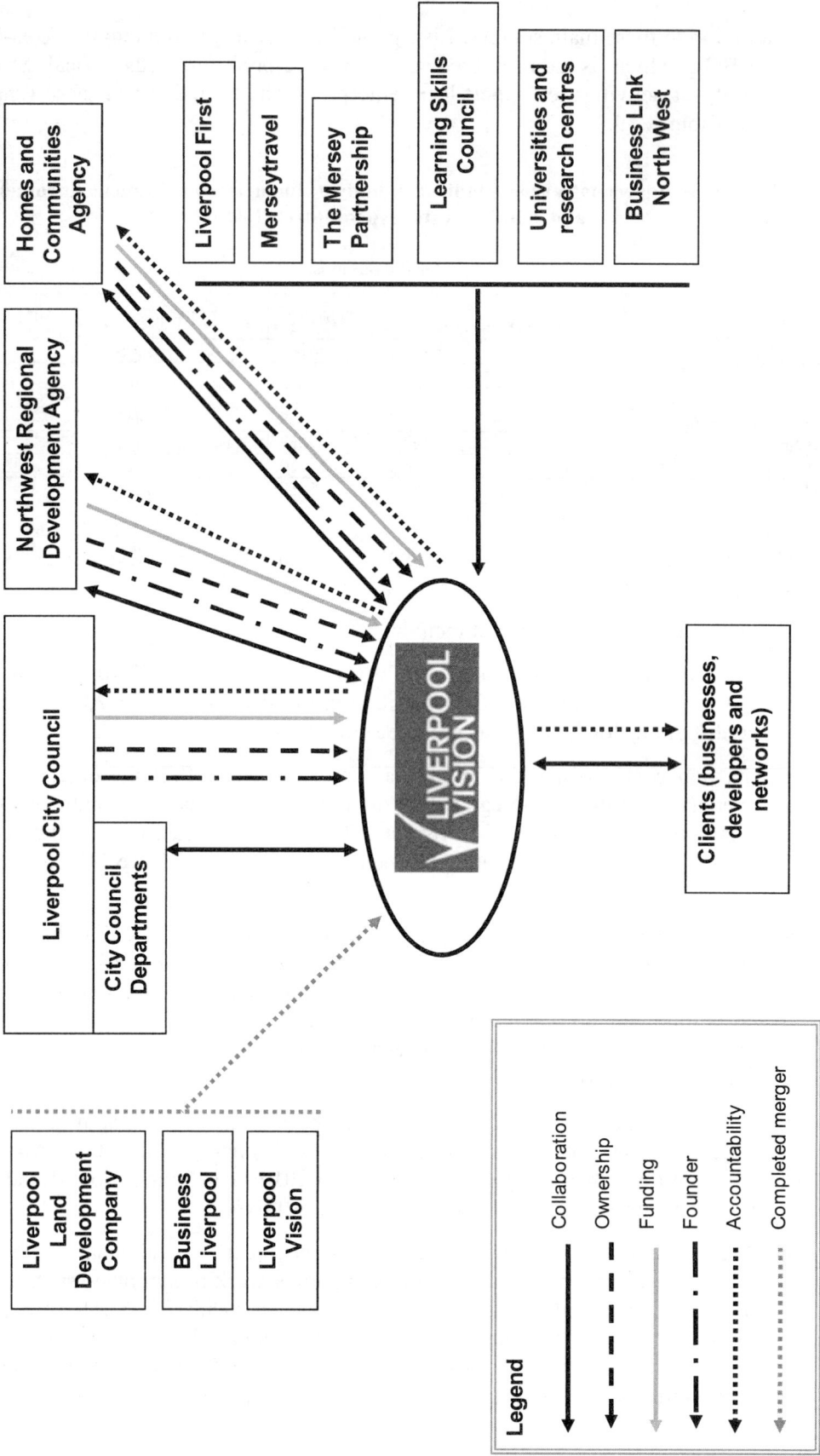

Legend

Collaboration
Ownership
Funding
Founder
Accountability
Completed merger

- The figures assume that Liverpool Vision is registered for value-added tax (VAT) so there are no costs of "irrecoverable" VAT (Liverpool Vision, 2008).

- Operating surpluses are redirected into programmes and particularly business support and investment.

In the face of declining public funding towards the future, Liverpool Vision is aware that it needs to find new methods of funding development activities in the city (Gill, 2009). Furthermore, in the context of an increasingly constrained public sector funding landscape, in addition to efficiency savings passed on to the company by Liverpool City Council, Liverpool Vision has also embarked on an organisational review to identify future operational efficiencies for the immediate term.

Wider programme budget

The 2009/10 Business Plan sets out current programme spending plans for that year and assumptions about future years' funding against a pipeline of priority projects (Table A.40).

Programmes have been defined as those projects or programmes where Liverpool Vision has a role in the delivery – directly or indirectly – of public sector resources.

Table A.40. **Liverpool Vision's funding sources and amounts for programmes, 2008-12**

In GBP millions

Proposed programme	2008/09	2009/10	2010/11	2011/12	2009/12
Northwest Regional Development Agency	2 523	12 675	15 330	11 807	39 812
European Regional Development Fund	733	7 218	9 405	6 531	23 154
English Partnerships / Homes and Communities Agency	-	-	-	-	-
Other public	-	7 100	13 100	2 324	22 524
Total	3 256	26 993	37 835	20 662	85 490

Source: Liverpool Vision (2008), "Business Plan, 2009/10", Liverpool Vision.

Who are Liverpool Vision's partners?

The partnership

The three key members of Liverpool Vision are: (1) Liverpool City Council (LCC); (2) the Northwest Regional Development Agency (NWDA); and (3) English Partnerships/the Homes and Communities Agency (EP/HCA). Each has agreed to work with and through Liverpool Vision in pursuit of their own objectives and the broader vision for Liverpool's economy.

Liverpool City Council

The LCC is the "senior" public partner in Liverpool Vision. Its role is:

- as appropriate, to apply its own resources in line with the vision and objectives set out in the Business Plan;

- to facilitate funding through the Working Neighbourhood Fund (WNF) and Local Authority Business Growth Initiative (LABGI), for projects which address the objectives of the Business Plan;

- to work with Liverpool Vision to establish planning policies and frameworks that will facilitate the vision and objectives of the Business Plan;

- where necessary and appropriate, to support the objectives of the Plan through use of its other statutory powers;

- to approve the Business Plan and to monitor progress against it through the Council's Regeneration Select Committee (twice a year);

- to provide operational and other support funding in particular for the Financial Assistance to Business scheme through the provisions of a services agreement.

The Northwest Regional Development Agency

The Northwest Regional Development Agency provides strategic leadership for the development of the regional economy and leads on the development of the Regional Economic Strategy, which sets priorities for the use of the agency's funds and the outcomes of its partners. Its role is:

- to approve the Business Plan and to agree a funding allocation to support delivery of relevant projects within it;

- to provide operational funding support;

- to provide indirect support to delivery of the Business Plan through its programme of business support, sector development and other programmes;

- as appropriate, to apply its own assets and resources in line with the vision and objectives set out in the Business Plan;

- where necessary and appropriate, to support the objectives of the Business Plan through use of its statutory powers.

The Homes and Communities Agency

Liverpool Vision is establishing a strong working relationship with the Homes and Communities Agency, which replaced English Partnerships from 1 December 2008. Its role is:

- to approve the Business Plan and to agree an investment programme to support delivery of the objectives set out in it;

- to provide operational funding support;

- as appropriate, to apply its own assets and resources in line with the objectives set out in the Business Plan;

- where necessary and appropriate, to support the objectives of the Business Plan through use of its statutory powers.

Liverpool Vision also works closely with other key organisations, which share its vision for the future of the city. They include:

- The Mersey Partnership, the "sub-regional partnership" charged with co-ordinating strategy and with inward investment; in marketing the city and city region, attracting inward investment and promoting Liverpool as a visitor destination;

- Merseytravel, as the partner responsible for providing an effective public transport system serving the key economic areas within the city;

- Liverpool Chamber of Commerce, as the main representative of small to medium business across the city.

Liverpool Vision also works with, and through, a wider body of partnerships and partners, including:

- Business Link NW, the key gateway for business to publicly funded business support products and services;

- the Learning and Skills Council, the national adult skills agency;

- The city's universities: the University of Liverpool, Liverpool John Moore's, the School of Tropical Medicine, Liverpool Hope and the Royal Liverpool Teaching Hospital;

- Alliance Fund Managers, managing Merseyside Special Investment Fund and related loan finance schemes for business;

- Liverpool Science Park, providing business support and links to the region's specialist experts for developing science and knowledge-based companies;

- Liverpool First, Liverpool's Local Strategic Partnership, co-ordinating the activities of partners to support the city's Sustainable Communities Strategy and Local Area Agreement;

- Registered Social Landlords, working within the framework of Liverpool's Housing Strategy;

- local organisations delivering skills and workforce development, enterprise and business support.

As the city's "business-facing" agency, Liverpool Vision works closely with business leaders and networks city-wide to facilitate partnership, engagement and dialogue with the business community. It acts as a bridge between the city's businesses and those public sector programmes and services which directly support a thriving business environment. The mechanisms to achieve this include "Business Leaders Forums" in the main business locations across the city and a wide range of other business and sector networks (Liverpool Vision, 2008).

How is Liverpool Vision governed?

Board level

The Liverpool Vision Board currently comprises ten individuals. Michael Parker is the chair of Liverpool Vision (Liverpool Vision, 2009c).

Staff

There are currently 54 staff employed by Liverpool Vision. Because the organisation was formed from the merger of three organisations, it has had to undertake a process of integration. A number of actions have been taken to help bring staff together within the new company and to establish an effective staff communications mechanism, including staff "away days" and an internal communications group.

In consultation with staff, the company has developed a new single set of terms and conditions of employment: a Staff Consultative Committee has been established; a new salary structure has been agreed based on a (limited) number of salary bands; a performance management scheme has been launched.

The main elements of the initial structure included:

- Three departments, each headed by an Executive Director: Investment and Enterprise; Development and Infrastructure; and Corporate Services.

- Within the Development and Infrastructure Department, an "area-based" focus reflecting the priority investment areas, with support from a specialist project management team as required. The area development teams work closely with colleagues in Investment and Enterprise, particularly with the relevant area managers. In particular, the North Liverpool team works through a number of cross-departmental task groups, such as the Northshore Masterplan, and the work programme is established.

- The Marketing, Finance and Programme Management resources of the three previous organisations have been merged and rationalised, and the heads of each section appointed following an internal "ring-fenced" competition.

In addition, a single Human Resources (HR) Committee of the Board has been established. The HR Committee has overseen the integration process and made final recommendations to the February 2009 meeting of the Board of Directors (Liverpool Vision, 2008).

How is Liverpool Vision governed?

Board level

The Board of Directors brings senior executive experience from significant public and private sector organisations. In particular, the board offers specialties in management and business, politics, skills and lifelong learning, law, accountancy and social exclusion.

All have a thorough working knowledge of Liverpool and are bound together by an interest in regeneration and urban development.

What are Liverpool Vision's key services and programmes within the system of local development and investment promotion?

The programme of activities for the Business Plan period (2009/10 and 2011/12) is described by a wide range of individual projects and programmes in which Liverpool Vision will take the lead, either in facilitation and management or direct delivery, ranging from enterprise promotion and support to small businesses, to large-scale, high-cost physical development and infrastructure projects.

The organisation's four key strategic pillars have been formed on the back of both opportunities and obligations highlighted in the Liverpool Economic Prospectus and from research and strategy development. Some of these include: (1) finance for business; (2) new financial instruments for development, regeneration and economic development; (3) the internationalisation agenda; (4) developing a greater critical mass of knowledge- and science-based economic activities; (5) the economic opportunities of the "Green" Agenda; (6) a business-led workforce skills programme; (7) Liverpool – the best place for the skilled, entrepreneurial and talented to live; and (8) maintaining the momentum of 2008 (Liverpool Vision, 2008).

By gathering and feeding intelligence into its programme of activities, Liverpool Vision has a mechanism to ensure its working agenda is relevant and responsive to the situation on the ground in the city. This effort involves:

- ensuring that Liverpool Vision's activities are underpinned by a robust economic evidence base and monitoring/evaluation processes;

- identifying economic opportunities and constraints on growth;

- understanding and responding to changing market and policy conditions;

- influencing and informing economic and urban policy and legislation in support of Liverpool's priorities (Liverpool Vision, 2008).

Strategic objectives with example initiatives

Strategic objective 1: Quality of place

Develop an outstanding quality of place, making the most of Liverpool's distinctive assets and potential as a maritime cultural centre, optimising its role as the economic, transport, knowledge and cultural hub of the city region, developing a premier built environment, public realm and effective transport connectivity for business, residents, workers, tourists and visitors. (Liverpool Vision, 2008)

- Driver 1. Liverpool: the Core City and Regional Business Centre

  – Action 1a: Expand quality, value for money physical business environment and infrastructure, and key business service sectors.

  – Action 1b: Realise the potential of Northshore and regenerate North Liverpool.

- Driver 2. Liverpool: The Cultural Hub

  – Action 2: Become the number one City for Culture outside London; a top international, national and regional visitor destination and convention centre.

- *Example initiative*: Work with NWDA (as landowner), NCP (as landowner) and English Cities Fund (as preferred developer to NCP) to further proposals for the development of Pall Mall as a major extension of the commercial core; determine by end March 2009 whether the NWDA element of the site should be progressed separately; produce an appropriate implementation plan and secure funding.

Strategic objective 2: Vibrant economy

Create the conditions for a larger city economy which delivers higher up the value chain; supporting a dynamic business space which attracts and retains more leading edge firms, and supports vigorous indigenous growth; optimising and expanding the knowledge and creative economy. (Liverpool Vision, 2008)

- Driver 1. Enterprising and Productive Liverpool

  - Action 1: Create an environment for enterprise and business success.

- Driver 2. Innovative and Creative Liverpool

  - Action 2a: Become an international knowledge centre with top university and private sector expertise, research and development (R&D) centres of excellence and quality digital and physical infrastructure.

  - Action 2b: Create an entrepreneurial, innovative culture from school room to board room.

- *Example initiative:* Undertake research and intelligence to secure a better understanding of the city's business base, and the opportunities and barriers to growth experienced by business, including through the Business Satisfaction Survey 2009/10.

Strategic objective 3: Global connectivity

Developing strong, new international relationships around trade, investment and knowledge, and visitor and tourist markets, strengthening and marketing the Liverpool brand world wide. (Liverpool Vision, 2008)

- Driver 1. International Liverpool

  - Action 1a: Image, brand and marketing.

  - Action 1b: International trade and investment.

  - Action 1c: Knowledge, learning and innovation.

  - Action 1d: International visitors.

- *Example initiative:* Launch and implement the Liverpool brand and image action plan and work with UKTI, NWDA and TMP to promote and position Liverpool in national and international markets.

Strategic objective 4: Thriving people

Growing human capital, learning creativity and innovation, embedding learning and skills on the passport for sustainable economic growth for the city and lifelong employability for individuals: attracting skilled and entrepreneurial residents to the city; ensuring economic inclusion through skilled working communities; supporting and celebrating cultural, racial, faith and gender diversity. (Liverpool Vision, 2008)

- Driver 1. Inclusive, Skilled and Talented Liverpool

- – Action 1: Build a larger, highly skilled and flexible workforce for the needs of today and the future.
- Driver 2. Inclusive, Diverse and Cosmopolitan Liverpool
  - – Action 2: Celebrate and increase diversity in a 21st century international city.
- *Example initiative:* Strengthen Liverpool Vision's capability to engage directly with business on the skills agenda and work with Business Link NW in recruiting and directing the work of two "Train to Gain" skills brokers dedicated to Liverpool.

What role has Liverpool Vision played in the system of local development and investment promotion?

Table A.41 summarises the role Liverpool Vision has played in the system of local development and investment promotion.

Table A.41. **Conceptualising the role of the Liverpool Vision**

	Direct delivery	Facilitation and co-ordination	Strategic support and programmes	Creating capacity elsewhere
Depth and breadth of role	✓✓	✓✓	✓✓✓	
Specific example	• North Liverpool / Northshore: transformational interventions within the area to exploit the opportunities for a step change in economic growth.	• Strategic leadership: Liverpool Vision is Liverpool's business-facing organisation mobilising businesses and public sector resources behind a joint vision for the city's economy.	• Branding: Liverpool Vision works with the NWDA and TMP to improve Liverpool's international profile and position, and to attract increased inward investment into the city.	

What enables Liverpool Vision to contribute to the local development and investment promotion system so effectively?

Inherited credibility and expertise

With over 15 organisation years' collective experience, a track record of delivery and established relationships with investors, developers, businesses and key public agencies, Liverpool Vision is strongly placed.

One-stop shop for development

Liverpool Vision co-ordinates key developments in the city with a specific economic development role and function, and works in close collaboration with the City Council's physical development services and functions.

Clean slate

Liverpool Vision, although the product of an amalgamation of existing agencies, is nevertheless a new entity, developing a new strategic vision for the city, encapsulated in "People, Place and Prosperity" – Liverpool's Economic Prospectus.

Comprehensive approach

The integration of physical development, business support, marketing and investment helps to generate increased outcomes from public investment and a clearer, simplified agency landscape for the business community to relate to.

Capital of Culture

Liverpool's delivery of European Capital of Culture 2008, supported and enhanced by the completion of some of the most important physical infrastructure of recent times, has repositioned Liverpool as a vibrant, successful European city.

Intelligence-based approach to urban development

An economic intelligence-based approach to strategic planning keeps Liverpool Vision relevant and responsive to the city's economic development agenda.

Pro-active board with a private sector outlook

The Liverpool Vision Board is notably constituted by individuals with a private sector orientation. The board is consequently good at reaching out to, and engaging, and collaborating with, key private sector players in the city to facilitate the aims and aspirations of Liverpool Vision.

What constraints make Liverpool Vision less able to effectively contribute to the local development and investment promotion system?

Reducing public funding context

The acute global economic crisis coupled with very high levels of government borrowing make it likely that Liverpool Vision, along with many other development agencies, particularly in the United Kingdom, will have to operate with lower volumes of conventional public funding.

How have, or how are, the approached/approaching these problems?

Reducing public funding context

Liverpool Vision has responded to the global and national economic downturn, credit crisis and reducing levels of public funding by reviewing priorities for the city; refocusing some of its activities on stronger support for business through difficult times; actively exploring new funding mechanisms for physical development and working with partners to identify how best to support the economic recovery and future economic growth. In 2009, Liverpool Vision undertook a rigorous review of its activities, priorities, resources, capacity and structures to prepare itself for the very different operating conditions that are anticipated over the following five years in the United Kingdom. The outcomes will be agreed by the company's board within the Business Plan for 2010/11.

How has Liverpool Vision performed in relation to its key performance indicators?

Liverpool Vision is developing a suite of key performance indicators reflecting changing programme priorities. It also has set a baseline against which it will monitor high-level outcomes and impacts of its programmes over a period of time (Tables A.42 and A.43).

Table A.42. **Liverpool Vision's proposed target outcomes indicators**

Outcome area	Indicator/source	Baseline	Target	
			2013	2023
Primary outcome target				
GVA per head	Cambridge Econometrics – LEFM (2005)	0.96 UK index (GBP 16 300 at 2003 prices)	1.07	1.15
Secondary outcome targets				
GVA (2003 prices)	Cambridge Econometrics – LEFM (2005)	GBP 7.3 billion	GBP 9.7 billion	GBP 12.7 billion
GVA per employee (2003 prices)	Cambridge Econometrics – LEFM (2005)	0.86 UK Index (GBP 28 600)	0.86	0.89
Employment	Cambridge Econometrics – LEFM (2005)	254 800	288 200	307 800
Business start-ups	DTI Small Business Service – VAT registrations (2005)	990	1 100	1 200
Business densities	DTI Small Business Service – business stock/Cambridge Econometrics population (2005)	19	22	25

Source: Liverpool City Council (2008), "Liverpool 'New Economic Development Company' Commencement Plan", Revised Working Draft, Liverpool City Council.

Table A.43. **Liverpool Vision's development programme targets**

Target themes	2009/10	2010/11	2011/12	Total
Jobs created	1 436	2 154	2 717	6 307
Jobs safeguarded	575	580	830	1 985
New floor space (thousands square metres)	11	24	42	77
Refurbished floor space (thousands square metres)	4	-	-	4
Brownfield land developed (Ha)	12	8	8	28
Business starts	826	827	564	2 217
Businesses supported	1 644	1 644	1 549	4 837

Note: These figures will be subject to programme funding.

Source: Liverpool Vision (2008), "Business Plan, 2009/10", Liverpool Vision.

Accountabilities, performance review mechanisms and best-practice sharing

Accountabilities

Liverpool Vision is accountable to its three member organisations: Liverpool City Council, the Northwest Regional Development Agency and the Homes and Communities Agency.

Performance review mechanisms

From the planning and incorporation phase of Liverpool Vision's development, monitoring and evaluation mechanisms have been built into the organisation's make-up.

The approach to monitoring Liverpool Vision is one that builds upon current best practice and guidance, while also taking account of the specific requirements of the organisation. To reflect both the wider regeneration impact of the proposed investment programme and the impacts of individual projects, the framework combines:

- a bottom-up (or micro) analysis of individual projects,

- a top-down (or macro) analysis of changes in strategic outcome indicators (Figure A.49).

Figure A.49. **Liverpool Vision's monitoring framework**

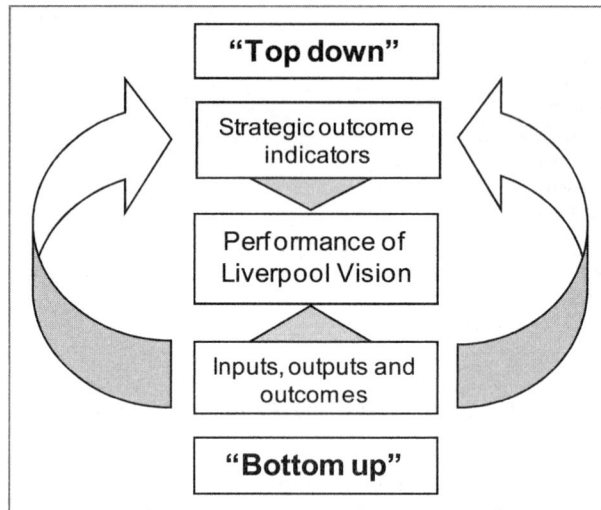

Bottom-up individual project monitoring

A clear and simple performance management system has been established to collect monitoring information for each individual project. This involves assembling and updating information on each project identified in the investment programme, including target/forecast data. The system produces the following information for each project:

- project name;

- description and key activities (including progress to date);

- aims and objectives;

- target geographical area and/or beneficiaries;
- key milestones/timetable (forecast and actual performance);
- costs, income and funding:
  - gross expenditure by source (forecast and actual),
  - receipts (forecast and actual),
  - net expenditure by source (forecast and actual);
- project outputs and outcomes (forecast and actual);
- key risk factors and mitigation;
- relevant comments.

Strategic outcome indicator monitoring

In addition to collecting the outputs and outcomes of individual projects, the monitoring framework involves monitoring changes in key strategic outcome indicators. This is used to measure progress against key objectives and to help assess wider impact of the Liverpool Vision Programme on the economy of the city. This top-down analysis considers changes in strategic outcome indicators (such as GVA and employment), where feasible, using historic information to identify long-term trends.

The evaluation of Liverpool Vision's individual projects and wider impact will comprise two components, as follows:

- ongoing evaluation, conducted "in-house" which will report on an annual basis (as part of the Annual Report) (Liverpool Vision, 2008);
- full evaluation, an independent evaluation of Liverpool Vision after the first-year cycle (Liverpool City Council, 2008).

Best-practice sharing

Liverpool Vision is committed to best-practice sharing. It is involved in a number of networks, such as the UK Economic Development Company Network and the Urban Regeneration Companies network, which meet regularly to discuss best-practice sharing.

It also seeks guidance from external advisors to gain advantage from a more comprehensive and global perspective on development agencies and their examples of excellent practice.

What progress has Liverpool Vision made?

As a recently incorporated agency, Liverpool Vision will be developing its track record from the time of writing this case study (July 2009). What is clear is that through the detailed and high-quality start-up strategy, Liverpool Vision is very well placed to deliver its agenda in the city.

What are Liverpool Vision's strengths, constraints, opportunities and challenges?

Liverpool Vision's strengths, constraints, opportunities and challenges are summarised in Table A.44.

Table A.44. **Liverpool Vision's strengths, constraints, opportunities and challenges**

Strengths	Constraints
• Proactive board and private sector outlook. • New organisation with a clean slate. • Combined expertise and capacities of three integrated organisations. • Strong collaborative relationships with private and public sector partners. • Economic intelligence-based approach to strategic planning keeps Liverpool Vision relevant and responsive to the city's economic development agenda.	• Slowdown in economic growth as the result of credit crisis and global recession. • Reducing levels of public funding at a time in the economic cycle when public intervention is needed to minimise the effects of the credit crisis and recession. • Constraints on private funding and investment.
Opportunities	**Challenges**
• Build on and continue the momentum of a decade of strong urban renaissance, economic growth, investor confidence in Liverpool and the Capital of Culture boost to the visitor economy. • Developing strong international economic relationships through Liverpool's presence at the World Expo in Shanghai 2010. • Developing the opportunities for building a carbon-neutral, knowledge-based economy through better use of the city's natural (tide and wind) assets and knowledge and creativity strengths. • Development of new funding mechanisms and financial arrangements to undertake hard and soft activities in the city.	• Protecting and maintaining the dynamism of the city's physical transformation and fast economic growth. • Securing greater outcomes from reducing levels of funding (private and public).

As Liverpool Vision is a relatively new organisation, the agency has undertaken a comprehensive risk assessment in order to fully evaluate future eventualities as it hopes to anticipate potential problems and react to them before they occur. It has further been completed to ensure that all stakeholders are aware of the climate in which this new organisation operates. See Table A.45 for full details.

Table A.45. **Liverpool Vision incorporation risk assessment**

Risk type	Risk name	Risk description	Combined impact	Probability	Overall score
Strategic	Reputation	Liverpool Vision fails to build and maintain a positive reputation within the private and public sector.	3	2	Medium – 6
Strategic	Leadership	Lack of leadership may reduce the benefits of Liverpool Vision.	4	3	Medium – 12
Strategic	Delivery focus	Focus and support is not maintained behind the delivery of the key early projects.	4	2	Medium – 8
Operational	Staff resources	Liverpool Vision is unable to recruit and retain the necessary quality and quantity of staff required.	5	1	Low – 5
Operational	Member consensus	Disagreements between members, resulting in uncertainties and delays to the delivery of the programme.	4	2	Medium – 8
Operational	Clarity of roles	Lack of clarity about roles and responsibilities.	3	3	Medium – 9
Operational	Partner engagement	Liverpool Vision does not engage effectively with other partners, resulting in reduced support for the programme.	4	2	Medium – 8
Operational	Governance	There is a failure to agree governance arrangements and reporting structures.	4	2	Medium– 8
Financial	Revenue funding	Revenue funding made available is insufficient to cover operating costs.	5	2	Medium – 10
Financial	Capital funding	The capital funding made available is delayed or insufficient to implement the proposed programme.	5	3	High – 15
Financial	Cost overruns	Project costs will overrun, leading to a shortfall of funding and/or delays in the programme.	3	3	Medium – 9
Financial	Cash flow	The timing of cash flows varies from that expected, resulting in operational and delivery difficulties.	3	2	Medium–6
Financial	Financial protocols	As a new company, does not comply with the necessary financial and operational protocols.	5	1	Low – 5
Financial	VAT	Liverpool Vision is unable to recover all or part of the input VAT associated with its activities.	4	3	High - 12
Implementation	Project implementation	Project-specific risks, such as ground conditions and land ownership, cause delays or cost overruns in the implementation of the programme.	4	3	High – 12
Implementation	Community support	Lack of community support for the proposals and opposition from local residents / businesses.	4	2	Medium – 8
Implementation	External capacity constraints	The external construction capacity to deliver the key physical development projects is not sufficient.	3	3	Medium–9
Implementation	Project management	Poor project management of the key projects, resulting in delays / cost overruns and reduced benefits.	4	2	Medium – 8
Implementation	Project feasibility	Elements of the programme cannot be implemented because of specific feasibility constraints.	4	2	Medium–8
Implementation	Statutory consents	Delays/failure in securing the necessary planning and other consents for the physical development proposals.	3	2	Medium – 6

References

BAK Basel Economics (2008), "Liverpool Employment Growth Between 1980-2006", BAK Basel Economics.

Gill, J. (2009), EDC Network Meeting, personal communication.

Liverpool City Council (2008), "Liverpool 'New Economic Development Company' Commencement Plan", Revised Working Draft, Liverpool City Council.

Liverpool Vision (2008), "Business Plan, 2009/10", Liverpool Vision.

Liverpool Vision (2009a), "About Us", *www.liverpoolvision.co.uk/aboutus/aims.asp.*

Liverpool Vision (2009b), "Development Map", *www.liverpoolvision.co.uk/changingcity /map.asp.*

Liverpool Vision (2009c), "Full List of Board Members", *www.liverpoolvision.co.uk/ aboutus/board.asp.*

¡MADRID!

madrid_GLOBAL

Madrid Global (Office for International Strategy and Action) Madrid, Spain

Organisation type

Madrid, the capital of Spain and the largest Spanish-speaking city in Europe, has established Madrid Global as a special office to take forwards its international relationships and positioning through municipal diplomacy, co-ordination of international projects and initiatives, and leverage of international activities by leading Madrid-based institutions and companies, including global firms, universities and research centres, and inter-governmental and non-governmental bodies.

Madrid Global is primarily an "internationalisation bureau" rather than a typical development agency. Madrid's Strategy and International Action Office (Madrid Global) was created as a response to Madrid's global aspirations and the City Council's recognition of the globalised nature of the world in the 21st century. The municipal government believed that Madrid must have a global and international outlook, both in its management and its strategy, and so the new body was born. Madrid Global collaborates with key public and private bodies to carry out strategic projects to improve international perception of the city based on its real strengths. It is dependent on the External Relations and Research Co-ordination Division, within the Deputy Mayor's Office. Madrid Global has opted for extending its own "traditional" international relations measures and projects, and has decided to complement them with new approaches, strategies, programmes and tools to ensure a solid international position for the city of Madrid in the coming decades (Madrid Global, 2009).

Mission statement

Mission

Madrid's Strategy for International Positioning states that Madrid Global has the task of "improving the international position of the Spanish capital by raising awareness of its competitive advantage and reality" (Madrid Global, 2008a).

Strategic objectives

If Madrid's Strategy for International Positioning is taken as the key guiding document for Madrid Global, then Madrid Global has four strategic objectives:

- Madrid, the third European metropolis,

- Madrid, "Main Plaza" of the Spanish-speaking world,

- Madrid, a nexus between cultures and continents,

- Madrid, an urban reference point for highly dynamic emerging cities (Madrid Global, 2008a).

The organisation's broader objectives are to join together all stakeholders around an international common project for the city; attract global events and international mass media exposure; active participation in international city networks and big international events *e.g.* universal expos; attract headquarters of international institutions; and support the Olympic bid as an engine of international projection and urban development (Madrid Global, 2008b).

Vision

Madrid Global's vision is to position Madrid in the scene of the great global cities as the third largest European capital; the leading city of the Spanish-speaking world; the bridge between the Americas, Europe and the Mediterranean; and a leading partner for Asian cities (Madrid Global and OPENCities, 2006).

History, origins and ownership

Elected in 2003 as Mayor of Madrid, Alberto Ruiz-Gallardón began the urban redevelopment process in Madrid by significantly extending the Madrid Metro, as well as other keynote urban development projects such as the *Calle 30* and *Madrid Río*, alongside the gentrification of dwindling historic downtown areas. By 2007, and following Ruiz-Gallardón's re-election, one of the main objectives outlined in the Mayor's Operational Programme for Local Government involved "positioning Madrid within the context of large global cities" (Madrid Global, 2008a).

The Madrid Global Office for International Strategy and Action was created in June 2007 as a dependency of the External Relations and Research Co-ordination Division. It had the express aim of responding to the need of improving the international position of the Spanish capital by raising awareness of its competitive advantage and reality.

According to Ignacio Niño, chief executive officer (CEO) of Madrid Global, whereas the last ten years has been spent improving the product, Madrid must now improve its positioning. He suggests, "There is a gap between perception and reality ... Madrid needs to improve its international image in order to be placed where it should be among the greatest global cities" (Madrid Global, 2008c).

It was for this reason that Madrid Global was created, to close the gap between how Madrid is performing and how it is perceived.

What does Madrid Global do?

One of Madrid Global's primary objectives is to establish and deliver upon a strategy for international positioning. As such, Madrid Global's core business and its specific projects predominantly fall in line with the city's 2008 Strategy for International

Positioning (2008-11). Madrid Global, therefore, employs a number of basic types of action to set this strategy in motion:

- international affairs and city diplomacy, *e.g.* participation with international bodies, liaising with other cities and international networks, strategic alliances involving international companies, and projects with the aim of strengthening the city's position and prestige at the international level;

- the management and execution of the international projection of the city, *e.g.* through commissioning major studies of the city, and the formation of catalytic projects such as the urban services cluster of leading firms headquartered in Madrid;

- the planning and development of international positioning plans and strategies, *e.g.* support of the 2016 Olympic Games bid;

- the fostering of public-private partnerships for internationalisation throughout Madrid, with a goal to leverage resources and know-how between partners in order to optimise the value of all international activities.

Madrid Global is not a typical city marketing agency. It undertakes key stakeholder liaison handling. Its core role is to foster strategic alliances, effective strategies and collaboration among companies and institutions already in Madrid with key organisations elsewhere in the world. Through this core activity, Madrid Global will raise interest in Madrid across the rest of the world, and position it effectively to contribute to global discourse and action (Madrid Global, 2009, 2008d).

What is the spatial scale of operation and influence of Madrid Global?

The main area of benefit is Madrid and its region. In terms of its operating area, the organisation works both within and outside the city to strengthen the city's reputation. This latter task can take the work of Madrid Global and its staff world wide.

How is Madrid Global financed?

As the Office for International Strategy and Action of Madrid City Council, Madrid Global was granted a budget of approximately EUR 8.48 million for 2009 by City Hall. It is likely that this budget will remain stable. Approximately EUR 3.1 million will be committed to human resources, EUR 3.9 million to existing projects, and EUR 1.4 million to operational costs.

These figures show that around 50% of this budget is already committed to existing projects. In effect this will involve a capital transfer to existing organisations. Examples of such projects with longer term partner networks and bodies include:

- Supporting "Houses", such as Asian House, Arab House and Israel House. These Houses promote and support cultural and international relations between the areas they represent and Madrid.

- Collaboration with the Union of Ibero-American Capital Cities (UCCI) network and the EUROCITIES network.

The remaining 50% of the budget, the majority in fact, is reserved for Madrid Global. This is a high proportion for such an agency to spend on its own costs. It shows that the

City Government is behind the venture and that attempts to internationalise Madrid are serious.

Madrid Global has also created the Madrid Global City 2010 Foundation to prepare and manage the city's participation in the 2010 Shanghai Expo. The Foundation is financed by Madrid Global, the City Council and private partners.

To maximise impact with the resources available, Madrid Global also pursues alternative finance from public-private partnerships (Vega, 2009).

What is the institutional context of Madrid Global?

The City Council sees Madrid Global as a "catalyst for mobilising all stakeholders towards a common goal and for implementing clear and focussed actions" (Madrid Global, 2008d).

The organogram that follows (Figure A.50) reveals the local development system within which Madrid Global operates.

Who are Madrid Global's partners?

City departments

Created by the City Council, Madrid Global is the Office for International Strategy and Action of Madrid City Council and works under the auspices of the External Relations and Research Co-ordination Division. Though Madrid Global has a high level of operational autonomy, relationships with City Hall and its departments are critical as it is funded and accountable to the City. Healthy relationships build trust and credibility as well as secure longer term funding and improved organisational effectiveness, *e.g.* the "Madrid 16 Foundation" (the office responsible for the candidacy of the Olympic Games). Specifically, Madrid Global works to engage partners and encourage them to provide financial support for the candidacy.

Government divisions

Madrid Global, however, is not the only organisation in the City's structures which supports the internationalisation of the city. For instance, all government departments within City Hall draw up and implement international projects. The Japan Project is an excellent example of Madrid Global operating in collaboration with government divisions to facilitate internationalisation.

Networks, international organisations and projects

Madrid Global continuously seeks out new non-domestic partners and new alliances. Gaining a wider network of partners gives the organisation more opportunities to participate in international events and projects. It also enables Madrid Global to engage with more stakeholders across the world, share best practices with other cities and develop new strands of activity and projects.

Figure A.50. **The position of Madrid Global in the system of economic development and promotion in Madrid**

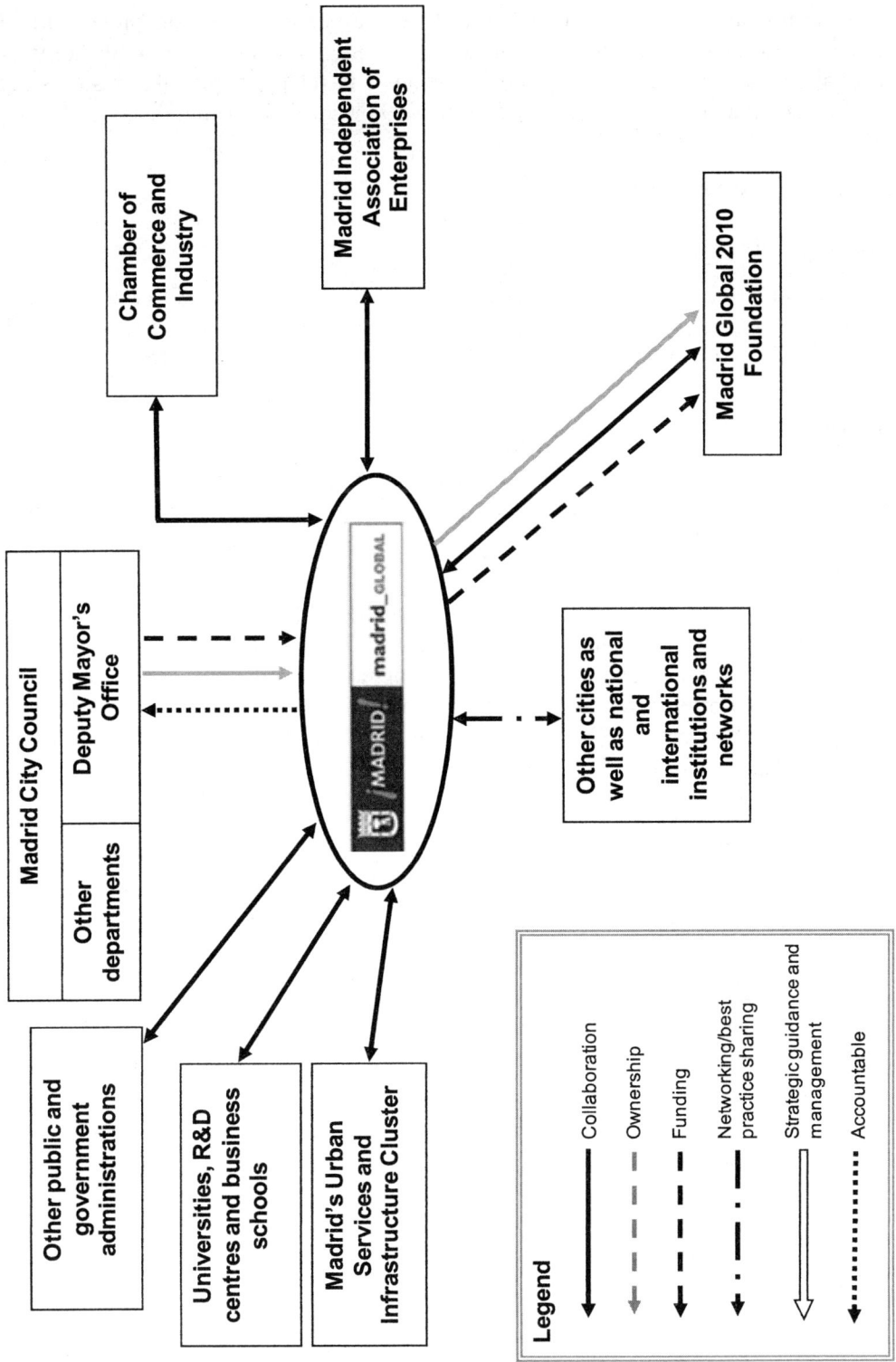

Madrid City Council

Deputy Mayor's Office	
Other departments	

Chamber of Commerce and Industry

Madrid Independent Association of Enterprises

Madrid Global 2010 Foundation

Other public and government administrations

Universities, R&D centres and business schools

Madrid's Urban Services and Infrastructure Cluster

Other cities as well as national and international institutions and networks

madrid_GLOBAL

MADRID

Legend

Collaboration

Ownership

Funding

Networking/best practice sharing

Strategic guidance and management

Accountable

The private sector

The private sector was instrumental to the urban revitalisation process in Madrid. They are, similarly, a key protagonist in the internationalisation of the city. Madrid Global pro-actively builds close collaborations and relations with the business sector to plan and deliver a range of projects (Vega, 2009; Madrid Global, 2008a).

How is Madrid Global governed?

Board level

The structure of the Board of Directors consists of one CEO (who has the direct support of four consultants) and three General Directorates. There is also a branch that provides direct administrative support to the three General Directorates.

Staff

Madrid Global has almost 45 employees, most of who are civil servants and have worked in other divisions of the City Council or other public administrations before joining the organisation. Most of the employees, no matter what their position, are university graduates and can speak at least two languages.

Divided into three General Directorates, Madrid Global has five deputy directors and eight service and department managers. The remaining staff members are assistants and secretaries. This top-heavy organisational structure is peculiar. It is due to the fact that Madrid Global often sends representatives to participate in international forums, events and projects. Because the CEO cannot be everywhere, other senior staff are required to fulfil this need.

In terms of business organisation, Madrid Global is organised into three General Directorates and one Deputy Directorate-General for Monitoring and Management:

- The General Directorate for International Relations is responsible for urban diplomacy and for establishing relations with cities and organisations with an international component.

- The General Directorate of Strategy and International Development is responsible for defining and implementing the Strategic Programme for the Internationalisation of the City of Madrid as a central axis for Madrid's international performance.

- The Directorate General for International Outreach and Partnership is responsible for establishing a stable public/private collaborative framework to boost the international positioning of the city of Madrid, developing joint measures, and promoting alliances with institutions and organisations that multiply the results of efforts made in this area (Vega, 2009).

How is Madrid Global led?

Board level

Direct communication channels between the board and staff have been established, offering the organisation a collaborative internal environment.

In terms of formal communication, there is a Direction Committee. It meets on a weekly or bi-weekly basis. At the same time, meetings with other departments take place on a monthly basis. These meetings help the process of strategic planning for the organisation. Each General Directorate also has a designated person who is responsible for sending project updates to the CEO and to the Strategy Area General Manager.

Chief executive officer

Due to his background in local government and European policy making and delivery, Ignacio Niño became head of Madrid Global on its incorporation in 2007.

As General Co-ordinator of Madrid Global, Mr. Niño is responsible for overseeing and co-ordinating the international relations of the City of Madrid, drawing up and overseeing a strategy to promote the city at the international level, relations with the Diplomatic Corps, planning and the development of plans and strategies in relation to international positioning in specific geographical areas (such as the City of Madrid's Japan Plan), and promoting public-private partnerships at the international level, in addition to any other matters that fall within the framework of the International Development of the City of Madrid (Vega, 2009).

Organisational style

Madrid Global can be characterised as tactical, strategic, a network builder, savvy and targeted in its approach.

What are Madrid Global's key services and programmes within the system of local development and investment promotion?

Madrid Global's core business and specific projects predominantly fall in line with the city's 2008 Strategy for International Positioning (2008-11). The overarching aim to position Madrid as a global city is supported by three main tiers of activity. The bottom tier is understanding the reality of the situation on the ground in Madrid. This information is then incorporated into a series of "vectors" for action, which then feed into four strategic priorities (Figure A.51). Charged with the implementation of this strategy, Madrid Global undertakes the following services and initiatives.

Figure A.51. **Developing the Madrid Global strategy for the internationalisation of Madrid**

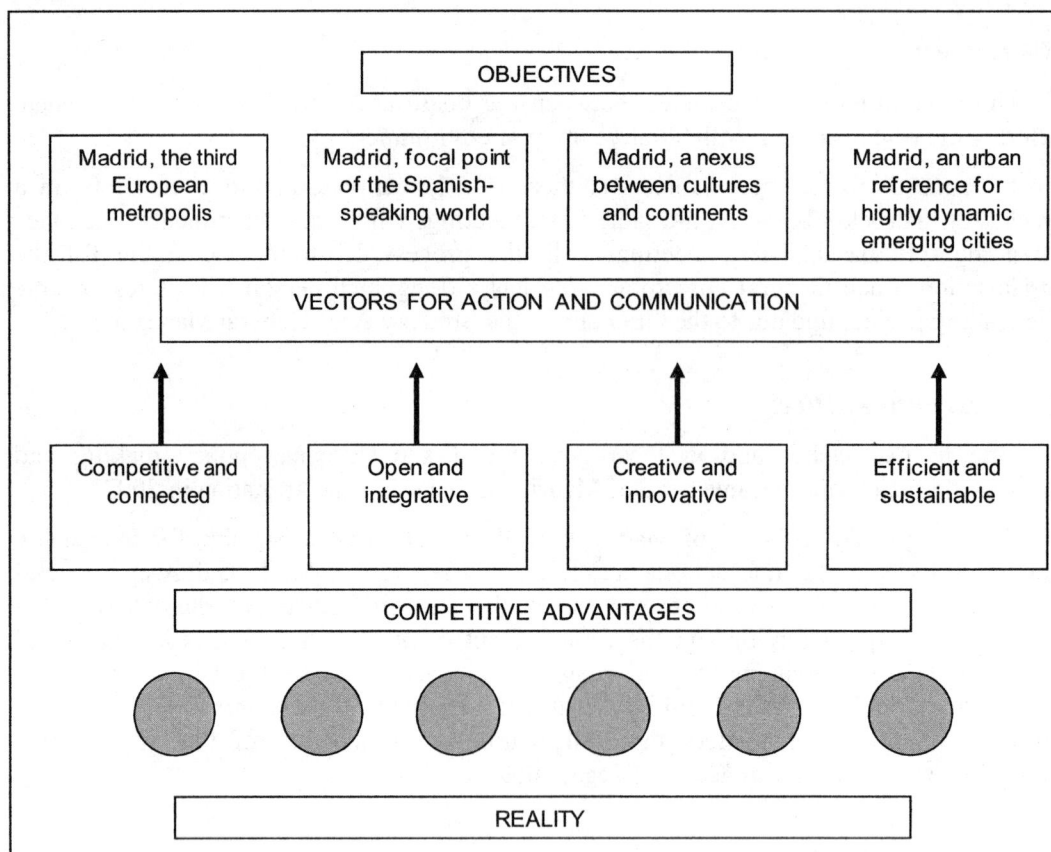

Services

Internal and external surveillance

The organisation constantly analyses studies, rankings and articles published on cities, to evaluate the perception of Madrid's international position. Madrid Global also continuously evaluates Madrid's internal operating environment to gain a better understanding of Madrid's competitive offer.

Internationalisation strategy development and delivery

Working from the Madrid's 2008 Strategy for International Positioning (2008-11), Madrid Global is charged with the development and delivery of the process of internationalising the City of Madrid. The strategy is based on an appreciation of Madrid's unique assets which through a series of "vectors for action and communication" are used to create four strategic objectives which include: (1) Madrid, the third European metropolis; (2) Madrid, focal point of the Spanish-speaking world; (3) Madrid, a nexus between cultures and continents; and (4) Madrid, an urban reference for highly dynamic emerging cities.

International affairs and city diplomacy

For example, participation in International Bodies, City Networks or strategic alliances involving international companies and projects, with the aim of strengthening the city's reputation at the international level.

Participation in global events

Madrid Global is a driver of Madrid's participation in international events raising Madrid's profile worldwide and promoting the city internationally.

Fostering public-private partnerships

Because of the importance of the private sector to development within the city and the attraction of talent and capital from outside the city, Madrid Global is charged with building effective public-private partnerships.

Participation in city networks

Madrid Global participates in networks such as the Union of Ibero-American Capital Cities, EUROCITIES, the Community of Ariane Cities, the Airport Regions Conference, the Union of Capitals in the European Union, United Cities and Local Governments, METROPOLIS, Mayors for Peace, the Ibero-American Organisation for Inter-Municipal Co-operation and the Ibero-American for Local Governments. Telling the Madrid story in influential networks such as these is an important mechanism to encourage the diffusion of Madrid's new brand across the globe.

Collaboration with international bodies

The OECD, Asia-Europe Foundation (ASEF), Asian Development Bank (ADB), Club de Madrid, European Investment Bank (EIB), the Council of Europe, the Committee of the Regions and the British Council all represent examples of the types of international bodies with which Madrid Global engages. This engagement, through meetings, conferences and projects, help to promote Madrid in the international arena.

Bilateral collaborations with other cities

Through twinning programmes, co-operation agreements and specific project collaborations, Madrid Global is facilitating the linkage of Madrid with influential city partners.

Urban public diplomacy

Madrid facilitates the dialogues between Madrid City Hall and key public sector organisations such as *Casa Asia, Casa Arabe, Casa Sefarad*, the Club de Madrid, the Cervantes Institute, the Spain-China Foundation and the Spain-Japan Foundation.

Strategic projects in collaboration with other bodies

Collaboration through projects is a very effective means by which Madrid global has engaged with influential individuals and bodies world wide.

Figure A.52 details the strategy for the international positioning of Madrid and the responsibilities of key institutions involved in its delivery.

Figure A.52. **Implementing Madrid's global city strategy**

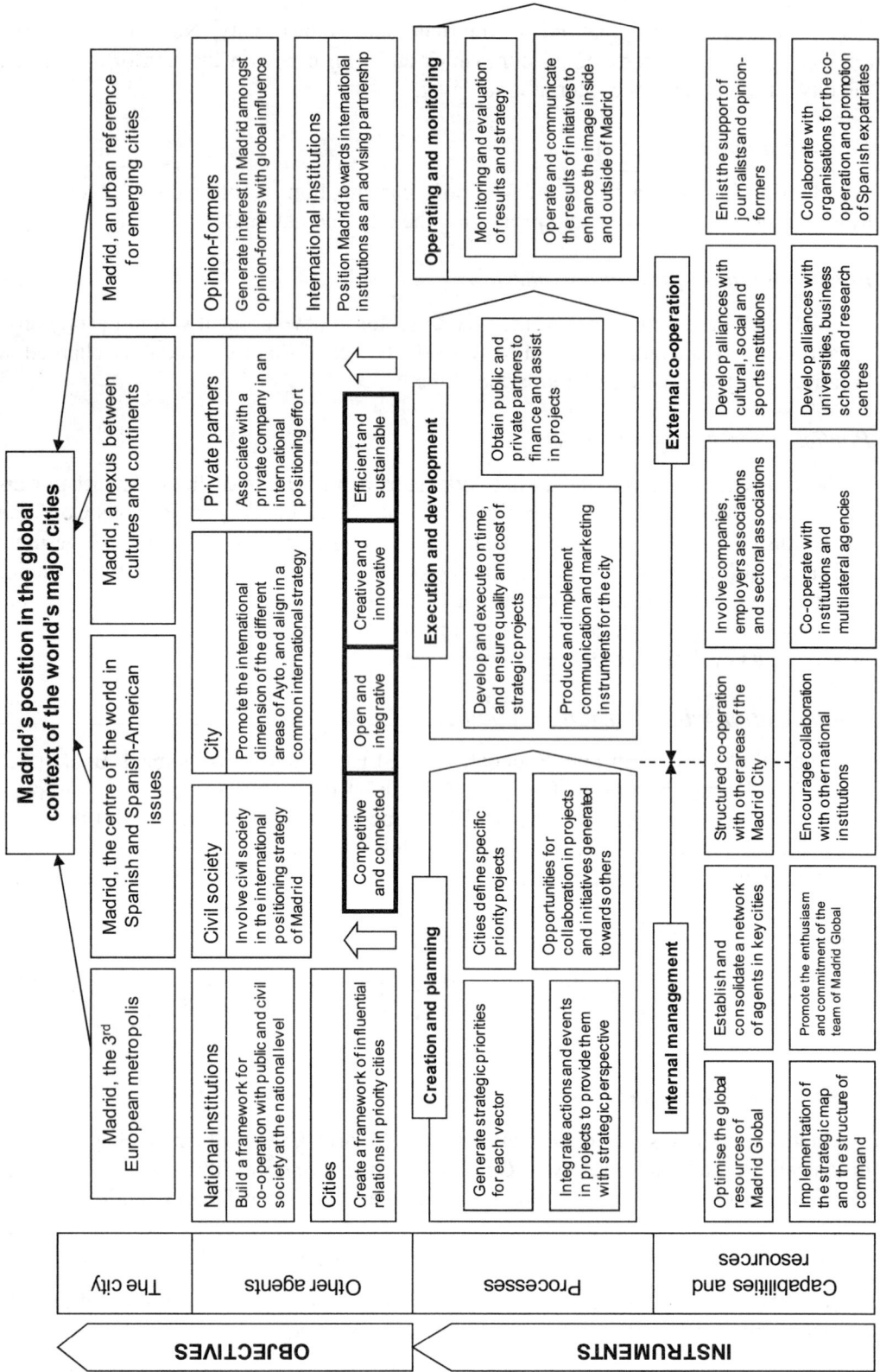

Madrid's position in the global context of the world's major cities

The city

Madrid, the 3rd European metropolis

Madrid, the centre of the world in Spanish and Spanish-American issues

Madrid, a nexus between cultures and continents

Madrid, an urban reference for emerging cities

Other agents

National institutions
Build a framework for co-operation with public and civil society at the national level

Cities
Create a framework of influential relations in priority cities

Civil society
Involve civil society in the international positioning strategy of Madrid

City
Promote the international dimension of the different areas of Ayto, and align in a common international strategy

Private partners
Associate with a private company in an international positioning effort

Opinion-formers
Generate interest in Madrid amongst opinion-formers with global influence

International institutions
Position Madrid towards in ternational institutions as an advising partnership

OBJECTIVES

Processes

Competitive and connected

Open and integrative

Creative and innovative

Efficient and sustainable

Creation and planning

Generate strategic priorities for each vector

Integrate actions and events in projects to provide them with strategic perspective

Cities define specific priority projects

Opportunities for collaboration in projects and initiatives generated towards others

Execution and development

Develop and execute on time, and ensure quality and cost of strategic projects

Produce and implement communication and marketing instruments for the city

Obtain public and private partners to finance and assist in projects

Operating and monitoring

Monitoring and evaluation of results and strategy

Operate and communicate the results of initiatives to enhance the image inside and outside of Madrid

Capabilities and resources

Internal management

Optimise the global resources of Madrid Global

Implementation of the strategic map and the structure of command

Establish and consolidate a network of agents in key cities

Promote the enthusiasm and commitment of the team of Madrid Global

External co-operation

Structured co-operation with other areas of the Madrid City

Encourage collaboration with other national institutions

Involve companies, employers associations and sectoral associations

Co-operate with institutions and multilateral agencies

Develop alliances with cultural, social and sports institutions

Develop alliances with universities, business schools and research centres

Enlist the support of journalists and opinion-formers

Collaborate with organisations for the co-operation and promotion of Spanish expatriates

INSTRUMENTS

Source: Madrid Global (2008a), "Executive Summary of Madrid: The Strategy for International Positioning, 2008-11", Madrid Global.

ORGANISING LOCAL ECONOMIC DEVELOPMENT: THE ROLE OF DEVELOPMENT AGENCIES AND COMPANIES © OECD 2010

Projects

The Madrid 2016 Olympics candidacy

Madrid Global has worked to engage partners and encourage them to provide financial support for the candidacy. Specifically, Madrid Global designed and implemented the Madrid 16 Sponsorship Programme, the promotion of Madrid Club 16 and Madrid 16 Sponsorship Return Programme. The candidacy offerered an opportunity to promote the city's new modern brand across the world.

The 2010 Shanghai EXPO

Madrid is one of only 15 cities worldwide to have its own pavilion at the 2010 Shanghai EXPO. Madrid Global aims to capitalise on this opportunity to underline the city as a competitive, dynamic and sustainable city. It will provide a unique opening to strengthen its image and consolidate its positioning in the international setting, particularly in relation to other European and global cities.

International positioning study

At the behest of Madrid Global, Strategy and Focus conducted a 2008 study into Madrid's current international position and its development. Madrid Global, in collaboration with Deloitte, has carried out a report about the different rankings, indices and classifications of the global cities in the world. The main objective of this analysis is to know the position that a city such as Madrid has in the global scene. More than 85 rankings and 27 global cities, including Madrid, have been taken in consideration.

OPENCities

OPENCities is a collaborative project involving various cities, including Madrid, led by the British Council, analysing the openness of cities as a variable indicating competitiveness. OPENCities aims to identify the links between migration and cities' competitiveness, with particular emphasis on internationalisation and population strategies that will pose migration as a competitive advantage for cities and, indirectly, help integration and cohesion agendas.

Dialogue Programmes between Young Urban Leaders of Asia and Europe

The first edition of the Dialogue between Young Urban Leaders of Asia and Europe Programme will be held in Madrid for the exchange of ideas, best practice and innovative experiments in the development of a new city management, for young rising stars in different national sectors of the member countries of ASEM (Asia Europe Meeting).

Madrid Global Chair for Urban International Strategy

Madrid Global and the IE Business School have founded the Madrid Global Chair for Urban International Strategy to reinforce the message of Madrid as an efficient, sustainable city, and to contribute to the co-ordination and mutual support of the efforts of Madrid and of its businesses. The Chair is centred on three functions: teaching; research and reports; and administration, with a fundamentally international scope (Vega, 2009; Madrid Global, 2008a).

What role has Madrid Global played in the system of local development and investment promotion?

Table A.46 summarises the role Madrid Global has played in the system of local development and investment promotion.

Table A.46. **Conceptualising the role of Madrid Global**

	Direct delivery	Facilitation and co-ordination	Strategic support and programmes	Creating capacity elsewhere
Depth and breadth of role	✓	✓✓	✓✓✓	
Specific example	• Socio-economic intelligence gathering in the city and outside the city.	• Positioning the international promotion agenda at the forefront of the Madrid development agenda.	• Participation in global-scale events. • Participation in collaborative international projects. • Fostering international dialogues among target groups.	

What enables Madrid Global to contribute to the local development and investment promotion system so effectively?

Highly motivated and qualified staff

Madrid Global's staff can be characterised as well-prepared, well-qualified, and motivated by the attainment of key objectives and the preparation of new proposals.

Operational independence

With respect to Madrid City Hall, Madrid Global enjoys a privileged position. Initially, the organisation was accountable only to the deputy mayor. This gives Madrid Global far greater independence to program and pursue its objectives.

Effective collaboration

Madrid Global maintains healthy professional relations with private and public of all kinds. This helps the organisation function with greater efficiency and add value to the work of local government more effectively.

What constraints make Madrid Global less able to effectively contribute to the local development and investment promotion system?

Newly created

Created in 2007, Madrid Global is a new organisation. As well as the internal challenge to ensure effective communication channels are open between staff and board members, and between different internal departments, it also faces external challenges. The organisation has had to be continually malleable enough to fit into the existing structures present in the city.

Political and funding cycles

Because of the four-year-long political terms, long-term planning is extremely difficult. Short-term planning is determined by annual budgets.

Bureaucracy

Though operational freedom is described as a strength, it should be noted that Madrid Global still experiences bureaucracy. The organisation is subject to administrative laws in many aspects of its work, which slows the rate at which the organisation can make and deliver ideas.

Budget constraints

In the current economic situation there are budget constraints that Madrid Global will have to tackle with imagination.

How has, or how are, Madrid Global approached/approaching these problems?

Newly created

Madrid Global has adapted extremely quickly to its operating environment. Despite its hierarchical structure, its internal operating model is direct and dynamic.

Bureaucracy

Madrid Global is well positioned and works to ensure that communication channels with City government are open and active.

Budget constraints

To cut costs in the face of the downturn, Madrid Global is working in collaboration with partners on projects that are already underway (Vega, 2009).

How has Madrid Global performed in relation to its key performance indicators?

Table A.47 summarises how Madrid Global has performed in relation to its key performance indicators.

Table A.47. **Key performance indicators of Madrid Global**

Theme (initiative)	Tangible impact	Intangible impact
Increased participation in strategic international events, networks and projects	• Madrid Global has been involved in the World Cities Summit, the Program of Urban Development ADB, the World Urban Forum Nanjing, OPENCities, The Dialogue between Young Urban Leaders of Asia and Europe (ASEF), and a number of others. • Madrid's engagement with international networks and partners, such as the committees and forums of the UCCI, Covenant BID and the dialogue between Toronto and Madrid has improved. • As part of the Shanghai 2010 Expo, Madrid has been selected to build a permanent structure. It is predicted that, over the six-month-long event, the structure could be visited by representatives from nearly 200 countries and international organisations – totalling some 70 million foreign and local visitors. • Through the *Árbol Bioclimático* and the Bamboo House at the Shanghai Expo, Madrid has the opportunity to promote its unique advantages to the Chinese market. • Up to 31 March 2009, Madrid Global was working on 40 projects. These projects were divided into 194 actions, of which 65 are still waiting to begin. A total of 103 were underway, with 26 finished.	• Improved international visibility and stature of Madrid. • Entry into the Eastern markets.
Formation of key alliances and partnerships	• Key alliances with institutions such as the Japan Foundation in Madrid, House Asia and Community of Cities Arianne have been forged.	• Credibility and trust is being generated between key partners.
Enhanced private sector engagement	• Improved co-ordination with private enterprises by Madrid Global has increased the number of sponsorship deals obtained for the 2016 Olympic candidacy. Two main groups include the Associates of "Club 16" and the Preferential Sponsors of Madrid 2016.	• Engagement with the private sector gains credibility and can improve access to finance.

Source: Vega, B. (2009), Written and telephone communication and interviews.

Accountabilities, performance review mechanisms and best-practice sharing

Accountabilities

Madrid Global, as with the rest of Madrid City Council, promotes a high level of both internal and external accountability for its activities. Across the city, a system to report the performance of city departments has been developed to make each accountable for its own activities, to the mayor and to the electorate. As a significant city department, Madrid Global uses the same system to report its progress against an agreed set of criteria at the beginning of a given period of activities. Madrid Global targets are agreed in conjunction with the mayor and deputy mayors to ensure that electoral promises are delivered upon.

Internally, Madrid Global operates a similar simple system. All targets and outputs are set out simply and made accessible across the organisation for scrutiny and/or praise (Vega, 2009).

Performance review mechanisms

As described above, Madrid Global reviews and refines its activities on a regular basis, using highly effective, modern and simple mechanisms. This performance review mechanism is the same used to ensure that the organisation delivers on behalf of the stakeholders to which it is accountable. Results are collated in accessible Microsoft Excel format, rather than complicated computer programs, and disseminated at open meetings on a monthly basis. Any actions which result from the discussions which take place are enacted the following month (Vega, 2009).

Best-practice sharing

Madrid Global participates in a number of international networks through which it shares best practice. It also undertakes city-to-city partnerships. For instance, the Madrid-Toronto collaboration agenda saw the two cities share expertise in strategic areas. Madrid learnt from Toronto's strengths in biotechnology and cultural diversity, whereas Toronto learnt from Madrid's strengths in urban infrastructure development, urban clustering and large-scale urban development projects (Vega, 2009).

What are Madrid Global's strengths, constraints, opportunities and challenges?

Madrid Global's strengths, constraints, opportunities and challenges are summarised in Table A.48.

Table A.48. **Madrid Global's strengths, constraints, opportunities and challenges**

Strengths	Constraints
• A great deal of political support from Madrid's mayor himself and the members of his City Government. • Highly qualified, motivated and young staff members. • A certain degree of self-sufficiency that allows Madrid Global to be relatively autonomous • Madrid Global designs and delivers cutting-edge and innovative projects. • Madrid Global has very powerful and well-regarded partners and allies. • Madrid Global retains much of its budget to undertake its own projects. • The organisation reviews and refines its activities on a regular basis, using highly effective, modern and simple mechanisms. • The organisation promotes high levels of both internal and external accountability for its activities. • Madrid Global performing well in Asia and is becoming a well recognised agent for Asian cities, countries and institutions.	• Madrid Global is a newly created organisation within a very old institution and needs to break some barriers and long-established inertias in order to fulfil its goals. • Some key stakeholders in the City, as well as within the City Council, are yet not aware of Madrid Global. • Madrid is not a well-known city and therefore Madrid Global must work doubly hard to achieve its goals relative to cities with a stronger international presence. • English is not widely spoken in Madrid and this makes it difficult sometimes for Madrid Global to achieve its goals and reach out to the world. • Madrid Global needs to be active in other world regions besides Asia to reach its goals.
Opportunities	Challenges
• Madrid's presence at the 2010 World Expo in Shanghai is a great opportunity for Madrid Global and for the whole city to implement its strategy in Asia. • The 2016 Olympic Bid as a catalyst to achieving global presence for Madrid. • Madrid Global has established a dense network of alliances with strategic partners. These links with other institutions and companies are an opportunity that needs to be developed to its full potential by starting up new co-operative projects. • There is still potential for working together in new projects with other departments in the City Council and with other public administrations working in internationalisation. • Madrid is the world capital of Spanish, a language spoken by millions in Latin America and the United States. This is an opportunity for Madrid Global to become a reference point for cities in the Spanish-speaking world.	• The current economic crisis is affecting the municipal budget and restrains in travelling and other costs are affecting some projects. If the recession does not end promptly, this could be a major threat. • Being a young organisation, Madrid Global is very active and sometimes tackles many projects and opportunities at the same time. This can be challenging. • Madrid is not yet fully recognised as a global city and this makes it difficult for Madrid Global to participate actively in some events and networks. • Other cities are very active in promoting their international image. In fact some are trying to place themselves in the same positions that Madrid wants to occupy. These direct competitors are a threat for Madrid Global's strategy.

References

Madrid Global (2008a), "Executive Summary of Madrid: The Strategy for International Positioning, 2008-11", Madrid Global.

Madrid Global (2008b), "Madrid Cluster in Urban Development and Management", *www.adb.org/Documents/Events/2008/Madrid-Urban-Management/manila.pdf.*

Madrid Global (2008c), "Madrid Public Infrastructures and Urban Services Cluster", *www.adb.org/Documents/Events/2008/Madrid-Experience-Sharing-Seminar/Bonifacio.pdf.*

Madrid Global (2008d), "Annual Meeting", *www.adb.org/annualmeeting/2008/presentations/jbravo-presentation.pdf.*

Madrid Global (2009), "Who are We?", *www.munimadrid.es/portal/site/munimadrid/menuitem.f4bb5b953cd0b0aa7d245f019fc08a0c/?vgnextoid=a70858fe026de11058fe026de1100c205a0aRCRD&vgnextchannel=8db7566813946010VgnVCM100000dc0ca8c0RCRD&idCapitulo=5211986.*

Madrid Global and OPENCities (2006), "Madrid Open and Integrating", *www.munimadrid.es/UnidadWeb/Contenidos/EspecialInformativo/RelacInternac/MadridGlobal/ProyectosEstrategicos/04_OpenCities/Ficheros/PresentacionEnglish.pdf.*

Vega, B. (2009), Written and telephone communication and interviews.

MILANO
METROPOLI
AGENZIA DI SVILUPPO

Milano Metropoli
Milan, Italy

Organisation type

Milano Metropoli is the Agency for the Promotion and Sustainable Development of the Metropolitan Area of Milan and aims to promote economic and social development in greater Milan. It was formed in early 2005 when the corporate purpose and structure of *Agenzia di Sviluppo Nord Milano* (ASNM) (North Milan Development Agency) were redefined. It is, however, not only the name which has changed. ASNM was essentially an urban redevelopment agency for the North Milan area, while Milano Metropoli's work not only encompasses a broader geographical area – the metropolitan area of Milan – but also has a wider remit, focusing on territorial marketing and promotion, supporting strategic economic sectors and carrying out reindustrialisation, urban regeneration and development projects.

Milano Metropoli is a joint-stock company and is comprised of mixed public and private capital, with public capital making up the majority. The agency is promoted by the Province of Milan and shareholders include the Province of Milan (majority shareholder), the Milan Chamber of Commerce, *Finlombarda* (the financial holding of the Lombardy Region), *ComuneImprese* (the Rhodense development agency on behalf of 11 municipalities), the municipalities of Sesto San Giovanni, Bresso, Cinisello Balsamo and Cologno Monzese, and private enterprises. All the municipalities in the metropolitan area of Milan, as well as any other public and private bodies interested in promoting the area's economic and social development, can become shareholders in the agency (Sala, 2009).

Mission statement

Milano Metropoli's mission is to promote sustainable development throughout the Milanese area through its actions, projects and services. These are designed to increase the competitiveness of local businesses, support growth in strategic industrial sectors and advanced services, and heighten awareness, both in Italy and abroad, of the skills, opportunities and centres of excellence available in the area.

Milano Metropoli's mission focuses on the following strategic areas:

- Territorial marketing: this involves national and international promotion of the territory, with a particular focus on attracting foreign investments and qualified resources. It also includes the creation of an integrated tourist offer and the planning and implementation of new tools and initiatives.

- Supporting strategic economic sectors: this includes support for and revival of trade companies, from the net economy, computer science and telecommunications areas to the creative industries.

- Special re-industrialisation, urban regeneration and development projects: the agency provides support to the local authorities for the implementation of the plans to upgrade redundant areas and to carry out actions to create a stronger production system (Sala, 2009).

History, origins and ownership

The legacy of Agenzia di Sviluppo Nord Milano *(ASNM)*

North Milan's development agency was a response by the local authorities to the deterioration of the area's socio-economic structure and, in particular, the problems faced by North Milan. In 1995, the Municipality of Sesto San Giovanni organised an OECD Local Employment and Economic Development (LEED) Programme socio-economic audit that helped to analyse the situation, draft local development guidelines and transform the industrial crisis into an opportunity (Pizzinato, 1997). In January 1996, Falck (an industrial company) closed the last steel factory in the area (pushed also by EU policies), making 1 700 workers redundant. Following OECD LEED Programme recommendations, the local administration promoted the North Milan development agency. The Province of Milan launched a "bottom-up experience of inter-municipal and municipal-provincial co-operation to bolster local economic development" (OECD, 2006).

The local municipalities and the Province of Milan set up a local development agency which operated on a voluntary basis and was known as *Agenzia di Sviluppo Nord Milano* (ASNM). This aimed to address problems related to de-industrialisation due to the delocalisation of many large firms and the dissolution of many traditional manufacturing firms. In order to help tackle these problems, ASNM promoted the restoration of brownfield sites by converting industrial areas into business incubators and sites for small firms, and also enhanced linkages between universities and business by financing innovative business ideas emanating from university professors and researchers.

From ASNM to Milano Metropoli

Due to its success, the agency increased its membership to other municipalities, important financial institutions and companies and, in 2005, was restructured as a public-private agency known as Milano Metropoli. Key partners now include the Province of Milan; the Milan Chamber of Commerce; four municipalities on the northern border of the city of Milan that share de-industrialisation problems (Sesto San Giovanni, Bresso, Cinisello Balsamo, Cologno Monzese); two financial institutions (*Finlombarda* and *Banca Dicredito Cooperativo di Sesto San Giovanni*); and several large companies (Falck, ABB, *Brollo-Marcegaglia, Edil-Marelli*) (OECD, 2006) (Figure A.53).

Figure A.53. **Ownership of Milano Metropoli**

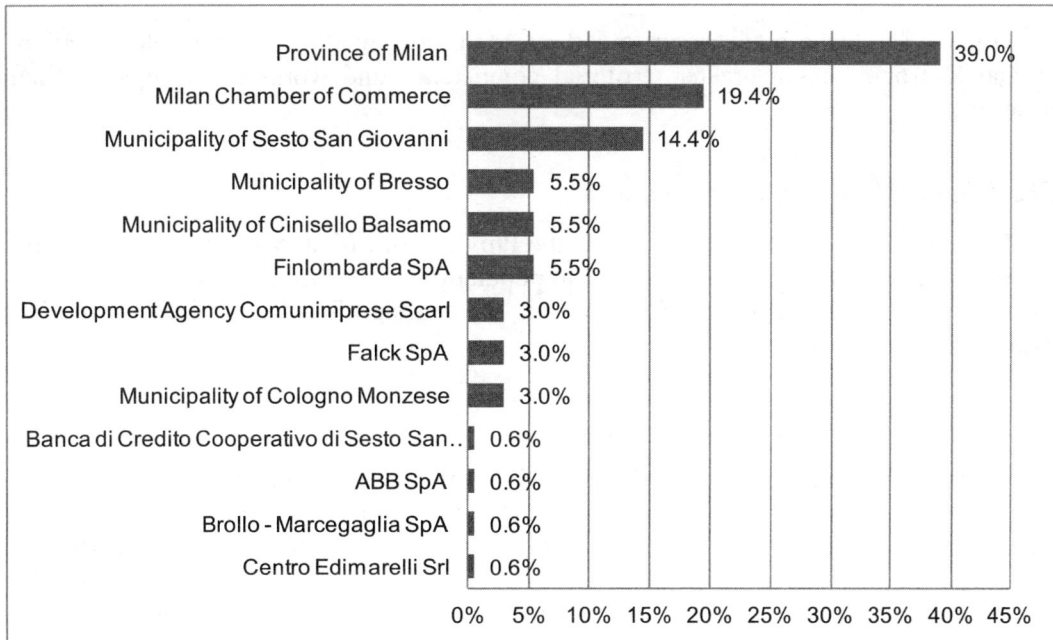

Owner	Percentage
Province of Milan	39.0%
Milan Chamber of Commerce	19.4%
Municipality of Sesto San Giovanni	14.4%
Municipality of Bresso	5.5%
Municipality of Cinisello Balsamo	5.5%
Finlombarda SpA	5.5%
Development Agency Comunimprese Scarl	3.0%
Falck SpA	3.0%
Municipality of Cologno Monzese	3.0%
Banca di Credito Cooperativo di Sesto San..	0.6%
ABB SpA	0.6%
Brollo - Marcegaglia SpA	0.6%
Centro Edimarelli Srl	0.6%

Source: Milano Metropoli (2009a), "Public and Private Institutions Together for Territory Development", *www.milanomet.it/en/chi-siamo/public-and-private-institutions-together-for-territory-development-2.html*.

What does Milano Metropoli do?

Milano Metropoli's strategic activities include:

- **Promoting the area.** The agency plans and develops territorial and communication marketing in order to heighten awareness – both at home and abroad – of local specialisations, skills and opportunities.

- **Supporting strategic economic sectors.** It devises schemes to support and re-launch businesses in economic sectors that are particularly important for the Milanese economy, such as biotechnology and creative industries.

- **Special re-industrialisation and urban regeneration projects**. The organisation supports local agencies which have developed plans to reclaim brownfield sites and take steps to boost the manufacturing system. Milano Metropoli creates integrated urban redevelopment schemes to improve territorial, environmental, social and economic interventions.

- **Supporting local agencies.** The agency devises and co-ordinates strategic planning and participation schemes to help local agencies work out a shared vision of development and improve territorial governance (Sala, 2009).

What is the spatial scale of operation and influence of Milano Metropoli?

While ASNM, the predecessor to Milano Metropoli, worked solely in North Milan, Milano Metropoli has a greater territorial competence and works at the metropolitan scale.

The Milano Metropoli operating area

This effectively corresponds in size to the Province of Milan, covering approximately 2 000 square kilometres. The area has a population of 3.7 million. There is a still, however, a particular focus on North Milan, an area significantly affected by the de-industrialisation process.

Tackling de-industrialisation in North Milan

In terms of actions taken in North Milan, following the Strategic Plan for North Milan (2001), the Pact for North Milan (2005) created a new territorial entity, a metropolitan area of 58 square km with over 310 000 inhabitants. The municipalities of Bresso, Cinisello Balsamo, Cologno Monzese and Sesto San Giovanni, which had launched the first Strategic Plan, were joined by the municipalities of Cormano, Cusano Milanino and Paderno Dugnano. Milano Metropoli and the Province of Milan co-ordinated these town councils to begin to work together on a joint local development process. Their aim is to build a common framework within which to start re-organising major public services in line with the demographic layout of the area and its infrastructure.

Actions taken include: the North Milan Area Plan to help organise services and functions such as infrastructure, transport, mobility and open spaces; the North Milan Housing Plan to provide new models for social housing; social and healthcare service improvement through the creation of a new type of healthcare company to cover the whole area; the creation of a local training and employment agency which aims to offer integrated job training in the area; and the creation of an integrated cultural system. Agenda 21 of North Milan is a co-operation process that promotes economic development in the territory while respecting the environment and people. It was started with the support of Milano Metropoli and the Municipalities of Bresso, Cinisello Balsamo, Cologno Monzese, and Sesto San Giovanni. It has defined a series of projects to be carried out by 2010 in order to better the environment and quality of life for citizens (Sala, 2009).

Building the economy in the wider Milan metropolitan area

In terms of efforts in other local areas, Milano Metropoli worked alongside the Como Chamber of Commerce to plan and set up a local development agency, the Como Development Agency (2006). Initially, various hypotheses were put forward for the type of agency required and the public relations work needed to gain local consensus for the project and engage key local players. Once the organisational and institutional schemes, and the financial viability of the new agency had been worked out, Milano Metropoli provided start-up support with tutoring and consulting on strategic planning and on the initial pilot projects to be launched.

In 2004, Milano Metropoli was commissioned by *Banca di Credito Cooperativo Trasimeno-Orvieto* to help implement a strategic plan for Valdichiana, an extremely well-endowed area from an environmental, cultural and historical point of view. The agency applied innovative planning methodologies to identify concrete projects and schemes that could sustain economic development, attract new businesses and discourage the younger generation from migrating away from the area. The agency has also carried out business incubator feasibility studies in cities, such as the Social Enterprise Incubator in Campobasso (2003-04), the network of micro incubators in Naples (2005) and the social enterprise incubator in Portogruaro (2006) (Milano Metropoli, 2009b).

How is Milano Metropoli financed?

Milano Metropoli is a joint-stock company, comprised of both public and private capital. The organisation receives no structural funding and its budget is totally covered by contributions and match-funding for the delivery of projects and services in its target area.

The turnover in 2007 amounted to approximately EUR 3 500 000. Some 70% of this budget originated from the match-funding of various sources, such as EU programmes and initiatives, the Italian national government and public local authorities. This capital was focussed on territorial marketing, supporting strategic economic sectors (including new entrepreneurship and the small and medium-sized enterprise [SME] value chain), and urban regeneration and area-development projects.

Some 30% of this budget came from the provision of services directly offered to promote new commercial and social entrepreneurship, boosting existing SMEs and heightening awareness of the importance of energy saving and social responsibility (for example, by managing an SMEs incubator in Sesto San Giovanni).

The clients of Milano Metropoli are SMEs, local municipalities, local agencies and other public bodies.

This 70:30, public-private funding ratio will partially change in 2008-10. Milano Metropoli has signed a co-operation agreement with a private not-for profit foundation in the Lombardy region, which has agreed to offer Milano Metropoli a three-year grant of EUR 1 500 000 for the crafting and delivery of development projects in the metropolitan area (Sala, 2009).

What is the institutional context of Milano Metropoli?

Milano Metropoli plays a key role in co-ordinating a diverse range of partners in the shared aim of the development of Milan. It also supports local agencies which are developing plans and aids in the definition and implementation of actions.

The organogram that follows (Figure A.54) reveals the local development system within which Milano Metropoli operates.

Figure A.54. **The position of Milano Metropoli in the system of economic development and investment promotion in Milan**

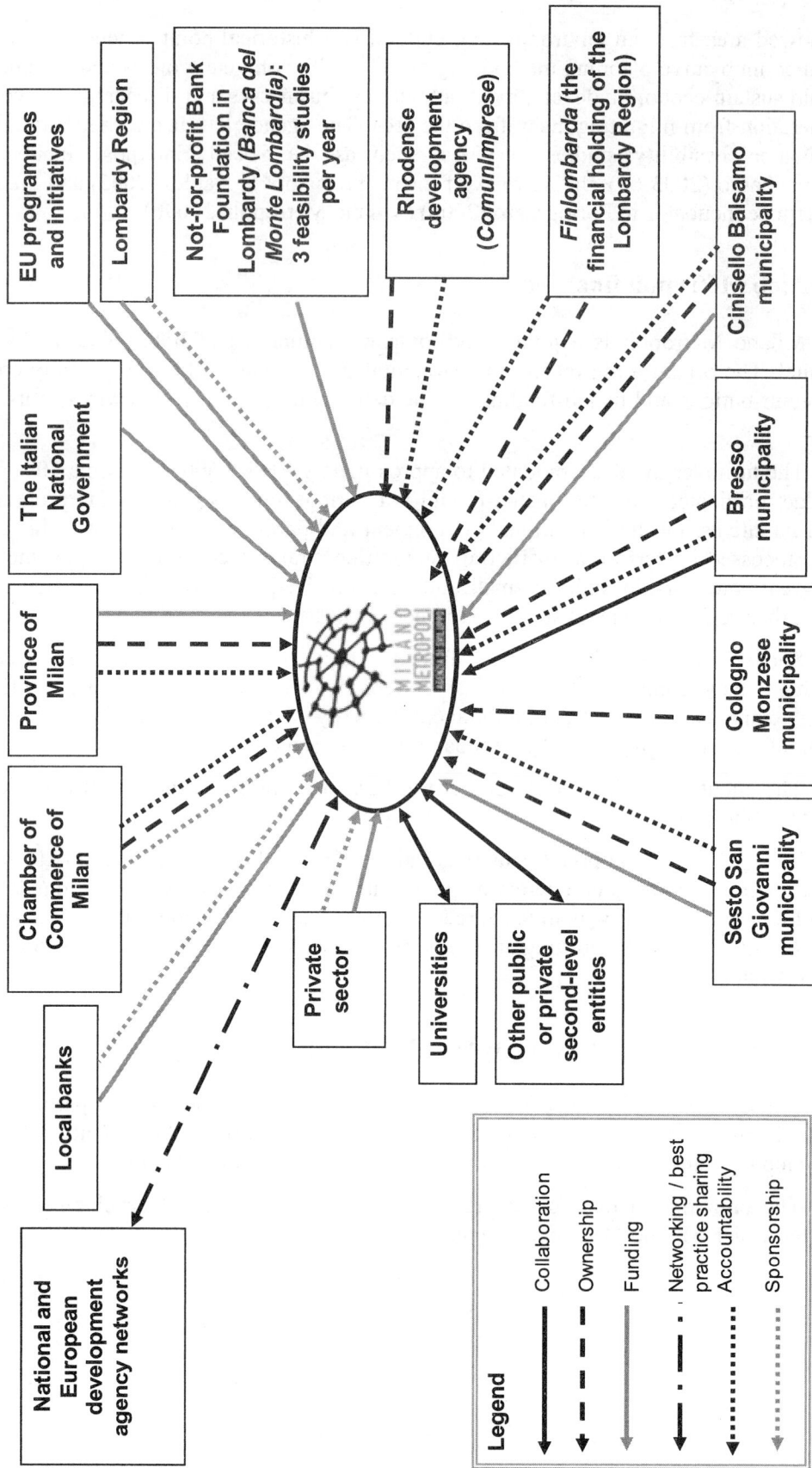

Legend

Collaboration

Ownership

Funding

Networking / best practice sharing

Accountability

Sponsorship

Who are Milano Metropoli's partners?

Milan metropolitan authorities

Milano Metropoli works closely with the public authorities operating in the metropolitan area of Milan and in partnership with local town councils and development agencies.

Third sector and further education

The agency also regularly collaborates with universities, research centres and not-for-profit organisations.

Business groups

Trade unions, the business community, banks and foundations are all critical to the effectiveness of Milano Metropoli.

International networks

The agency also relies on a far-reaching network of national and international contacts and partnerships, and takes an active part in numerous development agency networks, such as the Italian Association of Local Development and Territorial Marketing Agencies (AIDA), the European Development Agency Association (EURADA), the OECD LEED Programme and the European Learning Network (LNet), to name a few (Sala, 2009).

How is Milano Metropoli governed?

Board level

The Board of Directors is composed of representatives from shareholders and includes a Chair (Claudio Rotti), the chief executive officer (CEO) (Daniela Gasparini), six members and five auditors.

Staff

The agency has a very thin operational structure and employs around 35 people (Figure A.55). Half of these staff members do not work directly on specific projects, but rather within line-staff teams supporting project managers and taking care of the "LIB" – the business incubator it has managed since 2003. These staff specialise in:

- information technology (IT),
- secretariat,
- administration,
- marketing,
- communication and public and press relations.

Project managers work daily with the general manager and the CEO to develop projects and activities. They have a mix of competencies but, when needed, the agency can buy in the technical skills that it lacks (Sala, 2009).

Figure A.55. **Organisational structure of Milano Metropoli**

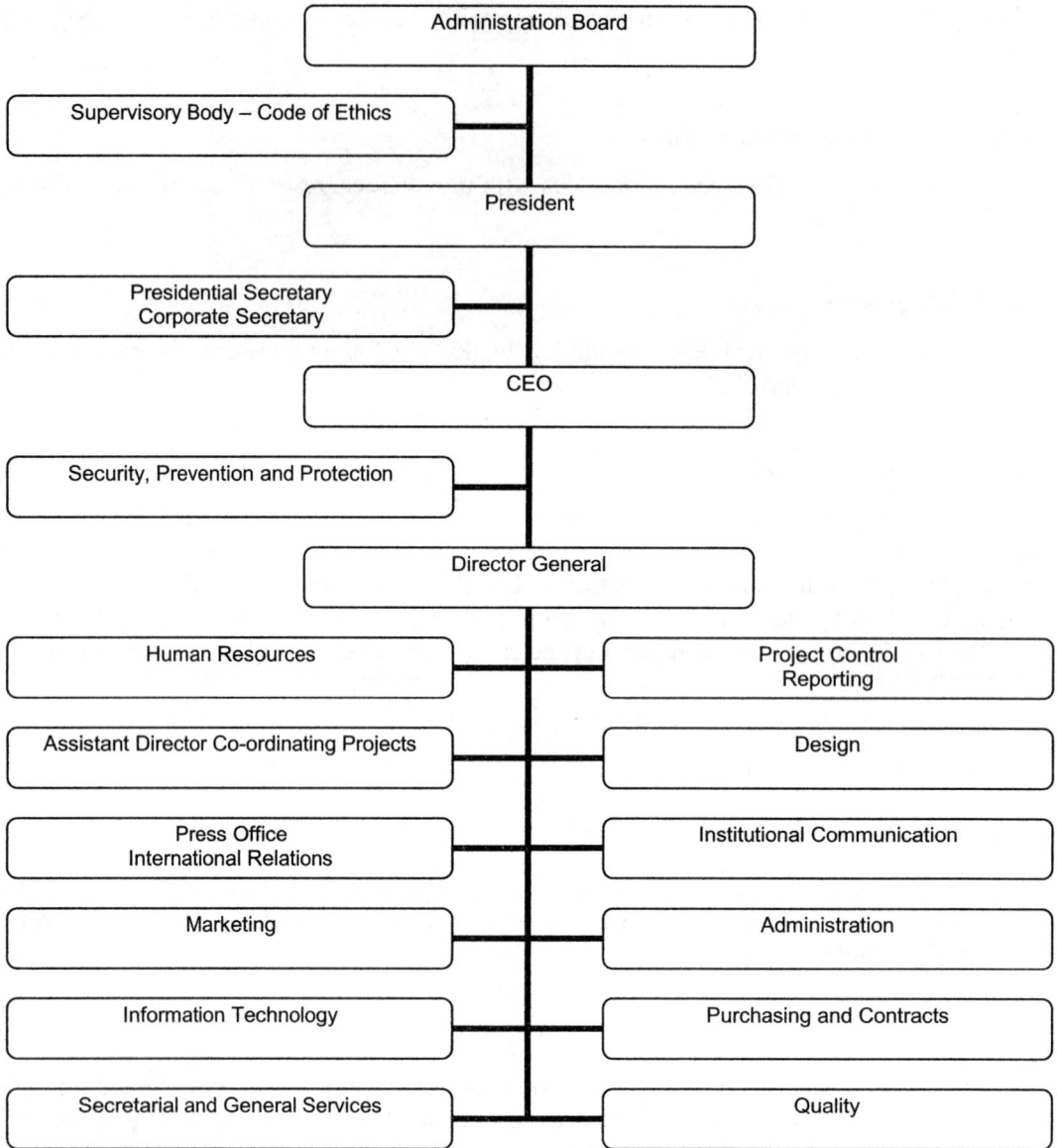

```
                    ┌─────────────────────────────────┐
                    │      Administration Board        │
                    └─────────────────────────────────┘
┌──────────────────────────────────┐
│  Supervisory Body – Code of Ethics│
└──────────────────────────────────┘
                    ┌─────────────────────────────────┐
                    │            President             │
                    └─────────────────────────────────┘
┌──────────────────────────────────┐
│      Presidential Secretary       │
│       Corporate Secretary         │
└──────────────────────────────────┘
                    ┌─────────────────────────────────┐
                    │              CEO                 │
                    └─────────────────────────────────┘
┌──────────────────────────────────┐
│  Security, Prevention and Protection│
└──────────────────────────────────┘
                    ┌─────────────────────────────────┐
                    │        Director General          │
                    └─────────────────────────────────┘
```

Human Resources	Project Control Reporting
Assistant Director Co-ordinating Projects	Design
Press Office International Relations	Institutional Communication
Marketing	Administration
Information Technology	Purchasing and Contracts
Secretarial and General Services	Quality

How is Milano Metropoli led?

Board level

Board members interact with staff only through bi-monthly presentations made by the general manager on the most strategic projects, and through bi-monthly controls on the working account.

Chief executive officer

Renato Galliano is the General Manager of Milano Metropoli and has worked for the agency since 1997. The CEO (Daniela Gasparini), who is also a member of the board, works daily with the staff and the general manager.

Organisational style

Milano Metropoli has been described as innovative, non-corporate, progressive and entrepreneurial.

What are Milano Metropoli's key services and programmes within the system of local development and investment promotion?

Territorial promotion and marketing

Milano Metropoli undertakes extensive work in the fields of territorial promotion and marketing. The agency helps local authorities and agencies to devise marketing tools and implement schemes that can improve and boost the identity, potential and centres of excellence of the Milan area. The agency helps local town councils develop joint ventures and strategic action plans, which allow local communities to work out a shared vision of development and to take strategic decisions to enhance their expertise and improve governance. Working closely with local authorities, Milano Metropoli is constantly looking for ways to better promote the area. These tools include local development participation and sharing processes (strategic planning, Agenda 21), and territorial marketing. In terms of territorial marketing, Milano Metropoli works to improve opportunities in the area and identify manufacturing and other jobs which can strengthen local identities. Various projects and schemes which aim to promote sectors of excellence include:

- MilanoMadeinDesign: this is a travelling exhibition which promotes the businesses, creative talent, local craftsmanship, training colleges and research centres of the Milan area internationally. It is sponsored by the Province of Milan, the Milan Chamber of Commerce and the City Council and is organised by the agency itself.

- PromoComune: this is a website designed to help potential investors find useful information on the economy, skills and opportunities in the 189 municipalities of the Province of Milan. The website was set up by Milano Metropoli on behalf of the Province of Milan.

- Milano Globale: this project, supported by the Province of Milan, is designed to publish information that could be of interest/use to potential foreign investors, through the use of a website and the organisation of schemes designed to promote Milan abroad (Milano Metropoli, 2009b).

Strategic planning

Milano Metropoli has undertaken extensive strategic planning with the aim of redeveloping local areas and giving them a new lease on life. Milano Metropoli works alongside local authorities and communities to identify problems and resources, define values, targets and strategies for the future, and create a local system. Milano Metropoli believes that strategic planning provides an informal, voluntary way for local communities to work out a shared vision for their future, and that it is also a process of social participation and interaction via which one or more towns can set and pursue common goals. The agency takes an active part in the key planning processes undertaken in the province of Milan. Some of the key strategic plans implemented include:

- Strategic Plan for North Milan (1999-2001): this involved four important towns in the metropolitan area - Bresso, Cinisello Balsamo, Cologno Monzese and Sesto San Giovanni.

- Strategic Project for the Milanese Urban Region, Città di Citta: this project was promoted by the Province of Milan, Milano Metropoli and the Milan Politecnico. The agency provided technical and planning support, in the form of making preliminary assessment and analysis of the projects taking part in the tender, supporting the promoters of the projects selected by the jury to implement them, and participating in developing the pilot projects.

- Territorial Plan for Provincial Co-ordination (PTCP): this is the general plan that defines the overall organisation of the Milanese area. Milano Metropoli works alongside the Province of Milan to arrange "who does what" and to draw up an in-depth study of the local economic system.

- Pact for North Milan (2005): the agency took charge of co-ordinating the second stage of the North Milan strategic planning process. Seven local councils – Bresso, Cinisello Balsamo, Cologno Monzese, Cormano, Cusano Milanino, Paderno Dugnano and Sesto San Giovanni – were involved in the process and were committed to meeting the new challenges presented by the local redevelopment schemes.

- Baranzate Strategic Plan: Milano Metropoli is helping Baranzate town council – a new administration in the province of Milan – to implement plans for a strategic vision of its own role in the broader area of northwest Milan.

- Special Programme for the Development of Integrated Green Systems and Social Housing: this is a research project, in which the agency is involved in defining an innovative urban-territorial project for the Lombard town councils. The idea is to find an organic approach to tackling two goals: the enhancement of the countryside (by creating new green areas and agro-environmental infrastructure) and more affordable housing. The scheme is being developed with the support of *Navigli Lombardi Scarl*, in partnership with *Centro Studi PIM* and with the direct involvement of the Lombardy Region (*DG Casa e Opere Pubbliche, DG Agricoltura e DG Territorio*).

- Rhodense Strategic Plan (2005): this involved 11 towns in northwest Milan and, promoted by ComunImprese, the agency experimented with an innovative way of using private resources to fund strategic projects for the economic and territorial development of the area.

The agency also helps provinces define and implement actions which come out of the *Forum per il Governo del Territorio Metropolitano*, a forum which discusses each province's Provincial Territorial Co-ordination Plan (PTCP) (Milano Metropoli, 2009b).

Development of strategic economic sectors

Milano Metropoli is committed to promoting economic sectors that are of strategic importance to Milan's industrial system, *i.e.* those that can create added value, innovation and jobs. These sectors involve both SMEs and social enterprises – key to Milan's competitive edge – and also sub-sectors of excellence such as fashion, design, publishing, biotechnology, IT and other activities linked to the creative industries. Some of the agency's activities in individual fields are outlined below:

- Creative industries: initiatives in this field are designed to generate new wealth and intellectual property.

- Design: the agency aims to devise innovative projects which bring the university and design world into contact with SMEs, and it acts to promote the sector.

- Biotechnologies: the agency has helped the Province of Milan and the Lombardy Region set up the BioMilano network of actors operating in the biotechnology sector in metropolitan Milan.

- SMEs: Milano Metropoli provides business incubators, facilities and advanced services to help SMEs, promoting new start-ups and helping them grow.

- Social economy: Milano Metropoli involves the social economy in territorial development processes and creates services to support and develop the not-for-profit sector. Milano Metropoli was one of the first agencies in Italy to engage the social economy in local development processes. The agency believes the not-for-profit sphere, and in particular social enterprises, are vital for promoting sustainable development compatible with the aims of social cohesion, as well as a strategic economic sector creating value and jobs for the province of Milan. Since 2006, Milano Metropoli has co-ordinated the Social Economy Round Table, devised by the Province of Milan to involve profit and not-for-profit organisations in working out effective and shareable strategies that help boost the potential of social enterprises. Service centres that work on behalf of the social economy promoted by Milano Metropoli include the *Centro Risorse per l'Impresa Sociale* (Resource Centre for Social Enterprise) and the *Centro Risorse per l'Economia Sociale* (Resource Centre for the Social Economy) (Milano Metropoli, 2009b).

General business services

Milano Metropoli is a majority shareholder in the business innovation centre, *BIC La Fucina* and the centre is dedicated to supporting both aspiring entrepreneurs with innovative ideas and SMEs wishing to develop their businesses. Support available includes business set-up and development, financing, internationalisation, innovation and technology transfer, and public administration technical advice. Milano Metropoli has also set up the business incubator *Laboratorio Innovazione Breda* (LIB), which provides space for entrepreneurs and innovative businesses. The new technology training centre, *Proxima*, provides space for businesses to learn about the most up-to-date technology, while the territorial animation centre, *Quarto Laboratorio* (with a business creation service centre, a social economy resource centre and an environment and energy space) allows local residents, entrepreneurs, associations and not-for-profit agencies to access information and services for new start-ups, support for the social economy and young entrepreneurs, access to credit, and information regarding responsible environmental behaviour. The Resource Centre for Social Business (CRIS) promotes local development projects with particular attention to issues such as employment, social inclusion and participation, with respect for citizens' rights (Milano Metropoli, 2009b).

Integrated projects

Milano Metropoli has become a benchmark for special projects aimed at preserving local identity, safeguarding the environment and promoting enterprise, innovation and social responsibility. Many of these projects are delivered through joint ventures and partnerships which see Milano Metropoli working alongside public administrations, local authorities, associations of town councils, territorial agencies, the business community and trade unions, banks and not-for-profit organisations. Some of these projects include:

- Re-industrialisation: Milano Metropoli helps local agencies to plan and implement brownfield conversions, promote the construction of new industrial premises and facilities for SMEs and artisans, and support innovative business start-ups and new territorial functions. The Province of Milan has asked Milano Metropoli to take part, on the technical side, in a pilot project entitled "Rethinking Industrial Districts" which is aiming to define a way of setting up eco-friendly industrial districts.

- Urban regeneration: this involves promoting business services, the social economy and the local population to redevelop and enhance areas and places in metropolitan Milan that have undergone profound socio-economic and urban change. The areas most affected by such change include Cinisello Balsamo and the municipalities around the new Rho Expo centre. Milano Metropoli plays an active role in urban redevelopment schemes such as *Urban Il Milano* and *Camfin Rho-Pero* integrated intervention area.

- Environment and energy: work in this area involves preparing projects and schemes aimed at individual businesses, and whole geographical and industrial areas, to heighten awareness of environmental issues and improve energy efficiency, not only in buildings but also in production processes.

- Social responsibility: Milano Metropoli is involved in implementing plans to generate a culture of socially responsible behaviour throughout the area and, in particular, in the fabric of SMEs (Milano Metropoli, 2009b).

Expo dei Territori: Verso il 2015

A key objective for Milano Metropoli has always been to foster the inclusion of a range of partners in the territorial development process. This is particularly significant in relation to the big drivers of transformation, such as global events and major infrastructure development.

With this aim in mind, the Milano Metropoli development agency and the Province of Milan, with the support of *Fondazione Banca del Monte di Lombardia*, promoted a competition entitled *Expo dei Territori: Verso il 2015* or "Expo of Territories: Towards 2015".

Milano Metropoli gathered, promoted and took forward projects and ideas from the Milanese urban region's most experienced players. They were all in line with the opportunities/requirements highlighted by the forthcoming universal EXPO 2015 that will be hosted in Milan.

The competition, which is meant to become an annual event for the Milan area, was very successful. It closed on 27 April 2009 in Milan with a prize-giving ceremony. In total, 42 projects were submitted by 170 organisations (local public authorities and not-for-profit organisations), and their many partners (524).

The project has been a success in a number of ways: its extraordinary attendance, quality of the projects submitted and the energy of the participants represent an opportunity for the area as a whole. In addition, the collection of ideas and projects will become a heritage asset for the whole Milanese urban region. Milano Metropoli is currently supporting the winning proposals to enable their delivery (Sala, 2009).

What role has Milano Metropoli played in the system of local development and investment promotion?

Table A.49 summarises the role Milano Metropoli plays in the system of local development and investment promotion.

Table A.49. **Conceptualising the role of Milano Metropoli**

	Direct delivery	Facilitation and co-ordination	Strategic support and programmes	Creating capacity elsewhere
Depth and breadth of role	✓✓	✓✓✓	✓✓✓	✓
Specific example	• Direct involvement in strategic planning. • Delivery of business services such as incubator centres.	• Co-ordinating diverse bodies throughout the city. • Managing and guiding local authorities' development plans.	• Territorial marketing and promotion.	

What enables Milano Metropoli to contribute to the local development and investment promotion system so effectively?

Partnership leveraging

Milano Metropoli's wide-ranging partnerships allow it to work in diverse geographical areas and across a wide range of economic sectors. Milano Metropoli puts a lot of energy into creating and sustaining co-operation agreements and networks at all levels (local, Italian and European).

Autonomous and nimble

Milano Metropoli is an "agile" and "ready-to-use" tool at the disposal of public authorities in its operating area. Its legal status as an organisation operating under private law, but with a clear public mission, makes it responsive and flexible enough to support local authorities in particular tasks.

Strong stakeholder buy-in

Milano Metropoli counts on the strong commitment of its shareholders. This makes it act, sometimes, as the operative arm of its public shareholders (in particular the Province of Milan) for the delivery of their development strategies.

Staff talent and commitment

The engagement of staff members, combined with their mix of skills, is essential to facilitate and drive the urban development process. The planning and delivery of local development action is both deep and requires a broad range of skills, from urban planning to facilitation, politics, communication and marketing, finance, brokering and project management.

Joining "bottom-up" and "top-down" approaches

Linking ideas and projects arising from the "bottom up" (*i.e.* from the players who actually live in the territory) with those coming from the top of the institutional processes is a crucial task for Milano Metropoli. It allows local and "global" ambitions to fuse together in a beneficial way.

What constraints make Milano Metropoli less able to effectively contribute to the local development and investment promotion system?

It is possible to identify three main constraints to the Milano Metropoli development agency model.

Sustainable finance

The question of how to assure real economic sustainability for the agency is in the forefronts of senior staff members' minds. The organisation is neither public nor private and this niche makes securing funding difficult, as it cannot compete effectively in private markets nor can it receive structural funds from public authorities. Moreover, its legal status (operating under private law but with a clear public shareholder majority) prevents Milano Metropoli from applying for public sources of grant funding or private contributions. For example, it cannot receive funding directly from private not-for-profit foundations. With no regular structural funding (*e.g.* funds to sustain, even partially, the costs of the structure itself) there is a real risk that Milano Metropoli will be forced to chase funding, rather than energe and inspire local policies and strategies. The current recession and the crisis of public finance are making the situation increasingly difficult.

Territorial complexity

The second challenge relates to the complexity of Milano Metropoli's operating area in terms of players, roles, responsibilities. These are not often clear and can overlap, making it harder for Milano Metropoli to make synergies where they should be found. It is also difficult for Milano Metropoli to help the governance processes on some issues that require, by their nature, a multi-stakeholder approach and an area-wide perspective. These can include, for example, public transport, public utilities, employment and local job market interventions.

National policy context

A third challenge relates to the role of national and regional policies for development. Over recent years, the importance of the "territory" and the "bottom-up" approach has been declining in favour of more centralised and sector-based policies. This is a challenge common to almost all Italian local development agencies.

How has, or how is, Milano Metropoli approached/approaching these problems?

Sustainable finance solution

A possible solution could consist of developing new forms of public/private partnership for territorial development. Links are being made with a bank foundation to pursue this. By trying to permanently involve as many important public bodies as possible, it is hoped that regular funding can be secured. It should also be noted that there has rarely been a strong collaboration with the Municipality of Milan. Indeed, Milano Metropoli has tended to focus on the regeneration outside the city's borders. Despite this, more and more energy has been invested in consolidating forms of co-operation between the agency and the Municipality of Milan, and it is hoped that a permanent co-operation will be established shortly.

How has Milano Metropoli performed in relation to its key performance indicators?

Table A.50 summarises how Milano Metropoli has performed in relation to its key performance indicators.

Table A.50. **Key performance indicators of Milano Metropoli in North Milan**

Theme (initiative)	Tangible impact	Intangible impact
Employment	• Unemployment has fallen by half and is now in line with the average for the metropolitan area of Milan.	
Businesses	• IT sector has grown by 400%.	
Redevelopment	• Physical redevelopment and conversion work has affected 67 270 square metres, and has led to the construction of four industrial parks for SMEs and artisan's workshops; two innovative business incubators; a Resource Centre for Social Enterprise and a craft/commercial workshop which has attracted 71 new start-ups and approximately 78 SMEs and artisan's workshops.	
Identity and Image		• New identity and image for North Milan.

Accountabilities, performance review mechanisms and best-practice sharing

Accountabilities

Milano Metropoli has an internal Board of Control, which consists of a member of the Board of Directors, a member of the staff and a member of the Board of Auditors. This Board of Control represents the accountability instrument of the organisation. Milano Metropoli also has an ethical code to which it adheres.

Performance review mechanisms

Each individual project also has its own specific performance review mechanism. It relates tangible performance indicators and budget to the terms agreed at project initiation, the nature of the project and the client's opinion. The organisation also publishes a report with its results at the end of each board mandate.

Best-practice sharing

Milano Metropoli was one of the key forces behind the Association of Italian Development Agencies (AIDA), set up at the end of 2003 to boost the role played by development agencies in the promotion and economic and social revitalisation of local areas. The agency also relies on a far-reaching network of national and international contacts and partnerships and takes an active role in numerous development agency networks. The organisation also shares best practice more locally, with its partners (Sala, 2009).

What are Milano Metropoli's strengths, constraints, opportunities and challenges?

Milano Metropoli's strengths, constraints, opportunities and challenges are summarised in Table A.51.

Table A.51. **Milano Metropoli's strengths, constraints, opportunities and challenges**

Strengths	Constraints
• Partnership leveraging. • Autonomous and nimble. • Strong stakeholder buy-in. • Staff talent and commitment. • Joining "bottom-up" and "top-down" approaches.	• Sustainable finance. • Territorial complexity. • National policy context.
Opportunities	Challenges
• The new political arrangements established from 2009 could assure a greater co-operation with the Municipality of Milan (the Province of Milan, Municipality of Milan and Region of Lombardy are now aligned).	• The recession will compound the organisation's financial uncertainties. • The recent creation of the Province of Monza and Brianza (comprising 50 municipalities and 780 000 inhabitants) will narrow the Milano Metropoli target area. Links are being built with the new Province of Monza and Brianza.

References

Milano Metropoli (2009a), "Public and Private Institutions Together for Territory Development", *www.milanomet.it/en/chi-siamo/public-and-private-institutions-together-for-territory-development-2.html.*

Milano Metropoli (2009b), "Milano Metropoli Brochure", *www.milanomet.it/en/nord-milano/brochure-nord-milano.-la-sfida-della-innovazione.-2000-2.html.*

OECD (2006), *OECD Territorial Reviews: Milan, Italy 2006*, OECD Publishing, DOI: *http://dx.doi.org/10.1787/9789264028920-en.*

Pizzinato, A. (1997), "Industrial Restructuring and Local Development - The Case of Sesto San Giovanni", *OECD LEED Notebook*, No. 24, OECD.

Sala, G. (2009), Written and telephone communication and interviews.

NYCEDC

New York City Economic Development Corporation

New York City Economic Development Corporation
New YorkCity, United States

Organisation type

The New York City Economic Development Corporation (NYCEDC) is "responsible for promoting economic growth throughout New York City through real estate development programmes, business incentives and more" (NYCEDC, 2009a).

The organisation works to promote economic growth in New York's five boroughs (the Bronx, Brooklyn, Manhattan, Staten Island and Queens) and to encourage investment in the city in a number of industry sectors. The NYCEDC is concerned with broadening the city's tax and employment base while simultaneously meeting the needs of both large and small businesses.

The aim is to achieve these goals in a socially responsible manner through the revitalisation of neighbourhoods, ensuring that economic development is not pursued to the detriment of local residents. The body is a key driver of the City's three-pronged economic development strategy:

- Make New York City More Liveable: improve the quality of life so that residents, workers and business owners want to be in New York.

- Make New York City More Business-Friendly: create an environment that gives businesses the tools to be competitive and create jobs.

- Diversify the New York City Economy: reduce the City's dependence on financial services and on Manhattan (NYCEDC, 2009b).

The NYCEDC is a local development corporation organised under Section 1411 of the Not-for-Profit Corporation Law of the State of New York. It is an effective public-private partnership and funding comes from a range of sources, but predominantly from the City of New York.

Mission statement

The organisation's mission statement is "to encourage economic growth in each of the five boroughs of New York City by strengthening the City's competitive position and facilitating investments that build capacity, generate prosperity and catalyse the economic vibrancy of City life as a whole" (NYCEDC, 2009c).

History, origins and ownership

The New York City Public Development Corporation, NYCEDC's predecessor organisation, was founded in 1966 to revitalise New York City's struggling economy. The organisation's primary objective was to retain and create jobs and generate revenue for the City by facilitating the sale and lease of City-owned property.

In 1979, the City created another organisation to focus specifically on the financial elements of the City's economic development initiatives outside of its real estate transactions. This organisation was eventually called the Financial Services Corporation of New York City.

By the early 1990s, New York City had six agencies devoted to economic development. They included the Office of Business Development; the Office of Economic Development; the Office of Labor Services; the Department of Ports and Trade; the Public Development Corporation; and the Financial Services Corporation. The City engaged the consulting firm McKinsey and Co. in the summer of 1990 to deliver recommendations on how to best promote economic development in New York City.

Following this period of consultation, during spring of 1991, Mayor David Dinkins and Deputy Mayor for Finance and Economic Development Sally Hernandez-Pinero announced that the City would consolidate the agencies into two groups: the New York City Economic Development Corporation (NYCEDC) and the Department of Business Services. While the merger was a priority for Mayor Ed Koch, Mayor David Dinkins, the Mayor's Management Advisory Task Force, and the City Council, it was Deputy Mayor Hernandez-Pinero who brought the consolidation effort to fruition.

The 1991 merger that formed the NYCEDC comprised of a number of small agencies, plus two large agencies. The two larger agencies included:

- The New York City Public Development Corporation (PDC). The PDC, created in 1966, was primarily charged with retaining and creating jobs and revenue for New York through aiding the sale and leasing of city-owned property. It also managed some of the city's industrial parks and undertook urban planning services.

- The Financial Services Corporation of New York City (FSC). The FSC was created in 1979 and was, at that time, known as the Economic Capital Corporation of New York City (ECC). It complemented the PDC's work and was concerned with overseeing the financial side of urban development work. The FSC acted to promote business expansion by administering finance programmes and overseeing work carried out by the New York City Industrial Development Agency (NYCIDA), a public benefit corporation which encouraged business expansion and employment growth in New York.

From 1991, the newly-formed body of the NYCEDC has assumed the services previously undertaken by the merged corporations, including overseeing programmes of the New York City Industrial Development Agency. NYCEDC also undertakes services previously performed by the City's Department of Ports and Trade (Olster, 2009).

What does the New York City Economic Development Corporation do?

To promote comprehensive economic growth, the NYCEDC's overarching actions are to stimulate investment, broaden the city's tax base and increase employment. To achieve these high-level goals, the NYCEDC concentrates its work in the following areas:

- It supervises transport and infrastructure projects which improve the efficiency of tri-state region transit. The corporation also manages redevelopment of freight lines, food markets and maritime and aviation facilities in order to allow better distribution of goods both internally and externally.

- The corporation promotes the city's central business districts to companies looking to relocate. The NYCEDC is able to sell or lease city-owned property and actively encourages those projects which will make use of under-utilised property for economic development purposes.

- The corporation is able to assist redevelopment projects by undertaking planning and feasibility studies, conducting financial analyses, helping companies through public approvals and outlining city programmes and incentives.

- The NYCEDC also offers incentives which enable eligible companies to meet their financing needs for acquiring property, purchasing equipment, undertaking renovation work, working capital and other matters through low-cost, tax-exempt bonds.

There is also a focus on revitalising communities by enriching neighbourhoods, publicising new areas of development and opportunity in the five boroughs, and creating local jobs.

The NYCEDC itself states that, "to carry out [our] mission, we play many roles - including real estate developer, asset manager, business advocate, policy analyst and program administrator. We also utilize design, urban planning and construction expertise to build many significant projects across the City" (NYCEDC, 2009d).

What is the spatial scale of operation and influence of the New York City Economic Development Corporation?

The NYCEDC works across all the five boroughs of Brooklyn, the Bronx, Manhattan, Queens and Staten Island. Its activities tend to focus in the city's central business districts (CBDs) and transport interchanges.

How is the New York City Economic Development Corporation financed?

As illustrated in Table A.52, the NYCEDC's revenue streams come from real estate sales, property rentals, tenant reimbursement, power sales, developer contributions, interest income, as well as grants from city, state, federal and private bodies, fee income and various other sources. In the three years of 2006, 2007 and 2008, by far the greatest level of revenue came from grants and reimbursements from the City of New York, with revenues from real estate sales and property rentals also providing a substantial amount of income.

Table A.52. **New York City Economic Development Corporation revenues and expenses, 2006-08**

In USD thousands

	2008	2007	2006	% change 2008-07
Operating revenues				
Real estate sales, property rentals	122 646	107 254	207 375	14%
Power sales	63 692	58 075	51 485	10%
Reimbursements and other grants from the City	589 728	381 283	300 896	55%
Fees and other income	72 682	46 805	62 175	55%
Total operating revenues	848 748	593 417	621 931	43%
Operating expenses				
Project and program costs	619 250	401 254	336 518	54%
Property-related expenses	37 776	35 306	34 863	7%
Utility expenses	62 867	58 101	51 278	8%
Personnel services	49 615	46 357	44 430	7%
Contract and other expenses to the City	44 350	33 395	139 691	33%
Office rent and other expenses	18 800	17 867	17 314	5%
Total operating expenses	832 658	592 280	624 094	41%
Operating income (loss)	16 090	1 137	(2 163)	1315%
Non-operating revenues				
Investment income	7 597	8 647	6 065	(12%)
Total non-operating revenues	7 597	8 647	6 065	(12%)
Change in net assets	23 687	9 784	3 902	142%
Total net assets, beginning of year	169 180	159 396	155 494	6%
Total net assets, end of year	192 867	169 180	159 396	14%

Source: NYCEDC (2008a), "Combined Financial Statements, 2008", New York City Economic Development Corporation.

What is the institutional context of the New York City Economic Development Corporation?

The NYCEDC operates under the guidance of the Deputy Mayor for Economic Development and counts city, state, federal and regional agencies, businesses and residents as partners. For instance, in the process of neighbourhood revitalisation, the NYCEDC works in partnership with city agencies, local officials and community members to harness the benefits of private developers. It establishes a development plan and executes that plan with a private developer to bring about lasting change in the communities in which it acts.

The organogram that follows (Figure A.56) reveals the local development system within which NYCEDC operates.

Figure A.56. **The position of the New York City Economic Development Corporation in the system of economic development and investment promotion in New York City**

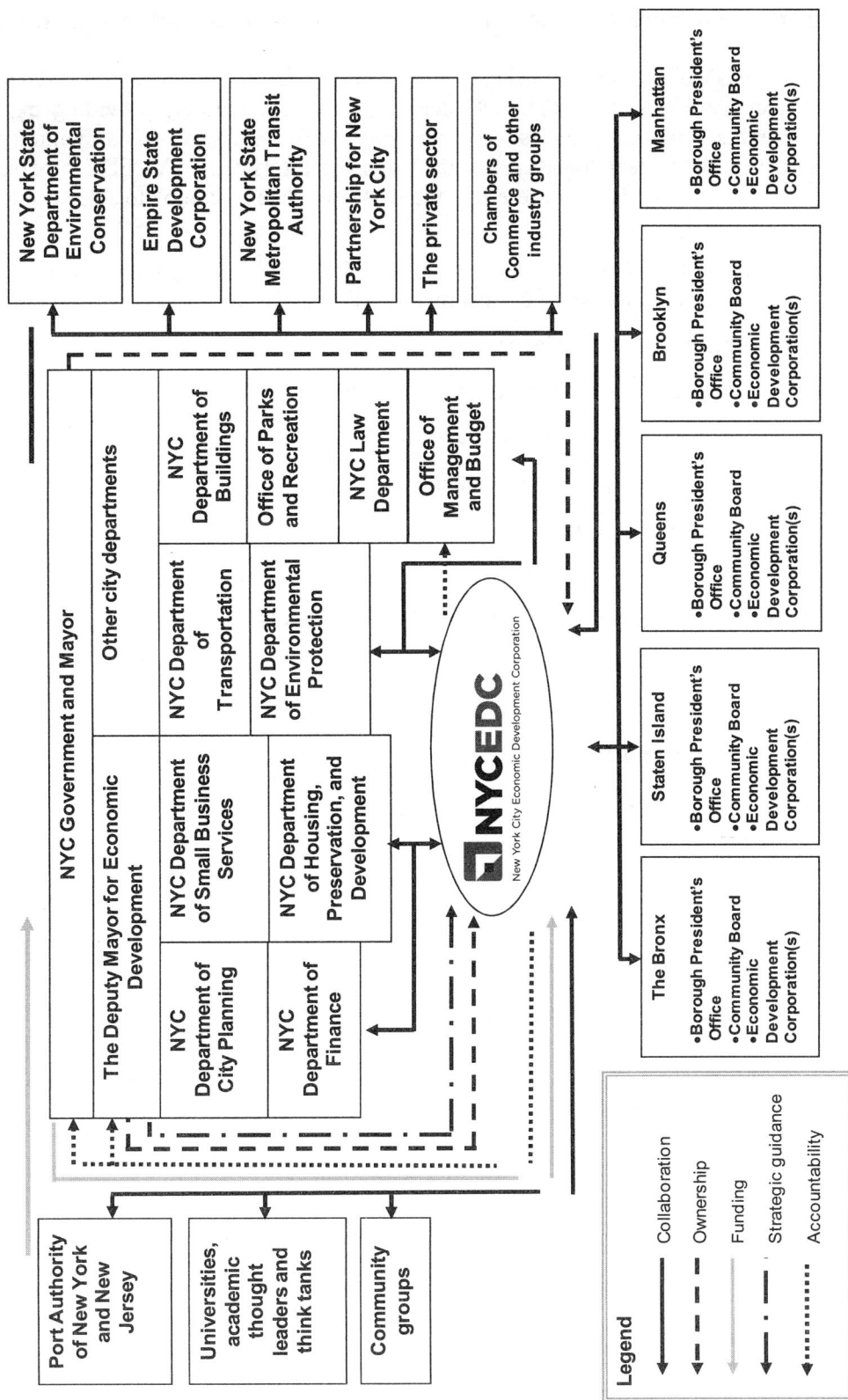

Who are the New York City Economic Development Corporation's partners?

The NYCEDC's relationships with the other agencies and actors vary from project to project. At times, the NYCEDC acts as a thought partner, providing expertise and research services to agencies. At other times, NYCEDC serves as a facilitator, bringing several stakeholders together to move a project forward. NYCEDC also serves as a project lead in situations where it is the best candidate to complete a project successfully and efficiently.

Though the NYCEDC has close working relationships with many organisations across the city, a number of critical relationships are listed below:

- the Office of the Mayor,
- the Deputy Mayor of Economic Development,
- the City's Department of Parks and Recreation,
- the Department of City Planning,
- the Office of Long Term Planning,
- the Department of Housing, Preservation, and Development,
- the Department of Information Technology and Telecommunications,
- the Department of Transportation,
- the Department of Small Business Services,
- the Department of Finance,
- the Office of Management and Budget,
- the State's Metropolitan Transit Authority,
- the Port Authority of New York and New Jersey,
- the Empire State Development Corporation (Olster, 2009).

How is the New York City Economic Development Corporation governed?

Board level

The NYCEDC is overseen by a president. The president reports to a Board of Directors which, as of March 2009, numbered 23. The mayor appoints NYCEDC's president and chair of the board, and its unpaid board includes representatives of City agencies, as well as appointees recommended by the borough presidents and the speaker of the City Council. There is substantial representation of businesses on the board (NYCEDC, 2009a).

Staff level

At the operational level, the NYCEDC is comprised of over 400 employees and a number of departments, including: the Asset Management/Capital Program; corporate communications (government and community relations, marketing and public affairs);

finance and administration (accounting, administration services, budget, compliance, contracts, human resources and management of information systems); general counsel (legal services and records management); planning and development (planning, development, maritime and Coney Island Development Corporation); strategy and policy (business development, economic research and analysis, energy and strategic planning); and transaction services(NYCEDC, 2009a) (Figure A.57).

How is the New York City Economic Development Corporation led?

Board level

NYCEDC's Board of Directors is responsible for the general management of the affairs of the corporation, and it and its committees approve most transactions and contracts into which the corporation enters. Staff members make presentations on matters for approval by the board and its committees and, at times, ask board members for advice and assistance. In order to make informed decisions on matters of general management, on specific questions or matters before a committee or the board, or in order to obtain additional information concerning activities of the corporation, board members at times will contact appropriate staff members. The Board of Directors adopted a protocol for contact between board members and staff in February 2009.

Chief executive officer

The current president is Seth W. Pinsky, who was appointed to the role by Mayor Bloomberg in February 2008 (NYCEDC, 2009a).

Organisational style

The NYEDC has been described as corporate, professional, lively, powerful and politicised.

What are the New York City Economic Development Corporation's key services and programmes within the system of local development and investment promotion?

Services

The NYCEDC offers a range of financing services including:

- Not-for-profit bond programme: tax-exempt bonds for not-for-profit organisations wishing to undertake major capital projects. They are issued by the NYCIDA.

- Manufacturing facilities bond programme: manufacturers of tangible personal property who wish to acquire, develop, renovate or equip facilities for their own use can make use of triple tax-exempt bond financing and real estate, mortgage and sales tax reductions.

- Industrial incentive programme: eligible industrial companies can take advantage of real estate tax reductions, mortgage recording tax waivers and sales tax exemptions on purchases of certain materials used for facilities.

Figure A.57. **The organisational structure of the New York City Economic Development Corporation**

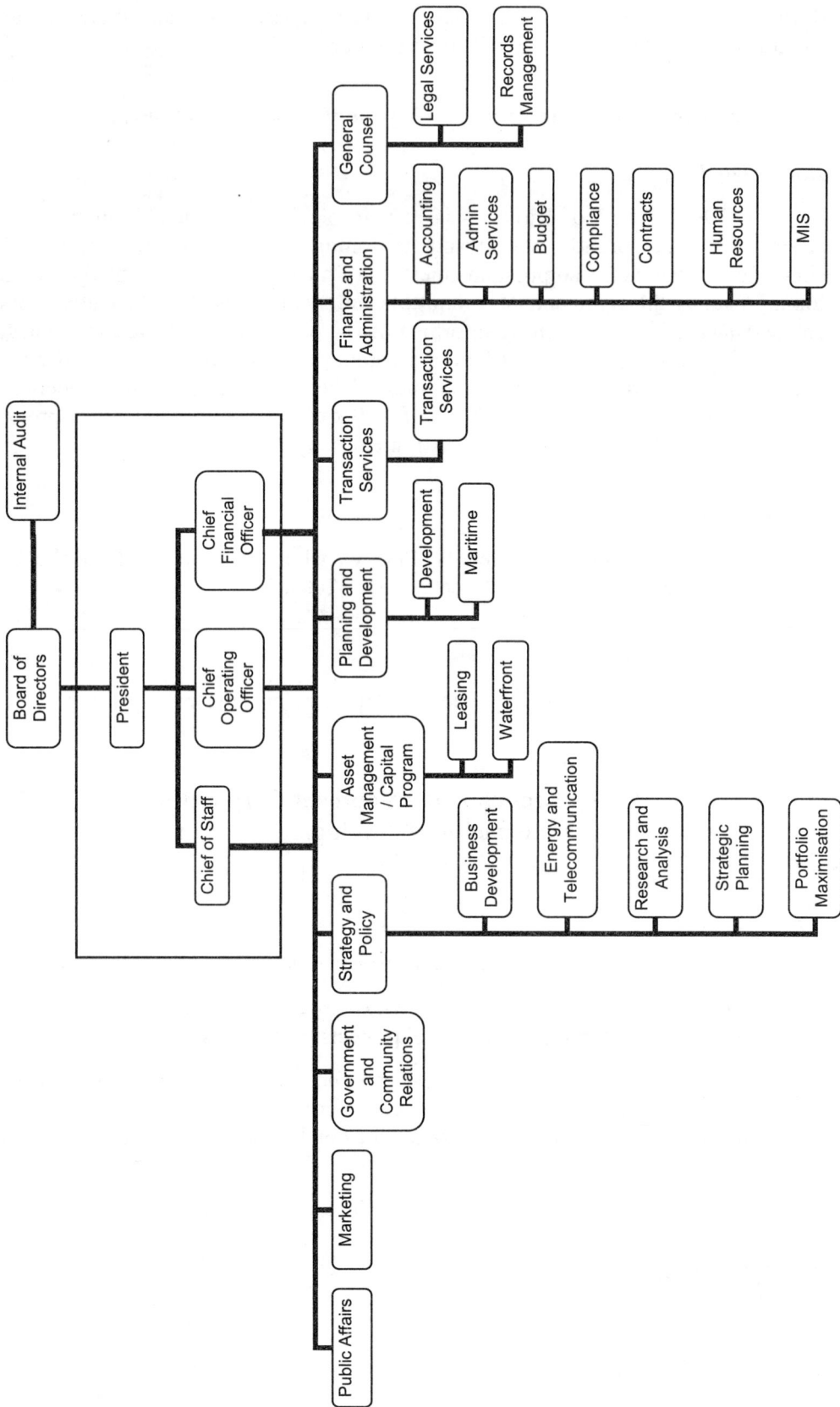

Public Affairs

Marketing

Government and Community Relations

Internal Audit

Board of Directors

President

Chief of Staff

Chief Operating Officer

Chief Financial Officer

Strategy and Policy

Business Development

Energy and Telecommunication

Research and Analysis

Strategic Planning

Portfolio Maximisation

Asset Management / Capital Program

Leasing

Waterfront

Planning and Development

Development

Maritime

Transaction Services

Transaction Services

Finance and Administration

Accounting

Admin Services

Budget

Compliance

Contracts

Human Resources

MIS

General Counsel

Legal Services

Records Management

- Industrial incentives for developers: companies developing industrial space in particular areas of the city can take advantage of tax waivers and exemptions on materials used for the facilities.

- Empowerment zone facilities bond programme: those companies carrying out capital projects in the city's Empowerment Zone can make use of tax-exempt bonds.

- Exempt facilities bond programme: those companies developing facilities on publicly owned docks and wharves or developing solid waste recycling facilities can access triple tax-exempt bond financing.

- Commercial tax incentives: companies who undertake projects which create significant levels of jobs for the city may be able to take advantage of a range of tax incentives.

- NYC Capital Resource Corporation (CRC/LEAP): lower cost financing is available for certain companies undertaking projects which provide sufficient benefits for the city.

- Liberty bonds: companies involved in the rebuilding of Lower Manhattan may be able to take advantage of tax-exempt bonds.

- New Markets Revolving Loan Fund: these funds aim to stimulate economic development in low-income communities and are available to small and micro-entrepreneurs.

- Energy saving: there are a number of programmes which act to reduce energy costs for companies, if certain criteria are fulfilled.

- NYCIDA: the NYCIDA aims to help companies and not-for-profit organisations undertake capital expansions and to become more competitive by locating within New York City or by expanding their existing operations. In particular, it helps companies access finance and take advantage of tax incentives to acquire or create capital assets.

- Other financing services include: the Locally Based Enterprise system, which works to ensure that local enterprises get sub-contracting preference for large City projects; the Procurement Outreach Program, which helps New York businesses successfully bid for public contracts at the city, state and federal level and includes counselling and review sessions; Foreign Trade Zones, whereby duties and barriers on imports and exports are reduced; and NYC Capital Access, which offers loan guarantees for small and micro-businesses (NYCEDC, 2009e).

Other services include the following.

Industry analysis and policy development

NYCEDC also employs several consultants and industry experts who analyse the needs of sectors like the financial services, media, bioscience and fashion to identify key growth barriers and develop policy recommendations to NYCEDC's executive staff, other city agencies and City Hall.

Business services

The NYCEDC provides industry expertise and financial resources, connecting business to information and opportunities, For instance, it produces a regularly-updated document which acts as a snapshot of the city's economy and promotes the advantages of doing business in New York.

The NYCEDC can advise companies on the New York market of potential opportunities, provide help in finding office space, help smooth the process of working with the City Government, and act as a medium between companies and business and community leaders (NYCEDC, 2009f).

Neighbourhood revitalisation

The organisation helps revitalise local neighbourhoods through the re-use of under-used and under-performing city properties. It works in partnership with city agencies, local officials and community members to harness the benefits of private developers. It establishes a development plan and executes that plan with a private developer. The NYCEDC also ensures that jobs are provided and communities enriched through the inclusion of community centres, recreational facilities and refurbished streetscapes in development projects.

To ensure the city remains attractive and sustainable, the NYCEDC co-ordinates various projects to incorporate green buildings and clean up the city, such as the Graffiti Free NYC programme and the Area Maintenance programme, which works to keep commercial and industrial parks free from debris.

Infrastructure services

The NYCEDC is involved in developing the City's infrastructure networks, including city-wide transportation, energy and communication systems. The body is Chair of the Energy Policy Task Force and, as such, leads a diverse group of stakeholders in a sustainable energy planning process for the City. The NYCEDC also manages planning and feasibility studies, provides analysis and makes recommendations to meet a variety of other infrastructure needs for the city.

The NYCEDC carries out strategic planning services to address the increasing demands placed on the City's transportation system. It identifies and supports new sustainable transit options, oversees the City's cruise terminals in Manhattan and Brooklyn and develops plans to improve aviation, maritime, rail freight and commuter facilities.

Key projects

A number of flagship projects have been undertaken by the NYCEDC, including:

- Ares Printing and Packaging: sale of underutilised land to Ares, which involved USD 8 million of private investment and created 100 permanent jobs.

- Battery Maritime Building: NYCEDC renovated this space in 2005 to encourage further development of the space.

- Bricktown Centre at Charleston: this project brings national retailers, such as Home Depot, to a previously underserved southern Staten Island market and aims to recapture sales tax revenues. The project is expected to create more than 630 construction jobs, 550 permanent jobs, involve USD 100 million in private investment and create a USD 76 million projected tax revenue.

- East New York Industrial Business Zone: since 1997, the NYCEDC has been involved in revitalising this 100-acre space. Some 25 formerly City-owned and vacant properties were sold to businesses, creating 600 jobs and generating more than USD 22 million in private investment.

- Greenwich Street Improvements: this project included streetscape and landscape improvements at a cost of USD 3.5 million. Work involved street/roadway rehabilitation, street lighting, traffic signals, water and sewer main work, and street-side amenities.

- Harlem Auto Mall: this development of a multi-dealer car mall has created roughly 175 jobs, generated USD 60 million in private investment to date and helped reintroduce economic vitality into Harlem.

- Keyspan Ballpark: in the summer of 2001, the NYCEDC completed the construction of this minor league baseball stadium in Coney Island.

- Pepsi Cola Bottling Company of New York: Pepsi purchased a vacant site from the City in which to create a new distribution facility, which should lead to approximately USD 30 million in private investment.

- Police Museum: in 2005, the NYCEDC completed the Police Museum's relocation.

- Staten Island Railroad reactivation: completed in 2006 at a cost of USD 80 million, this project was part of the City's plan for rail transportation of solid waste.

- Whitehall Ferry Terminal: in 2005, this project in Lower Manhattan was completed and involved USD 158 million worth of improvements to the terminal, including improved transit access, better pedestrian circulation and a new public plaza.

Current projects include the development of 125th Street in Harlem into an arts, culture and entertainment destination; the development of East River Waterfront; the Gateway Centre at Bronx Terminal Market to attract retailers to the area and create a new park that will reclaim open space for the public; Sherman Creek Neighbourhood Plan which aims to include re-zoning to establish more affordable housing and small retailers; South Bronx Greenway to improve waterfront access and provide more open spaces for Bronx residents and businesses; and Willets Point Development District to ensure that Willets Point becomes New York's next great neighbourhood, with retail and entertainment, hotel and convention centre, mixed income housing, public open space and community offerings (NYCEDC, 2009g).

What role has the New York City Economic Development Corporation played in the system of local development and investment promotion?

Table A.53 summarises the role the New York City Economic Development Corporation has played in the system of local development and investment promotion.

Table A.53. **Conceptualising the role of the New York City Economic Development Corporation**

	Direct delivery	Facilitation and co-ordination	Strategic support and programmes	Creating capacity elsewhere
Depth and breadth of role	✓✓	✓✓✓	✓✓✓	✓✓✓
Specific example	• Undertakes or oversees transport projects. • Sells or leases city- owned property.	• Conducts planning and feasibility analyses. • Performs financial analyses. • Works with private developers in the field of *e.g.* neighbourhood revitalisation. • Co-ordinates projects, *e.g.* Graffiti Free NYC programme and the Area Maintenance programme.	• Promotes the City's various CBDs. • Produces the economic snapshot of New York to promote the city. • Chairs the Energy Policy Task Force.	• Guides projects through necessary public approvals. • Packages City incentives. • Helps companies secure financing/ access capital, etc. • Provides support for projects.

What enables the New York City Economic Development Corporation to contribute to the local development and investment promotion system so effectively?

Highly talented and broadly-skilled staff

NYCEDC is able to effectively contribute to local economic development because of the broad range of expertise and commitment of its leadership and staff. NYCEDC has real estate professionals, engineers, management consultants, economic analysts and attorneys, among several other professionals on its staff, allowing it to look at a policy or real estate challenge across several different dimensions, which allows it to tackle economic development challenges in a thoughtful and innovative way.

501(c) 3 status

NYCEDC's 501(c) 3 status, which means that it is a non-profit corporation that performs economic development services for the City, allows it to complete its projects more efficiently because it is not bound by the same set of operational regulations and requirements as other New York City agencies. This status gives NYCEDC particular advantages around contract procurement.

Nimble

Relative to other agencies and government departments, the NYCEDC is a small, responsive and flexible organisation. The fact NYCEDC has small teams which are almost always constituted by members from different departments is hugely beneficial. It permits the cross-fertilisation of ideas, minimises bureaucracy and improves efficiency.

Strong revenue generating and maximising capability

NYCEDC has been able to successfully meet its increased financial commitment to the City, cut its expenses where possible and, with the help of its internal consulting departments, optimally leverage its assets to produce additional revenue.

What constraints make the New York City Economic Development Corporation less able to effectively contribute to the local development and investment promotion system?

Revenue cost balance during the recession

NYCEDC's property revenue has decreased, while its requested payments to the City to eliminate its budget gap have increased. In other words, NYCEDC has to contribute more to the City budget at a time when it's more difficult to generate revenue.

Balancing the needs of stakeholders

As with many other development organisations, the breadth and depth of the tasks in hand require the careful management of a variety of stakeholders. Despite diligent diplomacy, the complexity of certain circumstances means that some NYCEDC initiatives are slowed to ensure that stakeholder needs are met as best as they can be.

How have, or how are, the New York City Economic Development Corporation approached/approaching these problems?

Revenue cost balance during the recession

Because of NYCEDC's unique 501(c) 3 non-profit status and its significantly smaller size compared with other City agencies, the corporation has been able to flexibly respond to the changing economic climate. NYCEDC has taken aggressive steps to maximise its real estate portfolio's assets, while making strategic cuts to its budget. Prior to autumn 2008, NYCEDC had already engaged an internal team of real estate experts to examine how it could maximise the use of the City's real estate portfolio. The team has made several recommendations to NYCEDC's leadership and has identified ways to save the City and its taxpayers a significant amount of money.

Internal evaluation

Given the current pressures, NYCEDC recognises the need to be even smarter, faster and more flexible with its work. Over the past several months the organisation has intensely reviewed its internal operations to increase efficiency.

Enhanced stakeholder engagement

At this present time, the NYCEDC has taken the opportunity to reach out to community groups and ask for ideas. By improving the quality of its connections with its stakeholders, the NYCEDC hopes to improve the quality of the services it offers (Olster, 2009).

How has the New York City Economic Development Corporation performed in relation to its key performance indicators?

Table A.54 summarises how the NYCEDC has performed in relation to its key performance indicators.

Table A.54. **Key performance indicators of the New York City Economic Development Corporation**

Theme (initiative)	Financial year 2008	Financial year 2009
Transport-orientated development	• Introduced inter-modal train service on Staten Island Railroad for industrial transportation use, eliminating 58 000 truck trips in 2008 through the city. • NYCEDC is working to expand the railroad's capacity by 75%, which will create 200 new jobs and generate USD 50 million in wages.	
Physical urban development and revitalisation	• Completed Uniform Land Use Review Procedure (ULURP) approval process in November 2008 for the Willets Point revitalisation project, a 62-acre site which will be rezoned for 5 000 housing units; new retail, office and open space; convention center; and school will create 18 000 construction and 5 000 permanent jobs. • Certified into ULURP in January 2009 for the restoration and revival of Coney Island, a 27-acre amusement and entertainment district, which will create 4 000-5 000 units of housing, 500 000 square feet of new retail space, 25 000 construction, and 6 000 permanent jobs. • More than 15 major construction projects were substantially completed, and an additional 20 designs and construction projects were initiated. • Asset Management's Graffiti-Free NYC programme cleaned in excess of 15 million square feet of graffiti (NYCEDC, 2008b). • Worked to create nearly 20 million square feet of commercial, cultural, and open space. • Completed more than USD 225 million in capital projects.	• Received approval on five major developments. • Completed construction on almost ten miles of Streetscape Improvements throughout the city. • Completed construction on almost seven miles of plaza/open space.
Urban management and engagement		• Managed 60 000 square feet of gross property area. • Managed 20 000 square feet of buildings space. • Managed approximately 75 miles of shoreline, including 60 properties across all five Boroughs. • Removed 200 000 trucks from the road. • Participated in 276 community and strategic partnership meetings. • Reduced city-wide greenhouse gas emissions by 1 million tonnes annually by facilitating the procurement of cleaner energy for NYC. • Achieved 36% Participation Rate in Minority- and Women-owned Business Enterprise projects.
Leveraging private sector investment	• Real estate transactions leveraging almost USD 433.3 million in private investment were completed. These transactions project to create approximately 1 100 construction jobs and 850 permanent jobs (NYCEDC, 2008b).	

Economic diversification	• Announced numerous diversification initiatives, including:
	  o The Financial Services Initiatives, which will create an estimated 25 000 jobs for the city over ten years.
	  o Capital Access Revolving Loan Guaranty Program, which will provide USD 5 million to generate USD 14 million in new business activity, benefiting up to 400 businesses and 700 employees.	

Revenue generation and cost saving	• Achieved USD 24.64 million in land sales.	• Achieved USD 2.1 million in land sales. • Realised almost 20% in decreased operating expenditures.

Source: Olster, S. (2009), Written and telephone communication and interviews.

Accountabilities, performance review mechanisms and best-practice sharing

Accountabilities

Local Law 48 requires the NYCEDC to submit an annual report to the New York City Council, the mayor, the city comptroller, the public advocate and the borough presidents, containing descriptive data on a selected group of NYCEDC projects, the amounts of City assistance provided by NYCEDC to the businesses involved in these projects, and estimates of the tax revenues generated by these projects (NYCEDC, 2009h).

NYCEDC's leadership regularly reports to the Office of the Mayor and members of the City Council to ensure that it is fulfilling its mandate. NYCEDC also provides a list of achievements and accomplishments to the Office of the Mayor to prepare for the mayor's State of the City address and for the City Council's budget review (Olster, 2009).

Performance review mechanisms

NYCEDC is constantly developing, evaluating, and refining its goals and accomplishments. The corporation sets internal and project-based benchmarks and evaluates their progress based on meetings on those benchmarks every 90 days.

At the same time, NYCEDC's Strategic Planning and Strategic Operations departments regularly assess the effectiveness of the corporation's individual departments and city-wide policies, to propose improvements and solutions to inefficiencies.

As a custodian of City dollars, NYCEDC launched an internal research group to audit the company's real estate portfolio, to ensure that it is leveraging the City's real estate assets in the most responsible and advantageous way possible. The group has made several recommendations to the corporation that will save the City millions of dollars in tax revenue (Olster, 2009).

Best-practice sharing

NYCEDC consults with other economic development organisations to share best practices. Most of these instances are on an as-needed and project-specific basis. NYCEDC's Strategy and Policy division frequently communicates with other economic development organisations to gain insight into policy initiatives and programmes. In previous years, members of NYCEDC have joined the Office of the Mayor at the London New York Dialogues, sponsored by the Urban Land Institute (Olster, 2009).

What progress has the New York City Economic Development Corporation made?

Since its 1991 incorporation, NYCEDC has taken on additional economic development responsibilities on behalf of the City as additional needs arise.

Today, NYCEDC oversees transportation and infrastructure projects that make transit within the tri-state region more efficient. To help improve the distribution of goods within and outside the five boroughs, NYCEDC manages the redevelopment of the City's rail freight lines, food markets, and maritime and aviation facilities.

NYCEDC promotes the City's central business districts. When appropriate, they sell or lease vacant City-owned property throughout the five boroughs, often in corporate and industrial parks. They also encourage projects that strategically use under-utilised property for economic development purposes.

NYCEDC supports redevelopment projects by conducting planning and feasibility studies, performing financial analyses, guiding projects through public approvals, and packaging City programmes and incentives.

Their incentive programmes can help eligible businesses meet their financing needs for property acquisition, new equipment, renovation, working capital and other purposes through the use of low-cost, tax-exempt bonds. Double and triple tax-exempt revenue bonds are issued by the New York City Industrial Development Agency, an entity administered by NYCEDC, for various types of organisations and transactions.

NYCEDC also employs several consultants and industry experts who analyse the needs of sectors like the financial services, media, bioscience and fashion to identify key growth barriers and develop policy recommendations to NYCEDC's executive staff, other city agencies and City Hall.

While several other city and state agencies address similar issues, NYCEDC is uniquely positioned to complete projects quickly and efficiently because of the broad range of knowledge and expertise of its in-house staff and because of its unique capabilities as a 501(c) 3 non-profit public-private partnership (Olster, 2009).

What are the New York City Economic Development Corporation's strengths, constraints, opportunities and challenges?

The New York City Economic Development Corporation's strengths, constraints, opportunities and challenges are summarised in Table A.55.

Table A.55. **The New York City Economic Development Corporation's strengths, constraints, opportunities and challenges**

Strengths	Constraints
• World leader in city investment and reinvestment, promoting productive business districts and hosting global companies. • NYCEDC has been able to successfully meet its increased financial commitment to the City, cut its expenses where possible and, with the help of its internal consulting departments, optimally leverage its assets to produce additional revenue. • NYCEDC is able to effectively contribute to local economic development because of the broad range of expertise and commitment of its leadership and staff. • Relative to other agencies and government departments, the NYCEDC is a small, responsive and flexible organisation.	• Despite diligent diplomacy, the complexity of certain circumstances means that some NYCEDC initiatives are slowed to ensure that stakeholder needs are met as best as they can be.
Opportunities	Challenges
• Difficult economic circumstances can present once-in-a-lifetime development opportunities. In fact, the Empire State Building and Rockefeller Center were built during the Great Depression of the 1930s. With that in mind, NYCEDC recognises that there is great opportunity to improve the City during this economic climate.	• NYCEDC's property revenue has decreased while its requested payments to the City to eliminate its budget gap have increased.

References

NYCEDC (New York City Economic Development Corporation) (2008a), "Combined Financial Statements, 2008", New York City Economic Development Corporation.

NYCEDC (2008b), "Annual Report 2008", New York City Economic Development Corporation.

NYCEDC (2009a), "About Us", *www.nycedc.com/Web/AboutUs/AboutUs.htm.*

NYCEDC (2009b), "Annual Investment Projects Report", *www.nycedc.com/AboutUs/ FinStatementsPubReports/Documents/LL48_FY08%20_VolumeI.pdf.*

NYCEDC (2009c), "Mission Statement", *www.nycedc.com/Web/AboutUs/WhatWeDo/ MissionStatement/MissionStatement.htm.*

NYCEDC (2009d), "New York City: Make it Happen Here", *www.nycedc.com/NR/ rdonlyres/B36DE03D-3ECB-4D51-BD37-3801D68A9AEA/0/NYCEDC_brochure.pdf.*

NYCEDC (2009e), "Financing and Incentives", *www.nycedc.com/FinancingIncentives/ Pages/FinancingIncentives.aspx.*

NYCEDC (2009f), "Business in NYC", *www.nycedc.com/BusinessInNYC/Pages/ BusinessInNYC.aspx.*

NYCEDC (2009g), "Projects and Opportunities", *www.nycedc.com/ ProjectsOpportunities/Pages/ProjectsOpportunities.aspx.*

NYCEDC (2009h), "Annual Investment Projects Report", *www.nycedc.com/AboutUs/ FinStatementsPubReports/Documents/LL48_FY08%20_VolumeI.pdf.*

Olster, S. (2009), Written and telephone communication and interviews.

Prospect Leicestershire
Leicester, United Kingdom

Organisation type

Formally launched on 8 April 2009, Prospect Leicestershire is a new economic development company (EDC). Prospect Leicestershire was set up by the Leicester City Council and Leicestershire County Council to simplify the current economic development arrangements and to drive forward economic growth across the urban area of Leicester and its surrounding county. The new governance arrangements are underpinned by a GBP 1.36 million revenue budget with GBP 250 000 contributions each from the Homes and Communities Agency (HCA), the City and County Councils, GBP 125 000 from the districts and GBP 485 000 from East Midlands Development Agency (EMDA) (I&DeA, 2009). The organisation will primarily be focused on delivering regeneration, economic development and inward investment initiatives, as well as having steering functions. Prospect Leicestershire takes over the responsibilities of the Leicester Regeneration Company (LRC) and the inward investment arm of Leicester Shire Promotions. The majority of board members are from the private sector and legally the EDC is a company limited by guarantee whose founding members are the City Council and County Councils (Economic Development Company for Leicester and Leicestershire, 2008).

Mission statement

Prospect Leicestershire has the mission to "support investors, developers and businesses to improve economic prosperity across England's tenth largest city and the surrounding county."

History, origins and ownership

The creation of Prospect Leicestershire was in part the result of political change in the local economic development arena. In 2006, a Government White Paper regarding the creation of a new form of local economic development delivery vehicle – the economic development company – was presented.

Economic (City) development companies: a new approach to local economic development

The "State of the English Cities" report noted that, while much progress has been made by many English cities, most still need to make further progress in terms of disseminating success throughout the city and city region, strengthening economic rationales and becoming more globally competitive. Simultaneously, it was noted that there had been changes at the organisational level in English urban development. There had been a move towards bodies which were carrying out increasingly comprehensive and holistic functions in the field of economic development, consolidating the activities of many separate bodies and successfully liaising with the private sector. In particular, this more unified approach to urban economic development led to the suggestion of a new type of organisation, the EDC. The Government believed there could be a number of key advantages in establishing EDCs for English cities and city regions. In the consultation process for the White Paper, these were outlined as:

- As corporate bodies, EDCs better mirror the entrepreneurial approach and timescales of the private sector, facilitating a more responsive interaction with business, developers and investors than government or its agencies.

- EDCs provide an economic leadership role, setting out and co-ordinating delivery around an economic vision, enabling investment to be focused where there is potential for greatest impact.

- They reduce the number of players in the economic development arena, aggregating disparate roles and improving the efficiency of economic interventions through the succession, transition or integration of existing bodies' functions.

- EDCs are focused on the implementation of regional economic strategies and other relevant regional strategies at the city or city region level.

- They attract the specialist talent and skills that are key to economic development, including individuals involved in corporate finance, marketing, project management and physical regeneration and property development.

- EDCs are able to improve the quality of investment propositions generated by the city or city region for external third party, public-private and commercial financing.

- They increase the capacity of cities to bid for major projects that can have catalytic effects on economic performance.

- EDCs can increase the fit between economic development delivery and economic reality, by operating across local authority boundaries.

- They champion economic development needs in the development of other strategies.

The flexibility of this new form of local economic development body was made clear in the consultation process for the White Paper where it was stated that:

> *The Government does not intend to prescribe a single approach in relation to city development companies, nor does it intend to specify in which cities or city regions (including "polycentric" collections of cities and towns) this approach should be adopted. International evidence suggests it is appropriate to foster an evolutionary, bottom-up approach, led by local government and its partners within certain parameters set by national government. (Department for Communities and Local Government, 2006)*

Prospect Leicestershire

Prospect Leicestershire merges the bodies of the Leicester Regeneration Company (LRC), some of the delivery functions of the Leicester Shire Economic Partnership (LSEP) and the inward investment arm of Leicester Shire Promotions. This move will streamline economic development arrangements in the Leicester region.

Leicester City Council, Leicestershire County Council and the county's seven local borough and district councils will all participate in the new company. Councillor Patrick Kitterick from Leicester City Council stated that, "What we found when Labour came to power in 2007, was that the regeneration bodies in Leicester were confusing and it was difficult for any business person or investor to navigate … What we're hoping with [Prospect Leicestershire] is that by concentrating all our efforts and regeneration in one place, we are easier to do business with" (BBC, 2009).

In a meeting of the Cabinet in July 2008, the purpose of setting up Prospect Leicestershire was summarised as "to put in place an effective delivery vehicle to support achievement of the economic development and associated priorities of the County Council and Leicestershire Together as set out in the Sustainable Community Strategy (SCS), new Local Area Agreement (LAA) and emerging Multi Area Agreement (MAA)."

The new Leicestershire Sustainable Community Strategy (SCS) sets out the economic priorities for the County and, as such, sets the strategic policy context for the operation of the EDC. The priorities within the SCS are closely aligned with the Regional Economic Strategy (RES) which sets the economic policy context for the East Midlands. The priority outcomes are also set out in the new LAA and in the emerging sub-regional MAA. The priority outcomes are reduced worklessness, improved skill levels, improved business performance including start-up, survival and growth rates, and the provision of quality employment land and premises. It has been stated that the delivery of these priorities will form the bedrock of the activities of the new EDC.

Initial consultation of key stakeholders, undertaken by the consultants appointed to work on the Prospect Leicestershire project, highlighted a number of areas of consensus which shaped the approach to developing a new model, including:

- a shared appetite for change across key agencies;

- a shared concern to enhance overall economic performance;

- agreement that existing structures should be streamlined to enhance operational efficiency;

- recognition that private sector engagement will be key;

- acknowledgement that current arrangements risk undermining private sector engagement and confidence in economic development leadership in the sub-region;

- a shared view that the Leicester principal urban area (PUA) is the engine for growth of the sub-regional economy, but also that there are key assets (such as East Midlands Airport, Loughborough University and several large employers) which are located outside the PUA; cross-border working is required to support economic performance across the sub-region;

- recognition that there needs to be close alignment between the economic and housing growth agendas;

- need for closer integration between the physical development (supply) side and business investment activity (demand) side (Economic Development Company for Leicester and Leicestershire, 2008).

The cabinets of the City and County Councils formally committed to the new arrangements on 9 and 10 March 2009 respectively. On 18 March 2009 the members of the LRC met to undertake the business of transfer, which was legally completed the same day with the formation of Prospect Leicestershire Ltd.

Table A.56 articulates the city development company (CDC) framework set out by the government and the approach taken locally.

What will Prospect Leicestershire do?

Prospect Leicestershire will ensure that there is a co-ordinated approach to the delivery of business growth, investment and regeneration anywhere in Leicester and Leicestershire. This "no boundaries" approach is the first of its kind in the United Kingdom and was made possible by the agreement between Leicester City Council and Leicestershire County Council, with the support of all the district and borough councils across the county.

Prospect Leicestershire will focus on three principal delivery aims:

- **Regeneration and sustainable economic growth.** Delivering physical regeneration, renewal, environmental and infrastructure projects within the PUA of Leicester, its sustainable urban extensions and adjoining new growth points.

- **Inward investment.** Promoting both county and city as targets for mobile inward investment opportunities and enquiry handling. Links will be maintained with EMDA's regional investor development project which will co-locate into shared office space.

- **Business enterprise.** Ensuring continuity and integrity of business support provision across the county and city; acting as advocate for the private sector, joining up delivery of skills and learning activities at all levels, promoting enterprise development and innovation, particularly with the Universities of Loughborough, Leicester and De Montfort, and ensuring an adequate supply of serviced workspace and incubation facilities.

An operational plan for Prospect Leicestershire is currently under preparation. This covers core activities and relevant projects over the first three years of the organisation's operation (Economic Development Company for Leicester and Leicestershire, 2008).

Table A.56. **The city development company approach**

Urban development corporations, urban regeneration companies and city development companies	Leicester Regeneration Company (LRC)
Urban development corporations • Established under the Local Government, Planning and Land Act 1980. • Non-departmental public bodies funded by central government. Vested with statutory powers, including development control for strategic planning applications. • Aim to bring land and buildings back into effective use, encourage the development of new industry and commerce, and ensure housing and social facilities are available in the designated area. **Urban regeneration companies (URCs)** • Independent companies, limited by guarantee. The members comprise local authorities, regional development authorities (RDAs) and often English Partnerships. • Fulfil a co-ordinating role to deliver economic regeneration. Do not have statutory powers or hold assets. • Primary role is to address significant development opportunities by developing and managing implementation of a masterplan, and to build business confidence and realise a collective vision for the future of the area. **City development companies** • Local Government- and RDA-designed. • Independent companies, potentially (though not necessarily) limited by guarantee. Members would normally include local authorities, RDAs and other partners such as English Partnerships as appropriate. • Build on many of the characteristics of URCs, but tasked with responsibility for a wider agenda in driving economic growth across cities. This could involve greater geographical coverage, a broader range of functions, increased profile, and leverage over greater budgets.	LRC's job has been to define a Masterplan for the Physical Regeneration of Central Leicester and then to deliver it in partnership with the public and private sector. The company was set up in October 2001, and became operational in early 2002 as a response to the Government's Urban White Paper. It was one of 21 URCs in the United Kingdom. A key role of the LRC has been to attract developers and investors to Leicester by procuring development opportunities in accordance with the Masterplan and offering assistance and advice. The LRC also acted as a mediator between the public and private sectors to overcome any problems that arise in the development process. **Leicester Shire Economic Partnership (LSEP)** Set up in 2001, the LSEP was a not-for-profit company which was established by the East Midlands Development Agency (EMDA) to foster and promote economic development within Leicester and Leicestershire. LSEP's overarching vision has been to create the right economic conditions to improve the quality of people's lives and the environment within which local residents live. **Leicester Shire Promotions** Leicester Shire Promotions is the Destination Management Organisation (DMO) responsible for promoting Leicester and Leicestershire to visitors and investors. It was formed in July 2003 and is a private, not-for-profit company. Leicester Shire Promotions has been a partnership between Leicester City Council, Leicestershire County Council, East Midlands Tourism, EMDA and the Leicester Shire Economic Partnership.

Source: Department for Communities and Local Government (2006), "The Role of City Development Companies in English Cities and City-Regions: A Consultation", www.communities.gov.uk/documents/citiesandregions/pdf/154118.pdf.

What is the spatial scale of operation and influence of Prospect Leicestershire?

Prospect Leicestershire will operate at the city and county scale. The proposed model involves the "business enterprise and innovation" and "investor development and inward investment" functions operating across the whole of Leicester and Leicestershire. In contrast, the "urban development" function will focus on the Leicester principal urban area (PUA: urban Leicester and parts of Oadby and Wigston, Charnwood and Blaby Districts), but will be able to contract its services to support the delivery of housing and other physical economic infrastructure across the rest of the sub-region (Economic Development Company for Leicester and Leicestershire, 2008). It has also been recognised that the main urban areas outside the PUA (including Melton Mowbray, Market Harborough, Hinckley and Coalville) will also require assistance for economic development, infrastructure investment and housing growth and the resourcing of these areas is being considered.

How is Prospect Leicestershire financed?

Prospect Leicestershire has an initial revenue budget of around GBP 1.36 million per annum, although it is anticipated there will also be opportunities to generate additional income for expanded and new services (I&DeA, 2009).

What is the institutional context of Prospect Leicestershire?

Prospect Leicestershire will operate as a delivery body working within a strategic context provided by the County and City Sustainable Community Strategies, LAAs and the MAA. It will operate within a governance structure overseen by a sub-regional Leadership Group led by the County and City Councils (Economic Development Company for Leicester and Leicestershire, 2008).

The organogram that follows (Figure A.58) reveals the local development system within which Prospect Leicestershire operates.

Who are Prospect Leicestershire's partners?

The first year of the organisation will be a transitional year. In other words, it will take some time for the organisation to fully identify and establish its critical relationships. Nonetheless, a number of partners are likely to be significant as the organisation evolves.

City and County Councils

As founder partners and with strategic relationships with the Leadership Board, Leicester City and Leicestershire County Councils will be critical partners of Prospect Leicestershire.

Figure A.58. **The position of Prospect Leicestershire in the system of economic development and investment promotion in Leicestershire**

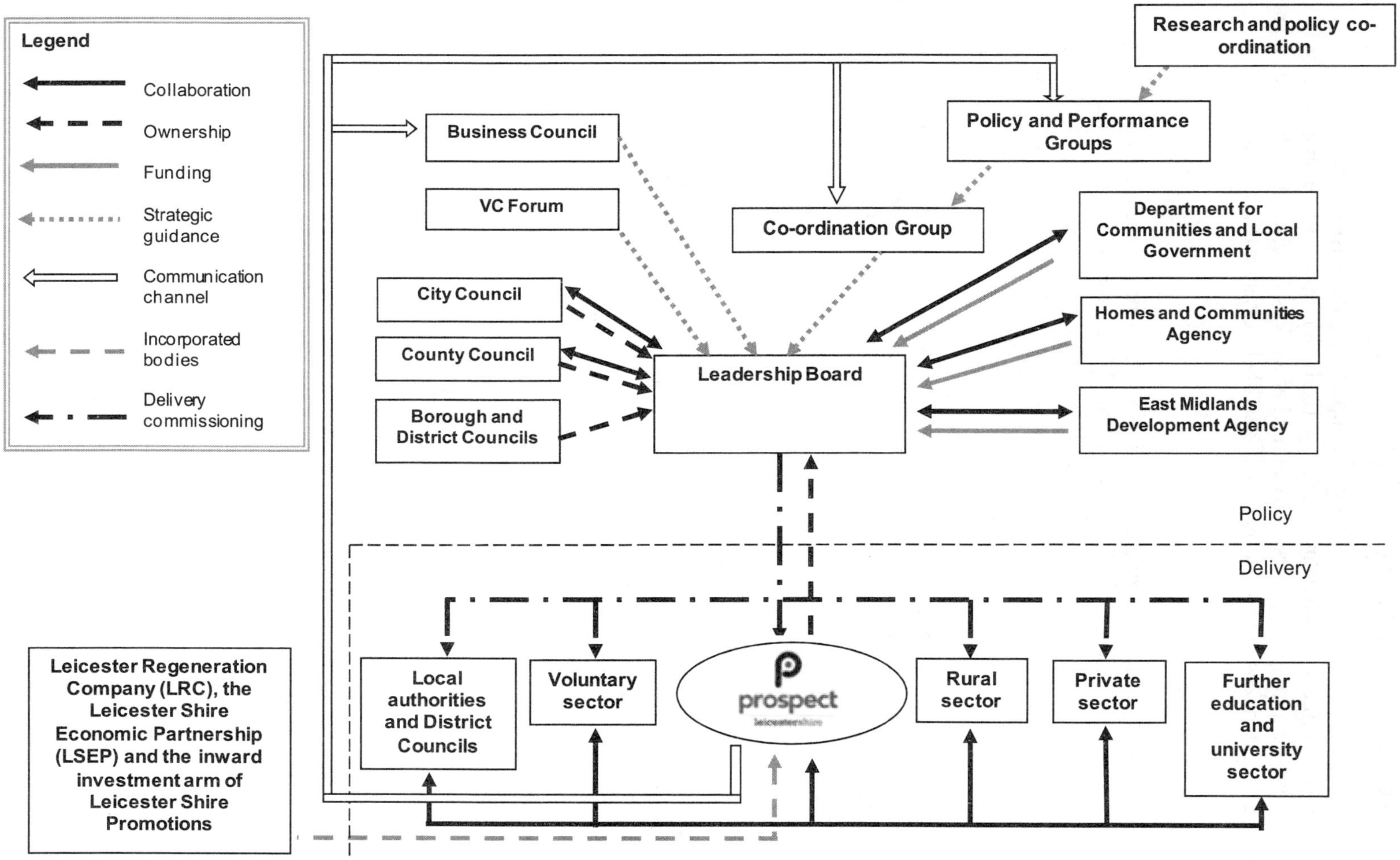

District and Borough Councils

As key collaborators with the Leadership Board, the District and Borough Councils will be key partners. At the same time, it is likely that they will be able to offer Prospect Leicestershire a more local perspective on what work is required and the effectiveness of any work undertaken. These partners will also likely assist in direct delivery.

Leadership Board

According to the Improvement and Development Agency (IDeA) Leicestershire Inquiry visit, "the role of the Leadership Board is to approve the sub-regional strategy, including the MAA, and to endorse a sub-regional investment plan (SRIP). The Leadership Board has no direct decision-making powers and decisions have to go back to the constituent bodies" (I&DeA, 2009). At the heart of the policy formation process across the county, the Leadership Board will be Prospect Leicestershire's key partner and Nick Carter, the Chair of Prospect Leicestershire is a member. It will both commission and communicate with Prospect Leicestershire on a regular basis. One question that remains is how the Leadership Board will commission delivery partners. Though the Leadership Board is setting out a commissioning framework, this issue has not yet been resolved.

The Co-ordination Group

The Co-ordination Group represents the executive arm of the Leadership Board. It comprises the chairs of the strategy and performance groups, David Hughes (the chief executive officer [CEO] of Prospect Leicestershire) and senior officers from the County and City Council. As IDeA suggests, the role of the group is to "provide the support function for the Leadership Board and oversee the preparation of the sub-regional strategy, the MAA and the SRIP and to consider projects for funding" (I&DeA, 2009).

Private sector

Prospect Leicestershire has many private sector partners. Not only is its board predominantly composed of private sector representatives; as part of the Multi Area Agreement, it partners with the Chamber of Commerce and Industry, Leicestershire Business Voice and ProCon (a property and construction network). The Business Council is also an important private sector partner. The Leicester Prospect chair sits on this council to ensure a clear communication channel is established and maintained.

Delivery partners

Prospect Leicestershire will be the chief delivery agent of the county. On many projects, however, it will work in collaboration with other delivery partners. For instance, Prospect Leicestershire meets the vice chancellors of the area's three universities to discuss plans and to bring additional skills and expertise to bear (Hughes, 2009).

How is Prospect Leicestershire governed?

Board level

In total, 12 directors have now been appointed to the company, including two continuing directors. There was a conscious decision not to include traditional key players from the property sector. It was thought that a clean slate with a large number of new board members would offer Prospect Leicestershire the best start.

Staff composition

Prospect Leicestershire has inherited 18 staff from the three incorporated agencies. Staff members are divided into three divisions, overseen by senior management (of two persons, the CEO and executive chair):

- Physical Development and Regeneration: five staff comprising planners, surveyors and project managers;

- Inward Investment: seven staff with marketing, finance and public/private sector experience;

- Finance and Administration: four staff with administrative and finance experience.

Though not included in this list, it is important to note that a personal assistant to the CEO and executive chair also joined the company on 1 May 2009 (Hughes, 2009) (Figure A.59).

How is Prospect Leicestershire led?

Board level

Nick Carter, former Editor of the Leicester Mercury, has been appointed to chair the organisation. The Board of Directors meets every month and has a transactional relationship with the operational arm of Prospect Leicestershire. More specifically, when the need arises, sub-groups will be formed and led by a relevant board member.

Chief executive officer

David Hughes has been appointed to lead Prospect Leicestershire. Hughes, 44, has 20 years' experience in regeneration and economic development and was previously a director of the national regeneration agency, English Partnerships (This is Business-East Midlands, 2009).

Ross Willmott, Leader of Leicester City Council, commented on the appointment of CEO David Hughes, "We are delighted with the appointment of David. He has a proven track record of delivering both regeneration programmes and economic improvement. This is a key post for Leicester, particularly regarding the new challenges we will face and I am pleased we have such an outstanding individual."

Organisational style

In terms of style, Prospect Leicestershire aims to be nimble, rapid, responsive and effective.

Figure A.59. **The organisational structure of Prospect Leicestershire**

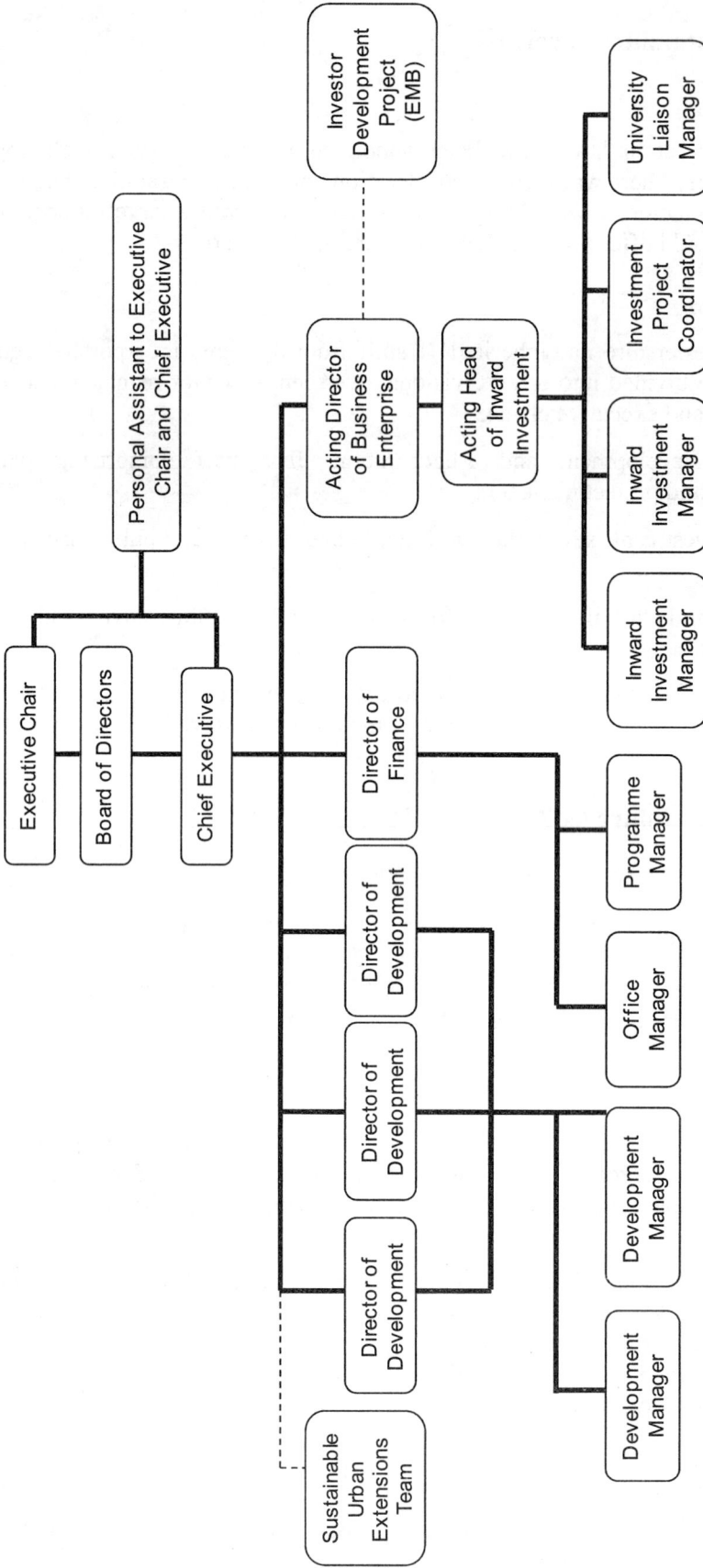

What are Prospect Leicestershire's key services and programmes within the system of local development and investment promotion?

Prospect Leicestershire key services include:

- **Regeneration and sustainable economic growth**. Delivering physical regeneration, renewal, environmental and infrastructure projects within the PUA of Leicester, its sustainable urban extensions and adjoining new growth points.

- **Inward investment**. Promoting both county and city as targets for mobile inward investment opportunities and enquiry handling. Links will be maintained with EMDA's regional investor development project which will collocate into shared office space.

- **Business services**. Ensuring continuity and integrity of business support provision across the county and city, acting as an advocate for the private sector within Prospect Leicestershire, joining up delivery of skills and learning activities at all levels, promoting enterprise development and innovation and ensuring an adequate supply of serviced workspace and incubation facilities. The Business Services Team will act as the research and development arm of Prospect Leicestershire, identifying and commissioning new projects, procuring resources, managing project roll-out and monitoring those projects (Economic Development Company for Leicester and Leicestershire, 2008).

Prospect Leicestershire key projects include:

- **New business quarter at Leicester Station.** This project is Prospect Leicestershire's highest priority flagship scheme. The current proposal is to reconfigure uses and buildings around the station to create a new public square, entrance hall for the station and development sites for the creation of 300 000 square feet of new office space, a hotel and a new multi-storey car park.

- **Developing new innovative workspace schemes.** In response to the shortage of quality workspace to support growth in key sectors such as creative industries and high-technology university spin-offs, Prospect Leicestershire is assisting public sector partners to develop workspace initiatives such as Science Park with Leicester City Council and the Universities, and an Innovation Park with Harborough District Council.

- **Leicester as a host city for the 2018 World Cup bid.** Leicester is bidding to be a host city in the campaign to bring the 2018 (or 2022) FIFA World Cup to the United Kingdom. There are considerable economic benefits in hosting one or more of the preliminary matches of the tournament, with potentially at least 200 000 fans coming to the area for each match. Host cities will form the spearhead of the United Kingdom's bid and attract significant national and international attention. Leicester's bid, a key element of which will be the partnership with the county, will be co-ordinated by Prospect Leicestershire and an application for support from the sub-regional fund is in progress.

- **Co-ordination of place marketing functions**. Development of a joint proposition to market Leicester and Leicestershire remains a key priority for Prospect Leicestershire, although not specifically within the company's brief (Economic Development Company for Leicester and Leicestershire, 2008).

What role has Prospect Leicestershire played in the system of local development and investment promotion?

Table A.57 summarises the role Prospect Leicestershire has played in the system of local development and investment promotion.

Table A.57. **Conceptualising the role of Prospect Leicestershire**

	Direct delivery	Facilitation and co-ordination	Strategic support and programmes	Creating capacity elsewhere
Depth and breadth of role	✓✓✓	✓✓	✓✓	✓✓✓
Specific example	• New business quarter at Leicester Station.	• Members of senior management sit on the Business Council, Co-ordination Group and Policy Performance groups.	• Co-ordination of the Leicester bid to be a host city for the 2018 World Cup.	• Assisting local authority partners to develop innovative workspace schemes.

What enables Prospect Leicestershire to contribute to the local development and investment promotion system so effectively?

Designated and expert project manager during start-up

The start-up process for Prospect Leicestershire was highly labour-intensive. The delegation of such fundamental groundwork as putting in place the computer systems, personnel, promotion and workspace to a project manager meant that the chair and CEO were able to build strategic relationships and build the vision of the organisation.

Multi Area Agreement / "No boundaries approach"

The "no boundaries" concept which Prospect Leicestershire has adopted, where all key players across the county work with one agenda, is key to the organisation's success. It avoids the negative effects of a lack of horizontal alignment and instead begins to build a united effort to achieve progress and sustainable development across the county.

High-level buy-in

Prospect Leicestershire has built and is nurturing relationships at the levels which enable action to be taken quickly and with minimum bureaucracy.

Board composition

The decision to inject fresh blood at the board level is a strength of Prospect Leicestershire. The new board members are enthusiastic, experienced in a range of fields relevant to the task in hand and don't bring with them any self-interest or tensions from the past.